# THE CREATION OF THE ANGLO-AMERICAN ALLIANCE 1937–41

## A Study in Competitive Co-operation

# THE CREATION OF THE ANGLO-AMERICAN ALLIANCE 1937–41

## A Study in Competitive Co-operation

### DAVID REYNOLDS ,1952 -
ɪ\|

The University of North Carolina Press
Chapel Hill

Published in the United States, 1982,
by The University of North Carolina Press

By arrangement with
Europa Publications Ltd.

Library of Congress Cataloging in Publication Data

Reynolds, David, 1952-
The creation of the Anglo-American alliance, 1937-41.
Bibliography: p. 373
Includes index.
1. World War, 1939-1945—Diplomatic history.
2. Great Britain—Foreign relations—1936-1945.
3. Great Britain—Foreign relations—United States.
4. United States—Foreign relations—Great Britain.

I. Title.
D750.R48  1982      940.53'22'41      81-16503

ISBN 0-8078-1507-1                    AACR2

Printed and bound in England by
Staples Printers Rochester Limited
at The Stanhope Press

To My Three Rs—L, M, and MP

*One of the principles of my politics will always be to promote the good under-
standing between the English speaking communities. At the same time alliances
nowadays are useless . . . As long as the interests of two nations coincide and
as far as they coincide – they are and will be allies. But when they diverge they
will cease to be allies. . . . Alliances uncemented by mutual interest are not
worth the papers they are written on.*

Winston S. Churchill, 1898


*[The United States] . . . will probably become what we are now, the head servant
in the great household of the World, the employer of all employed; because her
service will be the most and ablest. We have no more title against her than
Venice, or Genoa, or Holland, has had against us. One great duty is entailed
upon us, which we, unfortunately, neglect, – the duty of preparing, by a resolute
and sturdy effort, to reduce our public burdens, in preparation for a day when
we shall probably have less capacity than we have now to bear them.*

William Ewart Gladstone, 1878


*Time's wrong-way telescope will show
a minute man ten years hence
and by distance simplified.*

Keith Douglas, 1941

---

# CONTENTS

## PART III The Common-Law Alliance: Its Character and Development from Lend-Lease to Pearl Harbor, March–December 1941

# ACKNOWLEDGEMENTS

My interest in Anglo-American relations grew out of a year of study and travel in the U.S.A. in 1973–74. This book represents the fruit of over five years of subsequent work. The debts of gratitude I have accumulated during that time are too numerous to catalogue here, but I should like to acknowledge a few of them particularly.

In its preliminary states, as a Ph.D. dissertation, my work benefited from the wise counsel and careful reading of my supervisor, Professor F. H. Hinsley. I am also grateful to Dr J. A. Thompson and Dr H. B. Ryan for many hours of stimulating discussion, to Professor Frank Freidel and Dr Jonathan Steinberg for much kindness and advice, and to my dissertation examiners, Professors A. E. Campbell and H. G. Nicholas, for their helpful criticisms. Professor Donald Watt read an early version and gave me an opportunity to develop my ideas in seminar and conference papers, as did Professor Arnold Offner. Professors Warren Kimball and Bradford Lee scrutinized the final manuscript and offered many valuable suggestions.

Financially, I am grateful to H.M. Department of Education and Science for a three-year studentship, and to the Master and Fellows of Gonville and Caius College, Cambridge, who appointed me a Research Fellow in 1978. I have also been generously assisted by the Eleanor Roosevelt Institute and the Idlewild Trust. Two Harvard research institutes—the Center for European Studies in 1977 and the Charles Warren Center in 1980—have provided stimulating and hospitable bases for my work in the U.S.A.

In the course of my research I have visited numerous libraries and archives on both sides of the Atlantic. In each case I have found the librarians most helpful, but I should like to single out Dr William Emerson and his staff at the Roosevelt Library who make visits to Hyde Park so pleasant and worthwhile. For permission to quote from papers in their charge I am grateful to: the Baker Library, Harvard Business School; the Beaverbrook Foundation and the House of Lords Record Office; Birmingham University; the British Library of Political and Economic Science; Lady Ford; Lord Halifax and Major T. L. Ingram; Hon. John Harvey and the British Library; the Houghton Library, Harvard University; Lord Linlithgow; Lord Lothian; the Trustees of the National Maritime Museum, Greenwich; Mr P. E. Paget; Lady Catherine Peake; Reading University; Yale University. If there are any other copyright holders whom I should have contacted, I hope they will accept this apology. Extracts from Crown Copyright documents appear by permission of the Controller of H.M. Stationery Office.

I should like to thank those who allowed me to interview them, especially Aubrey and Constance Morgan for their interest, hospitality and friendship.

ACKNOWLEDGEMENTS

My appreciation also goes to Patricia Denault and Patricia McCullagh for their help in typing the manuscript.

My greatest debts are inadequately recorded in the dedication. My parents, Marian and Leslie Reynolds, have been an unfailing source of love and guidance over the years. My wife Margaret—who represents my more personal interest in Anglo-American relations—has encouraged me, borne with my preoccupations and subjected all that I have written to an invaluable critical eye, despite the pressures of her own work. To my 'three Rs' this book is gratefully dedicated.

# ABBREVIATIONS

The following abbreviations appear frequently in text or notes. For others
see bibliography, especially sections I and II.

| | |
|---|---|
| D/S | Department of State (U.S.A.). |
| F.D.R. | Franklin D. Roosevelt. |
| FO | Foreign Office (G.B.). |
| FO/A | Foreign Office, American Department. |
| FO/FE | Foreign Office, Far Eastern Department. |
| *FRUS* | *Foreign Relations of the United States.* |
| *HC Debs.* | House of Commons, *Debates.* |
| HMG | His Majesty's Government. |
| MEW | Ministry of Economic Warfare (G.B.) |
| MOI | Ministry of Information (G.B.). |
| NC | Neville Chamberlain. |
| NEI | Netherlands East Indies. |
| W.S.C. | Winston S. Churchill. |

Except for peripheral references, books and articles are identified in the
notes only by author and brief title. Full details of all works cited may be
found in the bibliography.

# INTRODUCTION

*[Churchill's] six huge volumes on the Second World War require the most careful assessment, and one not yet made: soon, however, the scholars must get to work, and what a task they will have!*

J. H. Plumb, 1969

*As the records become available the heroic simplicities of the Second World War crumble away.*

Michael Howard, 1978[1]

Since its publication between 1948 and 1954 Sir Winston Churchill's massive history, *The Second World War*, has guided the thinking of historians. As J. H. Plumb put it: 'They move down the broad avenues which he drove through war's confusion and complexity.'[2] One of Churchill's most important themes was that of a 'special relationship' between the British Commonwealth and the United States. He viewed their wartime alliance as the political expression of an underlying cultural unity—'the English-speaking peoples'—with the U.S.A. cast almost as the prodigal son within this great family of nations. The special relationship, according to Churchill, was the principal force for world order and peace. Despite their co-operation in the Great War, Britain and America had foolishly gone their separate ways in the 1920s and 1930s, thereby facilitating Hitler's rise to power. Their renewed alliance had been the basis of victory in 1945, and this time, Churchill argued, they must remain in partnership to secure the peace against the new totalitarian threat posed by Soviet Russia. In this way Britain could remain a great power, admittedly no longer in solitary splendour, but at least in concert with her kin across the seas.

In the last decade Churchill's interpretation of the War has been keenly scrutinized by a new generation of scholars, aided by the recently opened official archives, and, unlike Churchill, not protagonists in the events they describe. Their work may lack the immediacy of contemporary accounts but, as compensation, it displays a new detachment and sense of long-term perspective. For example, earlier writers on British foreign policy in the 1930s concentrated on the failure to control Hitler, often seeking to apportion blame for the 'folly of appeasement'. Recent historians have gone beyond these 'Eurocentric' and 'Guilty Men' preoccupations to show that the German problem in the 1930s was part of a global dilemma facing British leaders, that their response to it must be set in the context of Britain's gradual decline as a world power, and that, despite significant differences of opinion, appeasement was not the brainchild of a misguided few but the consensus of opinion in Whitehall.[3] Concurrently, U.S. historians have subjected the old myths about American isolation to close examination. During the inter-war years officials in Washington often used foreign econom c policy as their main instrument of diplomacy—one that seemed appropriate to America's limited overseas interests and to domestic political constraints. Much of this work has been on the 1920s, but studies of the 1930s have shown clearly the heightened commercial rivalry between Britain and the U.S., as the two countries adopted different policies in response to the Depression.[4] This undercurrent of transatlantic rivalry has also been discerned as a theme in wartime diplomacy. Another group of writers has examined the Anglo-American negotiations on such matters as grand strategy, economic policy and decolonization, noting the frequent arguments and revealing some of the limits of the Grand Alliance.[5]

This is the starting point for my own work. First, much of the recent research has focused either on the late 1930s or on the period 1941–45.[6] This book tries to fill the gap by offering an account of Anglo-American relations from the summer of 1937 until December 1941, and particularly from Munich to Pearl Harbor. Although not a comprehensive narrative—the archives are too vast for that—it discusses most of the major events, diplomatic, military and economic, drawing on my own research in British and American archives and on the studies of other scholars. This account constitutes the framework, secondly, for a deeper exploration of the nature of the relationship. Whereas earlier writing on the subject was prone to sentimentality, the recent work has emphasized and even exaggerated the hostility and suspicion between the two governments. We need to explore the areas of agreement *and* the areas of difference, trying to discern the basis of the evolving alliance. What did each country want from the other? How did they try to attain their ends? These are the questions running through the book. In trying to answer them, the historian cannot look simply at the bilateral, Anglo-American diplomacy. This only assumes its full significance in the light of several other considerations. One of these is the domestic pressure upon the leaders—the bureaucratic and party-political debates that shape foreign policy options. Another is the wider cultural framework, particularly the perceptions and misperceptions of the other country that grew out of the respective societies and their interwoven histories. It is also necessary to set the Anglo-American relationship within the context of each power's multilateral diplomatic ties and to keep in mind the changing international situation between 1937 and 1941. That requires sensitivity to the way events were seen at the time. We are so familiar with the milestones on the road to Pearl Harbor that we can easily forget that events now long in the past were once in the future. In a fluid diplomatic situation policymakers tried to avoid becoming committed to any one course of action, and in confronting an open future they drew on their own past, particularly on experiences of the Great War.

These are some of the themes of this book. We are dealing with a diplomatic relationship between two sovereign, independent states, of differing strengths and interests. Undoubtedly it had many special qualities, some of which recent work has tended to neglect. However, the co-operation rested not on some latent cultural unity, as Churchill claimed, but on certain similar geopolitical and ideological interests, which gradually assumed paramount importance for both countries in 1940–41 because of the international crisis. As this happened the conflicts of interest became less important, but they were not forgotten. The story, therefore, has two facets—the evolution of a unique alliance and, within that, the continual manoeuvring for advantage which was part of the shift of world power from Britain to the U.S.A.

# PART ONE

# Dual Policies

The Limits of Anglo-American Co-operation
during a Period of Diplomatic Uncertainty
May 1937–May 1940

*We are in the remarkable position of not wanting to quarrel with
anybody because we have got most of the world already, or the
best parts of it, and we only want to keep what we have got and
prevent others from taking it away from us.*
Admiral Sir Ernle Chatfield, First Sea Lord, June 1934

*You will remember that I warned you that while Roosevelt
desired the closest collaboration with England he would insist
on a true cooperation and would never accept a collaboration
similar to the collaboration between the automobile and the
chauffeur—with England in the driver's seat.*
William C. Bullitt to J. Ramsay MacDonald, February 1933

# CHAPTER ONE

## Doubts, Hopes and Fears

### The State of Anglo-American Relations
### in the Late 1930s

*Anglo-American concord will one day save the world, but that day has not yet arrived. There is still suspicion and hesitation on both sides.*
Frank Ashton-Gwatkin, Foreign Office, May 1938

*The British do regard us as a Dominion gone wrong, but if they frankly regarded us as a foreign country albeit a friendly one, relations would be far better.*
Jay Pierrepont Moffat, State Department, February 1939[1]

### A. The British predicament

British policymakers in the 1930s were preoccupied with the disparity between Britain's commitments and her capabilities.[2] As ruler of an Empire covering a quarter of the globe, she was responsible for the defence of dependent colonies and mandated territories, the great white self-governing Dominions and that jewel of the imperial crown—India. Furthermore, she was a major trading nation, heavily reliant on the import of primary products from around the world and on her own exports, investments and financial services. Yet, as the decade progressed, Britain seemed increasingly threatened by a potential coalition of hostile powers—Germany, Italy and Japan. In her state of relative disarmament she would have found war with any one of these states a stern test; in fact her leaders faced the nightmare of conflict against all three at once. Although Germany was identified as the prime danger, the two other powers posed grave and interconnected threats to Britain's global interests. In the Far East, the Sino-Japanese war, which flared up again in the summer of 1937, was damaging her substantial stake in China, while Japan's expansion potentially endangered the south-east Asian empire, including India itself. In the Eastern Mediterranean, Italy threatened Britain's dominant but shaky position, her oil interests and the security of the Suez Canal—the vital link between Britain and the eastern empire and Australasian Dominions. Were crises to arise simultaneously in these two sensitive areas, the Royal Navy did not have the capital ships to protect all Britain's interests, not to mention defending the British Isles themselves against Nazi Germany.[3]

The British Government could see no reliable allies at hand to help it confront this threat. France was politically divided, with one ministry following another; Russia was immersed in Stalin's purges of the bureaucracy and officer corps; and the U.S.A. was deeply isolationist and preoccupied with its grave Depression. Even the Empire presented problems, with isolationist sentiment complicated by ethnic divisions, especially in Canada and South Africa. Only New Zealand's unquestioning loyalty to Britain could be relied upon. Nor was there any way rapidly to increase Britain's own capabilities. It took time and organization to turn an industrial economy to war production—converting plant and tools, training skilled labour, developing an effective product. New weapons could not be created overnight— a battleship, for instance, might take up to four years to complete. In any case, British leaders agreed that the pace of rearmament had to be carefully controlled. High taxation seemed politically unacceptable, not least because of its deflationary effect on an economy still struggling out of depression. On the other hand, the Treasury, pre-Keynesian in outlook, warned that excessive borrowing would undermine confidence in sterling and raise Britain's export prices to uncompetitive levels. Both of these developments would exacerbate the acute balance of payments problem that had faced the Treasury since the financial crisis of 1931. But these arguments were not merely apposite to peacetime needs. It was axiomatic that Britain could only win another war if it were protracted and she had time to mobilize her global resources. She could not afford to dissipate those resources by over-hasty rearmament. The economy was therefore her 'fourth arm'—as essential to a future war effort as were the three services.[4]

The resolution of this dilemma seemed painfully clear, especially to Neville Chamberlain. As he wrote in January 1938, 'in the absence of any powerful ally, and until our armaments are completed, we must adjust our foreign policy to our circumstances . . .'.[5] Chamberlain assumed the premiership in May 1937 determined to end the drift and confusion of the Baldwin years and to reach agreements with Germany and Italy. To this end, and despite his very real detestation of Nazism, he applied all his considerable energy and skill. Contrary to popular mythology, Chamberlain did not envisage piecemeal concessions to buy off the dictators, but comprehensive and durable settlements of all outstanding grievances on both sides. Munich was therefore a desperate aberration from appeasement rather than its culmination. He also insisted that rearmament was the indispensable counterpart to conciliation—stronger defences would deter war while diplomacy removed its causes. The tone of diplomacy, too, was related to one's strength, for Chamberlain was sure 'that you should never menace unless you are in a position to carry out your threats'. And by the winter of 1938–39 he felt that Britain's position—both military and diplomatic—was strong enough to warrant a firmer line in negotiation with Germany.[6]

As the older myths about Chamberlain have been dispelled, some historians have gone as far as to imply that appeasement was largely an attempt to gain time until Britain was ready for war.[7] But this, it seems to me, is to overlook two fundamental, related assumptions of Chamberlain's policy—which will be recurrent themes of the first part of this book. For one thing, Chamberlain believed that allies could be liabilities as much as assets. He was concerned to preserve Britain's shaky position as a great power, and although Germany posed the principal threat almost every country was a rival in some respects. Alliances against Hitler would entail concessions and greater dependence. Thus, the French wanted British commitments to their alliance system in Eastern Europe, Russian Communism seemed a major if long-term threat to European stability, and, as we shall see, American help, even if it could be achieved, might involve too high a price. In any case, secondly, Chamberlain believed that costly alliances might not be necessary because total war could be averted. Unaware of Hitler's concept of *Blitzkrieg* warfare, he judged that Germany lacked the economic strength and political cohesion seriously to contemplate war and that she could be weaned from aggression by his blend of conciliation and firmness, carrot and stick. This conviction did not die with the German entry into Prague in March 1939, nor even with the declaration of war in September, but remained as a basis of Chamberlain's policy right up to his fall in May 1940.

The views I described above were associated particularly with Chamberlain, and also with the Treasury, over which he presided as Chancellor of the Exchequer from 1931 to 1937 and from which came his closest advisers, Sir Warren Fisher and Sir Horace Wilson. Not everyone in Whitehall completely shared their sense of possibilities and priorities. The Service ministries fought vigorously against the Treasury's efforts to co-ordinate and control their expansion programmes, while in the winter of 1937–38 Anthony Eden and some of his senior Foreign Office officials considered that Chamberlain exaggerated the unity and strength of the Axis and neglected opportunities for co-operation with Britain's friends. These disagreements were important, and, as we shall see, they were reflected in differences of opinion over policy towards the U.S.A., particularly in early 1938 and early 1940. But, when all the qualifications have been made, the attitudes just outlined were those of most British leaders. Defence planners such as Inskip, Chatfield and Hankey all accepted in principle that the economy was the 'fourth arm'; Eden and the FO objected more to the conduct of appeasement than to the policy itself and they never translated their doubts into a clear-cut alternative. And, for all the retrospective wisdom of memoir-writers, the parliamentary opposition remained muted and indecisive. Even Churchill advocated not war but negotiation from a position of strength. In short, within Chamberlain's dual policy of conciliation and firmness most positions could be accommodated. The arguments were usually about emphasis and balance—how much carrot? how much stick? All shared his concern to preserve Britain's fragile pre-eminence among world powers, and no one denied that war would be a disaster for Britain's interests, even if Chamberlain was more hopeful than most about preventing it. It is in the context of these shared assumptions that British policy towards the U.S.A. must be examined.

9

## B. British policy towards the U.S.A.—doubt, hope and fear

In the British Government's attitude towards the United States three recurrent elements may be discerned: deep cynicism about the likelihood of immediate, reliable help; a tendency to expect assistance in the long term and in time of war; and an undercurrent of anxiety that such help might compromise British interests and independence. The interplay between these three contradictory emotions of doubt, hope and fear is a major theme of this book.

In the first place, British leaders thought it quite unwise to treat the U.S. as an important and reliable factor in day-to-day diplomacy and planning. As Chamberlain told the Cabinet in December 1937: 'The Power that had the greatest strength was the United States of America, but he would be a rash man who based his calculations on help from that quarter.'[8] Few politicians and senior officials disagreed. According to contemporary clichés, often expressed with considerable bitterness and resentment, the Americans were good for words but not deeds, they would lead you up the garden path and then desert you. These judgements were based on a series of disillusioning experiences during the inter-war years, ever since what they termed America's 'betrayal' of the League of Nations in 1919–20. At least by the late 1930s there was little danger of reposing too much trust in the United States. The Administration rarely took an initiative in international affairs, and its occasional pronouncements were couched in isolationist language, reaffirming U.S. determination to avoid binding commitments. In the event of war there seemed little hope of American material help. The Johnson Act prohibited loans to governments that had defaulted on their Great War debts, and the Neutrality Act banned the sale of arms and the provision of credits to belligerents. British policy, then, was predicated on the experience of American unreliability and the assumption of American isolationism.

But there was no denying the U.S.A.'s potential as a great power. In principle, the British would have liked American help in three main ways. One was as a possible mediator, perhaps at the closing stages of negotiations or as host of an international conference. Another was through naval co-operation in the Far East, where American suspicions of the European powers were less pronounced. Finally, it was recognized that in the event of war in Europe Britain would again have to look across the Atlantic for munitions and money, if not for men. British policymakers hoped that if war did break out American support would be prompter than in 1914–18, especially if Britain were bombed. This would arouse American idealism and the sense of kinship with Britain. They therefore hoped that the U.S., though unreliable in the short term, might be 'educated' or 'wooed' into a realistic acceptance of its 'responsibilities' as a world power.

However, the process of education would still be prolonged, for American isolationism was a complex phenomenon. To British leaders, the fundamental problem was the excessive dominance of public and congressional opinion over the actions of a decentralized government. They judged the public mood to be overwhelmingly insular and isolationist, with a significant tinge of anglophobia, especially in the Midwest, which demagogues and a sen-

10

sationalist press were able to exploit. To a British élite brought up on the Burkean theory of representation, Congressmen seemed merely 'the obedient delegates of the sectional interests they represent',[9] lacking any wider sense of the public good. They agreed with Bryce that the political system was dominated by money and bereft of good leaders, and they viewed the Constitution as outdated and rigid—its eighteenth-century theories of balanced government hampering the exercise of firm, enlightened leadership. Within all these constraints, so foreign to a system of centralized parliamentary government with effective party discipline, it was clear that the Administration was isolated. British leaders did criticize Roosevelt for being timid, administratively disorganized and prone to gimmickry. But his intentions were not in doubt: '. . . I fully recognise that goodwill on the part of the U.S. Government is not wanting . . .',[10] wrote Chamberlain in January 1938. The real problem was the Administration's impotence in a fragmented political system dominated by an unrealistic public.

It was all very frustrating, for there seemed little HMG could do to improve the situation. Sir Ronald Lindsay, the British Ambassador in Washington, in an important despatch written in March 1937, set out the limits of diplomacy. He warned that U.S. neutrality must be accepted as 'something that it is useless to call in question'. That attitude 'and the native suspiciousness of foreign effort to influence it must dictate the action of His Majesty's Government. . . .' Where Congress was not involved, cautious, secret co-operation with the Administration was possible. But London should avoid taking any major political initiative or indulging in propaganda, towards which Lindsay had a rooted aversion. Nor could anything be done on the contentious issue of Britain's default on her war debts to the U.S.A., despite the ammunition this gave to 'the cheap orator'. In short, said Lindsay, 'America is the despair of the diplomat.' The only area in which significant action could safely be taken was on the question of an Anglo-American trade agreement, and this was only possible because the initiative had come from the U.S. Lindsay stressed that it would be 'most unwise' to reject any American offer of co-operation. The U.S., he wrote, 'is still extraordinarily young and sensitive. She resembles a young lady just launched into society and highly susceptible to a little deference from an older man.' Given Americans' 'famous inferiority complex' towards Britain, refusal to co-operate would be regarded as a snub. Lindsay drew particular attention to the widespread American belief that during the Manchurian crisis in 1931–33 the British had refused to co-operate with Henry Stimson, the then Secretary of State. They had felt rebuffed, and also believed that Britain's failure to follow an American lead had encouraged further Japanese aggression.[11]

The arguments Lindsay set out in this memorandum were both representative and influential. They prescribed a largely passive policy. Not only were the Americans uncooperative, but there was little that could safely be done about it. The British had to place their faith in what was sometimes called 'the educative power of events'.

But this policy rested upon deeper attitudes towards the U.S.A. as a whole. America seemed a land of 'eternal superficiality', bereft of civilization and integrity. Its people were either brash and vulgar, or else coated in a self-conscious veneer of culture. This '*de haut en bas* attitude', so resented by Americans,[12] was reflected in the frequent use by Lindsay and other British diplomats of terms such as 'educate' or 'woo', which betray the belief that America was like a youthful adolescent or a skittish belle who needed the guiding hand of John Bull. Often the guidance was seen as that of a parent to its child, because the Anglo-American tie was still conceived of by the British as fundamentally an extension of the colonial relationship. They considered the U.S.A. to be somewhere in status between a Dominion and a truly 'foreign' country. Despite its break with the Empire it still shared the language, traditions and culture, albeit in bastardized form, of the mother country. This sense of a community of ideals and values, expressed in the contemporary cliché 'the English-speaking peoples', helps to explain British hopes that the U.S.A. could eventually be drawn into effective co-operation. It also accounts for the depths of resentment felt at American isolation, which in his 1916 poem 'The Question' Kipling had gone as far as to liken to Peter's betrayal of the self-sacrificing Christ.[13]

This view of America as almost an errant Dominion can only be explained by reference to the pervasive British ignorance about U.S. life, not least among the ruling élite. For one thing America was relatively inaccessible, because regular transatlantic air services did not commence until just before war broke out and most journeys in the 1930s had to be made by lengthy and expensive sea voyage. Such contacts as did exist were usually with East Coast Republican and business circles, often of British stock and anglophile sentiments. Experience of the U.S. west of the Hudson was therefore rare, except for a minority in the artificial atmosphere of the commercial lecture circuit, and the immense ethnic diversity was rarely appreciated at first-hand or else was discounted. Most British leaders in the 1930s would have agreed with Lloyd George's comment in 1921: 'The people who govern America are our people. They are our kith and kin. The other breeds are not on top.'[14] Nor was much to be learned about America from the press. Geographically, coverage was concentrated on New York, Washington and Hollywood, where the correspondents and news agencies were based, and most attention was devoted to sensationalized 'human interest' stories such as the murder of the Lindbergh baby, the escapades of Al Capone and the life and death of Huey Long. Even more influential were the movies. Well over half the British population between the ages of 15 and 65 attended the cinema each week and American films took about 80 per cent of British screen time.[15] Although portraying only the eccentric, extravagant and violent aspects of American life, they provided a fund of basic stereotypes about the U.S.A. for British audiences. The education system offered no corrective to these distortions. Little American history, geography or literature was studied in schools and universities, and no serious steps were taken to rectify this until 1941. In short, the media only reinforced the image of America as a country in which, to quote Joseph P. Kennedy, the U.S. Ambassador to Britain from 1938 to 1940, little happened 'besides gangsters, shootings, rapes and kidnappings'.[16]

This blend of ignorance and condescension can be clearly seen in British reactions to the New Deal. Admittedly public works programmes attracted support from some union leaders and from Lloyd George in his 1935 campaign for a British 'New Deal', while among liberals of the centre—what Arthur Marwick has called 'middle opinion'—there was much informed interest in American experiments in planning, particularly the Tennessee Valley Authority.[17] But other American measures, such as the Agricultural Adjustment Act, were inapplicable to Britain, or, as in the case of unemployment insurance and social security, had already been achieved. Indeed, there was a general tendency to see the Roosevelt Administration as belatedly pulling the U.S.A. out of the era of nineteenth-century individualism and doing what the Asquith government had accomplished for Britain before the Great War. What stands out in British comment on the New Deal is the figure of Roosevelt himself—his personality and actions spotlighted and thrown into relief against the dark background of general ignorance about the U.S.A. The President's leadership also provided a convenient club with which critics could attack the National Government. However, British leaders were not impressed. Chamberlain and the Treasury were committed to balanced budgets and had no time for deficit financing. Whatever the achievements of Roosevelt's early years, Whitehall felt that by the second term he had lost his way. The foolhardy attack on the Supreme Court had mobilized opposition and produced political stalemate. The President had also lost the confidence of business, which was so important for American recovery, particularly in view of the new recession of 1937–38. The general feeling among British policymakers was summed up in this FO memo for the Cabinet in July 1938: 'The New Deal has restored order, but it has not established leadership.'[18]

$$* \qquad * \qquad *$$

These, then, are some of the attitudes towards the U.S.A. entertained in inter-war Britain. They underlie the first two elements of British policy—the hope that the U.S. might again provide help in the event of war, and the balancing doubts about American reliability. However, there is a third element, which has become clearer as the archives have been opened, and which is an essential part of British policy towards the U.S.A. This is the lurking fear that American help would prove more of a liability than an asset.

In a number of respects British and American interests conflicted in the 1930s, and this conflict generated considerable hostility and suspicion. For one thing, the two powers were economic rivals. Britain had been alarmed at American competition since the turn of the century, but the Great War and its aftermath was a crucial period, which British policymakers did not forget. It completely altered the financial position of the two countries. Britain liquidated some 10–15 per cent of her overseas assets, and struggled to attract short-term capital and to cover her persistent visible trade deficit, not least with the U.S. America became for the first time a net creditor nation and replaced Britain as the principal world source of new investment capital.[19] The result of this was an intensified rivalry for markets and raw materials, with the U.S. taking advantage of her 1914–17 neutrality and of Britain's preoccupation with the war and reconstruction to challenge British predominance in areas like Latin America. Britain's response was sluggish. Exports stagnated and she could not meet the American challenge in new industries such as telecommunications and oil. The rivalry intensified in the 1930s, as both countries tried to counter the effects of the Depression. In 1936–39 there was a bitter dispute, largely at the sub-ministerial level, over the ownership of tiny Pacific islands, which had assumed great importance because of the development of trans-oceanic aviation.[20]

As part of this rivalry, and in response to the Depression, the two countries began to follow divergent economic policies in the 1930s. In 1931–32 the National Government instituted a system of protective tariffs. Whereas in 1930 83 per cent of Britain's imports came in duty-free, the figure was only 25 per cent in 1932. Furthermore, under pressure from the Dominions, particularly at the Ottawa Conference in the summer of 1932, the Government discriminated against foreign goods, either through higher tariffs or import quotas. By 1937 23 more trade agreements had been signed with countries in Latin America, Scandinavia and Eastern Europe. This pattern of discrimination coincided with the beginnings of a 'sterling bloc' When Britain left the Gold Standard in October 1931 most of the Dominions and some other countries, all having strong commercial ties with Britain and large sterling holdings, followed suit and pegged their currencies to the pound. Many of the trade agreements of the decade were with these countries.[21]

The systematic character of these developments should not be exaggerated. The network of preferences grew up as an *ad hoc* response to the economic crisis and, whatever the expectations of the early 1930s, by 1937 most policy-makers including Chamberlain recognized that it solved few of Britain's problems. As for the sterling bloc, this was largely the formalization of existing payments patterns. A controlled Sterling Area, with exchange regulations and restrictions on currency convertibility, was a wartime innovation. Nevertheless, these developments were significant for three reasons. As we shall see, American policymakers *did* interpret them as part of a systematic effort to develop an imperial bloc, along the lines of Schacht's and Funk's programme for an autarkic German area. Secondly, the idea of imperial self-sufficiency, though rejected at the top, was strongly held by a number of prominent Tory back-benchers, notably Leo Amery and Lords Beaverbrook and Lloyd, who advocated a division of labour between the industry of Britain and the primary products of the Empire, encouraged by British capital and emigration. This 'imperial vision' no longer corresponded to the reality of Dominions industrialization, but it was proposed as the answer to Britain's problems, including that of American competition, and Amery, Beaverbrook and, briefly, Lloyd were to gain a new platform for their views after 1940 as members of the Coalition Government.[22] Finally, the framework of protective tariffs and imperial preferences commanded wide support from important business organizations, such as the Empire Industries Association, the Federation of British Industries, and the National Union of Manufacturers. These were well represented within the Tory party—the EIA, for instance, included 290 MPs, with Amery as its President—and they were an important influence on government policy.[23]

Commercial rivalry and divergent ideologies only reflected the changing power position of the two nations. British leaders vividly remembered the Great War and the haunting figure of Woodrow Wilson. In 1914–17 Wilson had been 'too proud to fight'—a phrase the British never forgot or forgave—yet increasingly he had tried to force a compromise peace upon the belligerents. Even after April 1917 the U.S. was an 'associate' rather than an 'allied' power, anxious to eliminate German militarism but also to liberalize the reactionary, imperialist tendencies of the Allies. To cap it all, they believed, Wilson had imposed an unrealistic peace settlement on the victors, without making sure that his own Congress would accept. Britain and France were left to keep the peace as best they could, without American help. This was, of course, a partisan view of Wilson—one drawn from memoir as much as memory—but as we shall see it was to colour British responses to American policies on numerous occasions during World War II.[24]

The controversy over Britain's war debts provided another instance of America's power and apparent selfishness. From 1916 the Allied war effort had been dependent upon American supplies and American credit. British debts alone amounted to over four billion dollars. In Britain and France it was felt that the debts should be written off—what the U.S. had provided in gold, they had given in blood. Whereas Americans considered Britain's default in 1934 as further evidence of her perfidy, in Britain the controversy, which dragged on throughout the 1930s, did much to establish an image of the U.S.A. as 'Uncle Shylock'.[25]

Britons discerned a similar, unfair and irresponsible assertion of power in America's conduct over naval limitation in the 1920s. The two countries had very different naval needs. For instance, as a major trading power Britain wanted numerous light cruisers to guard her extended supply routes; the U.S., economically much more self-sufficient and mainly concerned to contain Japan, desired a smaller number of more heavily-armed vessels. But beneath the clash of interests was a matter of national pride. The achievement of a 'Navy second to None'—of parity with Britain—had been a cherished goal of the U.S. Navy regardless of America's limited security needs and by the 1920s the U.S. had the power to insist on equality on its own terms. Britain's concession had been a recognition of this.[26]

Here, then, was the other element in British policy towards the United States. America was not merely a possible, if immediately unlikely, ally; she was also a potential threat to Britain's extended global position. As Chatfield recognized (epigraph to Part One), Britain's pre-eminence was still so marked—if now very shaky—that virtually every other nation was in a 'have-not' position relative to her in some respects. Of course, the conflict of interest was less direct and acute with the U.S.A. than with Germany, Italy and Japan. And, if a choice had to be made, as Gladwyn Jebb of the Foreign Office put it to a German diplomat in May 1939, he would infinitely prefer his country to become an American dominion than a German *Gau*.[27] But the hope and intent of British policy was that such a choice would *not* have to be made: that Britain could maintain her independence, and that of her Empire, against *all* the powers. Policymakers were therefore always inclined to count the costs as well as the blessings of possible American help. The example of 1914–20, as they interpreted it, figured large in these calculations. Preoccupied with war, and forced into increasing reliance upon the U.S., Britain had been unable to defend her economic interests or prevent the disastrous peace-

15

making of a bungling idealist. A new war would probably mean that once again the New World, in Thomas Jefferson's felicitous phrase, would 'fatten on the follies of the Old',[28] and would also intervene in Europe, to borrow the words used by Baldwin about the British press, with power but not responsibility. Such considerations strengthened HMG's determination to reach a settlement with the dictators.

*　　　*　　　*

British attitudes towards the United States were therefore an uneasy mixture of doubt, hope and fear. The basic recognition that Anglo-American co-operation was important, and would be vital in time of war, was tempered by the ingrained assumption of American isolationism and by the nagging anxiety that U.S. intervention, if it could be achieved, would mean inter-vention in everything. Of course there were differences of emphasis. Doubt tinged with fear was dominant in the case of Chamberlain, his leading Treasury advisers and a significant segment of Tory MPs represented by figures such as Amery. Some senior FO officials were similarly inclined, notably Sir Alexander Cadogan, the Permanent Under-Secretary. But in general the FO attached more importance to transatlantic co-operation and was more hopeful of attaining it, particularly Anthony Eden, Foreign Secretary until February 1938, but also his successor, Lord Halifax, backed by the American Department (FO/A) and by the Embassy in Washington. Their views were supported outside policy-making circles by liberals, such as Lord Lothian, and by a variety of figures across the political spectrum, ranging from Churchill to Harold Laski, whose overriding aim was an anti-fascist front among the Western democracies.

But, when all is said and done, these were differences of emphasis. Cham-berlain was not the crude Americophobe that is sometimes depicted; Eden and Churchill were both aware of the depths of American isolationism and that in some respects the U.S. posed a significant challenge to Britain's global interests. In short, these three conflicting considerations were present in the thinking of most policymakers, right through the war. How to reconcile them, how to strike a delicate balance, was the perennial problem. Chamber-lain's answer was formulated during the first nine months of his premiership.

### C. Chamberlain, Eden and the U.S.A., 1937–38

Sardonic comments about American unreliability litter Chamberlain's private papers. His maxim that 'it is always best and safest to count on nothing from the Americans but words' has become notorious.[29] Yet, as we have seen, most British leaders took a patronizing and sceptical view of the U.S.A., and, for that matter, of foreigners in general. That was the starting point for their diplomacy, not its conclusion. In other words it is not enough to cite Chamberlain's personal prejudices. One must look at what he *did*, or did not do, in order to determine his policy towards the United States.

Chamberlain came to power in May 1937 professing his keen desire to improve Anglo-American relations, and American observers such as the then Ambassador in London, Robert Bingham, believed him to be sincere.[30]

However, the outstanding Anglo-American problems, such as war debts and trade policy, were complex matters, involving many other powers. They were not susceptible of quick and simple solutions, and, given American isolationism and unreliability, there seemed no guarantee that their resolution would lead to closer transatlantic co-operation. In any case, Chamberlain's overriding goal was to reach a comprehensive settlement with the European dictators. This, he believed, could be achieved through bilateral negotiations rather than the frustrations of conference diplomacy. Every aspect of his policy towards the U.S.A. reflects this sense of priorities. For example, he agreed with Treasury officials that there was little prospect of resolving the war debts issue in the near future. The best hope was for some kind of international conference, perhaps called by Roosevelt, but *after* a European settlement had been achieved.[31] Similarly, he and the FO resisted F.D.R.'s pressure in the summer of 1937 for Chamberlain to visit the U.S.A. They argued that since the trip would attract publicity and arouse expectations it should not take place unless and until commensurate results could be anticipated. Chamberlain probably also feared that a visit, at the start of his premiership, would be taken by the dictators as further evidence of their encirclement by the democracies.[32]

A similar sense of priorities influenced Chamberlain's attitude to Anglo-American co-operation in the Far East.[33] In July 1937 hostilities between Japan and China flared up again and he and the FO pressed Washington in vain for joint mediation of the conflict. Their aim was to stabilize the situation in East Asia, so as to concentrate on European appeasement. They wanted action that would control but not provoke Japan, for fear of being faced with simultaneous crises in the Mediterranean and the Pacific. In October, therefore, Chamberlain, strongly backed by the Service departments, argued that sanctions against Japan would be pointless unless effective, and, if effective, would lead to war. Given worsening relations with Italy and the shortage of capital ships, Britain could only contemplate hostilities with Japan if she had firm guarantees of U.S. support. Even then, Chamberlain added, it was uncertain how long American public opinion would support its government.[34] The same desire not to provoke Japan, but to take limited, joint, deterrent measures if American support was assured, was apparent in December, after British and U.S. vessels had been attacked in the Yangtse. Chamberlain and his colleagues favoured a joint naval mobilization but not the American idea of financial sanctions. And when, in January 1938, Roosevelt suggested some limited, parallel naval preparations and manoeuvres these were rejected because of the absence of firm commitments and the importance of keeping the fleet in the Mediterranean to back up the impending talks with Italy.[35]

Thus Chamberlain wanted Anglo-American co-operation in principle, but only where it was consonant with his overall diplomatic goals and where U.S. support could be guaranteed. In practice these two conditions severely limited the chances of effective co-operation. But in the case of a trade agreement the conditions *could* be realized and here Chamberlain pushed forward with characteristic determination.[36] For months the U.S.A. had been pressing for an agreement and by the time he came to power Chamberlain

17

accepted the argument of Eden and Lindsay that this was the only avenue open for improving transatlantic relations. During the spring and summer of 1937 he convinced the Dominions[37] and his own Cabinet and also overrode the keen opposition of business and back-bench opinion, voiced by figures such as Amery and Sir Henry Page Croft, who argued that tariffs and imperial preferences were essential for Britain's economy and that they should only be modified, if at all, in return for substantial reduction of the U.S. tariff.[38] It is particularly significant that Chamberlain ignored this dissension within his own party when one remembers that similar business and back-bench resistance that spring had obliged him to abandon plans for a National Defence Contribution on the profits of arms manufacturers.[39] His motive in doing so was not support for the American aim of economic appeasement. By this time Whitehall agreed that the primary European problems were political and territorial. Nor did he expect significant commercial gains. As he explained in October:

> . . . the reason why I have been prepared (pace Amery and Page Croft) to go a long way to get this treaty is precisely because I reckoned it would help to educate American opinion to act more and more with us and because I felt it would frighten the totalitarians. Coming at this moment it looks just like an answer to the Berlin–Rome–Tokyo axis and will have a steadying effect.[40]

This tactic of eliciting American diplomatic support by limited commercial concessions was not a new one. It had been a familiar, if often fruitless, ploy of British leaders throughout the inter-war years, notably in the Debt Settlement of 1923. And Chamberlain had practised it as Chancellor before he came to power. In 1936 he had abandoned his earlier opposition to exchange rate stabilization except as part of an overall settlement of Anglo-American economic problems, including war debts, and had agreed to a limited tripartite agreement with the U.S. and France in the hope that this would facilitate political co-operation.[41] The search for a Trade Agreement also indicates another aspect of Chamberlain's attitude to the United States. He has often been interpreted, particularly by U.S. historians, as a Tory imperialist following in the footsteps of his father, Joseph Chamberlain, and seeking a self-sufficient imperial bloc.[42] Undoubtedly Chamberlain shared back-bench anxieties about American commercial competition and he favoured a selective protectionist policy. But, for all his expressions of filial piety after the Ottawa agreements, by 1937 he was not an imperial visionary in the manner, say, of Leo Amery. In a letter that November he stated clearly his belief that, despite the need to promote imperial trade, a deliberate diversion of trade to the Empire at the expense of foreign partners such as the U.S., Germany and France would be neither wise nor feasible.[43]

Chamberlain's fears of America were more political than economic. They related to the whole power position of the two countries, of which economic matters were only a part, albeit a very important one. Above all, he was reluctant to see the U.S.A. meddling again in the affairs of Europe. According to Ray Atherton, Counsellor at the U.S. Embassy in London, in the summer of 1937 Chamberlain felt that we were still a long way from being able to clean the slate; that in Europe he would like to see parallel action but that if it were a question of the United States going in and then going out he would rather that we never came in; what was really on his mind was a better understanding in the Far East.[44]

The comment about the U.S. going in and then going out surely refers back to the experiences of 1919–20. Chamberlain feared that American involvement in appeasement could be disruptive and unsettling, given American unreliability. Where he envisaged U.S. diplomatic help was in the final stage of negotiations. As he wrote in January 1938:

I have an idea that when we have done a certain amount of spade-work here we may want help from the U.S.A. It may well be that a point will be reached when we shall be within sight of an agreement, and yet unable to grasp it without a helping hand. In such an event a friendly and sympathetic President might be able to give just the fresh stimulus we required . . .[45]

Not surprisingly, therefore, Roosevelt's 'peace plan' of January 1938 thoroughly alarmed the Prime Minister. In a message sent via Lindsay, which arrived on 12 January, F.D.R. proposed that if the British agreed he would take a series of steps hopefully leading to international agreement on the fundamentals of world peace, including arms limitation, equal access to raw materials, and the rights and obligations of neutrals and belligerents in times of war. Roosevelt intended to announce the plan to the Washington diplomatic corps and to the world. If encouraged to proceed, he would then supervise the drafting of the agreement by delegates from the American states and European neutrals, and finally submit it for ratification either through diplomatic channels or at a world conference.[46]

Chamberlain could see numerous drawbacks. The whole idea, with its talk of fundamental principles and international conferences, must have seemed pure Wilsonianism to a leader bent on bilateral talks to discuss concrete political problems. The unaligned, mainly minor states, who would draft an agreement represented every view 'except those of the people who matter', noted Chamberlain.[47] Some aspects of the plan could only encourage the dictators, notably the emphatic reiteration of formal American isolationism and talk of the inequities of the Versailles treaty.[48] And its vagueness, together with the unexplained deadline for a British reply by 17 January, seemed another instance of American ineptitude.[49] But Chamberlain considered the plan not merely irrelevant and immature but positively dangerous. News of it had arrived at the crucial moment in appeasement. Vansittart, the obstructive and anti-German Permanent Under-Secretary at the FO, had just been replaced by the more sympathetic Cadogan. Italy was ready for conversations and hopes were high that Germany too would soon be prepared to negotiate. In short '. . . it was now or never and must be now if we were to avoid another Great War.'[50] Consequently, as the premier wrote privately, F.D.R.'s proposal came as a 'bombshell'.[51] In his diary he commented later: 'The plan appeared to me fantastic and likely to excite the derision of Germany and Italy. They might even use it to postpone conversations with us and if we were associated with it they would see it as another attempt on the part of the democratic bloc to put the dictators in the wrong.'[52] Once again it was a matter of balance and timing. Announcement of the trade negotiations, coming after the strengthening of the Axis pact, constituted a check to the dictators. Yet F.D.R.'s plan, just at the vital moment in appeasement, could drive them closer together.

Chamberlain's principal object was therefore to prevent this bombshell from exploding. But he was not indifferent to the effect of such action in Washington. He did not, as is often stated, reject Roosevelt's idea. Instead, his carefully drafted reply on 13 January explained HMG's plans for talks with Italy and Germany, suggested that the President's proposals might cut across them, and asked F.D.R. to postpone his initiative 'for a short while' to see what progress could be made by the British.[53] A week later, persuaded by Eden and the Cabinet Foreign Policy Committee who feared that F.D.R. might have been offended, he invited Roosevelt to go ahead, explaining to Lindsay that the American and British *démarches* could be seen as complementary—the one establishing general principles, the other dealing with concrete problems.[54] Thereafter the issue was in F.D.R.'s hands and for three weeks Whitehall expected him to launch the plan at any moment. Its eventual postponement was F.D.R.'s own decision. Throughout Chamberlain monitored the American reaction, as reported by Lindsay, with some anxiety. His annotations on the telegrams from Washington indicate his relief that the Administration was apparently not upset and indeed supported his efforts.[55] In other words, Chamberlain did not want the Americans involved in the detailed negotiations; but nor did he want to alienate them if at all possible. He seems to have felt that in his handling of the episode he had struck the right balance.

\*      \*      \*

During 1937–38 the main Cabinet opposition to Chamberlain's handling of Anglo-American relations came from Anthony Eden, his Foreign Secretary.[56] Eden had been the earliest Cabinet advocate of a trade agreement. He had pressed the U.S. on several occasions for joint action in the Far East—mediatory and later naval—and he favoured acceptance of F.D.R.'s limited naval measures in January 1938. In general, he was sympathetic to the feeling of some of his senior FO advisers, that the PM and Services tended to exaggerate the unity and strength of the Axis and to underestimate France and the U.S.A. as reliable allies.[57] When the news of F.D.R.'s initiative arrived Eden was away on holiday, but on his return he set out the issue starkly: 'The decision we have to take seems to me to depend on the significance which we attach to Anglo-American co-operation. What we have to choose between is Anglo-American co-operation in an attempt to ensure world peace and a piece-meal settlement approached by way of a problematical agreement with Mussolini.'[58] Eden was sure that HMG must choose the former alternative and therefore should strongly support Roosevelt's initiative. It was his advocacy, coupled with the threat of resignation, that mobilized the Foreign Policy Committee in favour of acceptance on 20–21 January.[59]

However, just as it is easy to overestimate the importance of F.D.R.'s initiative, so one can distort Eden's position in the episode. Despite his own remarks, it would seem an exaggeration to say that the issue between him and the PM was either 'to work for the appeasement of Europe or . . . to strive for an Anglo-American alliance with which to confront the dictators'.[60] For Eden, though less sanguine than Chamberlain, fully supported the idea of negotiations with Germany. He did not share the urgency felt by Chamberlain and the Services about detaching Mussolini from the Axis, but, even so, he was ready to let the talks with Italy commence, differing with Chamberlain only on how and when *de jure* recognition of the Italian conquest of Abyssinia should be given and on his condition that Italian 'volunteers' should be withdrawn from Spain before negotiations began. Chamberlain conceded most of Eden's demands. The argument, then, was more about priorities and conditions than about the principle of appeasement itself.[61] Admittedly, by the time Eden resigned on 20 February, the two men had convinced themselves that their differences were fundamental.[62] However, by that stage, working relations between them had broken down and Eden was close to nervous exhaustion. Halifax, who tried to mediate, could discern no fundamental differences, and judged that the crisis was the cumulative result of various irritants, including Eden's resentment at Chamberlain's personal diplomacy, magnified by his exhaustion and consequent lack of perspective.[63]

Similarly, over relations with the U.S., the rift seems shallower now than when Eden wrote his memoirs. On sanctions against Japan, for instance, he did not differ fundamentally with the PM. Eden agreed that these could not be contemplated unless the Administration guaranteed its help. However, contrary to Chamberlain, he felt that if such assurances were forthcoming then Britain should go ahead, trusting that they would be supported by the American public.[64] Nor, in 1938 or even in 1941, did Eden want the U.S. meddling freely and unchecked in Europe. When Lindsay suggested in mid-February that HMG might prefer Roosevelt to help in the direct conversations with the dictators rather than arrange another ineffective international conference, Eden approved his advisers' firm rejection. The danger of Lindsay's proposal was

> that the President would be associated in the conversations, although without responsibility, and would be free to make suggestions or press points on both sides. We are more susceptible to United States influence than are either Germany or Italy, and should therefore be at a disadvantage. In general, we do not want to have too much of a hand in shaping the President's course. It will be his plan—an American plan—and it seems to us that the main responsibility for it should be his.[65]

In fact, neither Eden nor Lindsay placed much faith in the plan itself, and readily admitted its difficulties from the British angle. Their main concern was that Britain should not reject any American initiative, however gauche, or even quibble too much about its details, for fear of alienating the U.S.A. (Lindsay's 'jilted woman' analogy), setting back the process of education and prejudicing the chances of American support in times of war.[66] Like Lindsay, Eden had the example of the 1931–33 Manchurian crisis very much in mind as an indication of how America would react if it felt the British would not follow if and when it led.[67] (The same historical precedent was to guide his

21

thinking over Far Eastern policy when Foreign Secretary again in 1941.) And it was on this issue—the danger of snubbing the Americans—that Eden gained support. We have seen that Chamberlain himself was not indifferent on this point. Similarly, Cadogan, Eden's Permanent Under-Secretary, who was no Americophile and had little liking for Roosevelt's 'wild ideas', was nevertheless adamant that 'what sticks out is American co-operation. We can't throw that away. . . . Whatever else may be decided, we *must not turn him down*.'[68] In the same way, when the Cabinet asked F.D.R. to go ahead, they stressed to Lindsay that they did so to prevent impairing cordial relations and that they did not want to be closely associated with a plan that seemed likely to fail.[69]

It would seem then that the depth and significance of Eden's rift with Chamberlain should not be exaggerated. They did not advocate clear-cut alternative policies. Like most statesmen they tried to balance conflicting considerations, keep open various options, apply the carrot and the stick. Given these qualifications, three areas of difference can be discerned in their approach to the U.S.A. In the first place, Eden was less optimistic than Chamberlain about the possibilities of a durable European settlement. At least he desired greater application of the stick, in the form of tougher treatment of Italy, more rapid rearmament and closer co-operation with potential allies including America. All this would serve both as pressure on the dictators and insurance in case of war. Secondly, in the latter eventuality, American help would be vital. Eden told his colleagues in December 1937 that 'it must always be our constant aim in peacetime to increase as far as possible the likelihood of the US giving us armed support in case of war'. He believed that such co-operation could be attained, that the U.S. could be educated. Chamberlain, on the other hand, did not think they could be educated in time. 'They would probably come in on our side eventually,' he observed, 'but they would probably come too late.'[70] Convinced that Germany could not sustain a long war, he believed that the first few weeks of any conflict would be crucial. Hitler would mount a great offensive, involving saturation bombing of British cities. If Britain survived then her superior economic power would tell in the long run. But in that initial assault, it seemed most unlikely that America would make any significant contribution. Thirdly, the two men differed on how America should be approached. Chamberlain took seriously the axiom that overt pressure would backfire and simply reinforce American isolationism; Eden was less cautious, and his anxious pressure, for example in Far Eastern matters in 1937, had the effect on the State Department that Chamberlain feared.[71] Such tactical differences obviously reflect the contrasting importance the two attached to wooing the U.S. Why, in Chamberlain's view, invest much time and energy in a fairly hopeless venture? But fear as well as doubt played a part. If the U.S. would do little in the crucial first stage of the war, and if thereafter the British Empire's prospects were good, significant U.S. help would not be necessary. And this would avoid concessions to and co-operation with a power that had proved herself to be a peacetime rival as well as a difficult and demanding ally in war. In short, although the appearance of Anglo-American co-operation might be a valuable additional pressure on the dictators to negotiate,

Chamberlain did not consider real American help to be likely, necessary or entirely desirable. After Eden resigned it was not until early 1940 that Chamberlain's approach to Anglo-American relations was again seriously questioned.[72]

## D. American images of Britain

What is striking about the U.S. in the 1930s, no less than Britain, is the basic ignorance about the other country and the prevalence of historically-rooted stereotypes. But whereas prejudices about the U.S. were strictly peripheral to Britain's national self-image, the inhabitants of the New World had defined their identity self-consciously by reference to the Old. As one historian has put it: 'It has been as hard for the American to see Europe realistically as it has been for him to see clearly his own country, because he has almost always understood himself only in relation to Europe.'[73]

This relationship was complex and ambivalent. On the one hand, Americans were fascinated by British traditions and institutions. When the King and Queen visited Washington in June 1939 the whole city stopped work. Even traditionally anglophobe newspapers such as the *Chicago Tribune* gave the event exhaustive coverage, well aware that, like the Abdication and Coronation, it excited enormous public interest.[74] This interest was facilitated by the common language and strengthened by the numerous ties of kinship with Britain, particularly in the South. American press and radio coverage of Britain was far fuller than the British media's treatment of the U.S.A. Although English history had virtually disappeared as a separate high school subject by the 1930s, it had been widely taught in the first quarter of the century, and about three-quarters of the books in literature courses continued to be by British authors.[75] There was also a strong sense that the two countries shared a common liberal political tradition, characterized by the rule of law and respect for the individual, which had originated in Britain. The British played shrewdly on this, for example making the Lincoln copy of the Magna Carta the much-publicized centre-piece of their exhibit at the 1939 New York World's Fair.[76]

On the other hand, there was a deep conviction that Britain was not a genuine democracy. Americans were ever alert to evidence of the 'class system'—the divide between what one commentator called 'cap-in-hand England' and 'old-school-tie England'[77]—usually contrasting it with the supposed 'classlessness' of their own country. And they tended to attribute most of Britain's failings, at home and abroad, to the machinations or ineptitude of the 'ruling class'.[78] There was also an insensitivity to the nuances of British politics. After talking with Chamberlain and Halifax in the spring of 1938 Herbert Hoover, hardly a radical himself, dismissed them as typical Tories in the mould of Palmerston and Salisbury.[79] This somewhat dated view of Britain, reinforced by the movies and classic novels, is not surprising. Ever since the Great War immigration from the U.K. had constituted 7 per cent of America's total, and in 1938 the figure was down to 3 per cent. In Chicago in 1940 it was estimated that nearly half the adult population did not generally speak English in their homes.[80] Not only were the living ties with

23

Britain weakening, they were also of diminishing political importance. In major cities like New York, Chicago and Boston, the old WASP political leaders had been displaced by representatives of newer, non-British ethnic groups of Irish, Polish or Italian descent, who achieved considerable prominence within the Roosevelt coalition. Some of these newer immigrants retained suspicions of Britain that derived from their families' European background, while, for others, hostility towards England was often bound up with opposition to the 'Anglo' political and financial interests which still exercised a disproportionate hold over national politics.

Anglophile or anglophobe, Americans could not escape their national past. As Henry Cabot Lodge had written in 1913: 'The colonial attitude of mind was displayed as clearly by the deep hatred of England which most Americans felt as it could have been by the most servile admiration.'[81] Just as the condescending British view of the U.S., as an immature but fundamentally British society, was still that of a mother country to her former colony, so American feelings towards Britain reflected the experiences of the Revolutionary era. Indeed, British visitors to the U.S.A. sometimes remarked that American perceptions had not evolved since 1776.[82] 'Tory' remained a historically and emotionally loaded word, associated with treason and privilege. It connoted Lord North, rather than, say, Disraeli, just as the 'British Empire' suggested the 'Intolerable Acts' and not the 1931 Statute of Westminster. The political turmoil in India, for instance, was usually treated as a contemporary analogue of America in the 1770s, with little appreciation of the problems of religion and caste.[83] Most Americans knew nothing about Britain's devolution of power to the white Dominions, and even to India in such matters as fiscal policy, and the moral connotations of 'Empire', which were part of the heritage of Britons raised on Curzon and Kipling, went largely unnoticed.

Interestingly, this ambivalence towards Britain is often found within individuals. The British did not always perceive this. They tended to categorize Americans as either anglophile or anglophobe. In fact, many were both—anglophile culturally and anglophobe politically. Woodrow Wilson was a good example. He loved the English countryside, immersed himself in English literature and often took English political institutions as a model. Yet he also entertained a deep distrust of the English ruling class and its self-interested, imperialist policies.[84] This combination is also characteristic of American policymakers in the 1930s, not least Franklin Roosevelt. Born in 1882, he grew up in a rich, cosmopolitan family in up-state New York at a time when the idea of an Anglo-Saxon race, with its distinctive character and responsibilities, had been fashionable. Although that racial concept died away after the 1900s Roosevelt continued to share the WASP sense of community with the British and often referred to them in private correspondence as 'cousins'.[85] During his years in Washington as Assistant Secretary of the Navy (1913–21) he had made a number of close British friends, and in 1919 had become a Vice-President of the English-Speaking Union, formed 'to promote good fellowship among the English-speaking democracies of the world'.[86] He also believed in the need for Anglo-American naval co-operation in the face of aggressive German militarism—a policy associated particularly with Admiral Mahan which was strongly held in parts of the U.S. Navy during the Great War.

But although discerning compelling reasons of ideology and strategy for Anglo-American co-operation, Roosevelt had no intention, as he put it in October 1937, of appearing to tie U.S. policy 'as a tail to the British kite'.[87] His dislike of British imperialism is well known, and by 1941 the British Embassy in Washington routinely warned any British visitor to the White House that the President's opening gambit would probably be some crack at the Empire.[88] He also shared the characteristic American suspicion of the British upper class, ascribing the failings of Britain's policy to 'too much Eton and Oxford',[89] and frequently criticized the selfishness of her diplomacy. In 1936 he observed that 'when you sit around a table with a Britisher he usually gets 80% out of the deal and you get what is left'.[90] Nor did Roosevelt have much affection for Chamberlain, of whom he commented at the same time: 'we must recognize that fundamentally he thoroughly dislikes Americans'. Reports during the winter of 1936–37 must have confirmed such opinions,[91] and it is unlikely that they were much altered by Bingham's more favourable comments when Chamberlain became premier. For Roosevelt, as for many 'New Dealers' of the 1930s, Chamberlain and the 'Birmingham crowd' were part of the pernicious Wall Street–City of London axis of capital and industry which they saw at the root of many of America's problems. In short, although anxious for Anglo-American co-operation, Roosevelt was determined that it would be co-operation on America's terms and to America's advantage, and not, as one of his emissaries put it, a relationship similar to that 'between the automobile and the chauffeur—with England in the driver's seat'. That was fundamental to his foreign policy.

### E. Towards a coherent foreign policy—the United States, 1937–38

To talk about 'the U.S. policy' towards Europe in the mid-1930s is somewhat misleading. It implies a unity and continuity of thought and action that did not then exist. This is particularly apparent if we compare Washington with London.

For one thing, foreign policy only becomes urgent and central when there is a widespread sense that a country's security is threatened. This was not the case in Britain until 1938, and in the U.S.A. until the summer of 1940. If the British were able to ignore the continent behind the security of the English Channel, how much more comfortable could Americans feel across 3,000 miles of ocean? For much of the decade, therefore, American politics turned on the Depression—graver than anywhere else except Germany—and on the New Deal's efforts to solve it. The great issues of 1937 were Roosevelt's ill-conceived attempt to reform the Supreme Court, and from August, the renewed recession. Foreign policy was not the subject of hard, sustained thought, and the old shibboleths of the isolationist tradition gained new sanctity in the mid-1930s from the danger of another European war and from American disillusionment with the previous one.

One must also remember the nature of the American political system. The legislature plays a crucial part in conducting foreign affairs, notably through

Congress' power to declare war and vote appropriations and the Senate's role in ratifying treaties and approving ambassadorial appointments. Not only are these powers jealously guarded, but, in a non-parliamentary system where party divisions are less important and party discipline less effective than in Britain, it is often difficult for an Administration to impose policy on a recalcitrant Congress. Major pieces of legislation are usually a compromise among various groups, rather than a direct expression of the President's wishes. This was clearly true of the Neutrality Acts which provided the framework for American diplomacy in the 1930s.

Nor is the Administration itself a monolith. Like most reforming presidents, Roosevelt learned that to control the country he first had to control Washington, but it was only in 1939 that his efforts at executive reorganization achieved even limited success, and this was in domestic affairs. The U.S. Cabinet had little of the collective decision-making function of its namesake in London, and there was nothing comparable to the British system of Cabinet committees and secretariats to formulate and implement policy. With only a tiny White House staff to monitor their actions, departments therefore tended to go their own way in their own domains.

In such a system much depended on the President himself, but Roosevelt was not the sort to promote coherence and decisiveness. He was a consummate politician, blessed with an outstanding creative political imagination and with an ability to dramatize a given situation in a vivid and appealing way. Lend-Lease provides a supreme example of these gifts. But he lacked Chamberlain's more prosaic but equally valuable capacity to examine a problem, formulate a solution and then put it into effect—a virtue which, admittedly, through Chamberlain's obstinacy, could become a vice. F.D.R. was notoriously indifferent to details—discussing policy with him, noted Henry Stimson on one occasion, 'is very much like chasing a vagrant beam of sunshine around a vacant room'.[92] He was also a casual administrator. In part, as apologists emphasize, he deliberately divided tasks between different, often antipathetic, individuals or departments so that only he would have overall responsibility for important decisions. But that philosophy of divide and rule often broke down because F.D.R. tended to divide without ruling effectively himself. We shall see on several occasions that he failed to 'tie up the loose ends' of policy at times of crisis.[93] Roosevelt also had a very cautious conception of presidential leadership, particularly in foreign affairs. As Robert Sherwood has written: 'The tragedy of Wilson was always somewhere within the rim of his consciousness.'[94] Whereas Wilson had adopted a very direct approach, modelled to some extent on the British parliamentary system, with the president giving a firm and decisive lead, Roosevelt, mindful of Wilson's rigidity and his failure to carry Congress and people with him in 1919–20, saw his role as that of spokesman rather than arbiter of the national will. He was the supreme exponent of consensus-building, keeping his goals flexible and vague, constantly modifying them to accommodate powerful pressure groups in the bureaucracy, Congress or country, often opting for messy, short-term compromises in the confidence that changing events and his own powers of persuasion would eventually ensure the desired outcome. But the caution of Roosevelt's diplomacy in the

1930s cannot be attributed wholly to his sensitivity to public opinion. As scholars have shown, the relationship of president and public in American foreign policy-making is complex and often circular.[95] Roosevelt tended to operate on a principle of 'selective inattention',[96] heeding those notes from the discordant noise of the *vox populi* that harmonized with his own inclinations. And those inclinations, particularly in the 1930s, were basically cautious and also uncertain—reflecting his great belief in keeping options open and avoiding binding commitments. As I shall argue throughout the book the ambiguities of F.D.R.'s foreign policy grew as much out of his own character and attitudes as they did out of his celebrated deference to the dictates of public opinion.[97]

For all these reasons, therefore—the unimportance of foreign affairs, the strength of isolationist sentiment, the fragmented nature of Congress and bureaucracy, and the personality of F.D.R. himself—American diplomacy in the 1930s approximates more to what political scientists call the 'bureaucratic politics' model of foreign policy-making than to that of the 'unitary agent'. According to the latter model a government's foreign policy can be understood on the analogy of an individual's purposive action—a deliberate choice of what seems to be the best means to reach a defined goal, after discussion of all the various alternatives. Clearly this was not true of Washington in the 1930s. Instead one finds a series of initiatives by rival government departments, supplemented by occasional forays by the President, largely uncoordinated, often at odds with each other and reflecting the different interests and perceptions of the individuals and groups involved. Moreover, in a confused diplomatic situation, there was no single defined goal, but a mixture of desiderata which U.S. leaders, and particularly Roosevelt himself, tried to keep in mind.[98]

\*     \*     \*

Perhaps the clearest view of the international scene was that of Cordell Hull, F.D.R.'s Secretary of State. Hull was an unreconstructed Wilsonian, convinced that disarmament, self-determination, non-violent change and the reduction of commercial rivalry were the foundations of world peace. In principle he also remained committed to collective security, but was slow to translate words into action, partly because he feared entanglement in British policy, partly because as an ex-Congressman he was acutely sensitive to opinion on Capitol Hill. Indeed, it was for political reasons that F.D.R. had chosen him as Secretary in 1933 and retained him until 1944. Hull's prestige on the Hill was often invaluable to the Administration, and it was enhanced during 1937–38 by his monotonous public preaching of the Wilsonian gospel. The goal of Hull's practical diplomatic efforts was peace through prosperity, by negotiating Reciprocal Trade Agreements to reduce tariffs and eliminate discriminatory practices in international trade. By the mid-1930s he saw the destruction of Britain's imperial preference system as essential for a liberal world economy.[99]

Hull loathed matters of administration and personnel, and beneath him the State Department had polarized into a protracted struggle between the self-styled 'realists' and those they termed 'idealists'.[100] The distinction was not that of isolationists and interventionists. 'Realists' were as concerned as any about German ambitions in the Americas, while no 'idealist' wanted the U.S. involved in another war. Nor was it a crude conflict between anglo-phobes and anglophiles, because the 'idealists' had little affection for Chamberlain and no desire to become a British satellite.[101] Nevertheless, this comment on Norman Davis, F.D.R.'s principal 'roving ambassador' of the 1930s, probably accurately summarizes the attitude of most of the 'idealists'. According to Moffat, Davis started 'on the premise that the existence of the British Empire is essential for the national security of the United States and that while we should not follow Great Britain nevertheless we should not allow the Empire to be endangered'.[102]

To the 'realists' such 'messianic' arguments seemed likely to bring the U.S. into another war on Britain's side. And by the spring of 1938 they had become established at the top of the Department, with the disgrace of Davis after the Brussels conference and the appointment of Adolf Berle as a new Assistant Secretary in March. The other principal 'realists' were Sumner Welles, the Under-Secretary, like Berle a Roosevelt appointee and friend, and Jay Pierrepont Moffat, head of the European desk again from July 1937, after a spell as Consul-General in Canberra. These men shared a deep and dated suspicion of perfidious Albion. Despite his impeccable WASP credentials Moffat resented intensely the British habit of 'treating us as their seventh dominion' and even repudiated the English cultural connection as alien and un-American.[103] All supported Hull's trade policy, but with a sharper sense of the commercial rivalry between Britain and the U.S. Ever mindful of the previous war, they were sensitive to evidence of Britain's entangling tentacles and felt sure she could not be trusted as an ally. Instead, they believed, the U.S. should pursue its traditional, independent foreign policy, based on a realistic and limited definition of its interests. And while the Germans posed a possible threat to the Americas, that could be met by hemisphere defence. Welles had pioneered the 'Good Neighbor' policy and he and Berle believed strongly in the concept of a separate, viable Western Hemisphere. By remaining aloof from the European turmoil, they also foresaw a possible role for the U.S. as leader of a neutral arbitrating bloc. As we shall see, Welles pressed this idea in 1937–38, and again in early 1940.

Hull's caution and his subordinates' 'realism' increasingly angered other members of the Administration, notably Harold Ickes, the abrasive Secretary of the Interior, and Henry Morgenthau, F.D.R.'s highly-strung Treasury Secretary. Both these men had begun to see world events in terms of a global contest between democracy and dictatorship. During the winter of 1937–38 Ickes was beginning to feel that the U.S. would probably have to fight for democracy at some point and that it would be better and safer to do so soon rather than too late.[104] Both men found State unbearably cautious: 'Hull has become so timid that he tries to walk without casting a shadow', wrote Ickes in September 1937.[105] And both were inveterate bureaucratic imperialists. They therefore used the powers vested in them to harass the fascists wherever possible—Morgenthau manipulating currency policy to aid China; Ickes fighting single-handed against the whole Cabinet, including, by May 1938, Morgenthau and Roosevelt, to prevent the sale of helium to Germany.[106]

Once again, neither could be termed a natural friend of Britain. Long-term, if not always central, aims for Morgenthau were the development of a U.S. currency bloc and the shift of financial power from Britain to the U.S.A.[107] But, given their sense of an overriding threat to democracy, they were readier for Anglo-American co-operation than the top echelon of State.

Perhaps the fundamental element in Roosevelt's own thinking on foreign affairs was his determination to avoid American involvement in another major conflict of the sort fought on the Western Front between 1914 and 1918. 'I am a pacifist', he told his Cabinet in September 1937,[108] and it would seem that he was being quite sincere when he spoke in vivid and emotional language about the horrors of warfare, for example in his celebrated Chautauqua speech of August 1936.[109] It is also clear that he subscribed to some parts of the revisionist argument about how the U.S.A. had entered the Great War. For Roosevelt, as for most Americans in the early 1930s, Wall Street and Big Business were the scapegoats for most foreign and domestic ills. The revelations of the 1934–36 Nye Committee, and of literary popularizers, encouraged the widespread belief that the U.S. had entered the war in 1917 to safeguard the vested interests of bankers and munitions manufacturers in an Allied victory. Roosevelt was sympathetic to this argument. He certainly favoured careful regulation of the arms industry and its profits. But he rejected the idea of an Administration–Wall Street conspiracy and seems to have ascribed the blame for American entry primarily to Wilson's extreme defence of neutral rights and to the consequent 'incidents' on the high seas. By 1935, in a complete reversal of his own wartime position, Roosevelt was saying privately that Bryan, Wilson's Secretary of State, had been right in 1915, and that he wanted legislation to prevent U.S. citizens and vessels from entering belligerent ports in wartime. Indeed, it was he who encouraged the Nye Committee to turn its hand to drafting neutrality legislation.[110]

Yet all this is not to say, as Robert Divine has argued, that Roosevelt was simply an isolationist in the mid-1930s.[111] Pacifism and the 'devil theory of war' were only two elements in inter-war isolationism.[112] Another was the Washingtonian conviction that peace was divisible and that the U.S. could remain safe within the Western Hemisphere even if the world was at war. Roosevelt, however, believed that the old oceanic barriers were no longer effective in an era of air power, and he was particularly anxious about Nazi subversion in Latin America. Nor did he share the isolationists' belief that international affairs were irredeemably amoral. Although his support for Hull's programme was sometimes tenuous, particularly in 1933–34, he fully agreed that disarmament and economic liberalization were fundamentals of world peace. From the summer of 1936 he toyed with various proposals for furthering these ends, particularly that of another international peace conference, perhaps at sea, convened under his own leadership. His intermittent overtures to individual European leaders, for example pressing Chamberlain to visit Washington in the summer of 1937, were part of this vague plan.[113] The problem was to find means that were effective abroad and acceptable at home, and by the 1930s he saw little point or possibility of America joining the League of Nations. To Wilsonian critics of this apostasy he insisted that his commitment to Wilson's ideals was unimpaired: he was looking for 'the best modern vehicle' to reach those ideals, more suited to contemporary circumstances.[114] How to maintain world peace and order, without becoming overcommitted or entangling the U.S.A. in another war—this was the fundamental problem.

One possible answer was provided by the Neutrality Acts. Roosevelt's attitude to this legislation was characteristically equivocal, and this equivocation, not always emphasized by historians, was central to his policy well into 1941. As we have just seen, he favoured restrictions on the movement of American citizens and vessels in time of war. His intent was to keep control of U.S. policy and not allow the country to be entangled in a conflict through 'incidents' provoked by the wilful or selfish acts of private individuals. But he also wanted discretionary powers so that he could apply an arms embargo only against the aggressor states in a war. In this way he would be able to align himself with any sanctions imposed by the League. He failed to get these powers in 1935, and indeed until the autumn of 1939, largely because he attached greater priority to domestic issues and would not risk a fight on foreign policy. But even in 1939, as we shall see, he deliberately maintained a balance—a discriminatory arms embargo *and* mandatory restrictions on travel on belligerent ships or into belligerent ports. Insulated against dangerous entanglements, the U.S. could safely co-operate in a limited way in international collective security.[115]

But by the autumn of 1937, after Abyssinia, the Rhineland, Spain and renewed Sino-Japanese conflict, collective security was clearly a dead letter and Roosevelt began to explore new methods of containing war without over-committing the U.S.A. In mid-September he suggested to Ickes that peace-loving nations might be encouraged to cut off trade with aggressor nations, thereby denying them vital raw materials. He stressed that he was trying to develop a policy for the future: nothing could be done about Spain or China.[116] In his celebrated speech in Chicago on 5 October, borrowing an analogy apparently suggested by Ickes, F.D.R. likened world lawlessness to an epidemic of a contagious disease and reminded his listeners that, in the case of physical disease, the community quarantined patients for the health of all.[117] But the President had no specific plan in mind. He was speaking to test and reassure public opinion—as he put it the next day to reporters, his address stated 'an attitude'; the Administration was 'looking for a program' by which to implement it.[118] He did not formulate that 'program' until mid-December, during the '*Panay* crisis' caused by the Japanese sinking of a U.S. gunboat in the Yangtse river. Pressed by the British to enter into naval staff talks and by the U.S. Navy to go to war, Roosevelt told his Cabinet that he wanted to control Japan but by means short of formal war. He spoke of a possible future Anglo-American naval blockade of Japan, together with economic sanctions. But, he added: '. . . We don't call them economic sanctions; we call them quarantines. We want to develop a technique which will not lead to war. We want to be as smart as Japan and as Italy. We want to do it in a modern way.'[119] He outlined the same ideas to Lindsay, the British Ambassador, as he took up the British suggestion of naval talks. Lindsay found the President 'in his worst "inspirational" mood',

30

and disputed his claim that a blockade would not mean war. But Roosevelt insisted that there was a new doctrine and technique as to what constituted war. His plan was within the constitutional rights of the Executive, he maintained, and there were precedents in U.S. history for the country being involved in hostilities without being formally at war.[120]

Little came of Roosevelt's 'inspiration' at the time. He had always talked of quarantine only as a possible technique for the future, and the *Panay* crisis was settled diplomatically by Christmas. In general, the Administration's public stance on Far Eastern problems, as indicated for example at the Brussels conference in November, combined stern moral condemnation of Japanese aggression with a pronounced determination to avoid being entangled in any international action. However, the episode was of considerable significance for the future. For one thing, as we shall see in the next chapter, the secret Anglo-American naval talks, which took place in London in January 1938, were the first tentative moves towards formal Anglo-American military co-operation. Moreover, the concept of quarantining the aggressors by sanctions and blockade was to prove a seminal idea. Roosevelt reverted to it on various occasions before Pearl Harbor, particularly with reference to the Far East, and it became the basis of his thinking on post-war peace-keeping in 1941 and after.[121] Of particular importance is his insistence that he could take such actions without becoming officially involved in war. The Italians in Abyssinia, the Japanese in China and the Germans and Italians in Spain had practised the doctrine of 'undeclared war', and Roosevelt argued that others could play the same game. The attraction of this modern technique was not simply that it would enable him to engage in collective international action while avoiding formal belligerency. The measures he envisaged could be taken on his own authority as President and Commander-in-Chief, without recourse to a hostile and isolationist Congress. To help quarantine the aggressors without involving the U.S. in war became the theme of F.D.R.'s diplomacy from Munich onwards, growing by 1941, as we shall see, into the tactic of limited, undeclared war.

All this should not suggest, however, that Roosevelt was seriously contemplating hostilities at this stage; for the winter of 1937–38 also saw the Administration's most determined attempt to secure an international settlement—the Roosevelt–Welles initiative presented to Chamberlain on 12 January 1938.[122] As we have noted, the idea of another international conference organized by the U.S.A. had been in the President's mind since the summer of 1936. It was revived by Welles and Berle in October 1937, as a way of giving substance to the ideas expressed in the Quarantine Speech. The plan illustrates again the Administration's basic Wilsonianism. Its core was disarmament and equal access to raw materials.[123] Neutral opinion would have a major role in preparing the agreement, and the whole process would culminate ideally in another great international conference. But increasingly F.D.R. modified this Wilsonian plan to make it complementary to British and French peace efforts.[124] Welles and Berle had wanted to announce it independently, without consulting the British, to maximize its impact and avoid being obstructed in London, as Wilson and House had been in 1916. Hull, however, was moving cautiously towards limited Anglo-American co-

31

operation, envisaging his coveted trade agreement as part of a loose under-standing with Britain which would provide a basis of strength from which to negotiate with Germany.[125] He insisted, and Roosevelt apparently agreed, that Welles' plan should receive British approval before it was presented to the world.[126]

Historians usually assert that Chamberlain's cool response 'sorely dis-appointed FDR',[127] but in fact it is quite likely that the President was never very enthusiastic about Welles' plan and only took it up because he was anxious to fill what seemed to be a very dangerous diplomatic vacuum in Europe. Washington knew little of Chamberlain's detailed preparations for talks with Italy and Germany. Indeed, it is significant that the main positive result of the whole episode was an agreement with Britain for a fuller sharing of political and diplomatic intelligence, particularly about Europe. The initiative for this came from Hull and Welles, which suggests that the Administration had become aware that it had previously been ill-informed.[128] Once apprised of British plans by Chamberlain on 14 January, F.D.R. 'readily agree[d]' to postpone action for a short time.[129] On 21 January, after Eden's intervention, HMG invited him to proceed and there was a period of nearly two weeks before Hitler's purge of the Berlin bureaucracy on 4 February, which finally killed the plan, during which the President could have gone ahead. The British fully expected him to do so.[130] It seems likely that as with the Quarantine Speech F.D.R. had no real programme[131] and that he was quite happy to let the British provide one.

What then was Roosevelt's attitude to British appeasement? Broadly speaking, he seems to have approved of its goals, while avoiding any public identification and expressing private doubts about the morality and prac-ticality of Britain's concessions. In March he wrote of Chamberlain in these terms, using a small-town analogy typical of the vernacular of American diplomacy:

> As someone remarked to me—'If a Chief of Police makes a deal with the leading gangsters and the deal results in no more hold-ups, that Chief of Police will be called a great man—but if the gangsters do not live up to their word the Chief of Police will go to jail.' Some people are, I think, taking very long chances . . .

As to whether Chamberlain would succeed, he told his Ambassador in Madrid: 'It is impossible to guess. But fundamentally, you and I hate compromise with principle.'[132] These mixed feelings were reflected in public policy. When the Anglo-Italian agreement was concluded in April 1938 Halifax indicated that favourable comment from Washington would be greatly appreciated. The U.S. response, drafted by Welles and approved by F.D.R., praised the fact that problems had been resolved by peaceful negotiation, while studiously refraining from comment on the contents of the agreement, including Britain's *de jure* recognition of Italian conquests in Abyssinia.[133]

In general, therefore, two observations can be made about Roosevelt's diplomacy in the winter of 1937–38. Firstly, he inclined increasingly towards carefully defined co-operation with the British. Quarantine began as an idea for all peace-loving nations to deny raw materials to the aggressor states and developed into the concept of an Anglo-American naval blockade of Japan. The Welles peace plan was transformed from a unilateral appeal to world opinion into an initiative parallel and then subordinate to British appeasement. Although both Roosevelt's schemes made little progress, they did result in each case in closer Anglo-American collaboration—through the naval talks and through a fuller exchange of diplomatic information. Secondly, F.D.R., like Chamberlain, was hedging his bets, hesitantly preparing for the possibility of war while working intermittently to preserve peace. On the one hand were the seminal ideas of quarantine and undeclared war; on the other was the new peace plan and then the acquiescence in British appeasement. Whatever F.D.R.'s private scruples, he had no alternative policy to offer, and he waited to see if Chamberlain could succeed. Like the British, Roosevelt was engaged in a diplomatic balancing act, trying to keep his options open as he peered into an uncertain future.

## F. The Czech crisis, March–September 1938

A brief glance at the Czech crisis will sum up many of the themes of this chapter and indicate the limits of the Anglo-American relationship in 1937–38.

In this polyglot state—'Czecho-Germano-Polano-Magyaro-Rutheno-Roumano–Slovakia', as Mussolini once called it—about a quarter of the population were Germans, the so-called Sudetens, and they were encouraged by Hitler in their growing demands for autonomy. HMG's aim was to avoid an international crisis by pressing the Czechs to reach an internal settlement with the Sudetens.[134] But in mid-September, the Sudetens broke off negotiations and declared for union with the Reich. Chamberlain obtained agreement from a divided Cabinet on the principle of an orderly cession of territory to Germany, together with a guarantee of the remainder of the Czech state. But the demands Hitler made at Godesberg, particularly on the speed of the transfer and on the lack of international supervision, were unacceptable to the French and to most of the Cabinet, and Chamberlain was obliged to concur. By 27 September war seemed certain. However, pressed by Mussolini, Hitler drew back from force and agreed to a four-power conference at Munich on 29–30 September, at which he achieved the substance of his demands under a more orderly façade.

Throughout the crisis the Roosevelt Administration had no intention of going to war.[135] However, the State Department in particular wished to avoid stating this publicly, otherwise American diplomatic influence would be largely negated. The U.S. tactic was therefore to 'embroider on the theme of the eternal question mark of American foreign policy'[136]—creating doubt in Britain that she could count on U.S. help and in Germany that she could rely on American isolation. The U.S., like the European powers that summer, was engaged in a diplomatic guessing game. Indeed, their tactic towards the British—which seemed typically irresponsible to London—was very similar to the evasive line the British had been taking with the French.[137] But, just as HMG was eventually obliged to commit itself to the Czechs and the French, so the Administration too was forced off the fence by events in early Sep-

33

tember, and particularly by British efforts, abetted by the U.S. Ambassador in London, Joseph Kennedy, to associate the U.S.A. with their policy. Consequently F.D.R. shelved tentative plans for possible economic action against Germany, and stated at a press conference on 9 September that reports of an Anglo-American-French front against Germany were 'about one hundred per cent wrong'.[138] With the guessing game over, the Administration stuck to what the State Department dignified as a 'policy of non-action', although it was disgusted by the 'betrayal' of Czechoslovakia, and F.D.R. talked privately about England and France washing 'the blood from their Judas Iscariot hands'.[139] Only during the stalemate over the Godesberg terms did F.D.R., pressed by Bullitt, his Ambassador in Paris, revive the idea of a conference, but the cautious Hull insisted that America should not be involved even as an intermediary. This reduced the initiative, as Hull's advisers admitted, to an appeal that the Europeans keep talking.[140] A similar message, again emphasizing formal U.S. isolation, was sent to Hitler on the 27th, and also a telegram urging Mussolini to use his influence to secure a conference.[141] Subsequently the Administration was anxious to claim great significance for its diplomatic *démarches*, especially the message to Mussolini, but in fact it played only a minor role in the crisis.

Certainly the British never placed much faith in the U.S. When the fundamentals of HMG's Czech policy were decided in March, the PM reminded his colleagues that he 'saw no reason to suppose that the United States were prepared to intervene in Europe'.[142] And in September, apart from Kennedy's efforts and the presence of two U.S. warships in British waters, the Cabinet found little in U.S. policy but the usual blend of fine words and minimal action.[143] Although, as Washington suspected, the British were not above using U.S. isolationism as a convenient scapegoat,[144] the lack of U.S. support at most confirmed the direction of British policy. The decisive reasons for their handling of the Czech crisis were the moral ambiguities of the Sudeten problem, the impossibility of defending Czechoslovakia now that Germany controlled Austria, the desire to avoid continental commitments particularly to France, and the continued hope of averting war through a comprehensive Anglo-German agreement.

In fact, the crisis only reinforced the basic British attitudes towards the U.S.A. which I have already outlined. In an important telegram on 12 September, Lindsay stated that Roosevelt was personally willing to provide everything except troops and loans, but that his actions would depend on the dictates of public opinion and domestic politics. Lindsay believed that if war did break out, the U.S. would become a belligerent in far less time than the two-and-a-half years that had elapsed before April 1917. However, he added, 'it will seem very long to us.'[145] Here again was the familiar combination of short-term doubts and long-term hopes that made it so difficult to calculate America's significance in international affairs. And, behind all this, the fear of American power was perhaps not entirely absent. At least one might infer so from the fact that in late September Hull felt it necessary to assure Lindsay that the U.S. would not take advantage of a European war to capture Britain's trade. 'The Ambassador', wrote Hull, 'seemed much moved and expressed his appreciation.'[146]

As far as Chamberlain and Halifax were concerned, probably the most important expression of American intentions came from the President himself. On the evening of 19 September he spoke with Lindsay, informing only Morgenthau and possibly Bullitt of his intentions, and then only in general terms. According to Lindsay, Roosevelt confessed himself impotent in the present crisis and 'spoke in a friendly and appreciative manner of the Prime Minister's policy and efforts for peace. If the policy now embarked on proved successful he would be the first to cheer.' He suggested that if war could be averted a world conference should be called to revise unsatisfactory frontiers along rational lines. He himself would be willing to attend, but only if the meeting were held outside Europe, say in the Azores. But assuming, as then seemed likely, that peace could not be maintained, F.D.R. urged the Allies to fight a defensive war, based on blockade. If they did so, and if the blockade were effective and acceptable to U.S. opinion, he might be able to recognize it and so assist the blockading powers. While he could not avoid applying the embargo on arms sales if war were declared, he stressed that this might not be necessary if a formal declaration could be avoided. In any case, he said, the Allies could legally import munitions parts from America into Canada, for shipment on to Europe. During the conversation, Lindsay found the President 'quite alive to the possibility that somehow' the U.S. might find itself again in a European war. But it seemed to F.D.R. almost inconceivable that he would be politically able to send American troops across the Atlantic, except, just possibly, if a massive German invasion of Britain led to a wave of emotion in the U.S.A.[147]

Roosevelt's comments reflected many of his underlying ideas: appeasement, conference, blockade, biased neutrality. In talking to Lindsay he was sticking his neck out a long way. He stressed the need for absolute secrecy and warned that if what he said leaked out he would probably be impeached. Some U.S. historians, conscious of the domestic enormity of the President's remarks, have criticized HMG for ignoring them.[148] In part, this was probably due to Roosevelt's own insistence on secrecy. The message was not seen by the FO's American or Central departments until after Munich, and probably only circulated at first among Chamberlain, Halifax and Cadogan, and their private secretaries. Lindsay had initially indicated that no reply was required. It was only on his later suggestion that Halifax sent a message of thanks.[149] Furthermore, as with F.D.R.'s other initiatives, there seemed to be numerous drawbacks. The idea of another conference to redraw the map of Europe got short shrift. The head of the FO's American Department later remarked that 'judging by the lamentable precedent of President Wilson, it would be the height of rashness for President Roosevelt to attend such a Conference in person, even if held outside Europe.'[150] And Halifax, in his reply to F.D.R., pointed out that an effective blockade of Germany could only be mounted at the risk of bringing Italy into the conflict. HMG might therefore have to choose between 'a neutral Italy with an ineffective blockade, and a hostile Italy with an effective blockade'.[151] Here was another instance of the complexity of HMG's position, and the invidious choices facing it at every turn. Moreover, Roosevelt's interpretation of the Neutrality Act did not square with that being implemented by the State Department. Reporting this at the beginning of November, Lindsay commented:

> Mr Roosevelt, of course, is notoriously inaccurate as to detail, especially where the detail hampers the progress of his pet schemes. I myself drew no particular hopes from this part of what he said, and I don't expect you did either, but he himself certainly, though erroneously, thought we could use Canada as an entrepot for unassembled munitions in time of war.[152]

One cannot, therefore, feel surprised at Chamberlain's apparent indifference. As we have seen, U.S. isolation was at the edge of his tangled web of problems. Even a sustained U.S. policy of benevolent neutrality would not have made much difference to his diplomacy. In any case, the qualifications in F.D.R.'s proposals, not to mention the secrecy and subterfuge with which they were advanced, can hardly have encouraged confidence in the likelihood of Roosevelt being able to translate words into actions. It was, in short, the perennial dilemma when dealing with even a well-disposed U.S. president. As a member of the Washington Embassy put it the following spring, the Americans effectively say: ' "Open your mouth and shut your eyes and see what I will give you." And that is not quite a fair attitude for one country to take to another in matters involving the possibility of war.'[153]

# CHAPTER TWO

## The Diplomacy of Deterrence

### October 1938–August 1939

*What the British need today is a good stiff grog....*
Roosevelt, February 1939

*... Roosevelt is saying Heaven knows what but anyhow something disagreeable to dictators....*
Chamberlain, February 1939[1]

### A. Britain's deterrent diplomacy

After Munich Chamberlain soon regretted his Disraelian talk of 'peace with honour'. But he was hopeful that with the Sudeten question settled Britain and Germany might eventually reach a comprehensive settlement, and the FO broadly agreed with him. By November, however, and especially after the anti-Jewish pogroms in Germany, it seemed that 'Rome at the moment is the end of the axis on which it is easiest to make an impression'.[2] But little was achieved, and New Year rumours of an impending German attack on the Low Countries led the Cabinet on 1 February 1939 to authorize staff conversations with France, thus reversing at last the principle of limited liability in a European war. After Hitler had annexed the rest of Czechoslovakia in mid-March, in violation of the Munich agreement, the Cabinet agreed to offer a unilateral guarantee to Poland and to double the territorial army. In early April Mussolini invaded Albania, and on the 13th further British guarantees were given to Romania and Greece. Later that month it was decided to institute conscription and to create a Ministry of Supply. In May Turkey was guaranteed and the Cabinet reluctantly agreed to Anglo-French negotiations for a triple alliance with Russia. After protracted haggling these talks broke down in August, while the secret, concurrent German–Soviet negotiations resulted in the surprise non-aggression pact of 23 August. With his eastern front secure, Hitler invaded Poland on 1 September and, after hesitating in the hope of another mediatory effort by Mussolini, Britain and France declared war two days later.

This, then, is the familiar story. With retrospective knowledge of the events of 1939–40 it may seem that Chamberlain and his colleagues had finally realized the impossibility of reaching an agreement with Germany and were belatedly preparing for war by diplomatic alliances and rapid rearmament. In fact, however, as recent work has shown, the reality is less simple.

Soon after Munich, Sir Alexander Cadogan, Permanent Under-Secretary at the FO, had posed the question: 'Can we take the initiative? Can we make the Germans guess, and so reverse the process, under which we have suffered for years, of the Germans "keeping us guessing"?'[3] The events of 1939 showed that his hopes had been completely vain. British policy remained erratic and uncertain. The 'decisions' taken were largely *ad hoc* responses to immediate crises. Thus, the January scare over Holland drove Britain into a continental commitment; in April, the French, fearful of an Italo-German offensive in the Mediterranean, forced her into a unilateral guarantee of Romania and into conscription. At other times, such as February and July, Whitehall lapsed into a mood of more or less cautious optimism.

However, in all this floundering, the fundamental aim of British and French policy remained the same, namely to reach a peaceful settlement with Germany. The 'diplomatic revolution' after Prague, although reversing traditional British policy of non-entanglement in Eastern Europe, was a shift of means rather than ends. Recent historians have emphasized that the guarantees were not a preparation for war but a show of firmness in a desperate effort to recover the initiative and deter Hitler from further aggression.[4] Although their military potential as the basis of a second front was subsequently explored, there was never any question of providing effective support for the new East European allies,[5] and only pressure from the opposition and the French pushed a reluctant Cabinet into negotiations with Russia—the logistic and military key to any effective eastern front. For, as Simon privately observed, 'we are not preparing for war, we are constructing a peace front'.[6] The Cabinet's object was not to exacerbate Germany's fears of encirclement but to make her pause, show her that aggression would not pay, and eventually bring her to the negotiating table. Not that this would happen immediately. Germany had to prove her good faith. This would take time; it would probably require the removal of Hitler. After Prague Chamberlain did not weaken in his new and outraged conviction that any undertaking by Hitler would be worthless.[7] But eventually, Britain's leaders believed, the search for an agreement would have to be resumed. Contacts with German 'moderates' were therefore maintained—and with them the hope of renewed economic discussions when Germany had shown that she had abandoned militaristic ambitions.[8]

Rather than adopting a new policy, therefore, Chamberlain was trying to maintain his uneasy balancing act. In the spring he shifted weight considerably, but he was still attempting to combine firmness with conciliation, the stick with the carrot, in the hope that war could be avoided. And with this hope went that fundamental consideration of policy on which it was based— the preservation of Britain's independence and position against all comers, not just Germany. This seems clear, for instance, in HMG's attitude to Russia.[9] Its reluctance to ally with Moscow was explicable on diplomatic and military reasoning alone. The Eastern European states Britain wanted to protect were deeply suspicious of Russian intentions; the Red Army was thought to have been decimated by the purges; and Chamberlain in particular feared that Berlin would interpret a triple alliance as further evidence of encirclement. But underlying all this was the premier's 'most profound distrust' of Soviet motives and expansionist aims[10] which increased as the summer went on and which reflected the feelings of the Tory right. He seems to have believed that if war could be averted then an alliance with Russia was neither necessary nor desirable.

Although the opposition groups had some success in these months, for example in helping push the Cabinet into negotiations with Russia, fundamentally Chamberlain's domestic political position remained secure.[11] The opposition was fragmented. Tory critics, some 20 in number, coalesced around Eden rather than Churchill, who, for all his public popularity, was regarded at Westminster as a spent elder statesman. Churchill's own following was small and purely personal—Bracken, Keyes, Boothby and Sandys. Immediately after the Munich debate, in which about 25 MPs ostentatiously abstained, there was talk of a popular front with Labour and the Sinclairite Liberals, but little came of the idea. Moreover, these critics were not far from Chamberlain's own position. They were demanding not war, but greater firmness. Bracken, despite all his contempt for 'the undertaker', judged in mid-May 1939 that if Britain pressed on with rearmament and avoided internal quarrels the chances of war were negligible, because the Nazi leaders had neither the stomach nor the resources for war.[12] Above all, Chamberlain's critics were trying to get themselves into his ministry. This was particularly true of Eden, the only possible alternative leader at this stage. In mid-October Chamberlain reported that Eden was saying 'he was 90 per cent with me on my last speech and when told that I had not found Hitler personally attractive declared that brought his agreement up to 100 per cent . . .'. And just before Prague the premier chortled that 'all the prodigal sons are fairly besieging the parental door'.[13] During the summer an intensive press campaign was mounted for Churchill's inclusion in the Government. To this, as to earlier pressure after Munich for broadening his Cabinet, Chamberlain remained unreceptive. In part he believed that to include outspoken critics of Germany, notably Churchill, would seem provocative to Berlin. But it would seem that, both then and during the Phoney War, Chamberlain's obstinacy in this matter is further evidence that in domestic as well as foreign policy he hoped to keep his options open and preserve the status quo.[14]

In fact, the most effective criticism came not from the opposition but from the Foreign Office.[15] During the winter there occurred a gradual but unmistakable shift in thinking among the permanent FO officials. After Munich they had agreed that further concessions to Germany would have to be made, in practice acknowledging her hegemony in central and eastern Europe, and that Britain should strengthen her contacts with France, the Empire and the U.S.A. But, rattled by the periodic crises, and especially the January scare over Holland, the senior officials came to feel that Hitler's aims were not limited, but encompassed the domination of Europe and even of the world. Prague only confirmed this viewpoint. As Cadogan minuted late in February: 'I have the profoundest suspicion of Hitler's intentions: . . . I believe what he would like best, if he could do it, would be to smash the British Empire.'[16]

During the winter Halifax, Eden's successor as Foreign Secretary, underwent a similar evolution, guided by his senior officials, to whom he was always very responsive. Halifax has often been dismissed as a light-weight—a gangling, pious, mild-mannered aristocrat, who, like Grey earlier in the century, would have been happier on his estates than in Whitehall. But, like Grey, Halifax was a complex character. Although a reluctant politician, prone at times to remarkable flights of naiveté, nevertheless he could be tough and tenacious, frequently using all his considerable charm, sincerity and shrewdness to get his own way. Not for nothing did Beaverbrook coin the punning nickname 'Holy Fox'.[17] During the winter, Halifax found his feet at the FO and developed deep doubts about continued appeasement of Hitler. In the September crisis Cadogan had swung him against the Godesberg terms, much to the discomfiture of Chamberlain, who relied heavily on Halifax's loyalty and support. And in mid-February Oliver Harvey, his private secretary, noted: 'I feel H. now sees his way much more clearly: he has mastered his subject and speaks and acts with greater confidence and boldness. . . . He is almost unrecognisable from the H. of a year ago. He says bluntly "no more Munichs for me" . . .'.[18] It was Halifax, prompted by his advisers, who led the Cabinet pressure for Anglo-French staff talks, for a continental expeditionary force, and for conscription. Similarly, although reluctantly, he accepted that co-operation with Russia could only be secured on Moscow's terms of a full military alliance. Again his decision tipped the balance against Chamberlain.[19] Halifax also saw himself as mediator and channel between Chamberlain and his critics, and he repeatedly urged the premier to broaden his ministry.[20] Like his advisers, of course, Halifax's mood was volatile, and, like them, he still hoped that firmness might prove a sufficient deterrent.[21] But together they moved faster and farther than Chamberlain, they were less sanguine, and they believed that a higher price would have to be paid if the policy of firmness were to succeed.

## B. American rearmament for Western defence, 1938–39

Washington's initial reaction to the Munich settlement was one of relief and hope. A State Department conference on 30 September agreed 'that an opportunity for real appeasement resting on solid economic foundations was at hand . . .',[22] and on 5 October F.D.R. cabled Chamberlain: 'I fully share your hope and belief that there exists today the greatest opportunity in years for the establishment of a new order based on justice and on law', adding that the premier's new personal contact with Hitler might prove an aid to resolving some outstanding problems.[23] But gradually disillusion set in, especially after the anti-Jewish pogroms in Germany in mid-November. These provoked such an outcry that the Administration recalled its ambassador in Berlin for consultation, reluctantly, but as a necessary gesture to satisfy public opinion.[24]

In any case, F.D.R. was by now certain that the Axis, and especially Germany, posed a real if not immediate threat to American security. His reasoning may be stated schematically as follows. First, there was the traditional Wilsonian belief that lawlessness and violent change anywhere in the world caused a dangerous rent in the all-too-thin fabric of international order. F.D.R. had stated this, for instance, in his Quarantine Speech, and he reiterated it in his annual message on 4 January 1939:

> We have learned that God-fearing democracies of the world which observe the sanctity of treaties and good faith in their dealing with other nations cannot safely be indifferent to international lawlessness anywhere. They cannot forever let pass, without effective protest, acts of aggression against sister nations—acts which automatically undermine all of us.[25]

More specifically, F.D.R. and his advisers were convinced, albeit erroneously, of the unity and close co-ordination of German and Japanese policies. F.D.R. had told Lindsay in September 1938 that he was sure that Tokyo was bound by a secret treaty to support Germany in case of war, while Berle noted in June 1939 that in the State Department all 'of us believe that a Japanese move is timed to synchronize with a German move in Central Europe. . . .'[26] This belief is an important element in American thinking right up to Pearl Harbor. But the main threat, of course, was felt to be Germany. By late 1938 F.D.R. clearly believed that Hitler was bent quite simply on world domination and that if the Germans subdued Britain and France they would turn on the U.S.A. Even by controlling a major part of Europe, Roosevelt felt, Hitler could isolate the U.S. by refusing to buy the economically crucial surplus primary products of Latin American states unless they accepted his dictates.[27] He and his advisers were also anxious about the growing Nazi propaganda and military and commercial penetration of South America. During 1938 American representation in key capitals was strengthened, and at the Lima conference in December Hull overcame suspicions of the U.S. to the extent that the American republics issued a joint declaration of solidarity and defence co-ordination.[28] Above all, F.D.R. feared that Germany might combine its subversion in Latin America with a direct invasion of the Western Hemisphere, perhaps after neutralizing the British and French fleets and securing European possessions in West Africa or the Caribbean. He was particularly conscious of the relative narrowness of the South Atlantic and of the potential for long-distance aerial attack on the U.S. from West Africa, via bases in South or Central America.[29] The problem was exacerbated by the lack of a U.S. Atlantic fleet. Since 1919 the American Navy had been concentrated on the Pacific coast, with only an antiquated training force in the Atlantic. But with the growing menace F.D.R. created an operational Atlantic squadron in September–October 1938, and the annual fleet manoeuvres the following February took place for the first time off the East Coast—the practice exercise being quite transparently to stop the German fleet from assisting a fascist-led revolt in Brazil.[30] Such developments only revealed America's defence weaknesses; they did little to correct them.

Given this German threat, and America's vulnerability, F.D.R. envisaged the European democracies as the U.S.A.'s front line. If war broke out he assumed that there would be an uneasy military stalemate on the ground and that the Allies would implement a tight blockade of the Axis by sea. The crucial struggle would take place in the air, where Germany had superiority both in current numbers and in production capability.[31] The U.S., F.D.R. believed, could help redress this balance by providing Britain and France with privileged access to the American arsenal. F.D.R. hoped that the embargo on arms exports to belligerents could be repealed, but, even if that proved politically impossible, he insisted that the British and French could legally purchase U.S. munitions parts for assembly in Canada.[32]

These strategic and diplomatic considerations underlay F.D.R.'s rearmament drive after Munich. Characteristically, his plans were clearer in principle than in detail. His fluctuating but grandiose production targets proved grossly unrealistic, as did his early talk about producing them largely in government plants. However, the discussions of late 1938 provide illuminating evidence about F.D.R.'s overall policy. First, to the alarm of his Army and Navy advisers, F.D.R. was not interested in balanced rearmament. His main concern was with the Army Air Corps rather than the Navy, let alone the Army itself. The alternatives, F.D.R. argued at a major meeting on 14 November, were either a huge air force now or a huge army as well as an air force later. 'He considered that sending a large army abroad was undesirable and politically out of the question. . . .' This aversion to another American Expeditionary Force remained fundamental to F.D.R.'s policy right up to Pearl Harbor. However, Roosevelt was not only, or even primarily, preparing for war. Like the British he hoped that rearmament might be an effective deterrent. Thus, he was not even interested in building up a balanced air corps, with adequate spares, reserves and trained pilots to sustain a war effort, but in the speediest possible increase in front-line combat aircraft.

> When I write to foreign countries I must have something to back up my words. Had we this summer 5,000 planes and the capacity immediately to produce 10,000 per year, even though I might have to ask Congress for authority to sell or lend them to the countries in Europe, Hitler would not have dared to take the stand he did.[33]

But, as this quotation indicates, F.D.R. not only wanted to rearm America but also to supply the western democracies. Leaving aside here the pregnant phrase about selling or *lending*, it is clear that Roosevelt was already thinking of the U.S.A. as what he later termed 'the arsenal of democracy'. Throughout 1938, and especially after Munich, he had encouraged the French desire to buy U.S. aircraft and also to construct factories in Canada which would draw on American labour, parts and machine tools. The French orders would help develop the U.S. aircraft industry. They would also assist the democracies in achieving vital air superiority over the Luftwaffe.[34]

F.D.R.'s main task that winter was to gain domestic support for his defence policy. Unlike Chamberlain he faced enormous problems of domestic disunity. These began within his own Administration, with the faction-ridden War Department particularly opposed to his policy of unbalanced rearmament and preferential treatment for French purchases. F.D.R. therefore turned to Morgenthau, increasingly active in foreign and defence policy since Munich, to co-ordinate American and French requirements. Publicly, he concentrated on two main goals—rearmament and repeal of the arms embargo—directing the attention of Congress to them in two important speeches in January. But his innate caution was reinforced by the furore in February when news of the French aircraft orders leaked out, together with a garbled account of his explanation to the Senate's Military Affairs Committee in which he was reported to have said that America's frontiers were on the Rhine. During these months Roosevelt still hoped that American and British firmness might deter Hitler from war. And, like the British, his own course was erratic. For instance, the U.S. had virtually decided on 13 March to send its ambassador back to Berlin, only to change its mind after the German entry into Prague.[35] But increasingly F.D.R.'s diplomacy was intended to educate American opinion rather than in expectation of real success. On 14 April, for instance, he appealed to the dictators to guarantee the integrity of 31 specified European and Middle Eastern states. Privately Roosevelt rated his chances of success as about one in five, but, as he wrote to the Canadian premier: 'If we are turned down the issue becomes clearer and public opinion in your country and mine will be helped.'[36] It was for similar reasons that F.D.R. arranged and closely supervised the royal visit of 7–11 June 1939—the first to the United States by a reigning British monarch. Ostensibly it was a purely ceremonial affair—F.D.R. firmly rejected Halifax's suggestion that he accompany the King and Queen in order to take the opportunity for talks with American leaders—but F.D.R. clearly had diplomatic goals in mind. He conceived of the visit as a safe but effective way of dramatizing Anglo-American amity for the benefit of the dictators and the American public, and as a chance to show off the British monarchy—the epitome in some ways of Anglo-American differences—in the best possible light. To this end he minimized the official functions in Washington and insisted that his guests spend some time at his family home in Hyde Park because 'the simplicity and naturalness of such a visit would produce a most excellent effect', enhancing 'the essential democracy' of the royal couple.[37]

In addition to 'educating' his own countrymen, F.D.R. did his best during the winter and spring of 1938–39 to spur the British and French into action. To British visitors he expressed his alarm at German air superiority and insisted that they must pull themselves together and take a firm line. To encourage them he spoke in the most optimistic terms about America's readiness to help. The President had no time for British protestations that they lacked the power and wealth to sustain their global responsibilities. He believed that the capacity of Britain and France to supply themselves with large quantities of munitions from America was very much underestimated, and claimed that Britain had some seven billion dollars of useable assets in the U.S.A.[38] He brushed aside the Johnson Act, which prohibited loans to defaulters on war debts, talking airily of money being able to 'seep through' to where it was needed.[39] It would seem, in fact, that F.D.R. attributed Britain's problems less to a lack of power than to a lack of nerve. He talked of her suffering from an inferiority complex, after diplomatic bungling and the follies of disarmament,[40] and of her upper class's dominant fear of Communism, which he found so evident in their handling of the Spanish Civil War. These were the insidious effects of 'too much Eton and Oxford'.[41] And he reacted violently to the idea that the U.S. should take over Britain's role as guarantor of world peace. 'What the British need today', he wrote in February 1939, 'is a good stiff grog, inducing not only the desire to save civilization but the continued belief that they can do it. In such an event they will have a lot more support from their American cousins. . . .'[42] These words clearly reveal F.D.R.'s limited conception of America's world role in 1938–39. The U.S. would act as democracy's arsenal, but she would not be pushed into a position of international leadership or dragged into another war. The primary responsibility for world peace lay on Britain's shoulders, and, once the backbones of her timorous leaders had been suitably stiffened, he hoped that their shoulders would be equal to the task.

## C. British policy on U.S. involvement in Europe

During the winter of 1938–39 the Foreign Office became aware of some important but not entirely welcome developments in U.S. opinion. Reports from various sources indicated that even in the Midwest Americans were greatly interested in European affairs, and, especially after the pogroms, evinced strong antipathy to the dictators. But they were bitterly disillusioned with Munich and considered Chamberlain and his colleagues cowardly and even pro-fascist.[43] The Washington Embassy also warned that Americans believed Britain was doing nothing to help herself,[44] and it regularly reported F.D.R.'s reiterated anxieties about the West's weakness in the air.[45] Even Roosevelt's private letter about the British needing 'a good stiff grog' got back to the FO.[46]

In trying to improve Britain's image in America, however, HMG ruled out one line of action completely from the start. There was virtually no dispute that an overt campaign of propaganda would prove disastrously self-defeating. The FO and Embassy had taken very much to heart the American 'propaganda phobia' of the 1930s, associated with the revelations of how cunning British propagandists and lecturers, backed by a large official publicity machine, had supposedly helped to lure the U.S. into the Great War. Consequently, the only official publicity organization in the U.S.A. was the British Library of Information (BLI) in New York, which was simply a reference library and agent for government publications. Not only would overt propaganda arouse American suspicions, HMG believed, it would also be ineffective. The British Government clearly could not compete with the U.S. media, and particularly with radio, which the Czech crisis of September 1938 had established as the principal source of prompt vivid news.[47] 'The principle upon which we should proceed', the BLI's director, Angus Fletcher, therefore advised in September 1938, 'is to leave to existing agencies, especially commercial agencies, the work of supplying American needs, and concentrate upon improving facilities for those agencies rather than attempt to set up any organization on the models of 1914–1918.'[48] This policy of assisting rather than duplicating the U.S. media and relying upon them to educate American opinion was broadly accepted in London and proved the basis of British publicity policy in the U.S.A. throughout the war. Admittedly it was upheld by Lindsay and Fletcher with a particular and probably unreasonable intensity. Both were hypersensitive on the subject of propaganda and opposed even minor efforts to improve the flow of information, such as the FO's suggestion in February 1939 to set up branches of the BLI in some other U.S. cities.[49] But, fundamentally, the FO was in full agreement with the 'no propaganda' policy and enforced it firmly during the spring of 1939 on the planning staff of the embryo Ministry of Information.

In the FO's view, the best way to educate American opinion and to wipe away the stain of Munich was by demonstrably conducting a firm foreign policy 'on the high moral plane'. This was an increasingly common argument in the FO that winter, but it was advanced with particular persistence by David Scott, the Assistant Under-Secretary with oversight of the American Department. Scott's thesis was that a succession of events from Manchuria to Czechoslovakia had undermined American confidence in Britain's integrity and had blurred the simple moral issue, which every American understood, of democracy versus dictatorship. If Britain could highlight this issue she would counter America's cynicism about European power politics and assist F.D.R.'s efforts to educate his countrymen into an active foreign policy. In short: 'Any compromise by us with the Dictators over a fundamental principle or moral issue would do this country untold harm in the United States.'[50] Scott was backed, of course, by the American Department and by the Washington Embassy.[51] But, especially from April, his argument was taken up by other senior officials, such as Harvey and Vansittart, the Chief Diplomatic Adviser, who stressed the need for idealistic diplomacy to recover Britain's lost prestige and position around the world.[52]

The principal sceptic within the FO was Cadogan, Vansittart's successor as Permanent Under-Secretary. He found American demands that Britain should 'fight for the right' irritating and unfair. Idealistic banners were a luxury for the strong. They could hardly be afforded by a weak and hardpressed Britain, who still remembered the gibes about her war aims in 1914–18.[53] Wearily he confessed, 'I am afraid that, taught by experience, I have little faith in America', and he had no time for speculation as to how the U.S. might 'act' in the event of war—'I am only too afraid that the word is intended in its histrionic sense'.[54] In most situations Cadogan had to weigh real threats against hypothetical American reactions. Thus, during the Albania crisis in late March, on receiving reports that the U.S. would enter a war within three weeks if, and only if, it were fought on clear ideological lines, without Italy on Britain's side, Cadogan minuted: 'Then we have got to balance the strategical advantage of having Italy on our side against the "ideological" disadvantages of it. If I was convinced that the U.S. would come in on our side I know which way I should vote. But I'm not so sure.'[55] HMG continued this balancing act well into 1940. But even the cynical Cadogan believed that the U.S. had to be wooed, even if she might not be won. Back in January 1938 he had urged a quick acceptance of the Roosevelt initiative, and after Munich he noted America's valuable deterrent role in the Pacific and judged that an Anglo-American trade agreement 'would be worth considerable material concessions'.[56] In other words, he supported the basic FO line that winter, which was effectively to concede German domination of Central and Eastern Europe while strengthening British ties with France, the Empire and the U.S.A.

This was also the view of Halifax.[57] Despite his advocacy of Anglo-French co-operation in 1938–39, however, the Foreign Secretary's inclinations were basically 'Atlanticist'—he was sceptical of continental commitments and felt happiest with closer ties between the English-speaking peoples. Knowing little about the complexity of U.S. society and politics—as is apparent from his incredulous letters from Washington when he went there as Ambassador in 1941—he tended to be persistently hopeful that the U.S.A. could be educated into effective co-operation. Perhaps the most striking testimony to Halifax's concern to improve Anglo-American relations is his single-handed campaign to secure the appointment of Lord Lothian as the next Ambassador to Washington.[58] Lindsay had held the post since 1930 and in May 1938 he made clear his desire to retire soon. He had been an excellent ambassador in the traditional sense—a career diplomat who had earned the respect and trust of the White House and State Department while deliberately avoiding press conferences, speech-making and travel. This low profile reflected not only Lindsay's acute shyness but also his inveterate antipathy to anything that might smack of propaganda. After reviewing the eligible career men, Halifax decided to go outside the diplomatic service for someone who would take a more forward line and would appeal to the American public rather than merely liaise with the Administration. His old friend, the Liberal peer Lord Lothian (Philip Kerr), seemed well qualified. Unusually among the British élite, Lothian knew and liked America and its people, having toured the country extensively over many years as Secretary to the Rhodes Trust. He also had good contacts with the President and other U.S. leaders, which dated back to his days as Lloyd George's private secretary at the Paris peace conference. He was an experienced journalist, capable of dealing easily and informally with the American press, and was extremely aware of the importance of press and public opinion in the making of American policy. Above all, Lothian had for years displayed a belief in the need for Anglo-American co-operation that was both passionate and unqualified. Far more than most British leaders—far more than Halifax and the FO, let alone Chamberlain and the Treasury—he felt that Britain's days as a supreme world power were over and that only with U.S. support could the democracies preserve control of the seas in the interests of world peace and stability.

Despite these impressive credentials, however, Lothian's appointment was strongly opposed by senior FO officials. In part, as usual, they simply wanted to keep a plum diplomatic post within the service. But they also pointed to Lothian's naive and well publicized support for appeasement and to his notorious lack of judgement and discretion. This latter failing was amply demonstrated during Lothian's visit to the U.S.A. early in 1939, at a time when his appointment had been decided upon in Whitehall but not revealed publicly or even to the Administration. In Washington Lothian had pressed his view of Anglo-American relations and Britain's need for U.S. help so insistently upon the President that F.D.R. had taken it as another instance of Britain's spineless reluctance to defend herself. His comments on Lothian got back to the FO, as F.D.R. had intended—hoping that they would help his campaign to stiffen Britain's backbone. But in London Cadogan used them as new ammunition against Lothian's selection as Ambassador-designate. Nevertheless, despite the reservations of Chamberlain and the King, Halifax succeeded in pushing through the appointment, after ascertaining that F.D.R. did in fact approve.[59] Lindsay stayed on to oversee the royal visit and Lothian finally took up his post on 30 August, just before the war began. As we shall see he would fully merit Halifax's trust.

But it was not only the FO that took an increased interest in the U.S.A. in early 1939. Contrary to the conventional view of Chamberlain as incorrigibly indifferent to the U.S.A., he too displayed a greater concern for Anglo-American relations in these months. During the winter London accumulated encouraging evidence of F.D.R.'s determination to supply the British with munitions and aircraft, or at least aircraft parts. As we saw, F.D.R. had emphasized this to Lindsay on 19 September, and he did so again later that month to the British air attaché.[60] A conversation on 21 October between Roosevelt and his old friend Arthur Murray proved particularly influential. In this F.D.R. outlined his plans in detail and stated firmly that, in so far as he was able to achieve it, Chamberlain would have 'the industrial resources of the American nation behind him in the event of war with the dictatorships'. Murray reported his talk fully to Chamberlain in mid-December.[61] Equally gratifying were Roosevelt's New Year speeches. In his annual message on 4 January F.D.R. emphasized the impracticability of isolation in the modern world, and, while reiterating America's determination to avoid war, stressed that American opinion could be brought to bear on the aggressors by 'methods short of war', notably rearmament and amendment of the neutrality laws.[62] British diplomats critical of Chamberlain felt Roosevelt was providing the world with the moral leadership that Britain had failed to give.[63] Chamberlain, of course, much closer to the German threat, was not able to speak with such impunity,[64] but he promptly issued a public statement welcoming the speech 'as yet another indication of the vital role of the American democracy in world affairs and its devotion to the ideal of ordered progress'. This was an unusual and unexpected step, which aroused great interest in diplomatic circles. The German Ambassador in London reported that the initiative for the statement had come from Chamberlain himself, and that it was probably made for four reasons: to thank F.D.R. for his support, to emphasize the similarity of Anglo-American ideals, to improve Britain's moral image in the U.S., and to answer criticism that the PM had been neglecting Anglo-American relations.[65]

Encouraged, the FO urged that F.D.R. should be fully informed in mid-January about the apparent threat to the Netherlands—a suggestion strongly supported by Horace Wilson, Chamberlain's closest adviser.[66] HMG hoped for another U.S. pronouncement before Hitler delivered a major speech scheduled for 30 January, and it was further encouraged by press reports that Roosevelt had told senators that the U.S. would give the democracies every possible help in a conflict, short of declaring war and sending troops to Europe. After Hitler's feared speech had proved an anti-climax, Chamberlain wrote on 5 February: 'At last we are getting on top of the dictators.' He went on to give four reasons, the first three being Britain's rearmament, the aroused state of public opinion, and Germany's poor economic situation.

> Point four is that Roosevelt is saying Heaven knows what but anyhow something disagreeable to dictators and there is an uneasy feeling that in the case of trouble it would not do much to bring U.S. in on the side of the democracies.
> These points all add to the weight on the peace side of the balance and they

are sufficiently heavy to enable me to take that 'firmer line' in public which some of my critics have applauded without apparently understanding the connection between diplomacy and strategic strength which nevertheless has always been stressed by the wisest diplomats & statesmen in the past.[67]

Here is one of the best statements of Chamberlain's conception of diplomacy.

In January and February 1939, therefore, HMG showed a new sensitivity to the United States. This reflected the need to build a diplomatic front against Hitler and the encouraging evidence of a firmer U.S. policy. However, at this stage Chamberlain was still hopeful that he could do business with Hitler. Indeed, in February and early March he was 'going about with a lighter heart than for many a long day', certain that like a latter-day Pitt he alone could save his country.[68] As we have seen, however, Prague brought the premier's view of Hitler in line with the FO's, and with this new consensus the need to strengthen Anglo-American ties became yet more pressing. Throughout the spring Halifax reminded his Cabinet colleagues that they must be attentive to opinion in key neutral countries, particularly the Balkans and the U.S.A.[69] His advice was taken seriously, as several examples will demonstrate. For instance, Kennedy was told of the Polish guarantee in advance so that he could brief the American press and inform the President, and Chamberlain was clearly pleased with F.D.R.'s favourable response.[70] Similarly, when F.D.R. sent his surprise 14 April message to the dictators, HMG immediately welcomed his 'statesmanlike initiative' which offered 'a real opportunity of averting the catastrophe which overhangs Europe'. Privately the FO was less credulous. Cadogan clearly thought the appeal amateurish and worthless and Sargent, the Deputy Under-Secretary, pointed out its 'obvious shortcomings', namely that they could never trust Hitler's promises again and that he could destroy countries' independence by other means than invasion. Chamberlain, however, divined Roosevelt's intentions and welcomed the message:

I think the appeal is very skilfully framed and has put H. & M. into a tight corner. I have no doubt they will refuse to play, though I cannot say whether it will be a polite, an evasive, or a rude refusal. But world opinion & particularly American opinion will have been consolidated against them and their own people will be disappointed and alarmed.[71]

Finally, later in April, it was French and American pressure that pushed the British into introducing conscription, the French having enlisted the aid of Bullitt, who told the British Ambassador in Paris that F.D.R. felt it absolutely essential that Britain announce conscription before Hitler replied to Roosevelt's message on 28 April.[72]

The British Government was also sharing a good deal of important diplomatic intelligence with the U.S.A. during these months. Since the misunderstandings over the Roosevelt initiative in January 1938 the FO had been careful to provide the Administration with background information on the international scene and on British policy, treating the U.S.A. in much the same way as the Dominions and U.K. missions overseas.[73] In early 1939 it was particularly anxious to inform F.D.R. about the air position, since the figures he was quoting—Germany with 9,000 planes; Britain with 1,500—grossly exaggerated the disparity.[74] (In October the British Air Ministry had estimated the gap at 3,200 to 1,600 in front-line aircraft and 2,400 to 400 in reserves.[75]) Halifax therefore asked the Air Ministry to prepare a suitable memorandum, which Chamberlain approved, after deleting some of the more sensitive figures showing Britain's current weakness. The document, finally sent to Roosevelt in April, admitted that in a year's time Germany would still enjoy a 2 : 1 advantage in front-line aircraft, but stressed that by then the two countries would be equal in monthly production and that effective air power had to be measured in reserves and pilots as well as front-line planes—a point which, as we noted, F.D.R. was inclined to overlook.[76] To reveal such sensitive information shows the importance Whitehall attached to American opinion, and it would seem that its efforts had some effect. By July F.D.R. felt that the air situation was 'much better both in England and in the United States'.[77]

\*     \*     \*

During the spring, therefore, both Chamberlain and the FO were responsive to American opinion and tried to promote its education. The military planners took the same line. They urged that 'in peace, as later in war, all the resources of diplomacy should be directed to securing the benevolent neutrality or the active assistance of other powers, particularly the United States of America'.[78] But, despite the new hopefulness, the ingrained scepticism about the U.S. was still very apparent. The FO advised the military in February:

> Although there has recently been a marked increase in anti-totalitarian feeling in the United States of America it would be most imprudent to count on armed assistance from that country. Intervention on our side at a later stage, however, is possible and might even, if present trends continue, become probable; but it is suggested that we should not count on more than sympathy and either the repeal of the neutrality legislation or an interpretation of it favourable for the Allies.[79]

This assessment sums up British judgements of what they could 'count on' from the U.S.A. throughout the period before war began. What was important when facing a possible three-front war was not good intentions but firm commitments. Nevertheless, there was a natural tendency to speculate on the possible development of American opinion. John Balfour, head of the FO's American Department, suggested in a widely circulated minute in April 1939 that 'some spectacular act of violence' such as an indiscriminate air attack on London might cause 'an explosion of American feeling' resulting in the participation of the U.S.A. at an early stage.[80] Not all his colleagues agreed—one predicted that only east-coast anglophiles would be aroused[81]—but Lindsay and the FO tentatively explored the idea of arranging special facilities to broadcast an air raid live to America, before turning it down on grounds of practicality, taste and American sensitivity to propaganda.[82] There would seem to have been two reasons behind these expectations about the effect of bombing on American opinion. The first was the assumption

49

that war would begin with massive air raids which would cause great destruction and horrific civilian casualties. The other was the belief that because American opinion was so moral, emotional and volatile, and because her cultural ties with England were so close, the slaughter and destruction of historic sites would produce a major change in U.S. policy. Lindsay persistently alluded to the emotional element in American policy. 'If America ever comes into a European war', he wrote in March, 'it will be some violent emotional impulse which will provide the last and decisive thrust. Nothing would be so effective as the bombing of London, translated by air to the homes of America.' Even Scott, for all his anxieties about U.S. opinion, observed: 'It is fortunate, indeed, for us that in times of crisis the vast Anglo-Saxon element in the United States tends to ferment and come to the top and assert itself.'[83] Such beliefs should not be given too much weight. They are a reminder of the element of hope that balanced the habitual British doubt about the U.S.A., and of the conceptions of America on which they rested. Yet it is interesting to note that the Germans took a similar view of the effect of bombing, as did Kennedy, Walter Lippmann, the distinguished American columnist, and Roosevelt himself. After talking with the President in June 1939, George VI recorded: 'If London was bombed U.S.A. would come in.'[84] This expectation, and Churchill's use of it, took on great significance in the summer and autumn of 1940.

The point behind such speculation was that the British expected an all-out German offensive as soon as war began, of which the bombing would be a part. This, they assumed, would be the decisive period of the war. If the Allies could survive the initial onslaught, their naval and imperial resources would guarantee eventual victory. It was therefore essential that U.S. opinion evolve quickly, to be effective in this first, critical phase. Not surprisingly, Cadogan was doubtful. 'We shall want quick starters in the next war', he minuted, 'and I doubt whether even President Roosevelt can be quick enough off the mark. I think at least he won't hinder us, with the Neutrality Act. But I doubt whether non-Neutrality (if he can get it) will be enough.'[85] The proponents of the 'moral line', however, believed Americans *would* move rapidly, *if* the moral issues were clear. As Vansittart put it: 'I think they will not only talk but do a great deal, and do it quickly, if we have no more Munichs. We nearly lost the U.S.A. over that; but if we now make it clear that henceforth we really are going to stand up, we can have much confidence in the U.S.A. Anyhow,' he added lamely, and significantly, 'it is our only chance.'[86]

Chamberlain probably took Cadogan's view, and not that of Vansittart. There is no evidence that the premier altered his opinion of December 1937 that the U.S. would probably not enter a war in sufficient time.[87] Nor did he share Vansittart's gloomy belief that wooing America was Britain's 'only chance'. We have seen that he remained hopeful of ultimately reaching a settlement, if not with Hitler then perhaps at a later date with the elusive German 'moderates'. Thus, Chamberlain's increased interest and indeed satisfaction in Anglo-American relations that winter can only be properly understood if one also keeps in mind his continued doubts about effective U.S. intervention and his continued hope for peace.

For instance, there was consternation in Whitehall in early February at a parliamentary question asking if the premier would consider visiting the U.S.A. Chamberlain composed the reply himself, while the FO made frantic efforts to avoid publicity and to play down the question's significance to the U.S. Embassy. In his answers Chamberlain stolidly insisted that he could not be absent from the country for long without considerable administrative inconvenience.[88] This was a justifiable response, in an era before regular transatlantic air travel, and one that had been advanced before against a prime ministerial visit to America.[89] Nevertheless, it was surely not the reason for Whitehall's alarm. For one thing, Chamberlain was convinced, as he warned Labour leaders in June, that 'the sure way . . . to lose the Americans was to run after them too hard'. Overt pressure would only reinforce U.S. fears of European entanglements—a point, he felt, that critics such as Eden and Churchill did not properly appreciate.[90] Even more important, he still wanted to preserve a delicate balance between firmness and conciliation. He probably believed that a visit to the U.S., or even rumours of one, would exacerbate German fears of encirclement. In fact, what Chamberlain seems to have valued was the appearance more than the reality of Anglo-American co-operation. Thus, he particularly appreciated the form of words Arthur Murray had worked out with F.D.R. as being suitable for Chamberlain's public use, namely that 'Great Britain, in the event of war, could rely upon obtaining raw materials from the democracies of the world'. Chamberlain felt that this formula was very important, and might, in certain circumstances, have a 'properly deterrent effect' on the dictators. Similarly, leaks about F.D.R.'s sentiments were valuable regardless of their accuracy. 'I am sure', Chamberlain told Murray in February, 'that the reports of his communication to the Senate Committee will have a powerful effect in Europe.'[91]

To a large extent Chamberlain was interested in the appearance rather than the reality of transatlantic co-operation because he believed that only the appearance was attainable, in other words that Britain could not count on quick and effective U.S. help. But it is also likely that Chamberlain did not really *want* full-scale American help, with the dependence upon the U.S.A. that this implied. Certainly this was the contemporary judgement of Herbert von Dirksen, the German Ambassador in London, who repeatedly told Berlin that the British found U.S. friendship 'oppressive' and that they feared for their Empire and for their economic and political independence should they have to ally with the U.S.A.[92] Similarly, the State Department, long convinced of a 'tie-up' between Chamberlain and 'economic royalists' in the City of London and Wall Street, was morbidly suspicious of every hint of Anglo-German trade negotiations during 1939. Their fears were not unjustified. Undoubtedly Anglo-American commercial rivalry was much in the mind of Tory business and financial circles, and Dirksen's pen-picture fits very well the views of, say, Lord Londonderry, a Cabinet minister from 1931 to 1936, who saw co-operation between Britain, France, Germany and Italy as the basis of world peace, and repeatedly criticized the argument 'that everything must be sacrificed . . . in the hope of placating American opinion'.[93] Moreover, in his study of economic appeasement, Professor Wendt has suggested that during the winter before Prague Chamberlain himself entertained hopes of a European economic bloc directed against the U.S.A. and that he believed the European 'big four' should keep a definite distance ('eine gewisse Distanz') between themselves and Washington, to preserve their economic independence.[94]

This is a complex problem, on which more research is needed. But certain qualifications must be made. For instance, the German diplomatic correspondence cannot be read uncritically. It was, after all, a fundamental aim of German propaganda to drive a wedge between Britain and the U.S.A., by playing on their mutual suspicions, and Dirksen himself tended to distort reports of British official opinion in order to influence Berlin in the direction of a *rapprochement* with London.[95] Furthermore, while one can find talk of an anti-American economic bloc from British industrialists and even from senior civil servants such as Leith Ross at the Treasury, it is not easy to find Chamberlain talking in this vein.[96] We saw in chapter 1 (c) that he explicitly rejected such an idea in 1937. Whatever Beaverbrook or Amery might claim, Britain could not do without American trade. But neither could she, unlike the U.S., afford to forgo commerce with Germany. The economic negotiations between German and British industrialists prior to Prague and the subsequent informal contacts between businessmen and civil servants during the summer were therefore an expression of economic necessity. The details are uncertain, but apparently the British genuinely intended to draw the U.S.A. in, once progress had been made on outstanding Anglo-German problems, although it is difficult to see how an agreement on controlled trading, involving cartels and economic spheres of influence to minimize competition, could have been accommodated to Hull's aggressive Open Door principles.[97] There was probably also little justification for American suspicions that sterling was being allowed to depreciate against the dollar in 1938–39 so as to make British exports more competitive. The British Treasury had learned from past experience that devaluation only raised import prices, caused a lack of confidence in the pound and led to retaliatory measures by other countries which reduced the volume of world trade. In fact the Bank of England genuinely tried to defend sterling in the face of war fears and the consequent withdrawal of funds to the U.S.A. In the last few months of 1938 the reserves fell by nearly a quarter, and the need to allay U.S. suspicions obliged HMG to spend more of its vital 'war chest' of gold and foreign exchange than it would otherwise have done.[98]

Maurice Cowling is therefore probably correct to say that Chamberlain's hopes of reducing Britain's economic dependence on the U.S.A. may have been verbal rather than real.[99] Certainly, Chamberlain remained willing to make limited economic sacrifices for political and diplomatic gain. Thus, when the Anglo-American trade agreement was finally concluded in October 1938, after protracted haggling and last-minute British concessions, he felt that the price was too high but that after such prolonged negotiation it would have a bad effect internationally if no agreement were reached.[100] But it is probable that Chamberlain saw the trade negotiations with Germany as a counterbalance to the Anglo-American agreement and as a way of avoiding further concessions to the U.S.A.[101] And it is likely that, more generally, Chamberlain still hoped to keep his distance from the U.S.A., as Wendt and other German historians suggest.[102] His anxieties were about Britain's overall position as a world power, of which *economic* relations with the U.S.A. were only one facet, albeit an important one. Dirksen's general comment about the British is probably applicable to Chamberlain, namely that while 'association with the United States would be preferred to completely unstable relations with the most important European powers', that association would only be accepted 'most reluctantly', when all else had failed, because the 'sympathy of the U.S.A., which already is often enough found oppressive, would become a heavy burden' and Britain would be reduced to the role of a 'junior partner' in a full alliance.[103] Such judgements are difficult to substantiate. They relate to the deepest assumptions on which foreign policy is based—assumptions not often articulated let alone recorded. But evidence in the next chapter confirms that Chamberlain was more interested in the appearance than the reality of American help, and that he wanted benevolent neutrality but not U.S. belligerency, as long as he could keep his country out of total war.

Perhaps the best indication of how British doubts and fears about the U.S.A. reinforced each other can be seen in the question of Britain's war debts. HMG was often importuned by interested private citizens to resume token payments on the debt, in order to gain American goodwill. But although no one denied that ideally the issue should be settled,[104] it remained HMG's position that until there was hope of reaching a complete settlement the matter should not be reopened. Token payments would be insufficient to lift the Johnson Act's ban on credits to war debt defaulters, and in any case they would seem like an attempt to buy friendship and entangle the U.S. in war. Furthermore, the controversy no longer seemed vitally important. As Scott commented: 'I doubt very much whether the existence of the war debt question would, in a time of real crisis, influence public opinion against this country to more than a limited degree.'[105] These judgements were probably sound. When Eden visited Washington in December 1938 he and his party were surprised to find that the live issue from the past was not war debts but Manchuria. Roosevelt himself indicated that he did not want to revive the issue or to obtain token payments.[106]

However, there was more to HMG's policy than practicalities. It is instructive to compare the British attitude with that of France. During the spring of 1939 Daladier made a vigorous effort to secure an interim settlement of the French debt. The plan was to offer 10–15 per cent of France's gold reserves plus the sovereignty or lease of certain French Caribbean islands for use by the U.S. as defence bases. The French aim was not to repay the debt in full but to dispel some of the ill-feeling that existed. The plan was eventually rejected by F.D.R., but, as Anthony Adamthwaite observes, it shows the extent to which France was willing to go to obtain American support.[107] In April 1939 Lindsay broached the idea of a debts-for-bases settlement with HMG, concerned at agitation on the matter in Congress.[108] The Admiralty was agreeable—if the proposal came from the U.S., if it involved complete cancellation of the debt, and if the islands ceded were of no strategic value, adding that it might not be in Britain's interest to strengthen the U.S.' sense of security in this way. As the Deputy Chief of the Naval Staff put it: 'We want to make it difficult, not easy, for the U.S. to remain neutral in a war between Germany and ourselves.'[109] The Admiralty's conditional agreement effectively eliminated any feasible proposal. The Colonial Office was more direct. Standing squarely on earlier HMG statements, the CO stated that under no circumstances could any part of the colonial empire be handed over to the U.S.A. in settlement of the war debt.[110] Chamberlain fully agreed—he later dismissed the idea as 'outside the realm of practical politics'[111]—and there was no ground for American press reports in June 1939 that the Cabinet had decided to seek a complete settlement.[112] However, the debate suggests again the complexity of HMG's problem in wooing America. To reopen the debt question seemed on one level pointless, unwise and unnecessary. But, in addition, the British, unlike the French, were unwilling to pay a high price for the uncertain benefits of American goodwill.

## D. Roosevelt's failure to revise the Neutrality Act, summer 1939

During the summer of 1939 the aspect of American policy that most interested HMG was F.D.R.'s attempt to amend the Neutrality Act. As already noted, this legislation was a compromise mixture of often contradictory provisions. Since 1933 the Administration had periodically tried to limit American trade with 'aggressor states', and thus align the U.S. implicitly with the collective security efforts of the League. It had also shared the general American desire to regulate the arms industry and keep American citizens off belligerent vessels. However, in 1935–37 these measures were increasingly appropriated by Congressmen anxious to restrict drastically American neutral rights of travel and trade in order to insulate the U.S. from a future conflict. The Neutrality Act, as amended in 1937, obliged the President in wartime to place an embargo on the sale and shipment by Americans of arms, ammunition and implements of war to *all* belligerents—victims or aggressors. He was also required to ban all loans to belligerent governments or their agents. In addition, he was given power, at his discretion, to require that U.S. citizens transfer title of all exports before the goods left the U.S.A. and/or prohibit the carriage of goods and raw materials on American vessels. These 'cash and carry' provisions—designed to minimize the economic entanglements and naval incidents that had supposedly drawn America into the Great War—were for a two-year trial period, which expired on 30 April 1939. In the spring of 1939, therefore, HMG was anxious to see their fate, and that of the legislation as a whole, given F.D.R.'s repeated assurances that Britain could count on American supplies in war as well as peace.

Roosevelt's own preference was that 'the existing Neutrality Act should be repealed in toto without any substitute'.[113] However, he recognized that this was politically impossible, and his more realistic aim was the repeal of the arms embargo, coupled, if necessary, with the placing of all trade with belligerents on a cash and carry basis.[114] As we have already seen, F.D.R. felt that this would present no obstacle to the Allies—Britain 'had ample funds in the United States and anyhow money had odd but sure ways of getting to where it was most wanted'; similarly ships could easily be acquired.[115] Nevertheless, Roosevelt felt that the provision of a war zone, from which U.S. citizens and vessels would be excluded, 'might really be useful'.[116] This would minimize the risk of naval incidents, which, as we saw, he believed had led to American belligerency in 1917. In April 1939 Roosevelt told Morgenthau that if Americans entered the war zone and were killed he did not intend to treat that as *casus belli*.[117] If war broke out, therefore, F.D.R. hoped to aid the Allies without getting America involved. But, one should also note, F.D.R., like the British, still hoped to *prevent* war. His main argument throughout the neutrality debate was that repeal of the arms embargo 'would actually prevent the outbreak of war in Europe'. This probably reflected his belief that if Wilson had made clear American sympathies in the summer of 1914 the Great War might have been averted.[118] Deterrence was the State Department's goal too. Thinking there had evolved beyond a policy of keeping the Europeans guessing as to American intentions. It was now hoped that repeal of the arms embargo and placing of all trade with belligerents on a cash and carry basis would make clear to the British, French and Germans that the Allies would be able to obtain American supplies in time of war. 'A clear-cut clarification of our position in advance', wrote Moffat, 'might prevent trouble.'[119]

F.D.R., therefore, hoped to prevent war and, should it break out, to aid the Allies without American belligerency. But it was not easy to translate his aspirations into actions. He had to operate in a very different political situation from Chamberlain, who enjoyed a built-in Commons majority and muted, fragmented opposition. The relatively placid political situation during Roosevelt's first term (1933–37) was almost unprecedented in twentieth-century U.S. history. Congress had been remarkably co-operative, the Democratic party held together, and the Republicans were a negligible force. After the Supreme Court crisis of 1937 all these unusual features gradually disappeared. Congress reasserted its independence, conservative Democrats revolted against the growing influence of the urban–liberal/labour wing of the party, and the Republicans re-emerged in the 1938 elections. By the time the 76th Congress met in January 1939, F.D.R. faced an effective coalition of conservatives from both parties, capable of defeating the Administration on controversial New Deal legislation. It was not merely the open reverses that worried the Administration. Its opponents were veteran Democrats from the south and west whose positions of leadership on the floor and in key committees enabled them to defeat or at least delay and amend Administration measures.[120]

However, the situation was not unmanageable. The coalition was loose and brittle, and it had been formed almost entirely around domestic issues. On foreign affairs alignments were more fluid, and, although there was general agreement on keeping out of war, opinion was divided on how far America should use its influence to preserve peace. The 1937 Neutrality Act had been a compromise between very different viewpoints. Some Congressmen, such as Borah, were belligerent isolationists, favouring the assertion of most traditional neutral rights of trade and travel in time of war. Others, notably Nye and Vandenberg, wanted to curtail these to avoid economic or emotional entanglement in a European conflict. Yet others, such as Senator

Thomas of Utah, sought an arms embargo to discriminate against aggressor states.[121] In this confusion lay the opportunity for a determined Administration. However, F.D.R. had not grasped it in the mid-1930s for two main reasons. One was his readiness to compromise on foreign policy goals, because he attached higher priority to domestic issues. This was particularly apparent in 1935 and 1937 over the neutrality legislation. But, secondly, F.D.R. also failed to give effective political leadership. He kept in the background, made tactical errors, and often entrusted Administration measures to inept managers on the Hill.[122]

In 1939, too, F.D.R.'s failure to amend the Neutrality Act cannot simply be ascribed to isolationist sentiment. Admittedly the fear of war was very strong and the Act had become a shibboleth—a talismanic symbol of American determination to remain at peace. Domestic politics also played a significant part in F.D.R.'s defeat. On the neutrality votes in June the House Republicans were solidly against him, supported by about a quarter of the Democrats, mostly conservatives already bitterly distrustful of the President. Nevertheless, even in the 1939 session, the opposition to F.D.R. can be exaggerated. It is surely an over-statement to say that 'Congress was moving aggressively to dismantle the New Deal'.[123] Although both houses did prune F.D.R.'s relief appropriations, they still gave him all but $100 million of the $825 million he requested, while the massive defence appropriations, almost twice those of the previous year, were granted quickly and largely intact. Much of the legislation that F.D.R. lost—the housing bill, for instance— failed because of lack of time at the end of a session that started extremely slowly.[124]

In other words, one must attribute the failure of neutrality revision in part to poor Administration leadership.[125] F.D.R. and Hull avoided direct, public involvement in the issue, advised by Pittman, the erratic and cautious chairman of the Senate Foreign Relations Committee (FRC), that this would be counter-productive, and alarmed by the furore over the annual message and the French aircraft orders. After considerable delay Pittman introduced a cash and carry bill in March, but meanwhile Senator Thomas had proposed a discriminatory arms embargo against the aggressors. Internationalist pressure groups were divided, uncertain of the Administration's attitude. In this confusion, which to Berle seemed typical of the last phase of a second-term administration,[126] the isolationists were able to mobilize opposition. Eventually, after further temporizing from Pittman, the Administration introduced its own bill in late May, but F.D.R. still stayed publicly aloof, fearful of arousing the personal hostility towards him. By this time the opponents were well organized, the internationalists bereft of Administration leadership, the session well advanced, and the bill's managers, Pittman and Bloom, ineffective. The House passed a mangled version of the bill on 30 June, while on 11 July the Senate FRC voted to defer consideration of it until the next session, which would not begin until January 1940. The voting was close—12 to 11—and the majority included five Democrats, four of them conservatives whom F.D.R. had either opposed or refused to support in the 1938 elections.[127] Thus, the arms embargo remained while the cash and carry provisions lapsed, thereby allowing American citizens and vessels to trade freely in time of war. It was another confused and contradictory result—'a negative compromise', as one commentator put it, 'between isolationism, collective security, Washington heat, and partisan politics'.[128]

Like F.D.R., the British and French were interested in repeal of the arms embargo primarily as a deterrent measure. In May Bullitt reported from Paris that HMG 'considered it of the highest importance that the modification of the Neutrality Act should if possible be brought about in the near future. Such a modification ... would end all chance that Ribbentrop might persuade Hitler to risk immediate war' on the grounds that Britain and France could not even count on American supplies. This warning, and repeated French comment in the same vein, helped push the Administration into introducing its own bill in late May.[129] Undoubtedly Roosevelt's eventual failure did have a deleterious effect on European opinion. It was seen in Italy as proof that the U.S. need not be taken seriously in the event of war, and the French were deeply depressed.[130] London, however, was less disturbed. The FO believed that the result did not reflect American public opinion, and that if war broke out F.D.R., as he had stated, would call a special session of Congress to repeal the embargo. Halifax, reported Kennedy on 5 July, thought 'that as long as the papers say that America will act if there is trouble and that is brought to the front, that will be satisfactory'. And on 20 July Kennedy cabled that Chamberlain was 'fairly optimistic about the outlook for the next 30 days'—being sure that Britain's defence measures had now convinced Hitler that she would fight if need be and that he was too intelligent to want world war.[131]

The neutrality fiasco, therefore, did not completely undermine Chamberlain's diplomacy of deterrence. However, it certainly exacerbated British cynicism about the Americans. In order to keep them sweet at a crucial time the Cabinet had agreed to negotiate a barter deal—trading rubber and tin for surplus American wheat and cotton. There was no evident economic value in the deal for Britain, and Kennedy reported that of the principal British policymakers only Chamberlain and Halifax were willing to push it. As usual the hope was that HMG might purchase political goodwill by economic concessions. This was the bait dangled by Kennedy and the State Department. But by mid-June there was stalemate, and it was anxiety about the effect of a collapse of the negotiations at a delicate moment in the House neutrality debate that impelled Chamberlain and the Cabinet to make last-minute concessions to the hard-bargaining Kennedy.[132]

Meanwhile the farce on Capitol Hill was played out to its denouement. Even the enthusiasts for Anglo-American amity were bitter at the result. Lindsay called the events in the House 'a lamentable display of incompetence, partisanship and log-rolling'. 'A picture of the democratic machine at its very worst' was David Scott's judgement. Those habitually less well disposed to America were even more scathing. The members of Congress, exploded Chamberlain, 'are incorrigible. Their behaviour over the Neutrality Legislation is enough to make one weep, but I have not been disappointed for I never expected any better behaviour from these pig-headed and self-righteous nobodies.' And, in a rare outburst of passion, R. A. Butler, Parliamentary Under-Secretary at the FO, informed the American Department:

I cannot tell you what a deplorable impression this news makes on my mind. In my political life I have always been convinced that we can no more count on America than on Brazil, but I had led myself to hope that this legislation might at least be passed.

In any of your contacts with Americans you should not minimise the dismay with which my political colleagues watch America, who landed us with the League and then quitted, and now deliberately encourages 'aggression' in our hour of need.[133]

Some of these comments were obviously written in the heat of the moment. But they are no less instructive or significant for that. They again reveal something of the bitterness that lay beneath the surface of British attitudes to the U.S.A. Butler's minute, with its disparaging reference to America and the League, is a particularly good expression of back-bench Tory opinion. Furthermore, the episode repeated what for Britain seemed the familiar pattern—American words without actions, British concessions without rewards. It also did little to enhance confidence in F.D.R. His breezy assurances throughout the winter had come to nothing. In short, the neutrality fiasco cannot have made Chamberlain more inclined to build his European policy around the U.S.A. Only in the Far East was the outlook a little more hopeful.

### E. The problem of Japan, 1938–39

It had long been an axiom of British policy that the U.S. was less isolationist and potentially more co-operative in the Pacific than in Europe. Indeed, British Far Eastern policy was based on the expectation of American help. In 1921 Britain had conceded naval parity to the U.S.A. and had terminated the Anglo-Japanese alliance, largely because of American pressure. Thereafter, her Pacific strategy rested on two foundations—the Singapore base and the hope of U.S. naval assistance. Neither was particularly well grounded. HMG had decided in 1921 to build a base at Singapore for the use of the main fleet in a Pacific war, but, because of the 'stop–go' policies of successive governments, the facilities were not completed until February 1938. As for the U.S.A., '. . . the British government was in fact replacing a formal alliance with Japan by a mere understanding with the United States, and assuming that the latter's interests would be served by defending the security of the Pacific dominions, and Britain's own territorial and commercial interests in the Pacific'.[134]

In fact, the two countries had very different interests in the Pacific. The U.S. had no major territorial stake there, with the exception of the Philippines, which were scheduled for independence, whereas Britain's possessions included Australasia, India, Burma, Malaya and Singapore. British commercial interests were also enormous. Shanghai and Hong Kong were two of the world's leading entrepôts and business centres. China attracted some six per cent of total British overseas investment, compared with a figure of one per cent for the U.S.A. In general, Asiatic trade was of little importance to the U.S. economy. It was persistently imbalanced and amounted to only half the value of her transatlantic trade, whose terms were always favourable.

Despite important interests in China, she had larger total investments in Japan. Japanese anti-foreign feeling was directed at Russia and Britain. Not until 1941 did Japan see her differences with the U.S.A. as fundamental.[135]

Thus the United States had no vital interests in the Far East, and such interests as she did have dictated a conciliatory policy towards Tokyo. However, for various reasons, American policymakers showed a keen concern for events in Asia and increasingly opposed Japanese expansion. A Japanese move southwards would threaten America's supplies of key strategic raw materials. Although in general very self-sufficient, the U.S.A. obtained 90 per cent of its crude rubber and 75 per cent of its tin from Malaya and the Dutch East Indies.[136] But much of America's concern for East Asia sprang from confused moralizing rather than a hard-headed assessment of U.S. interests. American leaders continued to believe that the U.S. should play a special protective role in China and that the China market had enormous potential. Moreover, they rarely formulated their Asia policy upon a careful evaluation of Asiatic problems, as the U.S. Embassy in Tokyo urged. Instead, events there were usually seen in a global perspective, as part of a growing polarity between democracies and totalitarians. This tendency was accentuated by the conviction, already noted, that Berlin and Tokyo were hand in glove.

Although opposed to Japan's expansion, the Roosevelt Administration was nevertheless unwilling and politically unable to take effective action, or to engage in commitments to Britain. Throughout the 1930s, U.S. policy was passive—verbally upholding moral and legal verities while providing little beyond minor financial aid to China.

> Roosevelt was never able to establish goals in the Far East which reflected the nation's limited interests, its lack of available strength, and its desire to avoid war. Nor could he, at any price, create a world which conformed to established American principles. No available policy, in short, could bridge the gulf between the nation's limited power and its unlimited objectives in the Orient.[137]

British policy from 1937 to 1941 had to take shape within this gap between America's words and actions. In the words of the best study of British East Asian policy between 1937 and 1939: 'London adhered quite consistently during this period to a middle course that favored China by giving her moral support and limited material aid but nonetheless aimed to prevent a breakdown in Anglo-Japanese relations.'[138] In general, Britain's military weakness and over-commitment, together with a lack of firm American commitments, ruled out vigorous action in East Asia. On the other hand, HMG made no real effort to appease Japan: the May 1938 Customs agreement and the interim Tientsin settlement in July 1939 were isolated concessions. Admittedly, London did not like the idea in principle—there was a general belief that Japan was incorrigibly aggressive, whereas German grievances were viewed with some sympathy and even guilt. But, again in contrast to Germany, it seemed that appeasement of Japan would definitely offend the U.S.A. This was the reply given to Sir Robert Craigie, the Ambassador in Tokyo, who urged such a policy in December 1938, on the grounds that HMG was simply falling between two stools in irritating Japan without really helping China. Craigie's criticisms prompted the FO to review its policy, but in the end his advice was rejected. As Cadogan wrote: 'the overriding consideration is the danger of alienating the U.S.'[139]

China policy was but one aspect of the general problem of Far Eastern strategy. Britain's prime interest was to secure firm American promises of naval help, in case of a three-ocean naval war. Fortunately for London, Washington was becoming better disposed to the idea of limited collaboration. Inter-war American strategy had been based on a series of contingency plans for wars against individual countries, with Japan as the principal potential enemy. But by late 1937 American planners had to work on the hypothesis of conflicts on two fronts, against Germany as well as Japan. Therefore, like the British, they were anxious to explore the possibilities of Anglo-American co-operation. Pressed by the Navy, and alarmed by the *Panay* incident, F.D.R., as we saw, accepted the British suggestion of staff talks. The conversations, which took place in January 1938 between the two directors of naval plans, Royal Ingersoll and Tom Phillips, were of limited immediate value, but they did permit an exchange of information on fleet sizes, strategy and technical matters—all of which was an essential precondition for effective naval co-operation.[140] The Americans were careful to stress the non-committal, purely hypothetical nature of the discussions, and their caution was accentuated by the furore in Congress when news of Ingersoll's visit leaked out. But the British were greatly encouraged by this unique instance of the U.S. engaging in pre-war staff conversations, however tentative, with a possible ally. Common action with the U.S. in the Pacific was now within the realms of possibility, and this was an important development.[141]

By early 1939 Britain's need for U.S. support had become acute. Franco-Italian relations had deteriorated to the point where war between them seemed a real possibility. The planners had therefore to prepare for the possibility of conflict against three foes. Such a situation, the Chiefs of Staff warned in January, would place Britain in 'a position more serious than the Empire had ever faced before. The ultimate outcome of the conflict might well depend upon the intervention of the other Powers, in particular of the United States of America.'[142] Moreover, Britain's naval strength was totally inadequate. The Admiralty reported in late February that until the end of September no more than ten capital ships would be immediately available in an emergency. Six of these would have to remain in home waters.[143] If crises developed simultaneously in the Mediterranean and the Pacific Britain would have to choose which theatre to abandon. Previously British Far Eastern strategy had been based on repeated assurances to the Australasian Dominions that in the event of war with Japan, and regardless of the Mediterranean situation, a fleet would be sent to Singapore. The Admiralty had been aware that such categorical promises were unjustified,[144] but they were diplomatically necessary and had been made against the background of HMG's hope that Italy could be appeased. By early 1939 it was clear that Britain must decide on her priorities between the Pacific and the Mediterranean, and during March and April there was a protracted debate in Whitehall. Chatfield, the new Minister for the Co-ordination of Defence, insisted that Britain must send a major battle fleet to the Far East in the event of war, even if that meant abandoning the Mediterranean, while Stanhope, the First Lord, argued that only a token force could be despatched. The same argument occurred within the FO, with, not surprisingly, the Far Eastern department agreeing with Chatfield, and the Egyptian and Co-ordination departments siding with Stanhope.[145] Whether the Far East or the Mediterranean should have priority was an abiding problem for Britain, and one that recurred again in 1941.

This debate assumed a new urgency in mid-March with the take-over in Czechoslovakia, the scare over Romania and the growing Italian threat to Albania. War with Germany and Italy seemed a real possibility, and the Australians were anxious to know how Britain would deter Japan from exploiting the European crisis. The result was two simultaneous overtures to the U.S.A. At a meeting of ministers on 19 March it was agreed to suggest to the U.S. that 'if we were involved in war with Germany and Italy, America should despatch a fleet to Honolulu', and two days later both Halifax and Chatfield made this point to Kennedy.[146] The main U.S. fleet had been in the Atlantic temporarily, for the Caribbean manoeuvres, but F.D.R. had postponed its return to the West Coast in view of the European crisis. The British request prompted him to review that postponement. He did not want Britain to send a fleet to Singapore, arguing that if they lost the Far East they could always recover it, whereas without the Mediterranean they had nothing.[147] On 16 April, the day after F.D.R.'s message to the dictators, Washington therefore announced that the fleet would return to San Diego. It departed on 26–27 April, leaving behind a strengthened Atlantic squadron.[148]

Also on 19 March, the FO invited the U.S. to resume the 1938 naval conversations. Two days later Roosevelt agreed, provided that the talks were held secretly in Washington to avoid press comment which might jeopardize the amendment of the Neutrality Act. The FO request was apparently sent as a panic measure, in the midst of the war scare. The Admiralty only heard about it later, and saw little value in further conversations because the Ingersoll–Phillips talks had been updated the previous January.[149] Once the scare died down there was a hiatus in April, but, when the planners agreed on 2 May that HMG could no longer be sure when or in what strength a fleet would be sent east in the event of war with Japan, they also decided to inform the U.S. of this new development in British strategy.[150] The idea of naval talks was revived and Commander T. C. Hampton arrived in Washington in mid-June to brief senior American naval officers.

Two points in particular emerged from Hampton's report.[151] Firstly, British and American thinking was broadly complementary. In the event of European war the U.S. intended to concentrate its main fleet at Hawaii to deter Japan, while offering limited cruiser assistance and patrolling in the Western Atlantic. This was exactly what the British wanted. Furthermore, Leahy, the Chief of Naval Operations, expressed his personal opinion that in the event of an Anglo-American alliance against Germany, Italy and Japan, the U.S. fleet should move to Singapore, adding, however, that this would only be acceptable to American opinion if the British sent an 'adequate token force' as well. The Admiralty considered this a gratifying advance on the 1938 talks. It felt that two or three battleships would be a sufficient 'token'.[152] Secondly, Hampton emphasized the Americans' fears of press leaks—the talks had been held in Leahy's own home and no agreed record had been made—and of possible inquisition by congressional committee. It was also evident that American thinking was still tentative and that although both F.D.R. and Leahy were, in Hampton's words, 'extremely pro-British', the U.S. had no detailed plans for co-operation. The general feeling in the FO was that, in view of these considerations, the U.S. naval planners had gone about as far as they could.

The broad features of Hampton's report prefigure the character of the Anglo-American relationship in the Far East throughout the period 1939–41. First, there was general agreement on a division of labour between the British and French in the Atlantic and Mediterranean, and the U.S.A. in the Pacific. Although queried in mid-1940 and modified from spring 1941, basically this arrangement was maintained up to Pearl Harbor. Secondly, HMG faced an abiding problem of whether the Administration would make firm commitments and of whether those commitments would be repudiated by Congress and the American people. Thus, in June 1939, when the Tientsin dispute arose with Japan, the Cabinet dismissed the idea of retaliation against Japan, including sanctions, for the familiar reason that no such action could be effective without U.S. help and that this was impossible with the present delicate state of the neutrality debate in Congress.[153] Finally, there was the more specific problem, if and when firm co-operation with the U.S. could be attained, of whether the U.S. could be prevailed upon to protect specifically British interests, and particularly to move its fleet to Singapore. Policymakers in London tended to be hopeful about this. In a way, they had no choice, since their Far Eastern strategy was bankrupt without it. However, they were indulging in wishful thinking. Despite Leahy's encouraging remarks, Washington opinion generally remained determined not to pull Britain's imperial 'chestnuts' out of the fire.

This last problem did not become acute until 1941–42. For the moment, in the summer of 1939, Japan was placated by the interim Tientsin settlement, and then perturbed by the announcement in July from the Roosevelt Administration, in response to congressional pressure, that the U.S.–Japan trade treaty would not be renewed after it expired the following January.[154] In August the Nazi–Soviet pact, coming after months of negotiations for a strengthening of the Berlin–Tokyo axis, temporarily discredited the extremists in the Japanese Army. It left Japan diplomatically isolated and also exposed her to possible Russian aggression should she become too deeply involved in China or South-East Asia. For Britain, therefore, the danger of a Pacific war receded—until the summer of 1940.

# CHAPTER THREE

# Between Peace and War

## September 1939–May 1940

*An elderly statesman with gout,*
*When asked what this war was about,*
*Replied with a sigh:*
*'My colleagues and I*
*Are doing our best to find out.'*
     American limerick, current during Phoney War

*Heaven knows I don't want the Americans to fight for us—we*
*should have to pay too dearly for that if they had a right to be*
*in on the peace terms—but if they are so sympathetic they might*
*at least refrain from hampering our efforts and comforting our*
*foes.*

     Chamberlain, January 1940[1]

## A. A phoney war?

Contrary to British convention, the Second World War did not really begin on 3 September 1939. Only in 1941 did the conflict become global in scope, with the involvement of Russia, and then the U.S.A. and Japan. In 1939 Russia stayed on the sidelines, helping to carve up Poland and Finland, but officially a neutral—as were the U.S., Japan and Italy. What began in September 1939 was therefore another European war—'the last European war' in the words of one historian[2]—involving Britain, France, Germany and, briefly, Poland.

The limited extent of the war was in fact a major achievement for Britain. This is another unconventional point, but one worth emphasizing.[3] For some four years British policymakers had faced the nightmare possibility of simultaneous war against three major powers. Their confused mixture of conciliation and firmness had been designed to avert that disaster. In September 1939 there was consequently considerable relief that Italy and Japan remained outside the conflict. Admittedly, their neutrality was 'malevolent', but it was clear that both powers were waiting on events and that their future actions would be determined largely by the course of the European struggle.

It therefore remained a major goal of British policy to deter Japan and especially Italy from war, without surrendering crucial British interests or weakening the war effort against Germany.

The conflict also seemed unusual because of the lack of action, except intermittently at sea. Despite periodic scares about a German offensive against France, the Western Front remained quiet. The Russo-Finnish war (30 November–12 March) involved the belligerents emotionally but not militarily, and it was not until the German invasion of Scandinavia in early April that serious fighting began. All this is, of course, very familiar. However, retrospectively we tend to see the Phoney War as preparatory to an inevitable German offensive, which eventually occurred in May 1940. It should therefore be emphasized that this was by no means so apparent in Britain and the U.S.A. at the time. The frustrating, enervating game of guessing Hitler's intentions and assessing German strength went on. The German failure to mount an immediate, devastating air attack on London, which everyone had feared, seemed an encouraging sign. As the days of inactivity lengthened into weeks and months, there were many, particularly in Britain and notably Chamberlain, who felt that they were experiencing not the calm before the storm but the overture to the German *Götterdämmerung*.

As in 1937–39, British policy towards the U.S.A. in the Phoney War is only explicable within these wider assumptions about strategy and diplomacy. During that uncertain winter the two countries grew closer together. Yet their co-operation remained hesitant, with each trying to define the relationship on its own terms and according to its own interests. In the next two sections of this chapter I try to determine the nature and limits of that relationship by looking particularly at Britain's use of the American 'arsenal' and at America's tentative efforts at peacemaking. The fourth section examines the place of Churchill in British policy and in Anglo-American relations. Finally, I argue that by the early months of 1940 there was growing criticism of HMG's equivocal policy towards the U.S.A., from various quarters of Whitehall including Churchill, and that, even before the German offensive of May, Britain was being forced into greater dependence upon America.

## B. Washington—the politics and diplomacy of double-edged neutrality

Initially Washington expected that as soon as Hitler had subjugated Poland, he would mount a major offensive on the Western Front. The State Department viewed the prospects with gloom. Hull foresaw the defeat of the Allies and the development of closed economies in Europe and the Far East. Moffat and Breckinridge Long—a veteran Democratic politico who had recently been appointed as another Assistant Secretary—both felt that Stalin would be the ultimate beneficiary of the conflict, while Berle predicted possible Nazi–Soviet domination from the Rhine to the Pacific. He concluded that the U.S. should concentrate on defending the Western Hemisphere rather than supporting the Allies.[4]

Roosevelt, however—intent as usual on keeping his options open—still hoped to do both. This is apparent from his idea for a Western Hemisphere Neutrality Zone, which was in many ways an adaptation of the quarantine/

blockade concept of December 1937. Pressed by the U.S.A., the American republics issued a declaration in early October stating that belligerent vessels should keep out of a zone about 300 miles in breadth, drawn around the Americas with the exception of the waters off Canada and European possessions. It was intended that the U.S. Navy would ensure that the zone was respected. In one sense this policy was an extension of neutral rights within the intellectual framework of the Monroe Doctrine. Roosevelt wanted to keep the war out of the American hemisphere and protect the Panama Canal and the vulnerable South American states. On the other hand, as he made clear to Morgenthau in April 1939, and to George VI and Lindsay in June, he also intended that it would assist the Allies. He believed that they would respect the zone, while the Germans would not—thus accentuating the important moral contrast between the belligerents. He also suggested that the Royal Navy could leave this area of their blockade to the Americans, thereby releasing much-needed vessels for service elsewhere.[5] It was because the neutrality zone and patrol were apparently to be operated in the Allies' favour that HMG was willing 'to discuss the application of a scheme which seems not only to infringe some of the established principles of the International Law but to be inherently impracticable'.[6] To facilitate its operation they had granted F.D.R.'s secret request for the lease of land on the islands of Trinidad, St. Lucia and Bermuda to build naval and air bases. When F.D.R. first advanced the idea, on 30 June, Whitehall found it typically Rooseveltian—grand and helpful in scope but glossing over numerous legal difficulties. The President, for his part, considered the British reply characteristically nit-picking and insensitive to his own domestic constraints.[7] Nevertheless the British recognized the importance of the scheme. Some officials felt that its operation in time of war would make it impossible for the U.S. to keep out of hostilities.[8] HMG therefore completed the arrangements for the leases by December. In the event, the U.S. Navy made little use of the new facilities that winter, mainly because it had insufficient vessels to patrol effectively,[9] but the episode constituted a precedent for the 1940 destroyers–bases deal.

The amendment of the Neutrality Act provides an even clearer instance of F.D.R.'s balancing act. When war began he issued the mandatory proclamations, but he made clear to the British his reluctance to do so, and, after allowing public opinion to crystallize, he called a special session of Congress in late September for the purpose of amending the Act.[10] The political situation differed in at least three respects from that of the summer. First, the outbreak of war had come as a considerable surprise to many Congressmen, making them more ready to accept presidential leadership in time of crisis. Secondly, F.D.R. belatedly began to conciliate his principal opponents, wooing Southern Democrats and giving them management of the bill, and also making overtures to Republican leaders on the Hill. He even considered taking Landon and Knox, his opponents in the 1936 election, into the Cabinet.[11] Finally, he led a clear and vigorous Administration campaign on behalf of the bill, enlisting prominent Republicans such as Thomas Lamont of J. P. Morgan's, and the Kansas editor William Allen White, at the head of an effective pressure group. Opinion was still divided but the Administration's clear lead mobilized support and gave Roosevelt 'his first experience of what it meant to be an *opinion maker* in foreign affairs'.[12] The revised Neutrality Act of 4 November repealed the arms embargo and placed all trade with belligerents on a cash and carry basis. These measures would clearly benefit the Allies, with their superior sea power and foreign exchange, but, much to the fury of his critics, F.D.R. represented them simply as a return to international law to keep America at peace. Nevertheless, the President was not entirely disingenuous. For, as he requested, the new act also gave him discretionary power to define combat areas around Europe from which U.S. citizens, ships and aircraft were excluded, and he immediately issued a proclamation to that effect.[13] This was not merely a sop to the isolationists. We saw in the previous chapter that F.D.R. believed that a combat zone 'might really be useful'. As with the Western Hemisphere Neutrality Zone, Roosevelt was trying to prevent repetition of the naval incidents of 1915–17 that had helped draw the U.S.A. into the Great War. He was willing, as Wilson was not, to restrict American neutral rights in the hopes of safeguarding her neutrality. He was also willing to pay the price in consequent losses to American merchant shipping which would be effectively excluded from the transatlantic carrying trade. U.S. exporters and shippers, who lobbied strenuously against these provisions, estimated that about 90–100 vessels—nearly a third of the U.S. oceanic merchant fleet— would have to be laid up.[14]

Roosevelt was also determined that the Allies should exploit the American arsenal in his way and not theirs. In the Great War British purchasing had been handled by J. P. Morgan and Company, the major New York banking house. In September 1939 New Dealers were alarmed at F.D.R.'s *rapprochement* with the Republicans and big business. Berle thought that this had 'a terribly suspicious 1914 ring about it' on the grounds that it was 'the Morgans, the Harvard New Englanders and the like who really influenced our entry into war in 1917', while Ickes, Cohen, Corcoran and Bob Jackson were all afraid that 'Wall Streeters and economic royalists' would march back into Washington, as they had in 1917, and reverse the New Deal's reforms. F.D.R., however, assured them that he was 'watching everything with an eagle eye'.[15] He made it clear to the Allies that they were not to work through Wall Street but in conjunction with Morgenthau and the Treasury. They should set up government purchasing missions, and leave their accounts with the Federal Reserve Bank of New York. There Morgenthau would be able to scrutinize their purchases and ensure that these did not conflict with U.S. needs. The British were quite ready to co-operate, primed by their Embassy and by Lord Riverdale, who had visited the U.S. that summer to assess the situation.[16] By the end of 1939 an Anglo-French purchasing mission, headed by Arthur Purvis, a Canadian businessman, was operating in New York, in close liaison with the U.S. Treasury.[17]

In these ways, F.D.R. sought to aid the Allies without the entanglements which, he believed, had drawn the U.S.A. into the previous conflict. His neutrality was double-edged—cutting both at Germany and at excessive ties with Britain and France. Admittedly he sometimes spoke as if he wanted and expected early American entry. The King, for instance, was greatly encouraged by F.D.R.'s bellicose comments in June, when Roosevelt told him that his neutrality patrol would shoot U-boats on sight and that if London were bombed the U.S. would come straight in.[18] More experienced 'Roosevelt-watchers', however, were used to F.D.R.'s moods and his tendency to exaggerate. The FO was not impressed, therefore, by reports in the early weeks of the war that F.D.R. expected that Hitler would soon arouse America's moral indignation and wound her national honour so that she would quickly enter the war. They ascribed them to his tendency to wishful thinking and to loose and optimistic talk in private. This was probably correct.[19] Moreover, such comments were usually made by Roosevelt to British listeners, and it is likely that they were part of his continuing effort to stiffen the Allies and convince them of American support. (We shall detect the same tendency again in May–June 1940.) In any case, all such forecasts by F.D.R. were predicated on the assumption of aggressive German acts affecting American ideals, interests or honour. Without such acts he felt he would not be able to overcome domestic opposition to belligerency. This remained the cardinal feature of his foreign policy right up to Pearl Harbor. For his part, Hitler was determined to avoid such incidents until he had dealt with European matters. He therefore restricted German propaganda in the U.S.A. and kept Admiral Raeder's U-boats on a tight rein to avoid incidents on the high seas.[20]

Whatever Roosevelt's inclinations, therefore—and they were probably less warlike than he averred to the British—he felt himself bound by political chains. In these circumstances, he seems to have convinced himself that he had done enough to prevent a German victory. Although feeling that the chances of an Allied defeat were fifty-fifty,[21] he anticipated a quick war, probably over before June, by which time Hitler would either have won or else have been overthrown.[22] He therefore probably derived encouragement from the successive postponements of the German offensive, which allowed the Allies a further winter to strengthen their defences. Fundamentally, Roosevelt's confidence rested as before on his assumptions about Allied power and wealth. These assumptions were not shared by his ambassadors in London and Paris. Kennedy filled his messages in September with gloomy reports about Britain's financial position and in November Bullitt told the Administration categorically that in about twelve months France and England would have exhausted their foreign exchange resources. However, Roosevelt considered Kennedy an inveterate defeatist and Bullitt an erratic reporter, excessively influenced by the mood of his most recent confidant.[23] Furthermore, the U.S. Treasury had no such doubts. As late as the end of the winter it stated that the Allies had 'liquid foreign exchange resources greatly in excess of sums needed for 1940', and that an 'Allied request for credit at this time is wholly unwarranted'.[24] Consequently, Roosevelt saw no reason in the autumn of 1939 to change his opinion that they had the means to take advantage of the benevolent neutrality the U.S. now offered.[25]

\*     \*     \*

During the winter of 1939–40, however, relations between HMG and the State Department became particularly strained, largely because of British economic warfare.[26] Britain was a major customer for several persistently surplus crops from the South and Midwest, such as cotton, fruit and tobacco —taking a quarter of the latter, for instance—and the Department was disturbed by the reduction in British purchases once war began. Frequently this contravened the 1938 Trade Agreement, and Hull feared that Congress might refuse to renew the Trade Agreements Act in the spring. The blockade, too, caused problems and many of the historic tensions between belligerent and neutral rights, which had so inflamed relations in 1916, soon recurred. Mail censorship was again particularly resented, and British diversion of neutral shipping for inspection at contraband control bases disrupted American trade. In the case of the Scottish base at Kirkwall it also meant that U.S. vessels were being compelled to enter the combat zone designated by F.D.R. Furthermore, it seemed that the British were deliberately discriminating against the U.S.A. Italian ships were less troubled by contraband controls, and, although cutting back on agricultural imports from the U.S.A., the British announced in December and January that they would be taking more from Greece and Turkey. Finally, the British export drive of early 1940 seemed highly suspicious, especially in Latin America. A few prominent businessmen went as far as to say that British competition was a greater threat to America than a German-dominated Europe.[27]

These developments gradually confirmed the darkest suspicions of the State Department's 'realists'. It should be stressed that this dominant group, centring as we have seen on Welles, Berle and Moffat, began the war with the intention of quietly assisting the British blockade wherever possible. However, they were also determined not to let Britain take advantage of American goodwill. According to Moffat their slogan was 'No help to Germany but no Dominion status for ourselves'.[28] And they became increasingly concerned at the implications of British policy. The curtailment of agricultural purchases seemed like an attempt to blackmail Americans into extending credit.[29] They believed that the navicert system acted as a covert black list, aimed partly at U.S. firms, and that economic intelligence gleaned by the censor was being used to Britain's commercial advantage.[30] Finally, the shift in tobacco purchases reinforced what Moffat described as 'the increasing evidence that Britain was planning a huge trading orbit within the pound–franc area designed to exclude us'. Similarly, by early 1940 Berle believed that 'the hard-boiled element in the British government is getting into an ascendancy in all trade matters' and trying to create a great closed Anglo-French trading area which would be little different from the German *Gross-raumwirtschaft*.[31]

The British failed to respond to U.S. notes of protest, and, when the tobacco and censorship controversies grew more heated in the New Year, the State Department decided that something had to be done 'to jolt the English into a fairer frame of mind and to satisfy the public that this Government was not a mere appanage of the British Government'.[32] In mid-January the official notes, and the feelings that had inspired them, were made known to the press, Hull called in Lothian to give him a lecture, and British officials were often reminded of the number of Southerners on key congressional committees that dealt with foreign and military policy.[33]

Most of the Administration found Britain's policy exasperating to some degree. However, there was a widespread feeling that State had lost its sense of proportion. Thus Bullitt told Moffat in February that although he found British behaviour 'very vexatious' they had to remember that America's primary interest was to help the Allies win the war and that any public dispute with the British only benefited the Germans.[34] This was also Roosevelt's opinion. He believed that with a few mutual concessions, including more flexibility by the British over mail censorship, diplomatic wrangles could be avoided. He also accepted that Britain had to conserve her exchange reserves to some extent. In early March Morgenthau reminded him that '... about a month ago you told me that if you were in the position of the allies you would buy only what you needed in this country and tell us to go jump in the Potomac if we didn't like it'.[35] What worried Roosevelt and Morgenthau was that the British were not even purchasing necessities, namely munitions and aircraft. The President was reluctant to mobilize American industry, and had been relying on Allied orders to encourage manufacturers to convert their plant and to stimulate rearmament. Furthermore, as he told his aides, 'these foreign orders mean prosperity in this country and we can't elect the Democratic party unless we get prosperity...'.[36] Above all, he considered the orders essential if the Allies were to resist the German offensive, which he, unlike Chamberlain, was sure would come in the spring. As one Treasury memo put it: 'Both England and France complacently assume that time is on their side. Time is on their side only if they make a vigorous use of all their resources and are prepared to make full use of their army and aviation as well as naval forces.'[37] Since the Allies were the U.S.A.'s front line their deteriorating position was undermining U.S. security as well as their own. F.D.R. and Morgenthau were therefore appalled at Allied inactivity and increasingly doubtful that they really knew 'what this war was about'.

\*     \*     \*

It was out of these various suspicions and anxieties in Washington that the Welles mission originated. Between 25 February and 19 March Welles visited Rome, Berlin, Paris and London as the personal emissary of the President, accompanied by Pierrepont Moffat. The visits to the Allied capitals were brief—they were only in London from 11 to 14 March—and most of their time was spent in Germany and on two visits to Rome. Even today the mission remains shrouded in mystery. It derived from talks between Welles and F.D.R. and in the end only these two really knew the thinking behind it. However, certain observations may be made.[38]

There is little doubt that the Welles–Berle–Moffat group within the State Department was seriously investigating the chances of a compromise peace. Their motives were complex, even contradictory. On the one hand, they agreed that Germany posed a potential threat to U.S. security and that the U.S. had a clear interest in seeing Hitler contained within Europe. Berle put the argument at its most hard-headed: 'We have no necessary interest in defending the British Empire aside from the fact that we prefer the British as against the German method of running an empire. But we do have a very real and solid interest in having the British, and not the Germans, dominant in the Atlantic.'[39] But they did not believe that commitments to the Allies were necessary. Despite lack of confidence in Britain and France, they certainly did not anticipate a sudden, total Allied collapse, which would leave the U.S.A. without time to rearm.[40] They were also determined to avoid being entangled in another war. It therefore seemed best to concentrate on hemisphere defence rather than to co-operate closely with the Allies. In any case, they were convinced that a total Allied victory was not in America's interests. Suspicious of British commercial policy and increasingly concerned about the effect of the war on the world economy, they saw the U.S.A., in Wilsonian vein, as defender of the rights of all peace-loving neutrals[41] and wanted to preserve her potential as a mediator, free from commitments to either side. By Christmas a Departmental committee was examining the foundations of a future peace, with a reformed League, large-scale disarmament and the elimination of economic rivalry as the central ideas.[42] Berle, like Harry Dexter White in the Treasury, tentatively envisaged the reconstruction of the world monetary system on the basis of a gold-backed U.S. dollar[43]—ideas that were to triumph at Bretton Woods in 1944—and Berle also expected that after the war much of the international economy, including Britain, would be dependent at least temporarily upon the U.S.A. for supplies, raw materials and finance. 'This', he concluded, 'is the outline of an unparalleled economic empire.'[44]

These ideas were common to many officials in the State Department. But it was their keenest advocates—Welles, Berle and Moffat's European division—who felt that the U.S. should seriously explore the admittedly faint chances of peace before the spring offensive.[45] Learning from the example of the House–Grey memorandum in 1916, and probably from the failure of the January 1938 initiative, they were determined not to work through London. As Berle put it, in a telegram approved by Hull and endorsed by Welles, '. . . we must of course perform no act or allow any impression to arise indicating that we are collaborating with the British for common peace terms. History has shown the dangers of such a course.'[46] For both Welles and Berle, as in the winter of 1937–38, the instrument of peacemaking would be the force of neutral opinion, led by the United States. Berle recorded on 11 January:

> We are about decided that the next thing to be done is to call a meeting of neutrals, in theory to discuss methods of maintaining their rights during the war period. But the real and inevitable discussion would be whether mediation could not be proposed, together with possible peace terms, and with an insistence that the neutrals sit at the peace table. This is an evolution of an idea which Sumner put forward several years ago.[47]

The meeting of neutrals was announced on 9 February. On the same day plans for the Welles mission were publicized. The coincidence was not accidental. Welles' European visit was an extension of this idea of mobilizing neutral opinion behind a compromise peace,[48] and Welles in particular believed that Mussolini could play a crucial role, as he had done in September 1938. It seems that Welles had vague plans for settling the frontiers of Central and Eastern Europe, and, as in 1937–38, he emphasized the importance of economic liberalization and disarmament, together, now, with the idea of an international police force.[49] In the end he concluded that the chances of a lasting peace were slight, but remained sure that Mussolini could prove invaluable when a real opportunity arose for peace-making.[50]

Roosevelt's thinking, as usual, is opaque and complex. Characteristically, he probably wanted to kill several birds with one stone. He told Breckinridge Long on 12 March that the main aim of Welles' mission was to help the Allies by delaying or even preventing the German spring offensive, thereby giving Britain and France longer to rearm and to obtain U.S. supplies. The other reason, he said, was to get the 'low down on Hitler and get Mussolini's point of view'. He already knew what London and Paris thought, he said— the visits there were only 'window dressing'.[51] Undoubtedly, these were both genuine considerations. As we have seen, F.D.R. was anxious about the Allied position and he also wanted information on the European leaders— probably all of them and not just Hitler and Mussolini. Welles' reports provided the vivid, gossipy pen-pictures that F.D.R. liked, and, more substantially, a corrective to the prevalent Washington image of Chamberlain as the naive, fussy, 'umbrella man'.[52]

However, F.D.R.'s comments to Long read like one of those disingenuous, retrospective, 'for-the-historical-record' statements that he was wont to make from time to time. In fact Roosevelt had spent considerable time that winter examining the possibilities of peace. His Christmas announcement of diplomatic relations with the Vatican—a politically delicate move which he had contemplated periodically since 1935—was designed, in part, in Berle's words, 'to lay something of the moral foundation for a lasting peace' by drawing on one of 'the great philosophical forces' of civilization.[53] The President was also behind the idea of a conference of neutrals.[54] Moreover, on 14 December he had a long ruminative conversation with Lothian about a future peace, in which he emphasized the importance of land disarmament and outlined the concept of the 'four freedoms'. Lothian told the FO that Roosevelt 'evidently hopes that before his time is up [presumably meaning before the end of his second term in January 1941] he may be able to intervene as a kind of umpire. He clearly does not want another Wilsonian peace conference. He rather seems to think that if he were appealed to he could lay down conditions for an armistice.' F.D.R. assured Lothian that the time had not yet nearly come for such a *démarche*, but 11 days before, according to Berle:

> The President told a couple of stories and then wound up by saying he would tell a stranger one. He proposed to make peace next Spring on the basis of having everybody produce everything they could; take what they needed; put the rest into a pool; and let the countries which needed the balance draw it as needed through cartels.[55]

From these fragments of evidence one can infer that F.D.R.'s comments to Long were a little too casual and that he had been seriously exploring the chances of peace. Suspicions of Allied economic policy were a less important motive for him than for Welles or Berle, but he *was* anxious about the deteriorating Allied military position and wanted to examine every means of containing Hitler peacefully. Nevertheless, Roosevelt was only interested in a durable peace—of at least a quarter-century—and not another compromise of benefit only to Hitler.[56] By 12 March his earlier tentative hopes had been proved vain—hence his rather disingenuous remarks to Long.[57] In addition to a serious interest in peace, F.D.R. had probably had domestic opinion very much in mind. His political fortunes were at their lowest ebb and favourable publicity for the Welles mission could help combat Republican attacks on Democratic warmongering as the presidential primaries got under way. On a more elevated level the visit would dramatize the war to a nation that was still complacent about its security. It was probably in part an answer to the problem F.D.R. posed in December 1939—how 'to get the American people to think of conceivable consequences without scaring the American people into thinking that they are going to be dragged into this war'.[58]

One should not exaggerate the expectations Washington entertained about the Welles mission. However, the wider ideas about American peacemaking that lay behind it were significant and they reveal the underlying Wilsonianism of American policy. Wilson had sought to eliminate aggressive German militarism, while also preventing Britain and France from exploiting the war for their own 'reactionary', 'imperialist' ends. Both as a neutral and as an associate belligerent he worked for a peace settlement that would achieve these aims. He was particularly concerned to ensure disarmament, freedom of the seas, the liberalization of trade and an effective international organization. These would be the foundations of a peaceful, liberal world order, which would also, not incidentally, benefit American interests.[59] As we have seen, F.D.R. rejected some of Wilson's methods and in particular believed that the League was outmoded. Nevertheless, he and his advisers were fundamentally Wilsonian in outlook. Above all they feared the Nazi menace to world peace, but they were also determined that the European powers should not perpetuate their traditional rivalries for territory and wealth—the soil in which fascism had grown. They faced what Berle called 'the old Wilsonian dilemma'—how to prevent 'an idealist conception of co-operative peace' from being 'used as a cover for strictly nationalistic designs' as they believed had happened in 1919 when 'the Allied and associated powers remained untouched by the high moral considerations which they were applying to their enemies'.[60] Like Wilson in 1914–17, they hoped to achieve their goals without U.S. belligerency, intending that America should save her strength and authority for determining and imposing the peace settlement. However, the balance was a delicate one. They would all have agreed with William Allen White's comment to Roosevelt: 'I fear our involvement before the peace, and yet I fear to remain uninvolved letting the danger of a peace of tyranny approach too near.'[61] Early in 1940 the latter fear, together with State's concern about the economic war, encouraged F.D.R. to explore the possibilities of a negotiated peace, with Welles cast in the role played by House in 1916. The attempt failed, but Washington remained determined, as we shall see in chapter ten, that this time the New World would not only fatten on but would correct the follies of the Old.

## C. London: continued doubts, hopes and fears about the U.S.A.

Officially, British policy was to prepare for a long war, perhaps of three years' duration. The military planners acknowledged that they faced an enemy better prepared for war who would therefore enjoy initial superiority on land and in the air. They expected that Germany would immediately mount a strong offensive, either on the Western Front or perhaps directly against Britain. If the Allies could survive this, then, through propaganda, subversion and, above all, blockade—the traditional British war weapon— the enemy could gradually be worn down and forced to surrender. In the long run Britain's sea power and global economic resources would be decisive. The planners recognized that if Japan intervened the position would be much graver and 'the outcome of war would depend on our ability to hold key positions and on other powers, particularly U.S.A., coming to our aid'. However, for the moment, that threat had receded, and they concluded that, in a purely European conflict: 'Once we had been able to develop the full fighting strength of the Empire, we should regard the outcome of the war with confidence.'[62]

The Treasury, however, took a rather different view. In an important paper for the Cabinet, dated 3 July 1939, it emphasized that Britain's ability to fight a sustained war depended on what it quaintly termed 'the war chest'—the country's gold and foreign exchange reserves. After the panics of the previous 15 months these stood at £500 million in gold and some £200 million in securities that could be easily requisitioned and sold. In themselves, these figures were not too bad—gold stocks were substantially larger than in 1914 and negotiable securities about the same. However, in the Great War, Britain had been able to draw on the U.S. money market, obtaining over £200 million from private investors and £840 million from the American Government. The crucial difference, therefore, between 1914 and 1939 was that with the Johnson and Neutrality Acts there was no prospect this time of private or government loans from the U.S.A. 'Nevertheless', the Treasury concluded, 'unless, when the time comes, the United States are prepared either to lend or to give us money as required, the prospects for a long war are exceedingly grim.' The estimate of three years 'is very likely much too optimistic'.[63]

This was a devastating assessment. It effectively undermined the fundamental assumption on which British strategy was based. Logically there were two ways of criticizing it—two ways of giving hope for Britain to fight a war. One was to question the paper's view of U.S. policy, by arguing that Britain must purchase heavily in the U.S.A. and that the Administration must be trusted to help her out when dollar reserves were exhausted. This was the approach of the Foreign Office and the Service ministries. Alternatively one could question the assumption that the war would be a long one. If it were over quickly then U.S. help would not be needed. This was the line of argument favoured by Chamberlain and many of his political colleagues. In principle the two positions were not incompatible—Halifax, for instance, ever in search of the middle ground, combined them both[64]—but in practice they became part of a passionate argument about the conduct of the war which developed in February and March 1940. I shall discuss the views of the

FO and the Services later in the chapter, in the context of that crisis. For the moment it was the outlook of Chamberlain and the politicians that was more important.

A week after war began the PM told his sisters bluntly that there could be no peace until Hitler 'disappears and his system collapses'. 'But', he continued, 'what I hope for is not a military victory—I very much doubt the feasibility of that—but a collapse of the German home front. For that it is necessary to convince the Germans that they cannot win.'[65] His policy was therefore one of passive firmness: 'Hold on tight, keep up the economic pressure, push on with munitions production & military preparations with the utmost energy, take no offensive until Hitler begins it. I reckon that if we are allowed to carry on this policy we shall have won the war by the Spring.' Unlike his military advisers the premier did not expect a major German offensive. 'I don't believe they feel sufficient confidence to venture on the Great War unless they are forced into it by action on our part. It is my aim to see that that action is not taken. . . .'[66] What he really feared was a Nazi 'peace offensive'. A 'specious appeal' from Hitler, promising no further territorial aggrandizement, could cause disunity among the Allies and strong pressure from the neutrals. In such a situation what 'we ought to do is just throw back the peace offer and continue the blockade'.[67] On the other hand, Chamberlain remained alert for *genuine* peace signals—indications of a possible coup against Hitler. Thus he kept open contacts with Goering and the other German 'moderates', and he emphasized repeatedly that Britain's quarrel was with Nazism and not with Germany.[68] As autumn passed into winter, and the repeated rumours of imminent German attack proved groundless, his confidence increased: '. . . I have always held that Hitler missed the bus in Sept. 1938. He could have dealt France & ourselves a terrible, perhaps a mortal, blow then. The opportunity will not recur.' As late as 20 April he was still sceptical about a German western offensive. Yet he was also sure that Hitler could not survive another winter.[69] Time, in short, was on the Allies' side.

Once again, Chamberlain was more sanguine than many of his advisers. Few, for instance, shared his persistent disbelief about a German offensive. Nevertheless, as before, we find that his overall assessment was widely accepted, particularly by his political colleagues—the expectation of a German collapse rather than military victory, the tactic of firmness without aggression, the cautious sifting of real from spurious peace feelers. The general belief among ministers, expressed for example by Halifax and Chatfield, was that German economy and morale were fragile and that time was on the Allies' side. Retrospectively such thinking seems ludicrous. In fact it was prevalent throughout Whitehall and reflected a basic and persistent misunderstanding of Hitler's conception of warfare. No less than the Allies the Führer wanted to avoid another Great War. His strategy was therefore to prepare for a series of short, sharp wars involving only limited economic mobilization and consequently only limited hardship for civilians. The *Blitzkrieg*—a strategic and not simply a tactical concept—therefore enabled Germany to enjoy guns *and* butter. The British never understood this. They assumed that Hitler was preparing for a sustained and total war effort. On such calculations the

German economy already seemed overstretched and without large-scale economic and territorial gains they believed it would experience grave shortages of raw materials within 12 to 18 months. The inevitable domestic privations would help bring Hitler down.[70]

Such thinking underpinned Chamberlain's fundamental hopefulness about the war. It was not simply a matter of the politician's professional optimism: he was doing more than hoping for the best while preparing for the worst.[71] He was also *preparing* for the best—still keeping his options open and maintaining his balancing act between peace and war in a fluid and uncertain situation. As in 1937–39, so in the winter of 1939–40, Chamberlain's overall policy in Europe provides the key to understanding his handling of the U.S.A.

*　　　*　　　*

At the beginning of the war HMG's policy towards the United States was determined by the Treasury's gloomy warnings about Britain's external finance. The Chancellor, Sir John Simon, and his officials made every effort to conserve Britain's reserves, imposing tight exchange controls and eliminating all but essential purchases abroad. With apparently no possibility of credits from the U.S.A., because of the provisions of the Johnson and Neutrality Acts, British policy was therefore to treat America as 'a limited marginal source of war supplies'.[72] In practice this meant buying mainly foodstuffs and raw materials, rather than expensive manufactured goods. The main exception was machine tools, which constituted about 17 per cent of the $720 million HMG estimated in January 1940 that it would spend in the U.S.A. during the first year of war. These were crucial for mass production, and a major bottleneck in rapid rearmament.[73] Aircraft and engines, on the other hand, comprised less than 11 per cent of the total estimate. This neglect of the American potential caused some disagreement between Britain and France, but it was based on good logistic arguments, as Chamberlain explained to the Anglo-French Supreme War Council in December. Britain lacked the foreign exchange, and she could produce the necessary planes much more quickly than the Americans, in their backward state of mobilization, provided that the vital machine tools came through. Indeed, expenditure on planes would necessitate a cut-back in purchases of tools. Whereas Britain could reach peak production in 1941, the U.S. was unlikely to do so until 1942—by which time Britain's three-year allowance would be perilously near to exhaustion.[74] In fact, by late February 1940, the Treasury had privately abandoned that estimate. On present rates of spending, it warned, by the end of the second year of war the 'prospect at the very best is that we should have to contract our war effort to a vast extent'.[75]

Chamberlain fully supported the Treasury's restrictive policy and the pessimistic view of the U.S.A. on which it rested. He told the French on 5 February 1940 that there was 'little hope that the United States would provide, or even lend, dollars, even after the forthcoming Presidential elections' in November.[76] Basically, he still believed that American help could not be relied upon or that it would not come in sufficient time or abundance. However, he also maintained his conviction that the *appearance* of Anglo-American co-operation could help to undermine German morale. This was the value of the repeal of the arms embargo—diplomatic rather than logistic. Chamberlain said as much to Roosevelt himself in a letter of 4 October:

> My own belief is that we shall win, not by a complete and spectacular victory, which is unlikely under modern conditions, but by convincing the Germans that they cannot win. Once they have arrived at that conclusion, I do not believe they can stand our relentless pressure, for they have not started this war with the enthusiasm or the confidence of 1914.
>
> I believe they are already half way to this conviction and I cannot doubt that the attitude of the United States of America, due to your personal efforts, has had a notable influence in this direction. If the embargo is repealed this month, I am convinced that the effect on German morale will be devastating.

When Chamberlain wrote again, a month later, to acknowledge the repeal, he alluded to the 'assurance that we and our French allies may draw on the great reservoir of American resources' but gave no indication that they were going to do so, and dwelt mainly on the effects of the news on British, German and world opinion.[77] Although HMG did not intend to take advantage of the American arsenal, the fact that it *could* do so, Chamberlain believed, would have a sobering effect in Berlin.

However, there was more to Britain's treatment of the U.S.A. than purely financial considerations, vital though these were. For, while reducing its normal purchases of agricultural commodities from America, HMG was willing to buy from other neutrals whose goodwill it considered particularly important. For instance, at the beginning of the war the Treasury prohibited further use of foreign exchange for the purchase of U.S. tobacco. However, in December, HMG decided to conclude trade agreements with Greece and Turkey, to prevent them falling completely into the German economic orbit. To achieve this aim Britain had to take a proportion of their tobacco crops, which were a vital part of their export trades—50 per cent in the case of Greece.[78] When this decision was announced in mid-January, as we saw, it caused great anger in Washington. However, senior British policymakers were more concerned about the Mediterranean than the U.S.A. In particular they wanted to tighten the blockade and reduce Italian trade with Germany, by ending Italy's imports of German coal and her exports of agricultural commodities. Yet it was also considered vital to keep on good terms with Mussolini—to avoid extending the war and, it is worth noting, in the hope of purchasing Italian ships and guns. Consequently Britain would have to fill the gap caused by any reduction in Italo-German trade. Late in January the FO and Ministry of Economic Warfare (MEW) therefore argued that 'notwithstanding the obvious disadvantages of buying goods which we do not need in order to enable Italy to buy coal which we could without difficulty sell elsewhere, it is politically necessary to offer to make essential purchases of fruit and vegetables in Italy'.[79] This was precisely the argument Lothian, the FO American Department and parts of the Board of Trade were making with regard to the U.S.A.—that Britain must yet again make economic concessions for political ends. But although Halifax was concerned about American reactions if Britain again bought from other countries agricultural produce she would not purchase from America, his overriding goal was an agreement with Italy. Chamberlain agreed. He 'was disposed to think that at this stage of the war, the goodwill of Italy was so important to us that we should do whatever might be necessary to secure it'.[80] In the event, it became apparent that British hopes of a trade agreement and of Italian military supplies were hopelessly unrealistic. But the episode reveals HMG's diplomatic priorities in early 1940. Tightening the blockade against Germany and keeping the Mediterranean out of the war were more important considerations than wooing the U.S.A. Behind them lay the hope that passive firmness would bring quick rewards and make a long war unnecessary.

But financial and diplomatic considerations alone do not fully explain Chamberlain's policy towards the U.S.A. during the Phoney War. His two overriding aims were to end the Nazi threat to European security and to maintain Britain's position as a world power. The first aim did not require total victory; only the elimination of Nazism and a negotiated peace with guarantees. If, as he believed, there was a real chance of achieving this by a policy of passive firmness leading to a German collapse, then there was no need to jeopardize Britain's global position by a full-scale war effort. As Alan Milward has observed, in war

> The correct strategic synthesis will be that which only makes exactly those demands on the economy which are sufficient to achieve the strategic purpose. For example, the strategic aim of defence against an enemy is not served if the demands made on the economy change society and the political system so much that it is no longer the same as the one originally to be defended.[81]

Such thinking is surely part of the explanation for Chamberlain's opposition to, say, complete economic mobilization or to a coalition government.[82] Why substantially upset the status quo if the war might be won cheaply and quickly? Similar considerations lay behind HMG's purchasing policy. Restricted spending abroad, thereby conserving Britain's reserves, made sense in the light of the 'three-year war' strategy. But it also maximized Britain's chances of recovery if the war turned out to be brief.

For the same reasons, HMG was also anxious to prevent America from once again extracting economic advantage from her neutrality in a European war. Prominent Tory back-benchers warned of the U.S. threat to British trade, and the Washington Embassy feared that the wartime demise of British civil aviation would leave Pan American Airways in impregnable control of Atlantic and Pacific air routes by the end of the war.[83] And, as Pierrepont Moffat in the State Department suspected, some British officials were trying to use Britain's refusal to buy U.S. agricultural products as a way of forcing the Administration to extend credits. This was explicitly the intention of the Board of Trade's representative in Washington and of the Ministry of Economic Warfare.[84] However, Berle and Moffat were probably wrong to suspect Britain of trying to take advantage of the war to create a sterling–imperial bloc. Chamberlain still did not believe that the Empire could be self-sufficient or that Britain could do without European and U.S. trade, and in response to sustained pressure from Lothian, the FO and the Ministry of Information, he agreed to restate publicly Britain's commitment to multilateralism. In an address on 31 January Chamberlain referred to the 1938 trade agreement with the U.S.A., calling it 'the very negation of that too prevalent system of bilateralism, of exclusive advantages, of discrimination carried to a pitch which clogs the wheels of commerce and which promotes ill-feeling among the nations'. He stressed that the wartime purchasing measures were a response to the temporary emergency, and that when peace was restored Britain would be committed to the resumption of international trade along multilateral channels and to an ending of that 'vicious policy of economic nationalism and autarky which did so much to upset the last great peace settlement'.[85] This statement attracted much attention in the U.S. press and was publicly welcomed by Hull. It was still being taken by the Board of Trade as an authoritative expression of HMG policy in the summer of 1941.[86]

It seems important, therefore, that Anglo-American economic competition should not be exaggerated or misunderstood.[87] Britain was trying to hold on to what she had got rather than to expand even further. In this regard, it is revealing to look at the assumptions on which the Treasury based its assessment of Britain's financial position. As we have seen, it valued her negotiable foreign securities at some £200 million. It thereby excluded from the 'war chest' the bulk of Britain's overseas assets, which were generally estimated at around £3,000 million.[88] The U.S. Treasury, however, which made its own calculations about Britain's position in November 1939, included the assets of all the Dominions, together with British holdings and investments in the U.S.A., in other neutral countries and in the Empire. It admitted that these could only be realized rapidly at a fraction of their current value, and that such a sale would be a last resort, but it definitely considered them part of Britain's potential war finance.[89] These different criteria reflected a fundamental difference of national interests. The Administration wanted to contain Hitler at minimum cost to the U.S.A. This was primarily Britain's war and she should and could bear the burden herself, even if that meant selling off some of her imperial 'real estate'. American 'aid' would be limited to filling crucial gaps in supplies, on a cash basis. HM Treasury's very different attitude was equally understandable. Not only would the sale of securities and investments further weaken Britain's payments position and cripple the trade on which her economic survival depended, it would also directly benefit her American rivals, who would readily snap up British assets, particularly in Latin America.

HMG's economic policy was therefore part of its wider determination to defend Britain's fragile global pre-eminence. Chamberlain even spoke of not wanting American entry into the war, for fear of Britain becoming too dependent upon the U.S.A. On 27 January 1940 he sounded off to his sisters about the problems presented by various neutrals. After complaining about Norway and Romania, he went on:

> Then the U.S.A. goes right back on us because while we spend all our dollars on buying war stores from them we have none left to buy tobacco. And they declare that they are insulted when we examine the mails which are the vehicle of a carefully organised system of aid & relief to our enemies. Heaven knows I don't want the Americans to fight for us—we should have to pay too dearly for that if they had a right to be in on the peace terms—but if they are so sympathetic they might at least refrain from hampering our efforts and comforting our foes.

Obviously, one can make too much of a single letter, written at a time of stress.[90] Nevertheless, Chamberlain's comments are an excellent statement of the twin themes of British policy during 1939–40—the desire for U.S. help, but on a limited scale.

Thus, on the one hand, the British wanted America's benevolent neutrality. Chamberlain was only expressing a common feeling in Whitehall in early 1940 when he complained about America 'hampering our efforts and comforting our foes'. Washington's protests caused a backlash in FO/A, and in early February the Department's head itemized British grievances about the effect of the U.S. policy on a war effort it professed to support. The neutrality laws, the FO noted, forced Britain either to restrict her purchasing or sell her securities. The European combat zone strained her shipping resources and operated to Germany's advantage. The Pan American neutrality zone—sold to Britain as an assistance to her blockade—seemed mainly designed to keep war away from America and extend U.S. 'economic and political penetration in Latin America'. Cadogan, annoyed at America's 'tiresomeness', recollected that he had felt the same way, for the same reasons, during the Great War, while Vansittart wanted Lothian to make a formal protest to Roosevelt.[91] Even the mild-mannered Halifax was fed up. After talking with American press correspondents he noted: 'I lose no opportunity of telling these people politely something of our feeling at being the constant recipient of good advice from them, who themselves take no very active part.' Likewise, military leaders complained that after denouncing Britain's appeasement of Hitler, the Americans now did nothing to help the war, while Chatfield wrote to Lothian: 'They are not in much of a moral position and no doubt feel it. They will indeed fight the battle for freedom to the last Briton, but save their own skins!' Even the King, who had returned from the U.S.A. the previous summer with such high hopes, realized by March 1940 that there was more to U.S. policy than the facile promises of its genial President.[92]

Despite their irritation, however, many Britons did not, at this stage, want all-out American assistance. Ed Murrow, the London-based head of CBS's European operations, recalled in 1941: 'In the opening months of the war, one often heard the comment, "God protect us from a German victory and an American peace. Britain and her Allies propose to win this one alone." ' Similarly, as far away as Bucharest, the American Minister heard a British diplomat asserting, in what sounded to him 'like a mot d'ordre . . . that this time they did not intend to have a Wilsonian peace'.[93] Of course, not everyone felt this way. As in the Great War, British liberals saw American peacemaking rather differently. Some even cast F.D.R. in the role of messiah, as their predecessors had done with Wilson. Thus Harold Laski, the Labour intellectual, told F.D.R. in September to keep out of the war, because: 'At some early stage we must have vital mediation, and no one but yourself will then be in a position to suggest terms consistent with the preservation of international decency.'[94] Similarly, Lothian in Washington was speaking out about the future peace, alluding particularly to the importance of federalism in Europe and Anglo-American co-operation in policing the seas. However, such thinking was too radical for the FO and the Tory party.[95] Both had long collective memories, and they hoped to avoid, as they saw it, again being victims of an inept, hypocritical American peace. Of course, British policy-makers never denied that the U.S.A. would have a role to play in peacemaking. The mistake in the drama of 1919, they felt, had been that America had assumed the leading part and the post of director, but then had abruptly made her exit, leaving the other actors to keep the play going as best they could. They wanted her back on the stage; they did not want her running the show. Thus, in 1938, they felt that the U.S.A. might help clinch and guarantee a settlement, but they did not want her closely involved in the negotiations. Similarly, during the war, they wanted American help in preserving post-war security; but they feared American power when exercised without responsi-bility and against Britain's interests. Chatfield expressed the feeling well when he told Lothian:

> I do not believe those who have fought for these great principles and sacrificed their sons and money will tolerate neutral action in settling the peace, unless the latter are prepared much more than after the last war to contribute permanently to security. We do not need advice; we do need and will accept help in the sharing of world responsibility.[96]

*    *    *

From the British point of view, the most disturbing episode in Anglo-American relations in early 1940 was the Welles mission. Not only did this seem like further interference in Allied policy, it was also an early attempt to subject the belligerents to American peacemaking. The FO had been expecting such an attempt for some time. One report on U.S. opinion during the winter concluded: 'There is little desire for the United States to take responsibility for the settlement but much that she should influence it.'[97] In January the FO saw F.D.R.'s overtures to the Pope as an ominous sign,[98] and it interpreted the sustained U.S. fuss over trade policy as evidence 'that the State Dept.'s policy at the moment is to keep squeezing us in order to make us more malleable and responsive to a peace offensive'.[99] When Welles' mission was announced, David Scott prepared this shrewd analysis with which his superiors agreed:

> The President and those surrounding him think that we can't win.
> The United States can not afford to let us lose and would not like to see us defeated.
> The only way to prevent our defeat is either to come to our help and declare war on Germany—and this is the last thing they want to do—or to make us accept peace.
> If the President can somehow stop the war his own domestic position will be enormously strengthened. . . .
> He therefore has decided to send Mr Sumner Welles and even if we assure him that the mere mention of the visit will affect our interests injuriously he will no doubt, secure in his conviction that we can't win, disregard our remonstrances and feel that he is saving us from ourselves.[100]

HMG was therefore in no mood to co-operate with the Welles mission. When the U.S. Embassy asked for secret military information for Welles on the build-up of the British Expeditionary Force in France, the Cabinet decided to refuse, though 'with circumspection and courtesy'. Now that Britain was at war, they judged that the situation was very different from April 1939, when they had sent F.D.R. the important assessment of British and German air power.[101] Given their evaluation of the Welles mission, they presumably feared that information about Britain's weakness would add to F.D.R.'s determination to seek an immediate peace. Nor did they intend to reveal full details of Britain's financial predicament, as is clear from this telegram to Lothian about agricultural purchases:

> Offer of short term credit would be of no help to us. We think it essential that no suggestion for long term credit should be made from our side, but if such an offer were made from the United States side it would, of course, be very welcome. Generally speaking we do not want to create the impression that we are in acute difficulties about dollars and that we cannot win the war without borrowing from the United States. Our position rather is that we have considerable resources but in order to win the war must utilise these for buying aeroplanes and other essential war means.[102]

In part the reasoning here was tactical. Hints that Britain needed financial aid could drive the U.S. further into isolation. With 1917 in mind, Americans apparently considered credits as the inevitable prelude to American belligerency. However, it was also feared that appeals for money would only increase America's pessimism about the Allies' chances, leading them to conclude, in the words of a French memorandum, that the only possible alternatives were 'un effondrement social' or 'une paix de compromis'.[103] Here one has an excellent example of the mixture of doubt, hope and fear from which British policy towards the U.S.A. was composed. The tactical caution required to secure American financial help was reinforced by the anxiety that this help could lay Britain open to irresponsible American interference. Both considerations dictated a reticence for which HMG was, literally, to pay dearly in the totally different situation that obtained after the summer.

Not only was the Welles mission apparently designed to hamper Britain's efforts, it also seemed likely to comfort her foes. Chamberlain and his colleagues believed that Roosevelt was playing right into Hitler's hands. When the PM received advance word of the visit through Lothian, he promptly informed the President of his conviction that talk of a spring offensive was really part of the Germans' war of nerves, aimed at intimidating both the Allies and the unaligned neutrals.[104] As we have seen, Chamberlain believed that the Germans' only assault would be on the diplomatic front, through a peace offensive preceded by the war of nerves, in the hope of dividing and unsettling Allied opinion. Welles' mission, and F.D.R.'s explanation of it to Lothian, suggested that the Americans had swallowed the Nazi bait.[105] The visit would fuel Goebbels' propaganda, arouse false and divisive hopes in the democracies, and, as Chamberlain warned F.D.R. in a further, highly confidential message, encourage the Scandinavian neutrals to obstruct Allied efforts to send an expeditionary force to help the Finns.[106]

Chamberlain's two messages obliged F.D.R. to couch his initiative in more cautious language, and he agreed to avoid the words 'peace' or 'peace mission'.[107] By early March Chamberlain was assuring Joe Kennedy that his initial fears that Washington was 'putting over a peace plan' had been dispelled. However, this assurance was not sincere. On 13 March, while Welles was in London, Chamberlain told the Cabinet that he feared F.D.R. would make some attempt to bring the war to an end, even at risk of embarrassing the Allies. Vansittart minuted that he, Chamberlain and 'everybody that I know who also knows anything of the American situation' had concluded that 'Roosevelt is ready to play a dirty trick on the world and risk the ultimate destruction of the Western Democracies in order to secure the re-election of a Democratic candidate in the United States'.[108] To some extent the meetings with Welles helped to calm some of British policymakers' fears—another reminder of how little personal contact there had been between British and U.S. leaders in the 1930s. Halifax 'had expected to find him a very stiff, unsympathetic creature, and was favourably disappointed'. Similarly, Chamberlain felt he had 'established a personal relationship' with Welles and 'concluded that he was the best type of American I have met for a long time'.[109] Nevertheless, Chamberlain still believed Welles entertained an outside chance of an agreement with Hitler, while the FO considered him somewhat under the spell of Mussolini and dangerously deluded about Britain's weakness and his own plans for disarmament.[110] The British line was therefore to stress their determination and strength, and to disabuse Welles of any hopes of an easy, early peace. The King was carefully briefed for his talk with Welles, and seems to have played his part well; Chamberlain let himself go, with what Welles termed 'a white-hot anger', about Hitler's perfidy; and prominent political figures, sometimes in a rather heavy-handed and obviously orchestrated way, played variations on the official theme.[111]

Despite this performance for Welles' benefit, however, Chamberlain remained alert for *genuine* signs of a German collapse. R. A. Butler, Parliamentary Under-Secretary at the FO and a confidant of Chamberlain, played on this facet of British policy in an intriguing conversation on 13 March with Moffat, Welles' companion.[112] Butler observed that some aspects of Nazidom were here to stay, although their 'fiendish manifestations' must be eliminated. Churchill, Eden and the like were intransigent, but he wanted Moffat to know that there were other, more realistic elements in Whitehall. The best hope for peace, Butler argued, was for the Allies to help overturn the Nazi regime, but Moffat pointed out that this might be difficult unless they could 'convince all Germans that if the regime were changed, Germany would not have to go through a second Treaty of Versailles'. Butler replied that Chamberlain's recent speech in Birmingham had been carefully drafted to get precisely this point across. According to Moffat, Butler said he

> . . . expected a German peace offensive soon, and the great question that England must decide was whether this peace offensive was genuine or was merely a trap to gain more time to build up further German rearmament and ultimately to turn a blitzkrieg on the west. He might be talking too much—he probably was— but he was reaching the conviction that Germany would be sincere, but that no-one in England or France at present would believe it.

It is not clear how far Butler went out on a limb here. Cadogan considered him an inveterate appeaser, and it is likely that most of the FO would have disowned his words.[113] However, he may well have been speaking for a small group around Chamberlain. The PM remained hopeful that Germany would collapse from within if the Allies maintained unremitting economic and psychological pressure. An overt peace mission like Welles' could only assist the Nazis, by weakening the firm Allied front and encouraging spurious German peace offers. For Chamberlain, there must have been a painful sense of *déjà vu*. As in January 1938, Welles and Roosevelt seemed to be cutting right across the path of his own diplomacy.

### D. Churchill, Roosevelt and Chamberlain

By early 1940, however, Chamberlain's American policy was beginning to attract criticism from within Whitehall. One of the critics was Churchill, and to understand his significance we need first to look at his role in British politics in the 1930s and at his attitude to Anglo-American relations.

Churchill's criticisms of appeasement have passed into legend. His policy throughout the 1930s was fairly summed up in his speech to the Commons during the Munich debate: 'I have always held the view that the maintenance of peace depends upon the accumulation of deterrents against the aggressor, coupled with a sincere effort to redress grievances.'[114] These deterrents were of two main kinds: rearmament, particularly in the air, and close co-operation with friendly powers in collective security arrangements sanctioned under the League's Covenant. However, this policy of negotiation from strength did not automatically lead to conflict with British leaders during the 1930s. Churchill's principal clash was with Baldwin in 1934–36 over the air estimates. In 1937 he warmly welcomed the succession of the energetic and capable Chamberlain, who had already shown his appreciation of the need to rearm,[115] and he supported the new premier's policy throughout that year. The main period of disagreement with Chamberlain was from February 1938 to April 1939. In Eden's resignation and the premature opening of talks with Italy, Churchill detected a disturbing shift of policy from one of deterrence through collective strength to one involving 'great and far-reaching acts of submission' in the hope of preserving peace.[116] That spring he developed the idea of a grand alliance of peace-loving states against aggression, with guarantees of Czechoslovakia while the Sudeten question was settled by international adjudication. In the Munich debate, in which he abstained, Churchill criticized the Government principally for not adopting this policy and for not admitting that Britain and France had 'sustained a total and unmitigated defeat'.[117] However, Churchill intended that this criticism would not estrange him from Chamberlain but would oblige the PM to take him back into office, from which he had been excluded since 1929. Thus, even after Eden's resignation, which he later recalled in such apocalyptic tones in his memoirs, Churchill was in fact the fourth Tory to sign a round robin in support of Chamberlain's policy.[118] In the spring of 1939, when HMG announced its diplomatic guarantees and concomitant defence measures, Churchill proclaimed his full agreement, asserting, not unreasonably, that Chamberlain had come round to his point of view. The remaining differences, he announced, were only 'upon emphasis and method, upon timing and degree'. In mid-April Churchill was pressing hard for a Cabinet post, but it was not until war began in September that Chamberlain took him in—as First Lord of the Admiralty, the office he had held under Asquith in 1914–15.[119]

Just as Churchill in 1939 could support Chamberlain's dual policy, so too he shared the PM's broad conception of the war. Like Chamberlain he apparently hoped to wear the Germans down to the point when they would overthrow the Nazis and seek an acceptable peace. In October 1939, when HMG was considering its reply to Hitler's peace offer, Churchill drafted a possible answer, which, he told Chamberlain, did 'not close the door upon any genuine offer' from the Germans.[120] He did not share the premier's scepticism about a western offensive, but he did believe that its postponement through the winter was an 'important success', equivalent to winning 'the opening campaign of the war'.[121] Where Churchill differed with Chamberlain was over the conduct of the war. While agreeing that time was on the Allies' side, he was sure they could not adopt a purely passive policy. He was particularly interested in a peripheral strategy—a theme of his thinking in both world wars—and in the winter of 1939–40 he advanced a variety of schemes to control the Baltic or at least to deny the Germans their crucial supplies of iron ore from Sweden down the Norwegian coast. But these proposals got nowhere, and Churchill became increasingly frustrated at the 'tremendous array of negative arguments and forces' marshalled against 'positive action'. In mid-March, after the Finnish armistice, he informed Halifax: 'I am very deeply concerned about the way the war is going. . . . There is no sort of action in hand except to wait on events.'[122]

Churchill's attitude to Anglo-American relations is well stated in an article he published in 1935.[123] There he propounded his familiar thesis about the need for rearmament and collective security among the European democracies. However, he continued:

> . . . the first and surest of all methods for maintaining the peace of the world would be an understanding between Great Britain and the United States whereby they would together maintain very powerful air forces, and navies decisively stronger than those of other countries put together; and secondly that they would use these forces, as well as the whole of their influence and money power, in support of any state which was the victim of unprovoked aggression.

'Everyone', Churchill admitted, 'can see the arguments against the English-speaking peoples becoming the policemen of the world. The only thing that can be said upon the other side is that if they did so none of us would ever live to see another war. . . .' This belief in Anglo-American co-operation as the decisive, if elusive, element in world security was fundamental to Churchill's thinking from the Great War until his death. In his memoirs about World War I he had criticized Wilson for trying 'to bend the world—no doubt for its own good—to his personal views', rather than making 'common cause' with Lloyd George and Clemenceau.[124] In trying in the 1930s to educate the U.S. into recognizing this 'common cause', Churchill, like Eden, was ready to press the point more directly than Chamberlain would have wished. Thus, after Munich, he broadcast to America: 'We are in no doubt where American conviction and sympathies lie; but will you wait until British freedom and independence have succumbed, and then take up the cause when it is three-quarters ruined, yourselves alone?' Not surprisingly, therefore, he was much keener than Chamberlain in 1939–40 to see America in the war. Kennedy reported that while most of HMG understood that the U.S. should not be pushed, 'Churchill, however, wants us in as soon as he can get us there.'[125]

Churchill's belief in Anglo-American co-operation rested on two subordinate convictions. The first was that the two countries were linked by very special ties. Given his half-American descent Churchill naturally felt bonds of kinship and blood. His mother had been an ardent believer in 'Anglo-Saxonism' and had founded the short-lived *Anglo-Saxon Review*.[126] However, the idea of a special racial tie was peculiar to the turn of the century. For Churchill, by the 1930s, the special relationship was understood primarily in terms of the common tongue. As he wrote in 1938: 'The greatest tie of all is language.'[127] This belief was deepened—and romanticized—during the 1930s by Churchill's work on his *History of the English-speaking Peoples*. Not surprisingly, then, he was probably the leading British exponent of the view that German bombing of historic English cities would arouse America and bring her into the war. He expressed his conviction on several occasions during 1939, and, as we shall see, it assumed great significance in the summer of 1940.[128]

The other main reason for Churchill's emphasis on Anglo-American co-operation during the 1930s was his growing fear of the Nazi menace to world peace. This gradually became his principal preoccupation, overriding all other considerations. Thus, he temporarily swallowed his hatred and suspicion of Bolshevism to stress the need to draw Russia into the Grand Alliance against Nazism. It is important to note that a similar—though, of course, far less pronounced—process can be discerned in his attitude towards the U.S.A. For, despite his desire for Anglo-American co-operation, Churchill was far from oblivious to the competition between the two countries. In 1925, as Chancellor, he had been concerned about the threat to imperial interests posed by a dollar-dominated gold standard, and in the next few years he became increasingly angry at American policy over war debts and, especially in 1928, over naval disarmament.[129] He saw the U.S. as 'arrogant, fundamentally hostile' to Britain and out 'to dominate world politics'.[130] To some extent such remarks reflect Churchill's pugnacious but mercurial temperament. The naval controversies were settled in subsequent conferences and by the late 1930s Churchill's dominant aim was to enlist America in the struggle against Nazism. But he remained aware that although 'the ideals of the countries are similar, their interests are in many ways divergent', and he did not intend to surrender those interests, especially Britain's position as a world power. As he wrote in 1937: 'I want to see the British Empire preserved for a few more decades in its strength and splendour.'[131] In short, although he had a different sense of priorities from Chamberlain, Churchill's attitude towards the U.S.A. included the same elements of doubt, hope and fear—as we shall see again in later chapters.

*   *   *

During the Phoney War Churchill had relatively little to do with Anglo-American relations. His main involvement was through his correspondence with Roosevelt. The exchange began with a letter from F.D.R., dated 11 September 1939, which Churchill received on 4 October. This invited Churchill 'to keep in touch personally with anything you want me to know about'.[132] What was the motive behind Roosevelt's remarkable gesture— one that put a neutral head of state in touch with the most bellicose minister of a belligerent power? First, contrary to what was once believed in the U.S.A., neither man intended to work behind Chamberlain's back. On the same day F.D.R. also wrote to the PM, making the same suggestion and assuring him that repeal of the arms embargo was Administration policy which he was hopeful would be achieved. Meanwhile, Churchill had promptly forwarded his own letter to Chamberlain, noting that there were 'many things we want him to do for the Admiralty, & this offer to accord a liaison must be used to the full'.[133] Churchill's reply to this and to nearly all subsequent messages were discussed in Cabinet before despatch. Nor, secondly, were Roosevelt and Churchill close friends. They had met only once before, at a dinner in London in 1918. Of this meeting, F.D.R.'s biographer has observed: 'Obviously these two men made little impression upon each other at the time, since several months later Roosevelt did not record the meeting in his detailed recollections and Churchill entirely forgot the episode'—much to F.D.R.'s subsequent annoyance when this came to light at the Atlantic Conference in 1941. By the time he came to write his war memoirs, however, Churchill's memory had apparently improved considerably.[134]

Nevertheless, it would seem that Roosevelt took advantage of a slight personal acquaintance to open new lines of communication with a British Cabinet in whose leaders he had little faith. Personal contact was the key to F.D.R.'s political technique. He achieved his ends through knowledge of his opponents, intuitive 'feel' of a situation and use of his own persuasiveness and charm. Personal contact was even more important in foreign policy than at home.[135] Because of physical incapacity and political constraint F.D.R. had not visited Europe since 1919. This may well help to explain his slightly dated view of Britain, to which I have referred. It also limited effective diplomacy. Roosevelt relied on others to be his eyes, ears and even mouth—a method that had its strengths and its drawbacks, as the Welles mission illustrates. F.D.R.'s closest British contacts dated from his years in Washington during the Great War. Most of these friends—men like Arthur Murray and Arthur Willert—were on the fringes of power and F.D.R. knew none of Britain's leaders in the late 1930s. Since 1937 he had been unsuccessful in developing a personal relationship with Chamberlain, who had rejected all opportunities to visit the U.S.A., and Willert recalls that in conversations in March 1939 F.D.R. 'had no use for Chamberlain' or for Hoare and Simon.[136] It may well be that Roosevelt saw the royal visit as an alternative way of opening up top-level contacts with London and that the letter to Churchill was an extension of the same policy.[137]

Be that as it may, Roosevelt probably singled out Churchill for two reasons. First, he was the best known British opponent of Nazism. As Joseph Lash points out, F.D.R.'s two letters were sent on the day that he and Hull also warned Kennedy about his hopes of an immediate peace, and the notes, particularly the one to Chamberlain with its promise of repeal of the arms embargo, were typical of Roosevelt's back-stiffening.[138] Secondly, he probably wanted a 'hot line' to the minister in charge of British naval policy. This would have been sensible if only because of the prime importance of the war at sea, but F.D.R. may also have had in mind the operation of his Western Hemisphere neutrality patrol. We noted that he was upset by Whitehall's detailed questions when he first suggested the scheme, to which he attached considerable importance. He probably felt that he could cut through further red tape and ensure prompt British co-operation in this and other naval matters by going to the man at the top.

On the British side, Churchill accepted Roosevelt's invitation with alacrity. He already knew of Roosevelt's neutrality patrol from the Admiralty papers and from the King's account of his talks at Hyde Park.[139] After discussion in the Cabinet on 5 October, he sent off a cable about the neutrality zone and spoke with F.D.R. by phone about another naval matter. Eleven days later he minuted: 'I think I ought to send something more to my American friend in order to keep him interested in our affairs. . . . We must not let the liaison lapse.'[140] Even when there was no diplomatic need to correspond, Churchill, styling himself 'Naval Person', fed F.D.R. morsels of information, such as detailed reports of the *Graf Spee* action, which he thought Roosevelt would enjoy. However, one should not exaggerate the importance of the correspondence during the Phoney War. In the period up to 10 May 1940, when Churchill assumed the premiership, it amounted to three, brief, messages from F.D.R. and eight, including a phone call, from Churchill. (This imbalance was to be a feature of the correspondence.) All the messages were concerned with naval affairs. Furthermore, the correspondence was not unique. It has often been forgotten that Chamberlain also was in personal touch with F.D.R. in these months. Although the PM was disinclined to strike up a close liaison—he probably delegated the task to Churchill—he replied as promptly as the First Lord to Roosevelt's initial letter and wrote again later to express his appreciation that the arms embargo had been repealed. In the period from late August 1939 to mid-March 1940 Chamberlain sent six letters to F.D.R., including several of major importance.[141]

Both in 1939–40 and throughout the war, Churchill was determined that his correspondence with Roosevelt should remain a personal link. He preferred to send messages through Ambassador Kennedy and the State Department rather than the FO and Lothian, for fear that the latter channel would reduce them to mere official communications. Naturally the FO disliked being circumvented in this way. It pointed out that in October Lothian had been placed in an embarrassing position when Welles started treating a message from Churchill, of which the Ambassador was unaware, as an authoritative statement of HMG's policy on the neutrality zone.[142] The FO was also unhappy about the use of Kennedy, whom it detested. The U.S. Ambassador's doubts about the Allies' chances were notorious and the FO knew that F.D.R. had lost confidence in him.[143] After some months of wrangling it was agreed in January that messages should be transmitted simultaneously to Roosevelt via the U.S. Embassy and to the Washington Embassy via the FO, 'thus keeping Lothian fully informed while giving the President the feeling that he has a special line of information'.[144] Nevertheless, problems still arose. For example, Churchill was anxious to reduce U.S. irritation over the blockade and on 29 January he cabled F.D.R. off his own bat to say that henceforth no U.S. ship would be diverted for inspection into the combat zone around Europe. 'This will make the M.E.W. [Ministry of Economic Warfare] spit and swear!' minuted Perowne of FO/A. Scott added later: 'It did!' The following day Churchill was forced to cable again, considerably modifying his categorical assurance.[145]

Here in microcosm was the problem that Churchill posed in Whitehall during the winter of 1939–40. He was genuinely loyal to Chamberlain and indeed grew to like and respect the PM during these months as they worked more closely together than ever before. However, his dissatisfaction with the passive conduct of the war, together with his immense energy and stamina, led him far outside his own sphere of responsibility at the Admiralty and into frequent conflict with politicians and officials. In April there was a blazing row with the Chiefs of Staff over Churchill's attempts to act virtually as minister of defence. In effect Churchill was trying to run the war, without being allowed the necessary authority. For, as Eden put it, 'however much people admire Winston's qualities, that admiration is constantly balanced by the fear of him if he was loose!'[146]

### E. Towards greater reliance upon America

In the first three months of 1940 growing criticism developed within Whitehall of HMG's policy towards the U.S.A. This criticism must not be exaggerated. It came intermittently and from various sources—the American sections of the FO and Ministry of Information, the Washington Embassy, the Board of Trade and the Service ministries, especially Churchill. The critics were often at odds among themselves—the FO still cool towards Lothian, both of these engaged in bureaucratic tussles with Churchill and the MOI over the execution of British policy in the U.S. Furthermore, they all accepted the basic axiom of British policy—that the U.S. could not be pushed too hard. This made it difficult to advocate a clear-cut alternative policy.

Nevertheless, without being too neat, one can say that these critics made three main points. First, they were increasingly doubtful that Britain could win the war or maintain the ensuing peace without substantial and quick U.S. help. Simply to mobilize and conserve British and Empire resources would not be enough, nor would a system of purely European alliances. Secondly, the critics believed that Chamberlain and his advisers were treating the U.S.A. as if she were incorrigibly isolationist. They felt that America could and should be wooed. It would be a slow and frustrating process, but HMG should begin by taking greater account of U.S. interests and sensitivities, thereby dispelling some of the suspicions of Britain. In other words, thirdly, they maintained that American help would not be won by hard bargaining but by generosity and concession. Like it or not, Britain's position was no longer that of an equal with the U.S. She needed transatlantic cooperation far more than did America, and her diplomacy had to take account of this imbalanced bargaining position.

*　　*　　*

These criticisms came to the surface in the early months of 1940 over the question of Britain's purchasing policy in the U.S.A. At the end of January, as we noted earlier, Lothian and the FO pressed the Cabinet to resume token purchases of U.S. agricultural produce or at least to give a public assurance that it would do so as soon as possible.[147] The rationale for such action was stated most cogently by David Scott in the FO, who had been the clearest spokesman of the 'moral line' a year before. American goodwill, he emphasized, was essential for an Allied victory. Britain must help the Administration to help the Allies, which meant cultivating public opinion—the key to U.S. policy, particularly in an election year. 'Indeed', observed Scott, 'we cannot expect any bold or forward move by the Administration until the election is over, save as a result of some cataclysm in Europe. Until November is past everything will be judged by its probable effect on the election.' While in general Scott believed, with typical British condescension, that it was 'no good expecting logical reactions from a nation like the United States', he felt that the U.S. did have some justifiable complaints about British policy.[148] HMG had not yet faced up to the dislocation its war measures had caused to the American economy, nor to its eventual need for U.S. help—'certainly the Treasury, who see everything through a haze of dollars which obscures the imponderabilia, are very far from having done so'.[149] He argued that Britain would inevitably exhaust her exchange resources one day, and that measures such as restricting tobacco purchases could only postpone that day for a few months. Surely it was better for the financial crisis to come sooner rather than later, if Britain had a store of U.S. goodwill to draw upon instead of a residue of bitterness?

This argument struck at the roots of official policy. Scott called into question the hope that financial prudence would suffice, the desire to avoid dependence on the U.S.A., the belief that she was incorrigibly isolationist and the priority given to other neutrals. His critique had some effect, interestingly, even on Cadogan. The Permanent Under-Secretary's thinking that winter initially remained very similar to Chamberlain's. He did not attach much significance to repeal of the arms embargo—rather than indicating support for the Allies short of war, as Lothian argued, Cadogan suggested it 'may only mean making money out of munitions'.[150] He continued to 'feel sick' at the usual combination of inaction and 'lectures on the "high moral" plane', and doubted that U.S. help would make much difference.[151] In January he agreed with the Cabinet that Italy was more important than the U.S.A.— a balancing of priorities reminiscent of the one he had made during the Albanian crisis in March 1939.[152] And initially he found little attraction in Scott's suggestions about agricultural purchases, observing on 29 February that more tobacco simply meant fewer planes—which were essential for Britain's defences—and the hostility of American industry instead of American agriculture. He added, with characteristic bitterness: 'It is a fact— of which most people are unaware—that Americans are the most difficult people on earth to deal with. That is very likely due to their political system.' Yet by next day Cadogan was coming round to Scott's opinion. He minuted on 1 March that what he called the idea of bribing the American electorate with apples and pears 'may be a good gamble, and perhaps worth taking, however much it goes against the grain'.[153]

89

However, the British Cabinet was not a noted gambler, and its anti-American grain was pronounced. When Welles and Moffat were in London in March they got little satisfaction from the BOT or MEW.[154] Even the architect of the FO's Balkan policy, Frank Ashton-Gwatkin, who had visited the U.S.A. early in the year, urged substantial concessions, and not mere palliatives. 'If Turkey was worth £2 millions in sultanas and figs, are not the United States worth £10 millions in tobacco, cotton, corn, fruit, etc.?' he asked.[155] The Cabinet apparently thought not. Even when, in April, HMG issued a declaration about the eventual resumption of agricultural purchases, the commitment was vague and conditional.

The significant change in British purchasing policy at this time came not through a resumption of normal imports but from the massive Allied orders, confirmed in late March, for U.S. planes. Throughout the winter the British Treasury had been under strong pressure from the Service ministries to be allowed to fill the gaps in their equipment by buying in the U.S.A. As early as 18 September Churchill had told the Cabinet that he wanted to purchase American destroyers, and the Admiralty had developed an ambitious programme for the building of anti-submarine vessels in North American shipyards.[156] Although this was whittled down to virtually nothing, the Air Ministry proved more successful. By the beginning of 1940 British and French aircraft production programmes had completely absorbed the existing capacity of the two countries. Chamberlain and the Treasury fought doggedly, stressing the need to conserve dollars and to avoid jeopardizing the supply of essential machine tools. But after investigation in America, and under strong French pressure, it was decided that a large order from the U.S.A. was imperative. The details of the scheme were finally approved by the Anglo-French Supreme War Council on 28 March. In the year beginning 1 October 1940, 4,600 aircraft, complete with engines, were to be produced at an estimated cost to the U.K. of around $300 million, about $210 million of which would be incurred in the second year of war. Already the Treasury had begun to sell British-owned securities, though on a small scale. By the end of April 1940 about $34 million had been realized.[157]

Here was a significant change in policy. At a time when the Government's advisers were estimating that the country could only afford to spend around £225 million abroad each year[158] the Cabinet was committed to disbursing a quarter of that in the second year of war in the U.S.A. alone, for the purchase of just one defence item. Implicitly, Chamberlain's government was acknowledging that financial prudence would not win the war, and that major U.S. help, including credits, could not be avoided.

The aircraft orders coincided with a more forward policy in other areas as well, particularly Scandinavia. Chamberlain had long resisted the idea of operations in the Baltic. Although professing himself well disposed in principle, he always found practical objections, notably the need to obtain the consent of the Scandinavian neutrals. As usual he was also ready to cite U.S. opinion as a convenient scapegoat,[159] but one suspects that behind all his objections—justified or not—lay his continued belief that a firm but essentially passive policy of economic and psychological pressure would be sufficient to bring Germany to the peace table.[160] However, at the Supreme

War Council on 28 March—the same occasion as the decision on U.S. aircraft orders—Chamberlain agreed to the mining of Norwegian territorial waters. Again his mind had been changed by pressure from the Service departments, notably Churchill in this case, and from the French. It had become apparent that more aggressive measures would have to be taken to satisfy public opinion, especially in France where the Daladier government had fallen in mid-March because of dissatisfaction with Allied inactivity. However, news of the mining plan leaked out and its implementation was delayed by renewed Anglo-French arguments, allowing Hitler to speed up his own plans for intervention in Norway. By the time the first mines were laid on 8 April, the German invasion of Denmark and Norway had begun, to the total surprise of the Allies, who mounted a hastily-improvised operation of their own. By early May British troops had been driven out of central Norway and fighting was confined to the north, around Narvik. FO/A, arguing as ever that only events would educate U.S. opinion, called for a vigorous counterstroke to dispel American fears about the Allies' chances. As T. North Whitehead, recently arrived in the Department as a specialist on the U.S.A., minuted on 7 May: 'There is nothing to be done by propaganda, or by bold words, deeds alone will count.' But Cadogan, with customary sardonic briskness, reminded FO/A of the perennial British predicament: 'I agree too. I should like to be a "tough guy": I should like to go and "slosh" the Germans. Only, at present, I find it a little difficult in knowing exactly how to do it. Meanwhile, of course, the American Gods in the Gallery will naturally start booing and cat-calling.'[161]

* * *

In fact, the 'gallery' was despondent rather than abusive. In the middle of March Hull had been very glum, bemoaning what he considered the bungling way in which the Allies were managing their affairs. F.D.R. was gloomy too. After talking with him at the end of the month, Morgenthau noted: 'He said he was very pessimistic about Europe. Thought the war might burst loose at any time in the next 30 days.' The aircraft orders, therefore, were a welcome sign that the Allies were in earnest about the war. After hearing from Arthur Purvis that the orders were going through, Morgenthau called the White House.

> I got the President at six o'clock and told him approximately what Purvis told me. I told him I felt right along that the Allies were stalling on their purchases and I would not be convinced that they were really going to go ahead and fight until they placed this order for planes and the President agreed with me that it was good news that they were going to go ahead.[162]

The media were similarly impressed. The *New York Post* columnist, Sam Grafton, called the order and the sale of securities to pay for it:

> . . . the first outline for a hungry England after the war.
> These stocks and bonds have been her food and drink. They, more than lands, have meant England, seat of Empire. Now she is shoving those investments into the furnace of war. . . .
> This is a measure of the cost to England of stopping Hitler.[163]

However, the good effect of the aircraft orders was quickly counterbalanced by the Norwegian fiasco. On 10 April Morgenthau found Roosevelt 'hopping mad'. Where was the Royal Navy when the Germans invaded?—the President wanted to know. 'It is the most outrageous thing I've ever heard of.' By the end of April his anger had subsided into the depths of depression. He was afraid that Britain was going to be defeated, on present showing, and wanted somehow to prepare opinion in America for the worst. Admittedly F.D.R. was prone to periodic bouts of depression, and Morgenthau thought his defeatism 'entirely wrong'.[164] Despite his oscillations of mood, however, he was clearly very worried about the Allies' position, and his anxiety was shared by many other members of his Administration. Probably they would all have agreed with the publicist William Allen White:

> What an avalanche of blunders Great Britain has let loose upon the democracies of the world! The old British lion looks mangy, sore-eyed. He needs worming and should have a lot of dental work. He can't even roar. Unless a new government takes the helm in Britain, the British Empire is done.[165]

# PART TWO

# Commitments and Dependence

The Development of Anglo-American Relations
during a Period of Global Crisis
May 1940–March 1941


*. . . the possibility of some sort of special association with the
U.S.A. . . . ought, I think, to replace the idea of Anglo-French
Union among the various plans which we may make for the
future.*

Halifax, July 1940

*Willy-nilly, the United States holds one end of the Scales of Fate
on which balances precariously the future of the British Empire.
. . . The British Government is aware that it is not in a position
to resist quid pro quo demands from the United States. . . . The
British are not ready givers. . . . But the fact remains that they
will in the last analysis stand and deliver.*
Walton Butterworth, U.S. Embassy, London, December 1940

# CHAPTER FOUR

## Britain Alone

### May–July 1940

*I see only one sure way through now, to wit that Hitler should attack this country and in doing so break his Air weapon. If this happens he will be left to face the winter with Europe writhing under his heel and probably with the United States against him after the Presidential election is over.*

Churchill, June 1940

*You must pass the hat now, while the corpse is warm.*[1]
Joseph Kennedy, May 1940 (on Britain's need for U.S. help)

In Part One I argued that the limited extent of Anglo-American co-operation prior to May 1940 is not attributable simply to the depth of U.S. isolationism. Of course, Americans' opposition to European commitments *was* a major factor. Chamberlain and his colleagues entertained deep and justified doubts about the chances of quick, significant U.S. help; Roosevelt was constrained by the indifference of his countrymen and the suspicions of Congress, especially in the year before another presidential election. However, the evidence suggests that prior to May 1940 neither government *wanted* a full-scale commitment, or believed it to be necessary. HMG wished to avoid over-dependence on America; the Roosevelt Administration feared that the U.S. would be dragged into another war. Each wanted limited co-operation with the other, and hoped that this would be enough to counter the German threat.

But such thinking assumed that conflict in Europe could be averted or, if not, at least contained. In the summer of 1940, however, the 'totalitarian war' that Chamberlain had dedicated all his energies to avoiding finally broke out with horrific intensity. France collapsed in six weeks. Italy entered the war. Japan took advantage of the power vacuum in the Pacific to advance her own sphere of influence in South-East Asia. The British planners' nightmare of a three-front war seemed very near, with Britain defenceless and bereft of allies. Closer co-operation with the U.S.A. around the globe was therefore essential, and the Roosevelt Administration, conscious of its own weakness, gradually, if much more hesitantly, extended assistance to Britain.

But we shall see that even as the two countries became more 'mixed up together' the old doubts and suspicions remained.

## A. Britain looks to America as the French collapse

The familiar story of the fall of France needs only brief summary here.[2] Recent research has shown that the Allies' confidence in the French Army was not entirely unfounded. Contrary to earlier belief, the Germans were not overwhelmingly superior in military technology.[3] They simply used their resources far more effectively. Expecting the main German offensive through the Low Countries, the French were ill-prepared for the Panzers' drive on 10 May through the Ardennes—the weakest part of their front. However, had they rapidly concentrated their armour for a counter-attack they could have pinched out the German salient. Instead, a divided and dispirited high command, whose communications with its own troops were primitive in the extreme, allowed the German armour to reach the coast on the 26th, trapping the French, Belgians and British around Dunkirk. Belgium surrendered on 28 May, but by 4 June, to the amazement of all concerned, about 330,000 Allied troops had been evacuated, with the loss of most of their equipment. The new German offensive in France began on 5 June, and the crisis deepened further when Mussolini entered the war on the 10th. The British made frantic but fruitless efforts to keep the French fighting, culminating on 16 June in an offer of Anglo-French union, involving common citizenship and joint organs of government. France sued for peace on the 17th, and a few days later armistices were concluded with Germany and Italy. HMG feared that the French would surrender their fleet, and to prevent this the Royal Navy had to attack its former ally near Oran on 3 July. This action, coming after mutual recriminations over the Battle of France and Dunkirk, left relations between London and Pétain's new regime at Vichy in a state of bitter hostility.

10 May was also the day on which Churchill began his premiership. The circumstances of his elevation will be discussed in the next section. Here we are concerned with the effects of this change of leaders on policy-making. Sir John Colville, inherited by Churchill as one of the private secretaries at Number Ten, recalls: 'Seldom can a Prime Minister have taken office with "the Establishment", as it would now be called, so dubious of the choice and so prepared to find its doubts justified.' Colville goes on: 'Within a fortnight all was changed. I doubt if there has ever been such a rapid transformation of opinion in Whitehall and of the tempo at which business was conducted.'[4] Churchill's frantic pace, long hours and unorthodox methods galvanized a bureaucracy still accustomed to the smooth, regular peacetime routine of the Chamberlain era, and most of Whitehall soon came to admire and respect its new political master. Churchill also gained control at last over military policy. He took the title 'Minister of Defence' and presided over the two crucial new Defence Committees—for operations and supply. The first of these initially comprised both Chiefs of Staff and Service ministers, but during 1940 the latter lost influence, as did the War Cabinet itself, and decisions were taken increasingly by Churchill and the Chiefs of Staff. This 'dictatorship' was to attract growing criticism in 1941, but in the crisis of

1940 it was essential for rapid decision-making.[5] Finally, Churchill took overall control of foreign policy, treating Anglo-American relations and his correspondence with Roosevelt as priorities. His own rise to supreme power coincided with a shift of influence within the FO. With the Nazi conquest of Western Europe the Central Department lost its pre-eminence as well as its *raison d'être*. The principal neutral was now the U.S.A., and the American Department (FO/A) gained a new and commensurate influence, particularly its head, John Balfour, its American expert, T. North Whitehead, and its presiding Under-Secretary, David Scott. Lothian, too, earned increasing respect for his excellent reporting and for the close relationship that he had developed with Roosevelt.[6] During the summer Churchill evolved an effective working partnership with Lothian and FO/A. Nevertheless, he assumed overall command of Anglo-American relations in a way that Chamberlain had never done.

The U.S.A.'s new and central place in British policy can be seen most clearly in HMG's attitude to purchasing in the States.[7] Previously, America had been a marginal source, providing only vital supplies unobtainable at home or within the sterling area. But from mid-May the British pressed the U.S. to sell 'surplus' equipment, notably aircraft and destroyers, from its own ill-equipped forces to make good the gaps in Britain's defences. These requests became even more urgent after Dunkirk, when the bulk of the BEF's modern equipment was lost. HMG then had to appeal for even rifles and revolvers. In the crisis British production turned to the immediate needs of home defence—fighters, AA guns, and so on. It was hoped that the U.S. would take over the long-term plans for achieving superiority in a three-year war. HMG therefore decided 'to create in the United States of America a vastly increased productive capacity for those types of munitions and armaments which are most essential for the continuation of the war'.[8] Britain's involvement in American industry became even greater after the French collapsed, because she took over all the outstanding French orders, amounting to some $600 million.[9] All these developments brought to an end the old policy of financial conservation. Jean Monnet, head of Anglo-French purchasing in London, set out the new thinking clearly in a letter to Churchill on 20 May:

> Our present foreign exchange policy was based on the assumption that we must be able to continue to finance expenditure for several years and that if our own dollar resources became exhausted we should no longer be able to draw from the United States. The last week has, I suggest, changed both these assumptions. It is much more important now to convert dollars into military strength at an early date than to save them for a time to which without additional strength we may not survive. The risk that America would refuse to supply when we could no longer pay cash has perhaps become so much less as to be almost negligible.[10]

The old policy had already been undermined by the massive orders for U.S. aircraft agreed at the end of March. Furthermore, on 9 May, before the German *Blitzkrieg* began, the Chamberlain Cabinet had explicitly accepted that financial considerations should not impede the crash programme for improving Britain's defences.[11] Monnet's first point—that Allied wealth was more valuable translated into equipment rather than retained as reserves—was therefore effectively already accepted. However, the extent to which Britain ran down the gold and dollar reserves depended on the validity of his second point—that the U.S. would carry on supplying goods when the funds ran out. Officials at the Washington Embassy tried to elicit assurances from the Administration, and Churchill told Roosevelt directly on 15 May: 'We shall go on paying dollars for as long as we can, but I should like to feel reasonably sure that when we can pay no more, you will give us the stuff all the same.' In an otherwise helpful reply the following day F.D.R. simply ignored that invitation.[12] The British were therefore forced to continue on the hypothesis that American financial help would be forthcoming. This was the advice of the FO, who, as we saw, had been critical of Treasury policy in the winter. Scott minuted on 17 May: 'If we survive the present crisis, (as I am confident we will), I have no doubt that America will let us have everything we want and that when our dollars and gold run out there will be no difficulty about credits or gifts.' His superiors concurred, though with characteristic differences of emphasis. 'I have little doubt of it', noted Halifax confidently. Cadogan's agreement was more qualified. 'We must go ahead as if that were so, anyhow', he wrote.[13]

The Treasury, however, remained reluctant to take such a risk. Understandable prudence, combined with ingrained doubts about the U.S.A., led it to counsel the greatest possible caution in spending in North America until the Administration had committed itself to provide credits.[14] In the past, the balance of power and argument had lain with the Treasury. Chamberlain had shared its sense of priorities and its cynicism about the U.S.A. Churchill, however, had little time for the Treasury and high hopes of the United States. He endorsed Monnet's statement of assumptions, and assured the French on 31 May that 'steel and other essential materials should be ordered in vast quantities; if we were unable to pay, America would nevertheless continue to deliver'.[15] Furthermore, the whole balance of power in Whitehall had shifted against the Treasury. Until October the Chancellor of the Exchequer was even excluded from the new War Cabinet, which, by contrast, included a strong representation of ministers responsible for production. In short, whereas in the past financial considerations had dominated policy, now economic mobilization became the priority.[16] Here again the crisis situation and the changes of leadership combined to effect a major shift in policy.

However, Britain needed far more than U.S. supplies. The extent of her reliance upon America was laid bare in the contingency planning by the Chiefs of Staff for a French collapse. They stressed that their major assumption was that the U.S. 'is willing to give us full economic and financial support, *without which we do not think we could continue the war with any chance of success*'.[17] This was written on 25 May. When the French surrender became inevitable the Chiefs prepared an *aide-mémoire* for Lothian which revealed starkly that virtually all aspects of the British war effort now depended on the U.S.A. To tide her over the invasion crisis Britain needed aircraft (particularly fighters), destroyers, light naval craft, military equipment and supplies, together with volunteer personnel. In the Far East, where there was no intention of surrendering any of Britain's possessions, it was vital that the U.S. prevent any alteration of the status quo. Looking ahead, U.S. supplies of food, munitions and raw materials would be essential, probably on credit, now that European and Scandinavian sources had been cut off. To ensure eventual victory, the Chiefs argued, the blockade had to be tightened to stop at source all supplies to the enemy bloc, both directly and via the remaining European neutrals. Not only was the U.S.A. directly important here, but her diplomatic help could be invaluable in obtaining the co-operation of Latin American states, who were one of the weak spots in the blockade. This was a point on which the Chiefs laid particular emphasis. 'Without the full economic and financial co-operation of the whole of the American Continent', they warned, 'the task might in the event prove too great for the British Empire single-handed.'[18]

\* \* \*

Ideally, of course, the British wanted more than material assistance from the U.S.A. By mid-June it was generally, though not unanimously, agreed in Whitehall that Britain needed an immediate American declaration of war. The principal exception was David Scott in the FO, but even his reservations stemmed from a desire to maximize American material help rather than from the hope of avoiding dependence upon the U.S.A. Back in February Scott had argued that the advantages of U.S. belligerency would not be much greater than those of highly benevolent neutrality. If America was willing to provide credits, surplus equipment including destroyers, merchant shipping and volunteers, then her entry into the war and the provision of an American Expeditionary Force would probably be unnecessary. Furthermore, he argued, there were at least three ways in which U.S. entry could be a dis-advantage. First, it would probably dry up the flow of supplies to Britain because the American public would demand their retention for U.S. use. This was a point also made by Lord Tweedsmuir, the Governor General of Canada. Secondly, Scott feared that U.S. entry would complicate the eventual peace conference, especially because the U.S. would probably bring with her into the war many of the Latin American states. Above all, he argued, a firm and honest declaration from HMG that U.S. belligerency was not desired would dispel American terror that limited aid would start them on a slippery slope to war. Freed from that fear, Americans would maximize benevolent neutrality.

When Scott stated these ideas in February they got no farther than his superiors within the FO. Neither Cadogan nor Halifax believed the U.S. would push her 'un-neutrality' to the extreme lengths needed by Britain unless she went to war.[19] Nevertheless Scott was not deterred. During the spring he and FO/A developed a plan for a judicious, professionally-run publicity campaign to calm American fears of entanglement and thus maximize their material aid.[20] When Scott unveiled the idea in June, however, in telegrams to Lothian and the Dominion leaders, the reactions were hostile. Lothian, who had been amazed at the rapid change of U.S. attitude in May, thought it would be a mistake to pretend that Britain did not want U.S. entry. Already a small but influential minority of Americans were calling for a declaration of war. They were preparing the ground, Lothian explained, for the moment when, almost inevitably, Hitler or Mussolini would do something that patently challenged U.S. interests. Smuts, the South African premier, was also concerned at what he termed 'this sort of lip-service to isolationism'. U.S. entry was essential for Allied victory, he asserted. Furthermore, events were moving fast. America might declare war at any moment. 'Why arrest this process of conversion by the logic of events?' Smuts was the only Dominion leader for whom Churchill had real respect. His telegram was discussed by the War Cabinet, which ordered the FO to amend its plans. 'I entirely agree with General Smuts', Churchill minuted. 'It is vital to our safety that the United States should be involved in totalitarian warfare.'[21]

Scott remained unconvinced. He continued to argue his case, and a few other policymakers, for example Hankey, supported him on the grounds that U.S. entry would mean a disastrous cutback in supplies to Britain.[22] As we shall see, this was also the standard Administration reply to British requests for U.S. entry. But the consensus in Whitehall—explicitly stated by the military planners on 13 June—was that Britain now needed not merely America's full economic and financial support but also her early entry into the war.[23] Most policymakers were confident that if the U.S.A. came in supplies to Britain would be maintained, with, at worst, only a brief recession. Indeed, a full wartime emergency would enable the President to mobilize U.S. industry and dramatically increase output. No one expected an immediate American Expeditionary Force. The U.S.A. had only a tiny regular army of a quarter of a million and the idea of a draft was only just being mooted in Congress. In any case, British strategists still held tenaciously to the view that a large-scale invasion of the continent would be unnecessary, believing that blockade, bombing and subversion would be enough. The Chiefs of Staff therefore stated in late June that, although technical personnel from the U.S.A. would be of the greatest value, 'we are unlikely to require troops'.[24] The greatest immediate effect of U.S. entry would be on international opinion. As Churchill told Roosevelt on 15 June:

> When I speak of the United States entering the war I am of course not thinking in terms of an expeditionary force, which I know is out of the question. What I have in mind is the tremendous moral effect that such an American decision would produce, not merely in France but also in all the democratic countries of the world, and, in the opposite sense, on the German and Italian peoples.[25]

These, then, were the basic British arguments for U.S. belligerency—its immediate effect on morale and its long-term effect on production.[26] The old fears of dependence upon the U.S.A. had not completely vanished, but they were no longer a pressing consideration for policymakers. In the long term Britain might have to pay a price for American help. Without that help, however, she would not survive.

*          *          *

Interestingly enough, though, even in the summer of 1940, British policymakers *were* looking ahead into the post-war future, and envisaging, however tentatively, the nature of transatlantic relations after victory had been won. A catalyst here was a telegram at the end of June from Sir Stafford Cripps, the left-wing politician, newly appointed as Ambassador in Moscow. In Cripps' view, the hastily prepared plan for Anglo-French union highlighted the need to start thinking carefully about the future and Britain's place in it. 'The old conception of a balance of power *within* Europe has now disappeared', he stated. Britain could no longer act as the balancing agent, and there was no obvious successor for her role. After the war, Cripps predicted, international groupings would be on a much larger scale than in the past. At present Britain was part of the larger entity of the British Empire. However, the Empire, not to mention Britain herself, would only survive the war with U.S. help. In the longer term both would probably become parts of a larger, Anglo-Saxon grouping, which would face comparable European and Asiatic blocs. Gradually, Cripps felt, the centre of gravity within this Anglo-Saxon group would shift to the American continent, leaving Britain as its European outpost.[27]

Cadogan and FO/A felt that Cripps underestimated the strength of the isolationist tradition. While the U.S.A. would probably develop closer ties with the countries of the Empire, particularly if Britain fell, Balfour did not believe that in the event of a British victory the U.S.A. would accept any commitments in Europe. But there was general agreement in the FO that Cripps was right in predicting a broad trend towards Anglo-American co-operation. For instance, Ashley Clarke of the Far Eastern Department felt that any post-war settlement in the Pacific must provide for 'close association' with the U.S.A. The lack of any 'binding commitment' by America in the 1922 Washington agreements had, he noted, been a major reason for the instability of the inter-war years. There was also support for Cripps from the Foreign Secretary himself. In July Halifax formally agreed that the committee that had been set up under Hankey to examine ways of post-war collaboration with France was now redundant. In a letter drafted by Sargent, Halifax told Hankey:

It may well be that instead of studying closer union with France we shall find ourselves contemplating the possibility of some sort of special association with the U.S.A. on the lines suggested, and for the reasons given, in Cripps' telegrams. . . . But, as I pointed out in my reply to Cripps . . . this is a matter which cannot be rushed. This does not mean we ought not to bear it always in mind. Indeed, henceforth it ought, I think to replace the idea of Anglo-French Union among the various plans which we may make for the future.[28]

For Halifax, a 'special association' with the U.S.A. was much more congenial than one with France. In September 1939 he had perceptively outlined some of the similarities between British and U.S. foreign policy in the 1930s, based on a common dislike of commitments in continental Europe:

. . . I have never been tempted to be surprised at the isolationist movement, which is a first reaction to the insane behaviour of Europe. It is, I always think, instructive to reflect that it was only on February 6th last that we, on the fringe of this mad continent, formally assured France unconditionally of our assistance to her if she became the object of aggression from any quarter. We cannot expect the Government or people of the United States to evolve quicker than we did.[29]

As Halifax observed, British isolationism only came to an end in February 1939, and even then the continental commitment was reluctant and tentative. After the collapse of Belgium and France, British leaders were at once bitter yet strangely content. They no longer had to pamper difficult and unreliable continental allies, afflicted with strange languages and customs. In Hankey's words: 'In a way it is almost a relief to be thrown back on the resources of the Empire and of America.' Indeed, as Lothian observed, the French collapse made it easier to secure those resources, now that Britain was freed from the European entanglements that had always scared the U.S.A. to death.[30] Cripps' telegram therefore suited the prevailing mood in July 1940— an 'Atlanticist' conception of Anglo-American co-operation with minimal commitments in Europe. Thus R. A. Butler—often the spokesman of Tory suspicions of America—commented: 'I have felt for a long time—ever since I toured the Empire & saw how under-developed it is—that our future lies more over the oceans than in Europe. The more we can work in with U.S. in a world- & not a European conception of Foreign Policy the better.'[31]

## B. Churchill and the hope of imminent U.S. entry into the war

In the summer of 1940, then, a 'special association' with the United States became the principal goal of British policy. However, in some circles in London the old doubts and fears about America remained major considerations, providing support for those who argued, however tentatively, for a compromise peace. To combat them Churchill played on hopes of American help, arguing with persistence and skill that U.S. entry into the war was only weeks, or at worst months, away.

To understand the significance of this controversy, we must remember the relative insecurity of Churchill's political position in the early summer of 1940. There was nothing inevitable about his rise to supreme power.[32] When the Commons voted in the crucial Norway debate on 8 May, Chamberlain's majority was only 81 instead of his usual 200–220. The PM tried to draw Labour into a coalition, but without success. However, Labour would have served under Halifax, who was also the choice of Chamberlain, the King and most Tory MPs. It was Halifax's reluctance, and Churchill's desire for the premiership, that decided the outcome.[33] Even then Churchill's position was anomalous. He was a Prime Minister without a party, for Chamberlain remained the Tories' leader. Even on 8 May three-quarters of the Conservatives remained loyal. Churchill was well aware of these political realities. 'To a large extent I am in yr. hands', he told Chamberlain on 10 May.[34] Halifax and Butler stayed at the FO, Kingsley Wood, who had defected to Churchill on 9 May, became Chancellor, and Chamberlain was made Lord President, with effective control over all domestic policy. After Dunkirk, when the press, Labour and some Tory critics campaigned to remove the 'Guilty Men' responsible for Britain's failures, it was made very clear to Churchill that if Chamberlain was forced to resign, Simon, Kingsley Wood and Halifax would go too, taking with them several junior ministers including Butler. Calling on the press lords to desist from their campaign, Churchill gave striking expression to his sense of insecurity:

Churchill said not to forget that a year ago last Christmas they were trying to hound him out of his constituency, and by a succession of events that astounded him he was invited by the practically unanimous vote of both Houses of Parliament to be Prime Minister. But the men who had supported Chamberlain and hounded Churchill were still M.P.s. Chamberlain had got the bigger cheer when they met the House after forming the new administration. A General Election was not possible during a war and so the present House of Commons, however unrepresentative of feeling in the country, had to be reckoned with as the ultimate source of power for the duration. If Churchill trampled on these men, as he could trample on them, they would set themselves against him, and in such internecine strife lay the Germans' best chance of victory.[35]

Not that Churchill entirely resented Chamberlain's presence. Indeed, he, came to value the ex-premier's sound judgement and administrative ability and he was extremely grateful to be relieved of the burdens of domestic policy.[36] And in the long run, of course, Churchill established a position in the country and in Parliament far stronger than that enjoyed by Chamberlain even at the height of his popularity, as we shall see in chapter seven. In the early summer of 1940, however, Churchill felt far less secure at Westminster, and that is the period with which we are now concerned.

It is against this background that we must understand the Cabinet pressure in late May for HMG to ascertain Hitler's peace terms. The prime movers there were Chamberlain, and, above all, Halifax. Chamberlain's initial reaction to the German break-through was one of despair. On 19 May he wrote: 'Our only hope, it seems to me, lies in Roosevelt & the U.S.A. But unfortunately they are so unready themselves that they can do little to help us *now* while preaching at Hitler is not likely to be effective.' He could not see how Britain could fight on if France fell. She would be 'fighting only for better terms, not for victory'. 'It seemed to me', he wrote on 15 May, 'that if the French collapsed our only chance of escaping destruction would be if Roosevelt made an appeal for an armistice, though it did not seem likely that the Germans would respond.'[37] At this stage Halifax, too, saw America primarily as mediator rather than arsenal. Like Chamberlain, he was appalled at the disintegration of the French Army—the 'one firm rock on which everybody had been willing to build for the last two years . . .'. After talking with him on 23 May, Kennedy reported that Halifax was 'definitely of the opinion that if anybody is able to save a debacle on the part of the Allies if it arrives at that point it is the President.'[38] On or about 25 May Halifax acted on this belief. He drafted a possible message for Churchill to send to F.D.R., in the event that the Belgian and British armies were lost and France surrendered. The PM, Halifax suggested, should ask Roosevelt to tell Hitler that terms that would endanger British independence—such as those involving the surrender of the fleet or RAF—would encounter American resistance, or, even better, would ensure full U.S. support for Britain. Such a message from the President, Halifax argued, could ameliorate Hitler's terms.[39]

Nothing came of Halifax's suggestion, but the whole question of Hitler's possible peace terms was discussed in Cabinet from 26 to 28 May. The debate became sufficiently heated for Halifax, briefly, on the evening of the 27th, to consider resignation.[40] This time Halifax envisaged Mussolini as a possible mediator.[41] He strongly supported the argument of Reynaud that the Italians should be used to find out Hitler's peace terms. Halifax made it clear that he would fight to the end if Britain's independence was at stake, but that if terms could be secured that guaranteed this then he favoured acceptance to prevent further slaughter and destruction. It is interesting that in principle Churchill expressed agreement with Halifax. He said that he would not ask for terms, but if they were offered, then he would consider them,[42] and that 'if we could get out of this jam by giving up Malta & Gibraltar & some African colonies he would jump at it'.[43] In other words, despite his Commons statement of 13 May about 'victory at all costs', Churchill, too, did not rule out some kind of negotiated peace. However, he argued repeatedly that this was only conceivable when they had convinced Hitler that Britain could not be beaten. Even to enquire about terms would be a sign of weakness. On this point he was supported by the Labour members of the War Cabinet. Chamberlain's position was confused. Initially he agreed with Halifax that there would be no harm in eliciting Hitler's conditions, but during 26 May he came round to Churchill's opinion, writing in his diary: 'it looks as though it would be better for us to fight on in the hope of maintaining sufficient air strength to keep the Germans at bay until other forces can be mobilised perhaps in U.S.A.' Halifax was therefore in a minority, and Churchill took care to strengthen his hand by canvassing junior ministers on the evening of 28 May. Dismissing the idea that Britain could secure better terms now than by fighting on, he pledged himself to a heroic death rather than surrender, and was warmly applauded by his colleagues.[44] The Cabinet accordingly told Reynaud that this did not seem an opportune time to approach Mussolini. The French went ahead themselves, but their *démarche* was rejected.

This whole episode reflects the desperate circumstances of late May, when it seemed unlikely that Britain would have an army with which to defend herself. On 27 May Cadogan saw 'no hope for more than a tiny fraction' of the BEF at Dunkirk. On the 28th Chamberlain expected to save no more than 30,000–40,000, while that afternoon Churchill told his junior ministers that 50,000 could certainly be evacuated and that 'if we could only get 100,000 away, that would be a magnificent performance'. For a time it also seemed possible that Hitler's next step would be to mount an immediate invasion of Britain, rather than continuing the offensive in France.[45] Such was the alarm that the Treasury, urged on by a panic-stricken Chancellor, Kingsley Wood, rushed through arrangements to ship all the Bank of England's holdings of gold and securities to North America.[46] There also seemed no prospect of assistance from the U.S.A. On 27 May, during the debates about possible peace terms, Churchill observed bitterly, to the approval of his colleagues, that the U.S.A. 'had given us practically no help in the war, and now that they saw how great was the danger, their attitude was that they wanted to keep everything which would help us for their own defence'.[47]

By early June, however, the situation had changed dramatically: 224,000 British troops had been saved, thanks to the Admiralty and the RAF and also the decision of Hitler, confident that no evacuation was possible, to halt his armour for essential repairs and leave the mopping-up to the infantry and air force. It also became clear that Germany planned to finish off the French first, and, at last, there were signs that America was waking up to the Allies' needs. These developments gave new encouragement after the nerve-wracking days of late May. Despite a further panic as the French surrendered, confidence increased in July when it became clear that Hitler was ill-prepared to mount an invasion. There was therefore no further debate among ministers about whether Britain should fight on. Halifax dealt firmly with those who wanted HMG to find out Hitler's terms. Such enquiries would be futile, he insisted, and would 'only sow profound discouragement in all the quarters on which we have to rely for our strength'. And both he and Chamberlain briskly dismissed the German peace feelers accompanying Hitler's speech on 19 July.[48] However, the hope was still that, by fighting on, Britain could secure acceptable terms. Halifax and Butler were particularly emphatic on this point, fearing that Churchill would be carried away by emotion and bravado into prolonging the war unnecessarily.[49] In fact, in his private and less rhetorical moods that summer, Churchill may have recognized that victory seemed unattainable. He seems to have accepted Halifax's formula of terms not 'destructive of our independence', arguing, as before, that a firm reply to all Hitler's current overtures was 'the only chance of extorting from Germany any offers which are not fantastic'.[50] As Paul Addison says, Churchill's attitude 'seems to have been that while *he* would never agree to it, he recognized that others might negotiate an untreasonable peace'.[51]

Despite this renewed consensus within the War Cabinet, however, not everyone in political circles agreed that Britain should fight on. A group of some 30 MPs and ten peers, from all three parties, believed that it would be disastrous for Britain and Germany to continue the war. Whoever won, they argued, Europe would be ravaged, and the only beneficiaries would be the U.S.S.R. and the U.S.A. By fighting on Britain would become 'a sort of Heligoland on the shores of Europe—in a military sense an American island fortress holding not merely Germany but the whole of Europe at bay, while the Americans have time to arm'. Meanwhile, 'the economic and financial centre of the world is shifting before our eyes' to the U.S.A.[52] This group looked to Lloyd George as their potential leader. In fact, the former PM's attitude was broadly similar to that of most of the War Cabinet. He did not favour an immediate peace, but believed that Britain should seek favourable terms once the Battle of Britain had been won and she had proved her invincibility. But Lloyd George's assessment of Britain's prospects did differ in two important respects from established HMG doctrine. He did not believe that victory could be won by blockade alone. The Allies would have to re-establish themselves on the continent and then fight a prolonged war of attrition in order to defeat Germany. The whole process would probably take five to ten years, during which time Britain would have been ruined and the U.S., Japan and Russia would have captured her trade and wealth. Nor did Lloyd George see any prospect of early American help.

It is assumed that America will enter the War on our side with all her immense resources. This is an optimistic assumption. She will no doubt help us in all ways short of War. But I cannot foresee her sending another huge army to Europe. But supposing she ultimately decide[s] to come in, when will she be ready? She

105

is by slow processes raising a bigger and a more formidable Army. Judging by the experience of the last War it will not be an efficient fighting force for at least 2 years. It might then take the place of the French army in the last War—although that is doubtful.[53]

Today we think of Lloyd George in 1940 as an extinct volcano. In fact, senility did not set in until after his wife's death in 1941, and in 1940 he remained a national and international figure, whom many still saw as a great leader. In May and June Churchill tried on several occasions to entice him into the Cabinet. Initially, these efforts were frustrated by Chamberlain, whose intense hatred of Lloyd George dated back to the Great War. However, Churchill persuaded Chamberlain to withdraw his opposition as the price for calling off the 'Guilty Men' press campaign. Thereafter, Lloyd George was the obstacle, ostensibly because he would not serve with the 'architects of disaster', Chamberlain and Halifax.[54] This was not the only reason, however. As Chamberlain, Churchill and others suspected, Lloyd George also saw himself as a future peacemaking prime minister, ready to take the stage when the nation perceived the bankruptcy of the existing leadership with its avowed policy of total victory.[55]

*    *    *

From the evidence set out in the preceding paragraphs, it is evident that the question of a compromise peace was aired in Whitehall and Westminster in the summer of 1940. Furthermore, some of those who toyed with the idea— Halifax, Chamberlain and Lloyd George—were politicians whom Churchill had to take very seriously. One of the central arguments of those who questioned the wisdom of fighting on was that real American help would not be forthcoming. Not surprisingly, therefore, whenever he wanted to raise morale and stop talk of peacemaking, Churchill adopted an exaggeratedly optimistic view of the U.S.A., expounding his long-held belief that, if the Germans attacked Britain, the transatlantic bonds of blood and heritage, pulled taut by the force of moral outrage, would draw America rapidly into the war.

For example, Churchill took this line with the French in late May and June, as he tried to keep them in the war. At the Supreme War Council on 31 May, he assured them that the U.S. 'had been roused by recent events, and even if they did not enter the war, they would soon be prepared to give us powerful aid'. 'An invasion of England,' he added, 'if it took place, would have a still profounder effect on the United States, especially in those many towns in the New World which bore the same names as towns in the British Isles.'[56] By 13 June, when the Council met for the last time, at Tours, Reynaud was insistent that France could only fight on if there was 'light at the end of the tunnel', by which he meant 'definite proof that America would come in with sufficient speed and force'. He had appealed to F.D.R. on 10 June for an immediate public declaration of every possible moral and material support for the Allies, short of an AEF, and when Churchill returned home from Tours he found a copy of Roosevelt's reply awaiting him. In it the President confessed himself heartened by recent French and British declarations that they would fight on, and he promised that his Administration, already doing all it could to aid the Allies, would redouble its efforts. Today this telegram seems little more than hyperbole and exhortation—cheering from the sidelines—but when the Cabinet considered it, late on 13 June, Churchill convinced his colleagues, by then ready to clutch at any straw, that the message 'came as near as possible to a declaration of war and was probably as much as the President could do without Congress. The President could hardly urge the French to continue the struggle, and to undergo further torture, if he did not intend to enter the war to support them'.[57] Churchill then pressed Roosevelt to make his 'magnificent' message known to the world. 'If he will consent to have this published', noted Halifax, 'it pretty well commits America to war.'[58] F.D.R.'s prompt refusal to do so, and his emphatic denial of any military commitment to the Allies, came as a shock in London, but, in retrospect, what seems remarkable is Churchill's ability to persuade his colleagues that another example of American 'preaching' was tantamount to a declaration of war.

Churchill used similar arguments in many other situations that summer. When sounding out the opinions of junior ministers on 28 May, he predicted that if Britain had to fight on alone 'there would be an immense wave of feeling, not least in the U.S.A. which, having done nothing much to help us so far, might even enter the war'. The leaders of the Dominions were also anxious about the future, not unreasonably since Britain was almost completely concerned at this time with her own defence. Churchill offered reassurance. On 10 June he told Smuts that the U.S. would probably enter the war after the November elections, and on the 16th, in a telegram to all the Dominions premiers, he stated his personal belief 'that the spectacle of the fierce struggle and carnage in our Island will draw the United States into the war'. He spoke in the same vein to the Commons in a secret session on 20 June, as his notes clearly show:

> Attitude of United States.
> Nothing will stir them like fighting in England. . . .
> The heroic struggle of Britain best chance of bringing them in. . . .
> All depends upon our resolute bearing and holding out until Election issues are settled there.
> If we can do so, I cannot doubt whole English-speaking world will be in line together.

He also held out this hope to Britain's remaining Allies. In his memoirs, de Gaulle, the Free French leader, recalled:

> I can still see him at Chequers, one August day, raising his fists towards the sky as he cried: 'So they won't come!' 'Are you in such a hurry,' I said to him, 'to see your towns smashed to bits?' 'You see,' he replied, 'the bombing of Oxford, Coventry, Canterbury will cause such a wave of indignation in the United States that they'll come into the war!'[59]

*    *    *

Contrary to patriotic mythology, then, it was not inevitable that Britain fought on in the summer of 1940. In fact the alternatives were seriously discussed. Perhaps in the end the idea of surrender would have been instinctively repugnant, but the position in May and June was so grave that there had to be rational as well as emotional grounds for going on.

One reason for continuing the struggle was the persistent conviction that the Germans themselves could not go on much longer. Whitehall believed the German economy was already centralized and fully extended. It anticipated an economic crisis by the spring of 1941, stemming from shortages of oil, food and key raw materials. No one yet appreciated Hitler's *Blitzkrieg* strategy—the concept of short, sharp wars which made full-scale economic mobilization unnecessary.[60] Thus, Whitehead of FO/A, assuring his family in America 'how nearly the Allies pulled it off in France', emphasized that 'in the long run Germany is doomed, she can only win this year if at all'.[61] Even Halifax and Chamberlain agreed that Germany needed a quick victory.[62] This was one reason, despite the jitters of late May, for hoping that Britain could eventually secure acceptable terms.

The other, related, reason was the hope of imminent American entry. And it was Churchill, as much as anyone, who, with a blend of conviction and calculation, established this as a new axiom of British policy. His precise argument varied. Sometimes he suggested that the bombing of historic English cities would be enough. Sometimes he emphasized the effect of actual invasion. Increasingly, however, as the summer progressed, Churchill cited the November election as the turning-point.[63] Although FO/A was less sanguine, many British policymakers privately set their sights on that goal. Thus, Harold Nicolson, a junior minister at the MOI, told his wife on 19 June: 'I think it practically certain that the Americans will enter the war in November, and if we can last till then, all is well.'[64] In chapter six we shall see that this conviction rested on fundamental misapprehensions both about Roosevelt and about the U.S. political system. Right or wrong, however, this belief—and the confidence about German weakness—were essential illusions. Together they helped to maintain British morale during that long and lonely summer.

## C. Backing Britain—the debate in Washington

The summer of 1940 stands as a unique crisis in the American experience. Historically, the security of the United States had rested on three main conditions. One was her geographical position—separated from the other major powers by vast oceans which posed near-insuperable logistic and technical problems for any would-be invader. She also benefited from the continuance of an equilibrium among the major powers which made it unlikely that any one of them would be in a position to mount an invasion. And, by 1900, she had emerged as the world's leading industrial nation with the potential to create a greater war machine than any of her rivals. Americans therefore did not have to devote much of their domestic product to defence spending or indeed to invest much time or energy in foreign policy. 'By virtue of its superior potential, the United States had no need to fear any nation; by virtue of the character of military technology and the balance of power abroad it could afford to leave that potential largely unmobilized.'[65]

In the summer of 1940 those favourable conditions seemed to have disappeared. American leaders were no longer confident, in an emerging era of air power, that the oceans remained guarantees of security. In any case, many of them accepted the argument that throughout the nineteenth century the oceans had only been a barrier because the British fleet had policed the seas in the interests of peace. Furthermore, by June 1940, the European balance had been totally upset. A single, aggressive power dominated the continent and Britain's own ability to survive was in doubt. If Hitler secured her fleet and that of the French, then he might be able quickly to mount an invasion of the Western Hemisphere.

We know now that Hitler had no such immediate designs. But the German successes of May 1940 caused near-panic in America. Congress fell over itself to approve massive appropriations for national defence. But for the moment these were strictly irrelevant. As Bernard Baruch, who had supervised the U.S. war mobilization in 1917–18, observed, 'you cannot just order a Navy as you would a pound of coffee, or vegetables and meat, and say, we will have that for dinner. It takes time. It takes organization.'[66] In 1940 America would have to make do with what she had—a regular army of some 225,000 men with obsolescent equipment, and, effectively, a one-ocean navy presently based at Pearl Harbor. Roosevelt was therefore faced with a choice—something he hated—how best to deploy these limited forces? Should he abandon his limited liability policy in Europe and concentrate on the defence of the Americas? This would involve bringing the fleet back to the East Coast and effectively abandoning the Pacific to Japan. Or could he still safely continue to treat Western Europe as America's front line—particularly if only Britain were left?

Some historians have insisted that throughout the summer F.D.R. displayed an unswerving confidence that Britain would survive.[67] But that seems an interpretation based upon the wisdom of hindsight. In my judgement the evidence suggests that Roosevelt's thinking that summer went through three phases. In the first, up to the French collapse in mid-June, he did his best to help maintain a Western Front on the continent of Europe. Then, for the next six weeks, he trod water, uncertain that Britain could survive alone and sure that he could do nothing to help. During August, however, he came to the conclusion that Britain could and should be helped, and his new confidence and commitment were expressed in the Destroyers Deal concluded on 2 September. In this section I will examine the first two phases, leaving the last for chapter five.

*     *     *

The President's initial reaction to the German offensive of 10 May was to intensify his policy of helping Britain and France maintain the Western Front in Europe. Aided by Morgenthau he fought a hard three-week bureaucratic battle to secure the release from U.S. stocks of military equipment for the Allies. To get round the Neutrality Act the equipment was sold back to its manufacturers who then sold it to Britain and France. Among the material released in early June were 250,000 rifles, 130 million rounds of ammunition, 80,000 machine guns, nearly 900 75-mm. guns with ammunition, and some

140 bombers. This was a considerable achievement—the rifles, for instance, were invaluable for arming the British Home Guard in July.[68] On 10 June F.D.R. made a rousing speech at Charlottesville in which he denounced the Italian attack on France as a stab in the back and proclaimed with unprecedented clarity his dual policy of rearmament and material assistance to 'the opponents of force'. The Administration would 'not slow down or detour'. His motto was 'full speed ahead'.[69]

These actions were taken against the advice of many of his advisers, who favoured concentrating on hemisphere defence. Berle spoke for many in the State Department and military when he noted on 15 May: '. . . it seems plain that our job is to collect the strongest and solidest defense force we can, and not fritter away small detachments to the other side of the Atlantic. The outcome of the battle which will decide the fate of Europe obviously will be decided before anything can get across the Atlantic.'[70] The Department was not neutral in thought, but even Welles, who, like F.D.R., was emotionally deeply committed to the French, felt that the President's gratuitous insult to Italy at Charlottesville was unwise. As Long put it, the U.S. should not antagonize the Axis any further until it was ready to face them militarily, which would not be for two years.[71] Similar sentiments were expressed in the War Department. Harry Woodring, the Secretary of War, fought the President tenaciously throughout the spring to prevent scarce U.S. equipment being released for sale to the Allies. And by 22 May the War Department planners advised that henceforth the U.S. should confine herself to defending the American continent and U.S. possessions east of Midway.[72]

Roosevelt had therefore acted with considerable political courage. As Joseph Lash observes, he felt that the sense of national crisis gave him a new opportunity to influence events and exercise leadership.[73] He also used the situation to make the Cabinet changes he had considered the previous autumn. After prolonged negotiations it was announced on 20 June that Henry Stimson, formerly Taft's Secretary of War and Hoover's Secretary of State, would return to the War Department, and that Frank Knox, the owner of the *Chicago Daily News* and the Republican vice-presidential candidate in 1936, would become Secretary of the Navy. Typically F.D.R. was solving several problems at once. He put dynamic men into the two crucial defence departments. He finally ended the War Department feud between Woodring and Johnson, which had polarized and paralysed the Department for more than two years. He also cut the ground from under the Republicans, by taking into his Cabinet two respected GOP members and thereby posing as the leader of a bipartisan coalition, aloof from petty partisan politics. Above all the President tipped the balance of his Administration decisively in favour of his policy of aid to Britain and France. Knox favoured U.S. entry into the war, while Stimson advocated measures such as escorting that would soon lead to belligerency. The two of them quickly developed a good working relationship with Ickes, who also wanted the U.S. to go to war, and with Morgenthau, who did not adopt this position until May 1941 but who was the most energetic supporter of F.D.R.'s policy of material assistance to the Allies.[74] Together these four men constituted the Cabinet 'hawks'. More than any other U.S. policymakers they saw the international scene as a global battle between democracy and dictatorship in which the British Empire, for all its blemishes, was America's front line and effective ally. Their collective influence was soon apparent, for instance in formulating policy towards Japan and in the Destroyers Deal.

Did Roosevelt go as far as Ickes or Knox at this time and favour American belligerency? On 16 May, just after the German offensive had begun, he did hint to Morgenthau that the U.S. might be in the war by late summer. He had made similar predictions of early U.S. entry to the British in mid-September 1938 and early September 1939, when total war had seemed imminent.[75] But from Munich to Pearl Harbor F.D.R. was quite clear that the decision for peace or war depended not on his own judgement but on the force of events. He could only ask Congress for a declaration when Germany had aroused American opinion by an assault on U.S. interests, such as an attempt to occupy the Azores, or some flagrant violation of American ideals. He suggested to the British on several occasions that an attack on Britain, particularly if it involved the bombing of London, would act as a suitable catalyst. Some such provocation, Roosevelt believed, 'was the necessary precondition to make the United States enter the war with the necessary popular support'.[76] Implicit in all these comments seems to have been an assumption that the war would develop along the lines of 1914–18, albeit in a more barbarous form, with a stable if active Western Front in Europe. This would be the context in which Americans might be aroused by daily reports of carnage and destruction. Such expectations were dramatically falsified by the rapid French collapse.[77] American opinion *was* aroused—but the result was a panic about hemisphere defence rather than a demand to fight for a losing cause in Europe. Admittedly in late May and early June the President suggested to British officials that Hitler might very soon provide the necessary provocation to force America into war. But, as we shall see in a moment, these comments were made to strengthen British resolve, and it is likely that F.D.R.'s own feelings were always less bellicose than he led HMG to believe. When Reynaud and Churchill appealed in mid-June for U.S. belligerency, F.D.R. was therefore adamant that if he called for U.S. entry 'the immediate result would be [the] destruction of his Government politically'. Lothian reported that F.D.R. was believed to have been sounding out the opinion of Congressional leaders on a possible declaration of war and that the 'result has been distinctly negative'.[78]

The French collapse, culminating in surrender on 17 June, represented a distinct change in America's strategic situation, although historians have not always made this clear. In May and early June Roosevelt's purpose had been to keep a Western Front in existence in continental Europe. The sales of U.S. equipment were directed to this end rather than specifically to the assistance of Britain. And, as Robert Sherwood pointed out long ago, the Charlottesville address was largely a response to Reynaud's impassioned appeals—the farthest a humiliatingly impotent President felt he could go to keep France in the war. It was not so much a detailed statement of policy as an inspirational exhortation. Certainly the rhetoric of going 'full speed ahead' through all obstructions was not translated into action, as was apparent next day when F.D.R. indicated that he had no intention of seeking

111

repeal of the Neutrality or Johnson Acts.[79] France's surrender marked the failure of these efforts to keep the Western Front alive. The emotional urgency subsided, and there was time for sober consideration of a separate question—could Britain survive alone as America's front line?

Roosevelt's initial response was a typically breezy 'yes'. On 13 June he told the planners to operate on the hypothesis that by the end of 1940 Britain would still be intact and that the U.S. would be actively involved in the naval and air war. Four days later he told Morgenthau that the British should be given the same help as had previously been given to Britain and France.[80] But in reality for the next six weeks Britain received little assistance, and it is clear that in part this must be attributed to Roosevelt's doubts about her capacity to survive. On 27 June Lothian reported 'that there is a wave of pessimism passing over this country to the effect that Great Britain must now inevitably be defeated, and that there is no use in the United States doing anything more to help it and thereby getting entangled in Europe'. He added: 'There is some evidence that it is beginning to affect the President. . . .' Similarly, Jim Farley, F.D.R.'s erstwhile campaign manager, states that on 7 July Roosevelt told him that Britain's chances were 'about one in three'. Some historians have questioned Lothian's judgement and Farley's memory, but Thomas Lamont and William Allen White, both of whom were in close touch with the President, independently expressed similar views to those of Lothian.[81] We also need to bear in mind Roosevelt's fear that the Royal Navy might be sunk or surrendered and his reluctance to provide Britain with destroyers, which will be discussed in the next section. Furthermore, such doubts seem understandable, if we forget the patriotic myths about Britain's 'finest hour'. After Germany had overwhelmed the world's best army in only six weeks, no one could be sanguine that Britain, despite her 'moat defensive', could survive. And there was much justice in the repeated observation of Ambassador Kennedy that Britain's diplomatic and military record over the previous few years hardly recommended her as a reliable ally.[82] In short, it would have been imprudent for Roosevelt to put all America's eggs in Britain's basket.

Aside from his own hesitations, Roosevelt was also constrained in late June and July by the state of America's own armaments and by growing pressure from the military and Congress to concentrate on hemisphere defence. The sales of equipment in early June had severely depleted U.S. stocks, particularly of rifle ammunition and heavy guns. The 130 million rounds of ammunition, for instance, represented nearly a quarter of army stocks, at a time when current production was only four million a month.[83] Deeply concerned, Marshall, the Army Chief of Staff, and Stark, the Chief of Naval Operations, pressed F.D.R. on 22 June for a virtual ban on further sales to Britain. Roosevelt refused to be pinned down, but he did drop plans to sell 12 B-17 heavy bombers to the British and agreed that sales of current stock and new orders would only be permitted if Britain demonstrated that she could survive, if the equipment would significantly help her to resist until the end of the year and if U.S. procurement programmes were not thereby retarded.[84] His hands were further tied by the Walsh amendment, which he signed into law on 2 July. Despite the belated efforts of Administration supporters in Congress, this measure, proposed by the isolationist, anglophobe chairman of the Senate Naval Affairs Committee, prohibited the sale of U.S. equipment unless Marshall or Stark could certify that it was 'not essential for US defense'.[85] On that criterion, given the state of America's forces, hardly anything could be considered 'surplus', and the Walsh amendment significantly restricted F.D.R.'s ability to sell more equipment to the Allies.

Of course, the President could have refused to sign the amendment. But he rarely challenged a strong and determined pressure group in Congress, least of all when his political situation was so delicate.[86] For Roosevelt was in a political vacuum that summer—a second-term president with apparently only a few months left. Over several years he had evaded questions about his intentions in 1940. As usual he wanted to keep all options open, but it seems that until the spring he had probably intended not to seek an unprecedented third term. Like most politicians, however, his sense of the desirable was inextricably linked with his sense of the possible. The crisis of summer 1940 provided the opportunity, the reason and the justification for running again.[87] Yet the two-term tradition was a major obstacle. For reasons of conscience as well as politics Roosevelt wanted his nomination to seem like a draft. Publicly he expressed his desire to retire, but he did nothing to discourage the successful efforts of Harry Hopkins to manipulate the Chicago convention and secure his re-nomination on 17 July.[88] As his party's presidential candidate, Roosevelt was now in a stronger position. But throughout the summer he had to be extremely cautious in his diplomacy. Although Wendell Willkie, the Republican presidential candidate, was in basic agreement with Roosevelt's foreign policy, his party, particularly in Congress, was ready to seize on any imprudent action by the President as evidence of Democratic 'war-mongering'. Already criticized by conservatives for subverting the American way of life, and currently engaged in an attack on the most sacred of American political traditions—the two-term presidency—F.D.R. could not afford to encourage any suspicion that he was also challenging the shibboleth of 'no entangling alliances'.

For all these reasons—personal doubts, domestic pressures and election politics—F.D.R. provided little further assistance to Britain from mid-June until early August. That is not to say that he abandoned his policy of trying to maintain some sort of front line across the Atlantic. But he was unsure that Britain could survive alone, and he was certain that for the moment at least he could do little to assist her. As he told Admiral Stark in late June, in a different context: 'When I don't know how to move, I stay put.'[89] Not until August did he move towards a clear commitment to the British, more confident that they could survive and having discovered a politically practicable way of giving them support. That commitment, which I shall discuss in the next chapter, was the celebrated 'Destroyers-for-Bases' deal.

## D. American destroyers and the British fleet

Britain's pleas for U.S. destroyers and American anxieties about the future of the British and French fleets were the central issues in transatlantic diplomacy in May and June 1940. Examination of them provides an excellent insight into the hesitant character of the Anglo-American relationship during those uncertain weeks.

Washington's lack of confidence in the quality of Allied leadership did not end with Churchill's assumption of the premiership. For one thing, at 65 he seemed past his prime—one of 'the old war horses', in Berle's words, 'behaving as well as he can, but no longer the young Churchill'. There was also the ideological divide between the New Dealers and the Tory defender of Empire, with American friends who, as Kennedy put it to Roosevelt, 'definitely are not on our team'.[90] Widespread doubts were also expressed about the new PM's sobriety and balance. In July 1939 Kennedy had told F.D.R. that Churchill 'has developed into a fine two-handed drinker and his judgment has never been proven to be good' and Welles made similar comments in his report in March 1940.[91] On 5 May Berle noted: 'The rumor is going around here that Churchill is drunk all the time; and Welles said that on the first of the two evenings he saw Churchill he was quite drunk. I asked whether he saw, in his peregrinations, any indications of clear-cut leadership. Welles answered that he saw none. This', Berle concluded, 'is the real heart of the Allied difficulty. . . .'[92] Roosevelt too apparently shared these doubts. When news of Chamberlain's resignation arrived, Ickes noted: 'We assumed that Churchill would be charged with the duty of organizing a new Cabinet and the President said that he supposed Churchill was the best man that England had, even if he was drunk half of his time. Apparently Churchill is very unreliable when under the influence of drink.'[93] Perhaps this was one of F.D.R.'s gossipy asides. We shall see that the Administration's view of Churchill changed considerably during the summer. However, these comments are worth noting because most of them have been discreetly expurgated from the published record and because they show that the change of British leaders, although welcomed in Washington, was not initially seen as decisive.

On 15 May, in his first letter to F.D.R. as Prime Minister, Churchill put at the top of his shopping list of American supplies 'the loan of forty or fifty of your older destroyers to bridge the gap between what we have now and the large new construction we put in hand at the beginning of the war'. Destroyers were vital for patrols against invasion and for anti-submarine escorts in the Western Approaches, and as early as 18 September 1939 Churchill had told the Cabinet of his desire to obtain U.S. destroyers to fill the gap until mid-1941 when the new British vessels would become available.[94] On 16 May Roosevelt made it clear that Churchill's request could not be satisfied, at least for the moment. He set out what were to be his three basic arguments throughout the summer against the loan or sale of destroyers—such a step would require Congressional approval, which was unlikely; the vessels were needed for patrolling American waters; and, in any case, the transaction would take so long to complete that it could not affect the outcome in Europe. On the evening of 17 May Roosevelt repeated these arguments to Lothian, who in turn reminded the President that if the Royal Navy lost control of the Atlantic for want of U.S support America would be left with a 'one-ocean' navy facing threats in both the Atlantic and the Pacific. F.D.R. then suggested that if the worst happened and Britain fell the British fleet should cross the Atlantic to Canada or the U.S.A. That, responded the Ambassador, would probably depend on whether the U.S. had entered the war. He did not think British public opinion would entrust the fleet to a neutral America. Lothian reported that F.D.R. 'seemed impressed by this possibility'.[95]

These exchanges of 15–17 May set out the lines of transatlantic diplomacy for the next few weeks.[96] Although aware that the Empire could only survive a British collapse if the U.S. and British fleets were combined, HMG felt it was shrewd tactics on Lothian's part to suggest that this would only happen if the U.S. became a belligerent. Commented Scott: 'This is rather like blackmail, and not very good blackmail at that, but I think we are justified in planting the idea rather more firmly in Mr Roosevelt's mind.' And for the next few weeks Lothian continued to warn American leaders periodically that Britain would probably not bequeath her fleet to a neutral U.S.A.[97] Churchill took the argument a stage further, telling F.D.R. on 20 May that although his own government would fight to the end, if 'others came to parley amid the ruins, you must not be blind to the fact that the sole remaining bargaining counter with Germany would be the fleet, and if this country was left by the United States to its fate no one would have the right to blame those then responsible if they made the best terms they could for the surviving inhabitants.' He reiterated his point in other messages in May and June, and instructed Lothian to impress it upon policymakers in Washington. Occasionally he mentioned Oswald Mosley as a possible peacemaker, but he never revealed the pressure upon him from far more prominent politicians such as Halifax and Lloyd George.[98]

Roosevelt was fully sensible of these possibilities. As early as 25 May, with many of the Allied forces trapped around Dunkirk, he told H. L. Keenleyside, a senior Canadian diplomat, that 'any day' the French would be forced to surrender, leaving Germany free to attack Britain speedily with five-to-one air superiority. According to Keenleyside, Roosevelt and Hull 'were doubtful if England would be able to bear up under the attack, and the President has it from what he believes good authority from Germany that Hitler may make an offer of settlement', involving a guarantee of Britain's independence in return for the surrender of the fleet and, effectively, of the Empire. Even more disconcerting, on 27 and 28 May F.D.R. learned from Kennedy and from Knox's *Chicago Daily News* bureau in London that a part of the Cabinet was talking about the possibility of a negotiated peace.[99]

Throughout May and June, therefore, Roosevelt reiterated the point he had made to Lothian on 17 May—that the British and French fleets must not be sunk or surrendered and that at least part of them should be sent to North America if European waters became untenable. With the British increasingly arguing that such action would depend upon U.S. entry into the war, F.D.R. also hinted that this was very near. On 25 May, for instance, he told Lothian that 'it seemed likely that Germany would challenge some vital American interest in the near future, which was the condition necessary to make the United States enter the war with the necessary popular support and that opinion was rapidly changing as to what United States vital interests were.'[100] He also enlisted the aid of Mackenzie King, the Canadian premier, who naturally shared Roosevelt's anxiety about Atlantic security and whose advice would be less offensive to the British than that of an American. Through King F.D.R. assured Churchill that if the Royal Navy had to leave British waters, American ports would be opened to it and the U.S.A. would help defend the Empire. 'As soon thereafter as grounds could be found to justify direct and active participation (and neither Mr Roosevelt nor Mr Hull believe that this would be more than a very few weeks)' the U.S. would participate in a tight naval blockade of continental Europe and if the Germans tried to punish the British for letting the fleet go 'public opinion in the United States would demand active intervention'.[101] But these bellicose sentiments were for British ears. The uncertain diplomatic situation strengthened F.D.R.'s inclination to wait upon events and to limit the assistance given to Britain and France. In addition to the political difficulties with destroyers, he told Ickes on 4 June that: 'If we should send some destroyers across, they would be no particular use to the Allies but they might serve further to enrage Hitler. We cannot tell the turn the war will take, and there is no use endangering ourselves unless we can achieve some results for the Allies.'[102]

Thus both governments were engaged in an uneasy bargaining game that summer, exploring in a rather heavy-handed way how best to obtain support from the other. British tactics seem particularly 'maladroit', as James Leutze has argued—strengthening the Administration's anxiety about Britain's defences.[103] But we need to remember here HMG's ingrained doubts and fears about the U.S.A. and the desperate predicament of May and June. On 19 May the Cabinet concluded, on the basis of Lothian's reports, that although F.D.R. was well disposed to the Allies he showed no appreciation of the gravity of Britain's supply position. The President's apparent obsession with the future of the Royal Navy only increased HMG's resentment. Thus, on 25 May, the Cabinet felt that F.D.R. 'seemed to be taking the view that it would be nice of him to pick up the bits of the British Empire if this country was overrun. It was as well that he should realise that there was another aspect of the question.'[104] Five days later Lothian reported that over the previous week Roosevelt's anxiety about the fleet had apparently lessened, because, Lothian judged, he had persuaded himself that the Dominions could be relied upon to get the fleet across the Atlantic before it was too late. This, Lothian observed, was the President's 'paralysing illusion'—if F.D.R. were not so sure of getting the fleet he would be forced to give more active support to Britain. Shrewdly Lothian emphasized that Roosevelt was still practising a dual policy: 'The expert politician in the President is always trying to find a way of winning the war for the Allies, or, if he fails to do that, of ensuring the security of the United States, without the United States itself having to take the plunge into the war.'[105]

In view of British scepticism and of reports like this from Lothian, it is understandable that HMG continued to play on Roosevelt's fears about the fleet. The object was to make clear that the vital battle was taking place in Europe. If Americans did not provide full support for Britain and France, they would not have a second chance to defend themselves in the Western Hemisphere, reinforced by the British fleet. But it is important to note that

Churchill reserved such warnings for private communications with Administration leaders. In public he adopted a mood of indefatigable optimism to uplift morale at home and abroad, reiterating Britain's determination to fight on to victory and frequently hinting, as we have seen, that the U.S. would soon be in the war. Thus in his 4 June speech—'we shall fight on the beaches' —he assured the Commons and the world that, in the unlikely event that Britain fell, 'then our Empire beyond the seas, armed and guarded by the British Fleet, would carry on the struggle, until, in God's good time, the New World, with all its power and might, steps forth to the rescue and the liberation of the Old.' But the next day he cabled Mackenzie King, rightly expecting that his message would be shown to Roosevelt: 'We must be careful not to let Americans view too complacently prospect of a British collapse out of which they would get the British Fleet and the guardianship of the British Empire, minus Great Britain. If . . . America continued neutral, and we were overpowered I cannot tell what policy might be adopted by a pro-German administration such as would undoubtedly be set up.'[106] For the most part Lothian, too, maintained this public–private distinction. The only exception was a speech he gave at Yale on 19 June. Alarmed that Churchill's 4 June speech had strengthened Americans' 'paralysing illusion', he warned them bluntly that they would be very unwise to build their defences on the expectation of securing the British fleet. If Britain fell, most of the Navy would be lost in its defence and the remnants would probably go to the Empire rather than to a neutral U.S.A.[107] With this exception—admittedly an important one—Lothian, like Churchill, kept his gloomier warnings for the private ears of U.S. leaders.

There was, therefore, an interesting contrast between Churchill's public confidence about the U.S.A. and his private doubts and fears. For domestic consumption he stressed that U.S. help was imminent, yet in secret he remained disappointed at the lack of assistance, and even suspicious that America was waiting on the sidelines to pick up the pieces. The doubts and fears led him to advocate a tough, bargaining approach to the U.S.A., tailoring British concessions to tangible evidence of American help. By contrast Lothian and FO/A preferred a tactic of calculated generosity to balance the attempted 'blackmail' about the fleet. If the British made spontaneous offers of co-operation, they argued, this would encourage the Americans to respond in kind and would also promote that spirit of Anglo-American amity which they considered essential for the future of the world.

This fundamental difference over tactics recurred throughout the summer. For instance, Churchill was reluctant to make a spontaneous offer of Britain's military secrets. Although eventually agreeing in principle on 30 June, after repeated pressure from Lothian, the FO and the Service departments, the PM still held back in practice. In part this reflected his obsession with secrecy, but tactical considerations were also much in his mind. 'Are we going to throw all our secrets into the American lap; and see what they give us in exchange?' he minuted on 17 July. 'If so, I am against it. . . . Generally speaking, I am not in a hurry to give our secrets until the United States is much nearer war than she is now.'[108]

117

A similar argument developed over whether to offer the U.S.A. bases on British possessions in the Western Atlantic. This would greatly strengthen the defences of the East Coast and the Panama Canal and would also prevent the colonies in question falling into German hands as a result of a European peace settlement. Lothian was well aware of the Administration's concern on this matter and repeatedly urged HMG to make a spontaneous offer of facilities, to pre-empt a possible U.S. take-over and also promote goodwill. His first proposal was made on 25 May, when London was preoccupied with the Dunkirk evacuation and bitter at the lack of American help. Although the FO and the Chiefs of Staff supported Lothian, Churchill and the Admiralty, anxious for U.S. destroyers, felt no offer should be made except as part of a deal from which Britain benefited as well. The Colonial and Dominion Offices also feared that the bases would be the first step to U.S. domination in the Caribbean. The matter therefore lapsed until 23 June, when Lothian suggested offering the U.S. more limited facilities on three Caribbean possessions. Once again the FO was enthusiastic, but the Admiralty, CO and DO sought a quid pro quo such as destroyers or financial credits. For much of July the matter became bogged down in inter-departmental argument.[109]

Churchill was also slow to take up F.D.R.'s offer on 17 June, after repeated pressure from Lothian, of secret Anglo-American staff talks. He told Halifax on 24 June: 'I think they would turn almost entirely on the American side upon the transfer of the British Fleet to transatlantic bases. Any discussion of this is bound to weaken confidence here at the moment when all must brace themselves for the supreme struggle.' The FO took issue with Churchill, citing the Services' enthusiasm and the need to co-ordinate policy in the Pacific as reasons for acceptance. Halifax also reminded the PM that HMG should never reject any reasonably practicable U.S. proposal, for fear of retarding American education, and added that if one failed to take up a suggestion from Roosevelt his interest might cool (or be cooled) and then the matter could not be revived when one judged that the moment *was* ripe. These were compelling arguments and Churchill acquiesced on 29 June.[110] But his own hesitations were comprehensible and probably justified. At this stage F.D.R. envisaged largely naval conversations, to prepare plans for such contingencies as the sinking or surrender of the French fleet, Spanish entry into the war or an attack on the British Isles.[111] At the same time he was about to begin staff talks with Canada. These were held in mid-July and late August and they centred on the provision of U.S. bases in Canada and the formulation of contingency plans in case Britain lost control of the North Atlantic.[112] Historians have usually viewed the Anglo-American staff talks, which eventually took place in late August, as a step towards military alliance.[113] When Roosevelt proposed them, in June, he was probably more interested in strengthening hemisphere defence against the possibility of a British collapse.

Roosevelt's doubts about Britain would have increased in May and June whatever the British said. The President was well aware of the risks he was running in leaving the fleet at Pearl Harbor, and the débâcle in France confirmed all his worst fears about the Allies. But it is likely that Churchill's sinister warnings about the fleet unsettled him further and, contrary to their intent, probably strengthened his reluctance to provide destroyers. During May and June the Administration's confidence in Churchill grew, largely through his moving and defiant speeches. The reference on 4 June to the fleet fighting on in defence of the Empire was particularly reassuring.[114] But then F.D.R., as Churchill had intended, received a copy of the premier's 5 June telegram to Mackenzie King. According to Moffat this 'disturbed the President considerably', although he eventually decided that it must have been composed before the speech of 4 June, which was 'firmness itself'. At the end of June, after reading a paraphrase of another Churchill–King telegram in similar vein, Roosevelt felt 'that Churchill was telling neither Americans nor Canadians of his ultimate intentions but that if worse should come to the worst he was convinced that Churchill would remember that the Fleet belonged to the entire British Empire, and that the Empire would remember it likewise'.[115] But there remained the perplexing anomaly of Lothian's Yale speech of 19 June, warning Americans not to assume that whatever happened they would get the fleet. This address—the only *public* utterance by a British leader about the possible loss of the Royal Navy—made it politically more difficult to reinforce that Navy with U.S. destroyers. The speech probably strengthened F.D.R.'s determination to secure a definitive public statement of HMG's policy on the fleet as a condition for the transfer of the destroyers.[116]

To some extent the Administration was reassured by the British neutralization of the French fleet on 3–4 July, which involved the attack on French vessels near Oran. The French had previously been responsible for patrolling the Western Mediterranean and although the British created a token force at Gibraltar this was quite inadequate, at a time when Italy, with a hundred submarines, had entered the war. If the French fleet fell into enemy hands this would tip the balance of sea power even further against Britain and the U.S.A. Under the terms of the Armistice it was to return to peacetime stations, for disarmament under Axis supervision. The French asserted, sincerely as we now know, that they would not allow the fleet to be used by any foreign power—Allied or Axis—but the embittered British Cabinet was unwilling to take any risks. It is also likely that HMG was anxious to prove to America Britain's ruthless determination to win the war. Roosevelt had made the American position quite clear to Lothian on 1 July, stating that U.S. opinion would expect the French ships to be forcibly seized 'rather than that they should fall into German hands and that he would do everything in his power to help this solution'.[117] The British action, and Churchill's pugnacious defence of it in the Commons, were widely applauded in the U.S.A.

Nevertheless, this did not make F.D.R. any more inclined to provide Britain with destroyers. When Ickes raised the matter on 2 July F.D.R. repeated his familiar arguments about U.S. needs and political difficulties, adding that the latter had been compounded by the Walsh amendment. In a letter dated 6 July he also reminded Ickes: 'I always have to think of the possibility that if these destroyers were sold to Great Britain and if, thereupon, Great Britain should be overwhelmed by Germany, they might fall into the hands of the Germans and be used against us.'[118] Meanwhile, in late June Lothian had asked Churchill for a 'reasoned confidential statement showing not only our determination to fight to the finish but giving grounds for hope and confidence', which he could use to persuade the President to resume vigorous aid. But Churchill, while agreeing that Britain had 'not really had any help worth speaking of' from America so far, did not think 'words count for much now'. Lothian should constantly impress upon the Administration that if Britain were occupied a 'Quisling Government' would use the Navy to secure better terms, but what really mattered was 'whether Hitler is master of Britain in three months or not. I think not', the PM stated. 'But this is a matter which cannot be argued beforehand.'[119] For most of July, therefore, with F.D.R. deep in election politics, both governments waited upon events. Between 15 June and 31 July the two leaders exchanged no messages, except for one from Churchill about the Duke of Windsor. It was a chilling time for the British. As Churchill recalled it later, for six weeks after the Fall of France 'the Americans treated us in that rather distant and sympathetic manner one adopts towards a friend one knows is suffering from cancer.'[120]

*    *    *

After Roosevelt's death, Churchill told the Commons: 'When I became Prime Minister . . . I was already in a position to telegraph to the President on terms of an association which had become most intimate. . . .'[121] Such a statement distorts both the limits of the Churchill–Roosevelt correspondence during the Phoney War, and the hesitant, even suspicious, character of Anglo-American relations in May and June. We need to remember the Administration's lukewarm reaction when Churchill assumed the premiership and F.D.R.'s uncertainties during June about Churchill's real intentions concerning the fleet. We need to remember Churchill's attempted 'blackmail' in tying the future disposition of the fleet to American belligerency and F.D.R.'s disingenuous insinuations that America was on the verge of war. We need to remember the President's doubts that Britain could survive and Churchill's determination to drive a hard bargain. In the unprecedented crisis of mid-1940 mutual trust took time to establish.

# CHAPTER FIVE

## American Destroyers, the British Fleet and the Defence of the English-Speaking World

### July—October 1940

*. . . the future of our widely scattered Empire is likely to depend on the evolution of an effective and enduring collaboration between ourselves and the United States.*

Foreign Office memo, July 1940

*. . . essentially, Britain is a small country of 45 million population and may not be able to hold the far-flung empire together. Should it go under, it is a very fair question whether the United States might not have to take them all over, in some fashion or other.*

Adolf Berle, State Department, March 1940[1]

### A. The Destroyers Deal, August 1940

It was not until the beginning of August that the stalemate over British requests for U.S. destroyers was broken. Throughout that month Washington and London engaged in complex and difficult negotiations. Eventually an agreement satisfactory to both sides was concluded on 2 September. The British were to receive 50 World War I destroyers in return for granting the U.S.A. leases of land on eight British possessions in the Caribbean and Western Atlantic on which the U.S. could construct naval and air bases. In addition to the destroyers and bases, as James Leutze has recently reminded us, there was a third element: a public statement by the British Government that if Britain fell the Royal Navy would not be sunk or surrendered.[2] Thus the Destroyers Deal tied together what had been the three main strands of transatlantic diplomacy throughout the summer and symbolized the growing co-operation between the two countries. Exploration of the August negotiations provides an excellent insight into the changing nature of their relationship.

The first positive moves came from London. During early July Lothian's proposal of 23 June to offer the U.S.A. limited base leases in the Caribbean became bogged down in the morass of bureaucratic politics. The Admiralty and the Colonial Office still insisted on some kind of quid pro quo, such as destroyers, or credits, or landing rights for British aircraft at Honolulu to prevent Pan Am from dominating post-war civil aviation.[3] On several occasions Lothian returned to the issue, warning that HMG must move quickly to head off unilateral action by the Administration. Not everyone in the FO agreed. Vansittart felt that Lothian had 'lost his balance about this question' and that the Admiralty was right to demand a fair price for the leases. 'For once', he told Halifax, 'we are vis à vis of the U.S.A. in a position of bargainers and not suppliants. Lord Lothian apparently doesn't like this position. I do.'[4] However, Vansittart was an isolated voice. FO/A was firmly behind Lothian, and it now enjoyed significant influence. In mid-July the Foreign Office decided to cut through the protracted bureaucratic wrangling and force the issue back up to Cabinet level. The catalyst here was a prescient memo from Professor T. North Whitehead—FO/A's specialist on U.S. opinion—drawing on his extensive experience of the U.S.A. He stated the case for offering bases in a form that appealed to all his superiors, and Halifax asked FO/A to prepare a paper for the Cabinet embodying Whitehead's arguments.[5]

The resulting paper of 18 July was an outstanding statement of the FO's approach to Anglo-American relations.[6] Its basic thesis was that 'the future of our widely scattered Empire is likely to depend on the evolution of an effective and enduring collaboration between ourselves and the United States.' That was a novel and startling doctrine for Americans, the paper observed. Britain must do all she could to help them assume this new responsibility, which was a total break with their past. This, of course, was the familiar FO concept of 'education'. Less familiar, but equally characteristic of Lothian and FO/A in 1940, was the paper's additional argument—the need for a concomitant change in *British* attitudes. There had to be 'a generous recognition by us of the fact that a responsibility involves a right to the means for discharging it'. If Britain wanted U.S. help in defending the English-speaking peoples, she must allow America access to British defence facilities. The provision of bases would be a first step in that redistribution of power. FO/A then raised the question of tactics. It rejected the idea of driving a hard bargain over the bases. This would seem unreasonable in view of Britain's many unrequited obligations to America, such as war debts. Nor would it be good diplomacy, since, although hard bargainers, Americans responded well to generosity. In general, the paper observed, the habit of cordial co-operation, which must be HMG's immediate and long-term aim, could not be fostered by 'tit-for-tat' diplomacy.

*Pace* Vansittart, then, Lothian and FO/A were not advocating giving something for nothing. They held that a spontaneous offer of base facilities was the most likely way of achieving Britain's wider ends. But Lord Lloyd, the Colonial Secretary, still warned that this would be the thin end of a wedge that would eventually result in the loss of British sovereignty over the possessions in question. As he told Balfour of FO/A bitterly: 'All this is the doing of Philip Lothian. He always wanted to give away the Empire and he now has a perfect opportunity for doing so.' Most of his colleagues, however, did not take such an apocalyptic view. When the FO's paper came before the Cabinet on 29 July there was general agreement that the position had changed greatly since the previous discussion in May. The U.S. had supplied so much that it was difficult to deny them the modest facilities now proposed. The Cabinet therefore agreed in principle to offer Pan American Airways, as agents for the U.S. Government, leases of land to build airfields in British Guiana and Jamaica and a small store and radio station on Trinidad, and to allow the U.S. landing rights for military aircraft in those three colonies. These were the facilities identified by Lothian in his message of 23 June as being particularly desired by U.S. planners. Communication of HMG's decision was delayed until 2 August because of enquiries, at Lloyd's behest, about Pan Am's reported hostility to British interests. The formal offer therefore coincided, as we shall see in a moment, with the American demand that Lothian had been trying to head off.[7]

To some extent the Cabinet's decision represented a victory for the FO's tactic of calculating generosity—wooing the U.S.A. with unsolicited gifts. But the British concessions were of limited scope, and there is some evidence that the Cabinet believed erroneously that they had been explicitly requested by the Administration. In any case, it is clear that the decision taken on 29 July was very closely related to HMG's new efforts to obtain U.S. destroyers. Beginning on 22 July Lothian had sent London a series of cables urging it to reopen the matter now that the Democratic convention was over and American attention was reverting to the war. He himself reiterated Britain's needs on U.S. radio and in contacts with pro-Allied pressure groups. On 23 July Vansittart asked Churchill to address a new appeal to the President. Although promising on 25 July that he would send a message on that day or the next, Churchill did not take action until the 30th when Lothian advised him that this was the moment to send Roosevelt the 'most moving statement of our needs and dangers in respect of destroyers and flying boats'.[8]

With one minor exception, Churchill had not communicated with Roosevelt since mid-June. He had prepared a draft message about destroyers on 5 July, but apparently Kennedy had dissuaded him from sending it. The U.S. Ambassador had vigorously criticized the draft as being too pessimistic— which Halifax admitted—and had advised that 'if Churchill were going to send a message he had better send the facts as they were and not make them better or worse than they were in order to try and influence the President'.[9] When Churchill prepared a new message on 30 July, sure that this was the moment to 'plug it in', he may well have had Kennedy's admonitions in mind. His telegram was a reasoned statement of Britain's needs, providing the sort of detailed information that HMG now recognized was required to convince the Americans, and, contrary to Scott's advice, avoiding any mention of what might happen to the fleet if Britain collapsed for want of U.S. help. Churchill reminded F.D.R. that destroyers, MTBs and flying boats were vital to help repel invasion, guard supply routes and command the Mediterranean. Eleven destroyers, which he named, had been lost from service in the previous ten days, and U.S. vessels were needed to tide Britain over the next three or four months, until new British construction became available. Once through that critical period, Churchill could feel 'very hopeful' about the future. In short, 'the whole fate of the war may be decided by this minor and easily remediable factor'. With that sonorous dignity of which he alone was capable, Churchill pleaded: 'Mr President, with great respect I must tell you that in the long history of the world this is a thing to do now.'[10]

\*     \*     \*

Roosevelt's continued reservations about transferring the destroyers had been clearly stated on 22 July, in a memo to Frank Knox. He rejected the idea, argued cogently by his old associate Ben Cohen, that he could act without congressional approval. F.D.R. felt that this was doubtful in view of the Walsh amendment and he feared that Congress was in no mood at that time to authorize a sale. The only opening he could see was that a little later the Administration might seek Congress' approval for a sale of some destroyers to Canada, to be used only for hemisphere defence.[11]

But over the next week or so, F.D.R. gradually changed his mind. It may be that Churchill's telegram, reinforced by similar analyses from U.S. Naval Intelligence,[12] had an effect, for when the Cabinet met on 2 August there was general agreement that destroyers were crucial for Britain's survival. However, it was also agreed that they could not be transferred without legislation and that this would be difficult to obtain. F.D.R. stressed that 'in all probability the legislation would fail if it had substantially unanimous Republican opposition'. He also feared, as usual, that even 15 or 20 determined isolationists in the Senate—where there was no procedure for ending a debate—could filibuster indefinitely. It was therefore essential to secure 'molasses' to sweeten the pill—concessions from the British that would enhance U.S. security and placate the opposition. These took two forms. One would be an agreement whereby the U.S. could use British bases in the Western Hemisphere or obtain land to create such facilities herself. This idea was discussed only briefly and vaguely. More important to Roosevelt and his Cabinet was a public assurance that the Royal Navy would never be allowed to fall into German hands and would, if necessary, fight on from North America and the Empire. Hull pointed out that such an assurance might prove worthless if the Churchill government were supplanted. 'However,' as Ickes put it:

> this is a risk that has to be taken. The feeling was that the one preoccupying thought on the Hill is what may happen to the British Navy. If we could go up with a bill frankly saying that we were going to sell fifty reconditioned destroyers in consideration of the possible coming over here of the British Navy, and of the granting of basing rights in British naval bases, we would be submitting a proposition that might have pretty general support.[13]

Over the next ten days the Administration sounded out both the British and the Republican leadership. F.D.R. had not yet committed himself to a deal; he was examining its practicality. It was only on 13 August that he and his immediate advisers prepared a formal proposal which F.D.R. cabled to

Churchill. 'For the first time that I discussed the destroyers with the President,' Morgenthau commented, 'he seemed to have made up his mind.'

Several reasons may be adduced for Roosevelt's decision. The Cabinet 'hawks'—Stimson, Ickes, Morgenthau and especially Knox—played an important part. Knox had been anxious to reinforce the British fleet for some time and he probably used the opportunity of a three-day cruise with F.D.R. from 27 to 30 July to press his point. (Such cruises often enabled the President to recharge his batteries and take stock of a perplexing problem.) It was Knox who initiated the debate in Cabinet on 2 August, having first briefed Ickes and Stimson, and it was Knox, Stimson and Morgenthau who pushed F.D.R. to the decision of 13 August.[15] Of equal importance was the work of the 'Century Group'—a small pressure group of ardent interventionists based in New York.[16] After a major policy discussion on 25 July its members pressed the case for transferring destroyers on U.S. policymakers, seeing Roosevelt himself on 1 August. The Group performed two related functions—prodding the Administration and mobilizing public support through speeches and media pressure. In its public campaign it worked closely with the William Allen White Committee, whose leadership was less ready to push the President but anxious to secure support for whatever F.D.R. wanted.

Both White—a Republican—and Century Group members such as Lewis Douglas also played an important role in gaining the support of Republican leaders. On 13 August White was able to inform F.D.R. of his confidence that Willkie would not criticize the deal. From McNary, the Senate minority leader and Willkie's running mate, came word that he could not support action in the Senate but would not object if 'plausible grounds' were found for acting outside Congress. By that stage, 15 August, such a course seemed possible. At Ben Cohen's request, Dean Acheson, a Century Group member, and his law partners set out in a long letter to the *New York Times*[17] the case for selling destroyers by executive agreement. This public statement, coming in very different political circumstances from Cohen's personal memo four weeks before, had a decisive effect. For soundings in Congress had not been encouraging. Speaking to Lothian on 4 August, Hull put the odds at four to one against legislation passing, and a poll of Senators showed that 23 were irreconcilably opposed to the sale of destroyers to Britain—more than enough to mount the filibuster F.D.R. feared.[18] The lawyers' argument, backed privately by the influential Justice Frankfurter, provided the 'plausible grounds' F.D.R. needed to bypass Congress. By 16 August he had decided that legislation was not needed for the transfer of the destroyers.[19]

Throughout these weeks the Cabinet 'hawks' and the pressure groups were in close touch with the British. Lothian and Embassy staff were supplying them with detailed information on Britain's naval position, to an extent unknown in London where it would probably have appalled the security-conscious Churchill and the propaganda-sensitive FO.[20] This is not the place to discuss this episode in detail, although it shows again that the British were learning the importance of hard facts rather than emotional rhetoric when trying to secure American support. The point here is that this collaboration did not imply that the 'hawks' and pressure groups were the tools of British policy. Knox, for instance, an ardent supporter of aid to Britain, had long advocated the acquisition of the British West Indies to 'make the Caribbean an American lake', and he saw a destroyers–bases deal as a way of achieving both these ends.[21] Similarly, the pressure groups were motivated by an interesting mixture of democratic ideology, anglophilia and geopolitical 'realism'.[22] Both the White Committee and the Century Group saw the war as part of a global battle between democracy and dictatorship, to which the U.S. could not be indifferent. Furthermore their leaderships comprised mainly WASP, Eastern establishment figures, many of whom had close ties with and affection for Britain. But their democratic sentiments made them keen critics of the reactionary aspects of British life, and in any case they had no intention of giving Britain something for nothing. They advocated transferring the destroyers on the grounds that the British fleet was the U.S. front line. From the Century Group meeting on 25 July came the idea of assurances on the fleet and transfer of bases as quid pro quo for the destroyers, and it may be that F.D.R. took up this idea seriously as a result of his meeting with Century Group representatives on 1 August.[23] The outlook of the pressure groups was colourfully expressed by William Allen White. Many of his Committee, White wrote,

> . . . had no great love for the British ruling classes. We have not relented in our general theory that George III was a stupid old fuddy duddy with instincts of a tyrant and a brain corroded and cheesy with the arrogance and ignorance which go with the exercise of tyranny. Yet I think I am safe in saying that our whole group felt . . . that if Great Britain were inhabited by a group of red Indians under the command of Sitting Bull, Crazy Horse and Geronimo, so long as Great Britain had command of the British fleet, we should try to arm her and keep that fleet afloat.[24]

There was one other major reason for Roosevelt's change of mind on the destroyers. He and other American policymakers were becoming more confident that Britain would survive. This was a slow process, of course. Washington-based analysts in the War and State Departments were still pessimistic.[25] But informed observers with recent experience of Britain were more hopeful. By late July the general opinion among U.S. military attachés in London was that the Luftwaffe was unlikely to gain the necessary air supremacy to mount an invasion. According to Lothian, one of these observers, Capt. Kelsey, who had returned to Washington, had made a marked impression on the defeatism rampant in early July.[26] Of particular importance were the views of Col. William Donovan, who had visited England on a special mission from F.D.R. to see conditions and to liaise with British intelligence. Donovan had been given VIP treatment by the British—meeting most senior officials and touring defence installations in the invasion area. Predisposed to optimism, he returned to Washington in early August confident that the British could repel any invasion that year.[27] He pressed his opinions enthusiastically on the President, who still seemed anxious about Britain's chances and about the fleet. Donovan assured him that the destroyers would not fall into German hands and that they were vital for Britain's defence.

Both Stephenson, director of British special operations in the U.S.A., and Lothian believed that Donovan's contribution to the destroyers deal had been very significant.[28]

\*     \*     \*

HMG first learned that the Administration was contemplating some kind of deal early on 2 August. Lothian reported that Knox was going to propose a formal destroyers–bases swap to the U.S. Cabinet, and advised HMG to accept. After long consultations in Whitehall Churchill cabled Lothian around midnight on the 3rd that the Government was agreeable in principle, provided that the land for bases was leased rather than sold and that the destroyers and flying boats Britain wanted would be immediately released. These provisos were made at the insistence of the CO and Admiralty respectively.[29] In other words, at this stage HMG was willing to accept an explicit destroyers–bases deal, and hoped to confine the bases to the limited offer already proposed after the 29 July Cabinet meeting. But on 4 August London received Lothian's report of his meeting with F.D.R. on the morning of the 3rd, at which the President had explained the proposal formulated by the U.S. Cabinet on 2 August, involving not only bases but also a public declaration about the fleet. This, Churchill, encouraged by the Admiralty, considered quite unacceptable. He stuck to the position agreed with Lothian in July—from which Lothian now retreated in his anxiety to get the destroyers—namely that an assurance about the future of the fleet should be made dependent upon U.S. entry into the war.[30] Moreover, Churchill believed, such assurances would damage British morale and they were not warranted by the equipment being offered. Unlike Lothian, the PM did not consider the old U.S. destroyers as crucial to Britain's survival—'very serviceable, no doubt, but not vital', he told Balfour. The U.S. was asking Britain to go 'much too far. . . . It doesn't do to give way like this to the Americans. One must strike a balance with them.' He therefore instructed Halifax: 'We must refuse any declaration as is suggested and confine the deal solely to the Colonial bases.'[31]

Once again Churchill was expressing his belief that Britain should tailor her concessions to tangible evidence of American help. Throughout July he had been pressed by the FO and the Services to offer the U.S.A. details of Britain's military secrets—'I am sure that we have everything to gain and nothing to lose by showing ourselves as generous and expeditious over this as we can', Halifax told him in a characteristic statement of FO tactics. On 1 August Churchill finally approved arrangements to send a special mission to the U.S.A. under Sir Henry Tizard, but he would not set a date for its departure 'in view of the holding-back on the American side in the last three days'—apparently a reference to the destroyers. Only after renewed pressure from Whitehall, and in the light of Roosevelt's offer of a destroyers deal, did Churchill announce on 8 August that he was 'anxious that they should start as soon as possible and under the most favourable auspices. The check of Aug. 1 was only temporary.'[32] Likewise the British response to Roosevelt's proposed deal also reflected the PM's conviction that they must 'strike a balance' with the Americans, although Halifax did dissuade him from totally rejecting the idea of a statement about the fleet. As instructed, Lothian explained to the Administration on 8 August that while Churchill's 4 June speech still represented HMG policy, further public reference to the fleet would be difficult at the present time. He went on to confirm the offer of landing rights and bases for Pan Am on Jamaica, Trinidad and in British Guiana, stressing, in deference to the Colonial Office, that British civil aviation must be allowed access to these bases.[33] He also listed Britain's desiderata—96 destroyers, 20 MTBs, 50 PBY flying boats, some dive-bombers and 250,000 more Lee Enfield rifles.

Lothian had admitted that the list 'represents, of course, our hopes!', but the Administration found the whole response quite inadequate. Welles called the facilities offered 'restricted and entirely unsatisfactory' and 'the very ample statement of British desiderata . . . far greater both in scope and in kind than it would be possible to consider'.[34] The formal U.S. proposal of 13 August drove a much harder bargain. F.D.R. told Churchill that he might be able to provide 'at least 50 destroyers', 20 MTBs, five PBYs and five dive-bombers, but only if the U.S. Congress and public could be convinced that in return their security had been enhanced. He would therefore need an assurance that, if necessary, the fleet would fight on from Empire bases. This need not be a public statement—reiteration for F.D.R.'s benefit of Churchill's 4 June remarks would be quite sufficient. He would also need an agreement both to lease for 99 years sites on Newfoundland, Bermuda and five West Indian colonies for the construction of U.S. air and naval bases, and to assume defence of these British possessions if the American hemisphere was attacked by any non-American nation. He added that specific details of the leases could be left to subsequent 'friendly negotiation'. Only broad principles need be agreed at that moment.[35]

Naturally, the British Cabinet was disconcerted. Instead of accepting landing rights and commercial air bases in three colonies, the U.S. wanted very long leases for official bases in seven. Lloyd warned again that, even if no formal loss of sovereignty were involved, the colonies would fall under U.S. influence. The assurance about the fleet was also problematic. Even though ostensibly private, Churchill observed, it seemed inevitable that something would have to be said to Congress. He remained anxious to avoid anything that might dampen domestic morale, and the Cabinet was not inclined to surrender what seemed Britain's only remaining bargaining card. In return Britain was likely to get less than she had requested, although subsequent messages from Lothian and Mackenzie King stated that F.D.R. also intended to include 250,000 rifles.[36] In short, there was a feeling in Cabinet that this might be considered a hard bargain.[37] Nevertheless, the proposal was approved in principle, subject to the agreement of Canada and Newfoundland. The FO arguments set out in the paper of 18 July were now having an effect. Guided by Halifax, Churchill argued the case less on the level of tangible benefits than by reference to what the FO liked to call the 'imponderables'. Thus, the PM told his colleagues that such an unneutral act as the transfer of destroyers would be a long step towards U.S. entry into the war. And from various viewpoints, the Cabinet agreed that the proposal must be seen in a longer-term framework—as possibly the beginning of an Anglo-

Saxon bloc, as the precursor of a new development for the Empire, or as the basis of a trusteeship principle which might stand Britain in good stead against anti-colonial pressures at the eventual peace conference.

It was on this level of imponderables that Churchill couched his announcement of the base leases to the Commons on 20 August. Making no allusion to the destroyers, he portrayed the leases as a friendly gift to alleviate U.S. anxieties about hemisphere defence. In a justly famous passage Churchill explained that these 'important steps' meant

> that these two great organisations of the English-speaking democracies, the British Empire and the United States, will have to be somewhat mixed up together in some of their affairs for mutual and general advantage. For my own part, looking out upon the future, I do not view the process with any misgivings. I could not stop it if I wished; no one can stop it. Like the Mississippi, it just keeps rolling along. Let it roll. Let it roll on—full flood, inexorable, irresistible, benignant, to broader lands and better days.[38]

Churchill's oratory caught the mood of the House. Moore-Brabazon, a prominent Conservative back-bencher, considered 'the idea of the English-speaking races policing the world' to be very attractive, in view of the vast post-war responsibilities that Britain would face. And Hore-Belisha, a National Liberal who had been Chamberlain's Secretary for War until January 1940, suggested that if the new link with the U.S.A. 'should lead to the same kind of relationship as we hoped for in the case of France, the evils of this war will have been almost worth while'.[39] Similar welcoming noises came from the leaders of Liberal and Labour peers.[40]

For the moment the PM was content. He had now come round to the FO view that Britain should not drive a hard bargain, much to Halifax's private jubilation.[41] This mood was shattered by the Administration's demand on 19 August to make the whole package an explicit and self-contained deal, set out in a public exchange of letters between the two governments. This was necessary to salve the conscience of Admiral Stark, who had to certify that the destroyers were 'obsolete and useless'. Since this was patently untrue, Stark wanted a 'clear-cut trade' of bases for destroyers so that he could claim that U.S. security was definitely enhanced. Marshall agreed with him, and F.D.R., who had not initially sought to link the two elements publicly, recognized the importance of convincing Congress that the deal was to America's benefit.[42]

With the exception of Halifax, the British Cabinet was adamant on 21 August that a formal bargain was out of the question. There seemed no comparison between Britain's concessions and America's offer. An explicit deal would only focus attention on the inequality and might embitter relations. Churchill was particularly firm on this point, telling Roosevelt that the destroyers and the bases should be considered as separate and spontaneous gifts. 'Our view is that we are two friends helping each other as far as we can.'[43] Earlier in August, when it seemed that Britain could get away with an offer of limited facilities, HMG had been happy to link the two transactions. Now that the terms of the proposed bargain were so obviously in America's favour, the Cabinet wanted to avoid a formal deal and keep matters on the plane of altruism and English-speaking friendship. As on 7 August Churchill was again inclined to play down the significance of the destroyers, stressing that they were only needed to tide Britain over from September to February. HMG would not be justified in giving 'a blank cheque on the whole of our transatlantic possessions merely to bridge this gap through which anyhow we hope to make our way though with added risk and suffering'.[44]

There was more to this new Churchillian eruption than simply a sense of national pride. We need to remember the PM's anxiety about his own parliamentary position—a point emphasized in the previous chapter. Throughout the negotiations Churchill had encountered stubborn resistance within the Cabinet to the base leases from Lloyd—a long-time advocate of Imperial unity, not least against America.[45] Similarly, Beaverbrook, who wanted good transatlantic relations but on a basis of equality, repeatedly urged Churchill to strike hard, businesslike bargains with the U.S.[46] Lloyd and Beaverbrook were not alone. They represented a sizeable body of back-bench Tory opinion who accepted the need for Anglo-American co-operation but sought to minimize the sacrifice of British interests. Following Churchill's Commons address of 20 August, an 'early day motion' was put down welcoming the 'splendid conception of Anglo-American co-operation foreshadowed in the Prime Minister's speech' and the principle of leasing base sites, but urging that the leases be reduced from 99 years to a maximum of 21. As the motion's sponsor told Churchill, recovery of the bases after three generations 'would be extremely embarrassing'—a tactful way of saying that HMG was implicitly conceding the bases in perpetuity.[47] Obviously one must not make too much of this. The motion was never debated and rival MPs put down an amendment deprecating any attempt to put a time limit 'on this association of the great English-speaking democracies'.[48] Nevertheless, the fact that some 50 MPs, including four ex-ministers and several senior back-benchers, saw fit to criticize the terms of the deal was a sobering reminder to a Prime Minister without a party of the force of Tory opinion. On the political left, too, there were occasional signs of disquiet about the long-term future. The newspaper editor, Cecil King, wrote in his diary:

> I am sure the United States will be politically the Anglo-Saxon world power, with the British possessions in America in her orbit. Our position as a world power has depended on the retention of the trading conditions of the 19th century. Now that they are gone I cannot see our Empire, built up on sea power as it is and with a population of 50,000,000 at the centre, can be maintained in anything like its old form.[49]

Finally, after long deliberations on 27 August, the Administration adopted a compromise suggested by its legal advisers. The base sites would be split. Those on Newfoundland and Bermuda would be a gift from HMG while the six Caribbean sites would be given in exchange for destroyers. Although the Administration accepted that MTBs, aircraft and rifles were included in the deal, Hull explained that for legal reasons they would have to be dealt with separately from the destroyers, which were therefore the only British desiderata named in the formal agreement. On 31 August Lothian also told

London that Hull now wanted the assurances on the fleet in the form of an exchange of notes, for publication, instead of private telegrams between Roosevelt and Churchill.[50] To all these requests HMG reluctantly gave way, recognizing that the 'split deal' covered British and American difficulties and accepting what they understood from Lothian to be Hull's assurances that the other desiderata would be provided. Beaverbrook continued to grumble about an unfair bargain, and privately even the FO had its reservations, but in Cabinet Halifax still insisted that Britain could not miss this chance to secure a closer association with the U.S.A. Short of declaring war, he told his colleagues, America's association with the British cause could hardly go any farther.[51] Having retreated from most of its previous diplomatic positions, not least with respect to the future of the fleet, and with the 'ponderable' elements of the deal so clearly weighted against it, the British Government was increasingly ready to adopt the FO's 'imponderables' argument.

*    *    *

After the agreements were signed on 2 September, both governments handled the publicity according to their respective domestic needs. Roosevelt played down the value of the old destroyers and likened the acquisition of the bases, in one of his typically loose historical analogies, to Jefferson's Louisiana Purchase. The assurance about the fleet was given much attention, although privately the President acknowledged that it would be difficult to enforce if Britain were on the point of surrender.[52] In London, however, little was said about the fleet assurance and the Government did not print the *aide-mémoire* confirming it in the White Paper about the Deal. 'After all,' the Cabinet minutes noted disingenuously, 'this *Aide-Mémoire* only repeated the Prime Minister's statement in Parliament.'[53] When Churchill spoke to the Commons on 5 September he described the transfers of destroyers and bases as 'simply measures of mutual assistance rendered to one another by two friendly nations'. He acknowledged that they were 'linked together in a formal agreement' and claimed that 'only very ignorant persons' would suggest that the transfer of destroyers 'affects in the smallest degree the non-belligerency of the United States'. These remarks were in deference to the Administration's domestic difficulties, but it is likely that Churchill's concluding advice to the House not to pursue the matter further also reflected his own desire to stifle any new rumbles of back-bench discontent.[54]

Neither government gained immediate, tangible benefits from the Deal. As we shall see in chapter 7(a), the precise sites and terms for the base leases were not settled until March 1941, after protracted and sometimes bitter negotiation. Similarly, only nine U.S. destroyers were in service with the Royal Navy by the end of the year, and only 30 by May 1941—because the British lacked experienced crews and because the antiquated vessels needed lengthy refits for anti-submarine work.[55] The other desiderata became enmeshed in another Washington administrative tangle. The 250,000 rifles were not despatched until 22 September, the B-17s were periodically released during the winter, and the MTBs did not come through until March, as part of Lend-Lease.[56]

Undoubtedly the immediate significance of the Deal, as the FO and, belatedly, Churchill had argued, lay in its wider, 'imponderable' implications. As Churchill concluded in his memoirs, the decision to transfer the destroyers was 'a decidedly unneutral act by the United States'.[57] Because of the long transatlantic haggling since May, the old vessels had assumed a symbolic importance far above their military utility. They had become a touchstone of the Anglo-American relationship. And, given F.D.R.'s midsummer uncertainty about Britain's chances and about the fleet, his decision to reinforce the Royal Navy in this way was a public statement of his growing confidence in and commitment to Britain as the U.S.A.'s front line.

Yet, as with most of Roosevelt's diplomacy, the Destroyers Deal had more than one aspect. The base leases and the assurance about the fleet were not merely 'molasses' to sweeten domestic opinion. Bases in the West Indies and Newfoundland had been a long-standing aim of the U.S. Navy, facilitating patrols far out into the Western Atlantic and strengthening defence of the Canal Zone. The Deal must also be seen in relation to the U.S.-Canadian defence agreement, concluded by Roosevelt and Mackenzie King at Ogdensburg on 17 August, which set up a Permanent Joint Board of Defence. The first tasks of the PJBD were to arrange details of the base in Newfoundland and to prepare contingency plans for the possibility of a British collapse. As Berle commented: 'It is plain that the plans are made so that even in the event of a defeat in Great Britain the fleet would continue to go on fighting in the Atlantic.'[58] The bases, the fleet assurance and the PJBD all show that F.D.R. was still to some extent keeping his options open. Although more confident that Britain could survive alone as America's front line, he was also significantly strengthening the defences of the Western Hemisphere.

When Churchill described the Destroyers Deal in his memoirs as 'an event which brought the United States definitely nearer to us and to the war' he was both right and wrong.[59] Wrong, in so far as he implied that these were Roosevelt's intentions, for the President was still hedging his bets, responding pragmatically to events and probably still hoping to avoid American belligerency if he could achieve his ends by less extreme means. But what mattered internationally was not Roosevelt's intentions, but how his actions were perceived by Germany, Italy and Japan. For they saw the Deal in the context of concurrent Anglo-American co-operation in the Pacific—as part of an embryonic alliance between the English-speaking peoples. Their own response—the Tripartite Pact of 27 September—represented a significant stage in the transformation of the European conflict into a world war.

## B. The Pacific crisis and the drift towards world war

Since 1938 the publicly-stated goal of Japanese policy had been the creation of a 'New Order in East Asia'—a Japanese sphere of influence from which, implicitly, the colonial powers of the Old Order would be excluded.[60] The implementation of that policy had been impeded, however, by Japan's failure to end the protracted war in China and by differences within policy-making circles on the direction and methods for expansion. While the Army General

Staff had seen Russia as the main danger and had favoured a military alliance with Germany, civilian and naval circles were more concerned about southward advance and feared too close an association with the anti-Comintern powers. Their opposition had defeated army efforts, despite prolonged negotiation, to secure a German–Japanese alliance in the winter of 1938–39, and the army's strategy was thrown into total confusion by the Nazi–Soviet pact of August 1939. During the Phoney War the Abe and Yonai Cabinets pursued a non-aligned policy, aimed at achieving Japan's goals by diplomatic means through an understanding with the Europeans and the U.S.A. But their efforts were largely unavailing and in June 1940 the Yonai Cabinet was forced into a stronger foreign policy. Even so it was unable to survive politically against growing army pressure and after its fall on 16 July Prince Konoye was asked to form a new government, taking Matsuoka as his Foreign Minister. Behind this upheaval lay a new Army–Navy consensus— formalized in the conferences of 26–27 July—that Japan should take the opportunity presented by the European crisis to bring the 'China incident' to a speedy conclusion and to expand southwards, drawing South-East Asia, including the European possessions, into a 'Co-Prosperity Sphere'. A neutrality pact with Russia and a strengthening of the Rome–Berlin–Tokyo Axis were to be the main diplomatic goals, and it was hoped that these measures would deter the U.S.A. from involvement and thereby prevent a Pacific war. But behind this hope of achieving Japan's ends by diplomatic means lay the clear intention to use force if necessary.

In the late 1930s, as we saw in chapter two, the British had tried to keep the Far East quiet without sacrificing vital interests.[61] Convinced that she could not act effectively without firm U.S. support and preoccupied with the German threat, Britain pursued a three-pronged policy of avoiding a breakdown in Anglo-Japanese relations while providing limited support for China and also trying to keep in step with the U.S.A. During the Phoney War it had been possible to hold these three elements in some kind of balance, for Japan remained quiescent, but with the new Japanese pressure in the summer of 1940 a less equivocal policy became essential. Given Britain's impotence in the Far East, British leaders agreed in June 1940 that this meant forcing the U.S. off the fence. Instead of condemning Japan without doing anything, America would either have to help in an active search for a Far Eastern settlement or else join in firmer measures to deter Japan. During the summer Britain and America moved closer together, not least because Japan now threatened not just China, where British interests greatly exceeded those of America, but the stability of South-East Asia and the Western Pacific. But we shall see that behind the growing co-operation lay the old problems of whether the U.S. would make firm commitments and how far she would protect purely British interests.

\*　　　\*　　　\*

The gravest crisis arose in late June as a result of Japan's demands that the colonial powers terminate their support for the Nationalists in China. In Britain's case Japan formally demanded on 24 June that HMG stop the flow of supplies from Burma and Hong Kong into China and withdraw British troops from Shanghai. Sir Robert Craigie, the British Ambassador in Tokyo, urged prompt compliance, for fear, if not of war, at least of a blockade of Hong Kong and air action against the Burma Road. Craigie argued that Britain could 'depend on nothing more concrete than American goodwill and diplomatic support' and that except in 'irresponsible circles' the U.S. would not criticize acceptance of Japan's demands in view of Britain's grave predicament at home.[62] The Foreign Office's Far Eastern Department (FO/FE) believed that Craigie was underestimating America, both as potential helper and potential critic. Anxious to keep in step with the U.S.A., it secured the opinions of Hull and Roosevelt, both of whom clearly indicated their dislike of further 'appeasement' and advocated procrastination or at worst tactical withdrawals rather than prompt and irrevocable surrender. Armed with this advice Halifax told the Cabinet that Britain should try to call Tokyo's bluff, and on 1 July his colleagues were inclined to agree.[63] In response Craigie increased his pressure by sending gloomier warnings of the likely Japanese action should their demands not be met—a 50 per cent chance of war and a real danger that Japan would formally join the Axis.[64] These cables had a sobering effect. Both the Chiefs of Staff and the Cabinet agreed that Britain could not risk war with Japan. Churchill, supported by Chamberlain, wanted to ask the U.S. directly for firm commitments, if only so that 'the responsibility for the decision should be placed where it ought to lie', but the FO rightly believed that, in Cadogan's words, it was 'hopeless to do as Winston suggested—try to put the U.S. on the spot. They simply won't stand there.'[65] When approached by Lothian on 5 July Hull merely repeated his earlier advice, and despite Halifax's continued efforts to persuade his colleagues at least to test Japan's resolve, on 10–11 July the Cabinet gratefully accepted Craigie's compromise that Britain close the Burma Road for the next three months on condition that Japan make a special effort to secure a 'just and equitable peace' in Asia.

The Burma Road crisis had several interesting implications. Ironically, it saw Halifax, identified then as now as an archetypal appeaser, ranged against Churchill, the celebrated foe of appeasement, in opposing immediate surrender to the threat of force.[66] Churchill and his colleagues desperately wanted to avoid a three-front war at a time when Britain was facing invasion, and, given the advice from Craigie, their action was understandable. So too was their resentment when Hull publicly condemned the closure of the Road, blaming Britain for a decision that HMG felt it had had to take through lack of U.S. help. Chamberlain told his sister 'my blood boiled', while a member of FO/FE minuted: 'We must try to remember in future that America expects us to take all the knocks and to look as if we liked it.'[67] What HMG did not know, however, was that Washington had been given a less gloomy view of Japanese intentions by its own ambassador in Tokyo, Joseph Grew, than that provided by Craigie in his efforts to sway opinion in Whitehall. Grew informed Hull on 7 July that Craigie was under strong pressure from his friends among the Japanese moderates and that his fears of war were probably exaggerated—an interesting contrast with Craigie's report to the FO two days earlier that Grew fully supported his own arguments and was cabling Washington to that effect.[68] Whether Craigie was the victim, or, more probably, the perpetrator of deceit is less important here than the fact that these differing assessments of Japanese policy help in part to explain the different responses of the two governments.

Despite American indignation, however, the closure of the Burma Road was of limited significance. It was only for three months from 18 July and this coincided with the rainy season when the Road would be virtually impassable anyway. Nor did it reflect a fundamental change in HMG's policy—it was a tactical withdrawal, as Hull had advised, rather than a prelude to 'appeasement'. Admittedly in late June, at the height of the crisis, Lothian and Craigie urged HMG to work towards a comprehensive Far Eastern Settlement. But this was only a temporary aberration on Lothian's part—probably prompted by his fears at that time that Britain might be overwhelmed—while Craigie's expectations of the Japanese 'moderates' had long seemed too sanguine to FO/FE who recognized that 'moderates' and 'extremists' did not differ on fundamental aims.[69] Within the FO only R. A. Butler seems to have entertained serious hopes of working towards a settlement with Japan, and, despite customary irritation at America, even he accepted what was axiomatic for the American and Far Eastern departments, namely that Britain could not afford to offend the U.S.A. Hull had made it quite clear that he saw no sign of a fair and durable settlement, consistent with his cherished 'fundamental principles'.[70] In practice, then, the British Government saw little chance of a Far Eastern settlement. Its efforts in the summer of 1940 to force the U.S.A. off the fence were mainly directed at securing firm American co-operation in tougher diplomatic, naval and economic measures that would deter Japan from war.

Most important of these was the continued presence of the U.S. fleet at Pearl Harbor. With the collapse of France and Italy's entry into the war, the British were unable, at least temporarily, to envisage sending a fleet to Singapore in the event of trouble with Japan. Yet this had been the basis of its Far Eastern strategy since 1921. HMG was therefore more reliant than ever on American help. In the spring of 1940 the U.S. fleet had left its West Coast bases for manoeuvres in Hawaiian waters. But from 4 May its return was periodically postponed because Roosevelt believed that by staying at Pearl Harbor it would help deter the Japanese from aggression in South-East Asia. By the second half of June, however, following the French collapse, there was strong pressure upon the President from Marshall and Stark, supported by State Department officials such as Welles and Long, to bring at least a part of the fleet back to the East Coast in case Britain fell.[71] After discussing rumours of such a move on 20 June, the British Cabinet asked Lothian to take the matter up with the Administration. 'As you know', the FO cabled, 'the presence of United States fleet in Pacific is strongest deterrent against Japanese adventures. Withdrawal of any substantial part of the fleet might precipitate Japanese action.' Roosevelt and Welles assured HMG that it would certainly be consulted before any decision was made to withdraw from the Pacific, and that there was no question of such a move at present.[72] Such assurances concealed the real debate in Washington in late June, but the British action against the French fleet on 3–4 July relieved the pressure on F.D.R., and for the rest of the summer the U.S. fleet remained at Pearl Harbor.

Britain's naval weakness in the Pacific had wider ramifications. Her promise to send a fleet to Singapore had been the basis not only of her Far Eastern strategy but of the defence policy of Australia and New Zealand as well. In mid-June HMG explained to the antipodean Dominions that it was 'most improbable' that adequate naval reinforcements could be sent to the Far East in the event of Japanese aggression, with the Royal Navy trying to hold both the Mediterranean and home waters alone against the German and Italian fleets, and that they must therefore look to the U.S.A. for help.[73] The British claimed that war in the Far East was unlikely, but, as the Australian premier Robert Menzies had put it in April 1939: 'What Britain calls the Far East is to us the near north.'[74] Australia had already opened direct diplomatic relations with the U.S.A. in March 1940, by sending Richard Casey as its first Minister in Washington, and by July New Zealand had secured London's permission to set up its own legation there. Canberra in particular pressed the U.S. to co-ordinate plans for the Pacific and to send some naval vessels on a courtesy visit to Australia.[75] The significance of these developments should not be exaggerated. HMG stressed that it was only temporarily suspending its promise about the fleet, and the Dominions' new links with Washington did not impair their allegiance to the Commonwealth. In one sense, then, these developments gave added justification to Churchill's talk of a partial mixing up of the Empire and the U.S.A. and to the FO's vision of redistributing the burdens of Imperial defence. Even Berle, despite his suspicions of British imperialism, talked of 'this strange new world-wide group that seems to be in the process of formation'. Nevertheless, as Berle had observed in March, Britain was 'a small country of 45 million population and may not be able to hold the far-flung empire together. Should it go under, it is a very fair question whether the United States might not have to take them all over, in some fashion or other.'[76] Britain's naval crisis in the summer of 1940 loosened the ties of Empire and helped to force Australia and New Zealand, like Canada, into greater dependence upon the United States.

Not only did the U.S.A. maintain its naval strength in the Pacific, it also began to apply economic pressure upon Japan. In mid-July Washington received reports that Japanese oil purchases in America were increasing dramatically and ominously. Japan obtained about 80 per cent of her oil from the U.S.—thereby giving the Administration an important potential diplomatic lever—but the danger was that if the U.S. turned the economic screw too tightly it would drive Japan into attacking the Netherlands East Indies (NEI) in search of alternative sources of supply. With America's main interest being the survival of Britain she dared not provoke a Far Eastern war and could therefore apply only moderate sanctions as a deterrent against Japan. That at least was the analysis offered by one group of U.S. policy-makers, including Hull, Welles and the State Department's Far Eastern desk, backed by Ambassador Grew and Admiral Stark. State therefore proposed on 19 July to restrict Japan to normal peacetime imports of oil. However, the new 'hawkish' element in the Cabinet—Morgenthau, Ickes, Stimson and Knox—together with Stanley Hornbeck, State's political adviser on the Far East, recommended a total ban on all U.S. oil exports, on the assumption that Japan would be the main sufferer. With the possible exception of Hornbeck, they too agreed that, until Britain's survival was assured, Japan was a secondary consideration for the U.S.A. But they argued that moderation would be interpreted in Tokyo as a sign of weakness or vacillation. The history of the 1930s had shown that only tough action was an effective deterrent, especially when dealing with Japan and other 'orientals'. Roosevelt, however, sided with the moderates, arguing, to Morgenthau's disgust, 'in much the same vein as S. Welles. Namely we must not push Japan too hard as we might push her into taking Dutch East Indies.'[77] After a confused bureaucratic battle, with F.D.R. again somewhat casual in tying up the loose ends, it was therefore agreed that the U.S. would bring under government licence the export of high-grade oil and scrap metal. It was a typical Roosevelt compromise—the run on U.S. supplies was ended, the Administration had taken a stand, but Japan's oil position was hardly affected, since she switched to purchasing lower-grade petroleum, which could easily be refined for aviation purposes. Nevertheless, the argument delineated here as to the dividing line between deterrence and provocation was to be the abiding theme of U.S. Far Eastern policy through 1940 and much of 1941.

Throughout this bureaucratic debate the British were no more than anxious observers. In principle, they keenly desired U.S. co-operation in controlling the global flow of raw materials, but sanctions against Japan posed special problems. A total ban on U.S. oil exports would damage Britain's own war effort, for she relied upon the U.S.A. for certain essential petroleum products, especially lubricating oil. If Japan were provoked into an attack on the NEI this would endanger another source of supply—half the NEI's oil exports went to the British Empire. Moreover, this would start a Far Eastern war for which Britain had no guarantee of U.S. help and from which she and the Dutch, not the Americans, would naturally be the principal sufferers. Little wonder, then, that Churchill, backed by all departments of the FO, minuted that the hawks' ideas were 'most dangerous, and should immediately be put a stop to'.[78] But this was easier said than done, for, as usual, the FO dared not directly rebuff any American initiative. It was obliged in effect to wait upon the outcome of the bureaucratic battle in Washington, presenting the British view but enjoying little real influence.

Ironically, it was Britain's 'friends' with regard to European policy—the Cabinet hawks—whose proposals had posed a real threat to British interests in the Far East. This reminds us again of how misleading terms such as 'friendship' are in this context. Supremely among U.S. policymakers Morgenthau and his colleagues saw the international scene as a global confrontation between democracy and totalitarianism which had developed because Britain and France had lacked the courage to stand up to the dictators in the 1930s. A tough policy in Asia, they believed, would prevent repetition of the disaster in Europe. Obsessed with ideology and morality, they paid less attention to strategic realities and to the complexity of Britain's position. Knox apparently did not even appreciate the potential threat to the NEI until after the sanctions battle was over, and none of them was aware of the extent of Britain's reliance upon U.S. and NEI oil.[79] Convinced that

Japan would back down, they were unready to acknowledge that Britain might have to pay the price for America's firmness—rather as Poland had done for Britain in 1939.

Contrary to Washington's intentions, however, even limited economic sanctions proved a provocation. They strengthened the hand of influential middle-level army and navy officers who successfully pressed for an acceleration of Japan's southward advance.[80] In August the Japanese began negotiations with the Dutch companies in the NEI for an assured supply of oil, and with the French authorities in northern Indochina for air bases and a troop corridor into China. The oil negotiations dragged on into the autumn but the Japanese concluded an agreement with the French and moved into Tonkin between 22 and 25 September. By this time the Anglo-American destroyers-for-bases deal had been completed, and from about 20 September there were frequent reports in Tokyo that a similar agreement was imminent in the Pacific, perhaps involving an American take-over of responsibility for Singapore.[81] In fact, the FO had specifically ruled out a bases deal in the Pacific, recognizing that the U.S. had no direct security interest in Singapore in the way that it did have in the case of the Western Atlantic bases, but the reports followed a deliberate leak by Hull and Lothian that they were discussing the Far Eastern situation and the British in particular fostered the impression that some formal agreement was in the wind.[82] These rumours increased Japan's interest in strengthening the Rome–Berlin–Tokyo axis. Although the Army was now committed to using force against British possessions, the general hope was still that Japan could gain her ends by diplomatic means. The Axis pact was conceived of as a warning to the U.S.A., in view of its recent economic and diplomatic actions, to keep out of the Far Eastern crisis.

Japan's motives for the Pact coincided with those of Germany. By mid-September Hitler's plans for invading Britain, which had been hastily improvised after France's sudden collapse and the British rejection of his peace terms, had to be postponed because the Luftwaffe had failed to achieve the necessary air supremacy before the summer ended. During the autumn, before he finally decided in December to turn against Russia in 1941, Hitler was attracted by the 'peripheral strategy' advocated by Raeder and the Navy and the complementary 'continental bloc' diplomacy of Ribbentrop and the German Foreign Ministry. The object of these policies was to defeat Britain by strangling her imperial lifelines. In September and October, therefore, Hitler assiduously wooed Franco and Pétain in an effort to close the Mediterranean and secure bases in the Eastern Atlantic. He also encouraged Mussolini's offensive in Libya, which threatened Suez and Britain's oil supplies from the Middle East, and urged Russia and Japan to carve up Britain's empire in Asia.[83] The main threat to this strategy was America's growing help for Britain. The Destroyers Deal and the associated U.S.–Canadian agreement in particular persuaded Hitler to take a new interest in Ribbentrop's long-standing aim of a closer alliance with Japan.[84] Like the Japanese, Hitler envisaged this as a warning to the U.S.A. not to provide further help to Britain and her Empire.

Negotiations accordingly began in Tokyo on 9 September and the Tripartite

Pact was signed on the 27th. Under the crucial Article Three, Germany, Italy and Japan undertook 'to assist one another with all political, economic and military means when one of the three Contracting Parties is attacked by a power at present not involved in the European war or in the Sino-Japanese conflict'. Since Article Five affirmed that this in no way affected the signatories' existing relations with the U.S.S.R., it was clear that the Pact was primarily directed at the U.S.A. However, the published text was qualified by an exchange of secret letters. The most important of these, sent to Matsuoka by the German Ambassador in Tokyo but apparently never communicated by the latter to Berlin, confirmed that 'the question, whether an attack within the meaning of Article 3 of the Pact has taken place, must be determined through joint consultation of the three contracting parties'. The Japanese Navy had insisted on reserving Japan's freedom of action in this way as its price for accepting an agreement.[85] In reality, then, this was a very tenuous alliance, if any of the participants could decide when it should be invoked. But the full details of the secret agreements did not leak out, and it was the appearance rather than the reality of the Pact that mattered internationally.

British and American reactions to the Tripartite Pact reflected the changing situation in Europe. We saw in the previous section that Washington's growing confidence in early August about Britain's chances of repelling invasion had been an important factor in F.D.R.'s willingness to proceed with a destroyers deal. During the rest of the summer that cautious confidence continued to grow. Although Ambassador Kennedy kept painting a gloomy picture, by late August even the most pessimistic officials in Washington, such as Berle and the War Department's intelligence branch, were increasingly hopeful.[86] Authoritative confirmation came from two senior Army and Air Corps officers, Generals Strong and Emmons, who had spent nearly five weeks in Britain from mid-August. They reported to F.D.R. on 23 September that although Britain's financial outlook was 'dubious' and her shipping position 'serious', in the air things were 'not too bad' and the military situation was 'fair insofar as the British Isles was concerned. If invasion be delayed until after October 15', they added, 'the situation will improve decidedly during the winter.'[87] Accompanying this increasing confidence was a new admiration for the British, dispelling, at least temporarily, the usual mood of suspicion and mistrust. There was a feeling that belatedly Britain was living up to its historic tradition of courage and determination in the face of adversity: 'The epic performance of the B.E.F. is the Britain I know', wrote the fiercely anti-Nazi Frankfurter to Lothian after Dunkirk.[88] This attitude became more prevalent during the Battle of Britain when even the most anglophobe observers praised the fortitude of ordinary British citizens. The effect was greatly enhanced by sensational reports from U.S. journalists and broadcasters in London—virtually all of them keenly pro-Allied—which gave the impression that the whole city was ablaze. Equally important was the personality of Churchill, who seemed to epitomize this renascent British spirit. His broadcasts attracted as much attention as those of the President, and the initial Administration doubts about his capacity had long since vanished. Ickes noted in his diary after one such broadcast in mid-

September: 'I am more and more impressed that Churchill is a great leader.'[89]

Whitehall monitored the changing American mood with satisfaction—the FO in particular seeing it as vindication of its constant policy of avoiding propaganda in the U.S.A. and relying on the normal reporting of the American media. There was, however, some anxiety lest the Americans' new confidence revive their earlier complacency which, just as much as excessive pessimism, could lead to a reduction in support for Britain. As Perowne of FO/A put it: 'This is the razor edge along which we must learn to dance.'[90] But HMG was now sure that in this precarious balancing act it was better to err on the side of confidence than pessimism. It eschewed further warnings to the Administration about the implications of a British collapse, and, after rejecting offers of Swedish mediation in late August, the FO made a point of sending F.D.R. some of the relevant correspondence, stressing that 'we shall meet all attacks and blandishments with firm resolve to rid this world of this scourge.'[91]

By late September, then, both the British and American governments were in the position and the mood to take a tougher line in the Pacific. On 25–26 September, in response to the Japanese occupation of northern Indochina and to strong rumours about the impending Axis pact, the Administration announced a new loan for China and brought under government licence the export of all grades of iron and steel scrap. To the Administration and the American public the Pact itself seemed confirmation that Germany and Japan were hand in glove. Far from deterring the U.S. it revived the hawks' demands for a tougher policy against Japan, specifically for a total embargo on oil and the movement of the U.S. fleet to Singapore. In early October the Administration once again debated the questions of strategic priorities and the character of effective deterrence. Eventually the proposal for an oil embargo was shelved and although F.D.R. toyed with the idea of sending detachments of the fleet to reinforce Singapore and the tiny Asiatic squadron at Manila, this too was abandoned. Indeed, the President was under strong pressure from some senior naval officers, notably Admiral Richardson, the fleet's commander, to move it back to its proper bases on the West Coast. As in July, the argument of the moderates in the State and Navy Departments had prevailed. Tougher measures might prove provocative and the U.S. had no reason to risk war in the Pacific when her primary interest lay in the survival of Britain.

The British, too, felt able to adopt a firmer policy.[92] During September the FO and Lothian had argued that Britain must reopen the Burma Road when the existing agreement expired on 18 October, and their arguments gained added force with the need to respond to the Tripartite Pact and to keep in step with America's firmer line. Even Craigie agreed, and on 3 October the Cabinet accepted the FO's advice. But, like the Administration, HMG was anxious to strike a balance between deterrence and provocation, particularly where tougher measures would not involve greater American support. Thus, it was very keen to commit the U.S. to the defence of Singapore and Churchill personally invited F.D.R. on 4 October to send an American squadron there on a goodwill visit. On oil, however, the British were more circumspect.

Further restrictions on Japanese oil supplies might provoke retaliation which would be directed against the British and Dutch without any guarantee of U.S. help. The crucial question, therefore, remained whether the Administration could be induced to provide firm commitments to help defend specifically British interests. On 30 September, when there were real fears of Japanese aggression, Hull, at Roosevelt's request, suggested to Lothian that the Americans, Australians, British and Dutch should have 'private staff discussions immediately on technical problems which would be involved in common action for defence, though it must be perfectly clear that these conversations were to be technical and not to concern themselves with political policy'. The Cabinet and Chiefs of Staff jumped at the idea and both Hull and Welles urged prompt action. But then on 9 October Lothian found that extreme caution had replaced Hull's earlier keenness. He now deprecated the idea of any formal conference and suggested that information could be exchanged through existing channels in London and Washington. The FO was disappointed but not entirely surprised at this reversal. It was clear that fears about the election on 5 November were replacing anxieties about Japan, and so HMG relaxed its pressure on staff talks and on Singapore, deriving consolation from the Administration's periodic hints that further co-operation would be possible once the election campaign was over.[93]

\* \* \*

Apart from its effect on concrete British and U.S. policies in the Far East, the Tripartite Pact also led to an important clarification of British Grand Strategy on the question of possible U.S. belligerency against Germany and Japan. To take Germany first: the standard Administration response to British pleas for a U.S. declaration of war against Germany was that this would inevitably mean a marked reduction in supplies for Britain. This argument, often propounded by Kennedy in London, helped to justify the Administration's contention that America could be of at least as much help to Britain as a non-belligerent than as a fully-fledged ally, and undoubtedly a few sincerely believed this, such as Breckinridge Long in the State Department.[94] During the early autumn HMG officially went along with this argument, but, as American observers in London appreciated, this was mainly to reassure U.S. voters in the election campaign. After 5 November no more was heard of it. Ed Murrow, CBS head in London, told American listeners on 3 December that if they asked any MP or member of the government whether he preferred America neutral or belligerent, 'you will get only one answer. Some would express a preference for winning the war without American aid, but most would admit that it can't be done.'[95] Murrow was quite correct. V. F. W. Cavendish-Bentinck, FO Chairman of the Cabinet's Joint Intelligence Committee and a persistent critic of Wilsonian diplomacy, minuted in early November: 'I had hoped that we would win this war without the intervention of the U.S., but now, if Germany were to declare war on the U.S.A., I should gladly participate in a thanksgiving service and in the consumption of a Jeroboam of champagne.'[96] David Scott still advanced the 'supply argument' against U.S. entry, but Lothian and FO/A briskly dismissed it and on 27 September, perhaps at Churchill's behest, the Cabinet Secretary made a point of recording: 'There was no support in the War Cabinet for the view, some-times advanced, that the United States could lend us more help by staying out of the war.'[97]

However, the Tripartite Pact raised a separate if related issue—did Britain want the U.S. involved in a possible war against Japan? Here the FO felt that the 'supply argument' had some merit. As Vansittart asked: 'what reason is there for having a new enemy if it is to absorb the resources of our only friend?' The general FO judgement, as expressed by Clarke of FO/FE, was that British policy in the Far East 'should be to create doubt and hesitation in the Japanese mind so that force will not be required in the event. It is not in our interests that the United States be involved in war in the Pacific . . .' To this point, the FO told Lothian, it attached 'vital importance'.[98] Lothian, however, believed that if a Pacific war did break out America would adopt a largely defensive strategy, aware that its priority lay in supporting Britain, and that, even if there were some diversion of resources, 'on balance' it would be better to have the U.S. in a Far Eastern war because only entry into war would rouse the American public to sacrifice butter for guns.[99] Churchill was even more vehemently of this opinion. When he discovered that Craigie was apparently assuming that Britain did not want the U.S. in a Pacific war and that she would not necessarily become involved if war broke out between America and Japan, he sent Halifax a sharp and comprehensive minute about

. . . the very serious misconception which has grown up in Sir Robert Craigie's mind about the consequences of the United States entering the war. He should surely be told forthwith that entry of the United States into the war, either with Germany and Italy or with Japan, is fully comformable with British interests. That nothing in the munitions sphere can compare with the importance of the British Empire and the United States being co-belligerent. That if Japan attacked the United States without declaring war on us, we should at once range ourselves at the side of the United States and declare war upon Japan.

It is astonishing how this misleading stuff put out by Kennedy that we should do better with a neutral United States than with her warring at our side should have travelled so far. A clear directive is required to all our Ambassadors in countries concerned.[100]

Quickly the FO followed Churchill's instructions.

The Tripartite Pact had therefore provided Churchill with an opportunity to formalize British attitudes on the question of U.S. belligerency. It was now express HMG policy that it would welcome American entry into either the European conflict or a possible war in the Pacific, and that, if the U.S. were involved by herself in war with Japan, Britain would immediately join in. This is not to say that Churchill was angling for a Far Eastern war. He fully agreed with Craigie that Britain's hope and objective should be ' . . . for skilful Anglo-American diplomacy so to arrange matters that, if and when the United States decided to enter the war in Europe, Japan can be kept neutral, pact or no pact'. In that sense he and the FO agreed. But the FO was less confident than the PM that Japan could be contained. Military weakness and repeated capitulation to Japanese encroachments had greatly diminished Tokyo's fear of British and U.S. power, FO/FE warned.[101] Churchill, by contrast, remained confident that a firm Anglo-American front would deter Japan or at least ensure that if war did break out the Japanese would not attack British and U.S. interests. We shall see that Churchill's tendency to underestimate Japan was of considerable importance in 1941. However, the differences between premier and Foreign Office should not be exaggerated, for both felt increasingly that the questions of war in the Pacific and war in Europe were inter-related. The Tripartite Pact had apparently confirmed the unity and co-ordination of the Axis and tied events in Europe and the Far East together. For a long time Balfour of FO/A had been unable to see how the U.S. could be brought to enter the European war. But now that the Tripartite Pact had formalized the Axis and had aroused such a vigorous U.S. response towards Japan, it seemed quite possible ' . . . that America will find herself landed in a war with Japan in the prosecution of which she will not consider it necessary to concentrate her main energies, but rather on Japan's far more powerful co-belligerents in Europe'.[102] The FO had long held that it was easier to obtain American help in the Far East than in Europe. Now, with the Tripartite Pact, there was a growing hope that the Pacific might prove America's back-door into the European war.

## C. The changing balance

The period from July to October 1940 saw a remarkable Anglo-American *rapprochement*. FO officials were struck by the growing confidence in Britain's capacity to survive, by the increasingly pro-British tone of American public statements on the war and by the 'complete absence of carping criticism' of the British—'an almost unknown state of affairs'.[103] The new mood of confidence and co-operation had been symbolized by the Destroyers Deal, even though F.D.R. was still hedging his bets to some extent by also strengthening the defences of the Western Hemisphere through bases, a fleet assurance and the agreement with Canada. In the Far East, too, after the earlier controversy over the Burma Road, U.S. and British policies were falling into line by the early autumn, with both governments favouring tougher but deterrent measures to contain Japan until Britain's survival was assured. In the process, the international crisis was developing from a European conflict into a world war, with the Destroyers Deal and the Tripartite Pact as major stages in this development. This was not the intention of Berlin, Tokyo or Washington, but what one capital conceived of as a deterrent measure was treated by another as provocative, thereby intensifying the polarization.

Increasingly, therefore, as American leaders recognized, they were being drawn into supporting not only Britain but the British Empire as well. But behind this global co-operation significant changes in the balance of power were taking place. British concessions during the destroyers negotiations had indicated the weakness of HMG's bargaining position, and, as Tory back-benchers feared, the bases agreement presaged extended U.S. influence in the Caribbean. Moreover, with Britain demonstrably lacking the sea power to defend them, Canada, Australia and New Zealand were also being drawn into the American orbit. In the Far East, contrary to the claims of some historians,[104] the Anglo-American disagreements of the summer were not temporary, but reflected fundamental differences between the two countries' positions in Asia. Britain remained unable to secure firm guarantees of U.S. help or to ensure that the U.S. would defend specifically British interests, such as Singapore. We shall see that Britain would gradually achieve her goal of drawing the U.S.A. into the war, but at a heavy and lasting price for her imperial interests in the Far East.

# CHAPTER SIX

## Lend-Lease

### October 1940–March 1941

*How are we going to pay for it all? I suppose one hopes all the time that the United States, whether they come into the war or not, will find some means of helping us make our resources go further than they otherwise would. But if you ask me how, I am jiggered if I know.*

Lord Hankey, July 1940

*It gets down to a question of Mr. Churchill putting himself in Mr. Roosevelt's hands with complete confidence. Then it is up to Mr. Roosevelt to say what he will do.*

Henry Morgenthau, December 1940[1]

By the end of September even the most cautious intelligence analysts in London and Washington agreed that Hitler had probably postponed his invasion of Britain (Operation 'Sealion') for the winter. Through a mixture of courage, geography and good fortune the British had not gone the way of the French, and the United States was now providing increasing assistance to Britain and her Empire as its own front line. But Hitler's new 'peripheral strategy' posed a deadlier threat to Britain's security. If she were denied essential imports of food, raw materials and munitions, then she could be brought to her knees without the need for direct invasion. And from the summer of 1940 the U.S.A. had become, in potential at least, Britain's major external source of material help. During the winter of 1940–41, therefore, supply became the crucial issue in Anglo-American relations. The two countries were forced to extend and formalize the tentative commitments made in the late summer, in the process emphasizing ever more clearly the growing imbalance in their relationship. These are the twin themes of chapters six and seven.

### A. Waiting for Roosevelt, October–December 1940

The supply crisis broke down into three principal elements—production, finance and shipping. First of all, the British needed a large, guaranteed share

145

of U.S. raw materials and manufactured goods. Even before May 1940, while the U.S. was still being treated as a marginal source of supply and the Administration was engaged in only limited rearmament, there had been competition between British and U.S. programmes. With the massive increase in British orders, particularly for aircraft and ordnance, from mid-1940, and with the concurrent U.S. rearmament drive, that competition inevitably became acute. The problem was also exacerbated by the President's dogged determination not to put the economy on anything like a war footing, despite HMG's warnings from its own 'bitter experience' that you could not have 'more guns and enjoy a full supply of butter at the same time'.[2] Unwilling to create a production 'czar' who might undermine his own authority, fearful of public and union reaction to restrictions, particularly in an election year, and underestimating the enormity of the task ahead, Roosevelt did little to reduce production for civilian consumption or to impose controls over labour, raw materials and equipment. The British and the Americans were therefore competing with voracious appetites for a relatively small cake—a monthly output of planes, for instance, of only 550 per month in July 1940.[3] Even if it were agreed that Britain was the U.S.A.'s front line—and this was still a controversial idea in Washington—it proved inordinately difficult to determine the optimal allocation of vital but scarce equipment such as machine tools and aircraft engines.

But even if the U.S. economy could be galvanized into full production, and even if British requirements could be integrated into America's own defence programme, how could HMG continue to pay? It should be emphasized that Britain was not facing imminent and wholesale bankruptcy. She still had between £3,500 and £4,000 million in overseas assets around the world[4] and had been able to fund much of her war spending abroad by persuading creditor countries to run up large sterling balances in London. The problem was narrower, but no less acute—namely Britain's inability to go on financing purchases from the U.S.A. The dollar was a strong international currency, backed by the bulk of the world's gold supply, and the U.S.A. had long enjoyed a sizeable surplus on its visible trade with Britain. It therefore had no reason to run up a large sterling overdraft, unlike the Commonwealth and foreign countries of the Sterling Area who traded unfavourably with Britain and used London as a clearing house for their multilateral payments. During the Phoney War Britain's strictly limited U.S. purchases were financed mainly by using her gold reserves, but with the end of financial caution in May that clearly could not go on indefinitely. In mid-July Sir Frederick Phillips, a senior Treasury official, visited Washington to explain the position personally to Roosevelt and Morgenthau. The essence of his message was that probably within six months Britain would need help in realizing cash on her securities and that certainly not later than mid-1941 'massive assistance' in the form of U.S. credits would be required. But apart from 'general phrases about seeing it through', Phillips cabled, Roosevelt 'said nothing which could be regarded as a commitment'.[5] Like Lothian and the FO, Phillips concluded that, although the Administration would not make any promises before the election, if it were satisfied that Britain could pull through and that she had definitely used up all her resources, particularly investments in the U.S.A. and

Latin America, then the necessary help would eventually be forthcoming in some shape or form.[6] Although the Treasury endeavoured to restrict spending in the U.S.A. to absolutely vital needs until the Administration's position was clear, Churchill, the supply ministers and even Chamberlain accepted that Britain had no choice but to gamble on America's willingness to help.[7] In late summer large orders for aircraft and tanks further depleted the reserves and by mid-October the Treasury calculated that Britain would not be able to pay for her purchases from the U.S.A. after December.[8] Clearly, then, Roosevelt would have to act quickly once the election was over.

Assuming that the problems of production and payment could be surmounted, there remained the question of whether the supplies could be safely transported to Britain. The problem became acute from the summer of 1940 with the elimination of European sources of supply and the effective closure of the Mediterranean and the Suez Canal to merchant shipping. By the end of 1940 Britain's importing capacity had been cut to 40 million tons per annum (16 million being food), which was about two-thirds of peacetime requirements and the absolute minimum needed to maintain the war effort at its present pitch. Yet in the last four months of 1940 less than 12 million tons of goods arrived—which would mean an annual shortfall of some 5 million. This was mainly due to the disastrous increase in merchant shipping losses, which had risen dramatically in June and thereafter averaged 400,000 tons per month. Just three months' losses at that rate were the equivalent of the *annual* output of merchant shipping from British yards. The British therefore looked to the U.S.A. for the eventual provision of some 3 million tons of merchant vessels a year and for the repeal of those sections of the Neutrality Act that forbade American ships to enter belligerent waters.[9] They also desperately needed assistance for the hard-pressed Royal Navy, now responsible for the whole Mediterranean as well as the defence of home waters and the patrolling of the Western Approaches, which was therefore unable to provide anti-submarine escorts for Atlantic convoys except at the beginning and end of voyages. Throughout the winter of 1940–41 HMG asked repeatedly for American warships, particularly more destroyers, and, above all, for Roosevelt to use the U.S. Navy to escort transatlantic convoys.

* * *

It was clear, therefore, that the answer to Britain's threefold supply problem lay with the U.S.A. It was equally clear to British leaders that 'until after the Presidential Election, at any rate, decisions of major policy are not likely to be taken'.[10] During October many aspects of the British war effort were in suspended animation—not only the great problem of finance but minor matters such as plans to improve British publicity in the U.S.A. and the scheme to raise units of Jewish-American volunteers. Not that the British had much respect for the U.S. political process, with its decentralized government and year-long election campaigns. 'The Constitution is a disaster', Cadogan had minuted in April,[11] and most policymakers were inclined to agree with him after the frustrating delays over destroyers that summer. Even Lothian, the great apostle of federalism, shared this irritation. But even if it seemed, in Lothian's words, like 'the most unreal election the world has ever seen'[12]—a

147

remarkable display of fiddling while Britain burned—the British had no choice but to await its conclusion. To be dependent on the result of a foreign election was a humiliating and unprecedented fate.

Even to observers more detached than Lothian the 1940 election had an air of unreality. Roosevelt's Republican challenger, Wendell Willkie, had voted the straight Democratic ticket in 1938. He supported much of the New Deal legislation and was as outspoken an advocate of aid to Britain as the President. Indeed his foreign policy record during the inter-war years was more consistently internationalist than Roosevelt's. Willkie was a handsome and able Wall Street lawyer who had achieved national prominence during his five-year fight as president of a Southern utilities corporation against the monopoly powers of the Tennessee Valley Authority. His victory at the Republican convention on 28 June had been largely due to a brilliant marketing campaign by New York publishing and business interests.[13] In the early stages Willkie campaigned ineffectively while the President played the national leader, too busy with the world crisis for partisan politics. But from late September, pressed by Republican leaders, Willkie's attacks became more bitter. He claimed that the New Deal was incipient totalitarianism and that F.D.R. was edging America near to war. This forced Roosevelt off his apolitical perch and in the last fortnight of the campaign he made five outstanding speeches, combining inspiring rhetoric with sharp attacks on the Republicans, and including his famous promise in Boston on 30 October: 'Your boys are not going to be sent into any foreign wars.' Despite Willkie's efforts, however, the New Deal coalition held together and on 5 November F.D.R. was re-elected by 449 electoral votes to 82, with a margin on the popular vote of nearly five million.

In Britain the nomination of Willkie had been greeted with relief. Whoever won the election, it seemed, aid to Britain would continue. A Low cartoon showed Hitler watching from behind a tree as the candidates tossed a coin. The caption read: 'Heads we win, tails he loses.'[14] But the British naturally appraised the rival merits of the two men, and FO/A and staff at the Washington Embassy were somewhat taken with the suggestion of the commentator Walter Lippmann that Willkie, an experienced businessman and administrator, would be better able to galvanize U.S. industry than Roosevelt. This seemed an attractive argument to officials who had for years bemoaned F.D.R.'s failure to conciliate business and promote recovery. In the closing stages of the campaign, when a Willkie victory seemed quite possible, the MOI took great pains to prevent the press from depicting this as a setback for Britain.[15] But most political leaders desperately wanted Roosevelt to win—'It will be a disaster, I think, for us if he does not', noted Halifax tensely on 27 October—and in Whitehall, Westminster, Fleet Street and the country at large there was general jubilation at his victory.[16] Oliver Harvey of the MOI, formerly private secretary to Eden and Halifax, went so far as to call 5 November

> perhaps the most important date in the war . . . It will ring a bell throughout Europe. Our enemies will know that henceforward, even if they could succeed in wearing us down in a long war, there is a man across the Atlantic who would certainly bring America to our rescue, and would carry on the fight if we failed.

A whole new Continent ready to fight Hitler. I believe it will prove in the end to have broken the German morale.[17]

Harvey had been a long-standing fan of Roosevelt, but the elation he expressed was not atypical. It was a reaction to the weeks of waiting, a release of repressed frustration. Having steeled themselves from September to accept that the U.S. could take no significant decision on aid to Britain until after 5 November, British leaders tended to assume that thereafter the flood-gates would suddenly open. Whitehead of FO/A believed that U.S. policy would clarify 'in a week or two' of Roosevelt's re-election, and the Treasury anticipated a decision on credits within the same time span.[18] Even more significant, there was a widespread expectation that the U.S. was on the verge of formal belligerency. Churchill's morale-boosting talk throughout the summer had clearly had an effect, reinforced perhaps by the warnings of Willkie and the isolationist press to U.S. voters about F.D.R.'s warmongering inclinations.[19] To Admiral Ghormley, the U.S. 'Special Naval Observer' in London, it seemed 'that everybody in Great Britain expects the U.S. to enter the war within a few days after . . . the President is re-elected'. Churchill himself commented privately on 1 November that 'he was sure Roosevelt would win the election by a far greater majority than was supposed, and he believed that America would come into the war'. But perhaps the most interesting example was that of T. North Whitehead in FO/A. Throughout 1940, drawing on his considerable experience of America, Whitehead had warned his superiors that 'the English habitually overestimate interventionist sentiment in the U.S.'. But on 4 November, after reviewing the recent intelligence, even he concluded: 'All the underground signs suggest that if Mr. Roosevelt is returned to power tomorrow he will bring in the U.S.A. as soon as this proves possible.'[20]

Clearly extravagant hopes had got the better of traditional doubts. Fundamentally, British leaders assumed that the U.S. *ought* to help them—she was part of the English-speaking world—and once the political constraints of the election had been removed there seemed no justification for continued neutrality. More specifically, their hopes rested on two important misconceptions. First, they clearly overestimated F.D.R.'s readiness to enter the war. The President usually spoke in his most bellicose tones to the British, implying that but for domestic politics he would be in the conflict with them. As we have seen, however, this was largely to encourage them to fight on. To his advisers and in public he often sounded a rather different note. Deciding which was the authentic voice of Roosevelt is a perennial problem for historians, but most agree that it was not until at least the spring of 1941 that F.D.R. decided that the U.S. would have to enter the war. Be that as it may— and we will discuss the issue properly in chapter eight—it is clear that in the crisis of 1940 the British had taken F.D.R. too much at face value. Moreover, they had also cast U.S. politics in a British mould. Used to a cohesive political system with firm party discipline, they had assumed, consciously or not, that the election would give F.D.R. a clear-cut mandate and the legislative majority with which to execute it. Of course Roosevelt *did* enjoy greater freedom of action after 5 November. In the new Congress in January he would have increased 'overall majorities' of 268 to 167 in the House and 66 to 30 in the Senate.[21] But these figures had little significance for his congressional arithmetic. Many conservative Democrats remained deeply suspicious of the President, including senior southerners on key committees, and Roosevelt was forever fearful that even a small rump of determined opponents could obstruct policy and undermine national unity, as Wilson had found. The election did not relieve him of the painstaking task of creating a foreign policy consensus—as the debate over Lend-Lease was to show.

*     *     *

November was therefore a depressing month for the British. After the election Administration leaders went off for badly needed vacations and nothing was said or done about Britain's dollar crisis. As the weeks passed the mood of elated expectancy in London turned to one of anxious uncertainty. Even Churchill admitted on 2 December that he had been 'rather chilled' by the U.S. attitude since the election.[22] It was Lothian, back in London for nearly four weeks from 20 October, who filled this vacuum in policy. Almost alone among British policymakers he had not seen 5 November as a magic date. If anything he was inclined to underrate its significance, arguing that the principal value of a Roosevelt victory would be in preventing a 'lame-duck' hiatus before Willkie's inauguration on 20 January.[23] But at least he had no expectation that the U.S. was about to enter the war. He did not believe this would happen until U.S. rearmament had taken off and until her vital interests were attacked—perhaps not until 1942—although in the meantime she would probably move towards a state of undeclared hostilities.[24] He had also recognized for months that Americans did not properly understand Britain's needs and that it would take a long time to educate them into effective action. He told the FO in September:

> Public opinion here has not yet grasped that it will have to make far reaching decisions to finance and supply us and possibly still graver ones next Spring or Summer unless it is to take the responsibility of forcing us to make a compromise peace. Yet owing to the size of country and its constitution it is usually impossible to get important decisions taken without at least six months preparation.[25]

In Lothian's view, therefore, the election was important mainly because it permitted the British to renew their efforts to 'educate' the U.S.A. And it was to discuss those efforts that he had returned to London.

Lothian advised Churchill to set out Britain's needs fully and candidly in a personal letter to Roosevelt. He explained that 'there was an opinion in Washington that we were inclined to ask for more than was necessary. The only answer to this is a ruthless exposé of the strategic dangers.' The FO fully approved of this tactic—'putting all our cards on the table', Cadogan called it—but Churchill was not so sure. Lothian had first suggested this approach in late June, to help lift F.D.R. out of his depression after the Fall of France, but Churchill had advised him not to pay too much attention to the eddies of U.S. opinion, arguing that Britain must wait on events and on 'our best friend', the President.[26] In November, too, he seems to have adopted the same line. According to Lady Astor, Lothian 'had a very difficult time making the P.M. see what he wanted to do in America. He [Lothian] felt that it was imperative that a strong note should go to the President telling him of our dire situation, particularly financially. It took him two weekends, one at Chequers and one at Ditchley but he finally got it done.'[27] By the time Lothian left Britain on 15 November drafts had been prepared and discussed, but then Churchill allowed the matter to lapse for some ten days. It was only after renewed pressure from Halifax and the FO late in November that Churchill revised the drafts and circulated them around interested departments preparatory to despatch. But this was not the end of the matter, for Churchill wanted the letter 'to focus on shipping'. Lothian, by contrast, thought the financial problem was the most important, but, above all, he wanted the President to have a balanced and comprehensive view of all Britain's problems. According to Scott, Lothian's 'idea was that this letter should be continuously in the President's mind and that its existence and the knowledge that some day it might be published would act as a continual spur in meeting our requirements for fear lest it should be said in years to come "he knew, he was warned and he didn't take the necessary steps" '.[28] In the end, Churchill won. More than half of the 4,000-word letter was devoted to the shipping crisis, in addition to a detailed appendix setting out the losses for 1940, whereas finance took up a scant 400 words at the end. And Churchill made it clear to Roosevelt that, in his view, it was 'in shipping and in the power to transport across the oceans, particularly the Atlantic Ocean, that in 1941 the crunch of the whole war will be found'.[29]

Nevertheless, the letter still provided the synoptic view of Britain's problems for which Lothian had been striving. After stating HMG's assumptions about the 'solid identity of interest' between the two countries, Churchill summarized the developments of 1940 and set out the prospects for 1941. He discussed the three great interrelated problems of shipping, munitions and finance, drawing out Britain's requirements from the U.S.A. in each case. The letter went into considerable detail, but its gist was frighteningly clear and, as Lothian had wanted, it put the evasive Roosevelt firmly on the spot. Without U.S. escorts, extended patrolling and the use 'of every ton of merchant shipping' that America possessed, the Royal Navy could not keep open the supply routes to Britain and her battlefronts around the world. Without U.S. munitions, especially aircraft, Britain could not arm herself and her allies. Without financial aid from America, Britain would not be able to acquire the shipping and munitions she so desperately needed. 'Mr. President', Churchill concluded, 'this is a statement of the minimum action necessary to the achievement of our common purpose.' It was an arresting account of Britain's predicament—inspired by Lothian's draft, reworked by various government departments and given its final form and distinctive character by the Prime Minister. Not surprisingly Churchill called the letter 'one of the most important I ever wrote'.[30] It was cabled to Lothian on the night of 7–8 December and transmitted via the State Department to the President who was then on a fishing cruise in the Caribbean.

But more than two weeks before this, Lothian had already brought Britain's needs forcefully to the attention of the Administration and the American public. On arrival at New York's La Guardia seaplane base on 23 November he read a brief statement to the press in which he stressed that the coming year would be a hard one and that 'England will be grateful for any help. England needs planes, munitions, ships and perhaps a little financial help.' In answering questions afterwards he seems to have dwelled particularly on finance. Press reports quote him as saying that this matter was 'becoming urgent', that 'available gold and securities had been virtually used up and that this factor figured in the calculations for 1941'. Lothian told the FO later: 'I mentioned no figures of any kind but indicated that the question of how to pay for munitions would be one of the problems which would come up certainly in the next 6 months, as our resources including gold and securities were running low.'[31]

Lothian had acted entirely off his own bat, without permission from London.[32] Although the FO approved of his action, Churchill was unhappy and the Treasury was furious. For one thing, Lothian had not made it clear that he was referring only to Britain's ability to purchase from the U.S.A. and not to her overall financial position. Anglophobe newspapers seized on his remarks—'Envoy Lothian claims Britain is going broke' was the *Chicago Tribune's* headline—and German propagandists exploited the reports of Britain's supposedly imminent bankruptcy with glee.[33] But, apart from the content of Lothian's comments, the Treasury also questioned his whole approach. On 14 October Lothian had told Morgenthau that Sir Frederick Phillips of the Treasury wished to visit Washington again to 'raise the red light signal in connection with our finances'. Morgenthau had proposed that the visit should take place some time in late November, when Washington had recovered from the election, and after further delays the date of 4 December had been set for Phillips' arrival.[34] It therefore seemed sheer folly on Lothian's part to raise such a delicate issue in public when high-level discussions were about to commence. Churchill put the point directly to Lothian in his delicate but firm rebuke: 'I do not think that it was wise to touch on very serious matters to reporters on the landing stage. It is safer to utter a few heartening generalities and leave the graver matters to be raised formally with the President or his chief lieutenants.'[35]

In view of the rumpus in Whitehall, Lothian deemed it politic to eat humble pie. He apologized for not consulting the Treasury in advance and promised to see that 'this mistake is not repeated'. But he went on to defend his actions with a vigour that showed he was basically unrepentant:

> In this as in every other question the ultimate determinant is public opinion. That opinion is saturated with illusions to the effect that we have vast resources available which have not been disclosed, that it is possible for us to mobilise all the American assets and all the assets of our Dominions and our allies as well as our properties in the Empire and in foreign countries and make them available in dollars for paying for munitions and that we ought to empty this vast hypothetical barrel before we ask for assistance.[36]

Dispelling these illusions, which, he warned, even the President shared, would take time, and it is probably for this reason that Lothian believed HMG should pay particular attention to the financial issue. He was also acutely conscious of how slowly the U.S. political system worked, having been explicitly designed to impede rather than facilitate vigorous executive action. As Balfour of FO/A noted on 28 November: 'Lord Lothian pointed out to us during his visit that it takes the American public, on whom the Executive depend for getting their policies approved, at least six months to demand action on an idea from the time it is mooted. I am convinced that he had this consideration in mind when he made the remark . . . '[37] In short, Lothian had not made an emotional appeal for credits, as is sometimes supposed; his aim had been to start off a public debate on a complex problem so that the necessary actions could be taken in time. Moreover, there is little doubt that he succeeded in his aim. In the words of the British Press Service in New York, which made a special survey of media reactions: 'The interview precipitated realistic discussion of the purpose and implication of the whole so-called "Aid-to-Britain" policy, a question hitherto generally discussed in a vague if well-meaning manner.'[38] Phillips' arrival on 4 December kept it in the public eye until F.D.R.'s celebrated press conference on 17 December, at which he announced the principle of Lend-Lease.

What was the effect of Lothian's initiative upon the Administration itself? Although the wheels were moving slowly, British leaders were wrong to feel that Washington was insensitive to their problems. According to Felix Frankfurter, Roosevelt faced his third term not with elation but 'in a deep Lincolnesque mood', conscious only of the enormity of the task ahead.[39] On 8 November the President told his Cabinet and then the press that he favoured a fifty-fifty division of war materials with Great Britain, much to the displeasure of Marshall and the alarm of the State Department, who feared a hostile reaction at home and in Germany.[40] He also began to develop an idea that had been in his mind as early as November 1938. According to Ickes, he said 'that the time would surely come when Great Britain would need loans or credits. He suggested that one way to meet the situation would be for us to supply whatever we could under leasing agreements with England. For instance, he thought that we could lease ships or any other property that was loanable, returnable, and insurable.' It is therefore clear that a month before the arrival of Churchill's letter and two weeks before Lothian's press conference 'American leaders were thinking of how to relieve Britain's dollar problem.'[41] But it is also clear that at this stage F.D.R. did not think that Britain's dollar problem was urgent or that his leasing idea had more than specific application to merchant ships. On 8 November, according to Ickes, F.D.R. had prefaced his remarks by saying 'that England still has sufficient credits and property in this country to finance additional war supplies. He thinks that the British have about $2.5 billion here in credit and property that could be liquidated.' Moreover, the day before, Roosevelt had talked with Arthur Purvis of the British Purchasing Commission. He raised the question of Britain's dollar resources but clearly felt, Purvis judged, that the problem was still six months away. The President's principal anxiety was Britain's shortage of merchant shipping. He felt that the U.S.A. should build three hundred ships and then 'rent them' to Britain, who would also pay for the insurance. 'He indicated that this system might be extended to cover certain other items.'[42]

During November F.D.R. continued to mull over these ideas, for example with Thomas Lamont and Norman Davis on the 28th,[43] but his sense of priorities remained the same. On 1 December, just before he left for a two-week vacation cruise in the Caribbean, he went over the whole situation with Morgenthau. He still did not believe that Britain's immediate financial position was critical. After a cursory glance at a U S. Treasury estimate of Britain's dollar resources he threw it down on the desk and said, 'Well, they aren't bust—there's lots of money there.' He still believed that they had enough money or easily liquidated assets to cover their own orders. What worried him was that they could no longer provide the capital investment that had helped convert U.S. industry to war production without the intervention of the Federal Government. He believed that the Administration should now make a large investment in plant and new orders, and the British could pay for their share of the output. He still saw his loan idea as applicable mainly to merchant ships. Roosevelt also believed that this plan did not require congressional approval. The capital investment and new orders could be financed by funds already appropriated for the Reconstruction Finance Corporation, a New Deal relief agency. Although reluctant, as usual, to put this in writing and give his Cabinet officers the authority they wanted, it 'was apparent, however, from the comments and attitudes of the President that the United States should place the orders, the RFC should finance the capital investment and that then the individual items would be sold to the British on a unit basis payable upon delivery'.[44]

When F.D.R. left Washington for his cruise on 2 December, therefore, he still believed that Britain's problems could be met by an extension of existing Executive action, with the addition of some kind of loan arrangement for merchant shipping. By the time he returned, two weeks later, he had pulled together his ideas into a comprehensive if still vague programme for all Britain's supply needs, based on the loan idea and backed by congressional legislation. Undoubtedly the opportunity for rest and reflection provided by the cruise had been invaluable. Not only Lothian but also close associates of the President such as Welles and Bullitt testified that he had been unusually tired and depressed after the election and right through November.[45] A badly needed vacation gave him time to draw together various half-formed thoughts, and, as on other occasions, it proved the prelude to a major policy initiative. It is also likely, as contemporaries and historians have argued, that Churchill's letter had a considerable effect.[46] In view of what has just been said, however, about its contents and origin, what made an impact was probably not so much the comments on finance as the synoptic character of the letter and the way it brought out the interrelationship of Britain's problems. In other words, it did not arouse F.D.R. to the dollar crisis so much as make clear the need for a comprehensive solution to Britain's needs. Lothian's press comments were also significant. As Morgenthau admitted, they 'had forced the President and himself to deal with the cash problem immediately'.[47] This was not, it should be stressed, because F.D.R. changed his mind about Britain's immediate needs. As we shall see, he still believed that she had enough funds to cover payments until the spring, and throughout the early months of 1941 he and Morgenthau applied increasing pressure on HMG to sell off its U.S. assets. What Lothian *had* done was to generate anxiety and debate in Congress and the press, which forced the Administration to clarify its position. The anxiety had some unfortunate side-effects. It probably complicated Britain's financial position in the interim period before Lend-Lease took effect. It also concentrated the Administration's attention for the next four months on the financial problem to the exclusion of shipping, which Churchill and also many U.S. officials such as Berle, Stimson and Knox believed to be the crucial issue.[48] But Lothian was clearly right that the Administration had to be prodded into a new policy. With Britain nearing the end of her financial and shipping resources, the limits of F.D.R.'s cash and carry policy, which had governed his programme of aid to Britain for some two years, had finally been reached. To be effective a new policy required congressional approval and support—the evasions and subterfuges of 1939 and 1940 were no longer appropriate or acceptable. And, as Lothian anticipated, it took about six months to translate that policy from idea into reality.

*    *    *

But Lothian did not live to see the fruits of his labours. He died suddenly on 12 December from uraemic poisoning, for which, as a Christian Scientist, he would not accept medical treatment. 'Our greatest Ambassador to the United States', was Churchill's verdict. That may have reflected the hyperbole of the moment, but even those in the FO who had bitterly opposed Lothian's appointment, such as Oliver Harvey, agreed that he had proved 'a very great ambassador' who would be 'very hard indeed to replace'.[49] Of course, some of the fears expressed by Harvey and Cadogan in 1939 had been justified. Lothian lacked the career diplomat's discretion, balance and attention to detail. He was often swayed by his immediate mood into making important errors of judgement. His comments to the press of 23 November, for instance, could certainly have been more carefully phrased. But over all Lothian amply justified Halifax's original trust. Unlike most of the British élite, he knew and liked Americans. He understood their political system and appreciated the importance of public opinion and opinion leaders in the making of U.S. foreign policy. He was also an enthusiast for Anglo-American co-operation, arguing consistently that only by trusting the U.S.A. and by adopting a generous and open-handed attitude could ingrained American suspicion be overcome and U.S. help secured. The last weeks of his life, when he filled the post-election vacuum in British policy by master-minding the 8 December letter to Roosevelt and by 'going public' about Britain's problems on his return to New York, were the climax of his career. Although he never overcame Churchill's aversion to publicity, with the assistance of FO/A Lothian did help 'educate' the PM out of his preference for hard bargaining into a more candid and trusting approach to the United States. That, as we shall see, was to be a feature of Churchill's policy throughout 1941.

## B. 'An Act to Promote the Defense of the United States'

While Roosevelt was vacationing from 2 to 16 December, Morgenthau was engaged in discussions with Sir Frederick Phillips. The British Treasury had hammered out the basic negotiating strategy for Phillips' visit in a meeting on 31 October. Following in large part the suggestions of Keynes, it was agreed that Phillips should ask the U.S. Government to take over responsibility for

British purchases of war equipment from 1 January 1941. If agreement could not be reached by that date it should take effect retroactively. Phillips should do his best to resist the inevitable U.S. pressure for Britain to sell off her overseas assets, particularly in the Americas where they would be snapped up by U.S. competitors. He should also insist that Britain must retain a minimum gold reserve of £150 million ($600 million) in order to operate the Sterling Area effectively. If the Americans pressed too hard on either point they would imperil Britain's post-war recovery and the maintenance of a stable currency—both of which were vital for the economic health of the U.S.A. and the world.[50] Similarly, with the post-war world in mind, the Treasury wished to avoid any recurrence of the U.S. credits of the Great War, whose repayment had poisoned Anglo-American relations in the inter-war years. As Sir Richard Hopkins, Second Secretary at the Treasury, noted: 'we should say as little as possible about loans and as much as possible about supplies in a common cause.' One or two private citizens, notably Arthur Goodhart, a distinguished American who was a Professor of Law at Oxford, suggested some form of 'barter agreement' whereby Britain would repay the supplies in kind after the war.[51] But the Treasury could see no way of doing this without gravely burdening the post-war economy, and in any case there seemed little prospect of the U.S.A. reducing its tariff sufficiently to facilitate increased British exports to America. In short, HMG was hoping that somehow the United States would make a 'free gift' of the supplies Britain needed.[52]

When Phillips arrived in Washington on 4 December he did his best to play down the significance of his mission to reporters.[53] But in private he took the tough line outlined in his instructions—presenting Britain's position bluntly and leaving the ball in the Administration's court. Phillips was a formidable if rather colourless character, who used his taciturn manner as a way of intimidating those with whom he negotiated. This was not, however, the best way to deal with Morgenthau, a hypersensitive man who always took time to settle down with new British emissaries and whose indefatigable efforts to supply Britain were matched by a constant suspicion of perfidious Albion. What preoccupied Morgenthau, like F.D.R., that December was the state of Britain's assets. He wanted full statistics on their financial position and a serious effort to sell off securities and investments in the U.S.A. This proved to be a long-standing issue of controversy, which we shall discuss more fully later in the chapter. What is interesting here is the way Phillips swiftly modified his tactics once he appreciated the mood in Washington. His first two working meetings with Morgenthau, on 5 and 9 December, had been mutually frustrating. The Treasury Secretary plugged away on the subject of British assets, only to hear a list of all the difficulties involved. Exasperated, Morgenthau told Phillips: 'It gets down to a question of Mr. Churchill putting himself in Mr. Roosevelt's hands with complete confidence. Then it is up to Mr. Roosevelt to say what he will do.' This was also the line being urged on Phillips by financial staff at the British Embassy and the tactic exemplified, much to Morgenthau's satisfaction, in Churchill's 8 December letter. In a brief meeting on 12 December the log-jam broke. Morgenthau told Phillips that he favoured making Britain a gift of supplies rather than undertaking another war loan and that he was pressing HMG on its assets only to demonstrate to the U.S. public that Britain was genuinely in need of help. In response, Phillips agreed to provide Morgenthau with all the information he wanted. The Secretary felt he had made more progress in fifteen minutes than he had since Phillips' arrival in the U.S.A. Phillips told HMG that the 'fullest information and greatest practicable willingness to make our assets available will be necessary' to satisfy the Administration.[54] From then on he became a consistent exponent of the Lothian argument, also favoured by most British officials in Washington, that the best way to get U.S. help was not to adopt the reserved, hard-bargaining attitude of the Treasury but to lay Britain's cards on the table and trust to the Administration's goodwill.

Summarizing the state of Phillips' discussion on 16 December, Keynes surmised that the Administration had ruled out a loan as 'inadvisable' and that it would 'propose to Congress an "adequate free gift of munitions, aircraft and shipping" ', provided that 'we have first of all surrendered all suitable assets we possess'.[55] But on the same day the President returned to Washington, refreshed by his cruise and 'in a very good humor, very quiet and self-possessed'. Although 'very proud of the fact that he didn't look at a single report that he had taken with him from Washington', he told Morgenthau over lunch on the 17th: 'I have been thinking very hard on this trip about what we should do for England, and it seems to me that the thing to do is to get away from a dollar sign.'[56] He proceeded to outline the general concept of Lend-Lease, which, with Morgenthau's enthusiastic approval, he then aired publicly at his press conference that afternoon. There he stressed that he was 'talking selfishly, from the American point of view'—couching his argument for helping the British Empire in terms of her importance for U.S. security. The 'one thing necessary for American national defense is additional productive facilities', he told reporters. British orders helped create those facilities, so they had to be encouraged. Although Britain had enough money to pay for existing orders, he claimed, there might be a problem in the future. Suggestions that this could be solved by repealing the Neutrality and Johnson Acts or else by a straightforward gift he dismissed as 'somewhat banal'. What he wanted was to 'get rid of the silly, foolish old dollar sign'. Using a metaphor suggested by Ickes in August, he likened the situation to that of a householder when the house next door catches fire. It is clearly in the householder's interest to lend the neighbour his hose. He doesn't haggle over the transaction at the time; he simply expects that once the fire is out the hose will be returned or, if damaged, replaced. In summary, the basic idea was that the U.S.A.

> would take over not all, but a very large number of, future British orders; and when they came off the line, whether they were planes or guns or something else, we would enter into some kind of arrangement for their use by the British on the ground that it was the best thing for American defense, with the understanding that when the show was over, we would get repaid sometime in kind, thereby leaving out the dollar mark in the form of a dollar debt and substituting for it a gentleman's obligation to repay in kind.[57]

This was F.D.R. at his best and worst. His intention was to avoid re-creating the network of intergovernmental war debts which had bedevilled international relations in the 1920s and 1930s. He considered that an outright

157

gift to Britain was politically impossible, but he was determined to avoid raising the precise details of repayment until after the present crisis had been overcome. First put out the fire; then discuss the state of the hose. Indeed that homely metaphor was considered by some commentators to have won the battle for Lend-Lease then and there—translating an arcane and controversial problem into simple and comprehensible terms. Roosevelt now accepted that he would have to fight the battle in Congress, but he did not want to attack head-on the Johnson and Neutrality Acts which had become isolationist shibboleths. As usual he preferred to circumvent barriers rather than to crash through them. On the other hand, Roosevelt's press conference raised almost as many problems as it solved. As usual, F.D.R. had little time for details— these were for the lawyers to work out. But the press naturally persisted in their questioning, and they quickly put their fingers on several weak spots. Did he 'think this takes us any more into the war than we are?' 'No, not a bit', the President quickly responded. Could the British really pay for existing orders? 'Yes, I think so. They have plenty of exchange, you know.' And— perhaps most telling of all: 'Mr. President, before you loan your hose to the neighbor you have to have the hose.' To this and several other questions about the inadequacies of the U.S. production programme and the lack of centralized organization F.D.R. returned his customary bland and evasive replies. It is clear from his initial remarks to the press that in fact he saw Lend-Lease as an answer not only to Britain's dollar crisis but also to the slowness of the U.S. rearmament programme. As before, he envisaged the flow of Allied orders as a way of galvanizing U.S. industry into greater output.

Joseph Lash has suggested that Churchill and the FO 'failed to appreciate the significance of the president's proposal', noting that it was not until the New Year, after prodding from the Washington Embassy, that a message of thanks was sent. In fact, Whitehall grasped both the strengths *and* the weaknesses of Roosevelt's remarks. As Phillips observed, echoing the comments of numerous British officials over the years, the President's general intentions were 'extremely encouraging' but the details were 'singularly obscure'. According to Sir Richard Hopkins: 'Broadly the plan which the President proposes to put to Congress settles the long-term programme just in the way we could best have hoped, inasmuch as we do not borrow money but receive the loan of weapons of war.' But, even leaving aside the ultimate problem of repayment, Hopkins, like Phillips, was disturbed about two immediate questions—did F.D.R. intend to strip Britain of her overseas assets and what did he plan to do about the financial problem in the interim before his new proposals became law? In this connection Roosevelt's comments about Britain having plenty of exchange to pay for her existing orders seemed rather ominous.[58] If HMG had to suspend orders for several months that would have a disastrous effect on Britain's supply position in a year's time. London expected that the President would soon clarify these points, possibly in a reply to Churchill's 8 December letter. In fact, no written reply was ever sent, and F.D.R. said and did nothing more in public until the end of the month. Even then, his fireside chat on 29 December, in which he spoke of the U.S.A., in a phrase taken from Jean Monnet, as 'the great arsenal of democracy', was designed to educate public opinion in the generalities of his policy rather than to elucidate its perplexing details. Whitehall remained in the dark until the Lend-Lease bill was published on 7 January. In any case, the FO was anxious to do nothing that might embarrass F.D.R. Expressions of British gratitude, even from Churchill, might prove a godsend to the isolationists.[59] All in all, HMG's lack of public response is therefore hardly suprising.

In the meantime, however, the British had been given a disturbing indication of how the President planned to deal with the interim financial problem. On 23 December Roosevelt told Phillips that a U.S. warship was on its way to Cape Town to pick up £50 million of British-owned gold which would be used to cover some of Britain's immediate purchases in the U.S.A. 'This is very much the President's way of handling business', Phillips cabled home. 'Decision is taken and acted on before we are informed.' In fairness, it should be noted that the idea had originally come from Phillips himself on 19 December, acting on explicit Treasury instructions, to help spin out Britain's virtually exhausted reserves. By the 23rd the Treasury had gone off the idea, partly lest the Americans 'acquire a habit of demanding more from our distant nest egg', but by then it had been adopted by F.D.R.[60] But Beaverbrook, the Minister of Aircraft Production, was incensed. In a minute that summed up months of mounting frustration he told Churchill that the Americans 'have conceded nothing. They have exacted payment to the uttermost for all they have done for us. They have taken our bases without valuable compensation. They have taken our gold. They have been given our secrets and offered us a thoroughly inadequate service in return.' This present action should therefore be resisted 'very strongly', even at risk of a rupture in relations. 'The American Government . . . is asking for the moon and appears unwilling to pay sixpence.' But when the Treasury tried to reverse the President's decision or at least to reduce the gold shipped to £10 million, Phillips was 'terrified of the effect of your attitude on the President'. Roosevelt was only trying to help, he stressed, and the idea *had* originated with HMG.[61] Whitehall reluctantly accepted this advice, but Churchill's own sense of humiliation showed through in a draft message composed on 28 December. He likened the American attitude to that of 'a sheriff collecting the last assets of a helpless debtor . . . It is not fitting that any nation should put itself wholly in the hands of another, least of all a nation which is fighting under increasingly severe conditions for what is proclaimed to be a cause of general concern.' That message was not sent, but by the 31st the PM incorporated its sentiments in a more balanced cable drafted by the Treasury. This thanked F.D.R. briefly for his fireside chat and then went on to itemize several British anxieties, notably the Cape Town operation, the scope of F.D.R.'s proposals and the problem of interim finance. 'Remember, Mr. President,' Churchill warned grimly, 'we do not know what you have in mind, or exactly what the United States is going to do, and we are fighting for our lives.'[62] This litany of complaint got as far as the British Embassy in Washington, where the staff were horrified. They had only just dissuaded the PM from sending Roosevelt a list of the defects in the U.S. destroyers, only nine of which were in service because of the extensive repairs and refitting required. They now successfully persuaded Churchill to send an 'unclouded' message of fulsome praise for the fireside chat and to develop his anxieties about finance in a separate message. Churchill reluctantly complied.[63] It was only when the bill was eventually published that he recovered his verve and enthusiasm, claiming that this was 'tantamount to a declaration of war' by the U.S.A. or at any rate an open challenge to Germany to declare war if she dared.[64]

Roosevelt's relative inactivity from 17 December until the New Year is not easy to explain, but it seems that as usual he was waiting cautiously for public opinion to build up behind his proposals. He had followed a similar tactic in September 1939, waiting for three weeks after war broke out before he called Congress into special session to repeal the arms embargo. In the case of Lend-Lease it was only after favourable reactions to his fireside chat on 29 December that he began to move. What he wanted, he told Morgenthau the next evening, 'was authority from Congress to go ahead and build the necessary arms for this country plus England, and that he should have a blank authority to . . . say at the particular time what kind of munitions should go to a particular country'.[65] Accordingly, when he instructed Morgenthau to go ahead on 2 January, the Treasury lawyers proceeded to prepare a bill 'in the blank check form'. In the best, frantic tradition of Roosevelt's First Hundred Days drafts went to and fro around Washington. The finished bill, which was entitled 'An Act to Promote the Defense of the United States', authorized the President 'to sell, transfer, exchange, lease or lend or otherwise dispose of' defence articles to countries whose defence he considered 'related' to that of the U.S.A. Repayment terms would be left to him, and they could take the form of 'direct or indirect consideration'. No limit was placed on the total sum involved, or on the President's right to transfer surplus existing equipment as well as new munitions. F.D.R. approved the draft on 7 January, and three days later it was introduced into both houses of Congress.

As the Administration was painfully aware, this was only the beginning of a long and delicate process. Not only had the House and Senate to approve the bill itself, they then had to vote the necessary appropriations. Both pieces of legislation would inevitably involve well-publicized committee hearings and acrimonious debates on the floor of each house. In theory the Administration probably had the numbers to push the measures through. But F.D.R., as usual, was anxious to achieve the maximum possible consensus. This meant allowing a full debate and also being flexible about amendments. On the other hand, he had no desire to facilitate a wide-ranging examination of U.S. foreign policy. Thus Administration witnesses who testified before the two committees followed a standard line—insisting simply that the legislation was essential because Hitler was bent on world domination and that Britain and her Navy were the U.S.A.'s front line. Opponents of the bill, echoing the old attacks on the New Deal, claimed that it would give Roosevelt virtually dictatorial powers. In the Senate they also warned that it would get the U.S.A. into war. In defence against this latter argument the Administration increasingly claimed that the bill was actually designed to keep America out of war: material aid to Britain would obviate the need for full belligerency. To rebut the inevitable isolationist and anglophobe argument about John Bull taking advantage of Uncle Sam, Morgenthau used as the centre-piece of his testimony to both committees a full statement of Britain's dollar position over the coming year, supplemented by evidence of the heavy tax burden borne by British citizens. HMG had reluctantly agreed to this full disclosure—although the Treasury was determined not to let it become a precedent for a general U.S. financial review of Britain's war effort[66]—and its unwonted openness undoubtedly had the desired effect on U.S. opinion.

It was an unpleasant and unprecedented situation for the British. 'For the first time in its history the United Kingdom waited anxiously on the passage of an American law, knowing that its destiny might hang on the outcome. London waited with an imperfect knowledge of American legislative processes and little understanding of American public opinion.'[67] Apart from co-operating with the Administration, there was little that HMG could do to accelerate the process. The Ministry of Information had been pressing since the election, and particularly after Lothian's press conference on 23 November, for permission to mount a publicity campaign to educate U.S. opinion about Britain's needs. At the end of November Churchill asked the MOI to postpone action until Roosevelt had replied to his forthcoming letter, and when Ministry officials returned to the matter in mid-January, with the bill coming before Congress, they were told by the Minister, Duff Cooper: 'this is a very delicate moment . . . the less we say just now the better.'[68] As usual, the FO believed that it was best to rely on the pro-Allied pressure groups in the U.S.A. and on the American media to promote Britain's cause, for fear that direct British propaganda would play into the hands of the isolationists.

Gradually the U.S. legislative process, which HMG so despised, moved towards its conclusion. The House had handled the bill with dispatch, approving it with some amendments on 8 February. By this stage the Senate hearings were reaching their conclusion and the floor debate there began on the 13th. At the end of January Roosevelt had confidently promised Churchill that the bill should become law between 24 and 28 February,[69] but the Senate debate proved longer and more bitter than anticipated and it was not until 8 March that the vote took place. As in the House, the division was broadly along partisan lines—most Democrats supported the bill, most Republicans opposed it—but in each case the majorities were healthy ones which reflected the Democrats' legislative dominance: 260 to 165 in the House, 60 to 31 in the Senate. On 11 March a jubilant F.D.R. signed the Lend-Lease Act into law. Churchill was anxious to 'ram in' the effect of the event, and, with the FO's help, he prepared a statement for the Commons. Calling Lend-Lease 'a new Magna Carta' and 'the most unsordid act in the history of any nation', he told the House: 'The most powerful democracy has, in effect, declared in solemn statute that they will devote their overwhelming industrial and financial strength to ensuring defeat of Naziism in order that nations, great and small, may live in security, tolerance and freedom.'[70]

### C. Scraping the bottom of the barrel, March 1941

Behind the effusiveness, however, the middle of March actually proved another period of deep anxiety and resentment in London. Now that the Act had emerged from the legislative process it became apparent that it did not cover what HMG considered to be Britain's needs. The British Treasury, it will be remembered, had wanted the Administration to assume responsibility for British war contracts in the U.S.A. from 1 January 1941, and also, ideally, for certain advance payments already made. Noted one official in London: 'The reply to this request is the keystone to our financial position over the next year.'[71] Phillips and Purvis, who had been closely involved in the drafting of the bill in January, had repeatedly emphasized the importance of this matter to U.S. Treasury officials. For its part the Administration encouraged the British to go on placing orders, assuring them that the eventual act would be appropriately comprehensive. In particular the British were greatly influenced by F.D.R.'s personal emissary, Harry Hopkins, who insisted on 30 January that F.D.R. was going to obtain a 'blank check' from Congress and that there must be no timidity in British purchasing policy in the interim period. 'In general Mr. Hopkins' advice was that we should show full confidence in the President's intentions, whatever doubts we might feel about the wording of the Bill and however little indication we might in fact as yet have as to what the President would do.' Hopkins was, however, given a full statement of what the British felt the bill should include if it were to cover their needs, but he mislaid it and it was not until 19 March, after considerable prodding from Morgenthau, that the U.S. Treasury received the memo.[72]

This sloppiness is another example of the perils of F.D.R.'s predilection for personal diplomacy, but, even if Hopkins' habits had been more orderly, it is unlikely that the Treasury memo would have significantly affected the character of the Act. The Administration was more concerned about congressional politics than British desiderata. Long before it emerged from Capitol Hill Lend-Lease had lost its 'blank check' character. One sacrifice was the acceptance of a House amendment on 8 February which limited the total amount of existing surplus equipment (as distinct from specially-produced orders) that could be transferred to foreign countries to a total of $1.3 billion.[73] This severely limited the U.S.A.'s capacity to assume Britain's 'old commitments', but in any case Administration spokesmen had already effectively ruled out such a move by their statements to congressional committees. Morgenthau had told the hearings in January that 'given the time, by that I mean the balance of this year, they are in a position to pay for the orders already placed'. This would be done by selling all their U.S. securities and investments. Morgenthau assured the Senate Foreign Relations Committee: 'Every dollar of property, real property or securities that any English citizen owns in the United States, they have agreed to sell during the next 12 months, in order to raise the money to pay for the orders they have already placed, they are going to sell—every dollar of it.'[74] This pledge was repeated on 15 March by Harold Smith, the Budget Director, in testimony to the House Appropriations Committee. He said that none of the Lend-Lease appropriation would be used to pay for existing British orders, that Britain had sufficient dollar resources to cover these, and that remaining British assets would be given as security for Lend-Lease supplies. Phillips had been consulted in advance about the first two of these assurances and, with the

Ambassador's approval, had objected to the proposed answers, but in vain. He was not consulted on the question of using British assets as collateral. Explaining the position to London Phillips concluded: 'Comment seems rather superfluous.'[75]

It was only in mid-March, with Smith's testimony and the publication of the Lend-Lease Act, that these alarming realities became apparent to British leaders. As they pondered the question of how to pay for orders placed before 11 March, the Administration provided some distressing answers itself. For months Morgenthau had been pressing the British to sell off their assets, as a demonstration that they were doing all they could to pay for their U.S. orders. On 10 March, fearful that when he had to testify on the Lend-Lease appropriations bill he would be grilled about his earlier pledges on British sales, he gave Halifax, Lothian's successor as Ambassador, a virtual ultimatum, with Roosevelt's approval, that an important British company would have to be sold within a week, as an earnest of good faith. The only candidate was the American Viscose Corporation (AVC), a subsidiary of the British textile giant, Courtaulds. Convinced by Phillips and Halifax that the sacrifice would have to be made, HMG agreed very reluctantly and on 16 March AVC was sold to a syndicate of American bankers. The sum eventually received by the British Treasury was $54 million, but this was about half the estimated value of the assets and the Treasury eventually had to reimburse Courtaulds accordingly.[76] Meanwhile, the Administration had returned to the matter of Britain's gold reserves. During the Lend-Lease hearings Morgenthau had told the House Foreign Affairs Committee that he believed HMG should use any South African gold it received during 1941 to pay for U.S. purchases. In March, fearful that this pledge would also be picked up in the Appropriations hearings, he suggested to the British that a U.S. warship pay another visit to Cape Town. HM Treasury objected, but Phillips was told on 13 March that F.D.R. had already despatched a vessel to collect $120 million.[77] London was furious. The gold had already been assigned to cover other British purchases abroad, particularly from Canada, and the Treasury feared that after the December visit a precedent had been set for regular raids by the U.S.A. on Britain's remaining gold reserves. Once again, there was little HMG could do at such a delicate juncture. Churchill rejected Treasury suggestions that he take the matter up personally with Morgenthau— 'I do not know whether the President would like me to address particular American Departmental Ministers direct', he noted punctiliously—but he did express his deep concern about the whole interim finance question to Winant, the new U.S. Ambassador in London, and he cabled Halifax: ' . . . I am clear that this is no time for us to be driven from pillar to post . . . Remember that although they may not all realise it, their lives are now in this business too. We cannot always be playing up to minor political exigencies of Congress politics. Morgenthau may have a bad time before his Committee but Liverpool and Glasgow are having a bad time now.'[78]

Why had the Administration taken what seemed such high-handed and even selfish action? Few British leaders in London could appreciate the ordeal of testifying before a congressional committee. Even the most torrid Commons Question Time paled into insignificance against the exhaustive and exhausting inquisition to which Administration leaders were frequently subjected, usually in the full glare of publicity, by well-briefed and powerful committees on the Hill. Morgenthau had based his strategy for the Lend-Lease bill on proving Britain's good faith, by revealing statistics on their financial position and pledging that they would use their gold and assets to cover existing contracts. By March he was morbidly fearful that if the Appropriations Committees were not satisfied that the British had been honouring these pledges they would delay or reduce funds for Lend-Lease.[79] Moreover, as British leaders were also slow to grasp, there was widespread ignorance and suspicion about Britain's financial position. Even Hull and Knox found it hard to comprehend how Britain could be an imperial power with world-wide assets, and yet be unable to pay for her dollar purchases. The deeply-rooted suspicion of the wily British and bitter memories of how they had 'welched' on their Great War debts made Congress and many Administration officials reluctant to provide assistance until they were absolutely convinced that Britain had 'scraped the bottom of the barrel'.[80] It is therefore understandable that Morgenthau became so determined that Britain should prove her good faith.

Yet the British were correct to feel that the Americans were, to some extent, taking advantage of their predicament. Phillips reported in late December: 'Much of public agitation about direct investment which is worrying the Administration is inspired and paid for by United States insurance companies who are exceedingly anxious to obtain the property.'[81] Even the Administration was not exempt from this opportunism, as the sale of American Viscose demonstrates. Admittedly AVC was well suited to be the sacrificial victim to propitiate Congress. Unlike other British investments, such as Shell and Lever Brothers, it was not under partial non-British ownership and could therefore be sold quickly and easily. It was also the largest British holding in the U.S.A. But there were other considerations. In the 1930s AVC had gained a certain notoriety as a foreign-owned company with no U.S. shareholders or directors which, supposedly, had amassed 'fabulous' profits. In 1937 *Fortune* magazine called it 'one of the industrial miracles of our time—a phenomenon comparable to Standard Oil or the automobile empire of Henry Ford'. This was journalistic hyperbole, encouraged by AVC's secretive ways. In fact the company had by then fallen on hard times and tough competition, but it was the myth rather than the reality that mattered. Moreover, from 1934 to 1939 AVC had been engaged in a bitter battle over tax avoidance, which had eventually been settled out of court for $5 million—$35 million less than the U.S. Treasury had been claiming. There can be little doubt that such considerations were in Morgenthau's mind when he pressed for AVC to be sold. He wrote in his diary afterwards:

> So ends a victory of almost eight months' battle. It has been the most difficult fight I think I have waged against the vested interests and also the most significant, because the tie-up between the so-called 'City' in London and our own Wall Street is terribly close. I consider this a great New Deal victory.[82]

This is not to say that the Administration was engaged in wholesale economic imperialism. As Warren Kimball rightly observes: 'Had this been a conscious policy of the Roosevelt Administration, far heavier pressures would have been applied.' For the most part 'economic imperialism was a subconsious temptation rather than an actual policy'.[83] But it is also apparent that the Administration did not always resist that temptation, particularly where it reinforced long-standing New Deal aspirations. We shall discern the same tendency in chapter ten, in examining the question of the repayment terms for Lend-Lease.

There is, therefore, a certain justice in the observation made by Neville Chamberlain in 1934, with characteristic Dickensian allusion, that 'Congress (and in particular the Senate) are the Mr. Jorkins of American representatives'—by which he meant that Administration officials tended to justify a harsh policy that they privately desired by blaming it on the need to satisfy Congress.[84] The President himself clearly supported the tactic of squeezing the British over their U.S. assets. Admittedly he had a much better grasp of HMG's position than many of his Cabinet. He told Hull that their total assets world-wide amounted to nine or ten billion dollars (Hull had a figure of $18 billion firmly in mind), most of which were already earmarked to pay for purchases from the countries in which they were located, such as Canada and Argentina. Within the U.S.A. British assets totalled no more than $1.5 billion, he estimated, using Treasury figures, of which the last $500 million could probably not be liquidated quickly 'except at a very heavy and un-warranted loss'. This was a rather different figure from the $7 billion of useable U.S. assets that he glibly ascribed to Britain just before Munich.[85] Nevertheless, F.D.R. stuck to the belief he had expressed at his press conference on 17 December, that the British could and should pay for their existing orders, and on 10 March 1941 he told Morgenthau 'that he always had in mind that they would have enough money to last until the first of May'.[86] Moreover, when Harold Smith, the Budget Director, made his categorical statements to the House Appropriations Committee on 15 March he was acting not from ignorance, as has often been supposed, but on the explicit instructions of the President. Before testifying, Smith had discussed his statement with F.D.R., who told him that none of the Lend-Lease funds 'were to be used by the British to meet these pre-Lend-Lease commitments but the British were to liquidate these commitments out of their own dollar resources'. When Smith made this statement on the Hill he was asked to check it with the President, but Roosevelt reiterated it the following morning.[87] Yet this did not square with the commitment made by Morgenthau to the British in January, and confirmed in writing by F.D.R. on 10 March, that the Reconstruction Finance Corporation would assume some of the British advance capital investment in plant and the War Department some of their advance payments for munitions.[88] When Morgenthau belatedly learned in May that F.D.R. had personally authorized Smith's statement of 15 March, he concluded lamely that Roosevelt must have forgotten their own discussion five days before. Perhaps he was right—as we have seen, the President was better on the big issues than on details. But it is strange that Morgenthau had left that meeting on 10 March certain for once that Roosevelt really under-stood the position on British finances.[89] It therefore seems likely that F.D.R. believed that the British were not playing fair about selling their assets, and that he deliberately used Smith's statement, at a time when the Viscose sale was coming to a head, to increase the pressure on HMG.

How justified were Roosevelt's suspicions? There can be little doubt that the British Treasury did all it could to avoid selling off Britain's securities and direct investments in the U.S.A. That had been the strategy agreed in October, before Phillips' visit, and when the Administration increased the pressure in early 1941 the British negotiator, Sir Edward Peacock, tried to arrange loans on the collateral of British assets rather than sell them off. Yet the Administration had been harping on the matter since at least July 1940, when Phillips talked with F.D.R. and Morgenthau, and every British official in Washington, including Lothian and Phillips, had emphasized for months that the Administration saw the question as a critical test of British good faith. To a considerable extent, therefore, HMG had only itself to blame for the AVC crisis and for the losses it incurred as a result of the forced sale. Nevertheless, the situation was a complex one. The British were undoubtedly correct when they pleaded that they needed a minimum gold reserve of £150 million in order to operate the Sterling Area and to maintain a stable exchange rate. There was also much truth in their contention that American and world trade would suffer after the war if Britain were forced to sell off her overseas assets, which helped cover her persistent deficit on visible trade. And the fact that the Administration did not squeeze the British harder over their assets was in part a recognition of the justice of these claims. But, although acknowledging the overriding need for co-operation, each side was hoping to maximize its own advantage within the relationship. The British hoped to shift as much as possible of the financial burden of the war on to the U.S.A., so as to safeguard their post-war position. The Americans, equally naturally, resisted British efforts and at times used Britain's crisis to advance their own ends.

\*　　\*　　\*

It may seem that this is only an unseemly footnote to the 'most unsordid act'. But, as so often, historians have appropriated Churchill's compelling rhetoric, used for the purposes of wartime diplomacy and propaganda, as the sober language of historical description. Lend-Lease, it should be emphasized, was not outstandingly novel, or notably altruistic, or even particularly important *in 1941*. The idea of America as the 'great arsenal of democracy' was the logical extension of F.D.R.'s defence and foreign policy since Munich. For two years he had envisaged the Western European democracies as America's front line of defence. By encouraging their orders for munitions the U.S.A. would help contain Hitler without being involved in the war herself and would also accelerate her own rearmament, which F.D.R., no less than Chamberlain in the 1930s, was unwilling to galvanize by government decree. Lend-Lease itself also had these two aspects. It was a defence appropriation bill *and* a device to get round the Johnson and Neutrality Acts now that cash and carry neutrality was no longer sufficient—a request for seven billion dollars of funds for the production of munitions and a request for authority to allocate some of those munitions to countries whose survival benefited the U.S.A. The supplies were not a free gift. Repayment was simply postponed, not waived, and we shall see in chapter ten that the preliminary discussions about it later in 1941 showed clearly that the Administration had no intention of giving something for nothing. The 'consideration' would not be in money or even in kind, but in a commitment to America's conception of the post-war world economy. Nor, in 1941, did Britain receive any great benefit from the American arsenal. Given the inevitable production 'lead time', what counted was not the massive sums appropriated—some $14 billion by the time of Pearl Harbor—but the amount of munitions actually delivered, which was a little over $1 billion. In 1941 84 per cent of the munitions used by Britain, the Commonwealth and Empire came from Britain. Lend-Lease provided only one per cent of the total; a further seven per cent came from the U.S.A. under pre-Lend-Lease contracts for which the British paid cash. Stated in more concrete terms, this meant that in the last nine months of 1941 Britain received 2,400 aircraft and 951 tanks from the U.S.A.—the equivalent in each case of about six weeks' British output—of which 100 planes and 786 tanks came under Lend-Lease. The largest single category of U.S. supplies in 1941 was not munitions but food. By the end of May the first consignments of American tinned goods were arriving, and about one-fifteenth of Britain's food supplies in 1941 came from the U.S.A.[90]

For the British the situation was akin to the financial crisis of 1916–17, when they found themselves 'down on our knees to the Americans . . .'[91] Others, with a sense of historical irony, invoked the analogy of the eighteenth century, when Britain had paid continental allies to act as *her* mercenaries. 'If this bill goes through', Wilmott Lewis, the distinguished *Times* correspondent announced in a crowded Washington restaurant, 'we shall be playing the role of the Hessians.'[92] Such feelings were also expressed within the Cabinet. As during the Destroyers Deal, Beaverbrook repeatedly urged Churchill to preserve an equality in the Anglo-American relationship by minimizing unreciprocated concessions. The Treasury too kept Britain's long-term financial interests very much in mind. But the FO and the Washington Embassy laid their emphasis on the need to trust the Roosevelt Administration and to accede to its requests. Visitors to Washington from London quickly appreciated the delicate political situation there and adopted the FO line—Sir Frederick Phillips' rapid conversion from the Treasury view being a particularly striking example. And Churchill, too, although susceptible to Beaverbrook's influence and sharing his 'gut' preference for a tough line, nevertheless understood the priorities. On 19 February the Beaver had sent him yet another memorandum, phrased as usual like a *Daily Express* editorial, enjoining him to 'Stand up to the Democrats'. But the following day Churchill told the Cabinet that they would have to resign themselves to liquidating Britain's remaining American assets, as the Administration wished and the Embassy advised. 'A few weeks ago he would have doubted the wisdom of this course; but no longer did so, since it was clear that we should receive from America far more than we could possibly give.'[93]

It seems that for Churchill Lend-Lease marked a turning-point in U.S. policy. After the hesitant, often secretive help offered in 1940, F.D.R. had now assumed responsibility for Britain's long-term American purchases, thereby relieving HMG of an impossible burden and demonstrating his faith in Britain's chances of survival. He had also sought and received congressional approval for his policy, instead of acting on his own authority, which put it on a much more reliable footing as far as the British were concerned. Roosevelt had therefore proved that he could be trusted. Moreover, as with the Destroyers Deal, there was the 'imponderables' aspect to consider. Although it seemed in mid-March that Britain was 'not only to be skinned but flayed to the bone', Churchill judged it a small price to pay if Lend-Lease helped pull the Americans into the war. 'I would like to get them hooked a little firmer,' he told the Treasury, 'but they are pretty well on now.'[94] For the rest of 1941 the PM became the most fervent exponent of the argument originally propounded by Lothian and the FO—trust Roosevelt, acquiesce in his requests, do nothing that might complicate his domestic position, because this was the best way to get the Americans into the war. This was Churchill's line, for instance, during the difficult negotiations in early 1941 about the sites for America's new Caribbean bases.

# CHAPTER SEVEN

## Getting 'Mixed Up Together'

Anglo-American Diplomacy and Strategy
in Early 1941

*. . . these two great organisations of the English-speaking
democracies, the British Empire and the United States, will
have to be somewhat mixed up together in some of their affairs
for mutual and general advantage.*

Churchill, August 1940[1]

### A. The West Indian bases

The notes exchanged on 2 September 1940 had outlined in only the most general terms the areas from which the sites for the eight U.S. bases would be chosen. The U.S. would receive leases 'on the eastern side of the Bahamas', 'the west coast of Trinidad, in the Gulf of Paria' and so on.[2] They also said little about the rights the U.S. would exercise within the leased areas, except that she would have all powers necessary for their defence and control. This, Churchill had been at pains to assert in Parliament, did not mean any abrogation of British sovereignty. It was clear, therefore, that the allocation of sites and the determination of U.S. powers within them would raise some thorny questions, further complicated by the fact that one country was a belligerent and the other a neutral. Nor could colonial sensitivities be ignored, particularly in the Caribbean, where the Depression had sparked off violent disturbances in the mid-1930s about the appalling social and economic conditions in the islands.

As in the summer of 1940 it was Lord Lloyd, the Colonial Secretary—an imperial die-hard with corrosive suspicions of the U.S.A.—who proved Churchill's principal problem. Lloyd had always argued that base leases would be the thin end of an American imperialist wedge in the Caribbean and he stuck to his guns throughout the winter. As soon as the agreement had been concluded in September 1940 the Chiefs of Staff had drawn up their own list of the maximum concessions over sites the British would be willing to accept, but meanwhile F.D.R. had sent a mission to the Caribbean, under Admiral Greenslade, to make its own selection. Some of the sites were quickly and amicably agreed, but in a few cases—notably in Bermuda and

169

Trinidad—the large American requirements aroused opposition in the colonies concerned and disquiet in London, where privately the Cabinet agreed with Lloyd that the Americans were 'opening their mouths far too widely'.[3] In October the Greenslade mission revisited Bermuda and accepted a site at the east end of the island, away from the centre for tourism—Bermuda's main industry.[4] Trinidad, however, remained a problem. The U.S.A. had originally wanted only a naval and air base but subsequently she also requested some 18 square miles in the centre of the island for an army base for two divisions, some 20,000 men. The colonial government, reluctant to sacrifice its best land, was only willing to offer a site on the west of the island which would have required substantial and protracted drainage. Just after Christmas Lloyd brought the whole question before the Cabinet again, drawing together a variety of evidence to demonstrate that the U.S. was bent on supplanting the British in the Caribbean. He instanced the expansive U.S. demands for sites, the brusque and peremptory demeanour of the Greenslade mission, the concurrent mission under Charles Taussig which had been investigating economic conditions in the islands, and the revival of American agitation for sale of the British West Indies to the U.S.A. He even alluded to the long-standing wrangle over ownership of islands in the South Pacific and suggested that this was all part of an American threat to the British Empire as a whole. Privately Lloyd was even more intemperate. 'These people are gangsters,' he told David Scott of the FO, 'and there is only one way to deal with gangsters.'[5]

The general feeling in the FO was that Lloyd's paper was 'ill-conceived and petulant'. While the Americans were 'clearly out for as much as they can get', FO/A did not feel that British sovereignty was in danger. In any case HMG could not afford to start a major row about a relatively minor issue. Eden, the new Foreign Secretary, agreed with these conclusions but he took a grimmer view of the situation in the West Indies. His minute, dated 29 December 1940, deserves to be quoted at length because it shows that, as in 1938, Eden's enthusiasm for Anglo-American co-operation was tempered by a desire to maintain Britain's independence and power.

> By allowing U.S. to establish important military garrisons in most of West Indian islands & Newfoundland we have struck a grievous blow at our authority and ultimately I have no doubt at our sovereignty, in all these places. The consequences upon our position in the American Continent & that of the Dominion of Canada are likely to be most unhappy for those who believe in the value of the British connexion. We have received in return 50 old destroyers of which 2 have so far—at the end of four months—been made seaworthy.
>
> This might reasonably be regarded as a poor bargain, *but it has been made*, & we are powerless to go back upon it. I am therefore against Lord Lloyd's methods; as a result of which we can only lose more than we have lost already, & throw American goodwill out of the window after the British connexion.[6]

The Admiralty took a similar view. Although increasingly of the opinion that 'the U.S. have us in a cleft stick, know it, and intend to take ruthless advantage of it', it recognized that the American proposed site in Trinidad was the only practicable one and deprecated the Colonial Office's consistent support for the colony's 'parochial' outlook.[7] When the question came before the Cabinet on 30 December, Lloyd was therefore isolated.

> The general view of the War Cabinet was that, while it went against the grain to make further concessions in this matter, we must be ready to do so in order to avoid the risk of providing ammunition to the isolationist opponents of President Roosevelt in Congress in the discussions as to the extent of financial help to this country in providing munitions for the war. This issue was of overriding importance, and other matters must give way before it.[8]

Accordingly the Cabinet conceded the remaining U.S. demands about the sites, but it strongly requested that the terms of the leases should be decided by a formal conference to be held in London. The reasoning, of course, was that otherwise '. . . we should be driven by piecemeal concessions to give away all that the Americans were asking, so that in the end we should [be] told that there were no outstanding points and that all our bargaining power would then be lost'.[9] For similar reasons the State Department wanted to hold the discussions in Washington, but eventually Roosevelt reluctantly acceded to the British request. A three-man team of negotiators was sent to London and the Conference formally began on 28 January, in a room from which a portrait of George III had been hurriedly removed, in deference to possible American sensitivities.[10]

However, it quickly became apparent that the negotiations would be slow and arduous. Anxious to ensure full recognition of British rights and aware that they were making an agreement that would have to last for 99 years, the British negotiators presented an agenda that covered all possible contingencies. The items raised ranged from customs duties to traffic regulations and from questions of jurisdiction to the liability of U.S. vessels for local harbour dues. For its part the U.S. delegation had been given strictly limited negotiating powers and had to refer virtually every question back to the State Department for approval. There, as the FO suspected, the issue was being handled mainly by Welles, Berle and the European desk, none of whom was particularly well disposed to the British.[11] Moreover, the colonies involved, most of whom had sent delegations to London, were obstinately determined to safeguard their own rights, and this strengthened the Americans' desire to secure the fullest possible powers in order to avoid further delays and obstruction. By the middle of February little progress had been made and Halifax was asked by the FO to take up some of the major problems in Washington. The State Department, however, keenly resented this attempt to go round the back of its London delegation. It also made clear to Halifax its own displeasure at the lack of progress, emphasizing repeatedly the danger of upsetting Congress, and as early as 25 February the Department had drafted a personal telegram embodying these points for Roosevelt to send to Churchill.[12] The President, however, was anxious not to make 'mountains out of molehills'. Rather than send the cable he achieved the same effect by showing the draft to Halifax on 5 March and impressing upon him the political necessity of a speedy agreement on essentially the American terms.[13]

Churchill was not disposed to argue. Throughout the controversy he stuck to the position he had adopted when the original agreement had been

concluded: Britain would gladly allow the U.S. all rights and powers necessary to ensure the security of the Western Hemisphere, but there would be
no diminution of British sovereignty.[14] He insisted that these two fundamental principles of the agreement were quite compatible and that the issue
was really of minor importance in the whole scheme of Anglo-American
co-operation. His attitude is epitomized in this minute of 4 March to the
Colonial and Dominions Secretaries:

> You can easily have a first-class row with the United States of America about
> these matters, and this will be particularly vexatious at a time when the Lease and
> Lend Bill is on its passage. I am anxious therefore by one means or another to
> keep this business as quiet as possible till the Bill is through. We shall then have
> only the President to deal with, and not be in danger of giving ammunition to our
> enemies in the Senate.[15]

By this date the bill was on its final stages and Churchill wanted nothing to
upset the Administration. Moreover, John Winant had just arrived to take
up the post of U.S. Ambassador to Britain, and this meant that at last there
was an official in London with sufficient authority to lean on the American
delegation. Churchill therefore told Halifax on 4 March not to take further
action at the Washington end: 'I am hoping to get matters smoothed out and
clarified here with Mr. Winant before troubling the President and Mr.
Hull.'[16] For the same reason Churchill did not communicate directly with
F.D.R. about the bases until the problem had virtually been settled. Like the
State Department the FO had been pondering for some days whether 'to
fire off our own big gun' in the form of a Churchill–Roosevelt message,
but although the PM did essay some drafts between 6 and 8 March nothing
was sent until the 10th, the day before Lend-Lease became law.[17] In the
cable, which dealt mainly with the Balkans, Churchill explained that he had
been 'working steadily about the bases on turning the mountains back into
molehills' and invited Roosevelt to 'lend a hand with the shovel' if he could.[18]
In fact, most of the spadework was done at two long meetings between
Churchill, Winant and the two delegations on 5 and 12 March.[19] The Cabinet
approved the agreement on the 13th and the formal signing ceremony took
place a fortnight later.

On their own admission the British had 'given way on practically everything'. Winant told F.D.R. that the powers conveyed to the U.S.A. were:

> probably more far-reaching than any the British Government has ever given
> anyone over British territory before. They are not used to giving away such
> concessions and on certain points they have fought every inch of the way. While
> they have intended all along to give us everything we really needed—they could do
> no less and had no desire to do less—it was a real struggle for them to break
> habits of 300 years.[20]

To justify such concessions Churchill had insisted on a clause in the preamble which stated that the agreement 'shall be fulfilled in a spirit of good
neighbourliness' and that the 'details of its practical application shall be
arranged by friendly co-operation'. The specific articles of the agreement,
granting the U.S. a wide range of rights and powers in the base areas, all
stated that these powers were to be exercised 'in the spirit' of the preamble.

Without this, Churchill argued, the treaty would be more of a 'capitulation' than a friendly agreement between the two great powers and he could not possibly justify it to Parliament.[21]

This was as far as the Administration was willing to go in publicly and formally acknowledging that the bases were a further step in the 'mixing up' of the British and U.S. defence efforts. The British military had wanted to establish explicitly in the treaty that, if any of the territories was attacked, both countries would co-operate in its defence and that the ultimate command responsibility would lie with the colonial authorities. Naturally the State Department wished to dodge such embarrassing questions, arguing, in its usual non-committal vein, that they 'should be settled by separate agreement when such questions arise on the basis of conditions then existing'. For its part, HMG would not accept 'that reference to mutual defence might be embarrassing to the United States. In our view this was the main principle underlying the granting of the leases.'[22] In other words, the controversy had exposed the different justifications originally advanced in America and Britain for the destroyers–bases deal—the Administration had presented it as a shrewd piece of diplomatic 'horse-trading', whereas Churchill, aware that he had the worst of the deal, had placed it on the level of mutual gifts to strengthen common defence interests. In the end the British had to accept the saving clause in the preamble as sufficient guarantee. Once more it was a question of trust.[23]

The British also took comfort in the expectation that time and events would resolve many of the other complex problems that had not been settled to their satisfaction. During the winter, for instance, they had been much exercised by the State Department's unilateral announcement in September that the bases would be open to the navies of Latin American countries under the Pan American neutrality pacts, and then by its warning in December that the Royal Navy might not be allowed to use them since Britain was a belligerent. FO/A pointed out that the American position was largely for the purposes of hemisphere politics—the American states had negligible navies—but R. A. Butler, sensitive as ever to back-bench opinion, warned: 'N.B. Parliament will be enraged when or if they hear that Uruguay can use these bases and we can't.'[24] But again HMG decided not to push the issue. By March 1941 there was a general feeling that the 'mixing up' process had created several loopholes in the State Department's legalistic position—in various places in the Western Atlantic, including the U.S.A. itself, British and U.S. vessels were already using each other's port and repair facilities. It was also felt in the FO and the Service departments 'that as the U.S.A. were in all likelihood approaching a moment when they would enter the war, there seemed no point in raising this contentious issue, which would in that event automatically solve itself'.[25] The present situation, in which the two were quite literally 'mixed up', seemed like a temporary phase before a clear-cut alliance.

As these two examples demonstrate, the Bases Agreement of 27 March 1941, no less than the original Destroyers Deal of September 1940, was justified by HMG largely in terms of 'imponderables'—as the necessary price for smoothing the passage of Lend-Lease and as a way of drawing the

U.S.A. deeper into the war. It was on the level of 'imponderables' that the agreement was presented to Parliament. For years American suggestions that the West Indies should be ceded in return for a settlement of the war debt had aroused considerable indignation at Westminster, and, as we saw, there was a small but significant protest in August 1940 at the length of the base leases. Throughout the winter of 1940–41 the Government had been irritated by persistent questions from a small number of MPs, notably Richard Stokes—the Americophobe Labour businessman who had been at the centre of the group favouring a negotiated peace the previous summer—and Commander Sir Archibald Southby, a Tory die-hard. Their efforts to force a debate about the negotiations had all been firmly resisted—Government spokesmen retreated behind the constitutional principle that the House of Commons was free to repudiate the agreement but that until it was concluded the Government had a free hand.[26] When the treaty was signed the Cabinet therefore mounted a big public relations campaign, allowing press, photographers and the newsreels to be present and handing round souvenir pens, in the American manner, to the signatories.[27] Privately, the press was briefed to treat the agreement 'in its broadest aspect'—as part of the progressive 'union of thought and interest' between Britain and the U.S.A. on which the 'future of Western civilisation' would depend—rather than scrutinizing the individual provisions 'through a magnifying glass'.[28] For his part Churchill was punctilious about laying the full details before Parliament,[29] and he told the colonial governments, some of whom had made considerable sacrifices: 'these bases are important pillars to the bridge connecting the two great English-speaking democracies. You have cause to be proud that it has fallen to your lot to make this important contribution to a better world.'[30]

What of the Administration? How valid were the suspicions of the Colonial Office and some senior naval officers that the U.S. was trying gradually to take over these British possessions? Clearly U.S. business interests, such as Standard Oil, were alert to the prospect of economic gain.[31] Equally, Welles and Berle, architects of the 'Good Neighbor' policy, probably saw the agreement as an opportunity to extend American influence in the Caribbean, and there were many, including notable 'friends' of Britain such as Frank Knox, who believed that the West Indies were rightfully U.S. property.[32] Nevertheless, FO/A was quite correct that Roosevelt himself had no desire to take over the islands. On numerous occasions he observed that the U.S. did not want what he called 'two million headaches' in the form of the impoverished black population of the British West Indies.[33] The primary reason for the Administration's heavy-handed insistence on the fullest possible powers was its panic about U.S. security in the Caribbean. Long hyper-sensitive to evidence of German penetration in Latin America and acutely conscious of America's lack of defence in the Western Atlantic and Caribbean, it had nevertheless done little to remedy the situation. During the winter of 1940–41 there were disturbing signs that Hitler might be moving out into the Atlantic, via the Spanish and Portuguese islands, and the Administration conceived of the new bases, particularly Trinidad, as the key to the defence of the Western Hemisphere. In private, though not in public, it acknowledged that this required close co-operation with Britain.

Moreover, this co-operation involved economic as well as military policy. No less than the British West Indies, U.S. possessions in the Caribbean— Puerto Rico and the Virgin Islands—had been plagued by unemployment, poverty and social unrest in 1937–38. Just as the British had set in motion a major welfare and development programme in 1940, so the U.S. Government took its own steps to improve the situation. The Taussig inquiry—which Lord Lloyd had seen as sinister evidence of U.S. imperialism—was one of those steps. Its immediate task was to assess the probable impact of the bases on the islands, but more generally it surveyed the whole social and economic situation in the Caribbean. One of Taussig's main recommendations when he reported in January 1941 was that Britain and the U.S. should collaborate in confronting Caribbean problems—notably low commodity prices and disgraceful living standards—and out of the informal co-operation that developed during 1941 came the Anglo-American Caribbean Commission—an investigative and advisory body set up in March 1942.[34]

But in the end, as all concerned were aware, the Bases Agreement marked a major extension of American power and influence in the Caribbean. In the Atlantic West Indies—Bermuda and the Bahamas—the American connection had long been important, but during the 1930s it had been spreading into the Caribbean, and the U.S. bases, particularly in Trinidad, were inevitably a major force for Americanization. All this was part of a longer process—that of the gradual reduction of British power and influence in the Western Hemisphere—which had been going on since at least the mid-nineteenth century if not since 1776, with particular rapidity at certain times, notably in the 1890s and also World War Two.[35] Churchill might romanticize the recession of British power by talk about the mixing up of the English-speaking peoples; Eden, despite his keenness for transatlantic co-operation, was more realistic in his recognition that the Bases Agreement struck a 'grievous blow' at Britain's now tenuous position in the Americas.

## B. The changing texture of Anglo-American relations

It was not only the balance of the Anglo-American relationship that shifted during the winter of 1940–41. There were also important changes among those conducting transatlantic diplomacy in London and Washington.

On the British side the most significant of these was the choice of a successor to Lord Lothian. Churchill had first turned to Lloyd George and early on the morning of 15 December he sent a message asking Roosevelt 'quite informally' whether this would be acceptable. 'Choice will be entirely agreeable', the President replied. 'I knew him in world war. I assume that over here he will in no way play into the hands of the appeasers.' But F.D.R. had inferred that the appointment had already been decided, and his cable therefore did not reveal the extent of Washington's perturbation and dismay.[36] Frankfurter was deeply depressed and Breckinridge Long in the State Department found it difficult to fathom the reasoning behind this 'rather astonishing nomination'.[37] Roosevelt's own 'consternation' was made known to Richard Casey, the Australian Minister in Washington, who arranged for complaints to Churchill from all the Dominion leaders. The British Embassy itself was equally appalled. Even Nevile Butler, the Chargé d'Affaires, a career diplomat who rarely questioned his instructions, ventured to suggest that L.G. might be unsuitable because of his age and his reputation as an appeaser.[38] Casey claimed that his 'Empire Strike' had helped to prevent the appointment, but in fact it was Lloyd George himself, on his doctor's advice, who decided against on 16 December.[39] After further thought Churchill turned to Halifax, acting again initially through the intermediary of Beaverbrook. Halifax was horrified. He tried to persuade Eden to go, but Eden refused. His wife argued it out with Churchill on 20 December, but the premier appealed to all Halifax's best instincts of *noblesse oblige* and obtained his reluctant acquiescence. 'In war one can but do what one is told!' Halifax wrote gloomily on Boxing Day.[40] Ironically, his successor was Eden, whom Halifax had himself succeeded in February 1938.

Lloyd George and Halifax—what had these two in common to recommend them for the Washington Embassy? Both of course had held high office, and the selection of either could be represented as a great honour to the U.S.A. Indeed Churchill made much of this in his public statements about Halifax's appointment. But two other considerations surely mattered much more to the PM. As we saw in chapter four, Halifax and Lloyd George posed potential threats to his political position and both were in favour of an eventual negotiated peace once Britain had proved that she could not be defeated. Lloyd George did not conceal his ambitions to head a future peacemaking government—'I shall wait until Winston is bust', he told his secretary on 3 October—and he was marked down in Government circles as a would-be Pétain.[41] Halifax was more complex. As the events of 9–10 May had shown, he had no stomach for supreme power and his basic loyalty to Churchill was unquestioned. But he saw himself as a balancing agent—preventing Churchill, like Chamberlain before him, from erring towards the extremes of policy and politics. In 1937–39 he tried to keep open contacts between Chamberlain and his critics; in 1940 he envisaged his task as that of standing up to Churchill's more hare-brained schemes and not least in preventing the PM from fighting on unnecessarily and ruinously to an unattainable victory. For his part Churchill always believed that Halifax was basically an appeaser, and it is likely that he did not forget the tense days just before the Dunkirk evacuation when Halifax had urged the Cabinet to sound out Hitler's peace terms.[42] The premier was determined to conduct the essentials of transatlantic diplomacy himself. The Ambassadorship would be a figurehead—and a sort of high-class political dustbin.[43]

Halifax's appointment was part of Churchill's changing relationship with the Conservative party. In the summer he had been a Prime Minister without a party, reliant on Chamberlain and the Tories for his political base. But at the end of July Chamberlain was operated on for cancer. Churchill initially wanted him to remain in the Cabinet. The relationship between the two men had matured and deepened over the previous year and the premier valued Chamberlain as an efficient and loyal colleague who looked after domestic policy and thereby freed him to run the war. But at the end of September, after the fiasco of the expedition against Dakar had given rise to calls from the press and Parliament for a Cabinet reshuffle, Churchill accepted

Chamberlain's resignation from all his political offices.[44] The leadership
of the Tory party was now Churchill's for the taking, but he was uncertain and confused. His wife, who, unlike her husband, had never wavered
in her Liberal convictions, believed that it would undermine his position as
a national leader, but Bracken and Beaverbrook convinced Churchill that
he could not allow the previous anomalous situation to continue and on 9
October he became the Tory leader.[45] At the end of September Churchill
had also considered moving Eden from the War Office to the FO; Halifax
would either replace Chamberlain as Lord President or else swap posts with
Eden. But Halifax, as Churchill put it, 'had shown no inclination to move'
and was firmly opposed to Eden returning to the Foreign Office—'certain
embers still warm' he observed in a cryptic reference to the controversies
over appeasement. Moreover, Chamberlain had made it clear that the
Conservatives would see such a change as a condemnation of his own policy,
particularly if he were dropped at the same time.[46] Churchill heeded the
warning and the reshuffle proved an anti-climax. But after Chamberlain's
death on 9 November rumours were rife once more in Whitehall and the
press that Halifax would be replaced by Eden. By now Eden had finished
his much-needed reforms of the Army, and he and his advisers, who were
depressed at the apparent inertia and pre-war mentality of the FO, favoured
his return.[47] The opportunity came with Lothian's death and Lloyd George's
refusal. Halifax's banishment to Washington was the culmination of Churchill's consolidation of power and an insurance that any movement for a
compromise peace would have no potential political base.

Despite being chosen largely for reasons of domestic politics, Halifax had
certain credentials for the job of Ambassador. Like Lothian he was essentially
an Atlanticist. He wanted a close bond between Britain and the U.S.A.,
uncomplicated by commitments in continental Europe, and he believed that
the elimination of France from the war had simplified the eventual peace
conference. Indeed Lothian had said on his last visit to England that of all
British policymakers it was Halifax who best understood his 'idea' of the
Anglo-American relationship.[48] But Halifax's understanding was theoretical
rather than practical. He had none of Lothian's affection for the U.S.A. or
'feel' for its political system. His early letters from Washington are filled with
amazement at the deference paid by politicians to every ripple of public
opinion—'They seem almost as afraid of that as they are of the Germans'—
and at the lack of co-ordination imposed by the White House on the activities of the various Executive departments, 'who might almost as well be the
administration of different countries'. Characteristically Halifax resorted to a
hunting metaphor: 'I suppose it is rather like a disorderly line of beaters
out shooting; they do put the rabbits out of the bracken, but they don't
come out where you expect.'[49] These and many other remarks in the same
vein show how little Halifax had understood about American policymaking
before he came to Washington, and how much he had to learn. It is hardly
surprising that his first few months as Ambassador were marked by a series
of *faux pas*, notably his much-publicized fox-hunting expedition which
U.S. critics seized upon to prove his incorrigibly aristocratic and un-American
ways. He was also slow to get on to the necessary levels of informality with

the Administration—the use of first names and the telephone did not come easily. Not surprisingly, therefore, the FO received a string of reports throughout the spring that Halifax was a disaster—cold in private and stilted in public— the epitome of Old World values and a far cry from his democratic, free-and-easy predecessor. Halifax's American education was slow and sometimes painful.

There was also a change of ambassadors in London that winter. Joseph Kennedy had long since lost the confidence of both governments. Convinced that another European war would be an unmitigated disaster, he had thrown his support behind Chamberlain's peace efforts in 1938 with little reserve. Whereas Kennedy believed that clear signs of Anglo-American co-operation would strengthen Chamberlain's negotiating position *vis-à-vis* the dictators, the Administration, although equally keen to avoid war, was determined during the Czech crisis, as we saw, to avoid any entanglement in British diplomacy. The Ambassador was never forgiven. Once Chamberlain's peace efforts had failed, Kennedy concentrated on keeping the U.S.A. out of the war. After the French collapse he advised Washington that Britain could not survive alone and that America should devote herself to hemisphere defence. These unconcealed doubts about Britain, though not unreasonable, naturally did not endear him to British leaders, who looked down on him as a vulgar, pushy Irish-American politico whose only preoccupations were his investments and his precocious family. In the summer of 1940 Kennedy was therefore bypassed by London and Washington. He played no part in the destroyers deal, of which he strongly disapproved, and by October the word in the State Department was that if Kennedy 'says something is black and Lothian says it is white, we believe Lord Lothian'.[50] Bitter and frustrated, he returned to the U.S.A. before the election, determined to endorse Willkie. A large dose of the Roosevelt charm changed his mind, but when Kennedy, following the usual post-election procedure, placed his post in Roosevelt's hands on 6 November, there was little doubt that he would not be returning to London.

Naturally Roosevelt wanted a successor who enthusiastically supported his policy of growing assistance to Britain. He also wanted someone who would be content to play a minor role in a relationship that increasingly revolved around the direct Churchill–Roosevelt axis. On both counts John G. Winant was a suitable choice—a mild-mannered former progressive Republican who had become an ardent New Dealer and anti-Nazi. But there was another and probably more important reason for the appointment. For some five years Winant had served Roosevelt at the International Labour Organisation in Geneva, ending up as its Director from February 1939. In that capacity he had got to know many British Labour leaders and after Kennedy's departure some of them, notably Harold Laski and Ernest Bevin, urged F.D.R. to appoint Winant in his place. The President took their advice, and, as the Embassy's legal adviser, he selected the veteran New Dealer, Ben Cohen. He believed Winant and Cohen were well qualified to assess the social and economic changes going on in wartime England, and that they could build bridges with the Labour leadership, who, Roosevelt felt, would be the dominant political force in Britain after the war.[51] As usual F.D.R. was trying to extend his personal contacts and maximize future options. In 1939, disenchanted with Chamberlain, he had initiated the correspondence with Churchill, the most bellicose minister in the British Government. In 1941, as his relationship with Churchill was consolidated, F.D.R. stretched out a hand towards the British Left, which was already emerging as the principal domestic beneficiary of the war.

But neither Winant nor even Halifax was to play a major role in the emerging Anglo-American alliance. Increasingly the official ambassadors were being bypassed by personal emissaries dealing directly between Roosevelt and Churchill. The most important of these was Harry Hopkins, who paid his first visit to London from 9 January to 9 February 1941. Hopkins was a hard-bitten but deeply committed New Dealer, afflicted with a series of digestive ailments that would have reduced a lesser man to a bed-ridden invalid. In the 1930s he had concerned himself with relief programmes and political patronage, but after his resignation as Commerce Secretary in August 1940 he became F.D.R.'s principal political go-between, and it was in this capacity that he was sent to London in the New Year. Mulling over Churchill's letter of 8 December Roosevelt had commented that 'a lot of this could be settled if Churchill and I could just sit down together for a while'.[52] This was clearly impossible for the moment, and in the meantime Hopkins was to be F.D.R.'s eyes and ears, learning at first-hand the British situation and conveying the President's own thinking. In a sense he was doing what Sumner Welles had done eleven months before, except that Hopkins was now far closer to F.D.R. than Welles and a compromise peace was entirely out of the question.

But Hopkins was more than a general information-gatherer. He was also to sound out Churchill's attitude to Roosevelt and to the U.S.A. We have seen that in the inter-war years and in 1940–41 Churchill was often inclined to a tough, hard-bargaining approach to Anglo-American relations. In the 1930s he had also made some cautious criticisms of the way the New Deal had alienated business from government. Some of these comments had been used out of context by Willkie during the election campaign, much to HMG's embarrassment. It was decided to make no public response—'Less said soonest mended', Churchill advised—but, as Joseph Lash suggests, Churchill's failure to repudiate Willkie may have irritated the White House.[53] For his part, in 1940 Churchill was far less sure of his relationship with Roosevelt than he implies in his war memoirs. He anxiously awaited the President's replies to his cables, and there were often long gaps in the correspondence. Before the election Churchill had been particularly anxious not to trouble the President, but once F.D.R. had been returned to power the PM hastened to send a fulsome message of congratulation. He was most disturbed not to receive a reply, and pressed the British Embassy to ascertain what had happened. The official line from the White House was that the telegram had been lost in the deluge of post-election messages, which may actually have been true, but it is striking that in November 1944, when F.D.R. was re-elected for a fourth term, Churchill took the trouble to send him a copy of his 1940 message, 'as you may have forgotten it'.[54]

Churchill had been made fully aware of the importance of Hopkins' visit. Brendan Bracken, Churchill's right-hand man and one of the few British leaders with real knowledge and understanding of the U.S.A., had met Hopkins in 1937 and was able to instruct Churchill on his significance among F.D.R.'s entourage.[55] From Felix Frankfurter via Richard Casey came word that Churchill must convince Hopkins of his warm regard for the President.[56] When, at their first meeting, Hopkins challenged Churchill with typical directness about his supposed dislike of America and of Roosevelt, Churchill vehemently denied this, placed the blame on Kennedy and proceeded to show Hopkins a copy of his post-election telegram. Thereafter in public and private he went out of his way to pay tribute to the President. Hopkins was quickly convinced—'I cannot believe that it is true Churchill dislikes either you or America—it just doesn't make sense', he wrote Roosevelt on 13 January. He also rapidly abandoned his prior scepticism about Churchill's importance—'*Churchill* is the gov't in every sense of the word . . . I cannot emphasize too strongly that he is the one and only person over here with whom you need to have a full meeting of minds.'[57] To facilitate that meeting of minds, for which the premier was as anxious as F.D.R., the two discussed plans for a Roosevelt–Churchill summit in April. Hopkins also accompanied the PM around the country as well as holding long discussions with other British policymakers. He returned home primed with Britain's needs and passionately committed to the anti-Nazi cause. His farewell letter is an eloquent testimony to his new and burning enthusiasm for the country and its leader:

> My dear Mr Prime Minister
> I shall never forget these days with you—your supreme confidence and will to victory—Britain I have ever liked—I like it the more.
> As I leave for America tonight I wish you great and good luck—confusion to your enemies & victory for Britain.
>
> Ever so cordially,
> Harry Hopkins[58]

Hopkins' own description of his mission—'to be a catalytic agent between two prima donnas'[59]—sums up his role in Anglo-American relations throughout the war. Soon after his return he was put in charge of the Lend-Lease programme. This placed him in a key position astride the vital supply lifeline between America and Britain. From then on he became an invaluable intermediary between the two leaders, moderating their differences, explaining their problems. Often Churchill would communicate with him rather than with F.D.R., anxious not to overload the direct line but also aware, perhaps, that Hopkins shared few of the President's uncertainties about whether the U.S. should enter the war.[60] To expedite Lend-Lease at the London end F.D.R. sent W. Averell Harriman, the banker and businessman, who was a close friend of Hopkins. Harriman's brief was typically broad and general: 'Recommend everything that we can do, short of war, to keep the British Isles afloat.' After his arrival in London in mid-March, he set up a small but dynamic office, and he quickly became part of Churchill's intimate circle. Harriman enjoyed direct communication with the White House avoiding the State Department, and, despite his tact, his elevated status inevitably caused friction with Winant.[61]

The emergence of Hopkins and Harriman as the pre-eminent transatlantic go-betweens reflected major shifts in the balance of power in Washington itself. Since the tentative beginnings of F.D.R.'s rearmament programme in the autumn of 1938 Allied purchasing had been handled by Henry Morgenthau. With the passage of Lend-Lease and the appointment of Hopkins, Morgenthau lost his direct role in the conduct of Anglo-American relations, even though he remained an influential adviser to the President. Even more striking was the declining power of the State Department. For years F.D.R. had been bypassing the 'cookie-pushers', as he and Hopkins liked to call the career diplomats, but the winter of 1940–41 saw a marked acceleration in the process. There was considerable resentment in the Department at the way it was ignored on matters of high policy, the Lend-Lease bill being a notable example. In fact this was hardly surprising given State's coolness to the principle of the bill. It remained confused and ambivalent—aware that Britain and her fleet were U.S.A.'s front line yet fearful that too much assistance would entangle America in another war—and during the winter it became a bitter refrain within the Department, not only from Berle but from less obsessively anglophobe senior officials such as Jimmy Dunn, that the power behind the throne was now Felix Frankfurter, the anglophile, Jewish Justice of the Supreme Court.[62] Frankfurter has covered his tracks well but there is no doubt that he had his finger in many pies. He played an important part in the drafting of Lend-Lease, he was instrumental through his contacts with the British Left in persuading Roosevelt to send Winant and Cohen to London, and it was he who passed the word that Churchill must 'sell himself' to Hopkins. Nevertheless, in the end State's fears were exaggerated. Roosevelt was an eclectic. He listened to many advisers but was dependent on none. However, Hopkins and, to a lesser extent, Frankfurter, did become the major voices in the President's ear during 1941, and the State Department was increasingly cut out of the major questions of transatlantic diplomacy and supply. Nevertheless, it still retained considerable authority over peripheral matters impinging on Anglo-American relations. By virtue of its control over Western Hemisphere affairs it was able, as we have seen, to drive a hard bargain with the British over the Caribbean bases. It was also left in charge of post-war political and economic planning, with results that we shall examine in chapter ten.

The Foreign Office was more successful than the State Department in preserving general control over the British end of Anglo-American relations, but, inevitably, even its authority was being eroded. The threat came not only from high-level intermediaries but also from the plethora of specialist missions that were being exchanged. In Washington a confused network of overlapping agencies of HMG had grown up in the best traditions of British muddling. The British Purchasing Commission (BPC) under Arthur Purvis handled orders for all munitions except aircraft and aircraft supplies, which, at the insistence of Beaverbrook (the empire-building Minister of Aircraft Production), was the preserve of his own staff in Washington. The position was further complicated by the presence that autumn of a special mission from the Ministry of Supply under Sir Walter Layton. There were other agencies to liaise with the U.S. Government on shipbuilding, economic warfare, scientific research, oil, weapons types and naval orders, not to mention their subordinate bodies in New York and other cities, and various organizations to handle publicity and information.[63] Eventually Churchill forced through a major reorganization in early December, creating a British Supply Council in North America which would deal with 'all issues of policy concerning Supply'.[64] Pressed by Morgenthau via Mackenzie King Churchill appointed at its head Arthur Purvis, the able Scots-Canadian who got on far better with Americans than did most English officials, who seemed stuffy and reserved.[65] After Morgenthau's departure from the scene Purvis maintained good relations with Hopkins and his staff. His death in an air crash in July 1941 was universally and rightly regarded as a major tragedy. Nominally Purvis and all other British missions were under the authority of the Ambassador. But in practice of course their size and variety, not to mention their highly specialized functions, made them extremely difficult to control. The Ambassador was reduced to the role of an overseer, keeping sight of the general issues of high policy, eliminating friction, acting as spokesman and figure-head for his country—all important tasks but somewhat removed from the traditional conception of an ambassador. Lothian had been ideally suited to a fluid and uncertain period when Anglo-American contacts had been tentative, informal and often secret and the Ambassador had to be a jack-of-all-trades. Halifax, by contrast, a former Foreign Secretary and Viceroy of India, was well qualified to preside with patience and dignity over the mini-Whitehall now proliferating in Washington.

In short, the texture of the Anglo-American relationship was changing. No longer were contacts principally the preserve of Foreign Office, State Department and ambassadors. Although the FO and Halifax were much more successful than Winant and the State Department in keeping hold of the main threads, the fact was that virtually every department of the British and U.S. Governments now had some interest in the problems of Anglo-American diplomacy and supply in all their global ramifications. Undercut by the specialists, the diplomats also found that the two leaders were increasingly operating over their heads, both directly and through trusted intermediaries such as Hopkins and Harriman. The cords that bound the two countries were becoming thicker, more tangled and more secure.

## C. The ABC staff talks, January–March 1941

Perhaps the most significant of the 'specialist' contacts that winter was the conference between British and U.S. strategic planners held in Washington between 29 January and 29 March 1941.[66] For several years U.S. planners had laboured under two serious disadvantages, both of which stemmed from deep-rooted American traditions. One was the persistent lack of political guidance on the goals of national policy, which made it necessary to formulate grand strategy in vacuum.[67] The other was the absence of official contact with planners in countries which might prove eventual allies. Both these handicaps are ultimately attributable to the fact that for most of U.S. history foreign and defence policies have been peripheral concerns, because of America's privileged geographical and economic position. It was fear that the era of 'free security' had come to an end that had led Roosevelt slowly and hesitantly to formulate a foreign policy in the late 1930s. Similarly, the awareness that the U.S.A. might have to face enemies in the Pacific and the Atlantic had led to growing pressure from the military for contacts with planners in Britain, the U.S.A.'s most obvious potential ally in the event of a two-ocean war. This was the impulse behind the Ingersoll mission in January 1938 and the subsequent pre-war updatings, particularly Hampton's visit to Washington in June 1939. Such conversations, as the Americans repeatedly emphasized, were entirely hypothetical and non-committal. Their object had been simply to elicit information about British plans in order to make U.S. contingency preparations more realistic. From the summer of 1940 these contacts increased. Pre-eminent in American minds, as we have seen, was the future disposition of the British fleet. This had been Roosevelt's original motive for staff talks with Canada and, probably, with Britain. The talks with the British took place in London in late August, conducted by a three-man American delegation. Again the flow of information was largely one-way: the British talking, the Americans listening, learning and making no commitments. One member of the delegation, Admiral Robert L. Ghormley, stayed on in London as the Special Naval Observer, playing the same role in more detailed liaison with an Admiralty planning committee. Ghormley was in an invidious position and he repeatedly advised his superiors to enter into proper, two-way conversations. We saw in chapter 5 (b) that the Administration nearly took up the idea in October 1940, during the Far Eastern crisis after the Tripartite Pact, but it was quickly dropped as the election loomed nearer.

Nevertheless, it was now generally agreed in Washington that a proper definition of U.S. grand strategy was imperative. By the autumn of 1940 U.S. military and naval planners shared Roosevelt's opinion that it was worth diverting some of America's scarce munitions, if only because continued British resistance would give the U.S.A. longer to rearm. But they still were far less sure than HMG about Britain's ability to survive, and thus felt that the U.S.A. should concentrate its strength in the Atlantic. They were also worried that F.D.R.'s casual and informal policy of co-operation with the British would result in unwitting and unnecessary commitments to Britain's position and policy all over the world, regardless of America's own interests. Naturally the Navy was particularly anxious, because it was the Service most closely involved with Britain and because the Pacific Fleet was pushing to return to the West Coast. Lacking any clear guidance from the White House, Admiral Stark, the Chief of Naval Operations, tried to define America's strategic priorities. His celebrated 'Plan Dog' of 11 November 1940 postulated that the U.S.A.'s principal interest was the defeat of Germany. This could not be achieved by Britain alone. It would require not only the use of American economic and naval power, but also a large-scale invasion of the continent of Europe. Britain was important in the short term as an outpost of American defence and, looking farther ahead, as a base for the ultimate offensive. In order to concentrate on Germany, the U.S.A. should remain on a 'strict defensive' in the Pacific, if possible avoiding war and certainly not undertaking any major commitment of forces west of

Hawaii.[68] Stark's plan was quickly endorsed in principle by the Army and the President. It summed up the drift of U.S. policy over the previous two years and outlined what was to be the basic grand strategy of the wartime alliance.

Meanwhile, with the election over, the British renewed their suggestion of staff talks. On his return to Washington Lothian took the matter up with Hull and on 29 November 1940 he reported to the FO that Roosevelt had agreed.[69] Both sides prepared their positions carefully. During December HMG considerably restricted the amount of intelligence it was providing to U.S. attachés in London, mainly because Churchill had become more obsessed than ever about security but probably also because, as the Americans suspected, the British wanted to strengthen their negotiating position in the talks by giving the U.S. no time to prepare counter-arguments to British strategy.[70] For their part, the U.S. planners worked in grim earnest, aware that traditionally they had lacked the machinery for inter-Service and military–political co-ordination that had been developed over many years in Whitehall. They were determined not to be drawn into areas of mainly British interest. In particular, given the basic 'Atlantic First' strategy, they had no intention of moving part of the U.S. fleet to Singapore, as the British repeatedly suggested, and they believed that its retention at Hawaii would be a sufficient deterrent against Japan. They also kept in mind the lessons of the Great War, insisting, successfully, that in the event of a wartime 'association'— the word 'alliance' was amended on Roosevelt's instructions—[71] the U.S.A. would receive copies of any secret treaties the British had signed[72] and that her forces would be responsible for specific regions rather than being parcelled out under non-American commanders.

The American–British Conversations (ABC) were held in great secrecy and, as ever, the Americans emphasized that they were totally non-committal. Throughout, the discussions were about contingency plans that might come into effect if the U.S.A., against the present wishes of its people, was 'compelled' to resort to war. Nevertheless, both sides found them invaluable. There was fundamental agreement (ABC-1) that Germany was the primary threat to the security of both countries, that the defeat of Germany and Italy was the priority, that the Atlantic lifeline between Britain and the U.S.A. must be secured and that a purely defensive, deterrent policy should be maintained against Japan. Here was the core of Anglo-American co-operation—a commitment to mutual control of the Atlantic as the key to both countries' survival. Agreement was also reached (ABC-2) that Britain would have first charge on current U.S. aircraft production and would also receive the entire output of any new aircraft factories until such time as the U.S.A. might enter the war. From the British point of view these were gratifying developments. But significant areas of disagreement also emerged. Were the British wise to devote so much of their scarce resources to the defence of Egypt and the Eastern Mediterranean? Were they right that victory could be achieved by bombing, blockade and subversion without a major invasion of the continent? For the moment these questions were only tangential but we shall see in the next chapter that they became topics of serious debate in the summer of 1941. Another controversy, which *was* aired at length and with considerable bitterness, in the staff talks, concerned Far

Eastern strategy. Again this will be explained in detail later, in chapter nine, but it is necessary here to summarize the compromise reached by the two sides. The Admiralty delegates had continued to press the U.S.A. to send a fleet to Singapore. This the Americans resolutely refused to do, and Churchill, who, as we shall see, took a more complacent view of Japan than the Royal Navy, was adamant that they should not be pressed further. The eventual compromise was militarily complicated but diplomatically sound. Since the U.S.A. was pre-eminently concerned with the Atlantic and since it viewed South-East Asia as largely a British interest, the Americans would keep their main fleet at Pearl Harbor to contain Japan, but would transfer some units from it to the Atlantic, thereby relieving the pressure on the Royal Navy and permitting it to send a fleet to Singapore in accordance with traditional British policy. The British accepted this convoluted swap, aware as usual that they were not in a position to push the U.S.A. too hard and confident that Japan could be deterred from aggression. 'The first thing is to get the United States into the war. We can then settle how to fight it afterwards', Churchill instructed.[73] Britain was to pay dearly for this complacency, as we shall see.

The status of the ABC-1 agreement was ambiguous, and this ambiguity is typical of the state of the Anglo-American relationship in early 1941. Officially the conclusions were purely hypothetical—contingency plans in case the U.S.A. entered the war. Moreover, F.D.R. and, for the most part, the State Department had deliberately kept well out of the conference. Consequently the agreements had no necessary political significance, and this clearly limited their utility for both sides as a definition of policy. On the other hand, the absence of commitments and of political supervision allowed the U.S. delegation to explore strategic problems with a fulness and candour that would not otherwise have been possible. Furthermore, the ABC-1 agreement did have some immediate and important repercussions. One of its recommendations had been that in the event of war each country should set up a military mission in the other's capital, and it was quickly agreed after the conference that 'nucleus' missions should be exchanged at once. In one sense this only formalized existing arrangements but it did lead to a rapid increase in staff. For instance, in June 1939 the U.S. Naval Attaché in London had a staff of three assistant attachés, three enlisted men and four civil service employees. By the end of 1940 the complement of naval officers at the Embassy had grown to about 30 and by August 1941 the figure was 130.[74] Even more important, the strategic compromise set out in ABC-1 proved the blueprint for U.S. policy even before Pearl Harbor. During the spring and summer U.S. naval units were gradually moved from Hawaii to the Western Atlantic and this permitted the British, by the autumn of 1941, to prepare at last to send a small fleet to Singapore. Other U.S. actions, including the successive plans for naval escorts and the occupation of Iceland, followed the strategy agreed in ABC-1. In short, the staff talks epitomized the relationship between the two countries in early 1941—non-committal yet ever more complex, increasingly close yet forever wary, based on a narrow community of interest in the security of Britain, the British fleet and the Atlantic, beyond which lay a wide range of divergent interests around the world.

## D. Anglo-American diplomacy and the European neutrals

Of particular importance among those divergent interests during the winter of 1940–41 was Southern Europe. Hitler's peripheral strategy, designed to defeat Britian by severing her imperial supply lines, led to a major diplomatic and military effort to bring the Mediterranean under Axis control. Material and financial aid from America to Britain was thus not enough. It was also essential for the two countries to develop a co-ordinated policy towards the crucial European neutrals who were the target of Hitler's strategy. As Langer and Gleason observed: 'The issue of material support of Britain was simpler and more obvious, but for the long term the development of political co-operation was perhaps of greater significance.'[75]

During the autumn of 1940 Hitler concentrated his attentions on Spain and France. Influenced particularly by Admiral Raeder, he was anxious to secure bases for the more effective prosecution of the naval war against Britain. In the case of France, Dakar and the French fleet were the prizes. From Spain Hitler hoped to gain bases in the Canary Islands and facilities to mount Operation 'Felix' against the beleaguered British base at Gibraltar. It was generally believed that if Spain joined the Axis, Portugal would follow either voluntarily or under duress. Hitler could then secure control of the Azores, 900 miles west into the Atlantic on a line between Lisbon and New York, and the Cape Verde Islands off West Africa. Neither London nor Washington could contemplate such developments with equanimity. Although most of Britain's American convoys came across the North Atlantic via Halifax and Iceland, German control of the French fleet and/or the Atlantic islands, particularly the Canaries, would imperil Britain's vital north–south supply line around Africa and the Cape of Good Hope. This was the main route to the Middle East and Asia now that the Eastern Mediterranean was too dangerous for merchant shipping. By contrast, the Americans were more concerned about the east–west axis, and especially the Azores, because the South Atlantic from West Africa to the bulge of Brazil had long been identified by U.S. policymakers as the shortest and easiest route for a German invasion of the Western Hemisphere. But although their motives were slightly different, both governments clearly shared a common interest in maintaining Anglo-American control of the Atlantic. They were therefore agreed on the need to keep France and Spain out of the German camp, and, if possible, to draw them eventually into the war on the Allied side.

Despite these shared goals, however, the two countries disagreed about how best to achieve them.[76] British policy towards Spain resolved itself into an argument between Hugh Dalton, the aggressive Minister of Economic Warfare, who insisted on the integrity of the blockade, and Halifax, advised by Hoare, the influential British Ambassador in Madrid, who wanted to woo Franco with offers of badly-needed food and supplies. Hoare 'wants to keep them sweet; I want to keep them short' was Dalton's epigrammatic summary.[77] Although temperamentally Churchill and Eden were inclined to a tougher line, they and the War Cabinet accepted Hoare's repeated advice, and endorsed limited and carefully regulated aid. But the key to any effective policy lay with the U.S.A.; only she could provide the credits and the supplies, particularly wheat, cotton and oil, that Spain needed. After the election Churchill sent Roosevelt a personal appeal, suggesting that 'an offer by you to dole out food month by month so long as they keep out of the war might be decisive' and reminding him of the threat to the Western Hemisphere if Germany became established in Gibraltar and North-West Africa.[78] The U.S. agreed to a special shipment of relief supplies under Red Cross supervision, tying it to British acceptance of similar action to help Vichy, but the State Department, despite the advice of Alexander Weddell, its Ambassador in Madrid,[79] was never willing to countenance the British idea of a regular, controlled supply programme. Hull was acutely sensitive to press and Congressional opinion and insisted that any such aid must be conditional on public assurances of continued Spanish non-belligerency, whereas the British believed that only private ones were necessary or possible. At root the State Department did not share the FO's belief that there was a significant body of 'moderate' opinion in Spain that could be wooed away from collaboration with Hitler.

On Vichy, however, the positions were reversed. The British favoured a tough line, the Americans a more conciliatory one. In the summer of 1940, angry at France's surrender, Churchill had thrown HMG's support behind de Gaulle and the Free French, in the hope of rallying the French colonial empire to the Allied cause. But the fierce resistance encountered by the abortive expedition against Dakar in September showed that this hope would not easily be realized and that the French were determined to preserve some sort of independent existence. Consequently HMG backed away from its earlier commitment to de Gaulle and during the winter made secret and tentative overtures to Vichy and to General Weygand, the French Deputy General in North Africa. But the mutual bitterness engendered by the events of the summer proved very difficult to eradicate, and it was the U.S.A. rather than Britain that was best able to keep open contacts with Vichy. Unlike HMG, Roosevelt had maintained diplomatic relations. Indeed he sent Admiral Leahy, the former Chief of Naval Operations, as U.S. Ambassador in December. Through Washington, therefore, HMG could exert pressure on Pétain, and Roosevelt moved rapidly whenever Churchill asked him to do so—particularly to forestall possible movements of the French fleet.[80] But the London–Washington–Vichy channel was inevitably two-way. The Administration applied increasing pressure upon HMG to modify its blockade of unoccupied France—partly to satisfy domestic critics, notably ex-President Hoover, partly because they believed that Pétain was at the centre of a significant group opposed to the collaborationist line advocated by Laval and then by Darlan. Dalton, of course, resisted the U.S. pressure, but Halifax was sympathetic and Lothian openly enthusiastic—so much so that Dalton believed he was not representing HMG's views properly in Washington.[81] At the end of the year F.D.R. made a direct approach to Churchill, and, given the recent announcement of Lend-Lease and the fact that HMG wanted a similar policy with regard to Spain, the War Cabinet felt obliged to agree to the special relief shipment of essential supplies.[82] In March the British agreed to let another two ships carrying U.S. wheat through the blockade and they were unable to prevent the U.S. signing a supply agreement with Weygand, but, like State in the case of Spain, they remained opposed to a steady programme of aid without explicit French assurances, especially with regard to the fleet and its bases.

In the case of the Republic of Ireland, however, Britain and the U.S.A. found it easier to agree on both ends and means.[83] The crucial question here was whether De Valera would allow the British to use the three 'Treaty Ports' on the north and south-west coast of Eire. These had remained in British hands after Partition but Chamberlain had surrendered them as part of the Anglo-Irish agreement in 1938, on the grounds that a substantial military force would be needed to defend them and that the use of bases in France and Northern Ireland made them redundant.[84] But Churchill, who had been instrumental in ensuring the retention of the ports in 1921, was bitterly critical of the agreement, and the issue assumed a new importance in 1940, after the French collapse, when the air was thick with (German-inspired) rumours of an imminent Nazi invasion of the Republic. Prior to the November election the Roosevelt Administration was a moderating influence on HMG, warning against any pre-emptive strike and providing Eire with 20,000 rifles. But once the election was over—and with it the danger of an Irish-American backlash—F.D.R. and his Minister in Dublin, David Gray, became less tolerant of Irish neutrality. Despite impatience with Anglo-Irish quarrels and a basic sympathy for Irish aspirations, they shared HMG's immediate anxiety about the Treaty Ports. The bases would enable Britain to mount more effective guard over her American convoys in the North-West Approaches, much as the new U.S. bases in Newfoundland and the West Indies permitted extended patrolling of the Western Atlantic. Roosevelt and Gray backed HMG's appeals to Dublin on the matter, and when Churchill cut back on British supplies and shipping for Eire in December, Roosevelt refused to fill the gap, except for providing two ships in April 1941 as a token gesture.

Ultimately these Anglo-American debates about whether to woo or coerce the Western European neutrals were of limited significance for the future of the war. In each case the supplies sent were minimal both in quantity and in influence. De Valera's neutrality was unshakeable, while for Pétain and Franco the real determinant of policy was events. Nevertheless, these Anglo-American discussions throw further light on the nature of their relationship. Despite different diplomatic traditions, both governments had an immediate interest in keeping these neutrals out of the Axis camp to preserve Atlantic security. They differed on tactics, particularly over Spain and France, but in each case they managed to reach acceptable accommodations. Indeed their policies were often complementary—one providing the carrot, the other the stick—and despite periodic frustrations both governments recognized that this compromise had a certain validity and value.

*     *     *

By early 1941, however, the focus of Anglo-American diplomacy had shifted from Western Europe to the Balkans and North Africa. Despite Hitler's Grand Tour in October, it proved impossible to reconcile the rival territorial ambitions of France, Spain and Italy or to provide sufficient aid to pull Franco and Pétain completely into the German orbit. Meanwhile, Mussolini had resumed his empire-building with campaigns in Libya and Greece, and, as the Italians became bogged down, Hitler made his own preparations to intervene.[85] However, since the summer, he had also been considering plans for a possible invasion of Russia the following spring, and by the end of November, after a fruitless meeting with Molotov which highlighted the extent of German–Russian rivalry in East and South-East Europe, Hitler committed himself to this project, code-named 'Barbarossa', as his priority for 1941. The peripheral strategy against Britain was therefore abandoned. But it was still essential to stabilize the Balkan situation because of the threat it would otherwise pose to the right flank of 'Barbarossa'. In early 1941 Hitler consolidated his hold over Romania and brought Bulgaria within the Tripartite Pact. But similar pressure on Yugoslavia, an important source of raw materials and a bone of contention with Moscow, led to an anti-German coup in Belgrade on 27 March. This forced Hitler's hand, and on 6 April he launched simultaneous invasions of Yugoslavia and Greece. The Yugoslavs capitulated on 17 April and by the end of the month British troops had been forced out of Greece and the country was in German hands. The Germans were also successful in North Africa. In December and January General Wavell, the British Commander-in-Chief in the Middle East, had forced the Italians out of Egypt and had driven on into Libya, recapturing Tobruk and reaching Benghazi. In East Africa his forces also succeeded in driving the Italians out of Somalia. To help defend Libya Hitler had sent Rommel with, at this stage, a very small *Afrika Korps*, but in late March, against orders, Rommel mounted a surprise three-week offensive which pushed the British back into Egypt leaving only a beleaguered garrison in Tobruk.

In dealing with this two-pronged German threat to their position in the Middle East, the British had once again fallen between two stools. Until late January 1941 they had concentrated on Wavell's offensive into Libya, but then he was instructed to stabilize his front on Benghazi and prepare to transfer his best troops to the Balkans. Ideally HMG would have liked to send a force into Turkey, but Ankara did not want to provoke the Germans. The Greeks, however, already engaged with the Italians, were anxious for military support and on 24 February the War Cabinet formally decided to commit British and Commonwealth units in the hope of holding a line in central Greece. A sustained campaign there would obviously entail huge logistic commitments, and Churchill himself admitted that Greece was not strategically vital:

> The war turned in his opinion on our—(1) holding England (2) holding Egypt (3) retaining command of the sea (4) obtaining command of the air and (5) being able to keep open the American arsenals. The enterprise in Greece was an advance position which we could try to hold, without jeopardising our main position.

Nor was there much hope of military success. Churchill talked of the operation as 'a risk we must undertake', and the Chiefs of Staff argued that, while the 'risks of failure are serious', the 'disadvantages of leaving Greece to her

189

fate will be certain and far-reaching'.[86] What HMG feared was that if it did not help Greece then there would be no hope of drawing the Turks and the Yugoslavs into a Balkan front. Moreover, it was felt that world opinion, particularly in the United States, would react very badly to yet another failure by Britain to support her allies—Greece had been the beneficiary (should one say victim?) of a British guarantee in April 1939. But although Churchill and British policymakers regarded these considerations as decisive,[87] it remained an awful decision to make. Listen to Cadogan—veteran practitioner of the impossible art of matching Britain's resources to her responsibilities—wrestling with the pros and cons:

> *Monday, 24 February* . . . Read Chiefs of Staff report endorsing proposals for a Balkan expedition to help Greece. On all moral and sentimental (and consequently American) grounds, one is driven to the grim conclusion. But it *must*, in the end, be a failure. However, perhaps better to have failed in a decent project than never to have tried at all. . . . It's a nasty decision, but I *think*, on balance, I agree with it.[88]

In short, it was for diplomatic rather than military reasons that HMG embarked on the Greek campaign,[89] and American opinion was one of the considerations behind its decision, albeit a subordinate one. It is, however, clear that the British somewhat miscalculated the attitude of the U.S. Government, probably because they had taken too seriously the person and opinions of Col. Bill Donovan who visited London and then toured the Balkans in January and February as an unofficial observer for Frank Knox. Donovan, it will be remembered, had visited London in the same capacity in July 1940 and his optimistic report had helped convince Roosevelt that Britain could survive. Now he turned his persuasive talents on the wavering Balkan neutrals, stressing that they should form a common front against the Axis, that the U.S.A. was fully behind Britain and that she had no intention of letting Hitler win the war.[90] Eden told Churchill that the tour had been of 'very great value to us' and the PM thanked Roosevelt for Donovan's 'magnificent work' and his 'animating, heart-warming flame',[91] but if anything Donovan had greater influence in London than in South-Eastern Europe. He was convinced that Britain must make a major effort to keep the Germans out of Greece and British policymakers seem to have taken this as an authoritative statement of U.S. policy, which contributed to their eventual decision. Thus, in the crucial 24 February Cabinet meeting: 'It was recalled that Colonel Donovan had stressed in a telegram to the President the importance of the formation of a Balkan front. If we now forsake Greece it would have a bad effect in the United States.'[92] In fact, Donovan's conviction was based on a rather idiosyncratic strategic assessment, as is clear from the report he prepared for Knox in late February. He was sure that Hitler's basic aim was 'the overthrow of England' and that all his projects, including the Balkan campaign, were part of this grand design. Not only was a Balkan barrier of importance for British defence, but, he argued, it was also the key to ultimate victory. This could not be won by blockade and bombing alone: the German army had to be defeated in the field and the Balkans 'offer perhaps the only place for such a defeat'.[93] This analysis was at odds not only with British strategic thinking[94] but also with the priorities of the policymakers in Washington. Roosevelt himself said on 15 April that he did not regard the Balkans as vital but that he was a good deal troubled by Rommel's advance into Libya. U.S. military intelligence, an unsparing critic of British follies, called the decision to divide Wavell's victorious army and send troops to Greece the most disastrous interference in the conduct of military operations since Halleck pulled back the Union army from the environs of Richmond in 1862.[95] It therefore seems likely that HMG was misled by Donovan as to the importance attached by the 'sentimental' Americans to Greece. If so, it was not the first or the last time that one of Roosevelt's roving emissaries, armed only with a vague brief and strong personal convictions, had spread confusion as well as comfort in his wake.[96]

Aside from being a commentary on the hazards of personal diplomacy, this episode is of significance for a deeper reason. The differences on strategic priorities hinted at here were to become wider over the next few months. As the spring crisis deepened, with the German capture of Crete and mounting shipping losses in the Atlantic, U.S. policymakers increasingly questioned the wisdom of Britain's Mediterranean commitment and the basic principles of her peripheral strategy. More fundamental still, there were renewed doubts about Britain's ability to survive, and therefore about the future of the Royal Navy and the security of the Atlantic. It is to that crisis and its effect on the Anglo-American relationship that I now turn.

# PART THREE

# The Common-Law Alliance

Its Character and Development from
Lend-Lease to Pearl Harbor
March–December 1941

*The Webster's Dictionary definition of 'common-law marriage'
is: 'An agreement between a man and a woman to enter into the
marriage relation without ecclesiastical or civil ceremony, such
agreement being provable by the writings, declarations, or
conduct of the parties. In many jurisdictions, it is not recognized.'
That definition would seem to apply perfectly to the alliance
which existed between the United States and Great Britain
following the passage of Lend Lease.*
Robert E. Sherwood, 1948

*. . . we have to bear in mind that the American people total
130-odd million, and the United Kingdom 40-odd million, and
that numbers count. The tail can't swing the dog.*
Richard Casey, Australian Minister,
Washington, March 1941

# CHAPTER EIGHT

## War in Masquerade

### Roosevelt's Limited, Undeclared War against Hitler

*At least such subtle Covenants shall be made,*
*Till Peace it self is War in Masquerade.*
John Dryden, 1682

*... the failure of Roosevelt to speak clearly, or to act, is getting*
*people down. We are told that he must not get in front of his*
*own public opinion, but the question is will he get in front of*
*Hitler?*
Hugh Dalton, May 1941[1]

The spring of 1941 saw what the Foreign Office called 'the singular situation of two Great Powers ... actively entering upon an association before any serious attempt has been made by either to define ... the objective or the articles of that association'.[2] The relationship was not properly defined until the U.S.A. formally entered the war after Pearl Harbor (7 December), but during the intervening months its nature and limits became gradually more apparent. In the last part of the book I examine three of its principal facets—policy towards Germany and Europe, policy towards Japan and Asia, and preliminary planning for the post-war world. These are the respective themes of chapters eight to ten. In each case we shall see that the initiative within the relationship now lay increasingly with the United States. In 1937–40 (Part One) Britain had taken the lead; in 1940–41 (Part Two) relations were in a state of confused equilibrium. But 1941 marked the U.S.A.'s self-conscious assertion of her potential as a great power, even though she was not at war—a situation that often reduced the British Government to diplomatic impotence. In this chapter we shall see that, despite all HMG's efforts, Roosevelt remained reluctant to bring the U.S.A. into formal war, if he could still contain Hitler by proxy.

### A. The spring crisis

Not surprisingly, the reverses in Libya and Greece provoked rumbles of criticism in London. Churchill's position was never in doubt—the Government won an overwhelming vote of confidence on 7 May by 447 to 3—but there was growing dissatisfaction with his conduct of military operations. Critics said that the PM was surrounded by 'yes men'—'It is a complete dictatorship', Hankey told Halifax bluntly—and that only a major re-organization at the top could ensure an effective balance to Churchill's erratic brilliance. Some of those who complained were personal foes of the PM, but their opinions were shared by civil servants, visitors to London such as Menzies, and by the Chiefs of Staff themselves, one of whom observed: 'There is a great deal too much cigar stump diplomacy.'[3] Certainly Eden did not provide an effective counterweight. He shared Churchill's impatient desire for action—indeed he had been more responsible than the premier for the decision to send troops to Greece. In general, Eden's views were closer to Churchill's than Halifax's had been, and although both Foreign Secretaries suffered from Churchill's personal interventions in diplomacy Eden's response was a nervous, even petulant, irritation, in contrast to Halifax's calm resolution at times when he deemed his beloved *via media* to be threatened.[4]

The tense and gloomy mood in London deepened as May progressed. Three main threats emerged, at least as grave as the dangers of the previous summer.[5] First, there was the crisis in the Eastern Mediterranean. Having evicted the British ignominiously from the Balkans and Libya the Germans seemed ready in May to mount a pincer attack on the British position in the Middle East—with Rommel preparing a thrust into Egypt and Rashid Ali's pro-Axis coup in Iraq presaging a drive south to the Persian Gulf and Britain's vital oil fields. Prompt British action in Iraq expelled Rashid Ali by the end of May and a joint operation with de Gaulle secured Vichy-controlled Syria, but the Allied hold over the Eastern Mediterranean was further weakened by the successful if costly German airborne attack on Crete (20–30 May) where lack of RAF support for the Army and Navy once again revealed Britain's shortcomings in combined operations. Although Rommel's build-up was slower than expected, Wavell's premature counter-offensive, in response to badgering from Churchill, floundered as soon as it was launched in mid-June. Meanwhile, the British Isles were under increasing pressure during the spring. The regular night bombing of key cities intensified, with Plymouth, Liverpool, Glasgow and London experiencing some of the heaviest raids of the war.[6] Shipping losses also worsened from a winter average of 365,000 tons a month to 530,000 and 668,000 tons in March and April. If sinkings continued at that rate it would mean a net annual loss of a quarter of Britain's merchant fleet.[7] Although many of the spring sinkings occurred in the Mediterranean, the U-boat campaign in the Atlantic had been extended in late March to the east coast of Greenland and the depredations of German surface raiders forced the Admiralty to disperse nearly all the Home Fleet to protect British shipping. One of these raiders, the *Bismarck*, was destroyed on 27 May, but only after a desperate week-long chase in which Britain's premier battle-cruiser, the *Hood*, was sunk. Thirdly, there seemed a very real possibility that the Germans might gain control of French, Spanish and Portuguese possessions in the South Atlantic. In late April HMG feared an imminent German attack on Gibraltar, and Churchill made preparations for a pre-emptive strike against the Canaries, Cape Verdes and the Azores. As the Iberian situation eased in May, attention shifted to Vichy, where Darlan, following talks with Hitler, had proposed offering Germany bases and logistic support in Syria, and North and West Africa, including Dakar. On 15 May Pétain made his most collaborationist speech to date and it was not until early June that it became clear that Weygand had swung Vichy against Darlan's proposals.

Even those Americans who had been most confident in the summer of 1940 that Britain could survive invasion that year were less certain about her chances in 1941.[8] Throughout the winter senior U.S. policymakers were saying that the crisis for Britain would come in March or April, with Hitler's Balkan campaign and the continued bombings and sinkings providing a prelude to a massive attack on the British Isles accompanied by poison gas,[9] and Washington was profoundly doubtful in May that the British could hold the Middle East against the two-pronged Axis threat from Iraq and Libya. They are 'damned near licked in the Mediterranean Area', wrote Breckinridge Long on 22 May.[10] Throughout the spring, therefore, the Administration feared that Hitler would soon be able to turn back to Western Europe and threaten the U.S.A. in two ways. One would be via French and Spanish bases in the Atlantic, which would provide stepping stones for an invasion of the Western Hemisphere through unstable Brazil. The struggle in Vichy over Darlan's proposals was therefore a major worry in middle and late May. Berle, for instance, was convinced for a time that the French had capitulated completely and that Hitler would soon be using Casablanca and Dakar, and in mid-May an agitated Welles even urged F.D.R. to bring West Africa within the Monroe Doctrine.[11] The other anxiety was that Hitler might again prepare to invade Britain, or that, even if he didn't, the enormous pressure from bombing and shipping losses might lead to a revival of 'appeasement', the fall of Churchill and the search by a new government for a negotiated peace. When U.S. Army Intelligence criticized the British decision to divide Wavell's army and send troops to Greece, Stimson was furious:

> I pointed out that the success of the United States depended on the safety of the British fleet; that the safety of the British fleet and its preservation depended on the preservation of the Churchill government and the life of the promise made by Churchill last summer to keep the fleet at all odds; therefore, in circulating such a rumor or comment [critical of Churchill] they were attacking the vital safety of the United States . . .[12]

The mutterings of discontent in London about Churchill's handling of the war did nothing to allay these nagging fears. Even more sinister was the sensational arrival of Rudolf Hess, Hitler's deputy, in Scotland on 10 May. Although HMG quickly discovered that Hess was acting on his own, in a desperate one-man peace mission, rumour and speculation ran riot in the U.S.A. Even Roosevelt was not certain what was going on.[13]

\*     \*     \*

Throughout the spring, therefore, the security of the Atlantic remained of vital concern to the Roosevelt Administration. In March and early April, with Lend-Lease out of the way, the President had taken a number of steps to ease Britain's position. Urged on by Knox and Harriman he agreed to let British merchant and naval vessels be repaired in U.S. ports.[14] Ten coastguard cutters were despatched under Lend-Lease to Britain—a belated final settlement of the complicated Destroyers Deal—and British victories in East Africa enabled F.D.R. to take the Red Sea out of the combat zones prohibited to U.S. shipping. Most 'unneutral' of all were plans to construct two air and two naval bases in Scotland and Northern Ireland for use by the U.S.A. if and when she entered the war. Materials and equipment were obtained under Lend-Lease funds. The workmen were also American, but the British were responsible for their pay and for transporting labour and supplies. Construction began in late May.[15] But these and other actions—including the large shipbuilding programme now under way—were strictly irrelevant to the immediate problem, which was the protection of *existing* shipping. To borrow Stimson's metaphor, F.D.R. had to plug the leaks in the bath tub rather than pour in more water.[16] In early April, after Lend-Lease and another much needed vacation cruise, the President gave the Battle of the Atlantic his full attention. In mid-January he had ordered the Navy to be ready by 1 April to escort convoys all the way to Britain, and on 2–3 April he seemed ready to put those plans into effect. This would require a major reinforcement of the newly designated 'Atlantic Fleet'—really still an inexperienced squadron—and so he also agreed to transfer a carrier, three battleships, four cruisers and supporting destroyers from Pearl Harbor. But then Roosevelt backed off. By 10 April he was talking in terms of simply extending the Western Hemisphere Neutrality Patrol, which had been in existence since the beginning of the European war. He eventually settled for a line drawn north–south along the 26th meridian. This ran midway between Brazil and West Africa and included most of Greenland, where the U.S.A. had just acquired the right to construct bases. Within this area the Atlantic Fleet would report the movement of Axis vessels to the British, but would not escort convoys or shoot, unless attacked first. In mid-April F.D.R. also postponed his earlier fleet move, agreeing only to transfer one carrier and four destroyers, which passed through the Panama Canal on 6–7 May. The new scheme went into operation on 24 April, but as with Roosevelt's original patrol in the autumn of 1939, there were not enough ships to make it effective. 'So that is about the state of our convoy policy', wrote Long in the State Department. 'We have got a tadpole that some day may be a frog.'[17]

Why did Roosevelt back down? In theory he could have ordered escorts under his authority as Commander-in-Chief. However, it was generally accepted that escorts would be tantamount to war—as F.D.R. had admitted himself to the press on 21 January.[18] He seems therefore to have decided that in order to escort he would have to go to Congress—much as he had initially felt about the destroyers the previous summer—and he told his advisers on 10 April that if he did so at that time he would probably be defeated.[19] On 31 March Senator Tobey and Representative Sauthoff had introduced a joint resolution to prohibit the use of U.S. vessels for convoys or escorts. Stimson begged the President to bring the resolution to a floor vote and defeat it, but although Roosevelt at first seemed enthusiastic,[20] he was probably trying to get Stimson off his back, and in the end he preferred to have the resolution blocked in committee. Moreover, his mail, to which F.D.R. always paid particular attention, was overwhelmingly against escorts, in part because of the campaign sponsored in conjunction with the Tobey resolution by the isolationist 'America First' organization.[21] A further reason for F.D.R.'s change of mind was the Russo-Japanese non-aggression pact signed on 13 April. With her northern flank more secure, Japan was now freer to move south, and Roosevelt, urged strongly by Hull, felt that to weaken the Pacific Fleet at this juncture might encourage her to do so.

\*     \*     \*

Despite the disillusionment of November 1940, there seems to have been an expectation in London that the U.S.A. would enter the war in April or May 1941.[22] Roosevelt's timidity over escorts, coupled with the disasters in Greece, therefore left British leaders tense and anxious. Churchill was particularly discouraged by a cable from Roosevelt on 1 May. To his recent requests for U.S. diplomatic pressure on Portugal, Turkey and Vichy—key points in the worsening situation—the President had returned a sympathetic but essentially negative reply. More disturbing still, Churchill detected a note of complacency about the effect of a collapse in the Mediterranean on Britain's overall position. In short, it seemed to him 'as if there has been a considerable recession across the Atlantic, and that quite unconsciously we are being left very much to our fate'.[23] FO/A thought the PM was taking too gloomy a view of the cable and it dissuaded him from sending his draft reply, which had begun: 'Naturally I am depressed by your message in spite of all the kindness it conveys.' However, the FO did agree that Roosevelt needed a push: 'The President has always shown great skill in making it appear that his public was leading him rather than the reverse; he has not always shown an equal facility for coming out into the open and frankly leading them at a crisis.' Accordingly the message was rewritten in a more encouraging tone, but with an explicit request for the U.S.A. to enter the war—the first Churchill had made since 15 June 1940:

> Mr. President, I am sure that you will not misunderstand me if I speak to you exactly what is in my mind. The one decisive counterweight I can see to balancing the growing pessimism in Turkey, the Near East, and Spain would be if the United States were immediately to range herself with us as a belligerent power. If that were possible I have little doubt that we could hold the situation in the Mediterranean until the weight of your munitions gained the day.

In his cable F.D.R. had mentioned that he expected 'to go on the air within the next two weeks' and Churchill used this as a further opportunity to put him on the spot: 'I shall await with deep anxiety the new broadcast which you contemplate. It may be the supreme turning point.'[24]

Despite having given Roosevelt a veiled ultimatum that his forthcoming speech must be a declaration of war or something close to it, HMG still wondered what further pressure could be applied. On 9 May Eden, whose itchy desire to 'do something' was getting Cadogan down, wanted a further direct appeal to the President about escorts, in view of the recent shipping losses, but FO/A counselled patience—HMG must wait for the big speech and remember that Roosevelt could only move when he felt there was a consensus behind him.[25] But then came news on the 14th that the speech had been postponed for a fortnight because of F.D.R.'s ill-health. Eden returned to the charge, but there were no obvious avenues of attack open. Twelve months before, Churchill and Lothian had played on American fears that Britain might surrender. As we have seen, those fears recurred in May 1941, and Churchill was not averse to playing upon them a little by encouraging press speculation about Hess.[26] But even the fretful Eden felt that explicit threats of surrender and the loss of the fleet might backfire. Churchill told him on 15 May, five days after Hess's arrival: 'The master key to American action would be the knowledge that the British Empire could at this time get out of the war intact, leaving the future struggle with a Germanized Europe to the United States. But this you did not want me to say.'[27] An alternative tactic, also employed the previous summer, was likewise rejected. On 7 May, and again on the 21st, Halifax suggested that a new offer of bases in any part of the Commonwealth might impress U.S. opinion and draw it closer to Britain. But the FO warned that Americans would see through the ploy as another attempt at entanglement, and Churchill minuted: 'I don't think we ought to press them too much; and certainly this is no time for us to give more.' For his part, Eden entered another caveat about the desirability of global American intervention:

> Incidentally do we want to see U.S. bases established, say, at Auckland & in Fiji, at Takoradi, & Trincomalee? Some of these are a far cry for U.S., others are not, and I would not happily contemplate a wholesale extension of U.S. bases throughout the British Commonwealth.[28]

On one point of tactics, however, Churchill was quite clear. Any voluntary forward act by the U.S.A. in the Atlantic must not be discouraged, however inconvenient it might be for Britain in the short term. To cite one of numerous examples—in late April the U.S. Navy asked the British Military Mission in Washington, hypothetically, whether Britain could provide troopships if the U.S.A. should decide to send troops to Iceland. The Mission naturally pointed to the enormous demands on British troopships in the Mediterranean and expressed the hope that the U.S.A. would be able to provide them herself. Churchill, however, was incensed to learn of this reply: 'What does the convenience of our shipping mean compared to engaging the Americans in the war? A negative answer like this is chilling and ill-suited to our present purpose.'[29] This was to be his refrain throughout 1941. Get America into the war, by hook or by crook; all else was secondary.

Since Roosevelt was apparently waiting for his own public, British leaders also considered how best to give the latter a push as well, particularly after the slump in American opinion following the Balkan collapse. Despite considerable efforts, not notably successful, to improve British publicity in the U.S.A., and despite the importunities of the Ministry of Information, leading British policymakers remained convinced that an overt propaganda campaign would be counter-productive and that HMG's policy should still be one of presenting the facts for the U.S. media to disseminate as they saw fit. Nevertheless, facts could be presented in different ways—even apparently hard data such as shipping losses. On 28 April it seemed that the figures for that month would be much better than originally feared, and Churchill, keen as ever to restrict the circulation of sensitive information, argued in Cabinet that if unexpectedly low figures were now published American isolationists would question the gravity of Britain's predicament. Publication was therefore deferred, but even without it Vandenberg and others tried to belittle Britain's losses. When it also became clear that the April figures were after all very bad, the Cabinet decided on 8 May to publish them—but as part of a cumulative list of sinkings since May 1940 and without breaking them down according to theatre. This conveyed a sense of mounting crisis while concealing the fact that most of the increased losses in April had been incurred not in the Atlantic but as a result of the Greek campaign.[30] Behind this debate about publishing losses, which rumbled on through May and June, lay the perennial problem of whether Americans would be more affected by good news or bad news. Beaverbrook and Eden felt that Britain should cautiously encourage Americans' fears about their security, by adopting 'for their benefit rather a pessimistic attitude' and by dramatizing the Battle of the Atlantic to the U.S. press. Attlee and Sinclair, the Labour and Liberal leaders, believed that publicity should concentrate on Britain's successes, a view with which both Churchill and the Admiralty were inclined to agree. They feared that highlighting the abundant grim news would further dishearten domestic morale and they also believed that Americans should be educated out of the idea that they should only enter the war if Britain were at her last gasp.[31] Beaverbrook and Eden were invited to recommend improvements in British publicity, but they could suggest little beyond better treatment of the disgruntled U.S. press corps in London. And, as the Beaver admitted to Churchill, he could get no clear answer as to which kind of news to spotlight: 'the loss of the Hood or the sinking of the Bismarck?'[32]

In Washington, too, the pressure on F.D.R. was increasing. Stimson and Knox, supported by Hopkins, gradually wore down Hull's opposition to further fleet moves, and on 14 May, with the Far Eastern situation somewhat easier, Roosevelt agreed to transfer three battleships, four cruisers and 14 destroyers to the Atlantic. These duly passed through the Canal between 2 and 5 June.[33] In addition, F.D.R. responded to the crisis in Vichy by ordering the Army on 22 May to prepare expeditionary forces for possible pre-emptive strikes against the Azores and the Atlantic islands within one month.[34] But these moves were undertaken in great secrecy. The Cabinet 'hawks' wanted some dramatic public act to mobilize American opinion, which, they believed, was waiting for a lead from the White House. Even the loyal Frankfurter was disappointed at the President's lack of leadership.[35] There was also a growing feeling that the U.S.A. would have to become a full belligerent. Stimson, Knox and Ickes had felt this since the previous summer, the Navy had been expecting it from 1 April, and on 14 May Morgenthau told Hopkins that during the previous week or so he had concluded 'for the first time that if we were going to save England we would have to get into this war, and that we needed England, if for no other reason, as a stepping stone to bomb Germany. I told him that we also needed the British Fleet.'[36] Although State was characteristically more cautious, with

Hull and Long still feeling that the U.S.A. should not declare war until she was ready, Adolf Berle, previously the Department's most resolute and acute exponent of 'hemispherism', now believed that the country had to decide between entry into the war and a British compromise peace.[37] Roosevelt's response was a familiar one. As in June 1940, he remarked on several occasions during the spring, both to the Cabinet 'hawks' and to Halifax, that he was waiting for an 'incident' and that he expected one to come soon. Did he mean by this an attack on a U.S. ship or something much larger in scale? Did he envisage it as grounds for requesting a declaration of war or simply for escorting convoys? Was he talking honestly or simply trying to relieve the pressure upon him? No certain answers can be given to these questions. As usual, Roosevelt's remarks were oblique, and his listeners were left to interpret them according to their own predilections.[38]

*     *     *

May 1941 must have been one of the most miserable months of Franklin Roosevelt's long and turbulent presidency. Both the British Government and his own closest advisers were urging him to take the final step and go to war with Germany, for fear that otherwise Britain might soon be defeated or forced to surrender, thereby exposing the U.S.A. to attack across the Atlantic.[39] Yet F.D.R. judged that Congress was opposed to such a move and that the American people, whose whole-hearted commitment was essential for any durable war effort, still had no real grasp of modern war and the threat to U.S. security.[40] During the spring his health—never good—was undermined by a series of heavy colds, and for much of the first half of May he was in bed with a debilitating intestinal infection. Illness accentuated Roosevelt's tendency to procrastinate in the face of a big decision. He postponed the broadcast scheduled for 14 May and did not hold a Cabinet meeting for three weeks, but all this only increased speculation that something momentous was in the air.

The speech was finally given on Pan American Day, 27 May. It was a typically vigorous statement of the Nazi threat to the Western Hemisphere, which concluded with the announcement of a state of 'unlimited national emergency' to strengthen U.S. defences 'to the extreme limit of our national power and authority'. At a press conference the next day, however, the President indicated that he had no plans to escort convoys, to ask for repeal of the Neutrality Act or even to issue the specific Executive orders by which alone he could assume the additional emergency powers.[41] It seemed like the familiar pattern of fine words but minimal actions, reminiscent of the Quarantine and Charlottesville addresses, and the Cabinet hawks were bitterly disappointed. 'Exactly what does it mean?', officials in London wanted to know.[42] In fact, the speech was a typically adroit attempt by the President to keep his balance amidst the competing pressures upon him, and it seems that in addition to his usual aims of educating and sounding out opinion, he had two specific objectives in mind. One was to provide the lead for which the British and his own advisers had been calling, without outraging the isolationists. Attorney-General Bob Jackson told the U.S. Treasury that 'an unqualified national emergency was being proclaimed primarily for its psychological effect in impressing upon the country the threat of aggression and the need for strengthening our defenses in all respects'. It was hoped that the proclamation 'alone will in and of itself have the desired psychological effect' without recourse to the specific emergency powers. F.D.R. was surprised and elated by the telegrams he received. 'They're ninety-five per cent favorable!' he said. 'And I figured I'd be lucky to get an even break on this speech.'[43] Secondly, F.D.R. probably saw the address as a necessarily indirect way of announcing and justifying further action in the Atlantic. He would not go to Congress, as Stimson wanted, and seek explicit approval for using force to protect convoys. But his speech contained clear warnings about the importance of Britain, Dakar and 'the island outposts of the New World' for U.S. security, a statement that the delivery of supplies to Britain was 'imperative' and a reiterated promise that 'all measures necessary to deliver the goods will be taken'. The speech gave no indications of what measures he had in mind, but F.D.R. had probably satisfied his conscience that he had given the American people fair warning. Given the refractory state of Congress, it was a compromise between constitutional propriety and political discretion.

Moreover, F.D.R. had a specific move in mind, and he was at pains to spell it out to Halifax on 28 May, because of the need to give the British further encouragement. Within the next month, he said, he would send U.S. troops to relieve the British garrison in Iceland, if HMG and the Icelandic Government agreed. He envisaged Iceland as an eventual trans-shipment point for Atlantic convoys. This would enable U.S. merchant ships to take over responsiblity for the Western Atlantic, thereby assisting the British without entailing a 'dog fight with Congress' over repeal of the Neutrality Act.[44] All this could be done peacefully and with little more than an extension of the existing patrol zone. By contrast, the other option F.D.R. had been examining in May—a move in the South Atlantic—seemed much more hazardous. It was clear that France, Spain and even Britain's ancient ally, Portugal, would resist unilateral U.S. intervention in their possessions, and the U.S. Army, in addition to being unable to mount such an operation properly until the autumn, was adamant that morale would suffer disastrously if America's first campaign of the war was other than 'overwhelmingly successful'.[45] In any case, by the end of May the threat in the South Atlantic had receded, as the tide in Vichy ran strongly against collaboration and Hitler's immediate interest in Russia became ever more apparent. Roosevelt was therefore free to take a further step to relieve the British and satisfy the hawks, in a form that would not seem too outrageous to domestic opinion.

Although the 27 May speech did not go as far as HMG had wished, the impending move into Iceland was very encouraging. Furthermore, after analysing the speech and accompanying intelligence, FO/A decided that Roosevelt was now definitely eager for an incident and that the shooting would soon begin.[46] Indeed it seemed for a moment as if an incident had occurred. From 11 June news filtered through to Washington about the sinking on 21 May of an unarmed U.S. merchant ship, the *Robin Moor*, by a U-boat in the South Atlantic. Senior officials in the British Embassy, among them Purvis, Monnet and Keynes, saw this as a chance to force

Roosevelt's hand. On 12 June they gave Hopkins a memo suggesting that here was the opportunity and justification to turn the Atlantic patrol into a full-scale security patrol using force. They also pressed Halifax to suggest a direct Churchill–Roosevelt message on the same lines, arguing that F.D.R. knew he had to enter the war but was putting off a decision, apparently insensitive to the mounting crisis in the Middle East. Halifax, however, counselled patience, and in the end his views prevailed after Hopkins had agreed on the 13th to give F.D.R. a note, as from himself, embodying the points in the Embassy memo.[47] Roosevelt, however, was unmoved. On 14 June he froze German and Italian assets in the U.S.A. and two days later ordered them to close all their consulates from 10 July, but both these measures had been contemplated for some time and were really a response to growing Axis propaganda and espionage in the U.S.A. On the *Robin Moor*, the President contented himself by citing it to Congress as proof of his warnings about Germany on 27 May. Meanwhile, in what was clearly a hint, word was passed to the Embassy that F.D.R. was very grateful for HMG's 'admirable' restraint in not pushing him farther than he could go.[48]

Roosevelt's failure to exploit the *Robin Moor* 'incident' is not necessarily significant. The confused and belated news of the sinking was hardly likely to arouse American opinion. It may be that at times in the trough of May 1941 F.D.R. did genuinely hope that the Germans would provide a *casus belli* to get him off the hook.[49] But, as we shall see, he had good reasons for *not* wanting to get into formal war, and his long-held policy of containing Hitler by proxy was given new validity by the developments of midsummer. In addition to Britain he now had a second front line—Soviet Russia.

## B. Russia—respite or turning point?

'The longer the perspectives, the more does June 1941 appear as one of the great turning points in history.'[50] Forty years is hardly time for mature reflection, but there can surely be little quarrel with Vojtech Mastny's conclusion. Not only did the attack on Russia on 22 June (Operation 'Barbarossa') prove to be Hitler's fatal mistake—the one above all others that lost him the war—but it also provided both the opportunity and the justification for Soviet expansion, which is the main theme of the post-war era and probably of the second half of the twentieth century. In the medium term, the invasion of Russia had three profound effects upon the Anglo-American relationship. First, it gradually reduced the direct threat to Britain and thence to the U.S.A., enabling both countries to fight the war by proxy once more, at least for the moment. In consequence, readjustments in U.S. material aid had to be made, and these brought to the surface latent Anglo-American disagreements about strategic priorities. Secondly, the desperate fighting on Russia's western borders left Japan free to expand into South-East Asia. At the same time the reduced threat in Western Europe enabled the U.S.A. to take a firmer position, militarily and diplomatically, to contain this threat. From July 1941, therefore, a considerable shift in U.S. Far Eastern policy took place. Thirdly, the entry of Russia into the war altered the character of the Anglo-American relationship. The courting couple, one might say, became part of a *ménage à trois*. Three sets of national aims and aspirations had now to be harmonized—Britain's largely defensive, as befitted a satiated power in decline, unlike the expansionary goals of Russia and America, the two virile young giants on the international stage. The effect of 'Barbarossa' on the Far East and post-war planning will be discussed in the next two chapters. In this section and the next we shall concentrate on the consequences for logistics and strategy.

But it must be stressed that even these medium-term consequences were initially far from evident. In the spring and summer most British and U.S. policymakers felt that 'Barbarossa' would prove no more than a brief sideshow, whatever they claimed retrospectively.[51] Basically they assumed that Hitler's primary aim was to conquer Britain, and that all else was part of that plan. Even after Operation 'Sealion' had been called off in October 1940, brilliant German deception measures encouraged the belief that invasion of Britain was still intended. Similarly, German moves into the Balkans and Eastern Europe were interpreted for some time as part of Hitler's peripheral strategy against Britain's imperial lifelines. As early as February 1941 the State Department had received accurate intelligence about 'Barbarossa' through its commercial attaché in Berlin, but it was not until May that both governments accepted that Hitler's build-up was definitely directed against Russia. Even then it was generally assumed that this would be a brief diversion. The initial expectation was that Hitler would issue an ultimatum and Stalin would capitulate without a fight. When, in early June, most British and U.S. policymakers came round to the view that the Germans were going to mount a full-scale invasion of Russia, the general opinion was that it would take them only three to twelve weeks to achieve total victory. The military in both capitals were particularly pessimistic about Russian chances, and, although Roosevelt and Churchill were probably more hopeful, neither could afford to take any risks. It is therefore hardly surprising that on 25 June Churchill ordered Britain's defences to be 'at concert pitch for invasion from September 1'. This instruction was not withdrawn until 2 August.[52]

On the other hand, every week that Hitler was occupied in Russia would be a respite for Britain and, by extension, the United States. Swallowing his ideological antipathy for Communism, Churchill had told F.D.R. that Britain would naturally 'give all encouragement and any help we can spare to the Russians following principle that Hitler is the foe we have to beat'. On the evening of 22 June he made a worldwide broadcast to this effect. Through Winant F.D.R. had verbally promised that he would publicly support 'any announcement that the Prime Minister might make welcoming Russia as an ally', and this he duly did, albeit more cautiously, in a statement and a press conference on 23–24 June.[53] Churchill's pledge of 15 June accurately prefigured the lines of Anglo-American policy for the first month or so—'all encouragement' but little material help. A British Military Mission arrived in Moscow on 27 June, and on 12 July the two countries signed a declaration pledging mutual aid and no separate peace, Eden having first ascertained from Winant that this would not offend American, and particularly Catholic, opinion.[54] In Washington the Russians made a formal request on 30 June for massive material help, and negotiations about this proceeded cautiously for the next month. But by late July it had become apparent that, despite immense Russian losses, the Germans were not going to win a quick victory. The *Blitzkrieg* strategy of limited economic mobilization for lightning mobile war was inapplicable to a country of Russia's vast size, impenetrable terrain and huge manpower resources. Moreover, the Germans had grossly underestimated the quantity and quality of the Russian forces, and their own armies were ill-equipped for a long campaign. Once they failed in their principal task—the early annihilation of the main Russian armies west of the Dnieper and Dvina rivers—the campaign degenerated into a conventional struggle, with ill-defined objectives, in which Russia's superior capacity for total war could gradually be brought into play.[55] As the German advance slowed, HMG took the agonizing decision on 20 July to send the U.S.S.R. 200 fighters, and at the beginning of August F.D.R. intervened personally to accelerate the delivery of U.S. tools and aircraft. On the 2nd the U.S.A. and the U.S.S.R. formally signed their own mutual aid declaration. The mood of cautious confidence that Russia would be able to survive into the winter was given a boost by Harry Hopkins' brief visit to Moscow at the end of July. Hopkins never saw the Front, which was probably just as well. His optimistic reports were based on his assessment of Stalin and his advisers. He played a role similar to that of Donovan a year before—providing personal testimony, from a source F.D.R. trusted, that it was worth supporting an opponent of Hitler.[56]

As Britain and the U.S.A. became more confident about Russia and moved slowly from verbal to material support, so F.D.R. had less need to force the issue in the Atlantic. When 'Barbarossa' began, the initial reaction of most of his military and naval advisers, with Stimson and Knox in the lead, was that he should use 'this precious and unforeseen period of respite' to intensify U.S. naval support for Britain before Hitler turned back again on Western Europe. Hopkins too 'was particularly earnest that we should push the President for action during this precious time', Stimson recorded.[57] But F.D.R. would not be hurried. He remained adamantly opposed to moving a further quarter of the Pacific Fleet through the Panama Canal, and although he announced on 7 July that U.S. Marines had started to arrive in Iceland, instead of the candid statement of policy that Stimson as usual had wanted, the President simply said that he had ordered the Navy 'that all necessary steps be taken to insure the safety of the communications in the approaches between Iceland and the United States' and between the U.S.A. 'and all other strategic outposts'.[58] Behind this vague statement was a renewed debate about escorting. On 2 July the President had tentatively approved Hemisphere Defense Plan Three, setting out arrangements for the escort of all convoys between U.S. ports and Iceland and including provision for any allied or neutral merchant ships to join. Under this plan Axis vessels in the extended Western Hemisphere zone were 'potential threats' to be attacked 'as a measure short of war and one that may not necessarily lead to the existence of a formal war status'. But then, as in April, F.D.R. backed down. Plan Three was revised and a new version—Plan Four—was promulgated on 11 July. Under this the provision for escorting Allied or neutral shipping was only to come into effect upon the issue of specific orders, and Axis vessels would only be trailed rather than attacked on sight. Pressed by Knox, F.D.R. agreed to implement Plan Four from 26 July, but the orders to escort Allied and neutral shipping were not issued.[59]

Behind the President's vacillations can be detected the same mixture of motives that had obtained in April and May. Once more he was anxious about the Far East, now that Japan's northern flank was secure with Russia fighting for her life in the west, and he wanted to maintain a strong deterrent presence at Pearl Harbor. 'I simply have not got enough Navy to go round', he complained.[60] Congressional opinion was also unsettled. Hull and Welles had endorsed the idea of seeking repeal of the key sections of the Neutrality Act, so as to permit armed U.S. merchant ships to travel into belligerent ports, but the word from Senate leaders in early July was 'that, while in their judgment there would be an undoubted majority in both Houses in favor of revision of the act, they feel that the debate would be prolonged and that the isolationist group would filibuster on the issue'.[61] Even more disturbing was the resolution introduced by Senator Wheeler on 30 June calling for an investigation of charges that the U.S. Navy was already escorting Allied convoys and shooting at German submarines. This was buried in committee, following F.D.R.'s usual tactic, but it and the advice from the Senate leaders can only have reinforced the President's caution. In any case, he had less need to act vigorously. As long as the Russians held out, the pressure on Britain, and therefore the pressure by Britain on him, was reduced. Aid to Russia was politically easier than naval escorts, even allowing for American anti-Communist sentiments, and continued Russian resistance would also serve as a sort of deterrent against Japan. In short, the 'decision to aid Russia' was an ideal compromise for a President who preferred to contain Hitler by proxy rather than hurriedly to commit his country to formal war.[62]

\*     \*     \*

Despite sending the obligatory messages of effusive praise to F.D.R. for all that he was doing, Churchill and Eden both felt in late June that he was 'slackening up'.[63] Although shipping losses were less in June, the figures were still grave, and Churchill commented privately, and even obliquely to F.D.R., about the futility of a policy which allowed shipping to be sunk at a high rate and relied upon replacing the losses by future construction.[64] But once again HMG felt diplomatically impotent. In early July, Cripps, the Ambassador in Moscow, and Sargent, the Deputy Under Secretary at the FO, both wanted a direct request to F.D.R. for formal belligerency— Cripps for its effect on Russian morale, Sargent because he reposed little faith in Russia's capacity to resist. But FO/A, Eden and Churchill all felt that they must not seem to be 'fussing' the President, and Cadogan noted, acutely, that from the point of view of hemisphere defence—the avowed basis of F.D.R.'s policy of aid to Britain—there was now less need for immediate U.S. action. In the end Halifax was allowed to communicate the gist of Cripps's argument to Roosevelt, but the Ambassador was even more anxious than the FO not to harry the President, and his very circumspect remarks elicited only the usual reply: F.D.R., Halifax reported on 7 July, thought that the U.S. move into Iceland would mean that the 'whole thing would now boil up very quickly and that there would very soon be shooting'.[65] All HMG could do was to try to facilitate the shooting that F.D.R. professed himself so anxious to see. Churchill was therefore furious to learn that some junior British staff officers had given their U.S. counterparts the erroneous impression that HMG would prefer the U S. Navy to concentrate on escorting shipping in the Western Atlantic, rather than all the way to Britain. 'Whoever has put this about has done great disservice, and should be immediately removed from all American contacts', he instructed in an 'Action This Day' minute on 28 June. 'No question of Naval Strategy in the Atlantic is comparable with the importance of drawing the Americans to this side.'[66]

This sense of priorities governed Churchill's response to the U.S. occupation of Iceland. When his advisers raised the question of whether or not British troops should stay, and if so how many and for how long, the PM swept such matters aside as 'trifles the discussion of which should not obscure still less obstruct the proceedings. Nothing matters in this place in the first instance except the moral effect.'[67] Like Roosevelt, he had a domestic constituency to consider, and, as we have seen, one of his major justifications for fighting on had always been the expectation of imminent U.S. entry into the war. He felt it especially important 'to give the people some encouragement at this particularly grim and fateful moment' and consequently was determined to secure the maximum possible publicity for the U.S. action.[68] Roosevelt, eyeing his own public and Congress, naturally wanted to avoid this, but he had eventually agreed on 24 June that 'the best course might be to be prepared for leakage and let publicity immediately follow'. Churchill was not deterred. Referring to this comment about leaks, he told Eden: 'We must make sure of this and that it should come from Icelandic sources.' He instructed that the Ministry of Information should exploit the event to the full and gave the lead himself in a statement to the Commons which called it 'one of the most important things that has happened since the war began' and hinted, in language that cannot have pleased F.D.R., about the Hemisphere Defense Plan for escorting British and U.S. shipping.[69] It was therefore a great disappointment to HMG when Roosevelt insisted for several weeks that journalists, especially Americans, be kept out of Iceland, to avoid publicity about the size of the U.S. forces and the extent of Anglo-American co-operation there. It was even more galling when he also insisted that HMG and not the U.S. Government must take the blame for the news blackout.[70]

## C. Problems of strategy and supply

The German invasion of Russia and the sustained Russian resistance profoundly affected other aspects of the Anglo-American relationship, in areas where there were considerable differences not only between but within the two governments.

One of these was the question of the strategic importance of the Middle East. The May crisis had given rise to a sharp exchange between Churchill and the Chiefs of Staff. While agreeing with the PM that 'the loss of Egypt and the Middle East would be a disaster of the first magnitude', they reminded him that Britain could survive as long as she was not successfully invaded and did not lose the Battle of the Atlantic. Dill, the Chief of the Imperial General Staff, went further. He argued that if a choice had to be made Britain should sacrifice Egypt rather than Singapore—a position diametrically opposite to Churchill's. All the Chiefs feared in May that the premier's preoccupation with the Eastern Mediterranean might lead to an over-commitment of forces at the expense of the British Isles.[71] Their anxieties were shared by the U.S. military who saw the North Atlantic axis as crucial and who felt increasingly, like Dill, that reinforcing the Far East was next in priority. The U.S. Navy was more sympathetic to Churchill's Mediterranean emphasis, but the Army, and even some senior admirals, for example Kelly Turner, believed that Britain was weakening herself unnecessarily by trying to defend the whole Middle East. As they saw it, her vital interests lay in the Persian Gulf, which commanded the key oil fields and the access to the Indian Ocean, as well as being, from midsummer, a supply route to Russia's southern front. If, as seemed likely, the whole Middle East could not be held, this seemed the crucial area, rather than Palestine, Syria and even Egypt, particularly since shipping bound for the Far East was already going the long way around the Cape because Suez was unsafe.[72] Undoubtedly U.S. policymakers had a point. British leaders were reluctant to define their nebulous but expansive Middle Eastern interests very precisely. Of course, a plausible case could be made out for the massive effort to defend Egypt. It was desirable to engage the Germans wherever possible, and withdrawal from Egypt would entail massive losses of men and equipment as well as having a disastrous effect on morale in the Arab world. But essentially these were rationalizations. British strategy throughout the war was based on the principle of 'what we have, we hold'. Only for those few desperate days in late May 1940, just before Dunkirk, was the idea of cutting Britain's imperial losses aired in Cabinet. The war, in fact, had permitted the British to recover some of the ground they had lost in Egypt—to reassert a presence that had been eroded by two decades of Wafdist nationalism culminating in the 1936 Anglo-Egyptian agreement. It was only natural that military strategy should reflect underlying national political interests. But it was sometimes difficult to justify that strategy in purely military terms to a quasi-ally that did not share the same interests. This of course became even more apparent in 1942. In the Far East, Burma was subsequently to present a similar problem.

But, whatever their views on the importance of the Middle East, all U.S. officials were agreed that Britain must put her house in order there. This was the opinion of the U.S. Army Intelligence, of American diplomats in Egypt and even of the sympathetic Harriman, who toured the theatre in June and July.[73] In their view the disasters in Greece and especially Crete, followed by Wavell's abortive counter-offensive in mid-June, highlighted the need for an integrated command structure for British forces in the Middle East. Although the Army, Navy and RAF were well co-ordinated at policymaking level, through the Chiefs of Staff and Defence Committees in London, theatre operations were conducted by the three Services independently on a principle of consultation and co-operation. The U.S. Army, in particular, believed that this lack of an overall theatre commander helped to explain the British failures in combined operations, such as Crete, where the lack of air cover had been disastrous for both Army and Navy. This criticism in turn reflected deeper differences in military philosophy between the two countries. Since 1918 the British had had a separate Air Force; in the U.S.A., by contrast, until 1947 the air arm remained part of the Army, on the principle that its key role was to provide support for ground troops. The case for an independent air force was that it had a strategic rather than merely a tactical role—the argument that saturation bombing would prove a war-winning weapon in its own right. This became an axiom in British policy-making circles during the 1930s and in the U.S.A. it became unanswerable after the development of the A-bomb. But in 1941 the U.S. Army fought tenaciously against a separate air force, and it used the British débâcles in Crete and the Western desert as evidence for its case.[74]

In the summer of 1941 these arguments about strategy and command structure in the Middle East were not pushed to a conclusion. The Americans were well aware of Britain's sensitivity and intransigence on the question of holding Egypt—in discussions with the Americans in late July Dill loyally trod the Churchillian line—and the successful Russian resistance made it less necessary to establish strategic priorities. Roosevelt, who throughout the war was less willing than his diplomatic and military advisers to take issue openly with the British, was inclined to accept HMG's argument that the Allies should fight the Germans wherever possible.[75] U.S. leaders also took comfort from a shake-up in the British command structure in the Middle East, including the replacement of the unfortunate Wavell by Auchinleck, and the appointment of Oliver Lyttelton as Minister of State for the Middle East—a new post which, it was hoped in Washington, might provide a measure of overall co-ordination. For the moment it therefore seemed neither necessary nor tactful to push HMG too hard. But the Middle East was to prove a durable topic of disagreement between the two governments. In the spring and summer of 1942 the arguments about strategic priorities were revived as part of the controversy about a second front. And after the end of 1942, with Axis influence eliminated from North Africa and the Middle East, the U.S.A. developed expansionist ambitions of its own. Initially these were at France's expense but by 1944–45 America was out to replace Britain as the dominant power in Saudi Arabia and greatly to reduce British influence in Egypt, with the exception of the Canal Zone. In 1941–42 the need to co-operate against the Axis was paramount; thereafter the latent competition between the two powers came to the surface once more.[76]

\*       \*       \*

Apart from its anxieties about the Middle East, the U.S. Army was also unhappy in mid-1941 with the direction of F.D.R.'s strategy. Not only was it having to divert scarce munitions in increasing quantities to Britain and the Middle East, but from August it had to prepare for a regular supply programme to Russia. During August and September British and U.S. officials worked out independently what they could spare. They then thrashed

210

the issue out together in London in mid-September, before Harriman and Beaverbrook took a joint proposal to Moscow at the end of the month. Within both governments the polarization of opinion on Russian aid followed similar lines. The politicians, notably Roosevelt and Churchill, advocated quick and generous aid to convince the U.S.S.R. of Western sincerity and keep her fighting. The military and diplomats doubted Russia's capacity for survival and suspected that she might change sides as she had done in 1939. They therefore wanted to limit aid and to tie it closely to reciprocal concessions. In the end it was the politicians' tactic of generous, unconditional aid that won out in the Supply Protocol signed by Harriman and Beaverbrook on 1 October.[77]

But paper agreements were one thing; how would the goods be produced, especially given the failure of U.S. industry to reach F.D.R.'s optimistic production targets? The answer from the U.S. Army was that in order to supply Russia there must be a reduction in aid to the British—hence the disputes about the importance of the Middle East. From late July, U.S. strategy in the Pacific had shifted and the Administration was now trying to reinforce the Philippines with troops and heavy bombers. The military was also determined to complete its own minimum preparations—the Protective Mobilization Plan (PMP) for a fully equipped combat force of 1.8 million men by 30 June 1942. When the Army unveiled its proposals for limited material aid to Russia at Britain's expense during the Atlantic Meeting in August, British leaders were horrified—particularly about the cutbacks on existing agreements about the supply of tanks and heavy bombers. Their complaints were relayed via Harriman and Hopkins to F.D.R., whose response, typically, was simply to order that U.S. production targets should be increased. But that, of course, was no answer to the immediate problem. Roosevelt therefore forced the Army to give more to the Russians, while acceding to British requests that their own supplies should be maintained. Thus, the Army had offered only 795 medium tanks for Russia and 611 for Britain in the period up to 30 June 1942. But the Protocol committed Britain and the U.S.A. each to provide 2,250 tanks in that time, and the British also got most of the 1,500 light and 200 medium tanks they had requested from the U.S.A. A similar arrangement was made for aircraft.[78] Effectively, therefore, throughout the autumn the U.S.A. was providing aid to Britain and Russia at the expense of her own armed forces. In order to fulfil even its limited initial proposal for Russian aid, the Army had to reduce equipment for training post-PMP forces by half. That made it very difficult to expand beyond the 1.8 million minimum. And once the scope of F.D.R.'s aid programme became clear, even the previously sacrosanct PMP target was violated. On 22 September the War Department agreed that 75 per cent of total munitions production would be allocated to foreign aid from 1 March 1942, when the PMP force would be only 70 per cent ready.[79]

The controversy over aid to Russia revealed more clearly than ever the basic difference in strategic thinking between the Army and the President.[80] The Army had never been totally sold on F.D.R.'s policy of assisting the opponents of Hitler. Basically it believed that the U.S.A. should concentrate on the security of the Western Hemisphere. Not only was this America's

211

primary interest, but it was a fundamental axiom of military science to concentrate one's strength and exploit the advantages of interior lines rather than to package out scarce resources along extended and vulnerable lines of communication to allies of uncertain reliability. In so far as America's interest required the destruction of Hitler, Army strategists believed that this could only be accomplished by a gradual build-up of troops for a massive invasion of continental Europe. 'Guesstimates' in September 1941 put the possible figure at five million U.S. troops. The army had gone along with Roosevelt's policy of material aid to Britain because her continued resistance gave the U.S.A. time to rearm and because she would be an invaluable launching pad for the eventual continental assault. But essentially it saw the policy of fighting Hitler by proxy as a temporary expedient—in the autumn of 1941 it did not expect Russia to survive beyond the following summer and remained very sceptical of the adequacy of Britain's anti-invasion defences. Roosevelt, by contrast, had always seen U.S. rearmament more as 'an alternative to war' than as 'a preparation for' it.[81] Since the autumn of 1938 he had hoped to keep war away from the U.S.A. by arming Hitler's opponents, whatever the effect on his own armed forces. And he seems to have envisaged this as sufficient for victory as well. He had always said privately that it would be politically impossible to send another large American Expeditionary Force (AEF) to Europe,[82] but he also believed that the development of strategic bombing had made land warfare on the scale of 1914–18 unnecessary. Indeed, at the Atlantic Meeting in August Hopkins had told the British that the President was 'a believer in bombing as the only means of gaining a victory'. Similarly, just before he left for the meeting, Roosevelt told Morgenthau that the 'way to lick Hitler' was by breaking German morale, which could only be done by systematic bombing of small towns as well as military targets. These remarks, taken in conjunction with F.D.R.'s stabilizing of Army expansion in autumn 1941, suggest that his celebrated pledge to the 'mothers and fathers' of America in Boston on 30 October 1940—that 'Your boys are not going to be sent into any foreign wars'—was made sincerely. He seems to have genuinely believed that saturation bombing combined with the application of America's vast economic resources and her expanding sea power could be an alternative to another AEF.[83]

The Army Air Corps naturally shared F.D.R.'s faith in heavy bombing, but the Navy took the Army's view that another AEF was inevitable. In fact, Roosevelt's strategic thinking was closer to HMG's than to that of his own military. In private, British War Office planners were questioning the limited 'mopping up' role ascribed to the Army in the strategy for victory, but officially, as the Americans found at the Atlantic Meeting, the Chiefs of Staff still clung to the old formula of blockade, subversion and bombing—with the latter as the decisive weapon. Heavy bombers were therefore Britain's production priority, with no limit set on the eventual numbers required. At most the Army would accelerate the final victory by landing armoured forces on the continent to fight mobile war in liaison with indigenous liberation forces.[84] This was also Churchill's view. No less than F.D.R. he was anxious about the political acceptability of another Expeditionary Force, and in Britain's case, of course, memories of the Somme and Passchendaele still bulked large. His own famous appeal—'Give us the tools, and we will finish the job'—although primarily intended to help smooth the passage of Lend-Lease, was not entirely disingenuous. The PM did not expect that a U.S. declaration of war, which he so ardently desired, would result in another large AEF. As in 1940 he saw its value in terms of the effect on U.S. production and above all on international morale. Increasingly he had come to believe 'that this was a psychological war' and that the Allies had to convince Hitler's European vassals that they would soon be free, otherwise they would succumb completely to his New Order.[85] He and Roosevelt therefore both hoped to avoid a war of large armies. However, during the late summer and autumn, it gradually became apparent that FDR hoped to avoid formal U.S. entry into the war as well.

## D. Towards limited, undeclared war

Undoubtedly the most dramatic episode in Anglo-American relations in 1941 was the long-awaited meeting between Roosevelt and Churchill, which took place on 9–12 August in Placentia Bay in Newfoundland, offshore from the new U.S. base at Argentia.[86] The conference (code-named 'Riviera') reached several important decisions, notably the joint declaration on peace aims—the so-called 'Atlantic Charter'—and agreement on a warning to Japan. These will be discussed later. It also provided the accompanying staff delegations with an opportunity to discuss questions of strategy and supply, as we have just seen. But the main value of the occasion lay in the personal relationships established or strengthened. Most important of all was the encounter between President and Prime Minister, which, despite Hopkins' efforts, had been delayed, first by the Lend-Lease debate and then by the successive British reverses in the Balkans, Libya and Crete. Churchill had forgotten his only previous meeting with F.D.R. in 1918—a source of considerable chagrin to Roosevelt apparently—but the two men quickly hit it off, working and socializing together as they explored common problems and tested out each other's mettle and temperament.[87] A similar pattern was repeated at other levels of the official hierarchy, with the ubiquitous Hopkins acting as ever as intermediary. Cadogan and Sumner Welles accompanied their respective leaders to advise on diplomatic problems, and, on the suggestion of Halifax and FO/A, Cadogan did his best to penetrate the American's reserve and suspicion of British intentions.[88] Similarly, the military delegations became better acquainted with their opposite numbers—Marshall and Dill in particular laying the foundations of a diplomatically invaluable personal friendship—and the crews of the British and U.S. warships which hosted the conference also fraternized easily and freely. For many of the participants the most memorable moment was a combined service on the deck of the *Prince of Wales*, British and Americans intermingled, sharing in readings and prayers and in the singing of familiar hymns such as 'Onward, Christian Soldiers'. Both leaders were well aware that the service, which was fully recorded on film, would, in F.D.R.'s words, 'make great propaganda', but undoubtedly they were also genuinely affected by what

213

Churchill called 'a deeply moving expression of the unity of faith of our two peoples'.[89]

Nevertheless, the conference proved a bitter anti-climax for the British. To understand why this was so, we need to remember the mood in London that summer. Russia's continued resistance was obviously welcome, but it left a sense of post-crisis depression after the invasion fears of the spring. Nor was it clear, even if the U.S.S.R. survived into the winter, that she could withstand a new German offensive in the spring of 1942. The future was therefore still uncertain; the only sure fact was that the war would be a long one. The optimism about an early German collapse, which had sustained Britain through 1940, seemed increasingly misplaced. So too did Churchill's once-inspiring confidence about early U.S. entry into the war—the other main rationale for fighting on in 1940. British leaders were now getting fed up with having to flatter and entertain any and every visiting American, of whatever position, ability or charm, apparently to no avail.[90] The suspicion was also growing that F.D.R. was quite happy to stand on the sidelines, paying others to fight while reorganizing the world, in Wilsonian vein, to suit America's expanding interests.[91] Churchill was therefore reassured by the prospect of a meeting with Roosevelt. 'I must say', he told the Queen just before leaving, 'I do not think our friend would have asked me to go so far for what must be a meeting of world-wide importance, unless he had in mind some further forward step . . .'[92] What Churchill hoped for, of course, was a promise that the U.S. would soon declare war. But no such promise was forthcoming—and the Atlantic Charter, with its grand but vacuous phrases about the post-war world, was a poor substitute. When Attlee read out the text in a worldwide broadcast on 14 August the palpable sense of disappointment extended from the clubs of Mayfair to the wardroom of the homeward-bound *Prince of Wales*. Assurances from F.D.R. and the White House that the conference brought Americans no closer to war acted as further depressants.[93]

Privately, Churchill tried to offer some solace to British leaders. His accounts to the War Cabinet of his talks were couched in the most encouraging terms. According to the Cabinet minutes on 19 August:

> The Prime Minister gave his impression of the President's attitude towards the entry of the United States into the war. He was obviously determined that they should come in. On the other hand, the President had been extremely anxious about the Bill [for continuing the Draft], which had only passed with a very narrow majority. Clearly he was skating on pretty thin ice in his relations with Congress, which, however, he did not regard as truly representative of the country. If he were to put the issue of peace and war to Congress, they would debate it for three months. The President had said he would wage war, but not declare it, and that he would become more and more provocative. If the Germans did not like it, they could attack American forces.[94]

Churchill then explained that agreement had been reached for the U.S.A. to assume responsibility for escorting North Atlantic convoys within the U.S. defensive zone west of 26° West. He hoped that this 'unparalleled gesture of friendship by a neutral power'[95] would take effect by the end of the month.

The President's orders to these escorts were to attack any U-boat which showed itself, even if it were 200 or 300 miles away from the convoy. Admiral Stark intended to carry out this order literally, and any Commander who sank a U-boat would have his action approved. Everything was to be done to force an 'incident'.

This, Churchill argued, would oblige Hitler either to engage in naval war with the U.S.A. or else effectively to concede defeat in the Battle of the Atlantic. In addition, he told the War Cabinet

> that he had thought it right to give the President a warning. He had told him that he would not answer for the consequences if Russia was compelled to sue for peace and, say, by the Spring of next year, hope died in Britain. The President had taken this very well, and had made it clear that he would look for an 'incident' which would justify him in opening hostilities.

We shall see in a moment how good a guide to Roosevelt's policy is provided in Churchill's account. Suffice it here to say that some at least of his colleagues were unwilling to take it at face value. Kingsley Wood told Dalton that 'not everyone accepts the P.M.'s view that the President is a great man. There is another view that says he is a yes man to all who speak to him, and Keynes thinks he is also quite a sick man.'[96] The discontent was expressed in a long and difficult Cabinet meeting on 25 August. Beaverbrook, who had been in the U.S.A. on a supply mission, and Halifax, who was home on leave, said they had no doubt that F.D.R. and Administration leaders wanted to enter the war, but neither of them held out much hope of U.S. entry in the immediate future. It was felt in Cabinet, as in the FO, that Churchill's 'Give us the tools' speech was now a dangerous brake on American action. Moreover, the U.S.A. was not even providing the tools. Beaverbrook warned that there was no prospect of obtaining appreciable quantities of supplies under Lend-Lease in the near future and that even orders that Britain had placed on her own account before Lend-Lease were now being diverted by the U.S. authorities to China or Russia. Inconclusively but at length the Cabinet pondered how to improve matters, with Churchill very much on the defensive, insisting that he had said all that could be said to Roosevelt and reminding his colleagues of the U.S. plans for Atlantic escorts from which 'developments' might come.[97] The PM managed to head off any decision that day, but on 28 August he sent a plaintive cable to Hopkins reporting the 'wave of depression' in the Cabinet, caused by F.D.R.'s many assurances that the U.S. was no nearer to war, which, he feared, would be reflected in Parliament after the summer recess. He restated his fear that Russia might be knocked out by 1942, and said he saw no prospect of the Germans forcing a naval incident. 'Should be grateful', he told Hopkins, 'if you could give me any sort of hope.' Hopkins and Roosevelt discussed the telegram. They felt that Churchill was depressed and was taking it out on them. But, Hopkins recorded:

> I told the President, however, that not only Churchill but all the members of the Cabinet and all the British people I talked to believed that ultimately we will get into the war on some basis or other and if they ever reached the conclusion that this was not to be the case, that there would be a very critical moment in the war and the British appeasers might have some influence on Churchill.[98]

Here was another reminder to Roosevelt of the delicate balance he had to maintain between getting ahead of his own public and getting too far behind the British.

Churchill's message (and Hopkins' gloss) may have helped hold Roosevelt to his promise about escorts. Contrary to the impression given by Churchill (sincerely or not) to the Cabinet on his return, all that had definitely been decided at the conference were the detailed contingency plans for how Allied convoys should be escorted, *if* F.D.R. so ordered.[99] The President had clearly led Churchill to believe that the orders would quickly be issued, but he did nothing on his return to Washington. On other matters, indeed, he followed his usual pattern and backed down from his previous commitments—the stiff parallel Anglo-American warning to Japan was rapidly watered down by Hull. Churchill's cable of 28 August effectively warned Roosevelt that he could not afford to retreat from the pledge on escorts as well. But it seems likely that he would have honoured it by subterfuge and stealth—allowing Allied ships secretly to join U.S.–Iceland convoys as provided for in Hemisphere Defense Plan Four[100]—had an 'incident' not occurred. The U-boat attack on the U.S. destroyer *Greer* off Iceland on 4 September provided the opportunity and justification to announce publicly a clear-cut system of escort and protection.[101] In his fireside chat on 11 September the President deliberately distorted the *Greer* incident. He emphasized that the U-boat had fired first while saying nothing of how the destroyer had trailed the submarine for several hours. But the *Greer* was not the centre-piece of his talk. He linked it with other incidents, such as the *Robin Moor* in May, as evidence of the Nazi attempt to 'seize control of the oceans' and subvert the Western Hemisphere as part of Hitler's ultimate goal of 'world mastery'. He promised that the U.S.A. would not be intimidated from safeguarding its own shipping and the supplies of aid to Hitler's opponents. Therefore, naval patrols would now protect all merchant ships 'of any flag' within American defensive waters. If Axis warships entered that area they would do so 'at their own peril'.[102] On 13 September the appropriate orders were issued, to come into effect three days later. On 17 September the U.S. Navy began escorting its first British convoy and on the 25th the Royal Navy withdrew completely from the Western Atlantic, leaving escorting there to the Americans and Canadians. Although Roosevelt had not made this clear in his fireside chat, the inclusion of Iceland within the Western Hemisphere zone meant that 'American defensive waters' now extended in the North-East Atlantic as far as longitude 10° West—little more than 400 miles off the north coast of Scotland.[103] Within this vast area—roughly three-quarters of the North Atlantic—U.S. vessels were to escort all friendly convoys with the exception of British troopships and to eliminate any Axis forces encountered. Great was the relief in London. Churchill seemed vindicated. 'The President's speech is your reward', the chameleon Beaverbrook told him. 'It is the work of your genius. You have taught the Americans to take their first faltering footsteps, then to walk and shortly to run. For my part I gain lustre and glory from serving under you—like one of Napoleon's Marshals.'[104]

It had taken five months for F.D.R. to move via extended patrolling and the occupation of Iceland to full-scale escorts. Slowly and painfully the tadpole had grown into a frog. As with the Destroyers Deal it had not proved necessary, as he had first thought, to get Congress' approval. He had been able to exploit his powers as Chief Executive and Commander-in-Chief while keeping legislature and public informed in general terms. The *Greer* allowed him to bring the matter out into the open—much to the relief of the Navy.[105] Logically the next step in assisting Britain and Russia was to seek repeal of the Neutrality Act—now a complete anomaly. However, the very close House vote on 12 August renewing the draft by only 203 to 202 (with 65 Democrats against) had been a chilling warning of the state of Congress. It was therefore decided not to seek repeal of the whole act—which had become something of an isolationist shibboleth—but only of those sections that materially affected the Battle of the Atlantic. These were sections two (prohibiting U.S. vessels from entering belligerent ports), three (giving the President discretionary power to proclaim combat zones around belligerent countries) and six (prohibiting the arming of U.S. merchant vessels). Of these the least controversial was clearly the last, in view of the escorts now under way, and so F.D.R. and the State Department decided to test out opinion in the House, where opposition seemed stronger, by asking it to approve repeal of section six. If the result was favourable then the Senate would be asked to approve repeal of all three sections. Finally the Senate bill would be put, as something of a *fait accompli* it was hoped, before the House. Initially the strategy worked well. On 9 October Roosevelt asked for repeal of section six. He was not calling, he said, for a 'declaration of war any more than the Lend-Lease Act called for a declaration of war. This is a matter of essential defense of American rights'—part of 'the American policy to defend ourselves wherever such defense become necessary under the complex conditions of modern warfare'.[106] On 17 October the House voted to repeal section six by 259 to 138, with only 21 Democrats against. But on the same day the U.S. destroyer *Kearny* lost 11 men in a torpedo attack while on escort duty near Iceland, and on the 31st another destroyer, the *Reuben James*, was sunk in similar circumstances with the loss of over 100 crew. When the full package was put to the Senate the debate was bitter and the vote close—50 to 37—the smallest Administration majority on a foreign policy issue since the war began. Six days later, on 15 November, the House voted on the Senate resolution to repeal sections two, three and six. The result was 212 in favour and 194 against, with more Democrats in opposition than over Lend-Lease.[107] F.D.R. had got the key sections of the Neutrality Act repealed, but the voting figures made him more pessimistic than ever about opinion on Capitol Hill. In August he had told Churchill that if he asked Congress to declare war they would debate the issue for three months. But after the votes on Selective Service and the Neutrality Act he feared that a request for war would not merely meet a damaging filibuster but would actually be defeated, possibly by as much as two or even three to one.[108]

The deteriorating political situation therefore confirmed F.D.R.'s desire to avoid asking Congress for a formal declaration of war. Perhaps, as he had so often averred, he was still waiting for that elusive 'incident'—now aware that it would take more than attacks on U.S. vessels to arouse Americans from their desire to see Hitler defeated without themselves having to fight.[109] But it seems likely that this was still F.D.R.'s desire as well. In fact he said as much to the press on 3 November, when asked why the U.S.A. did not end the 'dishonesty' of continuing diplomatic relations with Germany. Talking 'completely off the record', the President explained:

> We don't want a declared war with Germany because we are acting in defense—self-defense—every action. And to break off diplomatic relations—why, that wouldn't do any good. I really frankly don't know that it would do any good. It might be more useful to keep them the way they are.[110]

There are several reasons for F.D.R.'s desire to avoid formal war. First of all, his overriding foreign policy goal was to provide material aid to America's front lines. Like the State Department, but unlike the British, Roosevelt feared that if the U.S.A. declared war on Germany, public opinion would demand a disastrous cutback in supplies to America's quasi-allies, with, F.D.R. feared, equally disastrous consequences for the U.S.A. herself. In mid-January, therefore, when he told the Navy to prepare for possible escort of convoys to England, he stressed that he did not want thereby to create the occasion for war with Germany. And, according to Churchill: 'At the Atlantic Meeting I told his circle I would rather have an American declaration of war now and no supplies for six months than double the supplies and no declaration. When this was repeated to him he thought it a hard saying.'[111] A second concern for Roosevelt was the Far East and the implications of the Tripartite Pact between Germany, Italy and Japan. At the beginning of November 1941 F.D.R. told Mackenzie King 'that he was convinced that if the United States came into the war against Germany, Japan would enter the war immediately on Germany's side. This was a consideration which had to be carefully weighed in determining policy.'[112] Not only would a Pacific war run counter to the basic Anglo-American strategy of averting or postponing conflict with Japan until Germany had been defeated, it would also lead to the domestic demands he feared for a reallocation of supplies. Thirdly, it seems probable that the President genuinely abhorred war, or, more exactly, he shunned the stigma of leading the country into another world conflict. In May 1941 Hopkins concluded 'that the President is loathe to get us into this war', and on 7 December, as news began to filter through about the attack on Pearl Harbor, F.D.R. talked at length about 'his earnest desire to complete his administration without war'. Japan, he said, had now taken the matter out of his hands. Perhaps this was another of Roosevelt's statements for posterity, but it does square with the hatred of war professed by him, apparently sincerely, on numerous occasions during the 1930s.[113] And finally, the President did not think that a formal declaration of war would make much practical difference. As we have seen, he believed that America's contribution to eventual victory would be through arms rather than armies, and he continued to feel, as he had said in December 1937 during the *Panay* crisis, that declarations of war were unnecessary and 'out of fashion'.[114] In short, there seemed little to be gained, and a good deal to lose, from trying to persuade Congress to declare war. It seems that

218

F.D.R. saw a state of limited, undeclared hostilities as a satisfactory alternative to formal war—particularly now that the U.S.S.R. had survived into the winter.

*       *       *

As autumn progressed, many well-informed British leaders concluded that Roosevelt did indeed hope to avoid all-out, formal war. This was the view, for instance, of General Beaumont-Nesbitt, British military attaché in Washington, who felt that Churchill had been taken in by Roosevelt, or at least had failed to allow for the inevitable American overstatement when listening to F.D.R.'s bellicose assurances. Similarly, Sir Ronald I. Campbell, Minister at the Washington Embassy, warned in November that 'personally I should have thought that it would be dangerous to base any decisions on the expectation of their coming in at all, much less in the near future'.[115] But the politicians at least believed that F.D.R. could not maintain his balancing act indefinitely. Halifax told Churchill that his conversation with the President on 10 October 'pretty well confirms my view, which I think is yours, that he is going to move to the undeclared war rather than the other, although no doubt things might change overnight if the right things were to happen!' For his part, the PM had recognized for some months that both Hitler and Roosevelt might prefer to ignore minor naval incidents in the Atlantic, but he remained confident that the Americans were an emotional, crusading people and that one day 'the fire would catch'.[116] Some HMG officials still hoped to provide a spark. British special operations in the U.S.A., under William Stephenson—the celebrated 'Intrepid'—went so far as to forge various documents purporting to demonstrate German designs on the Western Hemisphere. These were passed to the U.S. press and some were used by Roosevelt—perhaps without knowing their provenance—in a broadcast on 27 October, but with no discernible effect on American opinion.[117] In fact, the significance of Stephenson's activities in the U.S.A. has been exaggerated by sensationalist writers and broadcasters. In 1941 his organization, despite its close links with the neophyte U.S. intelligence agency under Bill Donovan, was at odds with both the FBI and the State Department, where Adolf Berle, suspicious as ever of Britain, kept a justifiably close watch. An inept plot by one of Stephenson's agents, called Paine, to 'get the dirt' on Berle, with a view to discrediting him, was quickly uncovered by the FBI and Stephenson was forced to get Paine out of the country post-haste.[118]

Roosevelt's actions in late November and early December 1941—often neglected by historians—provide further evidence of F.D.R.'s desire cautiously to aid Britain and Russia, rather than to provoke hostilities. With the crucial sections of the Neutrality Act repealed, F.D.R. was now free to send convoys of armed U.S. merchant ships under U.S. naval escorts right across the Atlantic. Hopkins and Roosevelt's naval advisers pressed for a decision, but, as with all his actions in the Atlantic in 1941, F.D.R. gave general approval while wishing to implement the decision slowly and discreetly. He felt on 22 November that on British and Russian routes 'the use of American flag ships must come very soon but should be worked into gradually'. His advisers tried to pin him down and eventually it was decided on 25 November that U.S. vessels travelling to Lisbon should not be armed, that U.S. merchant ships should go to Archangel as soon as they had been armed and otherwise prepared, and that 'Ships under the American flag go to Great Britain as they become available but that this procedure progress gradually with only a small number of ships being so routed in the beginning. This number may be increased at a later date if in accordance with Administration policies and instructions.'[119] Presumably these vessels would have been included in British convoys, thereby postponing a decision about whether to send a convoy of U.S. ships under U.S. escorts. Nor was the move publicized—at his press conference on 28 November F.D.R. announced the decision not to arm Lisbon-bound vessels but made no mention of Russia and Britain, and no questions were asked.[120] This was hardly the all-out effort to provoke war that Churchill believed or claimed that he had been promised in August—F.D.R. was apparently trying to protect the Atlantic supply line in the least provocative way. Of course, in the end it was Hitler who would decide what constituted provocation. But the Führer was still in no hurry to start a war with the U.S.A. while European problems remained to be settled. Indeed, after his invasion of Russia became bogged down, he issued even stricter instructions to his admirals to avoid incidents in the Atlantic. As late as 2 December, with the Neutrality Act in large measure repealed, he still refused to sanction any change in policy.[121] In short, it seems likely that the state of limited, undeclared hostilities between Roosevelt and Hitler might have continued for many months—if events in the Pacific had turned out differently.

## E. 'In the same boat'

Early in the morning of Sunday 7 December Japanese aircraft attacked and crippled the U.S. Pacific Fleet at Pearl Harbor. The following day F.D.R. went to Congress and secured a declaration of war on Japan with only one negative vote. Roosevelt, like Churchill, assumed that Germany would quickly follow Japan,[122] but politically he still had to wait for Hitler to fire the first shot. Meanwhile, in his fireside chat on 9 December, he tried to prepare Americans for a continued 'Germany First' strategy, whatever Hitler decided to do—insisting that the Japanese attack was part of a global Axis plot and that, in fact if not in name, Germany was as much at war with the U.S.A. as with Britain and Russia.[123]

As usual, Roosevelt exaggerated the unity of the Axis, but he was right about the German response. The Tripartite Pact was a tenuous *defensive* alliance—applicable only if one of the signatories was attacked—but on 4–5 December Hitler and Ribbentrop had agreed to Japanese demands for a treaty of alliance in the event of war with the U.S.A., regardless of who was the aggressor. They were not told of the imminence of war, let alone about the impending strike on Pearl Harbor, and seem to have accepted principally for fear that otherwise Japan might persist and succeed in her negotiations with the U.S.A.—thereby leaving Roosevelt free to move in the Atlantic. When called upon to honour the agreement far more quickly than he had anticipated, Hitler nevertheless had little hesitation. His motives will remain an endless source of debate. He had long regarded the U.S. as Germany's ultimate enemy, to be dealt with by the next generation once European and colonial hegemony had been achieved, and his caution in the Atlantic in 1939–41 was therefore a matter of tactics rather than principle. Apparently he decided that F.D.R. would provoke war in the Atlantic within the next few months, that it was better for domestic morale if Germany initiated hostilities, and that Japan would tie America down in the Pacific. But committing his country to war against a third power simultaneously made no sense, especially given Hitler's basic strategy of limited wars against single foes, and with this, as with many of the Führer's major strategic decisions, it would seem that he was carried away by his racist ideology and the surges of pathological hatred that flowed from it.[124]

Whatever the explanation, Hitler immediately let his U-boats off the leash on 8 December and on the 11th he and Mussolini declared war on the United States. Congress reciprocated, *nem. con.*, the same day. 'The dictator powers have presented us with a United America', minuted Whitehead in relief and amazement. 'Today all of us are in the same boat with you and the people of the Empire', F.D.R. cabled Churchill on 8 December, 'and it is a ship which will not and can not be sunk.' As for the PM, he was ecstatic. It was the consummation of nineteen months of lonely leadership, the attainment of his main diplomatic goal, the assurance of ultimate victory. 'England would live; Britain would live; the Commonwealth of Nations and the Empire would live.' Little wonder that the night after Pearl Harbor Churchill went to bed 'satiated with emotion and sensation' and 'slept the sleep of the saved and thankful'.[125]

# CHAPTER NINE

## The Road to Pearl Harbor
## And Singapore

*... I feel that about the worst mistake that we and the Americans can make at this juncture is to under-estimate the strength and resolution of this country [Japan] and its armed forces, in the event—perhaps now not far distant—that it may feel itself driven to desperation.*

*Our interests and those of the United States in the Far East, while very similar, have never been identical. In particular, I doubt whether the United States Government can be expected to work with any enthusiasm for the defence of our interests and position in the Far East, except in so far as these contribute directly to the defence and security of the United States.*

Sir Robert Craigie, British Ambassador in Tokyo,
November 1941[1]

Churchill never altered his opinion that Pearl Harbor was a godsend for Britain. Throughout 1941 he had been determined to avoid war with Japan until the U.S.A. was fully committed to the British cause, and in that sense the events of 7–11 December were a triumphant vindication of his policy. Yet those events also began a disastrous six months for Britain in the Pacific, from which her imperial power and prestige never recovered. Most humiliating of all was the surrender of Singapore—the symbol and keystone of her Asian empire—on 15 February 1942. To evaluate the Anglo-American relationship in the Pacific in 1941, we must keep both these aspects in mind. We need to trace not only the familiar road to Pearl Harbor,[2] but also the road to Singapore.[3]

### A. Containing Japan: strategy, January–June 1941

Since 1921 British policy in the event of 'serious trouble' with Japan had been to send the main fleet to Singapore. But between 1935 and 1940 that policy had been gradually undermined by Britain's naval commitments elsewhere, notably in the Mediterranean. After the French collapse in mid-1940 and the concurrent decision by HMG to try to hold the entire Mediterranean alone, any hope of sending the fleet east was abandoned, at least for the moment.[4] Yet Britain had no intention of abandoning Singapore. It was essential for her whole imperial strategy. North and west, in a vast arc around the Bay of Bengal, stretched her South Asian empire, from the Malay states—sources of vital tin and rubber—through Burma to India. Singapore also commanded another arc of interest, running south and east through the oil-rich East Indies to Australia and New Zealand. This, in turn, had a further ramification. Australia, New Zealand and India together provided most of the British Empire's offensive manpower in 1940–41. With Britain's own forces largely tied down in home defence it was their troops who bore the brunt of the campaigns in Greece, Crete and North Africa. If Britain could not guarantee the security of the Far East, then these forces would have to be withdrawn to protect their homelands, leaving the Middle East virtually defenceless.

Some kind of revised 'Singapore strategy' was therefore essential.[5] From the summer of 1940 it developed along three main lines. First, it was still the Admiralty's intention to send a fleet east as soon as Britain's naval circumstances permitted, and this became possible in October 1941.[6] In the meantime, they relied on the RAF and Army to defend Malaya, and hoped that the U.S. Navy could be persuaded to assume responsibility for defending the Far East.

*　　*　　*

Singapore was a relic of the sea-power era. It had been intended as a naval stronghold that could be held against seaborne attack. But by the mid-1930s British strategists began to appreciate that the Malayan jungle did not constitute an impenetrable barrier and that without air bases to the north the Japanese air force could render Singapore untenable. To hold it, particularly in the absence of a fleet, Britain also had to hold the whole of Malaya. These were the conclusions of the Chiefs of Staff in their major study of Far Eastern policy on 31 July 1940, which laid out the policy of relying, at least for the moment, on air power and the Army.[7] The paper was approved in principle by the Cabinet on 28 August and became the blueprint for Britain's revised strategy. By December 1941 the Chiefs' target of nine army brigades had been reached—but paper strength could not disguise the shortage of experienced troops and modern equipment. Front line air strength was only 158—less than double the 1940 figure and under half of the Chiefs' minimum of 336. Most of the machines were outdated—Buffalo fighters rather than Hurricanes, Blenheim bombers instead of Glenn Martins.[8] Within two days of the start of the Japanese offensive this frail air force had been virtually eliminated. Without it the Army could do little but retreat steadily south to Singapore.

What had gone wrong? Consistently the Far East had been starved of men and equipment in order to supply the Mediterranean. In large measure the responsibility for this was Churchill's. Again and again he insisted that Asia came third in Britain's list of priorities after the British Isles and the Middle East. If necessary HMG should sacrifice the Far East rather than the Mediterranean. But he also believed that this invidious choice would *not* have to be made. In his view the Japanese would only enter the war, like the Italians against France, if Britain was on the verge of total defeat. Even then, he argued, their military efforts would not be significant—naval raiding of trade routes rather than major offensives against British territory, with the exception of Hong Kong and Shanghai whose temporary loss was inevitable. And, whatever happened, he was confident that Singapore was a great 'fortress', capable of resisting siege for six to twelve months. Its defence was to be based on a strong local garrison and on the expectation that the fleet would arrive in time.[9]

Churchill therefore never really accepted the Chiefs' policy of defending the whole of Malaya. He was also far more obsessive about Egypt: as we saw, the War Office had a brief but sharp exchange with him on the subject in the spring of 1941. Furthermore, during that controversy, he explicitly assumed personal responsibility for the guidelines of Far Eastern strategy.[10] But, in the end, the blame was not Churchill's alone. His errors were those of all British strategists, writ large. The Chiefs of Staff accepted his emphasis on the Mediterranean and shared his contempt for the Japanese as the Asian equivalent of Italy. Their July 1940 paper about reinforcing Malaya set out long-term goals, not immediate priorities, and its estimate of forces required was considered quite inadequate by the local commanders. Raymond Callahan neatly sums up the difference between the PM and his military advisers: 'Like Churchill, the Chiefs of Staff were content with token forces for the Far East. Unlike him, they wanted the tokens in place.'[11]

For Churchill, and for the Admiralty, Far Eastern security remained essentially a problem of sea power. Lacking their own naval resources, the British turned more than ever in 1940–41 to the United States. Ideally they favoured a simple division of labour: the Royal Navy, with assistance from U.S. cruisers and destroyers, would patrol the Atlantic sealanes, while the bulk of America's capital ships would take care of Japan. To do this, they argued, the Americans should move some or all of their Pacific Fleet from Pearl Harbor in the Hawaiian Islands either to Singapore or else to reinforce the tiny U.S. Asiatic Fleet (which had no capital ships) at Manila in the Philippines, 1,500 miles north-east of Singapore. In Washington, however, this seemed an incredibly selfish and parochial point of view. As we have already seen, in 1940 and 1941 most U.S policymakers did not share HMG's official optimism about Britain's capacity to resist Hitler. To leave America's main fleet at Hawaii, 2,000 miles from the *West* Coast, was controversial; to move it 6,000 miles farther away would be treasonably irresponsible as long as Britain's future was in doubt. Sending a detachment to reinforce Admiral Hart at Manila would be almost as dangerous. To keep the fleet at Hawaii was therefore a tolerable compromise. It constituted a deterrent against Japan without being beyond range if a crisis developed in the Atlantic. In any case, the only significant U.S. territorial interest in Asia was the Philippines, and this the War Department had effectively written off in the event of war. In general, American forces were not to be committed seriously west of Hawaii, in view of the U.S.A.'s pre-eminent interest in the Atlantic. Yet the British were virtually asking the United States to look after their Far Eastern interests. They had no capital ships in the Pacific or Indian Oceans and their small force of cruisers and destroyers was based on Hong Kong not Singapore. Indignantly U.S. policymakers asked why the U.S.A. should shoulder the burden of defending Singapore when the British would do nothing themselves—especially when Britain's presence in South-East Asia seemed part of a dated imperialism from which the U.S.A. had self-consciously tried to distance itself throughout its national history.

Churchill and the Admiralty both wished to change this attitude, but they had a different sense of tactics and priorities. The contrast emerged before and during the Washington staff talks in January–March 1941. The British delegation to the talks, particularly Admiral Bellairs, the senior naval officer, wanted to challenge the American view directly. Churchill, however, minuted on 9 December 1940: 'There is no use putting before them a naval policy which they will not accept, and which will only offend them and make it more difficult to bring them into the war.'[12] The delegates were therefore instructed to defer to the U.S.A. on all matters of Pacific strategy. The Americans should simply be invited to use Singapore if they wished and the onus placed on them in discussion to prove that they could deter Japan from as far away as Hawaii.[13] Despite these instructions, however, Bellairs and his colleagues raised the Singapore issue repeatedly at the Washington talks. In part they did so out of disquiet at Churchill's complacency, but their main reason was the very real fear in British military circles in early February 1941 that Japan was about to push south into Indochina and risk war with the colonial powers.[14] The location of the U.S. fleet was therefore not merely a matter of contingency planning for a future, possible war, but an issue of immediate and critical diplomatic importance.[15]

Churchill was furious with Bellairs. Like the Americans, he did not take the February war scare very seriously. In his view the most important aspect of Anglo-American relations was Lend-Lease, and nothing should be done to upset the Administration or imperil the Bill's passage.[16] In any case, he considered the whole Singapore versus Hawaii debate to be irrelevant. As he had minuted in November: 'The Japanese Navy is not likely to venture far from its home bases so long as a superior battle-fleet is maintained at Singapore or at Honolulu. The Japanese would never attempt a siege of Singapore with a hostile, superior American fleet in the Pacific.'[17] He was also confident that if war did break out events would naturally draw the U.S. into a forward policy—a move west from Hawaii.[18] Consequently, there was no need to press for this at the moment. 'Our object is to get the Americans into the war, and the proper strategic disposition will soon emerge when they are up against reality, and not trying to enter into hypothetical paper accords beforehand.'[19] What such an argument assumed was that there would be time between the outbreak of a Pacific war and the start of a serious Japanese offensive for 'the proper strategic disposition' to be made.

Churchill's intervention came too late to prevent Far Eastern strategy from becoming a major issue at the Washington staff talks. James Leutze has shown that the discussions were vigorous and often bitter, revealing the deep differences of interest and policy between the two powers in the Far East.[20] What is less clear from his account, however, is that an agreement on

Far Eastern strategy *was* reached. This may be attributed in part to the renewed instructions from Churchill and the Chiefs of Staff on 19 February that the British delegation must accept whatever the Americans wanted in the Pacific.[21] But it was also because the Americans, despite their dislike of British policy, were not indifferent to the defence of South-East Asia. After the most heated discussion, on 10 February, both sides agreed that it was essential to formulate a compromise Far Eastern strategy, which took account of Britain's obsession with Singapore and of the U.S.A.'s determination not to divide the Pacific Fleet or commit it west of Hawaii.[22] The two sides therefore prepared position papers and the issue was thrashed out on the 26th. The final report (ABC–1) made clear that the U.S.A. would not reinforce the Asiatic Fleet or the Philippines, let alone base its Pacific Fleet on Singapore. Indeed the Americans cast doubt on the latter's ability to support and protect a battle fleet. But, while emphasizing the supreme importance of the Atlantic, the Americans acknowledged that it was very desirable to hold the 'Malay Barrier', which stretched south-east from Singapore through the East Indies to New Guinea and Australia. In the event of war the U.S. Pacific Fleet would attack the Japanese mandated islands in the Western Pacific (the Marshalls and Carolines) to divert Japan from the Barrier. This was U.S. Navy policy. More important, by gradually shifting the bulk of her naval strength into the Atlantic, the U.S. would relieve the Royal Navy and permit it to send a *British* fleet to Singapore. This was the suggestion of the U.S. Army. The basic principle was therefore that each country should be broadly responsible for its own predominant interests. But that did not rule out eventual co-operation. The agreement also provided for British and U.S. commanders in the Far East to 'make such arrangements for mutual support as may be practicable and appropriate'.[23] These were to be the subject of further, local staff conversations.

\*　　\*　　\*

Although British and U.S. interests were less easy to reconcile in the Far East than in the Atlantic, it had, however, been possible to formulate a compromise strategy at the Washington staff talks. In any case, ABC–1 was only a hypothetical, non-committal plan by the British and U.S. military. Roosevelt and the State Department had kept well clear of the talks,[24] and they attached greater importance to the Far East than did the military. The President was particularly conscious that Britain depended on South-East Asia for much of her oil, tin and rubber. Consequently, F.D.R. argued, if the U.S.A. had an interest in the survival of Britain, then she also had an interest in the survival of Britain's Empire, despite the traditional American distaste for imperialism.[25] In any case, tin and rubber constituted the Achilles heel of America's otherwise remarkably self-sufficient economy—a point that the military seemed sometimes to forget. The U.S.A. derived about 90 per cent of her crude rubber and 75 per cent of her tin from Malaya and the NEI.[26] Roosevelt and Hull also felt that there were wider diplomatic and ideological considerations to be kept in mind. Throughout the inter-war years the moral basis of U.S. foreign policy had been a refusal to condone violent change anywhere in the world. Japan's expansion had become the most important instance, partly because of the U.S.A.'s belief in a Sino-American special relationship, but also because F.D.R. and Hull had increasingly argued during the 1930s that peace was indivisible and that totalitarian aggression anywhere diminished the freedom and security of the United States. This argument was given greater force by the prevalent belief that Japan and Germany were acting in close collaboration.

In the opinion of Roosevelt and the State Department, therefore, the U.S.A. had a significant interest in the security of the Far East. The question, of course, was *how* significant: given the limits of U.S. military power in early 1941, dare America try to protect all her interests in different parts of the world? F.D.R. fully agreed that the Atlantic was America's vital theatre. There was also no dispute that the U.S.A. could not afford to reinforce the Philippines or the Asiatic Fleet, at least for the moment, let alone make any permanent commitment to the defence of Singapore. But he and Hull believed that there must be a sizeable Pacific Fleet at Hawaii if Japan was to be deterred from aggression. They also felt that the fleet should not stay cooped up at Pearl Harbor but, when possible, should send detachments on periodic visits to the Far East to show the flag and remind Japan of the range of U.S. sea power. But the idea of ships 'popping up everywhere' appalled Stark. He stuck to the basic Navy position that the Pacific Fleet should not be divided or committed west of Hawaii. As a compromise a detachment of cruisers and destroyers from Pearl Harbor paid a very successful visit to Australia in March 1941.[27]

The difference of emphasis between Roosevelt and the State Department on the one hand and the War and Navy Departments on the other became most apparent during the crisis of April and May 1941. As we have seen, in mid-April F.D.R. transferred a carrier and four destroyers to the Atlantic but he and Hull would not accede to Stimson's and Knox's pleas for a further move of three battleships, four cruisers and fourteen destroyers—in total a quarter of the Pacific Fleet. Hull's reluctance was decisive. Although the situation in the Mediterranean had deteriorated alarmingly, the State Department was also very anxious about Japan. Matsuoka, the Japanese Foreign Minister, was then touring Europe to strengthen the Axis. On 13 April he signed a neutrality pact with Russia, leaving Japan free to move south with impunity. At the same time, as we shall see in the next section, Hull had reached a very delicate point in his secret talks with Japanese emissaries. He therefore argued that any shift of U.S. capital ships into the Atlantic would be seen in Tokyo as a sign of weakness and as an invitation to attack or at least to take a more intransigent line in the negotiations. Not until mid-May, as the Far Eastern situation improved and the Atlantic crisis deepened, was Hull willing to approve the move of the three battleships.[28]

But even this did not satisfy Knox and especially Stimson. They argued that the U.S.A. should transfer most of the Pacific Fleet, leaving only three or four battleships, nine cruisers and thirty or forty destroyers at Pearl Harbor.[29] Stimson was not oblivious of the need to deter Japan. Indeed he considered himself an expert on the subject, based on his experiences as Hoover's Secretary of State during the Manchurian crisis of 1931–33. But he believed in the spring of 1941 that the Atlantic position was desperate,

227

and he also insisted that, even if the Pacific Fleet were reduced to three or four capital ships, the *psychological* effect of such belligerent U.S. action would act as a sufficient deterrent. In Japan, and throughout the world, he claimed, it would be interpreted as the prelude to U.S. entry into the war, and thus would discourage Japan from aggression for fear of ending up on the losing side.[30] But what of the security of the Hawaiian Islands? Stimson and the War Department argued that land and air defences were sufficient, regardless of whether any ships were present[31]—the American equivalent, one might say, of British strategy for Malaya.

In London, too, the spring crisis exposed and exacerbated the differences of emphasis in Far Eastern policy. At the end of April Churchill was depressed by the Balkan débâcle and by F.D.R.'s inertia. He seized on Stimson's proposal for moving most of the fleet to the Atlantic and expressed horror that British naval representatives in Washington had questioned it. Churchill's main concerns, once again, were to get the U.S.A. involved in the Atlantic war and, thereby, to swing international opinion behind the Allied cause. Backed by Beaverbrook and Attlee, he got the Cabinet's Defence Committee, very late on 30 April, to send a telegram supporting Stimson: 'Our opinion is that any marked advance by the United States Navy in or into the Atlantic is more likely to deter Japan from going to war than the maintenance of the present very large United States fleet at Hawaii, and further that it might exercise a profound influence on [the] present critical situation in Spain, Turkey and Vichy France.'[32] The following day, however, the Admiralty and FO combined to remedy what seemed to them one of the PM's more egregious 'midnight follies'. Commented Cadogan: 'He who was convinced Japan was coming into the war last year [and] insisted on closing the Burma Road (a capital mistake), is now determined that *nothing* will make them come in. And he suffers from the delusion that any cold water thrown on any harebrained U.S. suggestion will stop the U.S. coming into the war!'[33] The Admiralty stressed that Britain's main need in the Western Atlantic was not for capital ships but for cruisers and destroyers for escort and anti-submarine duties.[34] The U.S. should keep a minimum of six battleships and, equally important, two carriers at Pearl Harbor to deter Japan. The FO agreed. Eden had only made the point weakly on the 30th, but at later meetings, beefed up by his officials, he argued that a major U.S. fleet move would provide Japan with both the opportunity (Western weakness) and the pretext (aggression against Germany as covered by the Tripartite Pact) for going to war. With the agreement of Australia and New Zealand, who should have been consulted in the first place, a further cable was sent on 8 May emphasizing that the U.S. had to maintain a deterrent in the Pacific while creating one in the Atlantic—a very delicate balancing of scarce naval resources. One senses a certain malicious pleasure in London that the Americans were now experiencing the predicament that had become a fact of life for British leaders.[35]

*   *   *

In the end, the spring crisis abated, and with it the case for drastic remedies of the sort proposed by Stimson and endorsed for a while by Churchill. It became less necessary for Americans to talk about holding either the Atlantic or the Pacific, for the British to debate whether to sacrifice the Mediterranean or the Far East. The more limited swap of three battleships and accompanying vessels was a compromise acceptable to policymakers in London and Washington.[36] Furthermore, it indicated that the hypothetical alliance strategy agreed at the Washington talks was already being implemented before the U.S.A. had entered the war. This Pacific–Atlantic swap was the key to effective Anglo-American co-operation in the Pacific—as the failure of the Far Eastern staff talks later that spring made clear.

ABC–1 had envisaged 'arrangements for mutual support' between the British and U.S. commands in the Far East, and a conference was held for this purpose at Singapore from 21 to 27 April, in conjunction with Australian and Dutch representatives. However, its report (ADB–1) was rejected by the U.S. Chiefs of Staff in June. This was partly because the document contained implicit political commitments—notably the assumption that an attack on the possessions of one power would be regarded as aggression against them all. This highlighted once again the strictly hypothetical character of all Anglo-American strategic conversations. The Chiefs' other major objection was that, although HMG attached great importance to the defence of Singapore and the Malay Barrier, the report nevertheless entrusted their defence almost entirely to U.S. and Dutch forces, with no provision for a significant British naval presence at Singapore or elsewhere.[37] That was not what the Chiefs understood by 'mutual support'; it sounded more like passing the buck, which, in their view, the British had been trying to do for years in the Far East. The American military therefore reiterated the principles of ABC–1: each country had primary responsibility for the defence of its own Asian interests; that was the precondition for co-operation in areas of mutual concern, such as the Malay Barrier. Not until Britain was ready to send at least a token fleet of her own to Singapore would the Americans be willing to enter into serious discussions about Far Eastern co-operation.

In summary, then, the limited overlap between British and U.S. interest in the Far East did not make it impossible to evolve a common strategy. It did mean, however, that the strategy was necessarily a convoluted compromise. The gradual movement of U.S. naval units from the Pacific to the Atlantic would allow the Royal Navy to reinforce Singapore. This in turn would open the way for meaningful conversations about 'mutual support' in the Far Eastern theatre. The crucial factor in this complicated strategy was—time.

## B. Containing Japan: diplomacy, spring 1941

Gaining time was, of course, the task of the diplomats. During 1941 the principal diplomatic negotiations with Japan were conducted by the U.S.A.—the so-called Hull–Nomura conversations in Washington. Admiral Nomura presented his credentials as Japanese Ambassador to the U.S.A. on 14 February 1941. Between then and Pearl Harbor he met with Hull some forty-five times, frequently in secret at Hull's apartment. He also talked with Welles on six occasions and with Roosevelt on nine.[38] These conversations

229

began as talks about talks but gradually developed into an exploration of the possible foundations of a Far Eastern settlement. Throughout they revolved around three seemingly intractable problems—Japan's military presence in China; her adherence to the Tripartite Fact and the consequent threat to the U.S.A. in the event of an American–German war; and the whole question of Japan's sphere of influence in South-East Asia involving the exclusion of western commerce and the use of force. At stake, in Hull's view, were the most fundamental principles of American foreign policy— national sovereignty, peaceful change and non-discriminatory trade. For Japanese policymakers the issue was increasingly one of national survival.

*      *      *

The Hull–Nomura talks grew out of the activities of a small group of unofficial would-be peacemakers, to whom the State Department gave the soubriquet 'The John Doe Associates'. 'John Doe' was the pseudonym of James M. Drought, Vicar General of the Catholic Foreign Missionary Society. His principal associates were a Japanese Christian banker called Wikawa and Colonel Iwakuro, a War Ministry official from Tokyo who was attached from April 1941 to Nomura's staff. Through prominent Catholic members of the Administration, Drought, and his superior, Bishop Walsh, were in contact with Roosevelt and Hull, while Wikawa and Iwakuro had the general blessing of Konoye, the Japanese premier, and quickly brought Nomura under their wing. The John Doe discussions in March and April were therefore a convenient way for both governments to discover, without commitment, whether there was any common ground. Out of them emerged the so-called 'Draft Understanding'—largely the work of Iwakuro and in consequence favourable to Japan—which Drought presented to Hull on 9 April. The State Department had numerous reservations, but it was anxious not to close the door on talks. So, on 16 April, Hull asked Nomura to ascertain whether Tokyo wished to submit the document formally as a basis for discussion, and also whether it would accept a statement of the general principles that Hull considered fundamental. However, Nomura failed to follow this request. In transmitting the 'Draft Understanding' he implied that it was an official U.S. proposal, rather than a product of the John Doe Associates. He also neglected to report Hull's statement of principles. Whether Nomura's conduct was the result of ineptitude or deliberate intent is a matter of debate, but the result, as Robert Butow has shown, was to create a fundamental misconception which bedevilled the talks throughout 1941.[39] Believing that the 'Draft Understanding' was an official U.S. offer, the Japanese judged subsequent Administration proposals against it. Their reply, on 12 May, elicited in turn an American proposal on 21 June—in reality the *first* official Administration statement—which to Japan seemed like a considerable hardening of the U.S. position.

It was not until 16 May—over five weeks after Drought had presented the 'Draft Understanding' to Hull—that the Secretary of State even mentioned the existence of the talks to the British. He only did so then because Stimson had warned him that there were references to them in U.S. Army intelligence documents that the British were receiving.[40] Furthermore, Hull's account of the talks to Halifax was hardly candid. He pretended that he thought he had told the Ambassador about them before, claimed that he was merely listening to whatever Nomura might have to say and gave no indication that a written Japanese proposal was now under discussion. The whole business was of limited importance, Hull insisted, but he felt he could not afford to miss even a one in twenty-five chance of success. If there was any substantive progress he would naturally bring in the British and Dutch. These disingenuous disclaimers did not satisfy the FO, which was most concerned. It believed that the Japanese were trying to split the nascent Anglo-American alliance and deter the U.S.A. from further support for Britain—holding out the prospect of a settlement at China's expense and warning of possible war if the U.S.A. intervened against Germany. (At this time, it will be remembered, the question of escorts was being keenly debated in Washington and the FO entertained considerable hopes that America was about to enter the European war.[41]) But when Halifax conveyed HMG's anxieties in a blunt *aide-mémoire* of 23 May, Hull was bitterly resentful that his sagacity and good faith were apparently being impugned. He even referred to the sensitive Simon–Stimson controversy over Manchuria in 1931–33 in order, supposedly, to show that the U.S.A. understood Japan far better than HMG. Halifax hastily withdrew his *aide-mémoire* and Eden sent a suitably soothing telegram on the 26th.[42]

To some extent this had been a storm in a teacup—attributable, as the FO surmised, to Hull's guilty conscience and to Halifax's rather tactless exposition of British anxieties. But although surface calm had been restored, it could not conceal two basic problems—Hull's failure to keep the British informed about the talks, and, even more important, whether talks should take place at all.

In principle, the FO was only too pleased for the U.S.A. to assume the major responsibility for Western relations with Japan. With her predicament in Europe and the Mediterranean, Britain could not afford to take the initiative in the Far East, especially given the lack of any firm prior commitments of U.S. support in the event of war. Allowing the United States to lead was therefore both strategically wise and tactically sound—the U.S.A. was the only Western power presently capable of containing Japan and she would be less able to wriggle out of involvement if the talks failed and war came. What HMG had to do, the FO emphasized, was to follow promptly and fully whatever move the Administration made—Hull's reference to Manchuria, when the U.S.A. believed that Britain had not done so, was yet another reminder of a lesson that the FO and especially Eden had taken very much to heart. The problem in all this, as we have noted before, was that it was the British and the Dutch, not the U.S.A., who had the greatest Western interests in the Far East. They stood to suffer most if things went wrong. Although happy to let Hull take the lead in the talks, HMG was therefore most anxious to be kept fully informed about their content and progress. But even after the May contretemps Hull provided minimal information and the FO was naturally wary of pressing him further. In mid-June Halifax was asked to make a new inquiry, but Welles was not forthcoming when they talked on 22 June and Halifax desisted 'rather than trying to pull out unwilling teeth'.[43] The British simply had to wait and see. Hull's monopoly of the negotiations was yet another reminder of their dependence upon the United States.

Even more objectionable to the British was the fact that Hull was talking at all. To some extent their worries were the result of erroneous intelligence. Whereas Hull claimed, correctly, that Nomura was acting for a moderate group in Japan who favoured a peaceful settlement, HMG believed that he was simply the mouthpiece of Matsuoka in a scheme devised with Ribbentrop to drive a wedge between London and Washington.[44] Furthermore, although Hull had insisted he was just listening to Nomura, HMG gathered from intercepted Japanese–German telegrams that the U.S. had made a formal offer.[45] In fact, the British were wrong on both counts. Nomura and Matsuoka *were* following different lines of policy, and the intercepted cables were misleading because they reflected both Tokyo's misconception about the status of the 9 April 'Draft Understanding' and also Matsuoka's efforts to counter Nomura's *démarche* by persuading Berlin that all the peace moves were coming from the U.S.A. and not Japan But even if the British *had* been properly informed, they would still have expressed concern, for, with the possible exception as usual of R. A. Butler, the FO saw very little hope of a durable settlement with Japan. Even Sir Robert Craigie, the British Ambassador in Tokyo, who had been more optimistic the previous summer, agreed that nothing could be done as long as Matsuoka remained Foreign Minister.[46] Japanese foreign policy, in HMG's view, was monolithic— the American idea of trying to identify and strengthen a group of 'moderates' seemed a delusion. Worse still, the talks were dangerous in that they encouraged the Axis and divided the Western powers—the same sort of argument that had been advanced against the Roosevelt–Welles peace initiatives in Europe in January 1938 and February 1940.

The British claimed that the only way to contain Japan was by constructing a firm front among the ABD powers—America, Britain and the Dutch. This would comprise two complementary elements—a joint or parallel ABD warning to Japan against further aggression in South-East Asia and a pledge of mutual support if deterrence failed and Japan resorted to war. Eden and the FO suggested the idea of a warning during each period of anxiety about the Far East, such as the February war scare and the aftermath of the April Russo-Japanese neutrality pact. Ideally FO/FE wanted a public statement, for maximum effect on Japanese public opinion, but the Dutch preferred a private warning, for fear of being too provocative, and Eden was inclined to agree. But the British Chiefs of Staff opposed any kind of warning, public or private, unless the U.S.A. joined in, and whenever Eden and Halifax pressed Washington they were unsuccessful. Hull feared that U.S. involvement in a warning might provoke the Japanese extremists and would also give ammunition to isolationists at home.[47]

Nor was HMG able to secure guarantees of U.S. support. Without Congressional backing any such assurance by the Administration would be worthless, and F.D.R. had told Halifax on 8 February that he did not think American opinion would approve of a war against Japan if only British and Dutch possessions had been attacked.[48] This in turn undermined British co-operation with the Dutch. Repeatedly Dutch ministers in London asked Eden for guarantees of support if Japan attacked the Netherlands East Indies. Eden and the FO believed that the case for compliance was overwhelming: NEI oil was essential for Britain's war effort, the Dutch forces in the Far East were the equal of Britain's and would prove valuable allies in the event of an attack on denuded Singapore, and the two countries had already evolved detailed contingency plans for military co-operation if war broke out.[49] But despite Eden's persuasive memos, the Chiefs of Staff, and especially the Admiralty, opposed any formal commitment to defend the NEI unless the U.S.A. participated. And so, when the question of a British guarantee of the NEI came before the Cabinet in February and March, it was quietly pushed aside—Churchill in February reiterating his familiar instruction not to bother Roosevelt with anything until Lend-Lease had become law. In May the Cabinet did consider making a public statement that would have amounted to a commitment, but action was suspended in mid-June when Japanese–Dutch trade talks broke down and such action might have seemed provocative.[50] Although disliking the American negotiations with Japan, the British were therefore unable to implement their alternative policy—a firm ABD front—because of the lack of U.S. support. In consequence they treated the Dutch rather as the U.S.A. was treating them—co-operating, consulting, making contingency plans, but avoiding any firm commitments.

## C. Tightening the screw on Japan: the Indochina crisis, July–August 1941

Both the American and British governments were partially accurate in their perceptions of the situation in Japan.[51] As the State Department concluded, a rift had developed in Tokyo. By early 1941 Konoye and the military were disturbed both by Matsuoka's undisguised ambition and by his endorsement of German pressure for an attack on Singapore. Konoye was desperately anxious to avoid war with America and covertly encouraged the efforts of Nomura, Wikawa and Iwakuro. News of the Washington talks came as a shock to Matsuoka. Their continuance despite his opposition represented a distinct setback to his authority, which was further diminished by the German attack on Russia about which Japan had not been informed. This was a further indication of how tenuous the Axis alliance really was, but it did provide Japan with a new opportunity to expand south with impunity. Matsuoka, however, again following Berlin even though this meant repudiating the neutrality pact he had so recently signed with Moscow, argued that they should join Germany against Russia. The debate was formally settled at an Imperial Conference on 2 July, which agreed that Japan should concentrate for the moment on southward expansion while making every effort to avoid war with the U.S.A. Matsuoka was forced from office in mid-July.

But although the State Department had correctly discerned the power struggle in Tokyo, the FO was right to feel that ultimately the argument was about means rather than ends. What distinguished Konoye from Matsuoka was the former's hope that Japanese goals could be achieved without a potentially disastrous war against the U.S.A. But there was no dispute in Tokyo on the need for a sphere of influence, or that in the last analysis force would have to be used if diplomacy failed.[52] This had been reiterated in the 2 July decision. Concurrent with Matsuoka's fall, Japanese leaders therefore took advantage of the favourable international situation in July 1941 to move south again. In September 1940 they had acquired bases in northern Indochina; on 23 July 1941 it was announced that Vichy had granted Japan naval and air bases in southern Indochina and the right to move and manoeuvre troops. This brought Singapore within range of Japanese bombers. On the 29th an agreement was signed for joint Franco-Japanese defence of Indochina—in other words a Japanese occupation. Next on Tokyo's list was Thailand, Malaya's northern neighbour.

*     *     *

It was the American response to these developments that proved decisive. Through its MAGIC intercepts of Japanese cable traffic the Administration was quickly aware of the gist of the 2 July decision and of the mounting threat to Indochina, and therefore had time to prepare its reaction. Its principal diplomatic weapon was Japan's reliance on foreign imports of strategic raw materials, and in particular of oil—60 per cent of Japan's supplies in 1940 had come from the U.S.A. and another 30 per cent from the NEI and Caribbean.[53] As in July and October 1940 the Cabinet hawks—Stimson, Morgenthau, Knox and Ickes—argued that a total embargo was the only effective deterrent, whereas Hull and most of his officials, together with the senior admirals, feared that this would be provocative and favoured only a substantial reduction in Japan's oil supplies. Once again the President sided with the advocates of caution. In Cabinet meetings on 18 and 24 July it was agreed that if Japan moved into Indochina the Administration would freeze all her assets in the U.S.A.—in other words making their use for each commercial transaction subject to Government approval. This would be a dramatic warning to Japan. But, as F.D R. made clear, although U.S.-Japanese trade would be substantially reduced, approval was still to be quietly given for the export of some oil and gasoline, because a complete oil embargo would probably precipitate a Pacific war. To preserve flexibility and to keep the Japanese guessing for the moment there would be no public announcement as to how severely the freezing order would be implemented. The Japanese would be left to find that out for themselves.[54]

The freezing order came into effect on 26 July. At the same time a major revision of U.S. Far Eastern strategy was under way.[55] Throughout the 1930s the War Department had been convinced that no serious effort could or should be made to hold the Philippines—a vast archipelago of 7,100 islands, most of them minute, sprawled over some 1,100 miles of ocean. To defend even the largest ones, notably Luzon which included the main naval base at Manila, would require a vast commitment, with no guarantee of success, and in any case by 1940–41 American priorities had been clearly determined: concentration on the Atlantic, no major commitments west of Hawaii. But the crisis of mid-1941 precipitated a radical reappraisal. Russia's preoccupation with her European front and Japan's new moves in Indochina made it necessary, U.S. policymakers believed, to increase American strength in the Far East. A new U.S. Army command was created in the Philippines under General Douglas MacArthur, who had been responsible for training the Filipino army in the 1930s. On 31 July Marshall stated that the defence of the Philippines was official U.S. policy and over the next few weeks an emergency programme was prepared to make this possible. Its central feature—and the principal reason for the new American optimism—was the B–17 bomber (Flying Fortress). Based on reports of B–17 operations with the RAF in Europe, Stimson and the War Department quickly convinced themselves that a sizeable force of B–17s in the Philippines would act as a deterrent not only against direct attack but also against Japanese aggression anywhere in Asia. They would threaten any expeditionary forces sailing south or east and even menace Tokyo, it was believed, if Japan considered attacking Russia. The B–17 'has completely changed the strategy of the Pacific', Stimson wrote jubilantly in his diary.[56] From August 1941 the War Department's top priority was therefore to reinforce the Philippines—with men, equipment, fighters and above all heavy bombers.[57] The build-up was to be complete by February or March 1942. By that time 165 B–17s—about half total U.S. strength—would be based in the Philippines.

The United States now had a very definite interest in playing for time, to permit this new strategy to come to fruition. Firm but unprovocative economic restrictions were one answer; the other was to spin out the diplomatic negotiations as long as possible. In line with the shift in War Department strategy, Stimson now became one of the keenest supporters of the Hull–Nomura conversations. These had been terminated on 23 July when Nomura was told that, in view of Japan's move into Indochina, Hull saw no basis for further talks.[58] But at the Atlantic meeting Roosevelt explained to Churchill that he intended to resume the talks in the hope of gaining time. Just before the Japanese move he had suggested, off the cuff to Nomura, the possibility of an international agreement to neutralize Indochina. The Japanese had picked up the idea, though with unacceptable conditions, Roosevelt said, and he intended to negotiate about these conditions and so gain 'say 30 days'. During the negotiations he promised that 'the existing economic measures' would be maintained in full force.[59]

Unfortunately, Roosevelt had no idea what those measures really were. He had intended only a partial, deterrent cutback in trade; in fact no oil at all was sold to Japan after 26 July 1941.[60] As Irvine Anderson and Jonathan Utley have shown, this was largely due to the actions of hawkish, middle-level bureaucrats. To understand what happened some administrative detail is necessary. After the freezing order, Japan's applications for oil purchases had to be approved by two separate bodies. The first was the Office of Export Control, which decided whether the oil could be spared from U.S. national needs. This it did under criteria established by the State Department. If an export licence was issued it was then the responsibility of the newly created, interdepartmental Foreign Funds Control Committee (FFCC) to decide whether to release the necessary frozen funds. By early August, in line with the Roosevelt–Hull policy, Export Control and the State Department had established the new criteria—a lower limit on the octane level of exportable fuel (to prevent Japan refining higher-grade crude for use in aircraft), and also general quotas designed to reduce Japanese oil imports from the U.S. to the 'normal' amounts of the mid-1930s. On 1 August Export Control notified the FFCC that Japan was entitled to 450,000 gallons of 'not so good' gasoline and issued licences for $300,000 of diesel fuel.[61] But the staff of the FFCC, especially Dean Acheson, the hawkish Assistant Secretary who was State's representative, took the toughest possible line. They insisted that no frozen funds would be released until the Japanese had used up their deposits in South American banks and the funds withdrawn from the U.S.A. before the freezing order. Japanese Embassy officials protested that this posed numerous problems. They persisted with their pressure on the FFCC and deadlock ensued. It was not until early September that Hull and Roosevelt (both of whom had been busy or away during August) appreciated what had happened. Rather than appear to back down, and thereby encourage the Japanese, Hull decided to institutionalize the FFCC's tactics.[62] By September 1941, therefore, the Administration was effectively enforcing a complete oil embargo against Japan. Because of F.D.R.'s casual administrative habits and the lack of an adequate White House secretariat to ensure that decisions were properly executed, U.S. diplomatic and commercial policies were badly out of line. Although its overriding goal was to gain time, the Administration was operating a foreign economic policy likely to force Japan to an early decision for peace or war.

\*     \*     \*

Throughout these developments the British Government remained an impotent bystander, much as it had been during the similar debate a year before. Its cardinal principle was to keep in step with the U.S. Government, and this it managed to do, despite the uncertainty as to what U.S. policy really was. Thus, in late July HMG adopted a very firm position, freezing Japanese assets in Britain simultaneously with the U.S.A. on the 26th, and planning very restrictive criteria for licensing exports and releasing funds for Japanese imports from the British Empire, including key raw materials from Malaya. When it became clear in early August that the U.S. intended only a partial embargo, British measures were somewhat relaxed in principle, but in practice Whitehall kept all trade with Japan on ice until U.S. policy on the release of funds had been clarified. Then, in September, as the FFCC's stalling became established Administration policy, the British and Dutch followed suit—confirming the trend towards a complete trade embargo.[63] This was not, however, the policy that Whitehall had originally advocated. During July reports from Washington about the Administration's intentions were very confused, but the frequent talk of a complete embargo was considered alarming in London. The FO, the Ministry of Economic Warfare and the interdepartmental Far Eastern Committee all agreed that such a move could well provoke Japan to war, contrary to the basic goal of British and U.S. policy. 'We should prefer, I think, that the screw be turned but not right home', minuted Ashley Clarke of FO/FE.[64]

Why, then, did HMG acquiesce in the *de facto* U.S. embargo? Partly because of its conviction that firm U.S. action was the key to successful deterrence—better that this action be too firm than not firm enough. Eden was particularly anxious to avoid any relaxation of the measures once they had been applied—that would have the worst possible effect in Tokyo.[65] But why did HMG not try to ensure from the beginning that the U.S. adopted and maintained a policy that accorded with Britain's attitude? That question had been faced and answered on 20 July in a lucid paper for the Cabinet by Eden and FO/FE. If the U.S.A. adopted a total embargo, the memo argued, Japan would either have to reverse her whole expansionary policy or else push south to secure her essential raw materials, thereby risking war with the British and Dutch. There seemed a real possibility that she would follow the latter course, hoping that the U.S.A. would not intervene in time. 'The question therefore arises whether we are prepared to go the whole way with the United States if they desire to take such drastic action; and, if not, whether we should attempt to restrain the United States.' Eden's response was unequivocal. He briskly dismissed the Chiefs of Staff's standard argument—do nothing to risk war until Britain had a firm pledge of U.S. armed support. Given F.D.R.'s constitutional and political position it was 'idle' to hope for a firm commitment. He also believed 'that the issue with Japan must be faced sooner or later and that the risk of the United States not intervening in a war between ourselves and Japan is small'. The only question in his judgement was whether to join the U.S. in forcing the issue at that time over Indochina or to wait until the Japanese posed a more direct threat (e.g. to Thailand) or provided a more favourable opportunity (if they attacked Russia). While the latter might be the best moment from HMG's point of view, Eden argued, the 'paramount' consideration was Anglo-American co-operation. HMG should on no account discourage the U.S. from firm action or do other than follow her lead. 'The risk of creating another Stimson–Simon incident and of seriously weakening the ties between us and America is real.'[66]

For Eden the Indochina crisis of July 1941 marked a potential turning point in Anglo-American relations in the Far East. As Foreign Secretary in 1937–38 he had tried in vain to draw the U.S. and Chamberlain into a common policy towards Japan. Now, at long last, the Americans were about to take firm and decisive action of some sort. He felt that if HMG quibbled at this point it could undermine the mutual trust and co-operation that had been created so laboriously over the previous few years. The Cabinet apparently agreed. On 21 July it approved Eden's recommendations after long discussion.[67] Effectively HMG was committing itself to whatever the U.S. decided, despite the acknowledged danger of provoking Japan, despite Britain's military weakness in the Far East, and despite the lack of American commitments. In view of the bellicose Japanese reaction to the *de facto* embargo—which I shall discuss in a moment—it was undoubtedly a fateful decision.

Clearly Eden did not believe that HMG was taking an unjustified risk. Like Churchill, he thought that Japan would probably not go to war with Britain, and certainly not with the U.S.A., and he was confident that the Americans would intervene if war did break out.[68] Others were not so sure. On being informed of the Cabinet's decision, the Australian Government asked HMG on 23 July to press for a firm U.S. commitment. Eden rejected this—any attempt to make British support of U.S. economic measures conditional upon such a commitment might deter the Americans from acting, he argued.[69] But Eden was not oblivious to Britain's exposed position. His view, as stated in the 20 July memo, was that *after* the ABD measures had been applied and Britain had thus proved her fidelity, HMG should press for 'the clearest possible indication' that the U.S.A would provide 'active armed support' in the event of an Anglo-Japanese war.[70] Meanwhile the Dutch had renewed their insistent requests for a comparable commitment from Britain if Japan attacked the NEI. The Chiefs were still opposed, as long as the U.S. stood aloof, and Churchill shared their opinion. He argued as usual that if war came the main danger would not be an attack on Singapore, which he considered most unlikely, but Japanese raiding of British trade routes. Since the Admiralty could not possibly provide adequate protection at this time, he felt it might be better to avoid being committed automatically, irrespective of the U.S. attitude, to a declaration of war if Japan attacked the Dutch.[71] The anxieties of the Australians and the Dutch in late July therefore forced HMG back yet again to the uncertainty at the core of its Far Eastern policy—what would the Americans do if war broke out? Moreover, war appeared distressingly close. It seemed that Japan was going to apply new pressure on Thailand for bases and military access. Could the Administration be induced this time to support a firm warning to Japan? Consequently, by the end of July Eden and the Cabinet had decided on a new and major effort to create a firm ABD front through a joint declaration against further Japanese aggression and mutual guarantees in case deterrence failed.[72]

On the advice of Ambassador Winant this *démarche* was made at the highest level—by Churchill in person at the Atlantic Meeting.[73] On 10 August the PM presented a proposal, drafted by Cadogan, for parallel British and U.S. notes to Japan. The American note would state that 'any further encroachment by Japan in the South-West Pacific would produce a situation in which the United States Government would be compelled to take counter-measures even though these might lead to war between the United States and Japan'. It would also say: 'If any Third Power becomes the object of aggression by Japan in consequence of such counter-measures or of their support of them, the President would have the intention to seek authority from Congress to give aid to such a Power.' (Winant had suggested this formulation as a possible compromise between British desires and Roosevelt's constitutional predicament.) To support his request Churchill resorted to scare tactics. If the U.S. did not present this note, he claimed, Japan would declare war and be able to 'seize or destroy' all British merchant shipping in Far Eastern waters, thereby administering an 'almost decisive' blow to his Government.[74] But Roosevelt and Welles were unmoved. When they all met again the next day, F.D.R. immediately made it clear that even Winant's qualified statement of intent was unacceptable.[75] The tactical differences on how best to deter Japan also became apparent—F.D.R. placing his emphasis on renewed talks, Churchill warning him of Japanese treachery and stressing the need for a firm ABD front. But the PM *did* secure a promise to maintain the existing economic measures and, above, all, what he understood to be Roosevelt's firm promise to issue a warning to Japan on the lines of the British proposal. Aware of F.D.R.'s evasiveness, and anxious to return home with something definite from the anti-climactic meeting, Churchill did his best to pin the President down. He was able to tell his Cabinet colleagues that Roosevelt had promised 'on more than one occasion' to use the British form of words and that he was 'confident that the President would not tone it down'.[76]

However, the PM's confidence proved sadly misplaced. Whether Roosevelt had deceived Churchill to get him off his back, or whether the President had genuinely intended to issue the direct warning and then was dissuaded by Hull is unclear. At any rate, once back in Washington, F.D.R. readily accepted State Department advice that the warning in its present form would be provocative and also too committal for U.S. opinion. The note he gave Nomura on 17 August therefore said that if Japan took any further steps towards the military domination of neighbouring countries the U.S.A. 'would be compelled to take immediately any and all steps which it may deem necessary toward safeguarding the legitimate rights and interests of the United States and American nationals and toward insuring the safety and security of the United States'.[77] The effect was further reduced by the fact that Roosevelt read the note before turning to the main part of the meeting—a statement about the resumption of talks—and by his mood throughout, which, if Nomura can be believed, was mild and affable. When the British finally obtained a copy of the U.S. note on 23 August they found it most unsatisfactory. There was no reference to possible war, the focus was on American rights and interests, and the warning covered all Japan's neighbours rather than the south-west Pacific. It therefore read more like yet another of Hull's general statements of principle than a firm deterrent against Japanese aggression against Thailand. Faced with its failure to commit the U.S.A. and with Hull's repeated advice to avoid provocation, the FO eventually decided to drop the idea of a parallel British note.[78]

All that HMG could do was to try to strengthen Britain's own position in the Far East in case war came. Here at least the Atlantic Meeting had been encouraging, for Roosevelt's promise of extended U.S. naval operations in the Atlantic allowed the Royal Navy at long last to consider moving ships to the Far East. But Churchill and the Admiralty were unable to agree in late August on the correct strategy. The Admiralty, in the person of Pound, the First Sea Lord, wanted to play safe. It would gradually send reinforcements into the Indian Ocean, based on Ceylon, and only when a balanced fleet had been created—in March 1942—would this move into the danger-zone at Singapore. For the rest of 1941 the Admiralty felt it could only move one Queen Elizabeth class battleship and then four R class battleships (all of World War I vintage). To release any of the modern battleships of the King George V (KGV) class from the Home Fleet would be most unwise, it felt, in view of the threat from the German battleship *Tirpitz*. Churchill, by contrast, wanted to send a small but powerful squadron, comprising an aircraft carrier and two modern capital ships (including a KGV) straight to Singapore as soon as possible. He dismissed the R class vessels as 'floating coffins' and ridiculed the Navy's excessive caution about the Atlantic. 'TIRPITZ is doing to us exactly what a K.G.V. in the Indian Ocean would do to the Japanese Navy. It exercises a vague, general fear and menaces all points at once.' He thought that Japan was unlike y to make a new move for at least three months and that his suggested force could prove 'a decisive deterrent'.[79]

In the end, it was the Admiralty's plan that was implemented. This is interesting in view of Churchill's determination to control all major naval dispositions and his usual dominance over Pound.[80] But perhaps the unusual resistance from a naval officer whom he respected made Churchill pause. In any case, the Thai crisis and the general threat to South-East Asia diminished during August and, just as after the February scare, British leaders again let Far Eastern problems slip from view. Supply priorities remained the Middle East, where a new offensive was planned, and Russia, in preparation for the Harriman–Beaverbrook mission in late September.[81] With Churchill's attention again elsewhere, Pound was left to implement the Admiralty's cautious plan as and when he felt able.

## D. Time runs out: autumn 1941

As moderates in London and Washington had anticipated, the *de facto* oil embargo brought the issue of peace or war to a head in Tokyo. The Navy's oil stocks would last for perhaps 18 months; the Army's for roughly a year. No further oil, it seemed, could be expected from the Western Hemisphere and the NEI, which together had supplied 90 per cent of Japan's needs. Other vital raw materials—cotton, rice, rubber and iron ore—were also being cut off. If Japan was going to have to fight to regain her sphere of influence, the longer she waited the weaker she would be. Climatic considerations were also important. The best time for amphibious operations in the South China Sea would be early November. December was also feasible, but thereafter the north-easterly monsoon would make conditions almost impossible until the spring. In short, if war was inevitable, it was in Japan's interests that it come within the next few months. Yet the Army and Navy still accepted that Japan should try to achieve her goals by diplomatic means. Konoye wished to stake all on a summit meeting with Roosevelt, and this became the main theme of Japanese diplomacy from August. Accordingly the Army forced a compromise which was formally approved at the Imperial Conference on 6 September. Preparations for war with the ABD powers would be completed by early October. If, at that point, no diplomatic solution had been reached, Japan would take the decision for peace or war.[82]

Nomura proposed a Konoye–Roosevelt Pacific meeting when he saw the President on 17 August, and Konoye urged it strongly in a personal message ten days later.[83] F.D.R. initially accepted. The idea accorded with his predilection for personal diplomacy and with his confidence in his own persuasive talents. The U.S. Embassy in Tokyo was also enthusiastic. Ambassador Grew believed that the fall of Matsuoka indicated a resurgence of the 'moderates' in Japan and offered a new, if slender, chance for agreement. He became the most ardent supporter in American diplomatic circles of the idea of a meeting, arguing that it should take place quickly and without prior conditions in order not to weaken further Konoye's already fragile domestic base.[84] But Grew's judgement no longer carried much weight in Washington, and Hull and his Far Eastern advisers took a very different view. A meeting of national leaders aroused public expectations, committed each country's prestige, and made it essential to return with some kind of agreement, however tenuous and unreal. They insisted, and F.D.R. eventually agreed, that no summit meeting should take place until basic agreement had already been reached. This of course was standard diplomatic precept, but Hull's attitude must also have been influenced by the President's recent Atlantic conference, when he stepped so far beyond the bounds of State's Far Eastern policy. Henceforth, Hull was determined not to give Roosevelt a long rein. During September the Department scrutinized Japan's latest proposal and discussed it with Nomura. Finally, in a note dated 2 October, it told Japan in effect that until she accepted America's fundamental principles there was no point in a summit meeting.[85]

Once again the British were perturbed spectators of this renewed diplomatic activity. Hull deigned to provide only occasional, vague reports, insisting all along that he was simply engaged in talks about talks, largely to gain time, and that none of his sacred principles would ever be violated. British frustration was general, but precise reactions differed. In Tokyo the British Ambassador, Sir Robert Craigie, shared Grew's conviction that the fall of Matsuoka offered a new opportunity for seeking a settlement. But whereas Grew's panacea was a Konoye–Roosevelt meeting, Craigie believed that full British involvement in the Washington negotiations was the crucial factor. He argued that Britain's Far Eastern interests were similar to America's but not identical, that the U.S.A. could not be relied upon to defend them in peace or war and that American diplomacy was inept and insensitive. He also insisted that both governments were underestimating Japan's war potential, and that there remained a chance of keeping her '*really* neutral' through skilful diplomacy. On various occasions that autumn he urged HMG to request, as of right, 'full and precise information' about the talks so as to help get them back on the rails.[86] But Craigie, like Grew, was largely discredited at home. FO/FE had long since abandoned hope of genuine Japanese neutrality. The most it expected was non-belligerency, and this, the Department believed, could be achieved, if at all, only by a firm ABD front in which the Americans took the lead. It feared that in the talks Hull and Roosevelt might be deceived by the Japanese into a position from which retreat might be difficult, particularly if a summit meeting took place.[87] Some members of FO/FE even suggested in the early autumn that it might be in HMG's interest to force matters to a head, because time was of more value to Japan that to the West.[88] Few senior policymakers shared this view, however, and the worst British fears about the talks were allayed by a conversation between Hull and Halifax on 4 October (*after* the U.S. reply to Japan) in which the Secretary belatedly explained State's attitude toward a summit meeting.[89] Commented Eden in a representative minute on 14 October: 'I see no harm in these American talks. The passage of time suits us & the Dutch.'[90] In any case, all the FO accepted the axioms that the

241

Americans called the tune in the Far East and that the talks helped commit them more deeply.

The American note of 2 October sealed Konoye's fate. The grace period was now at an end and army leaders were determined that the 6 September decision, to commit Japan to either peace or war in early October, should now be honoured. Konoye was forced from power and his War Minister, General Tojo, became premier on 18 October. But, in deference to the Emperor, Tojo agreed to re-examine Japan's policy. The climax of ten days of intense deliberations came in a prolonged conference on 1–2 November, which essentially decided to observe the 6 September decision but on a revised timetable. The diplomats would have until the end of November to complete an agreement. If they were unsuccessful by that date war with Britain and the U.S.A. would automatically follow. Even the new Foreign Minister, Togo, accepted this decision, which represented a considerable concession on the Army's part.

The Japanese submitted a new proposal for a lasting settlement on 7 November. This was still not congruent with American principles and Hull rejected it. On 20 November Nomura presented Japan's offer of a *modus vivendi*—a temporary agreement—which would effectively restore relations to the pre-26 July situation. In other words, Japan would withdraw from southern Indochina and the U.S. would end its freezing order and oil embargo. To this the Americans were more responsive. Although the suggested terms were unacceptable, the Administration favoured the principle of a temporary agreement that would give it another few months to complete its Far Eastern military build-up. Nine B–17s had arrived in the Philippines on 12 September and a further 25 during the first half of November. Large movements of aircraft and troops were planned for November and December but the whole programme would not be complete until February or March 1942. Roosevelt, Marshall and Stark were therefore anxious for Hull to gain as much time as possible. Accordingly State prepared an American *modus vivendi*. This called for a total Japanese withdrawal from Indochina, except for a maximum of 25,000 troops in the north, and a modified freezing order, permitting, for instance, supply of petroleum on a monthly basis for purely civilian needs. The agreement would last for three months. During that time both sides should make a new effort to reach a 'broad-gauge' settlement. To this end Hull intended to submit with the *modus vivendi* a new statement of principles and proposals for a comprehensive agreement. On 22 November he called in Halifax and the Chinese, Dutch and Australian envoys, outlined the proposed *modus vivendi* and asked them to obtain urgently their governments' reactions. Two days later he gave them further details but on neither occasion were they given copies to take away.[91]

As usual, HMG's ideal answer to Japan was a firm ABD front. On 5 and 30 November Churchill urged Roosevelt again to issue the blunt, parallel warning on which he had reneged in August. But Britain, like the U.S.A., had much to gain from a few months' extra time. In early October, relieved of Western Atlantic commitments by the extended U.S. naval patrols and escorts, the Admiralty had set in motion its plan for the gradual creation of an Eastern Fleet by March 1942, beginning with the movement of five older battleships to the Indian Ocean. But Churchill still wanted a small, modern force based as soon as possible on Singapore.[92] Eden agreed, concerned about the deteriorating situation after Konoye's fall, as did the other principal members of the War Cabinet. In two major meetings of the Defence Committee on 17 and 20 October the Admiralty was forced to back down. It was agreed that the *Prince of Wales* (a new KGV battleship which had carried Churchill to the Atlantic meeting), together with the battle cruiser *Repulse* and the aircraft carrier *Indomitable*, would converge on Singapore over the next few weeks. Later in the year the older battleships would join them, followed in 1942 by other capital ships, cruisers and destroyers.[93] The primary function of the initial nucleus—Force 'G' under Admiral Phillips— was to deter Japan—hence the decision to give the movements of the *Prince of Wales* the maximum possible publicity. It was also supposed to reassure the Australasian Dominions. But Churchill was probably also very conscious of the likely effect in the U.S.A. Raymond Callahan has suggested that he may have hoped that the move of precious British vessels to Singapore would embarrass the U.S.A. into a reciprocal gesture.[94] More likely, he had in mind the ABC-1 guidelines and the abortive ABD-1 agreement, which showed that only when the British had done their bit to reinforce Singapore would the Americans be willing to engage in serious consultation about the defence of the Malay Barrier.[95] Phillips' little fleet constituted the necessary catalyst for co-operation.

HMG therefore shared the Administration's interest in gaining time. This was particularly true of senior policymakers who were familiar with the whole picture—strategic as well as diplomatic. On the other hand, with memories of Hitler's progress in the 1930s, no one wanted a temporary agreement that allowed Japan to increase her strength. Thus the Ministry of Economic Warfare, as usual, argued that no realistic and enforceable distinction could be made between oil for civilian and military use, and general concern was expressed that nothing in the U.S. proposal prevented Japan from using its remaining forces in Indochina for a new drive into China. Churchill himself summed up the two considerations that governed HMG's response to the *modus vivendi* proposals: 'Our major interest is: no further [Japanese] encroachments and no war, as we have enough of the latter . . . I must say that I should feel pleased if I read that an American– Japanese agreement had been made by which we were no worse off three months hence in the Far East than we are now.'[96] The question was how best to reach such an agreement—and here the British felt strongly that Hull was adopting the wrong tactics. They assumed that Japan's proposal should be regarded 'as the opening move in a process of bargaining'. The Japanese had asked for much and offered little. The Americans should respond in kind. One way was to reject Japan's proposal, 'and (while making clear that a limited agreement is not ruled out) to leave it to the Japanese to produce a better offer'. This was FO/FE's suggestion. Eden and the Cabinet preferred a counter-proposal which stated America's maximum demands and offered the minimum concessions.[97] Such an approach was sound strategy for beginning any diplomatic negotiations; it coincided with HMG's conviction that Japan would respond to U.S. firmness; and it also took account of the mistakes of the 1930s. HMG's 'immediate reaction', communicated on 23 November, was therefore that it approved of the attempt to reach an interim settlement but that it favoured a tougher initial negotiating position, particularly on the question of China. This was confirmed by Churchill in a message to Roosevelt on the 26th and formally stated, as the considered decision of HMG and the Dominions, on 28 November.[98]

But two days before this Hull had decided to abandon the whole idea. The State Department cited Britain's 'half-hearted support' as one of the contributory reasons for its decision.[99] Probably HMG's messages could have been phrased with greater clarity and tact, particularly by giving as much space to HMG's basic agreement as to its specific reservations. The British, in turn, had reason to be angry that Hull gave them neither the time to make up their own minds, let alone consult the Dominions, nor the detailed information and documents on which to reach a decision.[100] But these irritations are symptomatic of a basic failure of communication between the two governments, for which Hull must probably bear the principal responsibility. HMG understood that the matter was urgent, but took that to mean weeks rather than days— hence its assumption that Japan's proposal was 'the opening move in a process of bargaining'. Hull's impatience was largely due to his knowledge from the intercepted Japanese cables that a deadline of 25 November (later extended to the 29th) had been imposed on the negotiations and that thereafter Japan would take aggressive action. The Administration conveyed to HMG its sense of urgency, but not, so far as can be determined, the evidence on which this was based. The failure to do so is understandable— the intercepts were an invaluable source of intelligence and very few U.S. policymakers were allowed to receive them for fear of leakage—but it prevented a proper understanding in London of why the U.S.A. wanted not advice but acquiescence. In any case, Hull was now at the end of his tether. He had been forced to take nearly two months off in the summer for nervous exhaustion, and by November he was in no state to tolerate criticism or questioning. The shrill objections from China, which, to Hull's weary and frustrated mind, seemed to have been endorsed disloyally by Churchill and the FO, together with the difficulties of justifying domestically any agreement that smacked of 'appeasement', made it clear that he would have to fight hard at home and abroad to get support for his proposal. The final straw was new intelligence on 25 November that a large Japanese expeditionary force had embarked at Shanghai and was moving south. The next morning Hull proposed to Roosevelt that the *modus vivendi* be abandoned and that the Japanese simply be given the U.S. ten-point plan for a general settlement. Earlier in the month the President had been as keen as any in Washington to win three or even six months' delay. But on the 26th he 'promptly agreed' to Hull's suggestion.[101] It would seem that he, like Hull, had concluded from the intelligence reports that time had finally run out.

Hull's ten-point note was not, as some have suggested, an 'ultimatum', but it was certainly a blunt and unconciliatory statement of the U.S. position on the question of a long-term settlement. When London belatedly received the news even FO/FE was unhappy that Hull had presented this general statement 'unsweetened by any concrete offer . . . This procedure must have produced a very unfavourable effect on the Japanese to no great purpose. The Japanese may even have concluded from this that there is nothing more to be gained from the conversations.'[102] But although disconcerted and displeased, HMG clearly did not consider the U.S. action disastrous. When Eden explained it to the Cabinet he expressed no particular anxiety, while hard-line elements in the FO and MEW decided, with much self-righteousness, that they had saved Hull from perpetrating a Far Eastern Munich.[103] Once again the assumption was that, even if Anglo-American co-operation was not of the best, and even if war did come, the Japanese could be contained at low cost. The important thing now was to consolidate the ABD front. Once more the FO, supported by Australia, called for British guarantees of the NEI and Thailand, the likely target for Japan's next move. Also at issue was whether HMG would give the British Commander in the Far East, Brooke-Popham, authority to mount Operation 'Matador'—a pre-emptive strike on the Kra Isthmus, joining Thailand with Malaya—if a Japanese threat materialized. The Chiefs of Staff still argued that until firm U.S. commitments had been made HMG should take no action, save in defence of Britain's vital interests, that might precipitate war with Japan. That maxim, in their view, ruled out the guarantees and 'Matador', even though they admitted that an attack on Kra could only be intended as a springboard against Singapore.[104]

Churchill sided with the Chiefs. He saw the Far East as part of a global drama—for which there were four possible scenarios:

1 U.S.A. in the war against Germany; Japan neutral
2 U.S.A. at war on the Allied side; Japan at war on the Axis side
3 U.S.A. and Japan both out of the war
4 U.S.A. out of the war; Japan in it.

The first of these would be best for Britain; the last had to be avoided at all costs, Churchill told the Cabinet.[105] This fear of having to fight a Pacific war without American help preoccupied Churchill in the autumn of 1941. Despite his official directives to this effect, and unlike the FO, he was not willing to base British policy on the assumption that the U.S.A. would automatically enter an Anglo-Japanese war.[106] Like the Chiefs he therefore opposed any action that might provoke Japan without the assurance of U.S. support, or that might lead Americans to believe that Britain was trying to drag them into her war. On the other hand, it was equally important to avoid arousing the old suspicion that Britain would not support a U.S. lead. Thus, significantly, the only prior commitment that Churchill made was to the United States. Stating publicly what had been established privately as HMG policy back in the autumn of 1940, he announced in speeches on 24 August and especially 10 November that in the event of a U.S.–Japan war 'the British declaration would follow within the hour'.[107] Thus, Churchill wanted a Pacific war to be an American–Japanese conflict, which Britain would immediately join, rather than an Anglo-Japanese conflict, to which the U.S. attitude would be uncertain. He was willing to forgo early military advantages in order to ensure this.[108] In any case, Churchill was probably playing for higher stakes than the Far East, which had never been at the centre of his attention. His supreme goal was an Anglo-American alliance against

Germany. By November 1941 there seemed little likelihood that the confused state of undeclared war in the Atlantic would crystallize quickly into a formal U.S.–German conflict. On the other hand, Churchill, like F.D.R., assumed that the Axis alliance was much tighter than it actually was.[109] It must therefore have seemed to him that a Far Eastern conflict, *if* properly engineered, might prove America's back door to world war.

To understand these considerations, we must remember that Pearl Harbor came as a total surprise. After the failure of the *modus vivendi* negotiations, Washington and London were prepared for a Japanese attack—but in the form of an offensive against Thailand and perhaps the NEI.[110] In late November 1941 the crucial question, therefore, remained—what would the U.S.A. do if non-American territory was attacked? F.D.R. and his military advisers had agreed on 28 November that the U.S.A. would have to fight if Japan invaded British or Dutch possessions, but the State Department remained evasive in the face of British questions.[111] On 1 December, however, Roosevelt discussed the Far Eastern situation with Halifax. The Ambassador reported: 'At one point he threw in an aside that in the event of an attack on ourselves or the Dutch, we should obviously all be together. . .' During the conversation F.D.R. also indicated, according to Halifax, that if Japan attacked the Kra Isthmus 'we could certainly count on their support, though it might take a short time, he spoke of a few days, to get things into political shape here.' In addition, the President said that although, for constitutional reasons, he could not make a guarantee to Thailand, HMG could be sure that any British commitment would have full U.S. support.[112]

The conversation was typical of Roosevelt—the momentous presented casually as the obvious. The FO was naturally delighted, but two decades of British disillusion could not be obliterated by a few genial words. When the Cabinet's Defence Committee met to discuss Halifax's telegram, the PM was still unwilling to take further action until 'he was quite sure of the American attitude'. Accordingly Halifax was instructed to pin the President down. Did Roosevelt mean 'armed support'? Yes, F.D.R. confirmed on the evening of the 3rd, he did. Of course, there was still no certainty that Congress would deliver, but the British left that problem for Roosevelt to solve. They now had the commitment they had sought for so long, and on which their Far Eastern policy depended. When the Cabinet met on the evening of the 4th Churchill quickly agreed that HMG should now give the Dutch a formal guarantee of armed support, that Brooke-Popham should be granted discretionary authority to mount 'Matador' if the Kra Isthmus was threatened, and that HMG should now prepare to guarantee Thailand.[113] On the spot, too, Anglo-American co-operation was improving. Force 'G' had now arrived at Singapore, and Admiral Phillips flew to Manila to discuss strategy with Admiral Hart, commander of the U.S. Asiatic Fleet, on 6–7 December. They agreed that defence of the Malay Barrier was of 'great importance' and formulated preliminary plans for mutual support. Hart ordered one of his destroyer divisions to Singapore and Phillips agreed that by April 1942 the British fleet would move north to Manila—a more suitable base for offensive operations against Japan.[114] And the ABD diplomatic front was also becoming firm. At last Roosevelt had decided to issue the warning that Churchill wanted—albeit as part of a process designed to educate U.S. opinion and ensure its support for a war in defence of non-American territory. On 6 December F.D.R. sent a message to the Emperor expressing his grave concern at Japanese movements. If no answer was received, he intended to issue a warning against further aggression. This would take the form of an address to Congress on the 9th, explaining why South-East Asia was of vital concern to the U.S.A. Only after that, on the 10th, should the British and Dutch warnings be sent.[115]

In the event, Japan struck at Pearl Harbor and the Philippines, thereby solving Roosevelt's and Churchill's problems. America was brought by the back-door into world war and Churchill's Grand Alliance became a reality. Yet Pearl Harbor was merely the prelude to a daring and comprehensive assault on Western power in the Far East—a pre-emptive strike to eliminate the only naval force capable of restraining Japan's offensive. During the next few months the British lost Hong Kong, Malaya, Singapore and most of Burma. Concurrently the Philippines and the U.S. Pacific islands, together with the Dutch East Indies, also fell to Japan. By the spring even India and Australia seemed in danger. In time, of course, the lost territory was recovered. Japan lacked the economic strength to fight a long war against the fully developed Western nations. But her victories in 1941–42 had undermined European power and prestige in Asia, encouraged nascent nationalist movements, and accelerated Britain's retreat from empire. Two years to the day after victory in the Far East had been won, Britain granted independence to India—the jewel of her imperial crown. The only Western beneficiary of the war against Japan was the United States. She replaced Britain as the principal power in China and, by her dominance of Pacific operations during the war, extended her influence throughout Asia and Australasia.[116] In short, Churchill was both right and wrong about the significance of Pearl Harbor: Britain would live, but her Empire was doomed.

### E. Conclusion

Had there ever been a chance of realizing Britain's and America's ideal—Japanese neutrality? Both Craigie and Grew, the men closest to events in Tokyo, believed so, and they developed their views in post-Pearl Harbor reports and memoirs. But in reality both ambassadors were too close to events for objectivity. They continued to rely on a moderates-versus-extremists pendulum view of Japanese politics, which was no longer adequate.[117] As we have seen, there was basic agreement in Tokyo that Japan needed a sphere of influence and that force would be used if diplomacy failed. Given the determination of the British, Dutch and Americans to preserve their own territorial and economic interests in the Far East it is difficult to discern grounds for basic agreement by 1941.[118] This is not to say that accommodation was totally impossible earlier in the 1930s, or to suggest that Hull's diplomacy was above criticism. He insisted on reaching agreement about basic principles before discussing concrete problems. He was adamant that Japan must abrogate the Tripartite Pact. And he was obsessed with the question of Japanese withdrawal from China—the rock on which hopes of agreement often seemed to founder.[119] But this only indicates that for the U.S.A. as for Japan national policy was a mixture of ideology and interests. China was a test case for Hull of whether Japan would accept the canons of Wilsonian liberalism—peaceful change, the Open Door, national sovereignty and territorial integrity.[120] These were regarded as the foundations of peace and prosperity for America and the world, as Roosevelt and Hull had said again and again. In order for the U.S. and Japanese Governments to have reached agreement in 1941, one of them would have had to abandon completely its conception of national identity and purpose.

But what of the suggestion that a *modus vivendi* in November would have delayed Japan until the spring of 1942, by which time German reverses in Russia and growing Western strength in the Far East might have deterred her from war? This was the argument advanced by Craigie in his final report in 1943 and echoed with variations by some historians.[121] Clearly Hull's handling of the *modus vivendi* was rigid and intemperate. Furthermore, although the Pearl Harbor task force had left Japan on 25 November, the attack on Hawaii, together with those on the Philippines and Malaya, could have been halted theoretically at any time up to 24 hours beforehand. [122] On the other hand, after a certain point any military operation acquires a momentum of its own. It can only be reversed with devastating effect on the morale of the forces concerned. Similarly, Japan's leaders had now convinced themselves that war was the only alternative to national degradation, and that they had to strike before the winter monsoons. They had no real strategy for ultimate victory—only the hazy hope that their initial gains might prove a suitable bargaining counter—but felt they had no alternative. Given such 'non-rational' thinking, it is difficult to imagine them being diverted by temporary U.S. concessions or growing Allied strength. But, even if November may have been too late, what of the oil embargo in July? Neither Craigie nor Grew criticized this, but it clearly obliged Japan to set a deadline for the end of diplomacy and the resort to force. Moreover, its significance is heightened by the recent work showing that F.D.R. intended only moderate controls but that a total embargo was implemented by bureaucratic hawks. If Roosevelt's intentions had been followed, would that have retarded the slide to war until such time as Japan thought twice or the Western powers had built up an adequate defence?[123]

Such speculations, although fascinating, are ultimately fruitless. But they do remind us that American diplomacy in July and November conflicted with the overall goals of Anglo-American policy in the Far East, and that U.S. actions did not necessarily serve Britain's interests. The Americans would not concentrate their naval strength in the Far East, let alone at Singapore. They excluded the British from the talks with Japan and from decisions on matters of vital interest to Britain, notably the oil embargo and the *modus vivendi*. On both these issues senior British leaders, if not the FO desk officers, favoured a firm but cautious line—to avoid provoking Japan in July, to gain time in November—but their views were given little attention in Washington. Yet throughout 1941 British leaders, particularly Churchill, argued that they must simply support whatever the Americans chose to do, even though Britain had more to lose from a Pacific war than the U.S.A.[124]

Keeping in step with the U.S.A. appeared the only way to avoid fighting Japan alone, and, given the presumed unity of the Axis and the stalemate in the Atlantic, the best chance of getting the Americans into the global war. Churchill remained sure that the realization of this stratagem had outweighed all else. As he wrote in a savage minute of September 1943, ordering the FO to suppress Craigie's final report, he considered it 'a blessing that Japan attacked the United States and thus brought America wholeheartedly and unitedly into the war. Greater good fortune has rarely happened to the British Empire than this event which has revealed our friends and foes in their true light, and may lead, through the merciless crushing of Japan, to a new relationship of immense benefit to the English-speaking countries and to the whole world.'[125]

HMG therefore felt it had little choice but to defer to the Americans. In any case, the inadequacies of Anglo-American co-operation in the Far East should not be exaggerated. Though weaker that in the Atlantic, it was far from ineffective. By 7 December the compromise strategy evolved at the Washington staff talks was being implemented. A British fleet had arrived at Singapore, initial agreement had been reached for combined operations with the Asiatic Fleet, and the firm ABD diplomatic front had finally been achieved. The basic mistake, common to London and Washington, was to underestimate Japan. Although concerned about the oil embargo and the failure of the *modus vivendi*, the British did not feel that either was fatal in view of their conviction that American firmness was more likely to prove a deterrent than a provocation.[126] HMG assumed that the Japanese were unlikely to declare war, and that, even if they did, little would happen beyond trade raiding. There would consequently be time to tie up the loose ends of Anglo-American co-operation if and when a Far Eastern war began and the U.S.A., as Churchill liked to put it, was up against reality. Such complacency was fatal. Far from conducting themselves like the 'Wops of the Pacific', [127] the Japanese struck with greater speed and effect than even Hitler in May 1940. Churchill's 'decisive deterrent'—the *Prince of Wales* and the *Repulse*—went the same way as much of the U.S. Pacific Fleet—sunk by Japanese bombers in two hours off Malaya on 10 December, with Admiral Phillips refusing to the end to request air cover, such was his contempt for the Japanese and for the effect of air power in naval warfare.[128] The B-17s in the Philippines—Stimson's wonder weapon that supposedly had revolutionized Pacific strategy—were destroyed on the ground on 8 December, while the RAF in Malaya—the other prop of Britain's rickety Far Eastern strategy—was eliminated within two days. The firmness that HMG believed would deter Japan only served to provoke her, while failing to provide adequate defensive protection.

Thus Craigie was right that Britain expected too much of the U.S.A. and too little of Japan. But even if HMG had been more realistic, would this have made much difference? Could Malaya have been properly reinforced; could the Navy have sent a balanced fleet east in 1941? Of course, more could have been done—particularly in providing modern aircraft, and here Churchill must bear much of the blame—but the overall answer is surely a negative one. Churchill himself admitted as much—after the fact—during the

Commons Vote of Confidence debate on 27 January 1942: 'There has never been a moment, there never could have been a moment, when Great Britain or the British Empire, single-handed, could fight Germany and Italy, could wage the Battle of Britain, the Battle of the Atlantic and the Battle of the Middle East—and at the same time stand thoroughly prepared in Burma, the Malay Peninsula, and generally in the Far East . . .'[129] Neville Chamberlain could not have put it better. It was the old problem of Britain's possessions outstripping her power, with no prospect of increased strength and a dogged determination not to relinquish voluntarily one inch of territory. When the crunch came in 1941 the British, in effect, had decided to hang on to the Mediterranean rather than the Far East. They therefore had little choice but to rely on the U.S.A. and to hope that Japan would not call their bluff.[130]

# CHAPTER TEN

# A New Deal for the World?

## Planning the Post-War Order, 1940–41

*This war will never be won by force. It can only be won as a by-product of carrying the New Deal to the world . . . This is the Democratic revolution we must preach and practice everywhere. But it ought to be first agreed to by Britain . . .*

Rex Tugwell, April 1941

*A close association between the British Commonwealth and the United States of America after the victorious conclusion of the war is essential for the establishment and maintenance of a tolerable international order and for the safeguarding of peace. How is it possible to ensure that the United States will shoulder this task . . . and that the partnership shall be as nearly as may be equal . . . ?*

Halifax, October 1941[1]

Long before the bombs began to drop on Pearl Harbor and Singapore, American and British leaders were speculating about the post-war world and their countries' respective places within it. Despite the paramount need to defeat the Axis, and the desire of both Roosevelt and Churchill to avoid any detailed planning, neither government could afford to neglect its long-term interests. One set of issues was political in character—what were the Allies' war and peace aims and what kind of international security system did they envisage to replace the League of Nations? These are the subjects of the first two sections of this chapter. But more contentious in 1941 were issues of long-term economic policy, which became part of the negotiations over Britain's repayment for Lend-Lease, as we shall see in section (c). Behind these problems lay a preliminary attempt to come to terms with the changing balance of the Anglo-American relationship. In 1941 the U.S.A. belatedly began to realize her potential as the world's leading power, partly because of anxiety about her own security in the face of developments in Europe and Asia, partly because of a renewed conviction that her ideals were essential for the well-being of mankind. The British reaction, not surprisingly, was ambivalent. They welcomed America's apparent acceptance of a 'responsible' international role, but sought to channel her new interventionism into forms compatible with the maintenance of British power, prosperity and leadership.

## A. First discussions of war aims, 1940–41

As we saw in earlier chapters, Roosevelt, his principal advisers and the State Department were Wilsonians as far as the goals of U.S. policy were concerned. That is to say, they shared many of the fundamentals of the Western-Christian-liberal tradition as refined by American experience and formulated in the pronouncements of Woodrow Wilson. They believed that existing international relations were unjust and unstable, and that a new system and spirit of collective security was required. Deeply conscious of the mistakes of 1917–20 they were determined that this time the U.S.A. would play a leading part. But it also seemed essential to eradicate the root causes of war. Their top priority was disarmament, or at least large-scale arms control. Equally essential was the elimination of barriers to trade, which limited economic growth and created hostile commercial blocs. The right of self-determination was also important. This ruled out oppressive spheres of influence and also colonial regimes, particularly where native welfare was neglected and no provision made for progress to eventual independence. The experience of the 1930s had shown that unless governments were responsive to the needs of their peoples, instability and revolution would occur, and New Dealers in the Administration saw the American reforms of the previous decade as a model for other parts of the world.[2]

This was a radical critique of contemporary international relations. It was directed primarily at Germany and Japan. They broke diplomatic agreements, resorted to force, created economic blocs, oppressed their own peoples and sought to subjugate others. But it was also applicable to those powers with whom the U.S.A. was co-operating to eliminate totalitarianism. Britain was one of the oldest practitioners of power politics, she had created her own economic sphere of influence and she was the world's major empire, with a chequered record in countries such as India. Domestically she was an imperfect democracy, enervated, as Roosevelt liked to put it, by too much 'Eton and Oxford',[3] and the appointment of Winant, as we saw earlier, was an attempt by the President to cultivate the forces of reform which he saw emerging in wartime Britain. Thus, co-operation with Britain did not mean identity of aims and aspirations. Like Wilson, Roosevelt and his advisers saw themselves as evangelists for a better world, in which the victors as well as vanquished would have to mend their ways.

In one sense American leaders were simply perpetuating the tradition, as old as the nation itself, that the United States had a unique duty as exemplar to the world. They believed that this example should be active not passive—instead of standing as an isolated beacon of liberty and democracy the U.S.A. should carry the torch boldly into a hostile world. But their world-view also clearly suited America's interests. It was easy to preach disarmament from the security of thousands of miles of ocean. The surrender of empire was no sacrifice for a power that had almost always eschewed territorial imperialism (outside the American continent). And the elimination of economic blocs was the natural response of a strong, competitive economy, anxious to expand, especially if the vast domestic market on which its growth was based remained protected by high tariffs. Moreover, 1941 marked the beginnings of a new assertiveness in American foreign policy. The chaotic international situation offered an outstanding opportunity to exercise influence and advance national interests. Lend-Lease symbolized this—at once a formal, public commitment by the U.S.A. to assist in the struggle against totalitarianism, and a dramatic demonstration that the world's greatest empire was now dependent on American power. The situation had been similar in 1917, of course, but this time American policy-makers saw their position of leadership as permanent. As Henry Luce put it in February 1941, this was 'The American Century' and Americans must 'accept wholeheartedly our duty and our opportunity as the most powerful and vital nation in the world'. Luce stressed that this did not mean policing the whole globe, nor imposing democracy on all mankind, but it did mean recognizing that the U.S.A. would be the single most decisive influence on the health, wealth and security of the world.[4] Luce was a Republican and a vehement critic of the New Deal. But in many respects his article was a representative statement of the thinking of the American interventionist coalition in 1941, blending idealism, self-interest and a new sense of national destiny.[5]

The State Department was anxious to translate these broad Wilsonian goals into specific blueprints. An early attempt had been made at the beginning of 1940, as background to the Welles mission and related efforts to secure a negotiated peace, and in February 1941 a special division of the Department was created to study post-war problems. Roosevelt was adamant that detailed planning was inappropriate until the international situation was much clearer. However, he encouraged tentative studies, as long as they were secret and non-committal, and he was also anxious to assert America's moral leadership in the march towards the new world. During the winter of 1939–40 he had talked privately to Knox and particularly Lothian about the Four Freedoms, which must be an integral part of the future peace. He developed his idea the following summer, and then included it in his State of the Union address on 6 January 1941. The 'four essential human freedoms'—freedom of speech and expression, freedom of worship, freedom from want and freedom from fear— were to be established 'everywhere in the world'. This, he emphasized, 'is no vision of a distant millenium. It is a definite basis for a kind of world attainable in our own time and generation.'[6] Roosevelt's statement, made at the time when he was launching the Lend-Lease bill, was part of his continuing campaign to mobilize informed support for aid to Britain. It was also a continuation of his work in the winter of 1939–40 to lay the basis of a future peace. By making this cryptic but inspiring statement of peace aims Roosevelt wanted to stake out his claim before the Allies. Wilson had tried to do the same 23 years before, with his Fourteen Points. A few weeks after the Four Freedoms had been announced to the world Hopkins warned the British that Roosevelt should be consulted before HMG made any statement of its war aims. 'He said that the President on these questions was rather touchy as he regarded the post-war settlement so to speak as being his particular preserve.'[7]

*    *    *

In Britain, too, thoughts were turning to the post-war world. Dunkirk had set in motion a distinct swing to the left in British attitudes, popular and official. The more egalitarian conditions of total war and the backlash of resentment against the Baldwin and Chamberlain governments encouraged the belief that this was 'a people's war', fought for a more caring and democratic society. This change was reflected politically in the rise to power of advocates of planned social reform—the Labour leaders who dominated domestic policy after Chamberlain's death and the intellectuals and journalists who provided the extra staff of wartime ministries. Their most notable early achievement was the acceptance of Keynes and Keynesian ideas by the Treasury in 1940–41.[8] Whereas the extreme left abhorred the U.S.A. as the embodiment of aggressive capitalism,[9] and the right feared her as a challenge to Britain's Empire and trade, these representatives of 'middle opinion' had frequently been influenced by the New Deal and inspired by Roosevelt's moral leadership during the dark days of Depression and appeasement. Like British liberals in World War One they looked to America for a lead in the struggle for a better world. The most striking example was Harold Laski, who urged Roosevelt to force Churchill into a British New Deal. But more representative of Labour opinion than the Marxist Laski with his sycophantic Roosevelt-worship, was Clement Attlee, the party's leader. In November 1940 Attlee was delighted at the 'magnificent' U.S. election result. Quite apart from preventing a disastrous hiatus in the American war-effort, Roosevelt's re-election meant the continuance in power of 'a man with a real understanding of European problems, strategic & economic as well as political & perhaps above all ideological. Only a man who sees the interrelationship between home policy & foreign policy can really give the hand required.'[10]

From the summer of 1940 there was a growing clamour from the left and liberal press for a statement of progressive war aims. This was echoed in Parliament by several back-benchers and supported in Cabinet by the Labour leaders—Attlee, Bevin and Greenwood—and by moderate Tories such as Halifax, Eden and Duff Cooper. This pressure became particularly acute during the winter of 1940–41, when it coincided with government anxiety about the success among European neutrals of German propaganda for a new economic order. In mid-November the FO and MOI both approached Keynes for material on which to base a rebuttal, and this action was approved by the Cabinet on 20 November when broad agreement was expressed about the value of a general statement of aims to appeal to opinion at home and abroad (not least the U.S.A.) It was also pointed out that if no official statement was made before the end of the year 'President Roosevelt might take the initiative in his Inaugural Speech in January 1941, and it would then be difficult for us to differ openly from that statement.'[11] But this meeting, and another on 20 January, showed how difficult it would be to reach a satisfactory statement. Anything too specific would be controversial at home and might commit Britain to policies that subsequently proved unwise. Yet a document that tried to avoid contentious issues would simply degenerate into platitudes. This was the fate of a draft declaration of war aims drawn up by Halifax in December 1940, which met with scarcely concealed derision from his colleagues.[12]

Churchill's answer was procrastination. Although the Cabinet minutes are unclear, it was probably he who suggested on 20 January that HMG do nothing until the Lend-Lease Bill had passed. In Parliament he dismissed all requests for an official statement as unnecessary, and established an informal ban on public discussion of war aims by ministers. His top priority was domestic unity. 'Party strife at the present time . . . would be disastrous', he told Bevin in late November 1940, after the latter had made a controversial speech about post-war nationalization. 'I have to try to keep all together till the Hun is beat.' The PM also agreed that premature commitments might prejudice the future. 'As you know,' he reminded Eden in May 1941, 'I am very doubtful about the utility of attempts to plan the peace before we have won the war . . . I do not think anyone knows what will happen when we get to the end of the war; and personally I am holding myself uncommitted.'[13] Behind these tactical considerations lay more personal reasons. Churchill was preoccupied with the conduct of grand strategy. He loved the excitement and heroism of war, and found economic and social problems dull and trivial by comparison. Moreover, his conception of the war was essentially conservative. It was not a crusade for a new order but an attempt to rid the world of an intrusive and fiendish ideology, thereby restoring an international status quo from which Britain was the principal beneficiary. Churchill was not opposed to social amelioration, but his views were those of a paternalistic Whig aristocrat with only the haziest notions about 'the common people'.[14] He saw no reason to destroy the fabric of what he called 'traditional Britain', and, as he said in November 1942, he had no intention of presiding over 'the liquidation of the British Empire'.[15] India had always been particularly important to him, and, despite pressure from Labour leaders and some of his own party in 1940–41, he refused to move beyond the vague promise of August 1940 to concede Dominion status 'with the least possible delay' after the end of the war.

But the Prime Minister could not suppress all talk of war aims. The major challenge came, interestingly, from Eden, who in 1941 felt ideologically closer to his Labour colleagues in the Cabinet than to the bulk of the Tory party and even talked privately about possibly changing parties after the war.[16] Like the Labour leaders Eden believed that the war was about a better order at home as well as abroad—that international security and social security were interdependent—and his outlook was therefore broadly similar to Roosevelt's. But Eden was also anxious that Britain should play a major part in planning and proclaiming the new order. One of his early tasks was to liven up the FO. When he became Foreign Secretary again in December 1940 he had been appalled at the 'deadness and woolliness' of the senior FO officials. With the exception of Sargent, they seemed tired, cautious, bereft of ideas and even anti-liberal. Working closely with Oliver Harvey, his confidant and former Private Secretary who was then at the MOI, Eden embarked on a major reshuffle of senior personnel, which was finally accomplished in June 1941. Reluctantly he retained Cadogan, whose disconcerting cynicism was counter-balanced by his coolness and experience. But Harvey returned to his old post, Richard Law replaced R. A. Butler as Parliamentary Under-Secretary, and several weary Assistant Under-Secretaries were packed off to British missions abroad.[17]

At the same time Eden was preparing a major statement of war aims to arouse opinion at home and abroad. Its basis was the economic material produced by Keynes in late 1940, which Eden and Sargent spent a good deal of time revising in early 1941. But there were several obstacles to overcome. The Treasury, complained Sargent, removed 'all the guts' of Keynes' statement, determined to keep Britain's options open on post-war economic policy.[18] And the PM sat on the text during February and March, while Eden was immersed in the Balkan crisis, and only gave grudging acquiescence in May when assured by his advisers that it contained nothing sensitive. Finally, following Halifax's advice, Eden wanted to square his remarks with the Administration. A draft was sent to Hull and Roosevelt, and Halifax and Keynes, then in Washington on Treasury business, discussed it with F.D.R. on 28 May, the day before the speech was to be given and the day after the President's address about a state of unlimited emergency. Basically, F.D.R.'s opinion was similar to Churchill's—although disliking detailed public discussion at the moment he disagreed on no major matters of substance. But he did object to the form of the statement. It sounded too much like Britain telling the world what *she* would do hereafter, he said, and the emphasis on Anglo-American co-operation should be complemented by references to the smaller states and particularly to Latin America. Eden revised his text accordingly, and added tactful passages praising F.D.R.'s recent speech and also the idea of the Four Freedoms. Indeed he introduced his outline of the new economic order as an attempt to discuss in more detail the goal of freedom from want. But despite the alignment of British and American thinking, the President's response to the draft, combined with Hopkins' warning in January, made Eden uneasy. As Harvey recorded, 'it seemed that Roosevelt was rather jealous of such utterances and A. E. [Eden] thought we should have to watch this.' 'Beggars . . . can't be choosers', Harvey responded, and Eden agreed, but his anxiety was soon to increase, as we shall see below.[19]

*　　*　　*

During early 1941 the question of war aims was a peripheral issue in Anglo-American relations. In the summer, however, it became a major concern—largely because of the activities of Adolf Berle. As we have seen, Berle combined one of the sharpest minds in the State Department with an obsessive suspicion of Britain. Convinced that in 1917–19 the U.S.A. had got nothing she wanted at Versailles because she had become an adjunct of the British, he was determined that this time the roles should be reversed. He believed that America had the strength, particularly economic, to determine the peace, and also the moral right, unlike the British whose foreign policy seemed to him not only inept but consistently self-interested. On 21 June Berle asked

Roosevelt for permission to begin tentative outlines of the post-war order, and F.D.R. agreed, stressing as usual that nothing must leak out and that Berle should concentrate on broad objectives rather than detailed methods.[20]

The specific reason behind Berle's request was probably his anxiety about British relations with Russia. On 14 June, with Hitler's invasion of the U.S.S.R. clearly imminent, Halifax had suggested to Welles that in order to win Stalin's trust and secure effective co-operation Britain would probably have to recognize Soviet control over the Baltic states she had conquered in 1939–40—Latvia, Lithuania and Estonia. Berle regarded the idea of 'appeasing' Russia in this way as a reversion to the traditional, selfish FO diplomacy.[21] His fears were strengthened when Russia entered the war and began signing alliances with the Eastern European governments in exile, notably the Poles, Czechs and Yugoslavs. Berle had been afraid from the beginning of the war that Stalin would be its ultimate beneficiary. He saw in these negotiations the basis of a Pan Slavic federation that would advance Soviet influence deep into Central Europe, and feared that the cynical British were ready to endorse Russian territorial goals to ensure Stalin's co-operation against Germany in war and peace.[22] This aroused memories of the now notorious Allied secret agreements of 1915–17, which had assumed a sacred place in American diplomatic demonology. Also disturbing was the inter-Allied conference on the post-war food and raw material needs of Europe. 'The obvious intent is partly humanitarian,' Berle observed, 'but it may be to channelize the trade and economics of this area through London when the war is over.'[23] During July he carefully monitored all these developments, and, on his own initiative, sent periodic reports to Welles, Hull and Roosevelt. His warnings, endorsed by State's European desk, led to a new Departmental Committee at the end of July to consider post-war planning. More important, they prompted Roosevelt to advise Churchill, both verbally through Hopkins and in a special telegram on 14 July, that Britain should make no political or economic commitments at this stage. These would be premature and also contrary to the principle of plebiscitary democracy. He suggested that a general statement from Churchill 'would be useful at this time, making clear that no postwar peace commitments as to territories, populations, or economies have been given'. He would then back up the statement 'in very strong terms'.[24]

This anxiety about possible Allied secret commitments was one of the main reasons for the Atlantic Charter. Receiving no reply to his message, Roosevelt was determined to commit Churchill explicitly to America's goal of self-determination. The other main motive behind the Charter was the American desire for a British commitment to the principle of economic liberalization, which had become a sticking point in the negotiations over the Lend-Lease Consideration. This will be discussed later. More generally, it is probable that for some time F.D.R. had envisaged his meeting with Churchill not only as a way of getting acquainted, but also as an opportunity to discuss and state their general war aims. By August he may well have hoped also that a dramatic and inspiring announcement would help arouse American opinion from its new complacency after the invasion of Russia.[25] And there was one other possible motive—which is less familiar and therefore deserves more discussion. That was the situation in India. On 1 August—a few days before the Atlantic Meeting—Winant had suggested that the U.S. press Britain to concede immediate Dominion status to India. He was strongly supported by Berle and the Division of Near Eastern Affairs, who had raised the issue unsuccessfully in May. Although dislike of colonialism was the underlying motive, their argument was couched in terms of the debilitating effect of Indian disunity on the Allied war effort in the Middle and Far East. In this, they emphasized, the U.S. had a significant national interest and therefore a justification for intervention. In May Hull and Welles had stood on the traditional U.S. policy that, although sympathetic to Indian nationalism, the Administration should not interfere in a sensitive British problem. But on 6 August they agreed that, while no official representations were appropriate, F.D.R. might wish to discuss the idea 'in a very personal and confidential way directly with Mr. Churchill'.[26] As far as can be determined, Roosevelt did not raise it explicitly at the meeting.[27] But it is likely, in view of these very recent discussions, that India was also in the minds of Welles and Roosevelt as they drafted the provisions of the Atlantic Charter.

F.D.R. gave the British no advance warning that he wanted to issue a statement of joint war aims after the Atlantic Meeting. Presumably he wished to maximize his diplomatic advantage, as well as to avoid bureaucratic argument. He suggested the idea at dinner on the first evening, 9 August, and invited Churchill and Cadogan to prepare a draft.[28] He and Welles then submitted a counter-draft on the 11th which was discussed at length that morning and during the afternoon. The two controversial points, to be discussed later, concerned post-war security and economic liberalization. The President was reluctant to include any reference to a future international organization, while Welles was determined to tie the British officially to the eventual abolition of Imperial Preference. Surprise had been F.D.R.'s tactical weapon. Churchill's was his claim that the Dominions must be consulted before any commitment on Preferences could be made. Just as Congress was the Americans' 'Mr Jorkins' so the Commonwealth was Britain's—a genuine constraint on freedom of action, but one that could be emphasized or played down as diplomatically convenient. Churchill knew that F.D.R. would compromise rather than delay issuing the declaration, and he was able to secure acceptance of his amendments on the disputed points.[29]

However, too much should not be made of these tactical differences. Both leaders were anxious for a mutually acceptable agreement, and what is particularly striking is Churchill's complete reversal on the question of war aims. Having previously resisted domestic pressure for an official statement, he now eagerly endorsed the idea of an Anglo-American declaration, as a way of identifying the U.S.A. more closely with the British cause. Back home, however, reaction was cool. The declaration of peace aims, quickly labelled the 'Atlantic Charter' by the press, seemed a poor substitute for the hoped-for U.S. declaration of war. Churchill appeared to have made 'great concessions' and 'sweeping pledges to Roosevelt without securing anything comparable in return'. Even as a statement of aims the Cabinet found that 'in certain respects' it 'fell short' of what they would have liked, and private dissatisfaction ranged across the political spectrum from Bevin, who was 'very critical', to Amery's condemnation of the document's 'meaningless platitudes and dangerous ambiguities.'[30] But for Churchill and Cadogan such comment missed the fundamental point. Neutral America had associated herself with belligerent Britain in a statement of common goals for war *and* peace, thereby making an implicit commitment to work for their realization. They stressed this 'astonishing' fact to the Cabinet afterwards and Cadogan was still alluding to it in 1943, when he asked FO critics of the Charter to remember 'that it had its genesis in an offer by the President' and that 'at that time (Aug. 1941) a joint declaration of any kind went beyond our wildest dreams'.[31]

Churchill and Cadogan were right to emphasize the diplomatic significance of the Atlantic Charter, but British critics were quickly vindicated in their warning about the dangers of hastily-drafted statements.[32] The first problem arose, surprisingly, not over commercial policy but over the applicability of the Charter to the decolonization of the British Empire. Point three had affirmed the right of all peoples to national sovereignty and self-government. Churchill had drafted this to satisfy American anxieties about secret commitments in Europe, but politicians in Burma, India and Ceylon quickly exploited its obvious implications for British colonial rule. Amery, Secretary of State for India and Burma, wanted a public statement indicating that the declaration applied primarily to those nations with whom Britain was at war or whom she intended to liberate, but that its spirit was the one animating British colonial policy, namely the 'development of self-governing institutions to the fullest possible extent' within the Empire. Even that was too categorical for the Colonial Secretary, Lord Moyne, and his officials. 'Some colonies are so small, or strategically so important, that complete self-government seems out of the question', Moyne told Amery. 'I cannot, for instance, imagine any conditions under which we would give Dominion status to Aden, Gibraltar, the Gambia or British Honduras.'[33] The Cabinet preferred to avoid such questions for the moment, and Churchill told Parliament on 9 September that point three was intended to apply primarily to the subject nations of Europe and that it enunciated the principles governing any future alteration of their boundaries. 'So that is quite a separate problem', he continued, 'from the progressive evolution of self-governing institutions in the regions and peoples which owe allegiance to the British Crown. We have made declarations on these matters which are complete in themselves, free from a[m]biguity and related to the conditions and circumstances of the territories and peoples affected.' Churchill's evasive statement seems to have accommodated Moyne's reservations, while making Amery's basic point about the Charter's European frame of reference.[34] But this could not dispose of the problem. Thereafter, the Charter was seen in Africa and Asia as having global applicability, and by the beginning of 1942 F.D.R. was taking the same line in public.[35] Indeed, given the debate about India just before they left Washington, it is likely that Roosevelt and Welles had *intended* point three of the Atlantic Charter to cover the British Empire and that Churchill and Cadogan had been outwitted.

Even the European aspect of the Charter disturbed Eden. When Hopkins and Winant had seen him on 21 July to convey Roosevelt's policy of no pre-determination of post-war boundaries before the peace treaty, Eden noted in his diary that 'the spectacle of an American President talking at large on European frontiers chilled me with Wilsonian memories'. This reinforced his earlier fears that F.D.R. saw himself 'as the man of the Peace Settlement', and further grist to the mill came when Harvey communicated these fears to Charles Peake, Halifax's publicity aide in Washington. Peake replied: 'I have little doubt that you are right in thinking that he intends to make the peace himself, and *that*, whether the U.S. comes in to the war or not.' Nor was Peake impressed with the President's idealism: 'I do not think that he believes very much in all the democratic slogans and catchwords which he and we think it our duty so constantly to repeat. He pays lip-service to them, as every American politician must do, but what he is out to do is to put the U.S.A. definitely on the top, and see that she stays there.'[36] Peake's letter reached London on 12 August, the day the FO first got wind of the Atlantic Charter. Eden felt 'that F.D.R. has bowled the PM a very quick one—such a document might well have been communicated in advance'. Harvey was less cynical about Roosevelt than Eden or Peake, but he felt that 'what is certain is that we are dealing with a headstrong man who means to monopolise the limelight at the Peace but whose political ideas are still those of 20 years ago'. The lesson was that Britain must start planning seriously the foundations of a realistic peace. On 6 October Harvey put the point directly to Eden. 'If we hadn't our plan all ready, Roosevelt would produce one of his own out of his pocket like the Atlantic Charter.'[37] Eden agreed, and during the winter of 1941–42 the FO and its research department began to prepare some preliminary outlines of the future peace settlement.

What made this issue particularly pressing was the state of Anglo-Russian relations. Administration suspicions of HMG in July had been exaggerated. At the Atlantic Meeting Cadogan gave Welles 'the most specific and positive assurance' that HMG had made no commitments about post-war frontiers, with the possible exception of a vague statement to the Yugoslavs in March 1941 about Istria. This satisfied Welles and the FO took care to provide supplementary information during the autumn.[38] But Berle was right to feel that a difference of attitude existed, at least between the State Department and the Foreign Office.[39] Ever since the German invasion began, Stalin had demanded not only logistic and military help from Britain, but also recognition of the U.S.S.R.'s 1941 boundaries, particularly in the Baltic. The official British position on this was that they could not define post-war aims in detail because the future was too uncertain and because the Americans 'have repeatedly asked us not to undertake during the war commitments which would bind us at the peace and after'.[40] This formulation satisfied Churchill and the Cabinet, most of whom, particularly the Labour leaders of union background, were vehemently anti-Communist. But, even before the failure of Eden's visit to Moscow in December, there was a growing feeling among FO officials that such a strict policy of 'no pre-determination' was unrealistic. They saw Stalin, in Eden's words, as 'a political descendant of Peter the Great rather than Lenin' for whom traditional Russian security concerns were more important, at least for the moment, than the spread of international Communism.[41] Reflection on past experience, particularly the disastrous failure of the 1939 Anglo-Russian negotiations, suggested that if his obsessive fears were not allayed Stalin might again seek agreement with Germany. In any case, the FO saw little hope of preventing Russia from controlling the Baltic states after the war, and its main post-war anxiety was to control a resurgent Germany. This required a strong and co-operative Russia. The diplomatic problem, as Eden put it, was therefore to harmonize 'amoral' Soviet policy with the policy of the U.S.A., which was 'exaggeratedly moral, at least where non-American interests are concerned'. Concretely, that meant trying to reach a tripartite agreement on preliminary aims, which would include recognition of Stalin's minimum demands for a sphere of influence over the Baltic states. Churchill was won over to the FO line in March 1942, but, after some wavering by F.D.R., the Administration stuck to its official position. In January Eden had written that if it became impossible to satisfy both the U.S.A. and the U.S.S.R. 'we should no doubt decide that Anglo-American co-operation is more indispensable and the more natural because it rests on broader and older foundations', but in early April HMG decided it was essential to reach agreement with the Russians despite U.S. opposition. Direct Anglo-American confrontation was only avoided in May when Stalin dropped Russian territorial demands from the Anglo-Russian treaty after receiving a vague promise from F.D.R. about a second front that year.[42] The details lie behind the scope of this study. What is interesting is that Eden was willing seriously to imperil Anglo-American relations in order to secure co-operation with Russia. To understand why, we need to look at Anglo-American thinking in 1941 about post-war security and at the continued mixture in Britain of hope, doubt and fear about the U.S.A. and its world role.

## B. The 'special relationship' and the problem of security

Although Roosevelt shared Wilson's vision of the world, as we noted in chapter 1 (e) he believed his predecessor had been profoundly wrong about means and methods. F.D.R. might be called a 'realistic Wilsonian',[43] using the adjective in both the common-sense and the more technical meaning. That is to say he felt that Wilson had been generally naive about diplomacy and politics, and that he had neglected the centrality of great power relations in an effective international order. Roosevelt's realism brought him into conflict with the more conventional Wilsonianism of the State Department. Welles, for instance, was talking in July 1941 of a new association of nations dedicated to the elimination of offensive armaments and of international economic discrimination—themes he had emphasized during his peace mission of 1940. Within the Department there was also continued support for the idea of an American-led neutral bloc. Early post-war planning papers had envisaged an international peace force under neutral control, and, even in 1941, there was a feeling in the Department that although Anglo-American co-operation was clearly important, America should continue to cultivate the smaller European powers who would be important in securing a continental settlement.[44] The President was not indifferent to these ideas. In early 1938 and early 1940 he had toyed with the neutral-arbiter approach, and throughout the war he insisted that the South American states must be associated with any U.S. *démarche* in foreign policy. But we have seen in the course of this book how his theory of international security between 1938 and 1941 placed increasing emphasis on the role of the great powers, particularly, from the summer of 1940, on a close relationship with Britain. And in late 1940 and much of 1941, before Russia's involvement in the war complicated the picture, he talked frequently in private about the importance of continued Anglo-American co-operation to secure the peace, especially in the critical reconstruction period before effective international institutions could be created.

Sometimes F.D.R. was indulging in his pastime of ruminating aloud. For instance, he suggested to Lothian in October 1940 that a permanent council should be set up in Washington, comprising representatives of the U.S.A., the American republics and the British Empire, to institutionalize political and economic co-operation in war and peace.[45] But on two points the President was clear and emphatic, as in a long conversation with Halifax and Keynes on 28 May 1941. The first was that this time the U.S.A. would not retreat into isolation at the end of the war. According to Keynes: 'He refused to consider the possibility that America would not take her full share of responsibility for the post-war situation in Europe, political as well as economic. The Europeans, on his view of the matter, are to be told just where they get off.' Secondly, although there had to be disarmament for the rest of the world, particularly the vanquished, he insisted that Britain and the U.S.A. should maintain sufficient military strength to enforce peace and stability. 'Whatever federal or other arrangements may be set up between groups of European states,' Keynes noted, 'he clearly contemplated that a British–American police force should take all the necessary responsibility for maintaining order for some time to come.' Moreover, this responsibility extended beyond the confines of Europe. In a conversation with Halifax on 6 April the President 'spoke with great emphasis about the importance of the United States and Great Britain retaining preponderance of sea and air power, in order to be in a position to enforce order on the world'. Roosevelt's difference of emphasis with the State Department became apparent at the Atlantic Meeting, when, to Welles' dismay, he 'said that he himself would not be in favor of the creation of a new Assembly of the League of Nations, at least until after a period of time had transpired and during which an international police force composed of the United States and Great Britain had had an opportunity of functioning'. Even if, as Welles suggested, the Latin Americans and European neutrals were associated with this policing role, F.D.R. stressed that the association would be largely cosmetic, since none of them would have the power to provide significant assistance.[46]

\*　　\*　　\*

Today such ideas may seem naive and even distastefully paternalistic, but they were very much 'in the air' in 1941 in both countries. In many ways, they were a natural extrapolation from the critical but unusually simplified international situation of 1940–41, when Britain and the U.S.A. were the only two major democracies left and therefore the only obvious basis for international security. But it was in Britain that the concept of a special relationship was particularly popular and also particularly prone to sentimentality. An obvious example is the vogue among intellectuals and politicians for the idea of eventual Union of the English-speaking democracies on the model of the abortive Anglo-French proposal of June 1940. Harold Macmillan was one of many MPs talking in this vein.[47] The lack of realism is apparent here in two respects. First, for many of its proponents, Union was a retreat from European commitments. We saw in chapter 4 (a) that the Fall of France led to a mood of relief that Britain could fall back on her kin across the sea in defiance of all those contemptible continentals, and this neo-isolationist reaction was still apparent in 1941. More fundamentally, the talk of Union and of 'the English-speaking peoples' betrays the continued tendency to imagine the U.S.A. as essentially a bastardized version of Britain, somewhere between the Dominions and a truly 'foreign' country. There was still little awareness in Britain of the ethnic dimension of American life, of the evolution of an eclectic but distinctive American culture, and of Britain's central place as a negative as much as a positive reference point in American national identity. In both these respects it is instructive to contrast British ideas about Anglo-American Union with similar schemes being advanced in the U.S.A., notably Clarence Streit's 'Union Now' movement which attracted some support from New York interventionist intellectuals. For Streit and his followers Union was not a retreat from Europe, but a first step in the federal union of the democracies of North America and the continent. Its unifying force was shared democratic values, exemplified by the U.S.A., instead of an exclusive Anglo-American culture, originating from Britain; and in form it would follow American precedents and American leadership, rather than being an extension of the British Commonwealth.[48]

British policymakers were not immune from some of these unrealistic conceptions about the relationship. FO/A, for instance, was enthusiastic about the idea of an Anglo-American bloc, largely detached from continental commitments, on the lines outlined by Cripps in June 1940.[49] But Churchill and most senior FO officials did not agree. For them the central, awesome post-war problem would be to create and maintain a Germany that was economically strong but militarily weak—able to ensure stability and prosperity for central Europe without being able yet again to dominate the continent. They also believed that this required Britain to accept some permanent continental responsibilities. Even during the Phoney War, Sargent, Harvey and others in the FO had been talking about a post-war association with France to preserve European security, and these ideas found expression in the Anglo-French declaration of March 1940 and the Union proposal the following June. For Churchill the goal was even grander—a Council of Europe comprising the five great European powers, plus regional federations of the smaller states.[50] This was a long-held ideal, growing out of his collective security concept of the 1930s. The problem, as Churchill and the FO saw it, was that Britain could not assume the burden of European security alone, particularly after the eclipse of her major ally—France.

263

As Cadogan remarked, in a typical minute, HMG had tried to live on bluff for too long—the late 30s in Europe, and half a century, he suggested, in Asia. Now '[a]ll bluffs have been called. . . Everything, it seems to me, will be dependent on the willingness & the ability of the U.S. to share our burden.'[51] And it was at this point—in their assessments of whether the U.S.A. *would* join in the police work—that Churchill and the FO parted company.

As early as 1935 Churchill had said that the ideal solution for international insecurity would be for the 'English-speaking peoples' to become 'the policemen of the world'. Nothing of the sort happened in the 1930s—in either country—and in his memoirs Churchill cited this as one of the fundamental causes of the war; but by 1940–41 Anglo-American co-operation was a reality and Churchill had no doubt that it was the key to the future of the world. He told the Anglo-American Pilgrims Society of London in January 1941: 'The identity of purpose and persistence of resolve prevailing throughout the English-speaking world will, more than any other single fact, determine the way of life which will be open to the generations, and perhaps to the centuries, which will follow our own.'[52] Even allowing for the hyperbole of such occasions, Churchill's words are a striking reminder that he was particularly prone to romanticize the relationship. Of course his deep conviction that the two countries were bound by indestructible ties of kinship and common culture had helped keep Britain going—particularly in the summer of 1940—but as the war progressed it often impeded a realistic perception of the relationship. For Churchill there was little tension between the Anglo-American alliance and the strengthening of European security. He seems to have believed that the U.S.A. could and would be 'educated' out of isolation into a sharing of continental responsibilities with Britain. In this connection the Atlantic Charter appeared to him particularly encouraging and significant, especially when contrasted with the mistakes of 1919–20. This time the aggressors would be disarmed, but not the Allies; on the other hand, there was no talk of reparations, which had crippled and embittered Germany in the 1920s, but only of helping *all* states, 'victors and vanquished', to achieve economic prosperity. For Churchill this was a real step towards the goal of a Germany that was 'fat but impotent'.[53] Moreover, the conference encouraged him to believe that this time the U.S.A. would really assist in the peace-keeping. F.D.R. had been emphatic about this in their discussions, with his talk of an Anglo-American police force, and Churchill told the Cabinet on his return that 'not the least striking feature' of the Charter was 'the realism of the last paragraph, where there is a plain and bold intimation that, after the war, the United States will join with us in policing the world until the establishment of a better order'.[54]

But the FO did not share Churchill's optimism about the U.S.A.—for several reasons. One was misperception of Roosevelt. Such was their fear of a replay of 1917–20 that they were somewhat slow to appreciate that F.D.R. was not a simple Wilsonian. Whereas Churchill, admittedly briefed by the President, returned home full of praise for the 'realism' inherent in the Charter, what caught the attention of even the sympathetic Harvey were the 'old clichés of the League of Nations period' which he took as evidence that Roosevelt's ideas were 'still those of 20 years ago'.[55] But the real problem was not the President's intentions but whether they would be expressed in national policy. The Democrats were now in power for a third term, but between 1896 and 1932 the Republicans had been the majority party, and the FO, not yet perceiving the transformation of American politics during the New Deal, believed that a Republican resurgence could not long be delayed. With it, they believed, would come renewed isolation and a high-tariff economic nationalism that would make even Wilsonianism seem like pure enlightenment by comparison. Moreover, whoever controlled the White House, there was no guarantee of a stable, consistent foreign policy. Again and again British officials returned in incredulity and even anger to their old bugbear—American politics. There were frequent complaints about the parochialism of Congressmen, the influence of the press and lobbyists, the volatility of public opinion and the consequent violent oscillations of policy. But the FO considered that the root problem was the lack of a parliamentary system, which harnessed the legislature to the executive rather than setting them at odds, as the Founding Fathers had deliberately done in the U.S.A. They found it hard to understand how a 'cumbrous' form of government could survive in the modern world. Commented Nigel Ronald: 'I regard the U.S. Constitution, impeding as it does rapid executive action, as one of the major menaces to international peace.'[56] However, the most fundamental obstacle to permanent co-operation, in their view, was simply the depth and persistence of the isolationist tradition. They assumed that this would inevitably reassert itself when the present conflict was over. For some this was a further damning commentary on American parochialism, but the more perceptive, such as Whitehead, recognized that America's stake in Europe, though real, was necessarily much less than that of Britain which was 21 and not 3,000 miles away from the continent.[57] Some also saw that the closeness of the Anglo-American relationship in 1940–41 was artificial, reflecting the uniqueness and gravity of the current crisis, and that 'once the danger of domination in Europe by a power other than Great Britain is past, there will be a tendency for the two countries to drift apart'.[58]

Despite Roosevelt's assurances, despite Churchill's optimism, the FO therefore remained sceptical that the U.S.A. would help police Europe. During the summer and autumn of 1940 FO/A and senior officials all stressed that although the Americans would probably assist in the 'convalescent' period immediately after the war, they were unlikely to assume any permanent responsibility for European security.[59] For some, Lend-Lease was an encouraging sign to the contrary, and in its aftermath the Washington Embassy speculated enthusiastically that American isolationism 'may well have gone for good', but FO/A officials still warned repeatedly against such complacency.[60] They envisaged continued U.S. responsibility for the Western Hemisphere, participation in a new international organization, a readiness to co-operate in controlling the Atlantic and Pacific, and the use of American economic resources in the post-war reconstruction of Europe. But, to quote Whitehead, who was particularly emphatic on the point:

It is safe to assume that in no circumstances will America accept responsibility for the territorial integrity of any country in Europe; nor is she likely to bind herself by any treaty which would automatically bring her into a future war outside the Western Hemisphere . . . [I]t would be sheer wishful thinking to suppose that America would ever be willing to underwrte the peace of Europe; that will be our task in conjunction with such help as we may be able to obtain from Europe itself.[61]

That is why in 1941–42 the FO was willing to go so far in courting the Russians, whatever the Americans might say. As Harvey put it in November 1941: 'Russia is fighting the war and America is not. We shall have to bear the brunt of the peace, even if we can get a measure of American cooperation.' With France in ruins, and the U.S. unlikely to assume permanent European commitments, a good relationship with Russia seemed essential as protection against German resurgence.[62]

But to fully understand the unwillingness of many British officials to rely completely on the Americans, we must also remember the continuing anxiety about the United States as a rival. On economic matters this was particularly apparent in the Treasury and the Tory right, and it will be discussed properly in the next section. But even within the FO there was a difference of emphasis between those such as Harvey and FO/A who saw the main obstacle to co-operation as American innocence and unreliability, and those who also detected a self-interested and expansionary impulse behind U.S. idealism. 'Americans are incapable of "thinking imperially" ', minuted Scott in March 1941. 'I am certain she will be so thinking within a decade', R. A. Butler responded.[63] Related to this disagreement was a difference in readiness to accept dependence upon the United States. FO/A did not dispute Henry Luce's conception of Britain as junior partner in the 'American Century',[64] but others were more hopeful of maintaining equality and a considerable measure of independence within the relationship. The most interesting argument was between Harvey and Eden. In the last section we saw that Eden was reluctant to concede to F.D.R. the moral leadership of the Allied cause and the right to arbitrate the destiny of Europe. We also noted in earlier chapters his fear of U.S. bases springing up indiscriminately all over the globe. In August 1941 Eden was unhappy about the possibility that the U.S. might occupy the Azores. Partly this was because he did not want to jeopardize relations with Portugal, but, as Harvey recorded, Eden was also 'rather isolationist where Americans coming into Europe is concerned. He wants us, not them to be the predominant partner.'[65] Harvey, however, believed that joint Anglo-American bases and policing were the answer to many international security problems, including the Middle East and Europe. 'Frankly', he told Eden, 'I don't believe in the bogey of American expansionism in Europe. I believe the far greater danger is American isolationism.' The British people would never agree to police Europe alone. 'But if it is an Anglo-American operation, then you will get what you want, and I am sure we can manage the Americans. They are children, simple, naif, yet suspicious.' Eden's rejoinder was sharp: 'I would not regard R[oosevelt] as either "simple or naif".'[66]

*     *     *

It is therefore apparent that in 1941 British attitudes towards the U.S.A. remained as complex as ever. Within the consensus on the vital importance of good Anglo-American relations there was a wide variety of attitudes and expectations. Particularly significant was Churchill's growing propensity to regard a permanent special relationship as not only attainable but also as a panacea for British problems, in contrast with the FO's reluctance to put all Britain's eggs in the American basket. What everyone agreed, however, was that HMG must *try* to create the closest possible relationship with the U.S.A. Not only would this maximize the chances of a durable post-war security system but it also offered the best hope of ensuring that U.S. power was harmonized with British interests. As Harvey put it: 'I think we can manage the Americans if we are "mixed up" with them, but I tremble for the consequences if we are on terms of suspicion and niggling concession.'[67] Whatever the doubts and fears, HMG had no real alternative but to hope that permanent and equal co-operation could be achieved. The problem, of course, was how?

Part of the answer lay in the web of personal acquaintance and friendship that was being spun in ever-increasing complexity across the Atlantic. We saw earlier how personal contacts between British and U.S. leaders had been limited in the 1930s, how visits such as those by Welles in 1940 and Hopkins in 1941 had helped to dispel misapprehensions, and how the main value of the Atlantic Meeting was that both sets of policymakers, from Churchill and Roosevelt down, became better acquainted. Visits to Washington were particularly instructive for British leaders. Like Halifax early in 1941, whose reactions were noted in chapter 7 (b), Keynes in the summer and Churchill and Dill in December all understood in a new way after a few weeks in Washington how complex and decentralized the U.S. political process really was and how difficult it was for F.D.R. to provide the decisive leadership for which they yearned.[68] But more important than these contacts at the top were those between middle-rank officers and bureaucrats who, as we saw in chapter 7 (b), were moving to and fro in increasing numbers between the two capitals. The friendships developed in the process helped to smooth relations during the war and to sustain co-operation in the years that followed, as those involved rose to positions of leadership in their respective hierarchies.[69] It was here that the shared language, stripped of all extravagant myths, proved particularly potent. It facilitated more extensive and more intensive personal relationships than would otherwise have been possible. Extensive—in that those capable of effective conversation were not confined to specialist linguists. Intensive—because only experts in a foreign tongue, versed in its nuances and masters of its vocabulary, can use it to penetrate beneath surface politeness and create a deep and many-sided relationship. That is what Shaw meant when he said that the British and Americans had the ability to understand each other's insults. One has only to compare the forthright intimacy of the ABC Staff Talks or the Atlantic Meeting with the strained artificiality of the Anglo-French Supreme War Councils of 1939–40, regulated by interpreters, to appreciate the value of the common tongue both in exposing disagreements and in helping resolve them. Paradoxically the fact that the two governments argued so frequently and directly is testimony to the specialness of their relationship.

Some British officials also recognized that building a relationship was a two-way process. This was a frequent refrain from FO/A, particularly

Whitehead, the only official with an intimate knowledge of New Deal America. 'Cooperation implies a sharing of ideas as well as labour & wealth etc.', he reminded his colleagues. HMG could not expect American material and naval help while dismissing her policies as unwarranted interference; nor could it expect America to mend her ways without doing some honest self-appraisal of its own.[70] Most FO officials acknowledged this latter point. They accepted that Britain's post-1919 isolationism, her handling of the war debts question and her economic policy in the early 1930s had all been short-sighted.[71] And on a more popular level the belated effort in 1941 to promote the study of American history in British schools, which got under way that summer with eight special training courses for 1,200 teachers, displayed a new recognition that the British had much to learn about America. As one Board of Education circular observed, it was important to correct the 'confused impression of American life and history' derived by children from the cinema and to 'rid ourselves of the tendency . . . to look at America for English traits and within a framework of English political ideas'.[72] But although accepting that *both* countries had to be educated into co-operation, most British officials had no doubt that America had far more to learn than Britain. R. A. Butler told Whitehead in March that 'our delinquencies over the debt are as nothing compared to the American betrayal over the League of Nations. We were landed alone with a European system fashioned by an academic American ideallist [*sic*].' He continued with sentiments characteristic of most British policymakers in 1941:

> Many here have an uneasy feeling that, if we study America, she may in her turn yet rat on us. This does not mean that we should despair. At present it seems that the Anglo Saxon (Rhodes) ideal is the finest before us. I feel this deeply yet I intend to approach this ideal realising that my country is, for the second time, doing America's fighting for her and that my country has more right than wrong on her side.[73]

No British official had any neat answer to this problem of how to 'educate' the U.S.A. The FO's best hope was that if close and comprehensive co-operation could be achieved during the war then it would be difficult for a new Administration or a change of national mood to reverse the process. The present Administration was clearly the best Britain could hope for. 'Roosevelt is our great opportunity of "mixing up with America",' Harvey reminded Eden. The future alternatives were horrifying—'Coolidges, Hoovers or even Lindberghs'. It was also clear that the current interventionist mood, born of deep security anxieties, was peculiarly favourable. 'Anything we can do to get America "entangled" in post-war settlement questions [now] will be to the good,' minuted Scott. 'After the war the forces operating in the other direction will be extremely strong.'[74] The Embassy, in a shrewd analysis, emphasized the significance of Executive agreements, such as the Destroyers Deal, to which the Roosevelt Administration was having increasing recourse. If arrangements for Anglo-American collaboration could be made in this form, even though their validity might sometimes be questionable, it would avoid the grave difficulties of securing the two-thirds Senate majority required for ratification of a formal treaty.[75] In particular all the FO, including Eden, believed that if real progress could be made towards a common economic policy this would allay many American suspicions and provide a bridge to fuller, political co-operation. This was an old FO argument—advanced for example in 1937–38 in support of a Trade Agreement—but it assumed a new significance in 1941 because of the growing controversy over post-war economic policy and the way this became wrapped up with the price Britain was asked to pay for Lend-Lease.

## C. Towards a new economic order

To understand the Anglo-American debates in 1941 about the post-war economy we need to recapitulate the economic history of the inter-war years.[76] During the 1920s a multilateral world economy had been painfully reconstructed, on the basis of stable exchange rates and a modified gold standard, only to fragment again after 1929 in the Depression and, particularly, the international currency crisis of mid-1931, which forced Britain off gold. The next five years were a time of almost unmitigated economic nationalism as the major powers grasped desperately for any weapon in defence of their currencies and trade. With the gold standard in ruins, monetary blocs coalesced around the four major currencies—sterling, the dollar, the franc and the mark. Germany's was the most regimented, in East and Central Europe, while Britain's looser bloc grew out of the role of sterling as a reserve currency for much of the British Empire (though not Canada) and a number of Scandinavian and Latin American countries heavily reliant on British trade and capital. Commercial policy followed a similar tendency to semi-independent groups of complementary national economies. This trend was again most pronounced in Germany and then Britain, with the 1932 Ottawa system of tariffs, quotas and preferences designed to promote intra-imperial trade and discriminate against rival imports from outside the Empire. Trade and currency blocs overlapped—Britain signed a series of preferential agreements in the mid-1930s with non-Empire countries within the sterling bloc. The trend was for countries to buy from those to whom they could sell, thereby minimizing the problem of payments settlements at a time when exchange rates were in chaos and gold in short supply.

The period 1936–39, by contrast, was one of relative stability which saw tentative attempts to re-create multilateralism. The tripartite monetary agreement of September 1936 provided for a degree of flexible stabilization between sterling, the dollar and the franc, and the Anglo-American trade agreement, concluded in November 1938, tried to reduce trade barriers between the world's two main trading nations. But these trends were soon reversed by the deteriorating international situation. The run on sterling for much of 1938 and 1939, and then the onset of war, forced Britain to consolidate the loose sterling bloc of the 1930s into a formal sterling area, protected by exchange controls, and to trade almost exclusively with those countries willing to run up large sterling balances in London instead of requiring payment in gold and dollars. Consequently, trade with the U.S.A. was cut to a minimum in 1939–40. It had to be revived, necessarily, after the Fall of France, but at the cost of Britain's remaining reserves, and it was only sustained in large quantities from mid-1941 because the U.S.A. was willing to supply the goods and defer the question of repayment.

The reaction to these developments differed in Washington and London. After an initial period of confused economic nationalism, the dominant theme of the Roosevelt Administration was the reconstruction of a multilateral world economy. Morgenthau and the U.S. Treasury advocated monetary stabilization and a return to gold, arguing that the instability of the 1930s stemmed largely from movements of speculative capital in response to fluctuating exchange rates. The problem seemed to them an extension of the New Deal struggle to combat the dominance of bankers and financiers over American economic life. Looking back over his years as Treasury Secretary, Morgenthau commented in 1946 that his primary object had been to 'move the financial center of the world from London and Wall Street to the United States Treasury and to create a new concept between the nations of international finance' under the control of 'sovereign governments and not of private financial interests'. The 1936 stabilization agreement had been a step in this direction, because in practice it operated as a loose dollar standard,[77] but the Treasury's main efforts were concentrated in the period after 1941, culminating in the Bretton Woods agreements of July 1944. More significant in the 1930s and in 1941 was the sustained campaign by the State Department to liberalize world trade. Hull and his colleagues believed that political conflict was caused largely by economic rivalry and that Wilson's neglect of economic issues at Versailles had been a major reason for the instability of the peace settlement. Ideally they wished to see the reduction of all trade barriers, including America's high protective tariffs, but their particular concern was with barriers that discriminated against certain countries in favour of others. Although German practices were the most extreme in this respect, Britain's network of Imperial Preferences and financial controls was more significant for world trade and easier to challenge. State faced an uphill battle at home as well, against Congress' traditional dominance over tariff policy and the interest of key manufacturers in continued protection, but it envisaged British concessions as a means of obtaining Congressional support. As with Morgenthau, considerations of national interest merged with a sense of the wider good: the dismantling of Britain's economic controls would benefit American trade and also stimulate world reform, prosperity and peace.

In Britain three lines of thought emerged among policymakers. A small group shared the American belief that a multilateral world economy could and should be quickly reconstructed, on the basis of Anglo-American currency stabilization and the elimination of all except a bare minimum of tariff barriers. This was the opinion, for instance, of Frank Ashton-Gwatkin, the FO's principal economic specialist during the 1930s, and officials in the Board of Trade were similarly inclined.[78] On the other hand, Leopold Amery led a small but influential group of Tory ministers, including Beaverbrook, Cranborne and Kingsley Wood, who believed that the retention of Imperial Preference would be the key to Britain's post-war economic security. Amery has often been caricatured as a reactionary, yank-hating imperialist, out to create an autarchic economic bloc. Undoubtedly he was alarmed about America's commercial expansion, and feared that her internationalist phase would not outlast the war. He was also emotionally committed to the vision of imperial unity, cemented by bonds of blood and language between Britain and the Dominions. But Amery believed passionately that it was Hull and not himself who was the reactionary. The Americans, he argued, were belatedly preaching the nineteenth-century gospel of *laissez-faire* individualism at a time when the world had moved towards planned economies and groupings of nation states. The larger group in which Britain primarily belonged was the Commonwealth, and what Hull, looking from outside, called 'discrimination', Amery saw from within, in positive terms, as co-operation between like-minded and now virtually sovereign states. He regarded the evolution of the Commonwealth as a model for the world at large, and as the basis of Britain's post-war future. This did not preclude continued co-operation with the U.S.A. On the contrary, Amery was 'anxious to cooperate with them after the war, in the economic as well as the political field, and on the basis of a liberal economic policy'. But it should be co-operation between the U.S.A. and the British Empire *as a unit*, free to develop 'such intra-Imperial cooperation as suits us' in the light of modern economic conditions.[79]

Both Amery and the free-traders were ideologues, for whom economic policy was but part of a broader vision of the world order. Most British policymakers, certainly the bulk of the Treasury and FO, took a much more pragmatic view, somewhere between these two extremes. For them financial controls rather than Imperial Preference were the paramount consideration. They interpreted the inter-war crisis largely as the result of America's failure to accept her responsibilities after the Great War as a creditor nation. The only way that Britain and other European powers could pay for their growing imports of commodities and manufactures from the U.S.A. was either by increasing their own exports to the largely self-sufficient Americans or else by settling payments deficits in gold, which had a deflationary effect on their own economies. Clearly neither of these methods was satisfactory, and in any case both were blocked during the late 20s and early 30s by America's ever-increasing tariffs, and by her accumulation of two-thirds of the world's gold reserves as she demanded payment of war debts and then cut back precipitately after 1929 on the foreign loans that had reflated the European economy in the 1920s. On this argument, Britain's bilateralist policies in the 1930s had been a protective response against American irresponsibility. A stable and prosperous multilateral economy would depend on the U.S.A. substantially reducing her tariffs and using her gold 'hoard' to increase international liquidity and finance post-war reconstruction. There seemed no sign in early 1941 that the U.S.A. would do this, and in any case Britain's own position after the war was likely to be far worse than the 1930s. With minimal gold reserves, vast sterling debts and the loss of many of her sources of invisible earnings—foreign investments, merchant shipping and insurance business—which had covered visible trade deficits in the past, it seemed clear that Britain would have no choice but to increase her exports dramatically and to buy primarily from those to whom she could sell. Multilateral

271

trade would only be possible among complementary economies which used sterling as a reserve currency. In other words, the Sterling Area, hopefully in an enlarged form, would be the basis of Britain's post-war economy. These arguments were elaborated most clearly by Keynes, as part of his work to counter German propaganda for a new order, but by the spring of 1941 they had been accepted through much of Whitehall, and, in a suitably vague form, served as the core of Eden's 29 May speech. For some these policies were a semi-permanent answer—the Bank of England, for instance, had long envisaged sterling's reserve-currency role as the guarantee of the City's now precarious position of international financial leadership—but most accepted them reluctantly, with a sense of no alternative, as a defence mechanism for the foreseeable future against continued American 'irresponsibility' and the supposedly inevitable post-war slump.[80]

What were Churchill's opinions? As Halifax once remarked, he was always 'pretty bored with anything except the actual war',[81] and for the most part preferred to leave economic matters to the appropriate ministries. Nevertheless, he held a number of deep convictions of his own, notably a long-standing belief in free trade. It was on this issue that he had joined the Liberals in 1904 and even after he returned to the Tory fold in 1924 he remained essentially a Liberal on economic policy. This is a point worth emphasizing in view of the frequent assumption that Churchill's defence of the Empire politically carried over into dogmatic support for Imperial Preference. 'My own view', he told the Treasury in August 1941, 'is that there can be no great future for the world without a vast breaking down of tariffs and other barriers', and he made clear his complete opposition to the Ottawa Agreements at the Atlantic Meeting and on other occasions in 1941. However, Churchill agreed that financial and commercial controls could only be relaxed in so far as the U.S.A., 'hitherto the worst offender in tariff matters', took the initiative herself.[82] Moreover, he was acutely aware of the domestic political issues involved. Protection and preferences had riven the Conservatives for four decades and the Ameryite rump had considerable support within the Party. Less important, but also of concern to the leader of a national coalition, was the divide on the left between moderate free traders such as Greenwood and those such as Dalton and Bevin who saw financial and commercial controls as a possible framework for a planned economy. All these considerations reinforced Churchill's dominant attitude towards the whole question of post-war planning, which as we have seen, was postponement. But in so far as this was not possible they also inclined him to repose particular faith in the judgement of Kingsley Wood. As Chancellor, Wood was spokesman for the Treasury experts. He was also an advocate of modified Imperial Preference, and, above all, he was Churchill's barometer and informal manager of Tory party opinion.[83] In handling questions of post-war economic policy in 1941 Churchill followed closely Wood's advice.

*    *    *

At first sight these questions of long-term economic policy seem remote from the central problems of Anglo-American relations in 1941—the Battle of the Atlantic and the confrontation with Japan. But they kept recurring as underlying issues in current diplomatic negotiations—for example Keynes' discussions in Washington that summer about Britain's pre-Lend-Lease 'old commitments', and the concurrent Anglo-American talks about a supplementary trade agreement. More significant was the public controversy sparked off by American press reports in June and July that the British were abusing Lend-Lease for commercial gain. The principal charge was that Lend-Lease goods, particularly metals, were being re-exported, or else used to replace similar British goods which were then exported, to compete with U.S. businessmen especially in South America. At this stage Lend-Lease had hardly begun to flow, and both the State Department and Hopkins' staff could find little to substantiate the allegations, but they were concerned that the criticism would damage chances of getting new Lend-Lease appropriations approved by Congress in September.[84] They pressed this argument on the British, who finally accepted an exchange of agreed notes on the subject, which were published in Britain on 13 September as a White Paper on Export Policy. The basic principles were that Lend-Lease goods were not and would not be exported, nor would goods similar to those supplied under the Act be used by British exporters 'to enter new markets or extend their export trade at the expense of United States exporters'. Furthermore, no materials of a type that was in short supply in the U.S.A. and that the British bought or received from the U.S.A. would be used for export, except in a few special cases.[85]

Strictly interpreted, these criteria of 'competition' and 'short supply' could severely and unfairly restrict Britain's export trade. This trade was important to pay for essential purchases from the Americas, including the 'old commitments' and items not covered by Lend-Lease. It was also vital if Britain wanted to balance her international payments when the war was over. American manufacturers, for their part, were very conscious that key raw materials were being restricted for government use in the U.S.A., and naturally wanted to preclude any possibility that they might be used by British competitors. However, they clearly encouraged the press furore in the summer of 1941 and stood to gain from the White Paper's provisions, while British manufacturers were most unhappy about HMG's concessions and often complained bitterly that the British were fighting America's war while she extended her trade at their expense.[86] What exporters in both countries were concerned about was their long-standing commercial rivalry in South America. The present war, like that of 1914–18, had enabled Americans to strengthen their position, as Britain concentrated her national resources on war and survival, and British manufacturers and exporters feared that the White Paper could be used to undermine further their markets and investments. The Roosevelt Administration was well aware of all this, but its primary concern, at least for senior policymakers, was not commercial opportunism but the propitiation of Congress. Hull and Winant were anxious for a fair agreement and the toughness of their demands is attributable in part to a failure to understand just how important Britain's export trade had been and would be for her economic future—in contrast with the U.S.A. where the domestic sector was the major market. At one point, the U.S. draft of the White Paper would have pledged Britain to 'concentrate her exports in the field of traditional articles, such as Scotch Whiskey, Harris Tweeds etc.'. The impression conveyed, one British Treasury economist sputtered indignantly, was that of 'a picturesque little nation whose trading reputation depends on a few specialities popular in fashionable circles in Boston and New York, but which had presumptuously, under the temptation of lend-lease, gone outside its "traditional" field to try its hand at real industry like metallurgy and the staple textile trades'. He suggested that the American negotiators be given 'an outline of the economic history of nineteenth-century Britain'.[87]

*   *   *

However, the Export White Paper was only part of a larger controversy over Lend-Lease. As we saw in chapter 6 (c), supplies for Britain and other countries were not provided free of charge: the Act simply deferred payment and authorized the President to negotiate the 'Consideration' the U.S.A. would receive in return. In mid-March and again in mid-May F.D.R. became worried for a time that Congress would demand an early agreement. By June he had decided that nothing definite need be announced until his annual report on Lend-Lease the following January, but it was nevertheless important that serious negotiations with the British about the 'Consideration' begin soon. These negotiations were complex and detailed. They also dragged on until February 1942. Nevertheless we need at least to dip into them, to see the main phases and the issues at stake, because they provide the clearest indication of where the two governments agreed and differed on economic policy, how they tried to achieve their respective ends, and how the process of negotiation first exacerbated differences and then diminished them.[88]

It took the Administration some time to determine the form it wanted the Consideration to take. In March and April the Treasury, to which F.D.R. initially delegated primary responsibility, produced some tentative drafts. These followed closely the basic 'loan' principle outlined by F.D.R. in December and confirmed by him during a long cross-examination by Morgenthau on 10 March: Britain would be asked to return surviving goods, and to reimburse the U.S.A. for goods used up or destroyed by providing 'an equivalent amount of similar defense articles' or else useful raw materials.[89] However, the State Department, which took charge of the question from May, argued that this would simply create another unpayable war debt—in goods not money. Its proposal was to write off *matériel* that was meant to be destroyed, such as bombs and shells, to require return of other equipment such as ships and guns that survived the war, and to ask for repayment in a non-economic form for other supplies such as food and merchant shipping. In particular, Welles, Berle and Acheson agreed that the U.S.A. should concentrate on securing a firm British commitment to abandon Imperial Preference and financial controls after the war, in return for a promise of radical reductions in U.S. tariffs. Unlike another war debt, this would be a meaningful quid pro quo, beneficial to the U.S.A. *and* to the world economy. They saw the leverage provided by the Consideration, at a time when Britain's bargaining power was greatly diminished, as their 'only chance to do it'.[90] And, after long discussions throughout the summer, the official draft submitted to the British on 28 July represented a victory for these State Department officials. Its seventh article contained a provision 'against discrimination in either the United States of America or the United Kingdom against the importation of any product originating in the other country'.[91] Since the U.S.A. had virtually no discriminatory tariffs, except on goods from Cuba and the Philippines, this clause was directed almost entirely at Britain and required a commitment to abandon Imperial Preference and probably exchange controls after the war.

That State was willing to use the Lend-Lease Consideration in this way as an instrument to promote its post-war goals is well known to historians. Less often noted, however, is the rather different attitude F.D.R. had adopted during the spring and summer. He agreed in principle with State's aim of economic liberalization, but had considerable reservations about trying to drive a hard bargain of the sort Welles, Berle and Acheson envisaged. So, too, had Hull—which is interesting in view of his notorious fanaticism about trade policy. Spring 1941, after all, was a time of great anxiety in Washington about Britain's ability to survive, and it seemed indelicate and perhaps diplomatically dangerous to push HMG too hard. At most, both felt that a general declaration of liberal aims could be required, rather than firm commitments.[92] Furthermore, by May the President was moving away from his original ideas of a quid pro quo and payment in kind, in search of ways to integrate the Consideration into his conception of post-war security. For instance, in the summer he was talking of getting the British to repay some of their Lend-Lease goods in the form of equipment for the post-war Anglo-American police force. However, such ideas would be highly controversial in the U.S.A., and could obviously not be stated in a published document at that time.[93] What Roosevelt wanted, therefore, was a preliminary agreement, outlining in general language the principles of the eventual settlement, including the return of surviving goods and the concept of mutual co-operation, and committing both governments to detailed discussions about the form that this co-operation would take. In the instructions he gave Acheson and Welles on 18 July the goal of economic liberalization was touched on only lightly, in a reference to 'the betterment of world-wide economic relations'.[94] Yet ten days later, when Acheson gave Keynes the tough U.S. draft, he said that F.D.R. had approved it. How can we explain this?

There seem to have been three principal reasons. One is that Roosevelt was probably not fully aware of what State had done. This was Keynes' belief, and Acheson virtually admitted as much. Keynes told London after talking with him: 'I understand that it [the draft] embodied ideas which had been approved by the President in conversation, and that he had signified concurrence with the wording of this paper read to him over the telephone, but had not had it before him in writing.'[95] It is difficult to believe that anyone could give serious consideration to a 750-word state document over the phone. Never one for administrative details, and lacking a proper secretariat to keep track of them, F.D.R. was preoccupied in late July with the freezing of Japanese assets and it is likely that State exploited the opportunity to re-introduce its pet idea.[96] However, it is also clear that Washington had been upset by the consistently negative attitude adopted by British leaders on the whole Consideration question. Ever since Hopkins and Acheson began to discuss the matter with Keynes in May, the official consensus in London had been that HMG should procrastinate, because of the complexity and divisiveness of the issues involved and because it was hoped that the U.S.A. would soon be in the war, thereby redressing the imbalance in the relationship and perhaps even eliminating any need for a Consideration at all. Even the FO, usually anxious to entangle the Americans in post-war questions, took this view.[97] In Washington, however, Halifax and particularly Keynes strongly disagreed. They argued that there was every chance of reaching an advantageous and indeed far-sighted basic agreement at the present time, whereas postponement might mean dealing with a Republican Congress or President less enlightened and well disposed towards Britain. Moreover, it was apparent that F.D.R.'s ideas were still fluid and that in the bureaucratic confusion of Washington it would be possible for HMG to influence significantly the policy-making process. 'It is vitally important that the President should give the right kind of instructions', Keynes told Halifax. '[I]f we draft the phrases, we can give them the turn we prefer.'[98] But when Keynes suggested this tactic to Churchill and the Treasury, he was sternly rebuked. All they wanted him to do was listen and report, still hoping that the problem would somehow go away, and when, in July, Keynes tried his hand at a mutually acceptable draft HMG emasculated it into a series of non-committal platitudes.[99] Not surprisingly, the British behaviour irritated F.D.R. and strengthened State's fears that they were really bent on an aggressive bilateralist policy. But what really confirmed these fears was Keynes' campaign, as he saw it, to teach Washington some rudimentary economics. Keynes was a man of great brilliance and charm. He also combined the irreverence of Bloomsbury with the arrogance of Cambridge—a combination that many Americans found insufferable on first acquaintance. During the summer his urbane, didactic manner had antagonized virtually every senior Administration official with whom he dealt, including Hopkins, Morgenthau, Acheson and even Roosevelt. In particular, Keynes had tried to get across the fact that a quick British return to multilateralism was unlikely, and that import and exchange controls would probably have to be maintained after the war. His tone became increasingly strident as he detected in every conversation with Administration officials the relics of classical economic theory—the gold standard, free trade and 'all that old lumber' which he termed 'the clutch of the dead, or at least the moribund, hand'.[100] Ironically—in view of Keynes' desire to reach an agreement—it is likely that his vehement criticisms of economic liberalism, as much as HMG's stone-walling, strengthened State's determination to commit Britain to ending discrimination. One might even call it 'The Diplomatic Consequences of Mr. Keynes'.

The account presented so far suggests, therefore, that despite policy differences between the two governments, and despite the desire of some senior State Department officials to use the Lend-Lease Consideration as a device to promote their ends, a direct confrontation over multilateralism could have been avoided if the British had been more tactful and forthcoming in their handling of the Consideration issue. It was their behaviour that led State, in partial defiance of F.D.R., to fight so hard and successfully for its draft of the agreement. From August 1941 the British had therefore to face the problem they had hoped to avoid—the policy differences had become a part of current diplomacy. The Treasury emphasized that continued import and exchange controls would probably be inevitable to balance Britain's payments, while Churchill was increasingly concerned about a possible split in the Tory party if Imperial Preference was not safeguarded, at least for the moment. Eden and the FO, despite their conviction that Anglo-American economic co-operation would help draw the U.S.A. into broader agreements, acknowledged the validity of both these concerns. The task, therefore, was to find a form of words that would satisfy the Administration without prejudicing Britain's future policy. A first attempt was made only a few days after the 28 July draft had been presented when Welles tried to insert State's formula banning commercial discrimination into the Atlantic Charter. Even though F.D.R. watered this down, the American version was still unacceptable to the British, and Churchill secured approval for his revision by warning that otherwise promulgation of the Charter would have to be delayed while the Dominions were consulted. Accordingly point four pledged both governments *'with due respect for their existing obligations'* to help all states enjoy equal access to trade and raw materials. But this negative formulation did not satisfy State,[101] and it was clearly insufficient for the Lend-Lease Consideration. After more than two months of intermittent debate and several reminders from Washington, HMG finally submitted its revised draft of article seven on 17 October. This set a commitment to end 'harmful discriminations' within a wider context of mutual obligations to create a balanced, expanding international economy. As compensation for the generalities of the language there was also a firm commitment to begin conversations 'at an early convenient date' to discuss ways of attaining these objectives. HMG's response was an authentic statement of British policy— that there could be no categorical and comprehensive commitment to ending controls and that progress on the matter could only be made if the U.S.A. was willing to move as well.[102]

The State Department considered this version for some six weeks. Of particular note is the fact that, although still determined to tie HMG to ending discrimination, State was increasingly sensitive to the British predicament. It acknowledged the need to 'avoid producing sharp political differences of opinion within the British Government at this time'.[103] More significant still, although the Department had always accepted the U.S.A.'s responsibility to reduce tariffs, Keynes' lectures and the British redraft had made it more aware that tariff reform would be only one of America's many responsibilities if balanced multilateralism was to be achieved. Accordingly, the Administration's December revision of article seven was significantly different from the version it had originally presented in July. HMG was no longer being required to make a unilateral commitment to end discrimination. The emphasis, instead, was on 'agreed action' directed to this end, to be determined by subsequent conversations and 'in light of governing economic conditions'. Furthermore, this was only one of several equally desirable goals identified in the draft—including the repudiation of tariffs and the expansion of production, employment and trade—all of which required substantial U.S. action if they were to be achieved. Finally, these goals were implicitly interdependent—if, say, Congress refused to reduce tariffs or failed to prevent a post-war slump, then HMG could reasonably renege on its own obligation to end discrimination. The largely one-sided draft of July had become a statement of mutual obligations; the quid pro quo had been subsumed in a blueprint for joint action to re-create balanced multilateralism. State still wanted Britain to give up Imperial Preference, and she was being asked to begin joint discussions with its elimination explicitly on the agenda. But the American second draft now assumed more of the form for which F.D.R. had searched unsuccessfully in the spring—with the emphasis less on what the U.S.A. could get back as on what both governments could contribute to the creation of a better world.[104]

*    *    *

The State Department's new version of article seven was presented to the British on 2 December 1941. Little was done about it until late January—for two reasons. One was that both governments were preoccupied with the crisis in the Far East and with the institutional arrangements for the new alliance. More fundamentally, most British policymakers hoped and believed that the Consideration would now be forgotten, although the FO and Washington Embassy warned that this was most unlikely. In particular, this was Churchill's conviction—for reasons to be discussed in the epilogue—and when in Washington in December he resisted F.D.R.'s efforts to raise the matter. But at the beginning of February 1942 State returned to the question, backed by a personal message from Roosevelt to Churchill asking for prompt acceptance of the American draft. The Cabinet agreed on 6 February, but wanted to issue an interpretative note elaborating the British position on multilateralism and indicating that it did not understand Imperial Preference to be included in the term 'discrimination'.[105] However, F.D.R. wanted to avoid a qualifying note, which would reduce the international impact of the agreement. He sent Churchill another cable on 11 February, stating that article seven did not contain a commitment in advance to abolish Imperial Preference, and acknowledging that HMG could not make such a commitment without consulting Parliament and the Dominions, just as he could make no commitments in his own right about reducing U.S. tariffs. All he wanted, the President insisted, was simply 'a bold, forthright and comprehensive discussion' about all post-war economic problems, from which, he stated twice, 'nothing should be excluded'. On the basis of these assurances Roosevelt asked Churchill to sign the Consideration agreement.[106]

Somewhat to the Americans' surprise, the President's message did the trick.[107] Part of the reason—astoundingly—is that Churchill misunderstood it, and believed that F.D.R. had said that the whole question of Imperial Preference 'should be excluded from our discussions'.[108] This misinterpretation was embodied in the Cabinet minutes, and was later to prove a source of controversy between the two governments,[109] but most of Whitehall did not fall into Churchill's error. More important was F.D.R.'s personal intervention, which showed that the Consideration was not State's private obsession, and his assurance that HMG was not committed in advance to abolishing Imperial Preference. This covered the Cabinet's main anxiety and, with all of them, especially Churchill, preoccupied in mid-February with the fall of Singapore, they had little incentive to argue further. In addition, the Treasury was now ready to compromise because F.D.R. was currently considering taking over Britain's pre-Lend-Lease commitments, to the tune of some $800 million. This would help enormously in bridging Britain's continued dollar gap and in the smooth operation of the Sterling Area, and it was clear that further haggling over article seven would be tactless. Indeed Keynes reported that Morgenthau had advised F.D.R. to make the take-over conditional on Britain's acceptance of article seven.[110] Given Churchill's reliance on Kingsley Wood, it is likely that the Treasury's advice was decisive. The Lend-Lease Consideration agreement was duly signed on 23 February 1942.

*     *     *

But to understand fully Britain's acceptance of article seven we need to appreciate that Whitehall was now more hopeful of finding common ground between the two governments on economic policy. Earlier I stressed that for most British policymakers the fundamental economic issue was not a dogmatic adherence to Imperial Preference, but a reluctant conviction that HMG would have to maintain exchange and commercial controls for the foreseeable future in order to protect its balance of payments. Bilateralism appeared the only alternative to the unbalanced multilateral economy of the inter-war years, with its debilitating trade deficits, fluctuating price levels and chronic domestic deflations. This negative, rather defeatist attitude was still being expressed in official Treasury documents during the autumn of 1941,[111] but behind the scenes in Whitehall this was a time of great intellectual ferment. Keynes was the leading agent, although other government economists, such as James Meade, were thinking along similar lines. What Keynes had tried to get across in Washington in the summer of 1941 was 'not necessarily that our policy would follow bilateral lines, and certainly not that this was the most desirable solution, but simply that we might be forced to move along these lines unless some other comprehensive solution was found'.[112] His talks in Washington made him aware that if this happened it would cause a major crisis in Anglo-American relations, and also that the Americans were conscious, albeit to what he considered a limited extent, of the need for the U.S.A. to modify its own policies before multilateralism could be restored. Keynes therefore returned to London determined to evolve a 'comprehensive solution' which combined the advantages and avoided the dangers of the two economic systems.[113] His first draft of the proposal for an 'International Currency Union' was circulated around the Treasury on 8 September; revised versions followed in mid-November and mid-December, after fruitful consultation with friends and colleagues, and it was submitted to the Cabinet the following April. The basic principles were to retain the discipline of certain exchange controls, to extend the practices of domestic banking on to the international level, and to require creditor nations to assume greater responsibility for expansion and stability. All exchange transactions would be conducted by national central banks, dealing through an international clearing bank with its own money of account pegged against gold. National payments surpluses and deficits would constitute credits and debits on the bank's account. Persistent debtors would be obliged to depreciate their currencies; persistent creditors to appreciate theirs and also to allocate their surpluses for loans, reconstruction and international policing.[114] On a much more sophisticated level this concept of responsible co-operation mirrored the attitude of F.D.R. towards the Lend-Lease Consideration during the summer. At the same time, independently, Harry White of the U.S. Treasury was also developing a plan to increase international liquidity and monetary stability. White's draft, which first appeared in early January 1942, was more modest in scope than Keynes'—essentially a fixed-assets stabilization fund, rather than an international clearing bank whose size depended on the volume of world trade—and by 1943–44 the differences between the two schemes became a source of controversy and conflict.[115] But in late 1941 the similarities were more significant than the differences. Both Treasuries were considering schemes to restore a multilateral world economy while ensuring stable exchange rates, payments equilibria and full employment. Within that context it was possible for HMG to be more optimistic about the eventual abandonment of many of the financial, if not commercial, controls adopted during the 1930s and the war. There now seemed a possible alternative to bilateralism.

## D. Leadership and the new international order

I have examined the negotiations over the Lend-Lease Consideration in some detail, partly because they have been neglected by historians but mainly because they provide an excellent illustration of the complexity of the Anglo-American relationship. On the one hand, we have seen the disagreement and rivalry about economic policy which underlay the growing co-operation in the military sphere. The Roosevelt Administration wanted an early return to a multilateral world economy. They saw the elimination of Imperial Preference as an important precondition, and had used the leverage provided by Lend-Lease to help force Britain to comply. By contrast, most British policymakers in early 1941 were reluctant bilateralists, who saw no alternative to maintaining exchange and commercial controls for the foreseeable future. Increasingly, however, at least for Churchill, the economic issues became less important than the political and diplomatic—the unity of the Tory party and the equality of the relationship. British intransigence strengthened the determination of State Department officials, and latterly of Roosevelt, to obtain an agreement. On the other hand, there was more to the story than an aggressive Administration exploiting Britain's predicament. The February 1942 agreement only committed HMG to discuss the possibility of ending discrimination, and even that commitment was ambiguous in view of Churchill's misunderstanding of F.D.R.'s message. More important, we have also seen that the policy differences between the two governments narrowed as 1941 progressed. From an apparently unbridgeable gap in the summer, dramatized by Keynes' harangues of Administration officials, London and Washington gradually moved closer together, as demonstrated by the successive drafts of article seven and by the independent but parallel outlines of a new monetary system. Fundamentally, most British and American policymakers agreed that multilateralism was desirable in principle. Britain was a nation unusually reliant on commerce and ancillary services for her economic stability and growth, and the idea of trading within a limited market was always second best. Whatever the more anglophobe State Department officials might believe in their gloomier moments, this consensus distinguished Britain and the U.S.A. from Nazi Germany, and as the Americans showed increasing readiness to assume their responsibilities as the world's major economic power, so HMG became less intransigent about moving away from defensive bilateralism. This is not to discount the subsequent argument about trade and financial policy, which rumbled on throughout the 1940s. But the issue, increasingly, was the practice rather than the principle of multilateralism—how far the new system, which they both desired, would accommodate their individual needs and aspirations.

This pattern—competition within a framework of co-operation—leads us on to some final points, on a more theoretical level. Many, though not all, economic historians agree that a stable and prosperous multilateral economy is not the automatic result of market forces, but must be underpinned by a single leading power. Otherwise the inevitable periodic political upheavals and economic cycles are difficult to contain and can easily unbalance and even undermine the whole system. In other words, the liberal economic order is actually liberal *and* 'imperial' or 'hegemonic'.[116] In the period from roughly the mid-nineteenth century until World War One the role of leader was assumed by Britain. She was the main guarantor of political stability, she acted as the principal source of investment and crisis capital, she kept open a free market for trade even at times of depression. In the quarter-century after 1945 these functions were largely taken over by the United States. But the period between the wars was one in which Britain was no longer able and the U.S.A. not yet willing to act as leader. The instability of the early 1930s, the drift to economic blocs and the depth and persistence of the Depression were in large measure the consequence of that fact. With Britain 'feeble' and the U.S.A. 'irresponsible', 'every country turned to protect its national private interest, the world interest went down the drain, and with it the private interests of all.'[117]

What is important here is the notion of a 'world interest', transcending yet encompassing the interests of individual nation states, of which the international leader is effectively the guardian. It reminds us of the ambiguity inherent in the position of a super-power—the complex mixture of self-interest and, quite literally, self-sacrifice.[118] On the one hand, the position of leader is a reflection of the political and economic dominance of a particular state, and the system the leader helps to shape is a way of institutionalizing that predominance. Thus, economic liberalization is in the interests of the world's leading manufacturer—Britain in the Victorian era and the U.S.A. after World War Two. Similarly, the classical gold standard rested on and confirmed sterling's position as the major reserve currency; just as Bretton

Woods reflected and reinforced the supremacy of the dollar. But, on the other hand, the rewards of leadership are balanced by the responsibilities. The system relies on the strength of the dominant power, and that strength must be exerted periodically if order and prosperity are to be maintained. But strength exerted is strength expended: the responsibilities of leadership are eventually debilitating. The cost of a strong military presence abroad is the most obvious example; another is the maintenance of the reserve status of one's national currency, as both the history of sterling and latterly the dollar have shown. Furthermore, the goal of the system is the expansion of world trade, and that inevitably means strengthening economic competitors and eroding one's own position. In short, there is a just irony about international leadership—it results from a position of dominance yet tends to undermine that position in the long run. To call the international leader 'imperial' is misleading if it connotes only benefits and not burdens.[119]

These insights are applicable to the British and American efforts in 1941–42 to reconstruct the world order—political as well as economic. The point at issue was not broad goals. Both governments wanted a stable international security system, and also, though consensus took longer to emerge, a balanced multilateral economy. They also envisaged Anglo-American co-operation as the lynch-pin of both the political and the economic orders. Their arguments were about how equal the relationship should be and who should lead within the new system. Even one as keen on Anglo-American co-operation as Eden was deeply concerned about these questions. The arguments reflect the shift in power from Britain to the U.S.A. and revolved around the latter's attempts to extend and the former's to preserve their respective positions. But they were not entirely selfish. Administration leaders believed passionately in America's mission as the harbinger of liberal democracy, as refined by the experience of the New Deal. The British concept of 'educating' the Americans embodied a long historical awareness that the roles of international 'policeman' and 'responsible creditor' did not come naturally—as American behaviour during the inter-war years had shown. We can only do justice to their arguments if we appreciate the idealism as well as the self-interest involved on both sides. In short, they were competing within a framework of co-operation, with the benefits and the burdens of international leadership as the gilded prize.

# EPILOGUE AND CONCLUSION

## Competitive Co-operation

*As long as England succeeds in keeping 'the balance of power'
in Europe, not only in principle, but in reality, well and good;
should she however for some reason or other fail in doing so, the
United States would be obliged to step in at least temporarily . . .
In fact we ourselves are becoming, owing to our strength and
geographical situation, more and more the balance of power of
the whole world.*

Theodore Roosevelt, 1910

*There is only one thing worse than fighting with allies, and that
is fighting without them.*

Churchill, 1940[1]

### A. Epilogue

Historians have sometimes been tempted to extrapolate from the circumstances of 1941—to see there the origins of a durable 'special relationship' or alternatively the turning point in Britain's inevitable decline into 'a warrior satellite of the United States'.[2] Whatever the truth of such verdicts, they tend to ignore the subsequent ebb and flow of the Anglo-American relationship, and this is worth a moment's comment.

Churchill's elation at the news of Pearl Harbor was matched by determined action. He immediately arranged a visit to Washington to 'review the whole war plan in the light of reality and new facts, as well as the problems of production and distribution'.[3] Particularly on the PM's mind was the continuance of 'Germany First' strategy now that the U.S.A. had been humiliatingly attacked in the Pacific. For a few days all Lend-Lease shipments were stopped, and the ABC-1 agreement, on which the U.S. military had placed such emphasis over the previous nine months, was soon in pieces as most of the Atlantic Fleet was rushed back to the Pacific leaving the British and Canadian Navies to cope again as best they could.[4] But underlying the specific issues was Churchill's conviction that the imbalance of the relationship, so apparent in 1941, had been redressed, and that problems that he had previously glossed over or compromised on to Britain's detriment could now be resolved more favourably in a situation of equality. The day after Pearl Harbor, when one of his Chiefs of Staff advocated a deferential attitude towards the U.S.A.,

Churchill 'answered with a wicked leer in his eye, "Oh! that is the way we talked to her while we were wooing her; now that she is in the harem, we talk to her quite differently!" '[5] Similarly, he believed that the concept of Lend-Lease had been practically superseded by the agreements reached in Washington for a series of combined bodies to oversee the allocation of raw materials, munitions and shipping, based on the principle that all the resources of the two countries were part of a common pool to be used for the best possible prosecution of the war. For Churchill the 'pooling' arrangements symbolized the equality of full alliance. 'This makes us no longer a client receiving help from a generous patron, but two comrades fighting for life side by side.'[6]

Churchill was undoubtedly right that 1942 saw a greater equality between the two powers. His own relationship with Roosevelt was at its closest during the eighteen months or so after Pearl Harbor, and the structure of the combined bodies to run the war effort, for all its inadequacies, was nevertheless a remarkable attempt at co-operation between two sovereign states and a notable contrast with 1917–18 when the U.S. had deliberately preserved its semi-independent 'associate' status. In other areas, particularly the vital ones of atomic weapons and Intelligence, the concept of partnership largely prevailed.[7] And, more generally, the period from Pearl Harbor to D-Day was one in which Britain's contribution in fighting manpower and key munitions was the equal of America's in all theatres except the Pacific and Australasia.[8] On the other hand, the differences of interest that had emerged during 1940–41 recurred within the full alliance. Strategic priorities in Europe and Asia, decolonization, the future of Imperial Preference, the form of the new international monetary system—all these problems became more contentious as the war progressed. And, as in the pre-alliance period, the U.S.A. was ready to exert its superior leverage to force agreement on issues it considered of particular importance—for example, linking British access to atomic secrets to Churchill's acceptance of American second-front strategy, or making Parliament's approval of the Bretton Woods agreement the quid pro quo for a post-war loan.[9] Furthermore by 1944–45 the balance of power and resources within the relationship had now shifted to the U.S.A. In 1944 America produced about 40 per cent of the world's armaments, and in the course of the whole war she contributed to the Allied cause a quarter of the manpower and half the munitions. The vast increase in war production was accompanied, uniquely among the belligerents, by a 12 per cent increase in consumer spending. The U.S.A. enjoyed both guns and butter, and her wartime boom not only pulled her out of the Depression but laid the foundations for her quarter-century or so of post-war industrial supremacy.[10]

This dual pattern—of short-term fluctuations and longer-term trend—was also apparent in the Anglo-American relationship after 1945, and both elements are again important. Some American historians have treated the post-war period as one of steadily increasing global confrontation between the U.S.A. and the U.S.S.R., with the world as their passive, largely impotent oyster.[11] It is therefore worth noting that Britain and the continental powers remained active and significant factors in international relations, and also that it was a primary object of U.S. policy that they should be so. Whatever

F.D.R. might have asserted in 1941, there was never any real likelihood in 1945 of a long-term U.S. military presence in Europe. The domestic pressures for rapid demobilization and for huge cuts in defence spending were far too strong. For the next five years the underlying philosophy of U.S. policy towards Europe was that of F.D.R. in the late 1930s—albeit on a much larger scale. Instead of military commitments the U.S.A. would again provide some of the financial, economic and diplomatic support needed to get the Europeans back on their feet and thus able to cope with their own security problems. Once more this placed the onus on France and particularly on Britain, who made a remarkable economic recovery during the 1940s.[12] Even NATO reflected America's desire for a limited commitment. At its inception in 1948–49 it was a multilateral defence pact designed to encourage greater defence spending and mutual co-operation by the Europeans. Not until 1950–53, in the global crisis created by the loss of U.S. atomic monopoly and the Korean war, was it turned into a military alliance with permanent, large-scale U.S. troop commitments in Europe and a U.S. commander. It was at this point, for the first time, that the U.S.A. became a *fixed* part of the European balance of power, instead of regarding the system as basically self-regulating except for occasional U.S. interventions to redress temporary imbalances. Even then the Americans remained anxious that their Allies should assume as much of the burden for their own security as possible, and, outside Europe, the continued British presence at key strategic points around the world was a welcome assistance in the global containment of Communism.[13]

The Anglo-American relationship after 1945 was therefore not as one-sided as some historians imply, and we need to be more sensitive to its eddies and currents. On the other hand, the tide was clearly running in America's favour. Her wartime growth and vast resources permitted, at least for a while, the very high levels of military spending and foreign commitments of the 1950s and 1960s. By contrast, Britain lacked both the economic and military power to sustain a vigorous global policy. That, of course, is apparent now, and we have seen that the problem was recognized in part by British leaders during the war. Indeed one of the themes of this book has been their awareness of the gap between Britain's responsibilities and the resources available to uphold them. But HMG's efforts to bridge that gap were directed not towards reducing the responsibilities but towards increasing the resources, in particular by trying to share the burdens with the U.S.A. Throughout the war, except for the momentary loss of nerve just before Dunkirk, HMG's motto was 'what we have, we hold'. And after 1945, despite the Attlee government's policy on India, what is striking in retrospect is the consensus among British leaders—Labour and Conservative, politician and bureaucrat—that their country could still afford the position of a World Power, albeit in third place to the U.S.A. and U.S.S.R.[14] No one seems to have appreciated the true costs of keeping a presence east of Suez, preserving the reserve status of the pound and neglecting the development of European unity.[15] Back in 1878 Gladstone had predicted that the U.S.A. would inevitably supplant Britain commercially, just as the British had previously displaced their Italian and Dutch rivals, and had sagely advised his countrymen 'to reduce our public burdens, in preparation for a day when we shall probably have less capacity than we have now to bear them'.[16] Perhaps such admonitions are always in vain. No empire has ever been relinquished voluntarily: the forces of self-interest, idealism, tradition and inertia are too strong. Arguably Britain's 'Recessional' was as gracious as any, but India, Suez and Rhodesia are among the reminders that it was still a violent, costly and painful business.

## B. Conclusion

Two themes have run through this book—the gradual creation of a unique alliance between two sovereign states and the rivalry within that embryonic alliance for advantage and increasingly for leadership.

The first phase of the story runs from Chamberlain's accession to the premiership in May 1937 until the end of the Phoney War three years later. During that time both governments hedged their bets in response to the uncertain international situation. Policy shifted to and fro between efforts to conciliate the dictators and efforts to contain them. Containment became dominant from the winter of 1938–39, but both leaders still had hopes of reaching a negotiated settlement right into 1940 and considered rearmament as much a deterrent as a preparation for war. This equivocation set the tone for the Anglo-American relationship during the period, which was one of growing but limited co-operation. In part the limits were imposed by the strength of isolationist sentiment in the U.S.A. and by the decentralization of the American political system which made firm executive leadership on the British model very difficult. The result was incessant caution on Roosevelt's part and profound scepticism in Britain that American diplomacy could ever be relied upon. As one senior Foreign Office official put it, predicting the course of U.S. foreign policy seemed 'as simple as trying to weigh a wild cat on the kitchen scales . . .'[17] But it is also clear that neither government *wanted* a close relationship in this period. F.D.R. had no desire to entangle his country in another war, when diplomatic and material assistance to Britain and France seemed sufficient to redress the European military imbalance and thereby eliminate any possible German threat to the United States. He regarded Britain's failure to 'stand up to Hitler' as evidence of a lack of nerve rather than a lack of power, and his efforts in the winter of 1938–39, in diplomacy and rearmament, were designed to 'stiffen their backbones' and make them face up to their responsibilities. Chamberlain, for his part, feared renewed 'Wilsonian' meddling in the affairs of Europe and the prospect of dependence on the U.S.A. He believed that genuine American help was unlikely, in view of American unreliability, unnecessary, in view of the continued hopes for peace, and undesirable, because of the American challenge to Britain's fragile pre-eminence. Consequently he was more interested in the appearance than the reality of Anglo-American co-operation—in signs of joint or parallel action, such as the Trade Agreement negotiations of 1937–38 or the repeal of the arms embargo in 1939, which might make the Axis readier to come to the negotiating table.

Of particular note is that this phase of the relationship did not end with the outbreak of the European conflict in September 1939, but extended through the Phoney War into the spring of 1940. Although Britain was officially preparing for a long struggle, Chamberlain and his political colleagues believed that the German economy was near to collapse and that a firm but passive policy might soon bring the German 'moderates' to the negotiating table. Benevolent U.S. neutrality would increase the diplomatic pressure on Germany, but Chamberlain did not want America to enter the war for fear of the price she would exact at the peace conference. The inertia of the Allies worried Roosevelt, and in early 1940 he made a serious exploration of the chances of peace, but throughout the Phoney War his basic policy remained that of allowing Britain and France preferential access to the American 'arsenal' so that they could serve as the U.S.A.'s front line.

These equivocations came to an end in the summer of 1940. Britain lost her main ally in only six weeks and had no choice but to turn to the Americans for every kind of help. Even Chamberlain acknowledged this, and it had already been foreshadowed in huge British aircraft orders placed in March, but the change in policy was accelerated by the change in leaders, as Churchill became Prime Minister and the Treasury, which had fully supported Chamberlain's policy, lost its dominant position in Whitehall. Nevertheless, Churchill was not as secure that summer as he later became. He was a premier without a party, because Chamberlain still led the Conservatives, and there were murmurings about a compromise peace among some back-benchers and also from potential rivals, notably Halifax and Lloyd George. Churchill's response was to insist with increasing vehemence that Britain should fight on because the U.S.A. was about to enter the war—perhaps when Britain was bombed, certainly after Roosevelt's re-election in November. This conviction helped keep Britain going through the lonely summer of 1940.

In the U.S.A. the end of equivocation came more slowly. Germany's astounding conquest of Europe left American policy in ruins as well, and there were real fears that if Hitler got control of the French and British fleets he would be able to mount an early invasion of the largely defenceless American continent. But although historians have argued that Roosevelt never lost confidence in Britain, the evidence presented in chapter 4(c) suggests that there were three phases to his policy in the summer of 1940. From 10 May until the fall of France six weeks later his object was to help keep a Western Front in existence on the continent of Europe. From mid-June to the end of July, with France gone, Britain facing apparently imminent invasion and his own political future undecided, he trod water, waiting on events, and provided little further help. Only in August, more confident that Britain would survive into the winter and enjoying greater room for manoeuvre politically, did F.D.R. finally agree to transfer 50 old destroyers which headed the list of British desiderata and which had become the touchstone of the relationship. Yet he was still hedging his bets—the eight base leases in the Caribbean and Western Atlantic, Churchill's reluctant promise that the British fleet would never be sunk or surrendered, and the staff talks with Canada to concert plans for that fleet's possible arrival in North America were all ways of strengthening the U.S.A.'s second line of defence in the Western Hemisphere in case Britain went the same way as France.

287

American fears of a British collapse were never completely allayed. The spring of 1941 saw a crisis of confidence in Washington almost as grave as that of mid-1940. But from the autumn of 1940 there was a broad Administration consensus that large-scale material support for Britain was the best way to keep the war away from America and give the U.S.A. time to rearm. In early 1941 F.D.R. responded to Britain's dollar crisis with Lend-Lease, whereby America would provide the supplies and waive repayment for the moment. During the summer and autumn he gradually extended and intensified U.S. naval operations in the Atlantic, and in November repeal of the crucial sections of the 1939 Neutrality Act gave him the right to send armed U.S. merchant ships to British ports. Some historians have seen these actions as deliberate steps along an inevitable road to war, which F.D.R. had to tread cautiously for fear of Congress and public opinion. And they have cited his bellicose remarks to Churchill at their meeting in August 1941—about wanting to provoke a German declaration of war—as confirmatory evidence. But the President often talked in warlike vein to British leaders at times of crisis—Munich, summer 1939, and especially May and June 1940—to encourage them to stand firm. And his own desire in 1941 was that America's contribution to the war would be in arms not armies—acting as the arsenal of democracy and the guardian of the oceans but not involved in another major land war in Europe. Moreover, as late as the autumn of 1941, Roosevelt could still see good reasons for avoiding formal U.S. entry into the war, at least for the moment. In particular, he was afraid that it would lead to a potentially disastrous cutback in supplies to the Allies as Americans demanded total concentration on U.S. rearmament, and that war with Germany would inevitably mean war with Germany's ally, Japan. If, as Roosevelt believed, he could do all that seemed necessary to assist Britain and Russia under his existing powers as Chief Executive and Commander-in-Chief, why be in a hurry to go beyond limited, undeclared war?

Although anxious for wide-ranging Anglo-American co-operation in war and peace, the Roosevelt Administration was therefore, quite naturally, determined that this should be on America's terms. It was also keen that co-operation should be to America's advantage, and Britain's overwhelming need for U.S. help after the fall of France gave the Administration additional leverage—as demonstrated by British concessions such as the quid pro quo for the destroyers, the sale of assets to expedite the passage of Lend-Lease, the West Indian base leases, and the 1941–42 Lend-Lease Consideration agreement. Roosevelt was usually less willing to drive a hard bargain than were his subordinates. They could afford to concentrate on a single issue, whereas he had to see the relationship as a whole. But he was sympathetic to their goals and in most controversies stepped in during the final stages in order to force an agreement on America's terms. In all these cases, of course, the Administration insisted that it was simply trying to placate anglophobes and isolationists on Capitol Hill. And undoubtedly the independence and power of Congress was a constant worry for American leaders, to an extent not always perceived by British leaders used to the coherence of a parliamentary system. But the conventional historiographical emphasis on Congress as a constant constraint on all aspects of F.D.R.'s foreign policy can be misleading if it suggests that the President was thereby forced to act in ways fundamentally contrary to his own inclinations. Just as F.D.R. had no desire to become involved in total war if he could satisfy U.S. interests and ideals in more limited ways, so the concessions extracted from the British as 'molasses' to sweeten Congress were all long-held goals of Administration policy—a lien on the British fleet, bases in the Western Hemisphere, economic liberalization. As Neville Chamberlain rightly said, Congress was the 'Mr. Jorkins' of American administrations—at once a genuine constraint on executive action *and* a convenient scapegoat for its own less palatable policies.

The British reaction to the imbalanced situation facing them from mid-1940 can be divided into two phases, epitomized by Churchill. The new PM placed the highest priority on maximizing U.S. help and on drawing her into the war. But for most of 1940, and particularly during the summer, he saw little sign of real assistance and remained anxious to protect British interests. Thus, in May and June he played on U.S. fears about the British fleet and, in contrast to the policy of generosity advocated by Lothian and the FO, tried to link all British concessions directly to significant American help. Although F.D.R.'s eventual authorization of the Destroyers Deal modified Churchill's doubts and fears, Lothian had considerable difficulty convincing the PM in November that they should put Britain's whole position candidly to Roosevelt, trusting that he would respond. What seems to have altered Churchill's attitude was the announcement of Lend-Lease in January 1941. After the secretive, hesitant help offered in 1940, the Administration was assuming responsibility for Britain's long-term American supply needs and was directly asking Congress to approve its policy of backing Britain. Thereafter Churchill's tactic was that HMG should put itself in Roosevelt's hands and do all it could to ease his domestic position. The overriding concern was to get the Americans into the European war. Arguments over peripheral questions, such as trade policy and naval dispositions in the Pacific, should be postponed or else settled temporarily in accordance with American wishes, because Churchill was confident that the balance of the relationship could be redressed once Britain and the U.S.A. were full and equal allies. Other British policymakers, however, were not so sure, and periodically bewailed the PM's tendency for 'appeasing the Americans'.[18] Particularly noteworthy was the attitude of Eden. He shared Churchill's desire for an Anglo-American alliance, and in the Far East was ready to tie HMG's policy blindly to that of the U.S.A. But, as in 1937–38, Eden did not want to see an unlimited expansion of American influence, nor did he intend to concede Roosevelt the leadership of the Allied cause. Churchill was not indifferent to these considerations, and as soon as the U.S.A. had entered the war he advocated a less compliant attitude, but as the war progressed he became increasingly prone to romanticize the Anglo-American relationship and to gloss over its limitations.

\*       \*       \*

What were the limitations of the relationship? What were its strengths? The core of the emerging alliance was a shared interest in the containment of Hitler. Nazi Germany was always less of a threat to the U.S.A. than to Britain, for reasons of geography, and this meant that there was always a difference in the intensity of the shared interest and in the urgency of the response. On the other hand, Britain, like the U.S.A., enjoyed a degree of immunity from European power struggles, conferred by her own insular position, and historically her policy towards the continent had been analogous to that of the U.S.A.—isolation from firm commitments and the deliberate encouragement of uncertainty as to her reaction in a crisis. This was particularly true of 1937–40, when both governments were trying to contain Hitler by redressing the continental imbalance. Each hoped to do this in a policy of limited liability, but the British, inevitably, were less successful as they were forced from early 1939 into growing military commitments to France. In the summer of 1940 the European balance collapsed completely and the German threat became acute. For Britain it was now a matter of national survival; for the U.S.A. the survival of Britain, and especially of her fleet, would mean the continuance of a front line of defence in Europe. By 1941 the focus had shifted to control of the Atlantic. The security of Britain's supply lines was of vital concern to both governments, given their shared interest in Britain's survival; in addition the U.S.A. was anxious to prevent Germany from commanding the oceanic approach routes to the American hemisphere. In each phase, then, we see a shared interest—the European equilibrium, the survival of Britain, the security of the Atlantic—albeit based on differing motives and felt with differing intensity. Unlike the British, the U.S.A. was able to maintain a policy of limited liability throughout the period 1937–41. It was no coincidence that the bitter French cry of the late 1930s—that the British were willing to fight to the last Frenchman—was adapted by the British against the Americans in 1939–41.

Elsewhere around the globe, British and U.S. interests were less close. Britain had a major territorial and commercial stake in the Middle East, for instance, whereas American interests in the area were limited at this time, and in consequence the two countries differed in 1941 about the strategic priority to be attached to the Mediterranean theatre. More significant, however, in this period was China. Again, Britain was the dominant power; again U.S. interests were minor, and between 1937–39 the U.S.A. had no reason to supplement her moralizing with firm action. But from mid-1940 Japan's southward expansion threatened to upset the balance of power in South-east Asia and jeopardized supplies of raw materials that were essential for Britain's survival and also important to the U.S.A. Both governments therefore had a similar interest in trying to contain Japan, and in doing so without resort to war, which would distract them from the main threat posed by Hitler. The basis of this common endeavour was an informal division of labour between the two navies. From the spring of 1940 Roosevelt kept the main U.S. fleet at Pearl Harbor—free to take this risk, against considerable criticism, as long as the Royal Navy held Hitler at bay in the Atlantic. Despite renewed American anxiety about the Atlantic in the spring of 1941, and consequent modification of the strategy, it remained the basis of Anglo-American co-operation up to Pearl Harbor and after. But the division of labour also meant that HMG was increasingly dependent on the

U.S. in the Far East. The Americans monopolized the diplomatic exchanges with Japan and determined Western policy on the supply of oil and key raw materials. The problem was that although the two countries agreed on the broad principles of Far Eastern policy, they still did not share the same specific interests. Britain had the possessions, but America had the power, and, given the secondary importance of Asia, the U.S.A. had no intention of committing scarce resources to defend purely British concerns, particularly if the British did nothing themselves. This divergence of interests was potentially dangerous for Britain, but it might not have been fatal had the two countries not grossly underestimated the Japanese. The speed and effectiveness of Japan's multi-pronged offensive in December 1941 left neither Britain nor the U.S.A. with time or resources to correct their mistakes and concert a proper defence.

Least compatible were the economic interests of the two countries and their long-term aspirations as world powers. Ever since the late nineteenth century the U.S.A. and Germany had been Britain's main commercial rivals, and America's size and resources alone made it almost inevitable that she would gradually dominate world trade. Even during the crisis years of 1939–41 these considerations remained in the minds of the two governments, and certain of their policies were clearly intended in part to benefit their commercial interests—British economic strategy during the Phoney War, for instance, or the U.S. pressure leading up to Britain's 1941 Export White Paper. But the decisive influence on the two countries' respective economic positions was simply the war itself. In order to mobilize all her resources to fight it, Britain liquidated foreign investments, accumulated huge sterling debts, lost export markets and surrendered her dominant position in commercial services such as shipping and insurance. In all these cases the U.S.A. was inevitably the major beneficiary—again able to fatten on Europe's follies but this time on an unprecedented scale. Chamberlain had foreseen all this; that is why he strove for so long—too long—to avoid total war. Similarly, Roosevelt's own limited-liability strategy—with the U.S.A. as the productive base for the Allied war effort—was clearly the one likely to maximize America's economic advantage.[19]

On a deeper level there was also a clash of economic philosophies. During the 1930s the British moved towards bilateral, controlled trade largely within a British-led bloc, while the Roosevelt Administration emerged as the new champion of economic liberalization and a multilateral world economy. This reversal of traditional roles reflected the changed commercial circumstances of the two powers—Britain now felt the need to protect her declining economy while the U.S.A. was strong enough to benefit from the principle of equal commercial opportunity. Just as Americans had protested in the mid-Victorian era about the imperialism of British free trade, so there was lurid talk in World War Two Britain about the Empire becoming 'the Lebensraum of American Pluto-Democracy'.[20] Throughout the period 1937–41 Britain's economic philosophy, and particularly Imperial Preference, was a persistent source of tension in Anglo-American relations, as shown by the 1937–38 Trade Agreement negotiations, the row over British purchasing policy in early 1940, and the Lend-Lease Consideration saga in

1941–42. But we have seen that the differences should not be exaggerated, and that Britain's bilateralism was in large part a defensive response to the unprecedented crisis of 1931–41. Whatever the fears of some State Department officials, most British leaders, including Chamberlain, repudiated the idea of a self-contained imperial bloc and believed in principle in multilateralism. By late 1941 they were cautiously exploring ways of reconstructing a balanced world economy, just as U.S. leaders were beginning to acknowledge the complexity of the problem and the need for radical action on their side as well.

What the two governments were arguing about, basically, was not the structure of the world economy but their respective places within it. The same is true with regard to the political order. Here too both governments wanted a balanced, interdependent international system, based on the great powers and particularly on Anglo-American co-operation. But in 1939 Roosevelt had insisted that Britain had the primary responsibility for saving civilization, whereas by 1941 he and his advisers saw the U.S.A. as the dominant partner in the relationship. Again, Chamberlain had foreseen this development, and his foreign policy had been designed in part to avoid it: once the sleeping giant was awakened it would inevitably dwarf its British ally. In 1940–41 British leaders cautiously welcomed America's acceptance of a great power role, hoping that she could be 'educated' into permanent, responsible international action through a special association with Britain. But they were anxious, within the imbalance of the relationship, to ensure that Britain's interests were safeguarded as far as possible and that her claims to continued great power status were not disregarded.[21]

*     *     *

The evolving Anglo-American alliance was therefore like any other diplomatic relationship—based on similar and divergent interests. But to analyse it solely in those terms is clearly insufficient. Defence of a common interest, by itself, is rarely an adequate basis for an alliance, for the disposition to see another country's power as a shield rather than as a threat depends in part on a sense of shared values.[22] And it is here, of course, that the richness and even uniqueness of the Anglo-American relationship is to be found. The common language facilitated communication between more Americans and Britons, in greater depth and complexity, than would otherwise have been possible. It also served as a constant reminder that America's eclectic culture had drawn, more than from any other single source, on English traditions, institutions and philosophy. This is the point at which the Anglo-American alliance and the earlier Anglo-French alliance, analogous in many respects on the level of interests, diverge markedly. Language and culture were a barrier not a bridge between London and Paris. The three-dimensional relationships developed between so many American and British leaders, from Churchill and Roosevelt downwards, would never have been possible between Britain and France, even if their alliance had not ended so abruptly and acrimoniously in 1940.

Nevertheless, the common Anglo-American heritage was a complex one, open to differing interpretations. In Britain the key concept was 'the English-speaking peoples'. Despite much condescension about America's supposed vulgarity and lack of culture, as stereotyped on the cinema screen, most British leaders viewed her as essentially English—a sort of illegitimate off-spring of the mother country, somewhere between the Dominions and truly foreign nations. Consequently, deep down, they tended to assume that the U.S.A. *ought* to help Britain and that the ties of common culture would eventually pull her into the war. This was the basis of Churchill's confidence in early U.S. belligerency, and the reason for the widespread disillusion, particularly after Roosevelt's re-election and the Atlantic Meeting, when an American declaration of war did not materialize. It was also the rationale for talk of a permanent 'special relationship', which, among its more senti-mental advocates, served as a fantasy to mask the harsh realities of Britain's decline. Some older U.S. interventionists, with close personal ties to Britain, did feel an emotional sense of solidarity, but for the most part the Anglo-American nexus of values was defined by Americans in terms of a shared democratic tradition. America was seen as the true home of liberal democracy, pioneered in Britain but always flawed there by the imprint of class and em-pire. Indeed the full flowering of democracy in America had been possible only after the break with Britain. The attitude of U.S. policymakers was therefore always ambivalent. They tended towards anglophilia culturally and anglophobia politically—deeply aware of the shared traditions yet self-consciously critical of British imperialism and ever-fearful that 'cunning' British diplomacy would once again entangle them in Britain's problems. This belief in New World innocence was long-standing—as one of Oscar Wilde's characters observed: 'The youth of America is their oldest tradition'[23]— and it was exacerbated by a somewhat dated image of Britain and her Empire, owing more to past history and literature than to present experience. This American 'inferiority complex', as British diplomats liked to term it, was very apparent in the hesitancy of their dealings with HMG in the late 1930s. But by 1941 it had been largely replaced by a new mood of self-assertiveness, as the nakedness of imperial Britain became more apparent. Increasingly, American leaders saw international events as part of a global struggle between the forces of democracy and dictatorship—foreshadowing already one element of the Cold War world-view. This perception helps to explain, for instance, why the U.S.A. became more involved in the Far East in 1937–41 than her economic and territorial interests alone would have warranted. And the increasing assertiveness of U.S. policy reflected the con-viction that her security was in large measure dependent on the 'quarantin-ing' and eradication of anti-democratic political strains and that Americans had the power and the right to lead the new democratic crusade.[24]

It was from these complex strands of interest, ideology and emotion that the Anglo-American relationship was woven. But it is important to stress, finally, that there was nothing inevitable about the wartime alliance. It was the result of the unprecedented crisis of 1940–41. Before mid-1940 neither government expected or sought a close relationship. This was only necessary when the European equilibrium tilted suddenly and dramatically against them. Likewise, it was only then that the latent ties of ideology and culture became important, as Britons looked to their 'kin across the sea' for help and Americans responded to the heroism of the Battle of Britain and the 'People's War'. And it was only in the peculiar circumstances of 1941, before the emergence of Russia and the reconstruction of Europe, when Britain and the U.S.A. were the sole remaining major democratic powers, that talk about a long-term Anglo-American world condominium made any sense. There was consequently something artificial about the closeness of the wartime alliance, reflecting the unique circumstances of its birth. The post-1945 relationship, by contrast, was a partial return to that of the 1930s, albeit with vastly increased American power, and when the U.S.A. again intervened militarily in European affairs at the end of the decade it was in a direct and permanent form. Subsequently Anglo-American relations have taken shape within the wider context of the U.S. relationship with Western Europe as a whole—first with NATO and then the EEC. In short, the wartime special relationship *was* special—had France not fallen it would have probably turned out, like many other things, very differently.

In conclusion, Britain and the United States were both developed Western powers, with similar cultural traditions and a shared interest in upholding the international status quo, of which they were the major beneficiaries, against the developing industrial nations, Germany Italy and Japan, who adopted alien and aggressive ideologies and demanded a position in the world commensurate with their economic power and military potential. They were thus in one sense 'have' states, fending off the assaults of the 'have nots'. This was the basis of Anglo-American co-operation. Yet in another respect the United States was also a 'have not', compared with the precarious but still dominant position of Britain. As the British First Sea Lord put it in 1934, with engaging candour, 'we have got most of the world already, or the best parts of it, and we only want to keep what we have got and prevent others from taking it away from us.'[25] This was the basis of Anglo-American competition. In 1940–41 the co-operative element was paramount. Both countries faced common military and ideological threats at a time when their strengths and weaknesses were unusually complementary, and the common-law alliance—like the state of 'matrimony' that followed it—undoubtedly constituted one of the closest diplomatic relationships in modern history. But even then it was a temporary marriage of convenience, with competition the persistent counterpoint to the melody of co-operation. Inside the framework of collaboration to sustain their common interests as established powers, Britain and America manoeuvred for advantage and pre-eminence. It was indeed a relationship of competitive co-operation.

# NOTES

## Introduction

1 Plumb, 'The historian', p. 147; Michael Howard, review, *The Sunday Times*, 26 Feb. 1978, p. 41. The epigraphs at the front of the book are from: Churchill to Lady Randolph Churchill, 22 May 1898, in Randolph Churchill, *Winston S. Churchill*, companion vol. I, part 2 (London, 1967), p. 937; William E. Gladstone, 'Kin Beyond Sea', *North American Review*, vol. 127, no. 264 (Sept.–Oct. 1878), p. 180; Keith Douglas, *Complete Poems*, ed. Desmond Graham (Oxford, 1979), p. 74. The Churchill and Douglas quotations appear by kind permission of William Heinemann Ltd. and Oxford University Press.

2 Plumb, p. 149.

3 E.g. Cowling, *Impact of Hitler*; Dilks, 'Appeasement revisited' and 'Baldwin and Chamberlain'; Gibbs, *Grand Strategy*, I; Lee, *Britain and the Sino-Japanese War*; Medlicott, *Britain and Germany*; Ovendale, *'Appeasement'*; Pratt, *East of Malta*; Roskill, *Naval Policy*, II, esp. chs. XI, XIV, and *Hankey*, III.

4 E.g. Parrini, *Heir to Empire*; William Appleman Williams, 'The Legend of Isolationism in the 1920s', *Science and Society*, 19 (1954), 1–20; Melvyn P. Leffler, *The Elusive Quest: America's Pursuit of European Stability and French Security, 1919–1933* (Chapel Hill, N.C., 1979); Costigliola, 'Anglo-American financial rivalry'; Hogan, *Informal Entente*; Gardner, *Economic Aspects of New Deal Diplomacy*; Rowland, 'Preparing the American ascendancy'; Gilman, 'Economic aspects of Anglo-American relations . . . 1937–40'; MacDonald, *U.S., Britain and Appeasement*.

5 E.g. on strategy, Leutze, *Bargaining for Supremacy*; Stoler, *Politics of the Second Front*; on finance, Kimball, 'Lend-Lease and the Open Door'; Van Dormael, *Bretton Woods*; on the Empire, Louis, *Imperialism at Bay*; Thorne, *Allies of a Kind*. For a discussion of some of these books, see Reynolds, 'Competitive co-operation' (review article).

6 An exception is Lash, *Roosevelt and Churchill*, which covers the period 1939–41 but from a rather traditional standpoint. The older studies of U.S. policy and international relations, 1937–41, by Langer and Gleason, *Challenge to Isolation*, and *Undeclared War*, remain invaluable.

## Chapter One

1 Ashton-Gwatkin, memorandum, CP 161 (38), 7 July 1938, CAB 24/277 (Public Record Office, London). Moffat, Diary, vol. 42, 16 Feb. 1939 (Jay Pierrepont Moffat Papers, Houghton Library, Harvard University). Epigraphs to Part One come from Chatfield to Sir Warren Fisher, 4 June 1934, CHT/3/1, p. 62 (Chatfield Papers, National Maritime Museum, Greenwich) and Bullitt (ed.), *For the President*, p. 30.

2 For background to this section see books cited in note 3 of the Introduction.

3 For example, in January 1939 the British Commonwealth had 15 capital ships; Japan possessed 9, Germany 7 and Italy 4—a total of 20. (Roskill, *Naval Policy*, I, Appendix B, p. 577.)

4 For these economic arguments see Peden, *British Rearmament*, esp. ch. III; also Shay, *British Rearmament*, Coghlan, 'Armaments, economic policy and appeasement' and Parker, 'Economics, rearmament and foreign policy'.

5 Chamberlain to Mrs Morton Prince, 16 Jan. 1938, quoted in Feiling, *Chamberlain*, p. 324. This and MacLeod, *Chamberlain*, are the standard studies. Until David Dilks' definitive biography is available the only recent accounts of Chamberlain's premiership are Beattie, 'Neville Chamberlain', Dilks, 'Baldwin and Chamberlain', esp. pp. 376–401 and Hyde, *Chamberlain*, chs. 3–4.

6 E.g. Neville Chamberlain to Ida Chamberlain, 11 Sept. 1938 (quotation), and to Hilda Chamberlain, 15 Oct. 1938 and 5 Feb. 1939, Neville Chamberlain papers, NC 18/1/1068, /1072 and /1084 (Birmingham University Library).

These weekly letters from Chamberlain to his spinster sisters are an invaluable source for the historian; but they have to be read with the personal circumstances in mind. Neville was the adored elder brother, and he maintains that position throughout, never confessing a mistake and ascribing most of HMG's successes to his own foresight and ability. Also, the letters were written at the weekend, often at Chequers. Chamberlain sometimes offers rationalizations for his actions during the week, rather than the more confused reasons that obtained in the heat of the moment.

7 E.g. Dilks, 'Appeasement revisited', p. 43 and 'Baldwin and Chamberlain', pp. 387–8. Cowling, *Impact of Hitler*, remarks that the question of whether Chamberlain expected to prevent war or just postpone it is a matter 'for guesswork', though he seems to favour the latter explanation (pp. 178–9).

8 CAB 23/90, Cab 46 (37) 10, 8 Dec. 1937 (PRO).

9 John Balfour, Head of the FO's American Department, memo, 14 April 1939, FO 371/22829, A2856 (PRO). The memo is a good example of these attitudes.

10 Chamberlain to Mrs Morton Price, 16 Jan. 1938, quoted in Feiling, *Chamberlain*, p. 322.

11 Lindsay to Eden, desp. 247, 22 March 1937, FO 371/20651, A2378. The despatch has been printed, with an introduction, in Hachey, 'Winning friends and influencing policy'.

12 Quotations from Nicolson, *Diaries and Letters*, I, 189, and Moffat, Diary, 17 May 1939.

13 *Rudyard Kipling's Verse* (Definitive edn., London, 1940), pp. 327–8.

14 Quoted in Louis, *British Strategy in the Far East*, p. 77.

15 Pronay, 'The newsreels', p. 112; Russett, *Community and Contention*, pp. 121–4. Cf. Heindel, *American Impact on Great Britain*, p. 337.

16 *The Times*, 19 May 1939, p. 18b.

17 Marwick, 'Middle opinion in the thirties', pp. 292, 295–8. For background to this paragraph see Pelling, *America and the British Left*, ch. VIII; Dizikes, 'Britain, Roosevelt and the New Deal'; Pear, 'The impact of the New Deal'; Malament, 'British Labour and Roosevelt's New Deal'.

18 Ashton-Gwatkin, memo, cited in note 1. See also FO 371/21546, A3440, and comments in Chamberlain to Ida, 12 Dec. 1937, p. 2, and 23 Jan. 1938, p. 3, NC 18/1/1031 and /1036.

19 Aldcroft, *Inter-War Economy*, p. 264, n.2; Potter, *American Economy*, pp.25–6.

20 Studies include Parrini, *Heir to Empire*; Tulchin, *Aftermath of War*, esp. pp. 30–7; Hogan, *Informal Entente*; Rabe, 'Anglo-American rivalry for Venezuelan oil'; Rosenberg, 'Anglo-American economic rivalry in Brazil'; Megaw, 'Scramble for the Pacific' and Gilman, 'Economic aspects of Anglo-American relations'.

21 More research is needed in this area. I have drawn on Aldcroft, *Inter-War Economy*, pp. 278–94; Drummond, *Imperial Economic Policy*, chs. 5–6; Drummond, *British Economic Policy*, p. 119.

22 On the 'imperial vision', see Drummond, *British Economic Policy*, ch. 2. Between the wars, the Empire's share of British trade increased, but 'foreign'

countries remained more important, especially for imports. In 1938 foreign countries took 53% of Britain's exports and provided 61% of her imports. The figures for 1913 were 78% and 80% respectively. But, over all, trade was less important to the economy than before the Great War. Exports constituted only 10% of national output in 1938 (20% in 1913) and imports only 17% of national spending (27% in 1913). Ibid., pp. 18–22.

23 Gilman, 'Economic aspects', p. 99. Cf. the FBI's influence on rearmament policy in 1935, particularly in limiting government intervention in industry. (Shay, *British Rearmament*, pp. 94–7.)

24 Several war memoirs were particularly influential: Keynes, *Economic Consequences of the Peace*, ch. 3; David Lloyd George, *The Truth about the Peace Treaties*, (2 vols., London, 1938), esp. pp. 152–7, 221–42, 1411–13; Harold Nicolson, *Peacemaking, 1919* (London, 1933), esp. pp. 195–209. See also Link, 'President Wilson and his English critics'.

25 Much work remains to be done on the war debts issue. For summaries, see Rhodes, 'Reassessing "Uncle Shylock"' and Burk, 'Diplomacy of finance' and 'Great Britain in the United States'.

26 See Roskill, *Naval Policy*, I, chs. viii, xiv, and II, chs. ii, x; also Gibbs, 'Naval conferences of the interwar years'.

27 Lord Gladwyn, *The Memoirs of Lord Gladwyn* (London, 1972), p. 90.

28 Merrill D. Peterson, *Thomas Jefferson and the New Nation: A Biography* (London, 1970), p. 398.

29 Feiling, *Chamberlain*, p. 325. Ironically, this oft-quoted remark was made at a time when Chamberlain *did* think the Americans would do more. When a U.S. gunboat was attacked on the Yangtse, he wrote to his sister: 'It is always best and safest to count on *nothing* from the Americans except words but at this moment they are nearer "doing something" than I have ever known them and I cant [*sic*] altogether repress hopes.' (N.C. to Hilda, 17 Dec. 1937, NC 18/1/1032.)

30 Chamberlain to Mrs Stedman Shumway Hanks, 10 June 1937, copy in Pittman papers (LC) box 148. Bingham to Hull, 6 July 1937, copy in PSF 46: Great Britain, 1937–8 (FDRL); cf. Bingham to Hull, tel. 387, 10 June 1937, *FRUS*, 1937, II, 39–40; Willert to F.D.R., 2 June 1937, PPF 4715.

31 T160/934, F13300/13 (PRO), esp. Chamberlain note, 16 March 1937, on Leith-Ross to Chamberlain, memo, 15 March 1937. See also Peden, *British Rearmament*, p. 86.

32 For published discussions of the visit proposal see Borg, *U.S. and the Far Eastern Crisis*, pp. 376–7; Kottman, *Reciprocity and the North Atlantic Triangle*, pp. 175–8; Ovendale, '*Appeasement*', pp. 17–19. For the British side see also material in PREM 1/261 (PRO), and Chamberlain to Ida, 4 July 1937, and to Hilda, 29 Aug. 1937, NC 18/1/1010 and /1018.

33 This paragraph draws particularly on Lee, *Britain and the Sino-Japanese Wars*, chs. 2–4.

34 CAB 23/89, Cab. 37 (37) 3, 13 Oct. 1937. The question of sanctions had been raised by Roosevelt's cryptic suggestion, in his Chicago speech on 5 October, that peace-loving nations might have to quarantine the aggressors. Chamberlain considered this another vague and irresponsible American action, made to test domestic opinion, and at variance with the State Department's evident anxiety to avoid trouble in East Asia. Nevertheless the speech was embarrassing because the Opposition could say that HMG was lagging behind the Americans. The only good point was that 'this sudden abandonment of America's attitude of complete detachment' would make the dictators pause. But, even then, it

was once again a delicate question of balance: the speech *could* drive them closer together. (Chamberlain to Hilda, 9 Oct. 1937, NC 18/1/1023.)

35 In addition to the discussion in Lee, pp. 85–95, see also Pratt, 'Anglo-American naval conversations'. The U.S. side of this episode is discussed below, section (e).

36 The principal accounts on which this paragraph is based are Kottman, *Reciprocity and the North Atlantic Triangle*; Schatz, 'The Anglo-American trade agreement'; and, for the British side, Gilman, 'Economic aspects of Anglo-American relations', pp. 96–123.

37 Rainer Tamchina, 'Imperial Conference of 1937', esp. pp. 90–3. Canada became the sacrificial victim—on which see the discussions in Kottman and Gilman. On Australia, see Esthus, *From Enmity to Alliance*, chs. 1–6; Megaw, 'Australia and the Anglo-American Trade Agreement'.

38 For examples of their pressure see Gardner, *Sterling-Dollar Diplomacy*, pp. 31–2, on the statement by 150 members of the Parliamentary Committee of the EIA; memo by that commt., March 1938, sent to all Cabinet ministers, copy in FO 800/324, H/XXXVII/1; FO 371/21492, A1525 on motion put down by 93 MPs in October 1937, though never debated; Amery to Chamberlain, 19 Nov. 1937, NC 7/2/74; and Sir Herbert Williams, House of Commons, 1 March 1938, *HC Debs.*, 5s, 332, 903–4.

39 Shay, *British Rearmament*, pp. 147–55. He eventually substituted an innocuous alternative.

40 Chamberlain to Hilda, 21 Nov. 1937, p. 3, NC 18/1/1029. The Italians had joined the German–Japanese Anti-Comintern pact early that month.

41 Rowland, 'Preparing the American ascendancy', pp. 206–10; cf. Drummond, *Imperial Economic Policy*, pp. 288–9.

42 E.g. Rowland, p. 205.

43 Chamberlain to Sir Edward Grigg, 8 Nov. 1937, Altrincham papers, Bodleian Library, Oxford, Ms. 1005. For similar judgements see Dilks, 'Baldwin and Chamberlain', p. 349, Cowling, *Impact of Hitler*, p. 154. See also Drummond, *Imperial Economic Policy*, pp. 32–3.

It is also worth noting, in view of American verdicts on Chamberlain, both then and now, as a Tory die-hard, that he deliberately avoided identification with the mainstream of the Conservative party. As he reminded Tories on becoming their leader, he stood for Parliament as a Liberal Unionist and he was proud of his Nonconformist, radical, Midlands manufacturing background which set him apart from the Anglican, Home Counties Tory élite. (See Dilks, 'Baldwin and Chamberlain', pp. 277–8, Ramsden, *History of the Conservative Party*, pp. 355–7.)

44 Jay Pierrepont Moffat, Diary, vol. 39, 29 July 1937. Moffat was reporting a conversation with Atherton.

45 Chamberlain to Mrs Morton Prince, 16 Jan. 1938, quoted in Feiling, *Chamberlain*, p. 324. Chamberlain had made the same point in a telegram to Lindsay a few days before. Chamberlain to Lindsay, tel. 36, 13 Jan. 1938, FO 371/21526, A2127. This may have been a draft: the version in PREM 1/259, p. 67, which does not contain the relevant sentence, seems like the final version of the message.

46 Lindsay to FO, tel. 37, 11 Jan. 1938, tels. 38–40, 12 Jan. 1938, FO 371/21526, A2127. This file, and PREM 1/259, are the main British sources. They are summarized and discussed in Ovendale, '*Appeasement*', ch. IV. See also Avon, *Facing the Dictators*, pp. 547–68 and FO 954/29A, pp. 55–9, 63–82.

47 Chamberlain, annotation on Washington tel. 77, 22 Jan. 1938, in PREM 1/259, p. 32.

48 Chamberlain to Lindsay, tel. 36, 13 Jan. 1938, PREM 1/259, p. 67.
49 'Woolly rubbish' was the verdict of Horace Wilson, Chamberlain's main Treasury adviser. (Quoted in Avon, *Facing the Dictators*, p. 562.)
50 Chamberlain to Hilda, 27 Feb., 1938, NC 18/1/1040.
51 He used this image in his letters to his sisters. See Chamberlain to Ida, 23 Jan. 1938, to Hilda, 30 Jan. and 6 Feb. 1938, NC 18/1/1036–1038. Possibly it was suggested by the so-called 'bombshell' message with which F.D.R. had supposedly blown up the 1933 London Economic Conference. Chamberlain had felt very strongly about this at the time: cf. Chamberlain Diary, 4 July 1933, NC 2/22, and Chamberlain to Ida, 15 July 1933, NC 18/1/836.
52 Chamberlain Diary, 19 Feb. 1938, NC 2/24A.
53 Chamberlain to Roosevelt, tel. 35, 13 Jan. 1938, FO 371/21526, A2127; copy dated 14 January printed in *FRUS*, 1938, I, 118–20.
54 Chamberlain to Roosevelt, tels. 58 and 60, to Lindsay, tels. 59 and 61, 21 January 1938, A2127. Only the brief conclusions of the crucial FPC meetings of 20 and 21 Jan. remain; the record of the detailed discussions was apparently destroyed. CAB 27/622, pp. 250–9; cf. Roskill, *Hankey*, III, 298–302. But see also Avon, *Facing the Dictators*, pp. 561–6; Harvey, *Diaries*, pp. 75–7.
55 E.g. PREM 1/259, pp. 5, 64.
56 For background see generally Ovendale, *'Appeasement'*, chs. III and IV.
57 E.g. Eden to Chamberlain, 31 Jan. 1938, PREM 1/276.
58 Eden to Chamberlain, 18 Jan. 1938, A2127, p. 87. This is a first draft of a letter which Eden eventually did not send, preferring to convey its contents orally to the PM.
59 Harvey, *Diaries*, pp. 75–7.
60 This is the conclusion of Ritchie Ovendale, *'Appeasement'*, pp. 115–16, after his valuable discussion of the evidence.
61 For recent discussions taking this line, see Cowling, *Impact of Hitler*, ch. 5 and Douglas, *In the Year of Munich*, pp. 6–16, 130–1. Douglas believes that Eden was the major obstacle to an Anglo-Italian *rapprochement*, which, had it come in time, might have averted the Austrian Anschluss, and that Chamberlain should have forced him out much earlier. See also Douglas, 'Chamberlain and Eden', where he shows that by late 1937 none of the senior permanent FO officials shared Eden's objections to negotiations with Italy.
62 Chamberlain, for instance, believed that 'at bottom Anthony did not want to talk either with Hitler or Mussolini'. (Chamberlain to Hilda, 27 Feb. 1938, NC 18/1/1040.)
63 'Record of Events connected with Anthony Eden's resignation, February 19th–20th, 1938', Hickleton papers, Churchill College, Cambridge, A4.410.11. Halifax still held this view three years later—and Malcolm MacDonald, another Cabinet member in February 1938, agreed with him. See Halifax Diary, 29 April 1941, Hickleton Papers, York, A7.8.8., p. 42. Exhaustion and loss of judgement were the reasons put about by the Government and the Tory Whips, much to Eden's fury (Dalton Diary, 7 April 1938, vol. 19, p. 3). It was also the line taken by Lindsay in talks with the State Dept. (Moffat Diary, 23 Feb. 1938 and Welles, memo of talk with Lindsay, 25 Feb., *FRUS*, 1938, I, 138).

Certainly Eden's subsequent political career casts doubt on his ability to cope with a crisis. Elisabeth Barker has written (*Churchill and Eden at War*, p. 17) that Eden 'lacked Churchill's extraordinary physical and mental energy, recuperative power and stamina'. A similar comparison could be made between Eden and Chamberlain.
64 CAB 23/89, Cab. 37 (37) 3, 13 Oct. 1937.

65 FO to Lindsay, tel. 126, 18 Feb. 1938, FO 371/21526, p. 34. This was based on a minute by Cadogan, 16 Feb. 1938, which commented, more bluntly, that the idea would mean 'an irresponsible interference in our negotiations' and cited the recent concessions over imports of U.S. films into Britain as an instance of HMG's particular susceptibility to American pressure. (Ibid., pp. 37–8.) For Eden's later views see chs. 7(a) and 10.

66 Eden to Chamberlain, 18 Jan. 1938, draft, ibid., p. 87; Harvey, *Diplomatic Diaries*, 19 Jan. 1938, p. 75; Lindsay to Eden, 7 Feb. 1938, FO 954/29A, pp. 80–1.

67 Kingsley Martin, memo on confidential press briefing, 16 Dec. 1937, Martin Papers, Univ. of Sussex, Sx. Ms. 11, 28/1. Cf. Avon, *Facing the Dictators*, pp. 523–4.

68 Cadogan, *Diaries*, pp. 36–9, makes this point on numerous occasions. Quotations are from, respectively, 12, 20 and 18 Jan. Cadogan was also anxious to allay U.S. suspicions that Britain was lukewarm about the plan, 'if only because of the risk that the President may one day say that he was discouraged from taking a useful initiative by the cool reception which we gave to his proposals'. (Minute [10 Feb. 1938], FO 371/21526, p. 50.)

69 Chamberlain to Lindsay, tel. 60, 21 Jan. 1938, A2127.

70 Quotations from record of Eden's and Chamberlain's remarks at Commt. of Imperial Defence, 2 Dec. 1937, in Colvin, *Chamberlain Cabinet*, pp. 65, 67.

71 Cf. Pratt, 'Anglo-American naval conversations', p. 749.

72 See below, ch. 3.

73 Strout, *American Image of the Old World*, p. ix.

74 *Moffat Papers*, pp. 242–4; Edwards, *Foreign Policy of Col. McCormick's Tribune*, pp. 101–2, 131; *Chicago Tribune*, 8 and 9 June, 1939.

75 See Russett, *Community and Contention*, pp. 103, 131–2, for press and education; on radio see Heindel, *The American Impact on Great Britain*, p. 334.

76 See FO 395/639, esp. P1865, P2134; cf. *New York Times*, 24 April 1939 and *New York Times* Magazine, 21 May 1939, p. 6.

77 Samuel Grafton, *New York Post* column, 8 Aug. 1939, in Grafton, *An American Diary*, p. 5.

78 E.g. George Henry Payne, *England: her Treatment of America* (New York, 1931): 'The fact is that the ruling class of England has ruled too long. America's troubles with England have always come from this class; they have never come from the laboring classes, or from the intellectual class, who have been our friends, fair, honorable, and helpful' (p. 289). 'Give the British people an opportunity to govern their own country and the prospect of war between America and England will forever vanish' (p. 293).

79 Henry L. Stimson Diary (Yale), 3 June 1938, vol. 28, p. 148.

80 Russett, *Community and Contention*, p. 117; Hutton, *Midwest at Noon*, p. 143.

81 Quoted in John A. S. Grenville and George Berkeley Young, *Politics, Strategy and American Diplomacy: Studies in Foreign Policy, 1873–1917* (New Haven, 1966), p. 205.

82 For instance, Bertrand Russell, 'Can Americans and Britons be Friends?', *Saturday Evening Post*, 3 June 1944, reprinted in Feinberg and Kasrils, *Bertrand Russell's America*, I, pp. 335–6.

83 A Briton, resident in the U.S.A. as a professor of business psychology, reported to the Foreign Office that India was 'commonly depicted as a fairly homogeneous country of intelligent asiatics prevented from enjoying the blessings of democratic self-government by the iron control of English regiments, kept there to fill the pockets of English merchants'. T. North Whitehead, report, 21 Sept. 1939, FO 371/22817, A7176.

84 Devlin, *Too Proud to Fight*, pp. 26–9, 499–500.
85 F.D.R. to Bingham, 11 July 1935, *Roosevelt on Foreign Affairs*, II, 554; F.D.R. to Roger B. Merriman, 15 Feb. 1939, PSF 46: Great Britain.
86 Dennis J. McCarthy, 'The British', in Joseph P. O'Grady (ed.), *The Immigrant's Influence on Wilson's Peace Policies* (Lexington, KY., 1967), pp. 90–1.
87 Norman Davis, record of talk with F.D.R., 18 Oct. 1937, quoted in Borg, *U.S. and the Far Eastern Crisis*, p. 407.
88 Admiral Sir John Godfrey, 'Memoirs', vol. V, 135–6 (Churchill Coll., Cambridge).
89 Sir Arthur Willert, memo of conversation with F.D.R., 25–6 March 1939, CAB 27/627, FP (36) 80, 20 April 1939; Halifax to Scott, April 1941, FO 371/26250, A3774. Cf. Barron, *Leadership in Crisis*, pp. 43–4.
90 Morgenthau Diary, 22: 155, 29 April 1936 (FDRL). A year later F.D.R. had increased the British norm to 90 per cent and felt that in the controversy over ownership of the Pacific islands they wanted even more than that. (See F.D.R. to R. Walton Moore, 15 Oct. 1937, quoted in Young, 'F.D.R. and America's islets', p. 215.)
91 Bingham to F.D.R., 13 Nov. 1936, *Roosevelt on Foreign Affairs*, III, 486; Bullitt to F.D.R., 5 May 1937, in Bullitt (ed.), *For the President*, p. 213; Jones, *Diary with Letters*, p. 338.
92 Stimson Diary, 32: 41, 18 Dec. 1940.
93 For a particularly sharp attack on F.D.R.'s habits see McFarland, 'Woodring vs. Johnson', on the long-running feud between the Secretary and Assistant Secretary of War, which F.D.R. not only tolerated but encouraged and which divided and increasingly paralysed the War Department from 1937–40. Perhaps the best account of F.D.R.'s administrative habits, from a sympathetic point of view, is in Arthur M. Schlesinger, Jr., *The Age of Roosevelt*, vol. II (Boston, 1958), chs. 32–5.
94 Sherwood, *Roosevelt and Hopkins*, p. 227.
95 E.g. Cohen, *The Public's Impact on Foreign Policy*; Leigh, *Mobilizing Consent*, chs. 1 and 6; May, 'An American tradition'. For examples in particular historical periods see Ernest R. May, *American Imperialism: A Speculative Essay* (New York, 1968); Thomas G. Paterson, 'Presidential foreign policy, public opinion, and Congress: The Truman years', *Diplomatic History*, 3 (1979), 1–18; Sidney Verba *et al.*, 'Public opinion and the war in Vietnam', *American Political Science Review*, 61 (1967), 317–33.
96 Leigh, *Mobilizing Consent*, p. 12 and, in general, ch. 2. See also Steele, 'The pulse of the people'.
97 It seems to me that there is a fundamental difference of emphasis in the historiography of F.D.R.'s foreign policy between those who attribute his largely isolationist policy in the 1930s to domestic political constraints and those who also stress his own personal inclinations and uncertainty. Among the former are Barron, *Leadership in Crisis*; Lash, *Roosevelt and Churchill*; Dallek, *Roosevelt and American Foreign Policy*. In the latter group are Langer and Gleason, *Challenge to Isolation* and *The Undeclared War*; Burns, *Roosevelt*; Divine, *Roosevelt and World War II*, esp. chs. 1–2.
98 For examples of the 'bureaucratic politics' approach as applied to concrete historical problems see Ernest R. May, *The Making of the Monroe Doctrine* (Cambridge, Mass., 1975); Reynolds and Hughes, *The Historian as Diplomat*, esp. ch. 7 (on the development of British policy on the question of the UN, 1942–5); Graham T. Allison, *Essence of Decision: Explaining the Cuban Missile Crisis* (Boston, 1971).
99 Drummond, 'Hull', and Pratt, *Hull*, are the principal studies.

100 Cf. Moffat Diary, 30 Jan. 1938, and Adolf A. Berle Diary, 19 March 1938 (FDRL). See also the discussion in Heinrichs, *Grew*, pp. 267–71.

101 Stimson Diary, 28: 155 (Herbert Feis); Offner, *American Appeasement*, p. 213 (George Messersmith).

102 Moffat Diary, 13 Nov. 1937.

103 Moffat Diary, 13 Dec. 1937 ('seventh dominion'). On the cultural tie see e.g. 11 Oct. 1938, where he deprecates the habit of spending two or three college years at Oxford, 'which is apt to ruin most Americans', and 28 Nov. 1938, on the new colleges at Yale: 'Unfortunately most of the architecture is transplanted English Gothic, and I never before felt so clearly how alien it was to all our American traditions.'

104 Ickes, *Secret Diary*, II, 18 Dec. 1937, 1 May 1938, pp. 276, 381–2.

105 Ibid., 19 Sept. 1937, p. 211.

106 Blum, *From the Morgenthau Diaries*, I, 204–28; Offner, *American Appeasement*, pp. 239–43.

107 Lloyd C. Gardner, 'The role of the Commerce and Treasury departments', in Borg and Okamoto (eds.), *Pearl Harbor as History*, pp. 274–5; Van Dormael, *Bretton Woods*, p. 211.

108 Ickes, *Secret Diary*, entries for 19 Sept., 9 Oct. 1937, pp. 211, 226, on Cabinet meetings, 14 Sept. 1937.

109 E.g. Divine, *Roosevelt and World War II*, pp. 7–10; Barron, *Leadership in Crisis*, pp. 20–1.

110 Divine, *Illusion of Neutrality*, esp. pp. 72, 86–7; Wiltz, *In Search of Peace*, pp. 174–8; Cohen, *American Revisionists*, pp. 161, 164–5.

111 Divine, *Roosevelt and World War II*, pp. 7, 23.

112 Cf. the definition in Jonas, *Isolationism in America*, p. 273.

113 See Loewenheim, 'An illusion that shaped history'; also Dallek, *Roosevelt and American Foreign Policy*, pp. 129, 134–5, 138–9.

114 F.D.R. to Robert Woolley, 25 Feb. 1932, quoted in Freidel, *Roosevelt*, III, 253n.

115 In my judgement the standard account on the neutrality legislation, Divine, *Illusion of Neutrality*, still gives the best sense of F.D.R.'s double-edged policy, e.g. pp. 120–1. (See also below, ch. 8, note 106.)

116 Ickes, *Secret Diary*, II, 213, recording conversation on 14 Sept. 1937.

117 Text in *FRUS, Japan, 1931–41*, I, 379–83; cf. Ickes, *Secret Diary*, II, 221–2.

118 Borg, *U.S. and the Far Eastern Crisis*, pp. 385–6. Both Borg, chs. XIII and XVI and Dallek, *Roosevelt and American Foreign Policy*, pp. 147–53 provide good accounts.

119 Blum, *Morgenthau Diaries*, I, 489, on Cabinet meeting for 17 Dec. 1937. Cf. Ickes, *Secret Diary*, II, 274–5.

120 Lindsay's record of the conversation, on the evening of 16 Dec. 1937, summarized in Pratt, 'Anglo-American naval conversations', pp. 751–2. Haight, 'Roosevelt and a naval quarantine of Japan', pp. 203–8, argues that F.D.R. had a clear-cut policy of blockade and sanctions as early as July but he did not put it into action because of unfavourable public reaction to his Chicago speech. Haight's evidence for this claim is largely drawn from the retrospective, published memoirs of Sumner Welles—never a very reliable source. Perhaps Welles' papers, when they are eventually available, will clarify the episode.

121 President Kennedy deliberately used Roosevelt's word 'quarantine' to describe the blockade of Cuba during the missile crisis of October 1962. (See Roger Hilsman, *To Move a Nation: The Politics of Foreign Policy in the Administration of John F. Kennedy* [Garden City, N.Y., 1967], p. 205.)

122 Principal secondary accounts are MacDonald, *U.S., Britain and Appeasement*, chs. 4–5; Offner, *American Appeasement*, pp. 190–4, 216–34; Loewenheim, 'An illusion that shaped history'; Langer and Gleason, *Challenge to Isolation*, pp. 15–32; Wallace, 'Roosevelt and British appeasement', esp. pp. 4–13. See also the documents in *FRUS*, 1937, I, 665–70 and *FRUS*, 1938, I, 115–48; Berle Diary, Oct. 1937–Feb. 1938 and British material cited in note 46.

123 Welles, as reported in Lindsay to FO, tels. 40, 44, 12 Jan. 1938, FO 371/21526, A2127.

124 Cf. the successive drafts in *FRUS*, 1937, I, 665–6, 668, and *FRUS*, 1938, I, 116.

125 Berle Diary, 7 Feb. 1938.

126 Welles, *Seven Major Decisions*, pp. 38, 40. Cf. *FRUS*, 1938, I, 115.

127 Quotation from Dallek, *Roosevelt and American Foreign Policy*, p. 156. The problem with discovering F.D.R.'s reactions is that he left the whole matter to Welles. Our principal source is therefore Welles' conversations with Lindsay and unfortunately the two men's records of these conversations frequently do not correspond.

It is perhaps worth noting that when Eden visited Washington as Foreign Secretary in May 1943 both he and Welles agreed that a great opportunity had been missed in January 1938. Halifax, by then Ambassador in Washington, examined the Embassy's files on the matter and concluded that it 'had not left the sore feeling in the minds of the U.S. Administration that might have been presumed from Welles' present attitude'. Soon afterwards, when the President was ruminating over the past history of Anglo-American relations, Halifax told Eden, '. . . I reminded him of this episode, not in detail, and said how annoyed you had been. He made no particular comment but went on to say that he thought history would judge Neville Chamberlain on Munich more kindly than he was judged at present, and then asked me whether I had ever seen the telegram that he had sent Neville when the news of Munich [actually the news that Chamberlain was going to Munich] reached him. He said it was the shortest telegram he had ever sent and only had two words, and these words were: "Good man". That perhaps is slightly co-operative evidence for what I would be inclined to feel, namely, that he had not been left in March [1938] with a feeling of resentment against Neville or H.M.G.' (Halifax to Eden, 21 May 1943, FO 954/30A, US/43/51.) Eden, naturally, did not agree, because the episode had long since become part of his justification for resigning, and Cadogan minuted: 'Americans, like elephants, never forget. They seem to nurse their grudges.' (8 June 1943, ibid., US 43/56A.) Halifax wrote in similar vein to Chamberlain's widow, after reading Churchill's greatly exaggerated account in his war memoirs. (Churchill, *Second World War*, I, 196–9; Halifax to Anne Chamberlain, 13 May 1948, Hickleton papers, A4.410.18.4, Churchill College, Cambridge.)

128 Cf. Lindsay to FO, tels. 72, 79, and 91, dated 20, 22, 26 Jan. 1938, PREM 1/259, pp. 37, 28, 26; Hull memo of conversation with Lindsay, 20 Jan. 1938, Hull papers (LC), 58/212. Horace Wilson, Chamberlain's principal adviser, took this invitation as evidence that F.D.R. had not been upset by HMG's initial coolness. (Wilson to Chamberlain, 23 Jan. 1938, PREM 1/259, p. 36.)

129 Welles told Lindsay he was pleased to hear of the detailed plans for European appeasement, adding that the President had been concerned to arrest an apparently increasing deterioration in the situation. (Lindsay to FO, tel. 51, 14 Jan. 1938, A2127.) In his reply Roosevelt told Chamberlain that the 'detailed information' about HMG's policy and preparations had been 'particularly helpful' and that in view of the considerations the PM had advanced 'I readily

agree to defer making the proposal' for a short time. According to Lindsay F.D.R. substituted the latter phrase for Welles' original draft: 'I am willing to agree . . . ' Lindsay took this as evidence that the 'President's disappointment had been distinctly felt', which seems a strange interpretation to put on the emendation. (Cf. Lindsay to FO, tels. 62 and 68, 12 and 18 Jan. 1938, A2127.)

130 It is possible that news of the British Cabinet split may have deterred F.D.R. This was fully reported by the U.S. Embassy in London in mid-February, drawing on a leak from the FO (Johnson to Hull, tel. 131, 15 Feb. 1938, *FRUS*, 1938, I, 136–7) but it would seem that Lindsay had been feeding Welles information on the political crisis since it began. (Cf. Welles, memo, 9 Feb., ibid., p. 125.)

131 As Offner concludes in *American Appeasement*, p. 232.

132 F.D.R. to John Cudahy, 9 March 1938, in Roosevelt, *Personal Letters*, II, 766; F.D.R. to Claude Bowers, 7 March 1938, PSF: Spain, 1938 (FDRL).

133 *FRUS*, 1938, I, 145, 147–8. Privately both F.D.R. and Welles, unlike Hull, believed that the U.S. would have to accord recognition eventually, although anxious about the effect this might have on their position in East Asia with regard to Japanese Manchuria. As Welles explained to Lindsay in January, they were ready to 'swallow . . . the unpleasant pill' with the British, but as part of a world settlement rather than a bilateral deal between London and Rome. (Cf. ibid., pp. 121–3, 133–4; Offner, *American Appeasement*, p. 191; Lindsay to FO, tels. 78 [quotation] and 106, 22 Jan., 2 Feb. 1938, A2127.)

134 Principal sources for British policy are Middlemas, *Diplomacy of Illusion*, chs. 7–13; Douglas, *In the Year of Munich*, chs. 2–6; and, on French policy, Adamthwaite, *France and the Coming of the Second World War*, chs. 11–13. For an excellent account of German policy see Weinberg, *Foreign Policy*, II, chs. 10–11.

135 The main discussion of U.S. policy is in Offner, *American Appeasement*, pp. 245–71. See also the now rather dated account in Haight, 'France, the United States, and the Munich Crisis'. On Anglo-American relations: Henson, 'Britain, America, and the Month of Munich'; Ovendale, '*Appeasement*', chs. V and VI; MacDonald, *U.S., Britain and Appeasement*, chs. 6–7.

136 Moffat Diary, 12 Aug. 1938.

137 Cf. Adamthwaite, *France and the Coming of the Second World War*, p. 206.

138 Blum, *From the Morgenthau Diaries*, I, 514–18; Presidential Press Conference 484, 9 Sept. 1938 (FDRL).

139 Moffat Diary, 16 Sept. 1938; Ickes, *Secret Diary*, II, 468, referring to F.D.R.'s comments on 16–17 Sept.

140 The appeal of 26 Sept. is printed in *FRUS*, 1938, I, 657–8. For the policy-making see Berle Diary, 26 Sept. and Moffat Diary, 25 Sept.

141 *FRUS*, 1938, I, 684–5, 677.

142 Cabinet Foreign Policy Commt., 18 March 1938, quoted in Ovendale, '*Appeasement*', p. 119.

143 Sir Thomas Inskip, Diary 12 Sept. 1938, INKP 1, pp. 8–9 (Churchill College, Cambridge).

144 For example in April Chamberlain was resisting French pressure to make military commitments to their security. As one of his objections he cited the U.S. neutrality legislation and the consequent uncertainty about munitions supplies from America. Daladier then reminded him that the French had recently placed an important aircraft order in the U.S.A. without difficulty. (Record of Anglo-French conversations, 28 April 1938, *DBFP*, 3s, I, 203.)

145 Lindsay to Halifax, tel. 342, 12 Sept. 1938, *DBFP*, 3s, II, 301.

146 Hull, memo, 28 Sept. 1938, *FRUS*, 1938, II, 57.

147 Morgenthau Diary, 141: 115, 19 Sept. 1938. Lindsay to Halifax, tel. 349, 20 Sept. 1938, FO 371/21527, A7504.

148 E.g. Harrison in 'Appeasement and Isolation', pp. 680–6; Lash, *Roosevelt and Churchill*, pp. 25–8.

149 Lindsay to Halifax, tel. 351, 21 Sept. 1938, and Halifax to Lindsay, tel. 640, 23 Sept. 1938, A7504.

150 Balfour, minute, 3 Oct. 1938, A7504.

151 Halifax to Lindsay, tel. 640, 23 Sept. 1938, A7504, conveyed to the White House as Lindsay to Roosevelt, 26 Sept. 1938, PSF 46: Great Britain, 1937–38.

152 Lindsay to Balfour, letter, 1 Nov. 1938, FO 371/21527, A8474.

153 F. R. Hoyer Millar, 'Vade Mecum' for the royal visit to the U.S.A., May 1939, p. 26, FO 371/22800, A3880.


## Chapter Two

1 Citations given below, notes 42 and 67.

2 Chamberlain to Hilda, 6 Nov. 1938, NC 18/1/1075.

3 Cadogan, memo, 14 Oct. 1938, in *Diaries*, p. 120.

4 Aster, *1939*, pp. 37, 143; Adamthwaite, *France*, pp. 300, 306; Cowling, *Impact of Hitler*, pp. 294–9; Gibbs, *Grand Strategy*, I, 803.

5 Aster, *1939*, pp. 94–5, 143–51; Gibbs, *Grand Strategy*, I, 703–7, 713–14.

6 Quoted in Colvin, *Chamberlain Cabinet*, p. 216.

7 Aster, *1939*, pp. 216–17; MacDonald, *U.S., Britain and Appeasement*, p. 158.

8 MacDonald, 'Economic Appeasement and the German "Moderates" ', esp. pp. 127–30. But see also Aster, *1939*, pp. 246–8.

9 For discussions of this topic see Gibbs, *Grand Strategy*, I, ch. XIX; Aster, *1939*, chs. 6, 10, 11; Manne, 'The British Decision for Alliance with Russia'.

10 Chamberlain to Ida, 26 March 1939, NC 18/1/1091.

11 For discussions of this topic see esp. Cowling, *Impact of Hitler*, chs. 7–8; Douglas, *Year of Munich*, ch. 8; Ramsden, *Age of Balfour and Baldwin*, pp. 365–8. Also Gilbert, *Churchill*, chs. 48–53.

12 Brendan Bracken to Lord Beaverbrook, 16 May 1939, Beaverbrook papers, HLRO, C/56. Cf. Lysaght, *Bracken*, ch. 13.

13 Chamberlain to Hilda, 15 Oct. 1938, to Ida, 12 March 1939, NC 18/1/1072 and /1089.

14 Chamberlain had made overtures to Lord Samuel in October 1938. (Douglas, *Year of Munich*, pp. 78–9.) Of Churchill he wrote: 'The nearer we get to war the more his chances improve and vice versa. If there is any possibility of easing the tension and getting back to normal relations with the Dictators I wouldn't risk it by what would certainly be regarded by them as a challenge.' Letter to Ida, 23 April 1939, NC 18/1/1095.

15 See esp. Newman, *March 1939*; Cowling, *Impact of Hitler*, pp. 271–83, 289–91, 294; Lammers, 'From Whitehall after Munich'.

16 Cadogan, min., 26 Feb. 1939, C/2/39/3, FO 800/294.

17 'Chips' Channon, Parliamentary Private Secretary to R. A. Butler, the Parliamentary Under-Secretary at the FO, was fascinated by the contradictions in Halifax's personality. After one talk with MPs Channon noted that Halifax 'was brilliant, he cajoled them, led them up the garden path, played with them, impressed them with his charm, sincerity and high ideals. He fascinates and bamboozles everyone. Is he saint turned worldling, or worldling become saint?' Channon, *Diaries*, 16 Feb. 1939, p. 184. See Birkenhead, *Halifax*, esp. chs. XXV and XXVI.

18 Harvey, Diary, 17 Feb. 1939, British Library Add. Mss. 56395.

19 However, to say that from the spring Chamberlain was reduced to 'a sort of public-relations man for the Foreign Office' (Newman, *March 1939*, p. 150) is a gross exaggeration.

20 One need not, however, go as far as Maurice Cowling in arguing that the major determinant of Halifax's new stand was his 'belief that the policy would have to be changed if the party was to be saved' (*Impact of Hitler*, p. 291) because appeasement was losing the Tories possession of the crucial middle ground of politics.

21 The day before Hitler attacked Poland, Euan Wallace, the newly appointed Minister of Transport, noted that Halifax 'was optimistic and even used the simile of "the first view of a beaten fox" in reference to the Führer'. Wallace Diary, 31 Aug. 1939, Bodleian Library, Oxford, MS. Eng. hist. c495, f. 14.

22 Moffat Diary, 30 Sept. 1938; Berle saw a good moment for the U.S. to revive the idea of a disarmament conference (Berle to Hull, 30 Sept. in Berle Diary for that date), but another Assistant Secretary, George Messersmith, one of the leading anti-appeasers, warned of the dangers of concessions to a government bent on world domination. (Messersmith to Hull, 29 Sept. 1938, forwarded to F.D.R., *FRUS*, 1938, I, 704–7.) The best detailed discussion of British and U.S. policy towards Germany in this period is MacDonald, *U.S., Britain and Appeasement*, chs. 8–12. On the U.S. rearmament programme see McFarland, *Woodring*, chs. 6–11; Blum, *From the Morgenthau Diaries*, II, ch. 2 and Haight, *American Aid to France*, chs. 1–4. On Germany see Weinberg, *Foreign Policy*, II, chs. 12–14.

23 F.D.R. to Kennedy, 5 Oct. 1938, quoted in Langer and Gleason, *Challenge to Isolation*, p. 138. On 11 Oct. he told the Canadian premier of his rejoicing that war had been averted and of his concern to prevent a new crisis by moves towards reducing armaments and trade barriers. (F.D.R. to Mackenzie King, 11 Oct. 1938, PSF 35: Canada, 1938–40.)

24 Moffat Diary, 29 Nov. 1938.

25 Roosevelt, *Public Papers*, 1939, p. 3. Cf. the 'Truman doctrine' speech of March 1947: '. . . totalitarian regimes imposed upon free peoples, by direct or indirect aggression, undermine the foundations of international peace and hence the security of the United States'. *Public Papers of the Presidents of the United States: Harry S. Truman*, 1947 (Washington, 1963), p. 178. The process by which the U.S. is felt to be threatened is the same in each case; in 1939 one can already see elements of the Cold War world-view.

26 Lindsay to FO, 20 Sept. 1938, FO 371/21527, A7504/64/45; Berle Diary, 17 June 1939. Cf. Iriye, *Across the Pacific*, pp. 202–5.

27 Ickes, *Secret Diary*, II, 568; Cf. Barron, *Leadership in Crisis*, pp. 33–4.

28 Langer and Gleason, *Challenge to Isolation*, pp. 40–1; Watson, *Chief of Staff*, pp. 89–91; Haines, 'Under the Eagle's wing', esp. pp. 373–9.

29 Barron, *Leadership in Crisis*, pp. 33–4; Berle Diary, 26 May 1939.

30 Abbazia, *Mr Roosevelt's Navy*, chs. 2–3.

31 Ickes, *Secret Diary*, II, entries of 18 and 23 Sept. 1938, pp. 469–70, 472–4.

32 As he had explained to Lindsay during the September crisis (see above ch. 1 [f]).

33 Quotations from Herman Oliphant, memo of White House meeting, 14 Nov. 1938, Morgenthau Diary, 150: 338. See also Pogue, *Marshall*, I, 339–40. Apparently F.D.R. deliberately excluded his Secretary of War, Harry Woodring, from this crucial meeting—because Woodring was a staunch advocate of balanced rearmament and an opponent of the heavy bomber. See McFarland, *Woodring*, pp. 164–7. In the end the military forced on F.D.R. a more balanced programme. See also Emerson, 'Roosevelt as Commander-in-Chief', pp. 185–7.

34 See discussion in Haight, *American Aid to France*, chs. 1–2.

35 Moffat Diary, 15 March 1939; cf. Offner, *American Appeasement*, pp. 272–3 and notes.
36 F.D.R. to Hitler and Mussolini, 14 April 1939, *FRUS*, 1939, I, 130–3; Morgenthau Presidential Diary, 1:81, 15 April 1939; F.D.R. to Mackenzie King, 16 April 1939, PSF 35: Canada, 1938–40.
37 F.D.R. to George VI, 17 Sept. 1938, PSF 49: Great Britain, King and Queen. For fuller discussion of Roosevelt's intentions see Reynolds, 'FDR's foreign policy and the British Royal Visit to the U.S.A. in 1939' (forthcoming).
38 Ickes, *Secret Diary*, II, 474, 470, comments by F.D.R. on 17 and 23 Sept. 1938.
39 Sir Arthur Willert, memo of conversations with F.D.R., 25–26 March 1939, pp. 3–4, Willert papers, Yale, 14/61.
40 Ickes, *Secret Diary*, II, 571, comments by F.D.R. on 28 Jan. 1939.
41 Willert, memo, p. 2.
42 F.D.R. to Roger B. Merriman, 15 Feb. 1939, PSF 46: Great Britain, 1939.
43 E.g. reports by Graeme Haldane, Feb. 1939, FO 371/22813, A1378, by Enid Laphorn, 25 Feb. 1939 and R. H. Bruce Lockhart, 15 April 1939, FO371/22829, A1451, A3017/1292/45.
44 E.g. Victor Mallet to David Scott, 26 Jan. 1939, FO 371/22827, A1143/1143/45.
45 E.g. Mallet to Cadogan, 23 Dec. 1938, FO 371/22956, C182/11/18, and Mallet to Scott, 10 Jan. 1939, FO 371/22962, C1063; cf. Harvey, *Diaries*, 25 Dec. 1938, pp. 229–30.
46 See FO 371/22827, pp. 332–3.
47 Kendrick, *Prime Time*, pp. 168–9; Culbert, *News for Everyman*, esp. pp. 5, 18–19, 73–6.
48 Fletcher, memo, 21 Sept. 1938, FO 395/616, P 2769/1157/150.
49 See FO 395/640, P340, P491, P1164/36/150. Although of considerable interest, the details of British propaganda policy are only peripheral to the main theme of this book and I discuss the subject here and later only briefly. I hope, however, to examine it more fully in a forthcoming article.
50 Scott, min., 4 April 1939, FO 371/22829, A2439/1292/45. For similar comments see mins. of 17 Nov. 1938, FO 371/21527, A8441/64/45; 8 Feb. 1939, FO 371/22827, A1143/1143/45; 25 March, 6 April, 11 May 1939, FO 371/22829, A2584, A2693, A3125/1292/45.
51 E.g. J. G. S. Beith, min., 22 Feb. 1939, FO 371/22813, A1378/98/45; Lindsay to FO, 4 April 1939, FO 371/22829, A2693/1292/45; 2 tels. of 8 May 1939, FO 371/22830, A3312, A3314.
52 Harvey to Halifax, memo 30 June 1938, and diary entry for 11 April 1939, Harvey, *Diaries*, pp. 435–7, 278–9. Vansittart to Halifax, 19 Oct. 1938, FO 800/314, p. 195; Vansittart, min., 9 April 1939, FO 371/22829, A2439/1292/45.
53 Cadogan, mins., 7 April 1939, FO 371/22829, A2439/1292/45 and 24 Feb. 1939, FO 371/22813, A1378.
54 Cadogan, min., 2 Feb. 1939, FO 371/22812, A660/98/45.
55 Cadogan, min., 27 March 1939, FO 800/315, H/XV/138.
56 Cadogan, memo, 14 Oct. 1938, quoted in Cadogan, *Diaries*, p. 119.
57 Kennedy to Hull, 12 Oct. 1938, *FRUS*, 1938, I, 85–6; Halifax to Phipps, 1 Nov. 1938, *DBFP*, 3s, II, 251–3.
58 For fuller discussion see Reynolds, *Lord Lothian and Anglo-American relations, 1939–1940*, esp. part I.
59 See Reynolds, 'F.D.R. on the British: A postscript'.
60 Hall, *North American Supply*, p. 106.
61 Murray, memo of conversations with F.D.R., 16–24 Oct. 1938, PREM 1/367; Murray to Halifax, 20 Nov. 1938, Elibank papers, National Library of Scotland, Mss. 8809, pp. 131–3. See also Elibank, 'Franklin Roosevelt'.

62 Roosevelt, *Public Papers*, 1939, esp. pp. 1–4.

63 Harvey commented that 'Roosevelt's splendid message . . . was the best news we have yet had. He had said what we ought to say and is at present the real spokesman of democracy. I wish A.E. [Eden] could speak out as bluntly as that.' (Harvey Diary, 5 Jan. 1939, vol. 56395.) In Washington, Moffat noted that Victor Mallet of the British Embassy was 'jubilant . . . His imagination was envisaging a power to do for England what the British Government had not been willing to do herself.' (Moffat Diary, 4 Jan. 1939.)

64 Cf. the comment by his sister: 'How nice at the moment to be an American, able to speak your mind freely. If you said as much as he said it might embitter relations and lead to war, but the Germans know they cannot hurt the Americans and the Americans can hurt them and under these circumstances a little plain speaking is likely to do them a lot of good.' (Ida to Neville Chamberlain, 6 Jan. 1939, NC 18/2/1105.) Chamberlain made a similar point to a Labour delegation in March. 'Asked about the possibilities of an economic boycott of Germany, he said that no doubt the U.S.A. could do this sort of thing and inconvenience Germany considerably and with impunity, but he had always taken the view that for European Powers economic sanctions against Germany, or Italy, would either be ineffective or, if effective, would lead to war.' (Dalton Diary, 23 March 1939.)

65 *The Times*, 6 Jan. 1939, p. 12a; Dirksen, political report, 9 Jan. 1939, *DGFP*, D. IV, 379–80. Arthur Murray told the FO that Chamberlain's statement would be welcomed in the U.S. where there had been discouragement at the lack of official British response or even interest at previous utterances by the President. (Perowne, min., 6 Jan. 1939, FO 371/22812, A114/98/45.) It is quite likely that Murray also told Chamberlain of this discouragement in the course of their meeting in December.

66 Cadogan, memo, 16 Jan. 1939, CAB 27/627, FP (36) 74; Cadogan, *Diaries*, 19 Jan. 1939, p. 140; FO to Mallet, 24 Jan. 1939, FO 371/22961, C939/15/18.

67 CAB 23/97, Cab. 3 (39) 1, 1 Feb. 1939; Chamberlain to Ida, 28 Jan. and to Hilda, 5 Feb. 1939, NC 18/1/1083–4.

68 Chamberlain to Hilda, 19 Feb. and to Ida, 12 March 1939, NC 18/1/1086 and 1089. He told Kennedy on 17 February that although Hitler was a fanatic, the only way to do business with him was to take him at his word, which to date he had not broken. Kennedy contrasted this viewpoint with the FO's conviction that Hitler was entirely untrustworthy. Chamberlain attributed Hitler's quieter behaviour to F.D.R.'s statement and to the U.S. rearmament programme, coupled with his own correspondingly firmer attitude. (See Kennedy to Hull, 17 Feb. 1939, *FRUS*, 1939, I, 14–17.)

69 E.g. CAB 27/624, FP (36) 38th mtg., 27 March 1939.

70 Aster, *1939*, p. 111; cf. Chamberlain to Ida, 2 April 1939, NC 18/1/1092.

71 Communiqué, 15 April 1939, FO 371/22969, C5431; Cadogan, *Diaries*, 15 April 1939, p. 174; Sargent, min., 15 April 1939, FO 371/22970, C5592. Chamberlain to Ida, 15 April 1939, NC 18/1/1094.

72 CAB 23/99, Cab. 22 (39) 3, 24 April 1939; MacDonald, 'Britain, France and the April crisis', pp. 166–7. F.D.R. objected to Bullitt expressing such direct advice on an internal British matter, but in fact he had given them similar advice a few weeks before via another old friend, Arthur Willert. (See Bullitt to F.D.R. and Welles to Bullitt, 19 and 20 April 1939, *FRUS*, 1939, I, 169–70; Willert, memo of conversations with F.D.R., 25–26 March 1939, circulated to the Cabinet's Foreign Policy Commt., CAB 27/627, FP (36) 80, 20 April 1939.)

73 Sargent, min., 22 March 1939, FO 371/23081, C3936/3936/18; FO mins., April 1939, FO 371/22829, A2693/1292/45; Ovendale, '*Appeasement*', p. 237; memos from British Embassy in FDRL, PSF 46: Great Britain, 1939.

74 Mallet to Cadogan, 23 Dec. 1938, C182/11/18; cf. Morgenthau Diary, 14 Nov. 1938, 150:337.

75 Gibbs, *Grand Strategy*, I, 584. The British figures were also exaggerations. The figure of 3,200 for German front-line strength was calculated in Aug. 1938; the correct figure at that date was 2,847. (Postan, *British War Production*, pp. 56–7.)

76 See docs. in FO 371/22956, C182, C3589, C4892/11/18; Kennedy to F.D.R., 6 April 1939, with enclosures, PSF 46: Great Britain, 1939.

77 F.D.R. to Arthur Murray, 10 July 1939, PSF(C) 53: Great Britain, Murray, 1936–9. In 1939 Germany produced 8,295 planes and Britain 7,490; in 1940 the respective figures were 10,826 and 15,049. (Overy, 'German pre-war aircraft production plans', p. 796.)

78 Report of Anglo-French staff conversations, AFC 7 (Revise), 11 April 1939, copy in CAB 16/209, annex II to SAC 17.

79 Chiefs of Staff (COS) European Appreciation, 20 Feb. 1939, Appendix I: FO Political Review, para. 316(i), CAB 16/183A, DP(P) 44.

80 Balfour, min., 14 April 1939, FO 371/22829, A2856/1292/45.

81 W. Cavendish-Bentinck, min., 17 March 1939, FO 371/23981, W4677/108/50.

82 See FO 395/647c, P2178/105/150 and FO 395/648a, P2820/105/150.

83 Lindsay to Rex Leeper, 17 March 1939, quoted in FO 395/648b, pp. 569–70; Scott, min., 17 Nov. 1938, FO 371/21527, A8441/64/45.

84 Hans Thomsen to German Foreign Ministry, 27 March 1939, *DGFP*, D, VI, 132; Halifax to Lindsay, tel. 619, 10 Sept. 1938, *DBFP*, 3s, II, 284–5. Lippmann, 'Today and Tomorrow' column, *New York Herald Tribune*, 23 March 1939, copy in FO 371/22829, A2439/1292/45. Balfour used some of Lippmann's phrases in his minute of 14 April. Wheeler-Bennett, *George VI*, p. 391.

85 Cadogan, min., 2 Feb. 1939, FO 371/22812, A660/98/45.

86 Vansittart, min., 9 April 1939, cf. Scott, min., 6 April, FO 371/22829, A2439, A2693/1292/45.

87 The comments in his 5 Feb. letter, quoted above, refer to German fears of U.S. intervention and not to his own expectations.

88 FO 371/22827, A1011/1011/45; *HC Debs.*, 5s, 7 Feb. 1939, vol. 343, 742–3.

89 For example, when it was suggested that the PM should personally visit Washington to sign the Trade Agreement. Mins. by Cadogan, 16 March, and Halifax, 19 March 1938, FO 371/21492, A1850/1/45; Chamberlain to Mackenzie King, 11 Nov. 1938, PREM 1/291.

90 Dalton Diaries, 28 June 1939; cf. George VI, memo of talk with Chamberlain, 19 Oct. 1938, Wheeler-Bennett, *George VI*, p. 357; Chamberlain to Hilda, 6 Nov. 1938 and 19 Feb. 1939, NC 18/1/1075 and 1086.

91 Murray to F.D.R., 15 Dec. 1938, Chamberlain to Murray, 2 Feb. 1939, Elibank papers, Mss. 8809, pp. 136–43, 165.

92 Dirksen to Foreign Ministry, 15 Oct. 1938, 3 Jan. 1939, 20 Feb. 1939, *DGFP*, D. IV, 311, 363–4, 413–14.

93 Cowling, *Impact of Hitler*, pp. 269–70; Londonderry to Chamberlain, 4 May 1939, cf. 1 Oct. 1939, NC 7/11/32/160 and /167.

94 Bernd Jürgen Wendt, *Economic Appeasement: Handel und Finanz in der britischen Deutschland-Politik, 1933–1939* (Düsseldorf, 1971), pp. 526, 529.

95 Cf. Aster, *1939*, pp. 256–8.

96 See *DGFP*, D. IV, 316, 375.

97 MacDonald, *U.S., Britain and Appeasement*, pp. 108–10, 130–1, 135–6, 165. See also MacDonald, 'Economic Appeasement', pp. 133–4.
98 Gardner, *Economic Aspects of New Deal Diplomacy*, p. 107; Peden, *British Rearmament*, pp. 85–6, 97–100; Sayers, *Bank of England*, II, 561–7; Rowland, 'Preparing the American ascendancy', p. 211.
99 *Impact of Hitler*, p. 299.
100 George VI, memo, 19 Oct. 1938, Wheeler-Bennett, *George VI*, pp. 357–8; CAB 23/96, p. 21, Cab. 49 (38) 9, 19 Oct. 1938.
101 MacDonald, *U.S., Britain and Appeasement*, pp. 109–10, 135. I am very grateful to Callum MacDonald for sharing with me his ideas and research on this question.
102 Cf. Hans-Dietrich Loock, '*Weserubung*', p. 68: 'If I interpret [British] appeasement policy correctly, it had as its objective the isolation of the Soviet Union and the exclusion of the U.S.A. from the quarrels of Europe so that the potential for independent political activity by the European powers could be maintained.' Similarly, Newman, *March 1939*, p. 6.
103 Dirksen, Political Report, 3 Jan. 1939, *DGFP*, D. IV, 363–4.
104 Cf. Sir Warren Fisher to Sir Horace Wilson, 15 May 1939, Fisher papers, BLPES, misc. coll. 461, file 2, p. 43.
105 Scott, min., 11 May 1939, FO 371/22802, A2766/85/45. For FO position see also Balfour, min., 6 March 1939, ibid., A1825/85/45 and mins. by Balfour, Scott and Cadogan, 10, 14 and 24 March 1939, FO 371/22829, A1451/1292/45. For Treasury comment see Leith-Ross to Hopkins, memo, 12 Jan. 1939, T160/934, F13300/13.
106 Moffat Diary, 13 Dec. 1938; Wheeler-Bennett, *George VI*, p. 392; Perowne, min., 5 June 1939, FO 371/22803, A4026/85/45.
107 Adamthwaite, *France and the Coming of the Second World War*, p. 342; for details see Bullitt (ed.), *For the President*, pp. 315–18, 326–7, 334–6.
108 Lindsay to Halifax, desp. 388, 5 April 1939, and accompanying papers, FO 115/3419, file 536.
109 S. H. Phillips to Balfour, 29 June, T. S. V. Phillips, min., 13 June 1939, ADM 1/9784.
110 A. H. Poynton to Perowne, 28 Aug. 1939, FO 371/22803, A5844/85/45; cf. Statement by Ramsay MacDonald, 6 March 1934, *HC Debs.*, 5s, vol. 286, col. 1650.
111 Chamberlain to Sir Leonard Lyte, 28 Jan. 1940, CO 323/1750, file 7019. He said it would raise such a political storm that 'no British Government could survive'.
112 E.g. *Washington Times-Herald*, 22 June 1939; cf. *Cong. Record*, 76/1, vol. 84, 7762.
113 F.D.R. to Hull and Welles, memo, 28 March 1939, in Roosevelt, *Personal Letters*, II, 873. For the text of the 1937 Act see U.S. Dept. of State, *Peace and War*, pp. 355–65.
114 E.g. State Dept. memo of 19 May 1939 meeting, quoted in Langer and Gleason, *Challenge to Isolation*, p. 138; cf. Berle Diary, 26 May 1939.
115 Willert memo of conversations with F.D.R., 25 and 26 March 1939, pp. 3–4, in Willert papers, 14/61.
116 State Dept. memo of 19 May.
117 Morgenthau Diary, 180:318–19, 20 April 1939. Cf. above ch. 1 (e).
118 State Dept. memo of 19 May. Cf. Ickes, *Secret Diary*, II, 481, entry for 30 Sept. 1938.
119 Moffat Diary, 25 January 1939, recording State Dept. meeting.
120 This paragraph draws particularly on Patterson, *Congressional Conservatism*

*and the New Deal*; see also Richard Polenberg, 'The decline of the New Deal, 1937–1940', in Braeman *et al.* (eds.), *The New Deal*, pp. 246–66; Otis L. Graham, 'The Democratic Party, 1932–1945' and George H Mayer, 'The Republican Party, 1932–1952', in Schlesinger (ed.), *History of U.S. Political Parties*, III, 1939–64, 2259–92.

121 Jonas, *Isolationism in America*, esp. chs. 2–3; Divine, *Illusion of Neutrality*, pp. 194–9; see also Maddox, *Borah*, pp. 225–32; Cole, *Nye*, pp. 66–132; Tompkins, *Vandenberg*, pp. 126–9, 158.

122 For a recent case study see Accinelli, 'The Roosevelt administration and the World Court defeat, 1935'.

123 Leuchtenburg, *Roosevelt and the New Deal*, p. 272.

124 See Riddick, 'First session of the seventy-sixth Congress', esp pp. 1035–6, 1043; Langer and Gleason, *Challenge to Isolation*, p. 130.

125 A point emphasized by both Divine, *Illusion of Neutrality*, ch. 8 and Schwar, 'Interventionist Propaganda and Pressure Groups', ch. 5, on which this paragraph is based. See also Porter, *76th Congress*, ch. 3, esp. pp. 45, 53.

126 A point he made on several occasions, e.g. Berle Diary, 7 March 1939; cf. Moffat Diary, 3 May 1939.

127 Patterson, 'Eating humble pie', p. 410.

128 Wilcox, 'The neutrality fight', p. 811.

129 Bullitt to Hull, tel. 920, 10 May 1939, *FRUS*, 1939, I, 184–5; Moore to F.D.R., 12 May, PSF 160: Neutrality, 1939–41; Divine, *Illusion of Neutrality*, pp. 260–1.

130 Bullitt to Hull, tel. 1253, 5 July 1939, Phillips to Hull, tel. 247, 5 July 1939, *FRUS*, 1939, I, 281–2, 663–4.

131 See FO 371/22815, esp. A4828, A4979, A5008, A5737; Kennedy to Hull, tels. 942, 1034, 5 and 20 July 1939, *FRUS*, 1939, I, 283, 287–8.

132 On the barter deal see Koskoff, *Kennedy*, pp. 195–8; Kennedy to Hull, tel. 763, 2 June 1939, *FRUS*, 1939, II, 248–9; Cab. 32 (39) 12, 14 June 1939, CAB 23/99 and Cab. 33 (39) 10, 21 June 1939, CAB 23/100.

133 Lindsay to FO, desp. 741E, 3 July 1939, Scott, min., 15 July, FO 371/22815, A4794. Chamberlain to Tweedsmuir, 7 July 1939, John Buchan papers, quoted in Pratt, *East of Malta*, p. 190, note 27. Butler, min., 3 July 1939, FO 371/22814, A4583.

134 Beloff, *Imperial Sunset*, I, 336. The major recent studies of British Far Eastern policy are Louis, *British Strategy in the Far East*; Lee, *Britain and the Sino-Japanese War*; Lowe, *Britain and the Origins of the Pacific War*. See also Callahan, 'Singapore, 1919–1942'.

135 Thorne, *Limits of Foreign Policy*, pp. 49–51; Nicholas Clifford, *Retreat from China: British Policy in the Far East, 1937–1941* (London, 1967), p. 16. Borg and Okamoto, *Pearl Harbor as History*, pp. 121–6, 359.

136 Thorne, *Allies of a Kind*, p. 17.

137 Norman A. Graebner, 'Hoover, Roosevelt, and the Japanese', in Borg and Okamoto, *Pearl Harbor as History*, pp. 25–52, quotation from p. 46; cf. Thorne, *Allies of a Kind*, p. 42: '. . . the 1930s saw no clarification of American Far Eastern policy as a whole, no reconciliation of cloudy, expansive aspirations with limited tangible interests, restricted means, and small readiness for sacrifice'.

138 Lee, *Britain and the Sino-Japanese War*, p. 212.

139 Craigie to Halifax, 2 Dec. 1938, and accompanying minutes, including Cadogan's of 16 Jan. 1939, FO 371/22181, F13984/71/23.

140 ADM 1/9822 and ADM 116/3922; U.S. Navy, Strategic Plans Division, Box 116 (Washington Navy Yard). See generally Leutze, *Bargaining for Supremacy*, pp. 15–28.

141 In October 1937, Chatfield, the First Sea Lord, was '. . . quite sure that if it ever comes to any trouble in the Far East the Americans will stand aside'. By the end of the year, with the Ingersoll talks imminent, although entering the inevitable caveat that '. . . one can never be sure what they will do so we cannot rely on them absolutely', Chatfield wrote that, if a British fleet had to go out to the Far East, 'I think we should be certain to have the American Fleet as well and that will make a great difference.' (Admiral Sir Ernle Chatfield to Admiral Sir Roger Backhouse, 8 Oct. 1937, CHT/4/1, p. 186, and to Admiral Sir Dudley Pound, 30 Dec. 1937, CHT/4/10, pp. 106, 108; cf. Chatfield to Sir Thomas Inskip, 25 Jan. 1938, CHT/3/1, p. 237 [Chatfield Papers, National Maritime Museum, Greenwich].)

142 Lee, *Britain and the Sino-Japanese War*, p. 168.

143 Strategical Appreciation Committee, esp. paper SAC 4 by First Sea Lord, 28 Feb. 1939 and SAC 1st mtg., 1 March 1939, CAB 16/209.

144 Roskill, *Naval Policy between the Wars*, II, 345–9, 351–3, 434–7.

145 Gibbs, *Grand Strategy*, I, 422–3; cf. FO minutes of March 1939 in FO 371/23981, W3784/108/50.

146 Mtg. of ministers, 19 March 1939, FO 371/22967, C3859/15/18; CAB 23/98 Cab. 14 (39) 2, 22 March 1939; Kennedy to Hull, 22 March 1939, *FRUS*, 1939, I, 88.

147 Berle Diary, 13 April 1939, reporting phone conversation with F.D.R. on evening of the 11th.

148 Abbazia, *Mr Roosevelt's Navy*, pp. 49–50; Lindsay to Halifax, tel. 130, 24 March 1939, FO 371/23560, F2942/456/23. See also ibid., F2693, F3017, F3889/456/23.

149 FO to Lindsay, tel. 131, 19 March 1939, and Lindsay to FO, tel. 124, 21 March, 1939, ibid., F2879, F2880/456/23. ADM 116/3922, esp. pp. 102–5; cf. Leutze, *Bargaining for Supremacy*, pp. 33–6.

150 CAB 2/8, CID 355 mtg., 2 May 1939.

151 Hampton's report, 27 June 1939, and FO minutes, FO 371/23561, F7010/456/23; see also memo in U.S.N., Strategic plans division, Box 116.

152 T. S. V. Phillips, min., 29 June 1939, ADM 116/3922, p. 110.

153 CAB 23/100, Cab. 33 (39) 3, 21 June 1939; cf. Cab. 35 (39) 8, 5 July 1939.

154 Langer and Gleason, *Challenge to Isolation*, pp. 157–9; but see also Tompkins, *Vandenberg*, pp. 162–7, Hosoya, 'Miscalculations in deterrent policy', pp. 98–100.


**Chapter Three**

1 Quoted in Lockhart, *Comes the Reckoning*, p. 78. For Chamberlain's comment, see below, note 90.

2 Lukacs, *The Last European War*, p. 3; Watt, *Too Serious a Business*, pp. 11–13, 55–6, made a similar point, adding that for contemporaries the 1939–41 conflict had the character of an ideological European civil war.

3 David Dilks draws particular attention to it in 'Great Britain and Scandinavia in the "Phoney War" ', p. 30.

4 Long, *War Diary*, 2 Sept. (Hull), 5 and 11 Oct. 1939, pp. 1, 24–5, 26–7. Moffat Diary, 1 Sept. 1939. Berle to F.D.R., memo, 18 Sept. 1939, PSF 94: State Dept., Berle; cf. Berle Diary, 4 Sept. 1939.

5 Berle Diary, 26 Aug. 1939; Berle to F.D.R., memo, 2 Sept. 1939, PSF 88: State, 1939. Morgenthau Diary, 180:319, 20 April 1939. Wheeler-Bennett,

*George VI*, pp. 391–2; Lindsay to FO, tel. 293, 1 July 1939, FO 371/23901, W10081/9805/49.

6 FO to Lothian, 2 Nov. 1939, FO 371/22763, A7279/5992/51.

7 Lindsay to FO, tel. 293, 1 July, FO to Lindsay, 6 July 1939, W10081; Lindsay to FO, tels. 304 and 305, 8 July, FO 371/23902, W10364, W10365/9805/49. For a recent examination of this episode see Baptiste, 'The British grant of air and naval facilities to the United States . . . in 1939'.

8 Fitzmaurice, min., 4 July 1939, W10081; Danckwerts, min., 10 July 1939, ADM 116/3922, pp. 163–4.

9 Abbazia, *Mr Roosevelt's Navy*, ch. 5.

10 The new act, of 4 Nov. 1939, is printed in State Dept., *Peace and War*, pp. 494–506. For discussions of the issue, on which this paragraph draws, see Langer and Gleason, *Challenge to Isolation*, pp. 218–35; Divine, *Illusion of Neutrality*, ch. 9; Schwar, 'Interventionist propaganda', ch. 6; Patterson, 'Eating humble pie'; Guinsberg, 'Ebb tide of American isolationism', esp. pp. 319–29; Johnson, *Battle against Isolation*, ch. II; Leigh, *Mobilizing Consent*, pp. 41–9; Porter, *76th Congress*, ch. 4.

11 Ickes, *Secret Diary*, II, 718–19, entry for 9 Sept. 1939.

12 Leigh, *Mobilizing Consent*, pp. 48–9.

13 In addition, the bans on travel by Americans on belligerent vessels, on loans to belligerents and on the arming of U.S. merchant ships were all retained.

14 See Divine, *Illusion of Neutrality*, pp. 319–24; Langer and Gleason, *Challenge to Isolation*, p. 232. I have also used the detailed discussion by John McAuliffe, President of Isthmian Steamship Lines, in a talk to the Council on Foreign Relations, 25 Oct. 1939 (CFR archives, New York, 'Meetings', vol. V). Until the act was passed U.S. vessels were free to carry all but arms anywhere in the world, because the cash and carry provisions had lapsed in May 1939 and the summer fiasco in Congress had meant that they had not been renewed.

15 Berle Diary, 30 Sept. 1939, pp. 1–2; Ickes, *Secret Diary*, II, 2 Sept., p. 710 and 9 Sept. 1939, pp. 716, 721 (F.D.R.); cf. Moffat Diary, 6 Sept. 1939.

16 Hall, *North American Supply*, pp. 60–8; Riverdale's report of 14 Aug. 1939 is appended to CP 177 (39) in CAB 24/288.

J. P. Morgan's, for its part, recognized that an overt role would be inadvisable, in view of the adverse publicity its Great War activities had attracted, but with its influential British contacts, notably Lothian in Washington and Lord Catto in London, the firm was able to press its services discreetly but insistently in other ways. See T. W. Lamont papers, Harvard Business School, file 84–19, esp. correspondence of Sept. 1939.

17 Blum, *From the Morgenthau Diaries*, II, pp. 101–3.

18 Wheeler-Bennett, *George VI*, pp. 391, 392.

19 Perowne, min., 9 Sept. 1939, on Phipps to FO, tel. 637, 6 Sept. 1939, FO 371/22816, A6085/98/45; Dalton Diary, 18 Sept. 1939. Berle believed F.D.R. was 'entirely sincere' about not wanting to go to war. (Berle Diary, 8 Sept. 1939, p. 2.)

20 See Friedländer, *Prelude to Downfall*, ch. 2; Hildebrand, *Foreign Policy of the Third Reich*, pp. 85–6, 100–1.

21 Leonard K. Elmhirst to F.D.R., 17 June 1940, PSF 46: Great Britain, 1940 (1): 'Do you remember warning me that it was a 50:50 proposition on this horse & not like the last war.' Elmhirst's last talk with F.D.R. had apparently been on 7 Sept. 1939—cf. Elmhirst to Missy LeHand, 23 Dec. 1939, PPF 4320. F.D.R. was offering similar odds in May 1939—see e.g. Langer and Gleason, *Challenge to Isolation*, p. 138.

22 Ickes, *Secret Diary*, III, 9 (entry for 16 Sept. about lunch with F.D.R. the day before).

23 E.g. Kennedy to F.D.R., Hull and Morgenthau, tel. 1873, 30 Sept. 1939, paraphrase in Morgenthau Diary, 214:213–15; Kennedy to F.D.R., 30 Sept. (letter 1), PSF (C)53: Great Britain, Kennedy; Bullitt to F.D.R. and Hull, tel. 2867, 30 Nov. 1939, *FRUS*, 1939, I, 524. For F.D.R.'s comments on Kennedy and Bullitt see Morgenthau Presidential Diary, 2: 317, 3 Oct. 1939.

24 White to Morgenthau, 5 Feb. and Puleston to Morgenthau, 18 March 1940, Morgenthau Diary, 239: 207 and 298:223.

25 Langer and Gleason's judgement still holds good: 'The only reasonable conclusion seems to be that the President considered repeal of the arms embargo a sufficient program for the moment, that he thought this measure about all the public would accept, and that he based his policy of military and economic preparedness on the belief that the Allies would be able to hold the fort in Europe at least for some time to come.' (*Challenge to Isolation*, p. 272.)

26 For more detailed discussions see ibid., pp. 280–8, 355–61; Medlicott, *Economic Blockade*, I, ch. X; Gilman, 'Economic aspects of Anglo-American relations', chs. 5–6.

27 Cf. Morgenthau Diary, 297: 74–5, 240, and 299: 18–20.

28 Moffat Diary, 12 Sept. 1939. For examples of their initial readiness to assist the British see entries for 26–27 Aug., 13, 22, 26 Sept., 19 Oct. and 6 Nov.

29 Ibid., 22 Nov. 1939.

30 Ibid., 2 Nov. 1939; on the black list see also 8 Nov. and 19 Dec. (A navicert was a certificate of clearance issued to a neutral ship at the start of its voyage by the British authorities at the port of loading. This saved it from further inspection en route.)

31 Ibid., 24 Jan. 1940. Berle Diary, 25 Jan. 1940 (quotation) and 2 Feb.

32 Moffat Diary, 24 Jan. 1940.

33 Ashton-Gwatkin, report, 17 May 1940, FO 371/25143, W8233/79/49.

34 Moffat Diary, 13 Feb. 1940. Within the State Dept. Herbert Feis took a similar view, leading Moffat and his deputy, John Hickerson, to liken him to Walter Hines Page—their ultimate censure. (Ibid., 20 Jan. 1940, and Berle Diary, 8 Dec. 1939, pp. 4–5.)

35 Lothian to FO, tel. 142, 2 Feb. 1940, FO 371/24417, C1839/285/18; Morgenthau Presidential Diary, 2: 423, 3 March 1940. It would seem that F.D.R. was not fully aware of the pressure that the State and Agric. Depts. were exerting on HMG and that he did not approve of this pressure when it was brought to his notice. (Ibid., also Morgenthau Diary, 250: 66, 2 April 1940.)

36 Morgenthau Presidential Diary, 2: 439, 12 March 1940. Morgenthau fully agreed.

37 Puleston to Morgenthau, memo, 20 Feb. 1940, Morgenthau Diary, 298: 127.

38 The main secondary accounts and interpretations are: Welles, *Time for Decision*, pp. 73–147; Langer and Gleason, *Challenge to Isolation*, ch. X, esp. pp. 361–75; Hilton, 'The Welles mission to Europe', critical of Langer and Gleason and arguing, unsuccessfully, I feel, that this was a piece of realistic statesmanship on F.D.R.'s part, which failed through no fault of his own; see also the valuable article by Offner, 'Appeasement revisited', esp. pp. 384–93. Dallek, *Roosevelt and American Foreign Policy*, pp. 215–18, is particularly good on the Welles mission. F.D.R. as usual committed little to paper and was careful in what he said to colleagues. Welles' papers remain closed and Moffat's own record— Diary, vol. 44, Section entitled 'Diary of Trip to Europe with Sumner Welles'— deliberately said nothing about Welles' secret conversations. According to the

editor of his published papers, Moffat kept a separate account of the confidential part of the visit, but this has not been traced. (Hooker, *Moffat Papers*, p. 291, n.62.) However, Berle's Diary provides valuable clues to Welles' and F.D.R.'s thinking. For background on State Dept. peace planning see Notter, *Postwar Foreign Policy Preparation*, pp. 18–28.

39 Berle Diary, 28 June 1939. The following March he complained that Britain failed to grasp that the U.S. acted for her own interests—the two were in no way Allies. 'However', he added, 'our interests may be parallel in certain respects; and there is, of course, the fundamental and underlying national interest that a German-Russian combination with megalomaniac means of world domination shall not break into the Atlantic and start corroding this Hemisphere.' (Ibid., 15 March 1940, p. 8.)

40 Berle, for instance, judged that 'undeniably' the British could maintain their blockade and the French defend the Maginot Line. Ibid., 3 March and memo of 23 March, 1940. Cf. Long, *War Diary*, 23 March 1940, pp. 71–2.

41 E.g. Berle Diary, 31 Oct. 1939, p. 7.

42 See e.g. ibid., 29 Dec. 1939, p. 1 (Welles' and Berle's support for some kind of League); cf. Long, *War Diary*, 19 Oct. 1939, p. 29, on the crucial problem of economic barriers.

43 Berle, text of speech at Yale, 31 Jan. 1940, p. 6, in PSF 94: State, Berle; and White, memo, 'A proposal for gold investment', 17 Nov. 1939, Harry D. White papers, 3/8h (Princeton).

44 Berle, memo, 'Possible study of post-war', p. 3 in Berle Diary for 8 Jan. 1940.

45 Moffat (like Berle) was kept in the dark about the Welles mission itself (cf. Moffat Diary, 13 Feb. 1940) and his own attitude is unclear. However, John Hickerson—his deputy on the European desk—was not ruling out the possibility of peace if Hitler could be removed. (Morgenthau Diary, 298: 199, 11 March 1940.) Others in the Dept. did not agree. Dunn and Hornbeck, the political advisers for Europe and the Far East respectively, considered hopes of peace to be delusory, while Hull himself had little time for the Welles mission and none at all for Welles. (Ibid., pp. 202 [Dunn] and 255 [Hornbeck]; on Hull's attitude see Hilton, 'Welles mission', p. 106.)

46 Hugh Wilson to Welles, draft tel., 29 Feb. 1940; Berle to Wilson, 1 March; Hull to Welles, 2 March; Welles to Hull, 11 March (D/S 121.840 Welles /106A–107).

47 Berle Diary, 11 Jan. 1940, p. 2.

48 This was the judgement of Herbert Feis (Stimson Diary, 29: 44–5, recording talk with Feis on 12 March); on 9 February Berle noted that Welles 'told me of the President's plan to send him to Europe—a variation on a procedure we have thought of before, since the explorations I had assumed would be carried on here'. (Diary, 9 Feb. 1940, p. 2.)

49 Offner, 'Appeasement revisited', pp. 385–6.

50 *FRUS*, 1940, I, 116–17. Cf. Bullitt to F.D.R., 18 April 1940, PSF: France, Bullitt; Ickes, *Secret Diary*, III, 216 (Bullitt on Welles) and 464–5 (Morgenthau, who told Ickes that when Welles had returned from Europe he had told Morgenthau that Mussolini was the greatest man he had ever met).

51 Long, *War Diary*, 12 March 1940, p. 64. Hilton rests much of his case for F.D.R.'s far-sightedness on the evidence of this conversation. See also note 57.

52 Welles wrote of his initial meeting with Chamberlain: 'He is one man who does not in the least look like his photographs. He is spare, but gives the impression of physical strength, and he seems much younger than his 71 years . . . In conversation one obtains none of the "puzzled hen" effect of which one hears so much, and which the photographs emphasize. The dom-

inating features are a pair of large, very dark and piercing eyes, and a low incisive voice.' (Report of 11 March, *FRUS*, 1940, I, pp. 74–5.)

53 Quotations from, respectively, Berle Diary, 13 Dec. 1939, p. 5 and 22 Dec., p. 3 (see also pp. 2, 4–5). Berle worked closely with F.D.R. on this *démarche*. For background see Flynn, *Roosevelt and Romanism*, pp. 98–115.

54 Berle Diary, 2 Feb. 1940, p. 4.

55 Lothian to Halifax, 14 Dec. 1939, FO 800/397, US/39/14. Berle Diary, 3 Dec. 1939.

56 F.D.R. to William Allen White, 14 Dec. 1939, in Roosevelt, *Personal Letters*, II, 967.

57 By then Welles had visited Rome and Berlin and had sent back gloomy reports about German intransigence. On 3 March Morgenthau recorded: 'I asked the President how the Welles thing was going and he said not so good. He said that he [Welles] did all right in Italy, but in Germany they just wanted everything. He shook his head two or three times and said "Not so good." ' (Morgenthau Presidential Diary, 2: 425, 3 March 1940.)

58 F.D.R. to White, 14 Dec. 1939.

59 See generally Levin, *Woodrow Wilson and World Politics*; the excellent article by Ambrosius, 'The orthodoxy of revisionism'; and Parsons, *Wilsonian Diplomacy*.

60 Berle Diary, 15 Nov. 1939 (first three quotations) and Berle to Upton Sinclair, 27 Dec. 1939, in diary for that date.

61 White to F.D.R., 22 Dec. 1939, White papers (LC), C-320.

62 Quotations from COS Sub-commt., 'European Appreciation', 20 Feb. 1939, CAB 16/183A, DP(P) 44; see also Hankey, memo, 12 Sept. 1939, Churchill College, Cambridge, HNKY 11/1; Gibbs, *Grand Strategy*, I, 657–67; Hancock and Gowing, *British War Economy*, esp. pp. 95ff.

63 Treasury, 'Note on the Financial Situation', 3 July 1939, CP 149 (39), CAB 24/287.

64 Cf. his comments about the Treasury paper on 5 July 1939, CAB 23/100, p 129, Cab. 36 (39) 2.

65 Chamberlain to Ida, 10 Sept. 1939, NC 18/1/1116.

66 Quotations from Chamberlain to Hilda, 8 Oct. 1939, NC 18/1/1124. For similar comments a month later see Kennedy to F.D.R. and Hull, 8 Nov. 1939, *FRUS*, 1939, I, 527.

67 Chamberlain to Ida, 23 Sept. 1939, NC 18/1/1122.

68 Cf. Cowling, *Impact of Hitler*, pp. 358–60; Woodward, *British Foreign Policy*, II, 183; MacDonald, 'Venlo incident', esp. pp. 455–6.

69 Letters to Hilda, 30 Dec. 1939 (quotation), to Ida, 13 April 1940 and to Hilda, 20 April, NC 18/1/1136, 1150 and 1151.

70 Letters to Lothian from Chatfield and Halifax, 26 and 27 Sept. 1939, FO 800/397, Ge/39/4 and 5. Cf. Milward, *War, Economy and Society*, pp. 23–30; Hinsley, *British Intelligence*, I, 63–73.

71 According to his biographer Chamberlain once told Halifax: 'Edward, we must hope for the best while preparing for the worst.' (Dilks, 'Baldwin and Chamberlain', p. 389.)

72 Hall, *North American Supply*, p. 112; for further background see pp. 105–15.

73 Sir Samuel Hoare, the Home Secretary, told Lothian that the speedy supply of machine tools from the U.S.A. was 'one of the key factors of the war'. (Hoare to Lothian, 25 Sept. 1939, Templewood papers, T/XI/5.)

74 CAB 99/3, pp. 7–8, mins. of SWC 4th mtg., 19 Dec 1939; see also Hall, *North American Supply*, pp. 118–19; Haight, *American Aid to France*, pp. 161–2.

75 Sir Frederick Phillips, min., 28 Feb. 1940, T 177/52.

76 CAB 99/3, p. 10, SWC (39/40) 5th mtg., 5 Feb. 1940. Perhaps Chamberlain was deliberately exaggerating a little. At this meeting he was marshalling every possible argument against the French plan to purchase U.S. warplanes. Typically, in different circumstances he could play a different tune. Thus, two weeks earlier, in the British Cabinet, when he was trying to stop Churchill's scheme to intervene in the Baltic without the permission of the Scandinavian neutrals, one of his arguments had been the bad effect of such action in the U.S.A., where it was 'essential to us, for financial and other reasons, to retain the support of public opinion'. (CAB 65/11, WM 16 (40) 9 C.A., 17 Jan. 1940.) As we have seen before, Chamberlain was quite capable of using the U.S.A. as an all-purpose scapegoat. Nevertheless, if one judges Chamberlain on actions as much as words, it does seem that his comments to the French provide a better indication of his views on the chances of American help than his remarks to the Cabinet.

77 PREM 1/366: Chamberlain to F.D.R., 4 Oct. and 8 Nov. 1939. For similar comments see report by Kennedy to F.D.R. and Hull, 18 Sept. 1939, *FRUS*, 1939, I, 440.

78 For background see FO to Lothian, tel. 161, 3 Feb. 1940, and BT memo, 19 Feb., FO 371/25052, W1394, W2721/2/49.

79 Joint memo, CAB 67/4, WP(G) 21 (40), 27 Jan. 1940.

80 CAB 65/5, WM 26 (40) 1, 29 Jan. For further details see Medlicott, *Economic Blockade*, I, ch. VIII; Woodward, *British Foreign Policy*, I, 147–54. The only sop to U.S. opinion was that, as the Board of Trade advised, no Italian apples were to be included in the deal.

81 Milward, *War, Economy and Society*, p. 21. Prof. Milward does not, however, apply his theoretical observation to Chamberlain's case.

82 Of course there was bitter antipathy between Chamberlain and the Liberal and Labour leaderships. But, as Paul Addison has suggested: 'Had Chamberlain been thinking in terms of another great war he would have set his course towards Coalition, with the aim of keeping events under the control of the Conservative Party. In fact, he expected a more limited war . . . Chamberlain must have imagined that, since the war was turning out to be a damp squib, it would be possible to get through it without any major upheaval in the pre-war order. The Conservatives, with at most token reinforcements from the opposition, would wind up the war on their own.' (*Road to 1945*, p. 63.)

83 Sir Patrick Hannon, Commons question, 14 Dec. 1939, *HC Debs.*, 5s, 355, col. 1321; Embassy to FO, desp. 197, 27 Feb. 1940, FO 115/3422 file 684/40.

84 E.g. Chalkley to Stirling, 27 Jan. 1940, BT 11/1401; Stirling, min., 28 March 1940, on inter-deptl. mtg. the previous day, BT 11/1411, noting views of Lindsay, then at the MEW.

85 *The Times*, 1 Feb. 1940, p. 10e. See papers in FO 371/25051, W1508, W1594/2/49; FO 371/25069, W1538, W1708/8/49.

86 See Shackle to Playfair, 11 July 1941, T160/1200, F15994/2.

87 There is a fuller discussion in Gilman, 'Economic aspects', pp. 263–303, but in my judgement he takes the State Department's suspicions too much at face value. Chamberlain's 31 Jan. speech, which Gilman seems to have overlooked, is an important piece of contrary evidence.

88 Hancock and Gowing, *British War Economy*, p. 116.

89 Harry White to Morgenthau, 21 Nov. 1939, and Glasser to White, 'Foreign Exchange Resources of England and France', 20 Nov., Morgenthau Diary, 223: 173–4, 175–82.

90 As usual Chamberlain was prone to self-righteous exaggeration—the comment about spending 'all our dollars on buying war stores' from America is non-

sense, as we have seen. Furthermore, these weekly letters to his closest relatives were a way of blowing off steam, and, as the letter makes clear, this particular week had been 'vile', with everything going wrong. (Chamberlain to Ida, 27 Jan. 1940, NC 18/1/1140.)

91 FO 371/24248: min. by Balfour, 19 Feb. 1940, A1285/434/45; mins. by Cadogan, 2 Feb. and Vansittart, 9 Feb., A1284.

92 Halifax Diary, 15 March 1940, Hickleton Papers, York, A 7.8.3, pp. 53–4. Ironside, *Diaries*, 23 Dec. 1939, p. 187; Pownall, *Diaries*, I, 290. (Ironside was Chief of the Imperial General Staff and Pownall Chief of Staff of the BEF in France.) Chatfield to Lothian, 27 Nov. 1939, Chatfield Papers, Greenwich, CHT/6/2, p. 164. Wheeler-Bennett, *George VI*, pp. 435, 436, citing diary entries for 3 and 13 March.

93 Murrow, address to CBS dinner, 2 Dec. 1941, Edward R. Murrow papers, 7-B-28, Tufts Univ., Medford, Mass. Frank Mott Gunther to F.D.R., 3 May 1940, PSF 90: State.

94 Laski to F.D.R., 5 Sept. 1939, PSF(C) 53: Great Britain, Laski.

95 See papers in FO 371/24246, file 301; for further details see Reynolds, *Lothian*, part II.

96 Chatfield to Lothian, 27 Nov. 1939, CHT/6/2, p. 166.

97 Chatham House, memo PAU 2, on U.S. unofficial opinion on peace aims from 1 Sept. 1939 to 15 Feb. 1940, 1 May 1940, copy in BLPES, misc. coll. 515/2.

98 Cadogan, *Diaries*, 24 Jan. 1940, p. 249; cf. Moffat Diary, 27 Feb. on similar fears by D'Arcy Osborne, British Minister to the Vatican.

99 FO 371/24418, C2124/285/18, mins. by Scott, 7 Feb. 1940, and Cadogan, 9 Feb.

100 Mins. by Scott, Sargent and Cadogan, all 7 Feb. 1940, FO 371/24238, A1309/131/45.

101 CAB 65/6, WM 58 (40) 6, 2 March 1940. Hankey recalled that no special military information had been given to House in the spring of 1915, but some Cabinet ministers had talked freely—perhaps too freely—about military questions.

102 FO to Lothian, tel. 499, 1 April 1940, FO 371/25139, W4893/79/49 (based on inter-departmental consultation).

103 Supplementary Note by Charles Corbin (French Ambassador in London), 6 March 1940, PREM 4/25/2, p. 94; see generally material in pp. 69–70, 92–9. At a similar point in the Great War—December 1916—President Wilson had made public his doubts about Britain's financial position—with disastrous short-term results for British credit in the U.S.A. Part of Wilson's intention in so acting was to make Britain less able to wage war, and therefore more amenable to his own peace efforts. (Burk, 'The diplomacy of finance', pp. 357–9.) The episode may well have been in the minds of British leaders in early 1940.

104 Chamberlain to Lothian for F.D.R., 4 March 1940, PSF 96: State: Welles 1940 (1).

105 Chamberlain told Lothian he feared 'that what the President now proposes is precisely what Hitler hoped he would do'. (Tel. 173, 4 Feb. 1940, FO 371/24417, C1839/285/18.) Cf. Colville Diary, 6 Feb. 1940, quoted in Colville, *Footprints in Time*, pp. 143–4.

106 Chamberlain to Lothian for F.D.R., 7 February 1940, PSF 96: State: Welles, 1940 (1).

107 Cf. Lothian to Chamberlain, 6 Feb. 1940, tel. 160, FO 371/24417, C1987/285/18.

108 Kennedy to Hull, tel., 9 March 1940, D/S 121.840 Welles /108. CAB 65/6,

WM 67 (40) 7, 13 March 1940. Vansittart, min., 18 March 1940, FO 371/24406, C3949/89/18.

109 Halifax Diary, 11 March 1940, Hickleton Papers, A7.8.3, p. 46. This conclusion, coming from Chamberlain, was not necessarily a great compliment to Welles (Chamberlain to Ida, 16 March 1940, NC 18/1/1147). For Welles' favourable reactions to Chamberlain see above, note 52.

110 Ibid.; FO to Lothian, tel. 472, 27 March 1940, FO 371/24407, C4564/89/18.

111 Notes for the King, n.d., FO 800/324, H/XXXVII/64; cf. Welles' account of their meeting, 11 March, in PSF 9: Welles Reports, 1940. See also his published report, 11 March 1940, in *FRUS*, 1940, I, 77 (Chamberlain) and 79–80.

112 Moffat Diary, vol. 44, 13 March 1940, pp. 35–8. Lothian had warned the FO that Moffat should not be neglected: Lothian to Scott, tel. 283, 29 Feb. 1940, FO 800/324, H/XXXVII/59.

113 Cadogan, *Diaries*, 23 Feb. and 30 April 1940, pp. 255, 275.

114 House of Commons, 5 Oct. 1938, in Churchill, *Speeches*, p. 6006. The standard studies are: Robert Rhodes James, *Churchill: A Study in Failure*, the single-volume biography by Henry Pelling, *Winston Churchill*, and the inter-war volume of the official biography by Martin Gilbert, *Winston S. Churchill*, vol. V, *1922–1939*.

115 See his speech formally moving that Chamberlain be elected the new party leader, Caxton House, Westminster, 31 May 1937, in *Speeches*, pp. 5856–7.

116 House of Commons, 22 Feb. 1938, in *Speeches*, esp. pp. 5915–16.

117 Speech cited in note 114, pp. 6004–13.

118 He stressed his support again in March. See Ramsden, *History of the Conservative Party*, pp. 366, 368. According to Churchill, throughout his premiership and even in the crisis of 1940, he was never unable to sleep, but on the night when he heard of Eden's resignation sleep deserted him and, as the dawn crept through the windows, he saw before him 'in mental gaze the vision of Death'. Churchill, *Second World War*, I, 201.

119 Quotation from speech of 21 June 1939 in *Speeches*, p. 6139; see also ibid., esp. p. 6091 (3 April) and p. 6142 (28 June). Chamberlain to Ida, 15 April 1939, NC 18/1/1094. On N.C.'s reluctance to include W.S.C. see above, ch. 2(a), note 14.

120 Churchill to Chamberlain, 9 Oct. 1939, PREM 1/395.

121 Quotations from *Speeches*, p. 6199 (Broadcast, 30 March 1940), p. 6188 (Speech, Manchester, 27 Jan.). On Churchill and the Phoney War see esp. Addison, *Road to 1945*, ch. III; Marder, 'Winston is back'; Dilks, 'The twilight war'. For a definitive account we must await the sixth volume of Martin Gilbert's biography.

122 Churchill to Halifax, 15 Jan. and 14 March 1940, FO 800/328, Hal/40/3 and /11.

123 'To end war', *Colliers*, 29 June 1935, in Churchill, *Collected Essays*, I, 347–53.

124 Winston S. Churchill, *The World Crisis: The Aftermath* (London, 1929), p. 450.

125 Broadcast to U.S.A., 16 Oct. 1938, in *Speeches*, p. 6016. Moffat Diary, 8 Dec. 1939.

126 Perkins, *The Great Rapprochement*, p. 94.

127 'The Union of the English-Speaking Peoples', *News of the World*, 15 May 1938, in *Collected Essays*, IV, 435–42, quoting from p. 438.

128 For 1939 examples see William S. Wasserman, memo of interview with Churchill, 10 Feb. 1939, PSF 73: Agriculture Dept., 1939–44; Churchill, 'Bombs don't scare us now', *Colliers*, 17 June 1939, in *Collected Essays*, I, 453; Churchill to Lothian, 24 Sept. 1939, FO 800/397, Ge/39/2.

129 Costigliola, 'Anglo-American financial rivalry in the 1920s', pp. 924–7; Hogan, *Informal Entente*, pp. 218–20; Gilbert, *Churchill*, pp. 304–5, 308.

130 James Scrymgeour-Wedderburn, Diary, 21 Sept. 1928, quoted in Gilbert, *Churchill*, p. 301.
131 Churchill to Marshall Diston, 3 Oct. 1937, and to Linlithgow, 3 Nov. 1937, in Gilbert, *Churchill*, pp. 871, 886.
132 F.D.R. to Churchill, 11 Sept. 1939, ADM 199/1928/5. The principal account of the Roosevelt–Churchill relationship is Lash, *Roosevelt and Churchill*. Their correspondence during the Phoney War is discussed in Leutze, 'The secret of the Churchill–Roosevelt correspondence'. A selection of the messages is printed in Loewenheim, Langley and Jonas (eds.), *Roosevelt and Churchill: Their Secret Wartime Correspondence*, and a comprehensive edition of the correspondence, prepared by Warren Kimball, will be published in 1982. His own general survey of the relationship is Kimball, 'Churchill and Roosevelt'. Most of the original messages for 1939–42 are either in FDRL, Map Room papers, boxes 1, 2 and 7a, or in PRO, PREM 3/467–470 (citations usually from latter collection).
133 F.D.R. to Chamberlain, 11 Sept. 1939, PREM 1/366. Churchill to Chamberlain, 4 Oct. 1939, NC 7/9/64.
134 Freidel, *Roosevelt*, I, 354; Sherwood, *Roosevelt and Hopkins*, pp. 350–1; Churchill, *Second World War*, I, 345, where Churchill claims to have been struck in 1918 by F.D.R.'s 'magnificent presence in all his youth and strength'. Cf. ch. 8(d), and note 87. There is some evidence that F.D.R. bore a grudge against W.S.C. for snubbing him at this first meeting. According to Joe Kennedy's unpublished memoirs Roosevelt said in Dec. 1939: 'I have always disliked him [Churchill] since the time I went to England in 1918. He acted like a stinker at a dinner I attended, lording it all over us.' Similarly, Kennedy claims that in Dec. 1940 F.D.R. told him that Churchill was 'one of the few men in public life who was rude to me'. (Beschloss, *Kennedy and Roosevelt*, pp. 200, 230.) Although Kennedy is not a reliable witness, his claim that F.D.R. spoke in this vein on two separate occasions cannot be lightly dismissed. Cf. ch. 7(b), and notes 53–7.
135 This point is stressed and developed in Watt, 'Roosevelt and Neville Chamberlain', esp. pp. 186–7.
136 Willert, *Washington and Other Memories*, p. 215. Willert did not include this in the memo he made at the time about the conversations (Willert papers, 14/61), but this may not be surprising since the memo was prepared for the British Government. Ovendale, '*Appeasement*', p. 318, concludes that 'Roosevelt had a high regard for Chamberlain'. This judgement seems to be based particularly on F.D.R.'s profession of 'real friendship' for Chamberlain, expressed to Arthur Murray in the winter of 1938–39 (cf. ibid., p. 202). However, as Murray's correspondence shows, British and American leaders always said the nicest things about each other in their letters to him, knowing full well he would pass the compliments on (Elibank papers, Mss. 8809, esp. pp. 105–40). Similarly, Welles told Chamberlain in March 1940 of F.D.R.'s deep admiration for him—Chamberlain to Ida, 16 March 1940, NC 18/1/1147—but I remain doubtful that such remarks, given their context, can be taken at face value.
137 Cf. Elliott Roosevelt and James Brough, *A Rendezvous with Destiny*, p. 230: 'As a practitioner of the arts of persuasion, Father wanted the welcome he planned for the King and Queen of England to act as a symbol of American affinity for a country whose present political leadership he did not trust.' Kennedy later claimed that in Dec. 1939 F.D.R. said he was cultivating Churchill 'because there is a strong possibility that he will become the prime minister and I want to get my hand in now'. (Beschloss, *Kennedy*, p. 200.)

138 Lash, *Roosevelt and Churchill*, p. 23.

139 Pound to Churchill and Churchill to Pound, 7 Sept. 1939, ADM 116/3922, pp. 254, 255.

140 CAB 65/3, WM 38 (39) 11, C.A., 5 Oct. 1939; Churchill to Pound, 16 Oct. 1939, ADM 199/1928/5.

141 Chamberlain to F.D.R., 4 Oct. and 8 Nov. 1939, PREM 1/366. Just before the war began Chamberlain asked the U.S. to release the Norden bomb sight for the RAF (Chamberlain to F.D.R., 25 Aug. 1939, PSF 46: Great Britain, 1939); he also sent two messages when informed about the Welles mission. The second mentioned the top secret British plan to send an expeditionary force to Finland (Chamberlain to Lothian for F.D.R., 4 and 7 Feb. 1940, PSF 96: State Dept.—Welles, 1940 [1]). See also Chamberlain to F.D.R., 13 March 1940, NC 7/11/33/142.

142 Cf. Lothian to FO, tels. 635 and 775, 19 Oct. and 17 Nov. 1939, FO 371/22764, A8146/5992/51.

143 Scott, min., 17 Oct. 1939, FO 371/22817, p. 269; cf. Koskoff, *Kennedy*, pp. 210–21.

144 FO 371/24248: Halifax to Churchill, 19 Jan. 1940, A434/434/45.

145 Ibid.: Churchill to F.D.R., 29 Jan. 1940 and mins. by Perowne and Scott, A711/434/45; Churchill to F.D.R., 30 Jan., A747.

146 Halifax Diary, 18 March 1940, Hickleton Mss., York, A 7.8.3, p. 56. A propos of the Churchill–Eden relationship it is interesting to note that in Feb. 1940 Churchill 'said he would rather have Chamberlain than Eden as Prime Minister by eight to one'. (King, *With Malice Toward None*, p. 22, 8 Feb. 1940, recording dinner party at the Churchills'.)

147 See esp. FO 371/25138, W2741, W2742/79/49.

148 Quotations from min. of 29 Feb. 1940, FO 371/24238, A1857/131/45.

149 Ibid., A1190, min. of 20 Feb. 1940.

150 Cadogan, min. [between 19 and 27 Nov. 1939], FO 800/317, p. 230.

151 Mins. of 25 Nov. 1939, FO 371/22818, pp. 15 and 176. In the latter he remarked: 'America seems to have put her money on us . . . It is too much to hope that America will contribute effectively any more to us winning than I can to the unambitious quadrupeds that I occasionally select.'

152 To FO/A he commented: 'I agree it is the business of the FO to put the American case before the other [Whitehall] Depts., and we must certainly do the best we can. But there are great difficulties, e.g. it is probably a fact that Italy *has* a potential nuisance value, at the moment, greater than that of the U.S.' (Min., 28 Jan. 1940, FO 371/25052, W1508/2/49.)

153 Mins. of 29 Feb. 1940, FO 371/24238, A1857 and 1 March 1940, FO 371/24248, A1285/434/45.

154 Moffat Diary, vol. 44, pp. 30, 32–5, 11 and 12 March.

155 Frank Ashton-Gwatkin, report, 17 May 1940, FO 371/25143, W8233/79/49. Cf. this emotional note from Beaverbrook to Churchill, 13 Dec. 1939: 'U.S.A. assistance, even in money and arms, to Scandinavia is far far more important to us than support from the Balkans, or sympathy in Italy. Is there any means of convincing Mr. Chamberlain or Lord Halifax? God help England.' (Beaverbrook papers, C/86.)

156 CAB 65/1, WM 19 (39) 2, 18 Sept. 1939; Hall, *North American Supply*, p. 116. The programme involved orders for 16 destroyers, 70 corvettes and 136 smaller vessels. It would have cost $132 million in the U.S.A. alone, most of it to be spent in the first year of the war.

157 CAB 99/3, pp. 20–1, SWC (39/40) 6th mtg., 28 March 1940; Haight, *American*

*Aid*, pp. 188–93, 217–19; Hall, *North American Supply*, pp. 116–24; Sayers, *Financial Policy*, p. 365.

158 £150 million from gold and foreign currency reserves, £70–80 million from the sale of easily-marketable overseas securities. Hancock and Gowing, *British War Economy*, pp. 115–16.

159 For instance: on 29 Feb. Chamberlain vetoed Churchill's plan to mine Norwegian territorial waters—taking what for him was the unusual step of speaking first and at length in order to kill it. One of the arguments he used was the danger that anti-British elements in the U.S.A. would exploit the mining—treating it either 'as an attack on neutral rights which might later prejudice their own interests' or as a snub to F.D.R. if it coincided with the Welles peace mission. (CAB 65/5, WM 55 (40) 1, 29 Feb. 1940.) Yet Lothian's assessment of the likely effect of mining on U.S. opinion, which Halifax had specially requested and which had been read to the Cabinet a few days before, had been non-committal. Americans, thought Lothian, might consider it an infringement of neutral rights *or* as a vigorous action of the sort needed to win the war. Much depended on how it was presented and justified. (Lothian to FO, tel. 257, 23 Feb., summarized for Cabinet in ibid., WM 50 (40) 1, 23 Feb.) Furthermore, back in December at a meeting of ministers when he was anxious to counter incipient criticism of HMG's passivity, Chamberlain brusquely rejected the suggestion that the Government remained inactive out of deference to neutral opinion. 'The Prime Minister said that we were certainly not deterred from more vigorous action by the fear of its effect on America.' (Mins. of mtg. of ministers, 7 Dec. 1939, FO 800/309, p. 104.)

160 For recent accounts of the Scandinavian question see Parker, 'Britain, France and Scandinavia, 1939–1940', and a special issue of the *Scandinavian Jnl. of History*, 2, 1977, esp. articles by Bédarida, 'France, Britain and the Nordic countries', Dilks, 'Great Britain and Scandinavia in the "Phoney War"' and Loock, '*Weserubung*—A step towards a Greater Germanic Reich'. I incline towards Dr. Parker's reading of Chamberlain's motives.

161 Mins. by Whitehead and Cadogan, 7 and 8 May 1940, FO 371/24239, A3171/131/45. Whitehead was the son of Alfred North Whitehead, the distinguished British philosopher, and he had been a professor of business psychology at Harvard during the 1930s. He returned to England at the beginning of the war and was recruited by Scott into FO/A early in 1940.

162 Long, *War Diary*, 15 March 1940, pp. 65–6 (Hull); Morgenthau Presidential Diaries, 2: 452, 31 March 1940. Morgenthau Diary, 250: 65, 2 April 1940.

163 Column for 19 April 1940, quoted in Grafton, *An American Diary*, p. 50.

164 Morgenthau Presidential Diaries, 2: 457, 10 April 1940. (The State Dept. was similarly incredulous: Berle Diary, 9 April, p. 8 and 11 April, p. 3.) Morgenthau Presidential Diaries, 2: 471, 29 April 1940. On 3 May F.D.R. told Stimson that Allied aircraft orders remained 'very disappointingly low'. (Stimson Diary, 29: 50, 8 May 1940.)

165 Johnson, *Battle Against Isolation*, p. 63, quoting from White editorial of mid-March. When Welles was in London, according to Björn Prytz, the Swedish Minister there, he had indicated 'that a British Government which included Liberals and Labour would go down better, and be more trusted, in neutral countries including the U.S.A.'. (Crozier, *Off the Record*, 30 March 1940, pp. 157–8.)

**Chapter Four**

1 W.S.C. to Smuts, tel. 209, 10 June 1940, PREM 4/43/B/1, p. 440; Halifax to Lothian, tel. 481, 13 May 1940, FO 371/24239, A3242. For sources of

epigraphs to Part Two see note 28 and Butterworth to Morgenthau, 13 Dec. 1940, Morgenthau Diary, 339:401.

2 Recent accounts, on which this paragraph draws, are Bell, *A Certain Eventuality*; Bond, *France and Belgium, 1939–1940*, which ends rather strangely at Dunkirk; Shlaim, 'Prelude to downfall: the British offer of Union to France, June 1940'.

3 E.g. Stolfi, 'Equipment for victory in France in 1940'.

4 In Wheeler-Bennett (ed.), *Action this Day*, p. 49.

5 Butler, *Grand Strategy*, II, pp. 180–1; Schoenfeld, *The War Ministry of Winston Churchill*, pp. 50–2.

6 Cf. Sir Ronald Lindsay (Paris) to Cadogan, 25 May 1940, FO 794/18, reporting comments of Bill Bullitt on Lothian's work in Washington.

7 Hall, *North American Supply*, ch.V, provides an excellent account of the supply crisis that summer.

8 FO to Lothian, tel. 870, 25 May 1940, FO 371/25142, W8010.

9 Hall, *North American Supply*, pp. 146–9; cf. FO 371/25143, W8408.

10 Monnet to Churchill, 20 May 1940, CAB 85/77.

11 WM 116 (40) 1, 9 May 1940, CAB 65/7.

12 Moffat, memo of conversation with F. R. Hoyer Millar (1st Secretary at the Embassy), 25 May 1940, D/S 841.51/1573; Merle Cochran, memo of phone conversation with Jerry Pinsent (Financial Secretary at the Embassy), 30 May, Morgenthau Diary, 267: 324; W.S.C. to F.D.R., 15 May, F.D.R. to W.S.C., 16 May 1940, PREM 3/468, pp. 208–9, 201–3.

13 Mins. by Scott, Halifax and Cadogan, 17 May 1940, FO 371/25142, W7890.

14 E.g. memo by Chancellor of Exchequer, 24 June 1940, WP (40) 218, CAB 66/8.

15 Bridges to Monnet, 21 May 1940, CAB 85/77; mins. of SWC (39/40) 13th mtg., p. 12, 31 May 1940, CAB 99/3.

16 For these changes, see Hancock and Gowing, *British War Economy*, pp. 93–4.

17 COS memo, 25 May 1940, 'British Strategy in a Certain Eventuality', WP (40) 168, CAB 66/7, para. 1. Italics in original.

18 COS *aide-mémoire* for Lothian, 13 June 1940, WP (40) 203, CAB 66/8; approved by Cabinet WM 166 (40) 10, 14 June, CAB 65/7.

19 FO 371/24239, A3242: min. by Scott, 28 Feb. 1940, including reference to Tweedsmuir's views, mins. by Cadogan and Halifax, 27 and 28 Feb.

20 See papers in FO 371/24228 and /24229, esp. A2033 and A3297.

21 FO 371/24239, A3171, Scott to Lothian, tel. 1003, 5 June 1940; A3316: circular tel. 237 to Dominion PMs, 7 June, Lothian to FO, tels. 922 and 931, 6 and 8 June, Smuts to Dominions Office, tel., 7 June. (Two weeks later, as Scott pointed out, Smuts took a diametrically opposite view, arguing that Britain wanted no more than benevolent U.S. neutrality. Smuts to Churchill, tel. 329, 22 June 1940, and Scott, min., 25 June, FO 371/25206, W8576.) WM 159 (40) 8, 9 June 1940, CAB 65/7; Churchill to Dominions Secretary, 9 June 1940, PREM 4/43B/1, p. 454.

22 Scott, min., 9 June 1940, A3316; Hankey to Lothian, 26 July 1940, FO 800/398, U.S./40/16.

23 Report by COS Joint Planning Sub-Commt., COS (40) 456 (JP), 13 June 1940, CAB 80/13.

24 COS (40) 496 (JP), 27 June 1940, para 29, CAB 80/13.

25 Whitehead, min., 8 June 1940, A3316; W.S.C. to F.D.R., 15 June 1940, PREM 3/468/126–7.

26 For a good statement from outside Whitehall, see the book by the veteran Labour intellectual H. N. Brailsford, *From England to America*, pp. 92–6. This was written in July.

27 FO 371/25206, W8602/8602/49, Cripps to FO, tels. 384 and 385, 29 June 1940; later circulated to Cabinet (CAB 66/10, WP (40) 310, 8 Aug. 1940).

28 W8602: esp. mins. by Whitehead, Balfour and Nichols, 2 July, by Clarke, 3 July and by Cadogan, 5 July; Halifax to Hankey 15 July 1940.

29 Halifax to Lothian, 27 Sept. 1939, FO 800/324, H/XXXVII/29.

30 Hankey to Hoare, 19 July 1940, Templewood papers, XIII/17; Lothian to Sir Abe Bailey, 1 July 1940, Lothian papers, 398: 465. See also Cairns, 'A nation of shopkeepers', pp. 742–3, and Thomas, *Britain and Vichy*, pp. 38–9.

31 Butler, min., 8 July 1940, W8602. On 'Atlanticism' see Watt, *Personalities and Policies*, p. 212.

32 For recent accounts of the political crisis, and the situation that summer, see Addison, *Road to 1945*, pp. 91-102, 104–12; Calder, *The People's War*, pp. 93–101; Cowling, *Impact of Hitler*, ch. 13; Dilks, 'Twilight war', pp. 78–86; Ramsden, *History of the Conservative Party*, pp. 371–6. For a detailed analysis of the Commons vote of 8 May, see Rasmussen, 'Party discipline in war-time'.

33 Fortunately, of course. Halifax was well aware that he could never have been an inspiring national leader, with his reserved manner and circumlocutory prose. As Angus Calder remarks: 'It is pleasant to imagine him saying, "This, on the whole, seems to have been their finest hour." ' Calder, *People's War*, p. 93.

34 W.S.C. to Chamberlain, 10 May 1940, NC 7/9/80. Interestingly, Chamberlain seems to have entertained hopes, until the onset of his fatal illness, of resuming the premiership after the war. (Cf. Chamberlain Diary, 9 Sept. 1940, NC 2/24A.)

35 Cecil King, diary record of talk with Churchill on evening of 7 June 1940, in King, *With Malice Toward None*, p. 50 (quoted by k nd permission of Sidgwick and Jackson, Ltd.). Generally see ibid., pp. 47–53 and Chamberlain Diary, 10 and 11 June 1940, NC 2/24A.

36 Cf. Dilks, 'Twilight war', pp. 85–6; Bracken to Hoare, 4 Aug. 1940, Templewood papers, XIII/17.

37 Chamberlain Diary, 19 and 15 May 1940, NC 2/24A.

38 Halifax Diary, 25 May 1940, Hickleton papers York), A 7.8.4., p. 139; Kennedy to Hull, tel. 1344, 24 May 1940, D/S 740.0011 EW 1939/ 3005 7/10.

39 Halifax, memo, c.25 May 1940, copy in Hickleton papers (Cambridge), A4.410.4.1. On 7 Dec. 1939 Halifax had told the Cabinet that 'if the French Government wanted to make peace, we should not be able to carry on the war by ourselves'. (Thomas, *Britain and Vichy*, pp. 7–8, 13.)

40 Halifax Diary, 27 May 1940, A 7.8.4, p. 142; Cadogan, *Diaries*, 27 May, p. 291. The fullest published accounts of these discussions are in Bell, *Certain Eventuality*, pp. 38–48, in Woodward, *British Foreign Policy*, I, pp. 197–208 and Barker, *Churchill and Eden*, pp. 140–6. The records are in the Confidential Annexes, CAB 65/13, WM 139 (40) 1, WM 140 (40) on 26 May, a.m. and p.m., WM 142 (40) on 27 May p.m., and WM 145 (40) 1 on 28 May p.m. In addition, there is an important and unique record of the meeting between Churchill, Halifax, Chamberlain, Attlee and Reynaud from 2.30 to 4.30 on 26 May in Chamberlain Diary for that date.

41 When talking to Kennedy on 23 May (see above, note 38) Halifax dismissed Mussolini as having no influence on Hitler. His change of view may have been caused by subsequent indications that the Italians might be ready to act as intermediaries.

42 WM 142 (40) C.A., 27 May 1940, CAB 65/13 p. 180.

43 Chamberlain Diary, 26 May 1940, NC 2/24A.

44 Dalton Diary, 28 May 1940, vol. 22, pp. 92–4. See also Dalton, *The Fateful*

*Years*, pp. 335–6, Churchill, *Second World War*, II, 87–8, and the account given by Malcolm MacDonald to Halifax five years later recorded in Halifax, *Fulness of Days*, p. 222.

45 Cadogan, *Diaries*, 27 May 1940, pp. 290–1; Chamberlain Diary, 28 May 1940, NC 2/24A; Dalton Diary, 28 May 1940, 22: 93. Bond, *France and Belgium*, pp. 159–67. Hinsley *et al.*, *British Intelligence*, I, 166–7.

46 T 160/1054, F17657/011, esp. Phillips to Kingsley Wood, 26 May 1940, with Wood's annotations.

47 CAB 65/7, WM 141 (40) 9, 27 May 1940.

48 Halifax to Duke of Buccleuch, 24 July 1940, Hickleton papers (Cambridge), A 4.410.33.1; Birkenhead, *Halifax*, p. 460. Chamberlain Diary, 10, 15, 19, 22 July 1940, NC 2/24A.

49 Woodward, *British Foreign Policy*, I, 204, note 1.

50 Halifax Diary, 6 June 1940, A7.8.4., p. 155; Churchill, draft reply to King Gustav of Sweden, 3 Aug. 1940, PREM 4/100/3, p. 131.

51 Addison, 'Lloyd George and compromise peace in the Second World War', p. 382.

52 Memo of meeting on 16 July 1940, esp. paras. 7 and 8, enclsd. in Richard Stokes to Lloyd George, 17 July, in Lloyd George papers (HLRO), G/19/3/12.

53 Lloyd George, memo, 12 Sept. 1940, Lloyd George papers, G/81. For his general position see the essay by Addison, cited in note 51; also Rowland, *Lloyd George*, esp. pp. 763–6, 779.

54 See Addison, 'Lloyd George', pp. 372–5; Dilks, 'Twilight war', pp. 82–4; Rowland, *Lloyd George*, pp. 770, 773–4, 775–7; A. J. Sylvester, Diary, in *Life with Lloyd George*, pp. 260–70; Chamberlain Diary, esp. 31 May, 4–7 and 10 June 1940, NC 2/24A.

55 Chamberlain Diary, 28 May, 11, 15, 18 June 1940; Sylvester Diary, 3 Oct. 1940, in *Life with Lloyd George*, p. 281. Cf. Lloyd George to Frances Stevenson, 4 Oct. 1940, in *My Darling Pussy*, pp. 237–9.

56 At the meeting on 11 June Churchill stated that, in the British view, the attack on Britain, when it came, 'would in all probability bring in the United States, who were already near the point of intervention'. CAB 99/3, SWC (39/40) 13th mtg., 31 May, p. 12 and 14th mtg., 11 June 1940, p.5. For earlier discussion of W.S.C.'s views see ch. 3(d).

57 CAB 65/7, WM 165 (40) 1, 13 June 1940. Even Chamberlain considered this a reasonable interpretation. (Chamberlain Diary, 13 June 1940, NC 2/24A.) F.D.R.'s message to Reynaud, 13 June 1940, is printed in annex I to WM 165.

58 W.S.C. to F.D.R., 14 June 1940, PREM 3/468, pp. 152–4; Halifax Diary, 13 June, A 7.8.4, pp. 167–8.

59 Dalton Diary, 28 May 1940, 22: 93. W.S.C. to Smuts, tel. 209, 10 June 1940, and W.S.C., circular tel. to Dominions PMs, 16 June, PREM 4/43B/1, pp. 440, 278. Churchill, *Secret Session Speeches*, p.15. Charles de Gaulle, *War Memoirs: I, The Call to Honour, 1940–1942*, tr. by Jonathan Griffin (London, 1955), p. 108.

60 See discussion in Hinsley *et al.*, *British Intelligence*, I, 232–48.

61 Whitehead to Myron P. Gilmore (Harvard), 22 and 27 June 1940. I am grateful to the late Prof. Gilmore for allowing me to read these letters from his father-in-law.

62 See comments on 26 May, CAB 65/13, pp. 148, 149.

63 He did not conceal this confidence from American observers. E.g. Kennedy to Hull, tel. 1603, 12 June 1940, *FRUS*, 1940, III, p. 37: 'Churchill said quite definitely to me he expects the United States will be in right after the election; that when the people in the United States see the towns and cities of England,

after which so many American towns have been named, bombed and destroyed they will line up and want war.'

64 E.g. Perowne, min. on tel. 950, 19 June, FO 371/24234, A3223/39/45. Nicolson to Vita Sackville-West, 19 June 1940, in Nicolson, *Diaries and Letters*, II, 96.

65 Warner R. Schilling *et al.*, *Strategy, Politics and Defense Budgets* (New York, 1962), p. 6.

66 Baruch to Walter Lippmann, 30 April 1940, Lippmann papers, 55/178 (Yale University).

67 E.g. Barron, *Leadership in Crisis*, pp. 61–2. This also seems to be the view of Lash, *Roosevelt and Churchill*, e.g. pp. 153, 167.

68 See discussions in Blum, *Morgenthau Diaries*, II, 138–58; Pogue, *Marshall*, II, ch. 3; Leighton and Coakley, *Global Logistics*, pp. 32–6. Churchill considered the rifle shipments so important that he gave them special protection in the Western Approaches, even though this meant weakening the anti-invasion patrols off the East Coast. (See PREM 3/372/1, pp. 18–20.)

69 Roosevelt, *Public Papers*, IX, 1940, 259–64.

70 Berle Diary, 2/629, 15 May 1940. Cf. Joseph E. Davies to F.D.R., 23 May 1940, PSF 90: State Dept., 1940 (1), predicting that short of a miracle Britain and France would be occupied or destroyed that summer.

71 Berle Diary, 10 June 1940, 2/696 (Welles); Long, *War Diary*, 13 June 1940, pp. 104–5.

72 McFarland, *Woodring*, ch. 12; War Dept. memo, 22 May 1940, D/S 740.0011 EW 1939/3168½.

73 Lash, *Roosevelt and Churchill*, p. 128.

74 See Kimball, *The Most Unsordid Act*, p. 59 (Knox); Stimson and Bundy, *On Active Service*, pp. 318–20; Ickes, *Secret Diary*, III, 209, 15 June 1940; Morgenthau Diary, 397: 301A, 14 May 1941.

75 On the evening of 16 May F.D.R. approved a further French aircraft order. 'Work it out in swap', he told Morgenthau, meaning that the French should be allowed to buy planes currently in service with the Air Corps while releasing for the U.S. their own orders scheduled for delivery in July. Then, according to Morgenthau: 'He said after all we will not be in it for *60 or 90 days*.' (Morgenthau Presidential Diary, 3: 545—emphasis in original.) For F.D.R.'s earlier comments see above chs. 1(f) and 3(b), esp. sources cited in ch. 1, note 147 and ch. 3, notes 18–22.

76 Lothian to FO, tel. 834, 26 May 1940, PREM 3/463, p. 189, reporting a conversation with F.D.R. the previous evening. Cf. Berle Diary, 21 Sept. 1939, p. 3 and 22 Sept., p. 2 (Azores); and the earlier comments cited in the previous note.

77 His comments to Morgenthau on 16 May were made just before the gravity of the French position became apparent. For his earlier views on the character of the war see above chs. 2(b) and 3(b).

78 Lothian to FO, tels. 1007 and 1006, 16 June 1940, FO 371/24311, C7294/65/17.

79 Sherwood, *Roosevelt and Hopkins*, pp. 143–4; Kimball, *The Most Unsordid Act*, p. 51; cf. Divine, *Roosevelt and World War II*, pp. 32–7.

80 Matloff and Snell, *Strategic Planning*, I, 13–14; Morgenthau Presidential Diary, 3: 585, 17 June, 1940.

81 Lothian to FO, tel. 1135, 27 June 1940, PREM 3/476/10, p. 531; James A. Farley, *Jim Farley's Story: The Roosevelt Years* (New York, 1948), pp. 244–5, 253. Cf. Lash, *Roosevelt and Churchill*, p. 167 and Langer and Gleason, *Challenge to Isolation*, p. 713, n. 10. Lamont to Lothian, 7 Aug. 1940, Lamont papers, 105–12 (Harvard Business School), in which he refers to the lack of confidence in Britain and says: 'I believe that even F.D.R. has been affected

by such talk.' In late July White believed that, since winning the nomination, F.D.R. 'had, as it were, lost his cud'. (Johnson, *Battle Against Isolation*, p. 100.) On 25 July F.D.R. estimated Britain's chances at about fifty-fifty. (Leutze, *Bargaining for Supremacy*, p. 141, and also p. 290, note 53.)

82 E.g. Kennedy to Hull, tels. 1211, 1579, 2535, dated 15 May, 10 June and 2 Aug. 1940, D/S 740.0011 EW 1939/2952, 3487⅕, 4929¾.

83 Leighton and Coakley, *Global Logistics*, pp. 34–5.

84 Watson, *Chief of Staff*, pp. 110–13. Cf. Moffat Diary, 2 July 1940.

85 See Langer and Gleason, *Challenge to Isolation*, pp. 521–2 and Schwar, 'Interventionist Propaganda', pp. 277–8.

86 It should be remembered that David Walsh was a prominent Irish-American politician and one of the leaders of the Democratic coalition in Massachusetts, whose support would be essential for bringing in the vote in the November election. See Lyle W. Dorsett, *Franklin D. Roosevelt and the City Bosses* (Port Washington, N.Y., 1977), ch. 2.

87 On Roosevelt's thinking see Lash, *Roosevelt and Churchill*, chs. 7 and 10, esp. pp. 114–16, 168–70.

88 See Ross, 'Roosevelt's third-term nomination'.

89 Quoted in Langer and Gleason, *Challenge to Isolation*, p. 597.

90 Berle Diary, 18 May 1940. Kennedy to F.D.R., 2 Nov. 1939, PSF(C) 53: GB, Kennedy.

91 Kennedy to F.D.R., 20 July 1939, ibid.; Welles, report, 12 March 1940, PSF(S) 9: Welles Reports, 1940. Welles began: 'When I was shown into his office Mr. Churchill was sitting in front of the fire, smoking a 24-inch cigar and drinking a whiskey and soda. It was quite obvious that he had consumed a good many whiskeys before I arrived.' Churchill then treated Welles to a speech lasting one hour and fifty minutes 'in the course of which he became quite sober'. (These passages are omitted from the text published in *FRUS*, 1940, I, 82–3.)

Through the U.S. Embassy the FO learned indirectly that Welles had said that Churchill was one of the most fascinating personalities he had ever met. The question was then raised—should Churchill be so informed? Cadogan, acerbic as ever, thought not: 'I feel some delicacy about asking the S[ecretary] of S[tate] (or the P.M.) to authorise our telling Mr. Churchill that he made a unique impression on Mr. Welles. I take comfort from the fact that Mr. C. will already have that conviction, so nothing is lost.' (Min., 30 March 1940, FO 371/24407, C4618/89/18.)

92 Berle Diary, 5 May 1940. (Again this passage is only reproduced in part in the published version of Berle's diaries—cf. *Navigating the Rapids*, p. 310.)

93 Ickes Diary, 12 May 1940, vol. 31, p. 4380 (LC). In the published *Secret Diary*, III, 176, this extract ends with the words 'that England had', and there is no indication that words have been omitted. (Cf. ch. 3, note 134.)

When F.D.R. met the Canadian premier in April, the two gossiped about Churchill being 'tight most of the time'. (Granatstein, *Canada's War*, p. 117.)

94 CAB 65/1, WM 19 (39) 2, 18 Sept. 1939.

95 W.S.C. to F.D.R., 15 May 1940, F.D.R. to W.S.C., 16 May, and Lothian to FO, tel. 759, 18 May, all in FO 371/24192, A3261/1/51.

96 There is a good discussion of some of these issues in Leutze, *Bargaining for Supremacy*, chs. 6–8.

97 Scott, min., 20 May 1940, A3261. For Lothian see, e.g., Long Diary, 21 May 1940, p. 100 (LC); Hull, memo, 11 June 1940, *FRUS*, 1940, III, 36; Lothian to FO, tels. 1007, 1011, 16 and 17 June 1940, FO 371/24311, C7294/65/17.

98 W.S.C. to F.D.R., 20 May 1940, A3261. For other instances see: W.S.C. to

Mackenzie King, 5 and 24 June 1940, PREM 4/43B/1, pp. 299–300A, 264–5; Kennedy to Hull, tel. 1579, 10 June 1940, *FRUS*, 1940, III, 35–6 (Mosley). Cf. W.S.C. to Lothian, tel. 1038, 9 June 1940, PREM 3/462/2–3, pp. 164–5 and tel. 1304, 28 June 1940, PREM 3/476/10, p. 528.

99 Pickersgill, *Mackenzie King Record*, I, 117. Kennedy to Hull, tel. 1400, 27 May 1940, D/S 740.0011 EW 1939/3018 4/10; memo for Early, 28 May 1940, PSF 82: Navy Dept., Knox.

100 Lothian to FO, tel. 834, 26 May 1940, A3261. On 28 May the Australian Minister in Washington reported that F.D.R. felt that it 'was far from impossible that some incident directly affecting the interests or the honour of this country might occur at any time and that this country might come in with us'. (Casey to Menzies, 29 May 1940, copy in PREM 4/43B/1, p. 467.) For similar comments see Lothian to FO, tels. 1007 and 1011 cited in note 97.

101 King to W.S.C., tel. 30 May 1940, PREM 4/43B/1, pp. 314–22. (Cf. Granatstein, *Canada's War*, pp. 119–22 and Pickersgill, *Mackenzie King Record*, I, 116–21.)

On 10 June F.D.R. gave clear instructions to Pierrepont Moffat, who was about to become the new U.S. Minister in Ottawa. According to Moffat: 'While talking to Canadian officials I was constantly to emphasize (a) that Canada should, for its own sake and not for ours, continue to seek assurances that the British fleet would never be surrendered, but be dispersed, with a part to North America, and (b) that the United States could give almost as much help as a neutral as if she became a belligerent. No one could tell if the United States would become a belligerent; obviously she would not unless an overt act were committed by Germany or Italy. Germany was clever and would probably avoid an overt act; Italy was foolish and might commit one.' (Moffat Diary, 10 June 1940.)

102 Ickes, *Secret Diary*, III, 199–200.

103 Leutze, *Bargaining for Supremacy*, pp. 77, 91–2.

104 CAB 65/7, WM 129 (40) 8, and CAB 65/13, p. 181, WM 142 (40) CA.

105 Lothian to FO, tel. 868, 30 May 1940, A3261.

106 Churchill, *Speeches*, VI, 6225–31; W.S.C. to King, 5 June 1940, cited in note 98.

107 Lothian, *American Speeches*, pp. 104–9; cf. Lothian to FO, tel. 932, 8 June 1940, FO 371/24239, A3316/131/45. For a fuller discussion of the speech and its significance see Reynolds, *Lothian*, part IV.

108 W.S.C. to Ismay, 17 July 1940, PREM 3/475/1, pp. 33–4. This file, and FO 371/24255, A2961/2961/45 and FO 371/24241, A3631/131/45, provide the background to this paragraph.

109 See esp. FO 371/24255–6, A3297, A3600/2961/45; also CAB 65/7, WM (40) 141/9 and 146/14, 27 and 29 May 1940.

110 Lothian to FO, tel. 1019, 17 June 1940; W.S.C. to Halifax, 24 June; mins. by Ronald and Scott, 26 June; Halifax to W.S.C. 28 June—all in FO 371/24240, A3582/131/45. Martin to Mallet, 29 June, and FC to Lothian, tel. 1331, 30 June in FO 371/24240, A3583/131/45.

111 As stated to Lothian—see tel. 1019 cited in previous note.

112 Stacey, *Arms, Men and Governments*, pp. 332–9, 349; cf. Berle Diary, 29 Aug. 1940.

113 Lash, *Roosevelt and Churchill*, p. 167, referring to F.D.R's offer of staff talks on 17 June, comments: 'That was not the move of a leader who lacked faith in British prospects.' I believe it could well have been—when judged in context.

114 E.g. Ickes, *Secret Diary*, III, 176, 185–6, 202.

115 Moffat Diary, 10 June and 5 July.

116 This was certainly the view of Mackenzie King. [Campbell to Machtig, 17

Aug. 1940, PREM 3/464/3, p. 83.) King felt at the time that the speech had been 'a great blunder' and other Canadian diplomats agreed. (Moffat, diary, 27 and 25 June.)

117 Lothian to FO, tel. 1206, 2 July 1940, FO 371/24321, C7553/839/17, read to Cabinet the next day (CAB 65/14, p. 16, WM 192 (40) 2 CA). Halifax had already told the Cabinet on 29 June that it seemed safe to assume that any action Britain might take in respect of the French fleet would be applauded in the U.S.A. (CAB 65/13, p. 359, WM 187 (40) 8 CA.) On 4 July Lothian forwarded a situation report to F.D.R., noting: 'You will see that Winston Churchill has taken the action in regard to the French fleet which we discussed and you approved.' (Lothian to F.D.R., 4 July 1940, PSF 50: GB, Reports.)

For background on the Oran action see Bell, *A Certain Eventuality*, ch. 7 and Playfair, *The Mediterranean and Middle East*, I, ch. 7.

The following March Churchill told W. P. Crozier, the editor of the *Manchester Guardian*, that he dated the 'decisive trend' of U.S. opinion towards Britain from the time of Oran. According to Crozier's paraphrase: 'The Americans appreciated ruthlessness in war and they were up to that time doubtful whether we could be ruthless in order to save ourselves. They were converted when they heard that we had gone for the French battleships and when they knew that we would *do anything* rather than go down.' (Crozier, *Off the Record*, 20 March 1941, pp. 210–11.)

118 Ickes, *Secret Diary*, III, 233 and F.D.R. to Ickes, 6 July 1940, OF 4044.

119 Lothian to FO, tel. 1135, 27 June 1940, and W.S.C. to Lothian, tel. 1304, 28 June, PREM 3/476/10, pp. 531, 528.

120 Cecil King, diary entry for 19 Feb. 1941, in King, *With Malice Toward None*, p. 109.

121 Churchill, *Second World War*, VI, 414.

### Chapter Five

1 For references see notes 6 and 76.

2 Leutze, *Bargaining for Supremacy*, chs. 6–8. Prof. Leutze is the first historian to explore this aspect in detail, although Langer and Gleason, *Challenge to Isolation*, e.g. pp. 490–1, and others have noted its importance. My own account, researched before the publication of Prof. Leutze's book, comes to similar general conclusions. I differ with him on points of detail, some of which are set out in the text, others in Reynolds, *Lothian*, part IV.

Other basic accounts of the deal are Churchill, *Second World War*, II, ch. XX; Langer and Gleason, *Challenge to Isolation*, ch. XXII; and Goodhart, *Fifty Ships that Saved the World*.

3 FO 371/24255, A3297/2961/45, esp. Lothian to FO, tel. 1086, 23 June; Scott, min., 26 June; mins. of mtg. on 1 July; draft CO/DO memo, 4 July; Adm. Godfrey to Cavendish-Bentinck, 4 July; Balfour to Poynton (CO), 5 July.

4 A3297, esp. Lothian to FO, tels. 1211, 1225, 1265, 1307, 1314, of 2, 4, 8, 10 and 12 July; mins. by Vansittart, 12 and 13 July.

5 A 3297, memo by Whitehead, 14 July; mins. by Balfour, Scott and Cadogan, 15 July, Halifax, 16 July.

On British hopes Whitehead commented: 'Under the stress of successive defeats in Europe our expectations with regard to American help have been mounting so rapidly that they have outstripped the surprising speed with which that country has been moving from the position of impartial neutrality towards one of frank material assistance. Because America has not yet given us all we want, we stand in danger of displaying to her the same petulant hostility that many Frenchmen are showing us as a result of our failure to give them effective assistance.'

6 CAB 66/10, WP (40) 276, 18 July 1940.

7 FO 371/24256, A3600/2961/45, esp. mins. by Cadogan, 18 July, Balfour, 26 and 30 July, Farquhar, 30 July; CAB 65/8, WM 214 (40) 4, 29 July; Balfour, 'Diadems askew', p. 176 (Lloyd quotation).

8 FO 371/24240, A3582/131/45, esp. Lothian tels. of 22, 25, 26 and 30 July 1940, mins. by Vansittart, 23 July, and Churchill, 15 July.

9 Churchill to Halifax, 7 July, and drafts of 5 July, PREM 3/462/2–3, pp. 151–2, 156–7, 158; CAB 65/8, WM 194 (40) 3, 5 July. Quotation from Kennedy to Hull, tel. 2001, 5 July, *FRUS*, 1940, III, 56.

10 A3582: Scott, min., 26 July; W.S.C. to Halifax, 30 July (quotation) and W.S.C. to F.D.R., 31 July. Beaverbrook may have had this message in mind when he told Kennedy on 31 July that the British were now trying to make 'the situation look as good as possible' instead of 'as black as possible'. (Kennedy to Hull, tel. 2486, 31 July 1940, D/S 740.0011 EW 1838/4929$\frac{1}{4}$.)

   Leutze, *Bargaining for Supremacy*, pp. 106–7, cites Churchill's cable and Beaverbrook's comment as evidence of a 'shift in British tactics', but he does not link them with Kennedy's advice on 5 July. Lash, *Roosevelt and Churchill*, pp. 205–6, though unaware of Beaverbrook's remark, does make the link.

11 Cohen to F.D.R., 19 July and enclosure, PSF 81: Navy, Destroyers-Naval Bases, 1940 (I); F.D.R. to Knox, 22 July 1940, PSF 82: Navy, Knox.

12 See two ONI reports of 25 July 1940, sent to F.D.R. on 30 July and 1 Aug., PSF 85: Navy, Shipping losses, 1940.

13 Main accounts of this meeting are F.D.R., memo, in *Personal Letters*, II, 1050–1 (quotations); Bell, memo, Morgenthau Diary, 288: 158–60; Ickes, *Secret Diary*, III, 292–4; and, more discreetly, Stimson Diary, 30: 57–8. See also F.D.R.'s account to Lothian in Lothian to FO, tel. 1606, 3–4 Aug., FO 371/24241, A3670.

14 Morgenthau Presidential Diary, 3: 635, cf. 643.

15 Schwar, 'Interventionist propaganda', p. 290; Ickes, *Secret Diary*, III, 283; Stimson Diary, 30: 55–6, 83–4; Morgenthau Presidential Diary, 3: 635.

16 For background see Chadwin, *The Warhawks*, ch. IV; Schwar, 'Interventionist propaganda', ch. 10; Johnson, *Battle Against Isolation*, ch. V; Agar, *Britain Alone*, pp. 151–3, 160.

17 See Stimson Diary, 13 and 15 Aug. and the good account in Lash, *Roosevelt and Churchill*, p. 210.

18 Lothian to FO, tel. 1610, 5 Aug., A3670 (Hull); provisional poll by Market Analysts, Inc., forwarded by Cohen and seen by Ickes on 8 Aug., Ickes papers, 371/5. The precise breakdown of the poll was: 7 probably in favour (including Byrnes and Connally), 39 awaiting word from F.D.R. or Willkie; 19 making no statement; 8 still to be questioned; and 23 opposed, mostly dedicated anglophobe proponents of hemisphere defence such as Nye, Taft, Bennett Clark, Hiram Johnson, Vandenberg, Walsh and Wheeler.

19 Lothian to W.S.C., tels. 1712 and 1727, 15 and 16 Aug. 1940, PREM 3/462/2–3, pp. 95, 94; Stimson Diary, 16 Aug., 30: 93.

20 See Reynolds, *Lothian*, part IV.

21 Schwar, 'Interventionist propaganda', p. 286; *Chicago Daily News*, 18 June 1940; Knox to Ickes, 18 June, Ickes papers, box 162; Lothian to FO, tel. 1307, 10 July, FO 371/24255, A3297.

22 See the good analysis in Chadwin, *The Warhawks*, ch. III and Schwar, 'Interventionist propaganda', pp. 194–210, 240–51.

23 Mins. of mtg. on 11 July, Lothian papers, 405: 519-21; memo of mtg. on 25

July, copy in Alsop papers (LC) box 32: Defence; Chadwin, *The Warhawks*, pp. 40–1, 84–6; Schwar, 'Interventionist propaganda', p. 288.

24 Johnson, *Battle Against Isolation*, p. 244, n. to p. 63, quoting from an unpublished article of Dec. 1940. Though exaggerated for popular consumption, the sentiments expressed were basically sincere.

25 E.g. Morgenthau Diary 301: 101; Stimson Diary, 24 July, 30: 33; Long, *War Diary*, 13 Aug., pp. 122–3.

26 Opinions of London attachés in Morgenthau Diary 287: 349–50; Col. Carl Spaatz to Gen. Arnold, 31 July 1940, Spaatz papers (LC) 7: Diary, Jan.–Sept. 1940. On Kelsey see Lothian to Clarence Dillon, 27 July 1940, Lothian papers, 400: 274; cf. Morgenthau Diary, 283: 290-5, 284: 44, 123.

27 Leutze, *Bargaining for Supremacy*, pp. 97–103, 112–13, provides a good discussion of Donovan's visit, emphasizing its importance. However, Donovan's optimism was not as unqualified as some accounts suggest. He believed that if the Germans tried to invade Britain in 1940, they would be repelled. But he was less hopeful if Germany delayed her attack until the spring. She would have time to prepare and British morale would inevitably have slipped from the high pitch of 1940. (Stimson Diary, 6 Aug. 1940, 30: 67.) This was a common fear in Washington, often neglected by historians. Spring 1941 was as much a crisis as June 1940.

28 Hyde, *Quiet Canadian*, pp. 38–9. Apparently Stephenson helped arrange Donovan's visit (ibid., pp. 33–9). In the absence of the official papers it is extremely difficult to know exactly how much importance to attach to Stephenson's undeniably invaluable activities. Hyde's book seems more reliable than Stevenson, *A Man Called Intrepid*—a sensationalized thriller of the 'how-I-won-the-war-single-handed' genre. Those claims and statements in the book that can be checked do not inspire confidence in the rest of it. For some examples see Lowenthal, 'Intrepid'.

29 Lothian to FO, tel. 1579, 2 Aug. 1940, FO 371/24240, A3582; FO to Lothian, tel. 1776, 3 Aug., FO 371/24256, A3600.

30 Lothian to FO, tel. 1606, 4 Aug. 1940, FO 371/24241, A3670; cf. Lothian to W.S.C., tel. 1244, 5 July, and W.S.C. to Lothian, tel. 1646, 24 July, PREM 3/462/2–3, pp. 153, 149.

31 Balfour, 'Diadems askew', pp. 185–6, on talk with W.S.C. late on 6 Aug.; W.S.C. to Halifax, 7 Aug. 1940, A3670.

32 See FO 371/24241, A3631, and PREM 3/475/1, esp. Halifax to W.S.C., 25 July 1940, W.S.C. to Ismay, 1 Aug., and Martin to Mallet, 8 Aug., pp. 28, 24, 13.

33 Halifax Diary, 7 Aug., A.7.8.5, p. 227; Halifax to W.S.C., 7 Aug. and FO to Lothian, tels. 1827 and 1848, 8 Aug. 1940, A3670. British Embassy to State Dept., 5 Aug., and Lothian to Welles, 8 Aug., *FRUS*, 1940, III, 63–5.

34 Lothian to Welles, 9 Aug. and enclosed list of 8 Aug., D/S 811. 34544/3⅓; Welles to Kennedy, tel. 2330, 14 Aug., *FRUS*, 1940, III, 66.

35 F.D.R. to W.S.C., 14 Aug. 1940, PREM 3/463/1, pp. 156–8. The five colonies were the Bahamas, Jamaica, St. Lucia, Trinidad and British Guiana. A sixth, Antigua, was included later by Britain as a goodwill gesture.

36 See Lothian to W.S.C., tel. 1727, 16 Aug., FO 371/24241, A3793/131/45, and Mackenzie King to W.S.C., 18 Aug. 1940, PREM 3/464/3, p. 104. This para. is based on Cabinet discussion of 14 Aug., CAB 65/8, WM 227 (40) 1.

37 Cf. Kennedy to Hull, tel. 2734, 15 Aug., *FRUS*, 1940, III, 67–8.

38 5s *HC Debs.*, 364: 1171.

39 Ibid., cols. 1186, 1195.

40 5s *HL Debs.*, 117: 304 (Samuel), 306 (Strabolgi).

41 Halifax Diary, 14 Aug., A 7.8.5, p. 237; cf. Cadogan, *Diaries*, 14 Aug., p. 321.
42 There is a good account in Leutze, *Bargaining for Supremacy*, pp. 117–19.
43 CAB 65/8, WM 231 (40) 1, 21 Aug.; cf. Halifax Diary, 21 Aug., A 7.8.5, p. 247. W.S.C. to F.D.R., 22 Aug., PREM 3/462/2–3, pp. 74–5.
44 W.S.C. to F.D.R., 25 Aug., ibid., pp. 51–2; cf. Cadogan, note, 23 Aug., FO 371/24259, A3917/3742/45.
45 See Colin Forbes Adam, *Life of Lord Lloyd* (London, 1948), chs. xv-xvi, and esp. p. 247.
46 See Taylor, *Beaverbrook*, pp. 438–9, 555; Kennedy to Hull, tel. 2948, 29 Aug., *FRUS*, 1940, III, 72.
47 PREM 4/43A/2, esp. Somerset de Chair to W.S.C., 26 Aug., pp. 48–50; cf. *Daily Herald*, 21 Aug. 1940, p. 1g.
48 *Daily Herald*, 23 Aug., p. 5e-f. Most 'early day' motions are not debated. They are put down to test the strength of parliamentary opinion on a particular issue, usually where back-benchers are at odds with their party leadership. In this case Churchill was helped by the fact that Parliament was conveniently in summer recess from 22 Aug. to 5 Sept.—the period between the deal becoming public knowledge and its conclusion.
49 Diary, 1 Sept. 1940, in King, *With Malice Toward None*, p. 72.
50 Lothian to FO, tels. 1853–5, 1857, 28 Aug., FO 371/24259, A3980/3742/45, and tel. 1886, 31 Aug., A4022.
51 CAB 65/8, WM 236 (40) 6, 29 Aug. 1940; cf. Balfour, min., 29 Aug., A3980.
52 Cf. Lothian to FO, tel. 1606, 4 Aug., A3670.
53 CAB 65/9, WM 239 (40) 7, 2 Sept. 1940.
54 5s *HC Debs.*, 365: 39–40.
55 CAB 65/10, WM 310 (40) 5, 27 Dec. 1940; W.S.C. to Halifax, 5 May 1941, FO 371/26148, A3496. See also Abbazia, *Mr. Roosevelt's Navy*, pp. 98–103 and Goodhart, *Fifty Ships*, ch. XIV.
56 See Blum, *From the Morgenthau Diaries*, II, 181–3; Hall, *North American Supply*, pp. 143–5. See also Reynolds, *Lothian*, part IV.
57 Churchill, *Second World War*, II, 358.
58 Stacey, *Arms, Men and Governments*, pp. 338–9, 349; Berle Diary, 29 Aug. 1940.
59 See note 57.
60 For background to the discussions of Japanese policy in this section see Butow, *Tojo*, chs. 6–7; Morley (ed.), *Japan's Foreign Policy*, esp. the essays by Crowley, Iklé and Iriye; Nish, *Japanese Foreign Policy*, chs. 11–12; Sato, 'Anglo-Japanese relations', chs. III and IV.
61 For background on British policy see Woodward, *British Foreign Policy*, II, 92–114 and Lowe, *Great Britain and the Origins of the Pacific War*, ch. V; on U.S. policy see Langer and Gleason, *Challenge to Isolation*, ch. XVII and *The Undeclared War*, chs. I–II and Feis, *Road to Pearl Harbor*, chs. 7–16.
62 Craigie to FO, tel. 1087, 25 June 1940, FO 371/24666, F3479/43/10.
63 Lothian to FO, tels. 1163–4, 29 June 1940, FO 371/24725, F3465/23/23 and tel. 1216, 3 July, ibid., F3545. CAB 65/8, WM 189 (40) 12, 1 July 1940.
64 Craigie to FO, tels. 1149 and 1196, 4 and 9 July 1940, FO 371/24666, F3544 and FO 371/24667, F3568.
65 COS memo, 4 July, CAB 66/9, WP (40) 249; CAB 65/8, WM 194 (40) 1, 5 July; Cadogan, *Diaries*, 5 July, p. 311.
66 An irony of which Churchill was well aware. See Crozier, *Off the Record*, 26 July 1940, p. 176.
67 Press release, 16 July 1940, *FRUS, Japan*, II, 101; cf. Hull, memo, 18 July, *FRUS*, 1940, IV, 53. Chamberlain to Ida, 20 July, NC 18/1/1166; Dening, min., 17 July, FO 371/24667, p. 283.

68 Grew to Hull, tel. 544, 7 July 1940, *FRUS*, 1940, IV, 40–1; Craigie to FO, tel. 1157, 5 July, F3544.
69 See FO 371/24725, F3465/23/23: esp. Craigie to FO, tel. 1068, 23 June 1940; Lothian to FO, tels. 1117 and 1138, 26 and 27 June; note by Brenan on Casey to Menzies, tel. 49, 28 June; and note by Dening on Clark-Kerr to FO, tel. 558, 5 July.
70 See FO 371/24708, F3633/193/61, various mins. of 23–26 July by Butler, Sterndale Bennett and Whitehead. In impotent frustration Butler warned: 'We may go to the grave chanting that we must be polite to America, but we shan't save our civilisation like this.' (23 July.) On Hull see Lothian tel. 1163, cited in note 63.
71 Quinlan, 'The United States fleet', pp. 157–62; Long, *War Diary*, 16 June 1940, p. 107 and Watson, *Chief of Staff*, p. 111.
72 CAB 65/8, WM 173 (40) 7, 20 June 1940; FO 371/24725: FO to Lothian, tel. 1222, 21 June, F3432, and Lothian to FO, tels. 1057, 1070, 1141, of 20, 21, 28 June, F3450.
73 DO circular tel. Z106, 13 June 1940, annexed to COS 180 (40), CAB 79/5; DO to Australian and N.Z. govts., 28 June and Ismay to Bruce, 4 July, CAB 21/893.
74 Watt, *Evolution of Australian Foreign Policy*, pp. 24–5.
75 Megaw, 'Undiplomatic channels'; Lissington, *New Zealand and the United States*, pp. 28–9 and PREM 4/43B/1, pp. 178–9, 183–4, 197, 420–1; Barclay, 'Australia looks to America', pp. 255–7; *FRUS*, 1940, IV, 156–7, 184.
76 Berle Diary, 2 Sept. and 21 March 1940.
77 Morgenthau Presidential Diaries, 16 Aug. 1940, 3: 644. This paragraph draws particularly on Anderson, *The Standard-Vacuum Oil Company*, esp. pp. 129–38.
78 FO 371/24741, F3634/677/23, esp. Kirsch, memo, and Churchill to Ismay, 21 July 1940; cf. Medlicott, *Economic Blockade*, I, 476–81.
79 Anderson, *Standard-Vacuum Oil Company*, pp. 140–1; Hornbeck, memo, 19 July 1940, *FRUS*, 1940, IV, 586–7; Lothian to FO, Arfar tel. 1637, 19 July, F3634. In fairness to the hawks, they had been misled as to the British Government's likely attitude by Lothian. At an Embassy dinner with the hawks on 18 July Lothian had encouraged the idea that if the U.S. embargoed all oil the British and Dutch would destroy their oil fields in the NEI. Although Lothian did favour a tough line on oil, he had been carried away during a particularly heated discussion and prudently did not reveal to London his part in the origins of the hawks' plan. For fuller discussion see Reynolds, *Lothian*, Part V.
80 See esp. Hosoya, 'Miscalculations', pp. 107–8.
81 E.g. Grew to Hull, tels. 877, 890, 893 of 22, 25, 25 Sept. 1940, D/S 841.34546D/127, 130. Cf. Berle Diary, 20 Sept.
82 See papers of mid-Aug. in FO 371/24259, A3958/3742/45; Lothian to FO, tel. 2307, 20 Sept. 1940, FO 371/24709, F4210/193/61; Long, *War Diary*, 9 Oct. 1940, pp. 138–9.
83 For discussions see Friedländer, *Prelude to Downfall*, ch. 3 and Van Creveld, *Hitler's Strategy*, chs. 2–3. See also ch. 7, n. 85.
84 Trefousse, *Germany and American Neutrality*, p. 69; Compton, *Swastika and the Eagle*, p. 191.
85 See esp. Hosoya, 'The tripartite pact', and text of agreements in Appendix 7.
86 Kennedy to F.D.R. and Hull, tel. 3063, 11 Sept. 1940, D/S 740.0011 EW 1939/5480½; Berle Diary, 28 Aug., 6, 11 and 16 Sept.; J. W. Alsop to Frankfurter, 21 Aug. 1940, Alsop papers, box 2 (LC).
87 Prelim. report of Strong and Emmons for F.D.R., 23 Sept. 1940, copy in Morgenthau diary 320: 168–74; Berle Diary, 25 Sept. 1940.
88 Frankfurter to Lothian, 3 June 1940, Lothian papers, 400: 622.

89 Ickes, *Secret Diary*, III, 317.

90 Perowne, min., 30 July 1940, FO 371/24241, A3628/131/45. Similarly see Sir Walter Monckton (MOI), notes for talk at Camberley Staff College, 15 Sept. 1940, Dep. Monckton Trustees 3/93.

91 Halifax to Lothian, tel. 2234, 11 Sept. 1940 and enclsd. tels., PSF(S) 4: Great Britain.

92 For general discussions of British and U.S. policy see books cited above, note 61, and also Leutze, *Bargaining for Supremacy*, pp. 162–9. The relevant FO files are FO 371/24709 and 24736; also, on oil, FO 371/25213, file W/9160/49.

93 Lothian to FO, tel. 2146, 1 Oct. 1940, FO 371/24736, F4495/626/23. For later developments see FO 371/24709, F4556, F4567, F4615, and FO 371/24710, F4732/193/61. As Leutze points out (p. 168) Hull's initial enthusiasm for the idea is deliberately concealed in his own accounts of the conversations, which can be found in Hull papers 58/213.

94 Both Hull and Welles, however, privately admitted that Germany would prefer the U.S.A. out of the war than in it. (Long, MS. diary, 12 Nov. 1940, p. 203.) For F.D.R. see above, ch. 4, note 101, and below, ch. 8 (d), esp. notes 110–14. For other examples see Bilainkin, *Diary*, 20 Aug. 1940, p. 189 (Kennedy); Lamont to Catto, 11 Oct. and to Halifax, 22 Dec. 1940, Lamont papers, 112–11 and 84–22.

95 Kennedy to Hull, tel. 3247, 27 Sept. 1940, *FRUS*, 1940, III, 48; Raymond E. Lee to Jeanette Lee, 16 Oct. 1940, in Leutze (ed.), *London Observer*, p. 95. Murrow, *This is London*, 3 Dec. 1940, pp. 216–17.

96 Min., 11 Nov. 1940, FO 371/24243, p. 217.

97 Mins. by Whitehead and Balfour, 7 and 8 Oct. 1940, FO 371/24242, A4453, and by Scott, 26 Oct. and 12 Nov., FO 371/24243, A4666. CAB 65/9, WM 260 (40) 5, 27 Sept. 1940.

98 FO 371/24709, F4290/193/61: FO mins., esp. those by Vansittart and Clarke, 20, 21 Sept. 1940, and FO to Lothian, tel. 2331, 21 Sept. For similar expressions see FO to Lothian, tel. 1262, 25 June 1940, FO 371/24725, F3465 and Halifax, min., 6 Nov. 1940, FO 371/24243, A4712.

99 Lothian to FO, tel. 2177, 3 Oct. 1940, FO 371/24736, F4553/626/23; cf. Moffat Diary, vol. 46, notes on Washington visit, 6–10 Oct. 1940, p. 6.

100 Churchill to Halifax, min., 4 Oct. 1940, FO 371/24729, F4634/60/23. See also CAB 65/9, WM 264/5 and 265/6, 2 and 3 Oct. 1940.

101 FO 371/24736, F4663/626/23: Craigie to FO, tel. 2006, 10 Oct. 1940, W.S.C.'s min. for Halifax, 13 Oct. and FO mins., esp. by Clarke, 20 Oct.

102 Balfour, min., 8 Oct. 1940, FO 371/24242, A4453.

103 Whitehead, min., 30 Oct. 1940, FO 371/24242, p. 140.

104 E.g. Feis, *Road to Pearl Harbor*, p. 71.


**Chapter Six**

1 Hankey to Lothian, 26 July 1940, FO 800/398, U.S./40/16; Morgenthau, to Sir Frederick Phillips, 9 Dec. 1940, in Morgenthau Diary, 337: 135.

2 British Embassy to State Dept., *aide-mémoire*, 3 July 1940, *FRUS*, 1940, III, 45.

3 Half of which were trainers. Kimball, *Most Unsordid Act*, p. 66.

4 Figures quoted in, respectively, Treasury memo., 21 Aug. 1940, CAB 66/11, WP (40) 324, and R. Hopkins, 'Note on paying our way abroad', 1 Jan. 1941, T 175/121.

5 Phillips to Sir Horace Wilson, tel. 1375, 18 July 1940, FO 371/25209, W8940/8940/49. According to Morgenthau: 'The President left a sort of vague im-

pression with Phillips that we might in some way help them borrow money against their securities.' (Morgenthau Presidential Diary, 3: 617, 17 July 1940.)

6  Phillips, report on U.S. visit, FO 371/25209, W9891/8940/49. Cf. Scott, min., 16 July 1940, FO 800/324, H/XXXVII/79.

7  CAB 65/14, WM 232 (40) 3 CA, 22 Aug. 1940.

8  Ibid.; cf. Phillips, memo on 'Gold Position', 17 Oct. 1940, T 177/52.

9  Statistics for this paragraph come from Roskill, *War at Sea*, I, 616; Lothian to Harry Hopkins, 8 Dec. 1940 and enclsd. memo, Hopkins papers, box 154: Britain; CAB 66/14, WP (41) 17, 29 Jan. 1941.

10  Hankey, memo, 3 Sept. 1940, Hankey papers, HNKY 11/3.

11  Cadogan, min., 2 April 1940, FO 371/24233, A2286/39/45.

12  Lothian to FO, desp. 386, 29 April 1940, FO 371/24239, A3202/131/45.

13  Ross, 'Was the nomination of Wendell Willkie a political miracle?' See also Johnson, *The Republican Party and Wendell Willkie*. The best accounts of the campaign are Burke, 'Election of 1940'; Divine, *Foreign Policy and U.S. Presidential Elections*, vol. I, chs. 1–2; Errico, 'Foreign affairs and the presidential election of 1940'.

14  Divine, *Foreign Policy and U.S. Presidential Elections*, p. 39. Willkie supported the destroyers deal, though attacking F.D.R.'s failure to consult Congress. Through Lothian he sent Churchill a secret message 'to say that he was personally in favour of doing everything possible to see that Great Britain did not get beaten in the war'. (Lothian to Churchill, 29 Aug. 1940, FO 800/398, US/40/22.)

15  FO 371/24234: A2862, A3502/39/45 (Willkie) and A4710 (MOI).

16  Halifax Diary, 27 Oct. 1940, cf. 6 Nov., Hickleton papers, A 7.8.6, pp. 321, 331; Nicolson, *Diaries and Letters*, II, 125. See also Channon, *Diaries*, 6 Nov., p. 273; Panter-Downes, *London War Notes*, 9 Nov., p. 113; Calder, *The People's War*, p. 266. In August Chamberlain had written: 'Personally I am for Roosevelt. We know where we are with him and we dont [*sic*] with Willkie who is very raw and inexperienced.' (To Ida, 20 Aug. 1940, NC/18/1/1166.)

17  Harvey, TS. diary, 9 Nov. 1940 (British Library Add. Mss. 56397).

18  Whitehead, min., 5 Nov. 1940, FO 371/24239, A4627/39/45; CAB 65/14, p. 103, WM 232 (40) 3 CA, 22 Aug. 1940.

19  E.g. Arthur S. Henning, *Boston Globe*, 17 Oct. 1940, p. 1: 'the widespread opinion in official circles is that if Mr. Roosevelt is re-elected it will not be long before the United States will be in the war.'

20  Ghormley to Stark, 11 Oct. 1940, U.S. Navy Strategic Plans Division, Box 117: Naval attaché, London (Washington Navy Yard); Colville Diary, 1 Nov. 1940, quoted in Colville, *Footprints in Time*, pp. 144–5; Whitehead, mins., 18 Sept. and 4 Nov. 1940, FO 371/24241, A3628 and FO 371/24243, A4712.

21  Edgar E. Robinson, *They Voted for Roosevelt: The Presidential Vote, 1932–1944* (Stanford, 1947), p. 25.

22  CAB 65/10, WM 299 (40) 4, 2 Dec. 1940. Oliver Harvey, ecstatic in early Nov. at F.D.R.'s election victory, wrote on 27 Nov. of the 'serious situation' in the U.S.A.—'there is no understanding of the need to do a great deal more for us if we are to win the war.' (Harvey Diary, BL Add. Mss. 56397.)

23  Dalton Diary, 24 Oct. 1940; Butler, *Lothian*, p. 290. For a fuller discussion of the material in the rest of the section, see Reynolds, *Lothian*, part VI.

24  Lothian to Hoare, 19 Oct. 1940, Templewood papers, XIII/17. See also Lothian to W.S.C., 29 Aug. 1940, FO 800/398, US/40/22.

25  Lothian to FO, tel. 2063, 21 Sept. 1940, FO 371/24246, A4534/301/45.

26  Lothian to W.S.C., 12 Nov. 1940, PREM 3/486/1, p. 299; Cadogan, *Diaries*, 11 Nov. 1940, p. 335. For the June exchange, see above, ch. 4 (e), note 119.

27  Lady Astor to R. H. Brand, 17 Jan. 1941, Nancy Astor papers, 3/14.

28 See FO 371/24243, A4790: esp. W.S.C. to Lothian tel. 3290, 30 Nov. 1940; Lothian to W.S.C., tels. 2915–17, 4 Dec. 1940; min. by Scott, 6 Dec. 1940. For details of the drafting process see PREM 3/486/1.
29 W.S.C. to F.D.R., 8 Dec. 1940, PREM 3/486/1, pp. 38–44.
30 Churchill, *Second World War*, II, 501.
31 See *New York Times*, 24 Nov. 1940, pp. 1:5 and 7:4; *Sunday Dispatch* (London), 24 Nov. 1940, p. 1:4; Lothian to FO, tel. 2753, 24 Nov. 1940, FO 371/24249, A4934/434/45. The account generally used by historians, in Wheeler-Bennett, *George VI*, p. 521 (and esp. as amplified in *Special Relationships*, p. 112) is seriously misleading.
32 As he admitted to Morgenthau on 2 Dec. 1940 (Morgenthau Diary, 342A: 1).
33 *Chicago Tribune*, 24 Nov. 1940, p. 1; Maling to Robertson, and Robertson to Waley, 27 and 28 Nov. 1940, T 160/1089, F16041/8.
34 Morgenthau Diary, 321: 325, 14 Oct. 1940; FO 371/25149, W11734/79/49.
35 W.S.C. to Lothian, tel. 3233, 27 Nov. 1940, FO 371/24249, A4935/434/45.
36 Lothian to W.S.C., tel. 2843, 28 Nov. 1940, T 160/995, F19422, p. 91.
37 Balfour, min., 28 Nov. 1940, FO 371/24243, p. 270.
38 BPS 79, 4 Dec. 1940, FO 371/24244, A4995/131/45.
39 Frankfurter to Laski, 27 Nov. 1940, Frankfurter papers, 74/1502 (LC).
40 See Long, MS. Diary, 12 Nov. 1940, pp. 200–1.
41 Ickes, *Secret Diary*, III, 367; Lash, *Roosevelt and Churchill*, p. 260. For Nov. 1938, see above, ch. 2 (b), esp. note 33.
42 Ickes, loc. cit.; Purvis to Salter, tel. Pursa 218, 10 Nov. 1940. FO 371/25149, W11700/79/49.
43 See Lamont papers, 127–25 (Harvard Business School).
44 Morgenthau Diary, 334: 1–4; Treasury memo for F.D.R., 28 Nov. 1940, Morgenthau Presidential Diary, 3: 720–7.
45 Lothian to FO, tel. 2802, 25 Nov. 1940, FO 371/24243, A4909/131/45; Moffat Diary, vol. 46, 'Washington Visit, 24–27 Nov. 1940', p. 12 (Welles); Ickes, *Secret Diary*, III, 374 (Bullitt). Cf. Casey, *Personal Experience*, p. 18; Sherwood, *Roosevelt and Hopkins*, p. 224.
46 See Kimball, *The Most Unsordid Act*, pp. 119–20.
47 Lothian to FO, tel. 2911, 4 Dec. 1940, FO 371/25209, W11960/8940/49. For similar judgements on Lothian's role as a catalyst see Langer and Gleason, *Undeclared War*, pp. 225–6; Kimball, *Most Unsordid Act*, p. 96.
48 Berle Diary, 1 Dec. 1940, p. 11, and 4 Dec., p. 2; Stimson Diary, 3 Dec. 1940, 32: 10–11.
49 W.S.C. to F.D.R., tel., 13 Dec. 1940, PREM 3/468, p. 5; Harvey, TS. diary, 14 Dec. 1940, BL Add. Mss. 56397.
50 T 160/1051, F17286, memos for 31 Oct. 1940 meeting, esp. Keynes, 'Notes for U.S.A.', 27 Nov. See also Phillips, memos, 2 and 23 Nov. 1940, T 160/995, F19422. (Keynes joined the Treasury in July 1940.)
51 T 160/1089, F16041/8: esp. Hopkins' note, 15 Dec. 1940, on Salter to Crookshank, 12 Dec., and Somervell to Bewley, 29 Nov. In a note on the latter Dennis Robertson, the distinguished economist then attached to the Treasury, dismissed the idea of a barter agreement: 'Alas we have so little to offer but negroes, of whom the Americans have so many already.'
52 Ibid., Kingsley Wood to Lyttelton, 9 Dec. 1940.
53 Cf. his prepared statement and notes of answers to possible questions, T175/121.
54 For meetings of 6 and 9 Dec. see Morgenthau Diary, 336: 147–73 and 337: 108–60 (Morgenthau quotation on p. 135). On 12 Dec. see ibid., 339: 208. See also FO 371/25209, W11960, W12403, and W12457/8940/49, esp. Phillips to Treasury, tel. 3094, 14 Dec. 1940.

55 Keynes, min., 16 Dec. 1940, T 175/121.
56 Morgenthau Presidential Diary, 3: 740, 17 Dec. 1940.
57 Presidential Press Conference 702, 17 Dec. 1940, in F.D.R., *Public Papers*, 1940, 604–15.
58 Lash, *Roosevelt and Churchill*, pp. 264, 271–3. Phillips to Treasury, tel. 3150, 18 Dec. 1940, FO 371/25209, W12593/8940/49; Hopkins, memo, 18 Dec. 1940, T 160/1056, F19425.
59 See mins. in FO 371/24244, A5251/131/45.
60 PREM 4/17/1: esp. Phillips to Treasury, tel. 3266, 25 Dec. 1940, p. 101; Kingsley Wood to W.S.C., 23 Dec. 1940, p. 114.
61 Ibid., Beaverbrook to W.S.C., 26 Dec. 1940, pp. 104–7; Phillips to Treasury, tel. 3286, 27 Dec. 1940, p. 95.
62 Ibid., W.S.C. to F.D.R., draft, 28 Dec. 1940, p. 86; and drafts and text of 31 Dec. message in PREM 3/469, pp. 562–70.
63 PREM 3/469: Butler to FO, tel. 3337, 31 Dec. 1940, p. 560; W.S.C. to F.D.R., tel. 19, 2 Jan. 1941, p. 557. On the destroyers see PREM 3/462/1 and FO 371/24242, A4437/131/45. For a fuller discussion of this period, published before the British sources become available see Kimball, 'Beggar my neighbor'.
64 Colville Diary, 11 Jan. 1941, quoted in Tree, *When the Moon was High*, p. 140.
65 Morgenthau Presidential Diary, 3:758. For what follows on the drafting and passage of the bill see Kimball, *The Most Unsordid Act*, chs. V–VIII.
66 Cf. Treasury–Bank of England comments in March, T 160/1051, F17286/01.
67 Hall, *North American Supply*, p. 259.
68 INF 1/872: esp. W.S.C. to Duff Cooper, 30 Nov. 1940 and Cooper, min., 15 Jan. 1941. Similar efforts by British officials in New York were also blocked. Aubrey Morgan and John Wheeler-Bennett of the British Press Service approached Russell Davenport, one of Willkie's election backers, to see if he could revive the organization that had been so successful in promoting Willkie and use it in support of the Lend-Lease bill. To do this Davenport required money, which Morgan and Wheeler-Bennett obtained from a prominent philanthropist, but meanwhile London had heard of the plan and had killed it. (Morgan, interview, 31 July 1977.)
69 F.D.R. to Hopkins, tel. 268, 26 Jan. 1941, D/S 121.841 Hopkins/10A; Hopkins to W.S.C., 27 Jan. 1941, PREM 4/25/3, p. 147.
70 See papers in PREM 4/17/2, pp. 196–202, 205–9, 217. The phrase 'a new Magna Carta' was Whitehead's.
71 T. H. Brand, memo, 17 Feb. 1941, PREM 4/17/1, p. 20.
72 T 160/1056, F19425: Horace Wilson, memo of talk between Kingsley Wood and Hopkins, 30 Jan. 1941, and Wood to Hopkins 1 Feb. 1941 enclosing *aide-mémoire*; Wood to W.S.C., 15 March 1941, PREM 4/17/2, p. 170; Morgenthau Diary, 381: 15, 12 March 1941, and 383: 339–42. Keynes, for one, had never been happy with Hopkins' breezy assurances 'that the President was obtaining a blank cheque and could be trusted to do everything to help us and to give the most liberal interpretation. But this does not adequately console me. I have never doubted that the President would use his powers to the full. The point is that the Bill is *not* a "blank cheque". Far from it. I doubt if the American authorities realise what large disbursement we have outside the specific contracts for munitions.' (Keynes to Robertson, 14 Jan. 1941, T 160/1089, F16041/8.)
73 Kimball, *The Most Unsordid Act*, p. 203. Originally the proposed amendment was to limit the transfer of existing equipment to 10 per cent in value of the total appropriation. It was Oscar Cox, the Treasury lawyer handling the bill's passage through Congress, who altered this to $1.3 billion. There is no evidence

that he acted on other than his own authority, although Morgenthau did approve after the fact. The figure of $1.3 billion apparently came from the Treasury's current estimates of Britain's outstanding commitments. (See Cox Diary, 8 Feb. 1941, and memo of Treasury conference on 14 Jan. 1941, Oscar Cox papers, FDRL, boxes 145 and 78: Aid to Britain, VI.)

74 U.S.A., House of Representatives, Commt. on Foreign Affairs, 77th Congress, 1st session, *Hearings on H.R. 1776* (Washington, 1941), p. 61; U.S.A., Senate, Commt. on Foreign Relations, 77th Cong., 1st session, *Hearings on S. 275* (Washington, 1941), p. 66.

75 U.S.A., House of Representatives, Commt. on Appropriations, 77/1, *Defense Aid Supplemental Appropriation Bill*, 1941, report no. 276 (Washington, 1941), pp. 4–5; Phillips to Treasury, tel. 1231, 20 March 1941, PREM 4/17/2, p. 159.

76 See published accounts in Sayers, *Financial Policy*, pp. 388–9; Blum, *From the Morgenthau Diaries*, II, 235–41; and D. C. Coleman, *Courtaulds*, II, ch. XV. See also correspondence in PREM 4/17/2. F.D.R. approved the ultimatum on 10 March (Morgenthau Presidential Diary, 4: 851).

77 Morgenthau Diary, 381: 268–70 and 382: 354; Phillips to Treasury tels. 1116 and 1143, PREM 4/17/2, pp. 190 and 185–6.

78 Ibid., W.S.C. to Wood, and to Halifax, tel. 1427 both 15 March 1941, pp. 176, 162–3. Cf. Winant to F.D.R., tel. 1060, 18 March 1941, Morgenthau Diary, 383: 199–202.

79 In the end Morgenthau was so afraid of being grilled on British assets and also on the tax increases required to pay for Lend-Lease that he persuaded Harold Smith, the Budget Director, to take his place. (Cf. Morgenthau Diary, 381: 94 and 382: 44–51.)

80 Cf. Kimball, *Most Unsordid Act*, pp. 143–4; Morgenthau Diary, 347: 233 (Knox); Ickes, *Secret Diary*, III, 409–11.

81 Phillips to Treasury, tel. 3282, 27 Dec. 1940, FO 371/25209, W12763/8940/49.

82 Morgenthau Diary, 382: 250, 16 March 1941. For the background on AVC in the 1930s see the excellent account in Coleman, *Courtaulds*, II, chs. XIII, XV, with whose analysis I concur.

83 Kimball, *The Most Unsordid Act*, pp. 237, 10.

84 Chamberlain, draft memo on relations with Japan, Sept. 1934, para. 11, NC 8/19/1. It was an apposite allusion. Mr Jorkins figures briefly in *David Copperfield* as the dreaded but unseen junior partner in the law firm of Spenlow and Jorkins. He was 'a mild man of a heavy temperament, whose place in the business was to keep himself in the background, and be constantly exhibited by name as the most obdurate and ruthless of men. If a clerk wanted his salary raised, Mr Jorkins wouldn't listen to such a proposition. If a client were slow to settle his bill of costs, Mr Jorkins was resolved to have it paid; and however painful these things might be (and always were) to the feelings of Mr Spenlow, Mr Jorkins would have his bond. The heart and hand of the good angel Spenlow would have always been open, but for the restraining demon Jorkins.' See *The Personal History of David Copperfield* (London, Gordon Fraser reprint, 1970), p. 324.

85 F.D.R. to Hull, 11 Jan. 1941, PSF 90: State Dept.; cf. Ickes, *Secret Diary*, II, 474.

86 Morgenthau Presidential Diary, 4: 852, 10 March 1941.

87 See account given by Smith to Morgenthau on 22 May 1941, Morgenthau Diary, 401: 17. Smith did not make a written record of the 15 March conversation. (See Harold D. Smith papers, FDRL, Box 13.)

88 Morgenthau Presidential Diary, 4: 851, 854.

89 'I know that the President got everything I said because I repeated most of the

things a couple of times, and I feel that as far as my financial relationship with the English is concerned he at least understands it, and that he won't be giving some orders through Hopkins or anybody else to change it without first talking to me. At least, that is my hope.' (Ibid., p. 852.)

90 For figures see Hall, *North American Supply*, p. 39; Pelling, *Britain and the Second World War*, pp. 118–19; Calder, *The People's War*, p. 266.

91 Lord Northcliffe, 1 July 1917, quoted in Burk, 'Great Britain in the United States, 1917–1918', p. 228.

92 Aubrey Morgan, interview, 31 July 1977.

93 Beaverbrook to W.S.C., 19 Feb. 1941, PREM 4/17/1, pp. 49–50; CAB 65/17, WM 19 (41) 6, 20 Feb. 1941; cf. Wood to W.S.C., 3 April 1941, PREM 4/17/2, p. 148.

94 W.S.C. to Wood, 20 March 1941, PREM 4/17/2.

### Chapter Seven

1 5s *HC Debs.*, 364: 1171, 20 Aug. 1940.

2 The eight British possessions in question were Newfoundland and Bermuda, where the leases were gifts, and the Bahamas, Jamaica, St. Lucia, Trinidad, Antigua and British Guiana, where the leases were the quid pro quo for the destroyers and other equipment. The only published account of the negotiations over the leases is in Goodhart, *Fifty Ships*, ch. XV, written before the official papers became available. The principal British documents can be found in CAB 98/6 and FO 371/24259–24263 and /26152–26159; a selection from the equally voluminous State Dept. papers in D/S 811.34544 is published in *FRUS*, 1941, III, 53–85.

3 FO to Lothian, tel. 2444, 1 Oct. 1940, FO 371/24260, A4285/3742/45.

4 Cf. 'Supplementary report on Bermuda', 26 Oct. 1940, in Adm. John W. Greenslade papers, 2/14 (LC).

5 CAB 66/14, WP (40) 485, 27 Dec. 1940; Scott, min., 11 Dec. 1940, FO 371/24263, A5125/5125/45.

6 FO 371/24262, A5203/3742/45: mins. by Scott, 18 and 28 Dec. 1940, Balfour, 26 Dec. and Eden 29 Dec.

7 Bailey, min., 7 Jan. 1941, ADM 116/4656, PD 09434/41; various mins. of Dec. 1940 in ADM 1/11200.

8 CAB 65/10, WM 311 (40) 7, 30 Dec. 1940.

9 CAB 98/6, USB 9 (40) 1, 20 Dec. 1940. See also FO 115/3422, file 2074, FO 371/26152, A53, A148/20/45 and *FRUS*, 1941, III, 53–8.

10 Cf. FO 371/26153, pp. 192 and 206.

11 Cf. Balfour, min., 8 Feb. 1941, FO 371/26155, A726/20/45, and memo by Capt. G. D. Belben, 12 March 1941, FO 371/26159, A 1749.

12 See FO 371/26157, A1262, A1263, and *FRUS*, III, 68–75.

13 See FDRL, Map Room Papers, box 1, esp. Hull to F.D.R., 1 March 1941, enclosing draft cable of 25 Feb., and F.D.R. to Hull, 7 March; Halifax to FO, tel. 1007, 6 March, PREM 3/461/3, pp. 17–19.

14 As stated for example in CAB 65/17, WM 12 (41) 6, 3 Feb. 1941.

15 W.S.C., min., 4 March 1941, PREM 3/461/3, p. 64. For similar statements see his annotations of 26 Jan. and 16 Feb. in PREM 3/461/4, p. 42 and PREM 3/462/1, p. 70.

16 W.S.C. to Halifax, tel. 1213, 4 March 1941, PREM 3/461/1, p. 7.

17 FO 371/26158, A1536; drafts in PREM 3/461/3, pp. 5–6, 20–5.

18 W.S.C. to F.D.R., tel. 1295, 10 March 1941, PREM 3/469, p. 521.

19 For a colourful account of one of these, probably that of 5 March, see Winant, *Letter from Grosvenor Square*, pp. 23–6.

20 Moyne to Hoare, 19 March 1941, Templewood papers, T/XIII/18 (Lord Moyne had become Colonial Secretary on 8 Feb., following the sudden death of Lord Lloyd). Winant to F.D.R. and Hull, tel. 1207, 27 March 1941, *FRUS*, 1941, III, 84.

21 *Agreement . . . relating to the Bases Leased to the United States of America*, Cmd. 6259 (London 1941); cf. Winant to F.D.R. and Hull, tels., 8, 9, 12 March 1941, *FRUS*, 1941, III, 77–82.

22 Quotations from Hull to Johnson, tel. 303, 29 Jan. 1941, ibid., p. 68; W.S.C. to Halifax, tel. 1185, 3 March 1941, PREM 3/461/1, p. 14.

23 Subsequently most of the detailed problems were resolved by the British military mission in Washington, thus confirming David Scott's prediction in January that eventually 'we shall have to arrive at some formula which will look all right to the outside world and settle the question by staff talks'. (Min. by Scott 21 Jan. 1941, FO 371/26153, A262; cf. FO 371/26161, A2802, A3228.)

24 Hull to N. Butler, 30 Dec. 1940, *FRUS*, 1940, III, 76; FO 371/26154, A405, and FO 371/26155, A726, min., R. A. Butler, min., 1C Feb. 1941.

25 See FO 371/26159, A2023—quotation from Balfour, min., 25 March 1941, citing comments of Squadron Leader Maurice Banks of Air Ministry.

26 See 5s *HC Debs.*, 365: 193–4, 19 Sept. 1940; 367: 396–7, 3 Dec. 1940; 369: 642–3, 766, 27 Feb. and 4 March 1941; 370: 254–64, 697–8, 19 and 27 March 1941; 371: 22–3, 22 April 1941. For HMG comments see FO 371/24262, A4883, A5009/3742/45; CAB 65/18, WM 23 (41) 6, 4 March 1941; FO 371/26159, A1944; FO 371/26160, A2230.

27 Cf. PREM 3/461/4, pp. 21–5.

28 'Confidential note for use with Editors and the B.B.C.', no date (*c*. 24 March), PREM 3/461/2, pp. 56–7; cf. FO 371/26159, A2139, Nicolson, *Diaries*, II, 153.

29 When the U.S. Embassy requested a last-minute delay in the signing ceremony so that F.D.R. could send a message to Congress, Churchill noted testily: 'The Americans should be told that I too have a Parliament to consider . . .' (W.S.C. to FO, 25 March 1941, PREM 3/461/2, p. 65.)

30 W.S.C. to colonial governors, tel., 25 March 1941, PREM 3/464/1, p. 26.

31 Cf. correspondence in Greenslade papers, 1/1, esp. E. J. Sadler to Stark, 5 Sept. and transcript of Sadler-Greenslade phone conversation, 30 Sept. 1940.

32 *The Daily Express*, 18 Jan. 1941, reported Knox as saying, in response to a suggestion that the U.S. should buy the islands outright instead of negotiating a 99-year lease, 'The British West Indies possessions are going to be ours some day, anyway, by willing consent; and I wouldn't attempt to drive a hard bargain with them while Britain is fighting for her life.' HMG decided to make no comment in view of Knox's importance as a supporter of aid to Britain. (Cf. FO 371/26154, A354.)

33 E.g. F.D.R. to Hull, 11 Jan. 1941, PSF 90: State Dept.; cf. Davis and Lindley, *How War Came to America*, pp. 74–8.

34 See Taussig to Hull, 12 Sept. 1940, and Welles to F.D.R., 5 Dec. 1940, Hull papers 48/138 and /141; Taussig's report in PSF 89: State Dept.; Welles to F.D.R., 5 April 1941, PSF 90: State Dept.; and generally Corkran, *Patterns of International Cooperation in the Caribbean*, chs. 1–3.

35 On these two themes see Lewis, *Growth of the Modern West Indies*, esp. pp. 33–5, 58–61, 211–12, 308–12, 413–15; Bourne, *Britain and the Balance of Power in North America*.

36 W.S.C. to F.D.R. and F.D.R. to W.S.C., 15 Dec. 1940, Butler to FO, tel. 3113, 17 Dec. 1940, FO 954/29A, pp. 93, 96, 97. See also D/S 701. 4111/1141½.

37 Morgenthau Diary, 15 Dec. 1940, 340: 1; Long, MS. Diary, 16 Dec. 1940, p. 222.

38 Memos by Berle, 20 Dec. and by Welles, 21 Dec. 1940, D/S 701. 4111/1179 and /1172; Casey, *Personal Experience*, pp. 46–7; Wheeler-Bennett, *Special Relationships*, pp. 117–18; Butler to FO, tels. 3108 and 3113, 15 and 17 Dec. 1940, FO 954/29A, pp. 95, 97.

39 Sylvester, *Life with Lord George*, 16 Dec. 1940, p. 282; Lord Dawson to Lloyd George, 16 Dec. 1940, Lloyd George papers, G/6/4/12.

40 Halifax to Hankey, 26 Dec. 1940, Hankey papers, HNKY 5/4/27; for background see Halifax, diary, A 7.8.7, pp. 365 ff., Birkenhead, *Halifax*, pp. 467–70, and Young, *Churchill and Beaverbrook*, pp. 170–5.

41 Sylvester, *Life with Lloyd George*, pp. 279, 281; Chamberlain Diary, 30 Sept. 1940, NC 2/24A.

42 As Elisabeth Barker suggests, *Churchill and Eden*, p. 146. In 1945 Churchill wrote of Halifax: 'At every step he sees a crisis which can be met only "by appeasement" .' (W.S.C. to Eden, 3 Jan. 1945, PREM 4/27/9, p. 588.)

43 Churchill was not the only PM to take this view. In May 1923 Stanley Baldwin had urged his predecessor as Tory leader, Austen Chamberlain, to take the post. Cf. Keith Middlemas and John Barnes, *Baldwin: A Biography* (London, 1969), pp. 175–6; Sir Charles Petrie, *The Life and Letters of the Right Hon. Sir Austen Chamberlain* (London, 1940), II, 221–2, also p. 145. Similarly, Margaret Thatcher pressed the Ambassadorship on Edward Heath in May 1979.

44 See Chamberlain Diary, 9, 24 and 30 Sept. 1940, NC 2/24A; Chamberlain–Churchill correspondence, Sept.–Oct. 1940, NC 7/9/97–103.

45 Lysaght, *Bracken*, pp. 181–2.

46 Harvey, MS. Diary, 30 Sept., 2 Oct. 1940, B.L. Add. Mss. 56397; Chamberlain Diary, 30 Sept. 1940, NC 2/24A.

47 Dalton Diary, 23:93, 97–9, 11 and 14 Nov. 1940; *Daily Herald*, 12 Nov. 1940, p. 2f; Harvey, MS. Diary, 24 Nov. 1940.

48 Morgenthau Diary, 352: 224, 29 Jan. 1941 (France); Lady Astor to Eleanor Roosevelt, 28 Dec. 1940, FDRL, PPF 192, and to Norman Davis, 15 March 1941, Davis papers (LC), box 2.

49 Quotations from Halifax to Eden, W.S.C. and Simon, 4 Feb., 13 and 21 March 1941, Hickleton papers (Cambridge), A4.410.4.15, 11 and 14. Generally see Birkenhead, *Halifax*, chs. XIX–XXII.

50 Moffat Diary, vol. 46, 'Notes on visit to Washington, Oct. 6–10 1940', p. 5— conversation with Jimmy Dunn; on Kennedy's ambassadorial career see Koskoff, *Kennedy*, pp. 114–295, and the brief note by Vieth, 'The Donkey and the Lion'. Also Beschloss, *Kennedy and Roosevelt*, chs. 6–7.

51 Cf. e.g. Long, *War Diary*, 15 Feb. 1941, pp. 180–1. On Winant's ambassadorship see Bellush, *He Walked Alone*, esp. pp. 157–81; also Whittemore, 'A quiet triumph'. I hope to discuss the background to Winant's appointment more fully in a subsequent article.

52 Sherwood, *Roosevelt and Hopkins*, p. 230. Ch. XI of this book provides the standard account of Hopkins' visit, based on his own papers.

53 See FO 371/24234, A4279/39/45, quotation from Colville to Whitehead, 4 Nov. 1940; cf. Lash, *Roosevelt and Churchill*, pp. 246–7.

54 W.S.C. to F.D.R., tels., 6 and 16 Nov., Lothian to FO, tel. 2864, 30 Nov. 1940, FO 371/24242, A4437/131/45; W.S.C. to Lothian, tel. 3233, 27 Nov. 1940, FO 371/24249, A4935/434/45. Cf. W.S.C. to F.D.R., and reply, 8 and 10 Nov. 1944, PREM 3/472, pp. 142–3, 137. F.D.R. thanked W.S.C. for 'repetition of your 1940 message which I certainly had not forgotten'. Churchill's

original message is to be found filed with the daily British military reports in PSF 51. Lash, *Roosevelt and Churchill*, pp. 245–7, 271–3, brings out well the part that suspicions about Churchill's attitude to the U.S.A. and to F.D.R. played in the origins of the Hopkins mission, although, in my opinion, he is somewhat insensitive to Churchill's own situation. On F.D.R.'s suspicions see also ch. 3, n. 134.

55 Lysaght, *Bracken*, pp. 183–4; cf. Bracken to Swope, 16 Jan. 1939, Hopkins papers, FDRL, Box 304: London visit (A), and Bracken to Hopkins, 25 Aug. 1940 and reply, 14 Sept., in Hopkins microfilm roll 19, box 301. Bracken was sent to meet Hopkins at Poole and escort him to London. Just before doing so he also had a long talk about Hopkins with the U.S. Chargé d'Affaires in London. (Cf. Herschel V. Johnson Diary, 7 Jan. 1941, Johnson papers, box 7, vol. 3, Univ. of North Carolina, Chapel Hill.)

56 See Casey to Bruce, and reply, Casey to Frankfurter, 6, 8, 10 Jan. 1941, Frankfurter papers, 257/743–5 (LC); also Casey, *Personal Experience*, pp. 51–2.

57 Hopkins Diary memo, 10 Jan. 1941, Hopkins micro. roll 19, box 302; Hopkins to FDR, 14 Jan. 1941, in Sherwood, *Roosevelt and Hopkins*, p. 243.

58 Hopkins to W.S.C. (8 Feb. 1941), PREM 4/25/3, p. 130. According to Oliver Lyttelton, President of the Board of Trade, 'at one stage of the Churchill–Hopkins Odyssey the evening finished rather late, at 2 a.m.'. Lyttelton 'crept to bed but was prevented from sleeping by Mr. Hopkins, who slunk into his room and ensconced himself in a chair in front of the fire, muttering at intervals "Jesus Christ! What a man!" ' (Cadogan, min., 29 Jan. 1941, FO 371/26179, A101/101/45.)

59 Given to Ed Murrow of CBS (Sherwood, *Roosevelt and Hopkins*, p. 236).

60 Ickes, talking with the journalist Bob Kintner in August, learned that Paul Smith, Editor-in-Chief of the *San Francisco Chronicle*, had been to Britain and 'brought back word that Churchill did not like Harry Hopkins. This was after Hopkins' first trip. However, Churchill hopes that Hopkins will go to England often. The reason is that Hopkins is a fluent promiser . . . Churchill's theory apparently is that is [*sic*—if] Hopkins keeps coming over and making bigger and better promises it will put a heavy obligation upon this country to deliver on the premises [*sic*—promises].' (Ickes, TS. diary, 2 Aug. 1941, p. 5818.) Whether or not it is true that Churchill's first reactions to Hopkins were unfavourable, as Ickes observed in February, 'if, as his personal representative, the President should send to London a man with the bubonic plague, Churchill would, nevertheless, see a good deal of him.' (Ickes, *Secret Diary*, III, 429.)

61 For background see Harriman and Abel, *Special Envoy*, pp. 3–27.

62 Moffat Diary, 31 Jan. 1941; Berle Diary, 12 and 17 March.

63 Cf. Bridges, memo, 'British Missions in the United States', 24 Sept. 1940, PREM, 3/477/1, pp. 21–4.

64 CAB 65/10, WM 304 (40) 6, 12 Dec. 1940; cf. PREM 3/483/5.

65 Cf. Pickersgill, *Mackenzie King Record*, I, 183–4; transcripts of Morgenthau–King phone conversations, 5, 9, and 14 Dec. 1940. Morgenthau Diary, 336: 41–4, 337: 104–7, 339: 426–7; W.S.C. to King, tel. 184, 13 Dec. 1940, PREM 4/43B/1, p. 31.

66 Standard accounts are Butler, *Grand Strategy*, II, 423–7; Watson, *Chief of Staff*, pp. 367–82; Matloff and Snell, *Strategic Planning*, pp. 32–43. There is also a useful background discussion in Leighton and Coakley, *Global Logistics*, ch. II. The fullest account, using British and U.S. sources and concentrating on the naval discussions, is Leutze, *Bargaining for Supremacy*, esp. chs. 13–15. This seems to me somewhat misleading, particularly with respect to Far

Eastern policy, as I have suggested briefly in my review article, 'Competitive Co-operation', pp. 237–8 and more fully below in ch. 9. Records of the meetings are in CAB 99/5.

67 Cf. Greene, 'The military view of American national policy, 1904–1940'.
68 A copy is in PSF (S) 5.
69 Lothian to FO, tels. 2802, 2851, 25 and 29 Nov. 1940, FO 371/24243, A4966/131/45.
70 Lee Diary, 29, 30 Dec. 1940, 2 Jan. 1941, in Leutze (ed.), *London Observer*, pp. 192–4, 197–8. Churchill also tried to crack down on information to the Dominions (who were never generously treated at the best of times): 'It is a pity we have to tell so much to so many', he minuted on 13 Dec. 1940 (PREM 4/43/B/1, p. 49).
71 F.D.R. to Knox, 26 Jan. 1941, PSF (Deptl) 80: Navy. The ABC-1 report referred throughout to Britain and the U.S.A. as 'Associated Powers'.
72 The U.S. delegates asked that HMG should agree 'That the United States and the United Kingdom furnish each other, under suitable safeguard, full texts and particulars of any treaties, secret or otherwise, or other commitments, which may affect either the action proposed in the enclosed report, or the peace terms to be agreed upon after the cessation of hostilities. If no such treaties or commitments exist, a categorical statement that none such exist should be made by both governments.' The Chiefs of Staff, in conveying this request, noted that the U.S. delegation attached particular importance to it, and the Cabinet's Defence Commt. agreed on 15 May 1941. (See CAB 80/27, COS (41) 284, and CAB 69/2, DC (O) (41) 30th mtg.) See also below, ch. 10.
73 W.S.C. to Alexander and Pound, 17 Feb. 1941, PREM 3/489/4, p. 57.
74 *Office of the United States Naval Attaché, American Embassy, London, England, 1939–1946* (unpublished TS. by Historical Section of Staff of Commander Naval Forces Europe, 1946) in U.S. Navy, Operational Archives, Washington Navy Yard, pp. 1–2, 5.
75 Langer and Gleason, *Challenge to Isolation*, p. 741.
76 The following discussion is based on Langer and Gleason, *Challenge to Isolation*, ch. xxi/5–6, and *Undeclared War*, chs. iii, xii; Woodward, *British Foreign Policy*, I, chs. xiii and xiv, II, ch. xxi; and esp. Thomas, *Britain and Vichy*, chs. 3–5; and Smyth, 'Diplomacy and Strategy of Survival: British Policy and Spanish Non-Belligerency'.
77 TS. note, 'Hoare and Spain', 1 Oct. 1940, Dalton papers, 7/2, p. 13.
78 W.S.C. to F.D.R., 23 Nov. 1940, PREM 3/468.
79 On whom see Halstead, 'Diligent diplomat'.
80 E.g. W.S.C.–F.D.R. correspondence of 10–18 Nov. 1940 in PREM 3/468, and 2–6 April 1941, PREM 3/469.
81 See Dalton Diary, 31 Aug., 2 Sept., 24 Oct. and 7 Nov. 1940. Dalton and Kingsley Wood agreed that Lothian's 'strong suit is high-minded ballyhoo. This may be quite useful in America so long as the policy of HMG has not to be too exactly based upon it.' (9 Nov.) Dalton attached even greater importance to the blockade of France than of Spain, because of the considerable leakage of supplies from Vichy to the German-occupied zone.
82 F.D.R. to W.S.C., 31 Dec. 1940 and W.S.C. to F.D.R., 3 Jan. 1941, PREM 3/469, pp. 579–83; CAB 65/17, WM 1 (41) 3, 2 Jan. 1941.
83 Basic accounts are Mansergh, *Survey of British Commonwealth Affairs . . . 1939–52*, pp. 58–75; Carroll, *Ireland in the War Years*, chs. 2–6; Dwyer, *Irish Neutrality and the U.S.A.*, chs. 3–5.
84 The three ports were Lough Swilly, Cobh (Queenstown) and Berehaven. Chamberlain always maintained that Dev had given him private assurances 'of

his intention to put them into a proper state of defence, to consult with us as to how that should be done and to buy his material in the U.K.' but that he would not agree to these being written into the 1938 agreement for fear of domestic criticism. (Cf. Chamberlain to Ida, 1 May 1938, NC 18/1/1049.)

85 Van Creveld, *Hitler's Strategy: The Balkan Clue*, argues (esp. pp. 33–9), contrary to established opinion, that Hitler knew of and approved in principle of Mussolini's plan to attack Greece. For British policy see Butler, *Grand Strategy*, II, chs. xvi and xix; also Cruickshank, *Greece 1940–1941*; Van Creveld, 'Prelude to disaster: the British decision to aid Greece'; Barker, *British Policy in South-East Europe*, esp. ch. 10.

86 CAB 65/21, WM 20 (41) 4, 24 Feb. 1941; COS report, quoted in Butler, *Grand Strategy*, II, 442–3. Privately, policymakers were even more pessimistic. Churchill 'thinks Greece is lost', Harry Hopkins noted as early as 10 January. Sir John Dill, Chief of the Imperial General Staff, took a similar view six weeks later. (See Hopkins diary memo, 10 Jan. 1941, Hopkins micro. 19/302; CIGS to VCIGS, 21 Feb. 1941, PREM 3/206/3, p. 173.) It was the advice of Eden, who had toured the Middle East extensively over the previous weeks, that helped sway the Cabinet.

87 According to the Cabinet minutes for 24 Feb., Churchill 'was in favour of going forward to the rescue of Greece, one of the results of which might be to bring in Turkey and Yugoslavia, and to force the Germans to bring in more troops from Germany. The reaction of the United States would also be favourable' (CAB 65/21, p. 27). Two months later Hoare wrote from Madrid to say that: 'I have always taken the view that we could not allow Greece to collapse without a vigorous attempt to save her. The moral effect of another collapse of this kind after Poland, Denmark, Scandinavia and the Low Countries would have been disastrous, particularly in the U.S.A.' (Hoare to Churchill, 21 April 1941, Templewood papers, T/XIII/16).

88 Cadogan, *Diaries*, 24 Feb. 1941, p. 358.

89 Cf. Cruickshank, *Greece*, pp. 143, 182–3; Van Creveld, 'Prelude to disaster', esp. pp. 91–2. It should however be remembered that it was not until early June 1941 that HMG was sure that Hitler had now turned his attentions on Russia. It therefore saw the Germans' Balkan campaign not as a flank operation but as part of their continued attempt to cut Britain's imperial lifelines. (See Hinsley, *British Intelligence*, I, chs. 8 and 11.)

90 Dykes to CIGS, tel., 5 Feb. 1941, FO 371/29795, R1005/1003/67. For similar reports by U.S. observers see e.g. MacVeagh to F.D.R., 19 Jan. 1941, PSF (Dip) 54: Greece. There is a good account, based on Donovan's papers, in Langer and Gleason, *Undeclared War*, pp. 397–400.

91 Eden to W.S.C., tel. 361, 22 Feb. 1941, PREM 4/25/5, p. 214; W.S.C. to F.D.R., tel. 1295, 10 March 1941, PREM 3/469, p. 521.

92 CAB 65/21, p. 29. Similar emphasis was placed on Donovan's opinion in CIGS to VCIGS, 21 Feb. 1941, PREM 3/206/3, p 173.

93 Copy of report for Knox in PREM 4/25/5, pp. 197–202. A précis was cabled to London on 21 Feb. (Lampson to FO, tel. 345, FO 371/29778, R1483/113/67). Presumably it was to this message that reference was made in the War Cabinet on 24 Feb. The description of it as a telegram from Donovan 'to the President' was perhaps a significant slip, reflecting HMG's uncertainty as to Donovan's status and importance.

94 Although it should be noted that Churchill was already attracted by this idea of the Balkans as the vulnerable soft under-belly of the Axis—and he was to press it repeatedly on the Americans in 1942–44. (See Barker, *British Policy in South-East Europe*, pp. 13–19, 101, 111–25.)

95 Stimson Diary, 15 and 17 April, 33: 160, 161, 167. In December 1940 the President had impulsively promised the Greeks 30 fighters, but it soon became apparent that all available planes were earmarked either for Britain or for the U.S.A. Embarrassed, F.D.R. and the War and Navy Depts. wanted to bury the whole business but State insisted that to renege would gravely damage the U.S.A.'s prestige in the Balkans. After a monumental bureaucratic battle the planes were released. They were just being packed for shipment as the Germans invaded Greece. (Langer and Gleason, pp. 116–18, 400–1.)

96 One thinks of Norman Davis at the Brussels Conference in Nov. 1937, the Welles mission of March 1940, and, in a minor way, Hopkins' contribution to the interim finance crisis mentioned above, ch. 6 (c).

## Chapter Eight

1 Quotations from 'Absalom and Achitophel', II, 268–9, in James Kingsley (ed.), *The Poems of John Dryden* (Oxford, 1958), I, 279; Dalton Diary, 24: 133, 26 May 1941, following conversation with Bracken. Epigraphs to Part Three come from Sherwood, *Roosevelt and Hopkins*, p. 270; Casey, *Personal Experience*, p. 62, diary entry for 7 March 1941, based on comments by General Raymond E. Lee, U.S. military attaché in London.

2 FO to Halifax, desp. 233, 10 April 1941, FO 371/28796, W3379/37/49.

3 Hankey to Halifax, 1 May 1941, Hickleton papers (Camb.), A4.410.4.5; Halifax to Hankey, 25 May 1941, Hankey papers, HNKY 5/4; Thorne, *Allies of a Kind*, pp. 63–4; Richard Stokes to Lloyd George, 14 May 1941, Lloyd George papers, G/19/3/27 ('cigar stump'). For further examples see Dalton Diary, 28 March 1941 (Oliver Stanley); 5s *HC Debs.*, 371: 880–1, 7 May 1941 (Lloyd George); Sir James Grigg to F. A. Grigg, 9 May 1941, P. J. Grigg papers, PJGG 9/6; Chatfield, *Sunday Times*, 15 June 1941, p. 4 (cf. Chatfield papers CHT/7/2).

4 According to Dalton, the word from the FO in early February 1941 was that although Eden wrote many 'peevish minutes' he was not really a strong man and that Churchill was taking much more charge of the FO than when Halifax was Foreign Secretary. Halifax 'had guns in reserve, which A.E. has not, and could sometimes give the P.M. the unmistakable impression that he regarded him as a very vulgar and ignorant person'. (Dalton Diary, 4 Feb. 1941.) Dalton never spared those whom he disliked, but it does seem that Halifax believed, almost as a matter of principle, that one should stand up to Churchill periodically. 'He hates doormats. If you begin to give way he will simply wipe his feet upon you', he told Dalton on 14 Nov. 1940.

5 For background see Butler, *Grand Strategy*, II, esp. chs. xx and xxii.

6 Collier, *The Defence of the United Kingdom*, pp. 278, 504–5. The raid on London on 10 May destroyed the Chamber of the House of Commons.

7 Roskill, *War at Sea*, I, 616; Conn and Fairchild, *Framework of Hemisphere Defense*, p. 101.

8 Cf. Donovan's comments in ch. 5, note 27.

9 See esp. comments of late Jan. and early Feb. 1941, e.g. Stimson Diary, 32: 133, 139–40, 33: 3; Ickes, *Secret Diary*, III, 422–3, 428–9; Berle Diary, 31 Jan. 1941. Administration leaders made much of these fears in testimony during the Lend-Lease hearings—cf. Kimball, *Most Unsordid Act*, p. 187.

10 Long, *War Diary*, p. 201.

11 Berle Diary, 26 May and 5 June; Long, *War Diary*, 12 and 22 May, pp. 200 and 201; cf. Long, MS. Diary, 4 June.

12 Stimson Diary, 33: 160, 15 April 1941. For other fears about British morale see Long, *War Diary*, 12 May 1941, p. 200 (Welles); Berle Diary, 4 and 5 June; Moffat Diary, 9 June (C.D. Howe).

13 Sherwood, *Roosevelt and Hopkins*, pp. 293–4; Berle Diary, 26 May and 5 June; G. Campbell to MOI, tel. 56 Empax, 19 June 1941, PREM 3/219/1, p. 4.

14 Cf. correspondence in PSF 80: Navy Dept. for 18 March—1 April. In addition to the general accounts of F.D.R.'s policy in the Atlantic, e.g. Langer and Gleason, *The Undeclared War*, esp. chs. xiv, xvii and xxiii, see the more detailed account in Kittredge, 'U.S.–British naval cooperation', esp. pp. 405 ff.; Abbazia, *Roosevelt's Navy*, parts III and IV; Bailey and Ryan, *Hitler vs. Roosevelt*, esp. chs. 9–15; Quinlan, 'The U.S. fleet', pp. 177–90.

15 See Ghormley to Pound, 21 April 1941, copy in PREM 3/460/1, p. 7; Stark, memo for F.D.R., 6 May 1941, and Hopkins to Welles, 11 June 1941, Hopkins papers, box 305: N. Atlantic bases.

16 Stimson Diary, 19 Dec. 1940.

17 Long, MS. Diary, 12 May 1941.

18 Cf. Bailey and Ryan, *Hitler vs. Roosevelt*, p. 110.

19 Stimson Diary, 10 April 1941.

20 'You can do so, can't you?' Stimson asked. Roosevelt replied, ' "We certainly can." He seemed to jump at the suggestion', Stimson recorded. (Diary, 22 April 1941.)

21 Cole, *America First*, pp. 156–7, and Nye, pp. 194–5. On the polls see Lash, *Roosevelt and Churchill*, pp. 303–4.

22 Sherwood, *Roosevelt and Hopkins*, pp. 263, 276–7. Sherwood suggested that Willkie's accusations to this effect during the election campaign, combined with memories of similar events in 1916–17 may account for this. More significant was probably the British discovery in February, during the Washington staff talks, that the U.S. Navy was working on the hypothesis that the U.S.A. might be in the war as early as 1 April. (This was part of its response to F.D.R.'s instruction to prepare for full escorts by that date.) See CAB 99/5, BUS (J) 5th mtg., 6 Feb. 1941, p. 5, and Bellairs for Chiefs, tel. 752, 17 Feb. 1941, FO 371/26147, A881/11/45.

23 PREM 3/469: F.D.R. to W.S.C., 1 May 1941, pp. 356–60, and W.S.C. to Eden, 2 May, with draft, pp. 350, 351–4.

24 FO 371/26147, A3359, esp. Whitehead, min., 3 May, based on FO meeting; W.S.C. to F.D.R., 4 May 1941, PREM 3/469, pp. 345–9. Cf. Winant to F.D.R., tel. 1787, 6 May 1941, PSF (S) 9: Winant.

25 Cadogan, *Diaries*, 9 May 1941, p. 376; FO 371/26150, A3773. Eden contented himself by explaining Britain's needs to Winant on 13 May. (FO 371/26148, A3375.)

26 Cf. Cecil King, diary, 15 May 1941, in *With Malice Toward None*, pp. 129–30; CAB 65/18, WM 51 (41) 9, 19 May 1941. Churchill's main aim was to exploit this rare chance of keeping the *Germans* guessing, but, although he gave F.D.R. a general account of Hess's statements (PREM 3/469, pp. 402–6), it seems likely that he was happy to unsettle the Americans a bit as well.

27 Martin to Stevenson, 15 May 1941, PREM 3/476/10, p. 493.

28 FO 371/26148: A3462, esp. Halifax to FO, tel. 2006, 7 May 1941, and W.S.C., min., 10 May, A3866, esp. Eden, min., 23 May.

29 W.S.C., min., 29 April 1941, PREM 3/230/1, p. 44.

30 CAB 65/18, WM (41) 44/4 and 48/9; PREM 3/385/2, esp. W.S.C. to A. V. Alexander, 8 May 1941, p. 146; Lee, diary, 10 May, in Leutze (ed.), *London Observer*, pp. 269–70. The tonnage losses by theatre for March and April were:

North Atlantic—364,689 and 260,451; U.K.—152,862 and 99,031; Mediterranean—11,868 and 292,518. (Roskill, *War at Sea*, I, 618.)

31  CAB 69/2, DC (O) (41) 31st mtg., 19 May 1941, min. 2.
32  FO 371/26184, A3893; PREM 4/25/7, pp. 339–41; Beaverbrook to W.S.C., 24 June 1941, Beaverbrook papers, D 417/92.
33  Abbazia, *Roosevelt's Navy*, pp. 172–3; Stimson Diary, 5–9, 11, 13–14 May 1941; Ghormley to Pound, 9 June 1941, ADM 205/9, file 3.
34  Morgenthau Presidential Diary, 4: 930–1, 22 May 1941.
35  See Ickes, *Secret Diary*, III, 486–7, 508, 510–13; Stimson Diary, 12 May 1941. Complained Ickes: 'we seem to have a leader who won't lead.' (Ickes to Tugwell, 24 April 1941, Ickes papers, 373/12.)
36  Morgenthau Diary, 397: 301A, 14 May 1941.
37  Long, *War Diary*, pp. 195–6; Berle Diary, 7 May (letter to Rudolf Berle) and 4–5 June 1941.
38  The following are the main pieces of evidence. On 24 March F.D.R. told Ickes: 'things are coming to a head; Germany will be making a blunder soon.' Commented Ickes: 'There could be no doubt of the President's scarcely concealed desire that there might be an incident which would justify our declaring a state of war against Germany or at least providing convoys carrying supplies to Great Britain.' Ickes noted later that F.D.R. indicated that he was waiting for the Germans to create an incident on two or three occasions during their fishing trip in late March. (Ickes, *Secret Diary*, III, 466, cf. 523.) When Bullitt talked with F.D.R. on 23 April the latter said he had just had an argument with Stimson about the problem of public opinion and the war. 'Stimson thought that we ought to go to war now. He, the President, felt that we must await an incident and was confident that the Germans would give us an incident . . .' (Bullitt, memo of 23 April 1941, in Bullitt (ed.), *For the President*, p. 512.) On 2 May Roosevelt told Halifax 'that he regarded the patrolling arrangements as an episode only. He expected that they would lead to an incident which it seemed would not be at all unwelcome. He spoke more freely about the possibility of the United States being in than I have yet heard him.' (Halifax to FO, tel. 1947, 2 May 1941, FO 371/26147, A3359.) On 17 May Morgenthau noted in his diary: 'When I saw the President at six o'clock this evening, he said, "I am waiting to be pushed into this situation." He had previously said that he thought something might happen at any time, and I gathered that he wanted to be pushed into the war rather than lead us into it. This is no doubt what he meant.' (Morgenthau Presidential Diary, 4: 929.) In Cabinet on 23 May F.D.R. said bluntly: ' "I am not willing to fire the first shot." So it seems', Ickes concluded, 'that he is still waiting for the Germans to create an "incident".' (*Secret Diary*, III, 523.) Stimson, anxious as ever for F.D.R. to be honest with Congress, was worried that 'the President shows evidence of waiting for the accidental shot of some irresponsible captain on either side to be the occasion of his going to war'. (Stimson Diary, 23 May 1941.) For further evidence and discussion see below, section (d), particularly Churchill's report of his Atlantic Meeting with F.D.R. in August.
39  The banker and erratic New Dealer James P. Warburg, now a fervent interventionist, told Roosevelt that many interventionists felt that the British will to fight on 'is now based upon the absolute belief that we are coming into the war with them. If this belief is shaken a collapse of British morale is almost certain. There is only a very short time left in which we shall either have to make their belief come true or face a breakdown of British resistance.' (Warburg to F.D.R., 6 June 1941, PPF 540.)

40 Cf. F.D.R. to Norman Thomas, 14 May 1941, in F.D.R., *Personal Letters*, II, 1156.
41 F.D.R., *Public Papers*, 1941, 181–95. Presidential Press Conference, 28 May 1941 (FDRL).
42 Charles A. Lockwood Diary, 28 May 1941 (LC). Lockwood was the U.S. Naval Attaché in London.
43 Morgenthau Diary, 402: 177; Cox to Rosenman, 26 May 1941, Hopkins papers, box 304: May 1941 file. Sherwood, *Roosevelt and Hopkins*, p. 298. Strictly, as a puzzled FO quickly discovered (FC 371/26265), there was no legal distinction between an 'unlimited' emergency and the 'limited' one F.D.R. had proclaimed in Sept. 1939. However, the move was not purely propaganda and cosmetic—a 'full emergency', Administration lawyers felt, might permit a broader construction of certain unclear or controversial powers, particularly in the field of counter-espionage. Cf. Cox to Rosenman, cited above, and Berle, memo, 27 May, Berle papers, box 67: F.D.R.)
44 Halifax to FO, tels. 2406 and 2407, 29 May 1941, FO 371/26148, A4071, and FO 371/26150, A4069.
45 See Stimson Diary, 26 May and 19 June; Steele *First Offensive*, pp. 9–18; Conn and Fairchild, *Framework of Hemisphere Defense*, pp. 116–26.
46 Whitehead, min., 28 May, FO 371/26150, A4159; cf. FO 371/26148, A5061. Minuted Scott on 11 June: 'it is common ground that the guns will go off as soon an as incident occurs and that the only question now is whether they should not be fired before there is an incident.' (FO 371/26261, A4529.)
47 See documents in Hickleton papers, A4.410.4.3 and 5; also Hopkins memo for F.D.R., 14 June 1941, Hopkins papers, box 308: 'Shoot on Sight'. The memo is printed in Sherwood, *Roosevelt and Hopkins*, p. 299, but without any indication of its source.
48 Casey, diary, 15 June 1941, in *Personal Experience*, p. 66. As Lash points out (*Roosevelt and Churchill*, p. 326) the 27 May speech contained a barbed sentence that may well have been directed at HMG as much as at Hitler: 'We in the Americas will decide for ourselves whether, and when, and where, our American interests are attacked or our security is threatened.' (*Public Papers*, 1941, p. 193.) Even the most anglophile of interventionists got very hot under the collar at British calls for the U.S. to enter the war. Wrote Thomas Lamont: 'It is astonishing to realize how many Englishmen forget that 160 years ago we fought England to gain our own freedom. Thirty years later we had to fight her again for a less worthy cause, but for the purpose of establishing our own final independence and freedom of the seas, and we almost had to fight her a third time eighty years ago when the British Government, even though perhaps not the people, were so hostie to the preservation of our Union. So that while we are doing more and more in our war effort, our active participation is going to depend primarily upon the danger in which so many of us see our own country involved, rather than upon any duty to the British people or instructions from them.' (To Lord Catto, 29 May 1941, cf. memo by Russell Leffingwell, 23 May, in similar vein, Lamont papers, 112–12.)
49 Langer and Gleason, (*Undeclared War*, p. 458) argued on the basis of the evidence from U.S. sources then at their disposal (in 1953) that 'his hope of a shot by an irresponsible captain expressed a fleeting mood of despair rather than a consistent objective or planned course of action'.
50 Mastny, *Russia's Road to the Cold War*, p. 307. This section draws on Beaumont, *Comrades in Arms*, chs. II and III; Woodward, *British Foreign Policy*, I, xviii, and II, xix; Dawson, *Decision to Aid Russia*, esp. chs. iv–x; Herring, *Aid*

to Russia, ch. 1; Levering, *American Opinion and the Russian Alliance*, chs. ii-iii; Erickson, *Road to Stalingrad*, esp. chs. 2–5; Lash, *Roosevelt and Churchill*, esp. chs. 20–1, 26.

51 This paragraph draws on Hinsley, *British Intelligence*, I, ch. 14, and Whaley, *Codeword Barbarossa*, esp. pp. 37–40, 172–4, 227–8. In his memoirs, for instance, Hull wrote that in June 1941 he 'could not believe' the claims of some military experts 'that Hitler would eliminate Russia from the war in a matter of a few weeks', and that he repeatedly insisted that the U.S.A. should give Russia 'all aid to the hilt'. (Hull, *Memoirs*, II, 967.) On 19 June 1941 Berle recorded in his diary that Hull 'believes that the Germans will make short work of Russia and then will go "all out".' (Berle agreed.)

52 W.S.C. to F.D.R., 1 July 1941, PREM 3/469, p. 212. Cf. Hinsley, *British Intelligence*, pp. 482–3.

53 Churchill, *Second World War*, III, 330; *FRUS*, 1941, I, 767–8; Presidential Press Conference no. 750.

54 Cf. FO 371/29467, N3603, N3607.

55 See Leach, *German Strategy against Russia*, esp. chs. 4 and 8. It is often said that Hitler's Balkan campaigns necessitated a crucial six-week delay in mounting Barbarossa. Leach (pp. 165–8) puts the delay at no more than three weeks; Van Creveld (*Hitler's Strategy*, pp. 170–6, 182–3) argues that the basic problem was lack of equipment and that, regardless of the Balkan diversion, the Germans could not have mounted Barbarossa before about the end of June.

56 Sherwood, *Roosevelt and Hopkins*, ch. 15; cf. Langer and Gleason, *Undeclared War*, p. 563.

57 Stimson to F.D.R., and Knox to F.D.R., both 23 June 1941, in PSF 106: War Dept., Stimson, and PSF 82: Navy Dept., Knox. See also Stimson Diary, 23 June, and Cox to Hopkins, 23 June, Cox papers, box 145.

58 Stimson Diary, 6, 18, 20 June, 3–8 July 1941; F.D.R., *Public Papers*, 1941, pp. 255–7.

59 Kittredge, 'U.S.–British naval cooperation', pp. 542–54; Stimson Diary, 21 July, pp. 2–3.

60 Ickes, *Secret Diary*, III, 567.

61 Welles to F.D.R., 9 July 1941, PSF 96: State Dept., Welles. On 11 July F.D.R. sent this memo to the two senators approached by Welles—George and Connally—asking for 'a little unofficial and private opinion as to what you think would be the best policy—try to put over now or hold over'. I cannot trace any written reply; presumably the advice was to 'hold over'.

62 I follow here the argument of Dawson, *Decision to Aid Russia*, pp. 144–7.

63 Harvey, *War Diaries*, 25 June and 6 July 1941, pp. 25, 26. There was some concern for F.D.R.'s health after his illness in May. (Cf. FO 371/26268.)

64 Wrote W.S.C. on 1 July: 'I know you will feel with me the pain that such vast masses of tonnage have to be sunk before being replaced by colossal American efforts.' (PREM 3/469.) Cf. CAB 69/2, DC(O) 45 (41) 1, 3 July 1941.

65 FO 371/26148, A5102, esp. Cripps to FO, tel. 691, 1 July 1941 and accompanying mins.; FO 371/29486, N3540: Halifax to FO, tel. 3162, 7 July, and mins. by Sargent, 9 July, and Cadogan and Scott, 10 July. On Halifax's desire to avoid appearing to press F.D.R. see also Stimson Diary, 24 June 1941, p. 2. Sir Noel Hall, a senior MEW official then in Washington, told the FO on 21 July that Halifax's calmness and patience that summer 'when everybody around him was urging him to put the Administration on the spot to get a final decision' had been invaluable. Scott took this as confirmation of other evidence that Halifax had now settled down and survived the worst of the criticism about him. Cadogan was pleased: 'I have got a copy, which I might

show to P.M.' 'Good', noted Eden. (FO 371/26144, A6182, mins. by Scott, 1 Aug., Cadogan and Eden, 2 Aug. 1941.)

66 Concluded Churchill: 'May I ask that this should be accepted at once as a decision of policy and that it should be referred if necessary to the Cabinet on Monday.' Not surprisingly, no such referral was necessary. (PREM 3/460/4, p. 10: W.S.C., minute, 28 June 1941; see also pp. 4–14 and Stimson Diary, 24 June 1941, pp. 2–3.)

67 PREM 3/230/1, p. 21: W.S.C., min., 7 July 1941.

68 Ibid.: W.S.C. to Eden, 7 July 1941, p. 18.

69 Ibid.: Halifax to FO, tel. 2941, 25 June, and W.S.C. to Eden, 25 June, pp. 27, 26; Churchill, *Complete Speeches*, 9 July 1941, VI, 6446–7.

70 At F.D.R.'s personal request three U.S. journalists, en route for Iceland, were removed from a train at Inverness. (See Eden to Halifax, 9 July 1941, FO 954/29A, p. 231; MOI Guidance Memos, 659 (4), 683 (3), 712 (2) in Dep. Monckton Trustees, Box 7.)

71 See Butler, *Grand Strategy*, II, 577–81; Churchill, *Second World War*, III, 373–7.

72 See accounts of Anglo-American meeting of 24 July in Hopkins Papers, Box 306: Harriman–Beaverbrook Mission (1); Lee, *London Observer*, ed. Leutze, pp. 304, 349–51; Churchill, *Second World War*, III, 377–9. Also account of meeting of 9 Aug. 1941 in CAB 99/18, COS(R) 5 and Wilson, *First Summit*, pp. 148–9. W.S.C. discussed the question at length in his letter of 20 Oct. 1941 to F.D.R. (see Map Room papers, box 1).

73 E.g. *FRUS*, 1941, III, 278, 284–7; Harriman and Abel, *Special Envoy*, pp. 162–76; Miles to Marshall, 29 Sept. 1941, copy in Hopkins Papers, box 307: Return to London (2); Stimson Diary, 30 Sept. and 1 Oct. 1941.

74 E.g. Stimson to F.D.R., 8 July 1941, and enclsd. tels., PSF(S) 9: War Dept.

75 According to Hopkins on 24 July (see memo in Hopkins Papers cited in note 72). F.D.R. probably also shared W.S.C.'s view that the Middle East was more important than the Far East, if Britain had to choose—that had been his opinion in April 1939, at least. (See ch. 2 (e) and note 147.)

76 See Baram, *Department of State in the Middle East*, esp. pp. 7, 54–5, 157–8.

77 For a recent account see Langer, 'The Harriman–Beaverbrook mission'.

78 For the same period the Army had initially offered Russia 1,200 planes. Under the October protocol, however, Britain and the U.S. were each to provide 1,800 (200 per month) and the increase in the U.S. commitment was taken initially from production for the U.S. Army rather than for Britain. On this see Leighton and Coakley, *Global Logistics*, pp. 99–101.

79 Ibid., pp. 89–104.

80 This is discussed in an excellent essay by Leighton, 'The American arsenal policy in World War II', esp. pp. 221–35.

81 To quote Emerson, 'Roosevelt as Commander-in-Chief', p. 187.

82 See above, ch. 1 (f), note 147, and ch. 2 (b), note 33.

83 CAB 99/18, COS(R) 12, II/5 (Hopkins); Morgenthau Diary, 4: 952, 4 Aug. 1941; Divine, *Foreign Policy and U.S. Presidential Elections*, I, 88–9. See also Sherwood, *Roosevelt and Hopkins*, p. 272, where greater emphasis is placed on F.D.R.'s belief in sea power. F.D.R. also seems to have feared that if official Allied strategy was to invade and crush Germany, this would harden the support of the German people for the Nazis. (Stimson Diary, 25 Sept. 1941, pp. 2–3.)

84 COS(R) Strategic Review, 31 July 1941, CAB 99/18, COS(R) 14, esp. paras. 28–9, 36–8. For Army dissent see Pownall, *Diaries*, II, 20 and 39, entries for 11 June and 20 Aug. 1941.

85 CAB 69/8, DC(O) 3 (41) 1, SSF, 12 Jan. 1941; Pownall, *Diaries*, II, 20; Churchill, *Complete Speeches*, VI, 6350, 9 Feb. 1941; King, Diary, 23 Aug. 1941, in *With Malice Toward None*, p. 139 ('psychological war'). W.S.C. elaborated on how armoured divisions would help speed up the end of the war in messages to F.D.R. on 25 July and 20 Oct. 1941 (Map Room Papers, Box 1). See also Sherwood, *Roosevelt and Hopkins*, pp. 239, 262, 272, 375.

86 The standard account is Wilson, *The First Summit*, written before the British official documents became available. Some of the latter are used in Lash, *Roosevelt and Churchill*, ch. 23.

87 In a cable to the Dominion PMs on 3 Aug., just before he left, Churchill said 'I have never had the pleasure of meeting President Roosevelt.' (FO 371/26151, A6944.) On F.D.R.'s chagrin see Sherwood, *Roosevelt and Hopkins*, pp. 350–1; also above, ch. 3 (d) note 134. After discussing the question at the conference both decided conclusively that they *had* met before (PREM 4/71, p. 88). Thomas Lamont spoke with F.D.R. on 16 Aug. in Maine. In his notes of F.D.R.'s remarks is the cryptic and intriguing sentence: 'W.C. surprised me very much.' No elaboration is given. In response to Lamont's question, F.D.R. said he felt more encouraged than he had been for many months. (Lamont Papers, 127–26.)

88 Cadogan, *Diaries*, pp. 397, 399; FO 371/28903, W9610/426/49, mins. by Whitehead and Balfour, 1 Aug. 1941.

89 Lamont, notes, point 15 (F.D.R.); CAB 66/18, WP (41) 202, IV/3 (W.S.C.) (much of which is reprinted in the account in *Second World War*, III, 384).

90 E.g. Dalton Diary, 25: 10, 10 July 1941 on the array of ministers, generals and diplomats assembled for a dinner at the Savoy Hotel in honour of the interventionist American broadcaster Raymond Gram Swing: 'just a little humiliating, though we shall soon get more and more used to this sort of thing'. Particularly striking are these comments from the Viceroy of India to Halifax, when the latter was home on leave: 'How glad you will be to be relieved for a little from the heavy labour of toadying your pack[?] of pole-squatting parvenus! What a country, and what savages those who inhabit it! My wonder is that anyone with the money to pay for the fare to somewhere else condescends to stay in the country, even for a moment! What a nuisance they will be over this lease-lend sham before we have finished with it! I shan't be a bit surprised if we have to return some of their shells at them, through their own guns! I love some clever person's quip about Americans being the only people in recorded times who have passed from savagery to decadence without experiencing the intervening state of civilisation! Mind you Edward! I know you don't say all this, but nothing will persuade me that you don't feel it, or that it will not do you a heap of good to read what I have written. Well, you must go on with your good work, & get from them all you can for goodness knows! we want it.' (Linlithgow to Halifax, 26 July 1941, Hickleton Papers, A4.410.23.2A. The 'lease-lend sham' is a reference to the negotiations then in train for the 'Consideration' the U.S.A. would receive in return—see ch. 10 (c).) Of course, Linlithgow was blowing off steam, but his letter, with its revealing last sentence, testifies eloquently to the frustration and damaged pride of British leaders.

91 See ch. 10 (a). Cf. Liddell Hart to Lloyd George, 10 Sept. 1941, on how the U.S.A. was currently 'playing the same hand that we did, in relation to Continental allies, in the 18th century' (Lloyd George Papers, G/9/3/67).

92 W.S.C. to Queen Elizabeth, 3 Aug. 1941, PREM 3/485/6, p. 16.

93 Lee, *London Observer*, ed. Leutze, pp. 240, 368–9, 375–6, 383; Wilson, *First Summit*, 223–4; F.D.R., *Public Papers*, 1941, p. 322.

94 This quotation, and, with the exception of note 95, all others in the paragraph come from CAB 65/19, WM 84 (41) 1, annex.
95 CAB 66/18, WP (41) 202.
96 Dalton Diary, 25: 54, 25 Aug. 1941; see also similar comments on pp. 54–5 by David Eccles, an MEW official who had been in the U.S.A. since early 1941. General Pownall, Vice-Chief of the Imperial General Staff, who attended the 19 Aug. Cabinet, also seemed somewhat sceptical of W.S.C.'s account (Pownall, *Diaries*, II, 37).
97 CAB 65/19, WM 86 (41) 3, annex.
98 W.S.C. to Hopkins, tel., 28 Aug. 1941, PREM 3/224/2, p. 37; copy dated 29 Aug. 1941 marked with F.D.R.'s request to Hopkins: 'Will you speak to me about this?' in PSF(S) 2: Atlantic Charter Mtg.; Hopkins, memo, 2 Sept. 1941, Hopkins Papers, box 308: Shoot on Sight.
99 Langer and Gleason, *Undeclared War*, say it was put into operation after the Atlantic Meeting, but give two different dates—20 Aug. (p. 665) and 26 Aug. (p. 742). The basic source—Kittredge, 'U.S.-British naval cooperation— seems confused on this point, but, so far as I can ascertain, a proper system of escort for Allied vessels was not instituted until 16 Sept.
100 Cf. his comments on Plan 4 in Kittredge, pp. 549–50
101 Next day F.D.R. told W.S.C. that he was planning to broadcast on the 11th about the attack and 'to make perfectly clear the action we intend to take in the Atlantic'. As in May, W.S.C. tried to underline for F.D.R. the importance Britain attached to his speech. 'We await' the statement, he said, 'with profound interest'. (Tels. of 5 and 7 Sept. 1941 in FO 371/26151, A7164.)
102 F.D.R., *Public Papers*, 1941, pp. 384–92. On the incident and F.D.R.'s treat-ment of it see Abbazia, *Roosevelt's Navy*, ch. 20, and Bailey and Ryan, *Hitler vs. Roosevelt*, ch. 12.
103 The operational area followed longitude 26° West as far north as 53° North. It then ran north-east to include Iceland before following 10° West from 65° North. (See Kittredge, pp. 588–9.)
104 Beaverbrook to Churchill, 13 Sept. 1941, PREM 3/474/1, pp. 11–12. ·
105 Cf. Little to A. V. Alexander, 22 Sept. 1941, ADM 1/14994.
106 F.D.R., *Public Papers*, 1941, p. 407. Notice again the expansive definition of American interests, characteristic of all F.D.R.'s speeches of the period on foreign affairs, and foreshadowing the orthodoxy of the post-war era of Ameri-can globalism. (Cf. above, ch. 2 (b) and note 25.) Part of F.D.R.'s reason for retaining certain provisions of the Act—particularly those regulating the rights of private citizens in dealing with belligerents (private loans, arms trade and travel on belligerent ships)—was his continued belief that the Administra-tion should be kept control over foreign relations. As we saw in chapter 1 (e), this had been one of his main reasons, with Wilson's cautionary example in mind, for accepting the neutrality legislation in the first place. And in his 9 Oct. 1941 message he said: 'I would not go back to the earlier days when private traders could gamble with American life and property in the hope of personal gain, and thereby embroil this country in some incident in which the American public had no direct interest. But, today,' he pointed out, 'under the controls exercised by the Government, no ship and no cargo can leave the United States, save on an errand which has first been approved by govern-mental authority. And the test of that approval is whether the exportation will promote the defense of the United States.' (Ibid., p. 410.)
107 There is a good discussion in Langer and Gleason, *Undeclared War*, pp. 750–9.

108 CAB 65/19, WM 84 (41) 1, annex, 19 Aug. 1941; note by Malcolm Mac-Donald of talk with Mackenzie King, 3 Nov. 1941, immediately after King's return to Canada from visit to Hyde Park, PREM 3/476/10, p. 413.

109 This seems to be the view of Robert Dallek, for instance (*Roosevelt and American Foreign Policy*, pp. 265, 285, 292, 530).

110 F.D.R., *Public Papers*, 1941, p. 463. Bailey and Ryan, *Hitler vs. Roosevelt*, pp. 209–10, draw particular attention to this.

111 Matloff and Snell, *Strategic Planning*, pp. 28–9; W.S.C. to Smuts, 8 Nov. 1941, PREM 3/476/3, p. 31. It is interesting to note that when Churchill was under considerable pressure during the Cabinet meeting on 25 Aug. he had mentioned his own remark about wanting a declaration rather than supplies, but *not* F.D.R.'s dispiriting reply (CAB 65/19, WM 86 (41) 3).

112 Note cited above, n. 108, PREM 3/476/10, p. 414.

113 Morgenthau Diary, 397: 301B, 14 May 1941; Hopkins memo, 7 Dec. 1941, Hopkins Papers, roll 19, box 302. For FDR in the 1930s see above, ch 1 (e), esp. notes 108 and 109.

114 Halifax to W.S.C., 11 Oct. 1941, PREM 4/27/9, pp. 713ff., on his talk with F.D.R. the day before: 'He said that if he asked for a declaration of war he wouldn't get it, and opinion would swing against him. He therefore intended to go on doing whatever he best could to help us, and declarations of war were, he said, out of fashion.' (For Dec. 1937 see above, ch. 1 (e), notes 119 and 120.)

Among other historians who have taken the view that F.D.R. may well have hoped right up to Pearl Harbor to avoid formal war, see Bailey and Ryan, *Hitler vs. Roosevelt*, esp. pp. 147, 166–7, 226–7, 260–4 (my own formulation is nearest to theirs); Abbazia, *Roosevelt's Navy*, e.g. pp. 278–9; Dawson, *Decision to Aid Russia*, pp. 290–1; Emerson, 'Roosevelt as Commander-in-Chief', p. 187; Divine, *Roosevelt and World War II*, pp. 40–8 (which stresses his personal hatred of war but makes no reference to the importance of the attack on Russia).

115 Lee, *London Observer*, ed. Leutze, 3 Oct. 1941, p. 415; Campbell to Little, 19 Nov. 1941, ADM 205/9, file 2.

116 Halifax to W.S.C., 11 Oct. 1941, cited in note 114; Crozier, *Off the Record*, 20 March and 2 Oct. 1941, pp. 211 and 239. To those such as Smuts who pressed him repeatedly that autumn to do something to end F.D.R.'s 'Hamlet-like' hesitation, the PM could only recapitulate Roosevelt's comments at the Atlantic conference and suggest that the U.S.A. would soon in fact if not in name be involved in 'constant fighting in the Atlantic'. He saw no way 'of helping lift this situation on to a higher plane' and in 'the meantime we must have patience and trust to the tide which is flowing our way and to events'. (Smuts to W.S.C., and W.S.C. to Smuts, 4 and 8 Nov. 1941, PREM 3/476/3, pp. 35, 31–2. For earlier pressure by Smuts see CAB 66/18, WP (41) 209 and Smuts–W.S.C. exchange of 13–14 Sept. in PREM 3/474/1, pp. 6–10.)

117 See Berle to Hull, 5 Sept. and to Welles, 27 Sept. 1941, Berle Diary, reel 3, pp. 308–9, 420–1; F.D.R., *Public Papers*, 1941, pp. 439–40; Hyde, *Quiet Canadian*, pp. 139–44; Stevenson, *Intrepid*, pp. 346–8; *Daily Telegraph*, 22 Aug. 1979.

118 Apparently the only 'dirt' Paine could dig up was a newspaper column reporting that the Berles had twin bath tubs in their house. (Berle Diary, 13 Feb. 1942, 3/1151–3; for early suspicions of Stephenson see Berle, note, late Jan. 1941, D/S 841.01B11/185.)

119 OF 1561/4: Neutrality, 1939–45, esp. F.D.R. to Hull, Knox and Land, 22 Nov., and Land to F.D.R., 25 Nov. 1941. Hull felt that the U.S. should go

slowly on sending U.S. vessels to Britain—see Watson to F.D.R., 19 Nov. 1941, PSF 188: Maritime Commssn.

120 Press Conference 787, 28 Nov. 1941 (FDRL); based on State Dept. draft enclsd. in Hull to F.D.R., 25 Nov., OF 1561/4. Herbert Feis, one of the few historians to discuss these decisions, implied that they would have led quickly to war with Germany. (*Road to Pearl Harbor*, pp. 313–19.)

121 See Compton, *Swastika and the Eagle*, ch. 11; Trefousse, *Germany and American Neutrality*, pp. 113–36; Friedländer, *Prelude to Downfall*, pp. 255–61, 290–5.

122 Halifax to FO, tel. 5668, 7 Dec. 1941, FO 371/27914, F13339/86/23; CAB 65/20, WM 125 (41) 1, 8 Dec.

123 F.D.R., *Public Papers*, 1941, pp. 522–30.

124 For discussions of Hitler's motives, see Friedländer, *Prelude to Downfall*, pp. 306–9; Trefousse, *Germany and American Neutrality*, pp. 137–51; Herwig, 'Prelude to *Weltblitzkrieg*', pp. 667–8; Hildebrand, *Foreign Policy of the Third Reich*, pp. 115–17; Weinberg, 'Hitler's image of U.S.', pp. 1014–17. Recent German historiography has stressed Hitler's 'rational' strategic 'Programme'. For a good emphasis on the importance of the 'non-rational'— of Hitler's racial dogma which was a blend of 'social Darwinism and pathological antisemitism'—see Hauner, 'Did Hitler want a world dominion?'.

125 Whitehead, min., 12 Dec. 1941, FO 371/26286, A1C104/10055/45; F.D.R. to W.S.C., 8 Dec. 1941, PREM 3/469, p. 13; Churchill, *Second World War*, III, 539–40. Churchill's physician noted that almost overnight the PM was rejuvenated by U.S. entry into the war. (Moran, *Churchill*, p. 9.)

**Chapter Nine**

1 Craigie to FO, tel. 2186, 1 Nov. 1941, FO 371/27911, F11672/86/23.

2 For standard works on U.S.–Japanese relations, see Feis, *Road to Pearl Harbor*; Langer and Gleason, *Undeclared War*, esp. chs. II, X, XV, XX, XXII, XXVI–XXVIII; Wohlstetter, *Pearl Harbor: Warning and Decision*; Butow, *The John Doe Associates*. Basic studies of Japanese policy are cited in ch. 5, n. 60. The important collection of essays *The Fateful Choice: Japan's Advance into Southeast Asia, 1939–1941* (ed. Morley) appeared after this MS. was completed.

3 On Anglo-Japanese relations see Woodward, *British Foreign Policy*, II, chs. xiii and xiv; Lowe, *Britain and the Origins of the Pacific War*, chs. VI and VII.

4 For earlier discussion see above, chs. 2 (e) and 5 (b).

5 On Britain's Far Eastern strategy from summer 1940 there are general accounts in Butler, *Grand Strategy*, II, esp. chs. xiv and xxi; Gwyer, *Grand Strategy*, III/1, ch. xi; and, in more detail, Kirby, *War Against Japan*, I, chs. iii–iv, x. The best recent account, on which I have drawn particularly, is Callahan, *The Worst Disaster*, esp. chs. 3–6; his argument is summarized in an earlier article, 'The illusion of security'. See also Barclay, 'Singapore strategy'.

6 In addition, HMG remained committed to sending a fleet east, *whatever* the circumstances in the Mediterranean, if Australia and New Zealand were in serious danger of invasion.

7 CAB 66/10, WP (40) 302, esp. Annex I, part D.

8 Kirby, *War Against Japan*, I, 162–3, 506–11.

9 These views were of long standing. For examples, see W.S.C., memo, 25 March 1939, PREM 1/345; W.S.C. to Ismay, 10 Sept. 1940 and 10 April 1941, and 'Directive by Prime Minister and Minister of Defence', 28 April 1941, PREM 3/156/6, pp. 281–3, 132, 138–9; W.S.C. to F.D.R., 15 Feb. 1941, PREM 3/469; CAB 69/2, DC(O) 30 (41) 2, 15 May 1941.

10 See 'Directive' of 28 April 1941 cited in previous note, and printed in full in Butler, *Grand Strategy*, II, 577.

11 Callahan, *The Worst Disaster*, p. 80. He also suggests that the Chiefs' failure to correct Churchill's repeatedly stated conviction that Singapore was a fortress 'is inexplicable except upon the damning assumption that they shared it'. (Ibid., p. 272, cf. pp. 60–1.)

12 W.S.C. to Ismay, 9 Dec. 1940, PREM 3/489/4, p. 82. Bellairs' draft of the brief for the talks had exposed with undiplomatic candour the gaping hole in Britain's Singapore strategy: 'On the one hand we shall say to the Americans that the whole safety of the Far East depends on the arrival of their battle fleet at Singapore. On the other hand we shall also have to say that we have not placed a garrison in Malaya sufficiently powerful to ensure that the base at Singapore will be intact when the United States fleet arrives . . .' (Butler, *Grand Strategy*, II, 489–90.) Not surprisingly, that was too much for the Chiefs of Staff.

13 CAB 80/24, COS (40) 1052, 19 Dec. 1940, esp. covering note by Hollis and special instructions for naval delegates.

14 See esp. FO 371/27760, F458, F540/9/61, and FO 371/27886, F674, F677/17/23.

15 As Bellairs clearly explained, e.g. CAB 99/5, BUS(J) (41) 6th mtg., 10 Feb. 1941, pp. 3–5. This is also why Halifax, on 16 Feb., gave Hull a copy of one of Bellairs' appreciations of the importance of the Far East—an action to which the U.S. delegation took great exception, arguing that it jeopardized the non-committal, non-political status of the talks and that the British were resorting to unfair political pressure. Undoubtedly the British were ready to exploit the crisis to strengthen their case, but their basic fears were genuine, and this seems to have been overlooked by the standard U.S. accounts of the episode which take a more cynical view. (See, e.g., Langer and Gleason, *Undeclared War*, p. 330; Herzog, *Closing the Open Door*, p. 117; Leutze, *Bargaining for Supremacy*, pp. 230, 238–45.)

16 CAB 65/17, WM 13 (41) 4, 5 Feb. 1941.

17 W.S.C., min., 22 Nov. 1940, PREM 3/489/4, pp. 84–5.

18 Ibid., p. 59: min. of 12 Feb. 1941.

19 Ibid., p. 55: min. of 17 Feb. 1941.

20 Leutze, *Bargaining for Supremacy*, chs. 14–15. The account in Herzog, *Closing the Open Door*, ch. 7, although based only on U.S. records, is clearer in this respect.

21 FO tel. 914, from Chiefs to Bellairs, 19 Feb. 1941, FO 371/26147, A875/11/45.

22 CAB 99/5, BUS(J) (41) 6th mtg., 10 Feb. 1941, p. 5.

23 Ibid., BUS(J) (41) 30, ABC-1 report, 27 March 1941, esp. para. 13 (d) and Annex III, para. 30. For Navy and Army thinking see Herzog, *Closing the Open Door*, pp. 106–8, 248–9.

24 In fact, a month after they had ended neither Roosevelt nor Knox had read the report (Stimson Diary, 33: 184, 24 April 1941). Apparently Churchill did not read it until after the Atlantic Meeting in August. (See PREM 3/489/1, pp. 2–3.)

25 E.g., in letters to Sayre, 31 Dec. 1940, *Personal Letters*, II, 1093–5, and to Grew, 31 Jan. 1941, PSF 59: Japan.

26 Thorne, *Allies of a Kind*, p. 17. Conversely, 75 per cent of Malaya's rubber and 90 per cent of her tin went to the U.S. and Canada. (Kirby, *War Against Japan*, I, 477–8.) The FO could not understand the apparent disregard for these facts on the part of the U.S. Navy and Army. See mins. by Scott, 19 Feb., and Ashton, 7 July, FO 371/26147, A748, and FO 371/27860, F8054/8054/61.

27 The differences of opinion were not always clear-cut. Stark was willing to countenance Far Eastern cruises by ships from the *Asiatic* Fleet, while in April Hull opposed *any* fleet moves in the Far East because Japan might find this too provocative. (See Quinlan, 'The U.S. fleet', pp. 172–5; Herzog, *Closing the Open Door*, ch. 9.)

28 Quinlan, 'The U.S. fleet', pp. 177–85, is a good discussion. See also above, ch. 8 (a).

29 These were the figures suggested to the British on 29 April. See Halifax to FO, tel. 1883, 29 April 1941, in CAB 65/22, pp. 141–2. Initially, Stark agreed with Stimson but then, on 6 May, he changed his mind and thereafter favoured only the smaller move of three battleships. (See Stimson Diary, 34: 13–14, 31, of 6 and 13 May 1941.)

30 Halifax to FO, tel. 1883.

31 Stimson Diary, 33: 181–5, 23–24 April 1941.

32 CAB 69/2, DC(O) (41) 21st mtg., 30 April 1941.

33 Cadogan, *Diaries*, 1 May 1941, p. 375.

34 Stimson's argument for moving most of the U.S. fleet rested on the rather different assumption that the survival of the Mediterranean and of Britain herself was in doubt and that the U.S. might soon face a major German move into the South Atlantic.

35 CAB 69/2, DC(O) (41) 22nd mtg., 1 May 1941; CAB 65/22, WM 48 (41) 2, 8 May 1941. For FO views see FO 371/27843, F3739, F3820/2967/61.

36 Cf. Danckwerts to Turner, 28 April 1941, PSF 80: Navy Dept.

37 Herzog, *Closing the Open Door*, pp. 129–32.

38 Butow, *The John Doe Associates*, p. 44. This book is the standard study of the negotiations and the following account is based upon it.

39 Ibid., chs. 11–13; originally stated in his article 'The Hull–Nomura conversations: A fundamental misconception'. As to Nomura's conduct: he was a retired admiral, not a professional diplomat, his command of English was shaky and he may not have understood Hull's request. Alternatively, it has been argued that Nomura deliberately deceived his government in order to get serious talks started, hoping thereby to isolate the pro-Axis Matsuoka, then touring Europe, and strengthen the hand of Konoye and his colleagues who favoured a peaceful settlement of Japan's differences with Britain and the U.S.A. Butow has alluded to this possibility, e.g. in his article p. 55, but the argument is stated much more firmly in the essay on Nomura by Hilary Conroy in Burns and Bennett (eds.), *Diplomats in Crisis*, esp. pp. 303–10.

40 Stimson Diary, 34: 38–9, 15–16 May 1941. Stimson feared that the British 'would not very much like the terms of the negotiations' and would accuse the U.S.A. of 'double-dealing'.

41 Cf. min. of 20 May by Balfour, FO 371/27880, F4187/12/23.

42 This paragraph is based on F4187, and FO 371/27908–09, F4430, F4570/86/23. For Hull's understandably bland and brief memos of the exchanges with Halifax see *FRUS*, 1941, IV, 197–8, 212 note 84. 233–4.

43 Halifax to FO, tel. 2992, 26 June 1941, FO 371/27909, F5655/86/23.

44 FO to Halifax, tel. 2727, 18 May 1941, F4187. On Hull's claim that Nomura was acting without Matsuoka's knowledge Craigie commented that the idea was 'remarkable even for Japan, though not impossible'. Ashley Clarke of FO/FE, however, was quite definite: 'He is acting on Mr. Matsuoka's Instructions.' (Craigie to FO, tel. 851, 23 May, and Clarke, min., 25 May 1941, FO 371/27908, F4379/86/23.)

45 Tel. 2727, F4187; cf. Welles, memo, 23 May, *FRUS*, 1941, IV, 210. Butow, *John Doe Associates*, pp. 394–5, notes that, thanks to Nomura and the assoc-

iates, by May 1941 the Japanese, British and German Governments all believed that the U.S. Government had offered an 'agreement' to Japan.

46 See Craigie to FO, tel. 656, 22 April 1941, and accompanying mins. by Butler and members of FO/FE, FO 371/27908, F3310/86/23; cf. Craigie to FO, tel. 865, 24 May 1941, FO 371/27880, F4457/12/23. See also above, ch. 5 (b), text and notes 69 and 70. Craigie moderated his views after Matsuoka's fall—see below, section (d).

47 For Feb. 1941, see FO 371/27886–87, F677, F741, F1001, F1184/17/23. For April–May, see FO 371/27775, F2919, F3164/54/61, esp. FO tels. 2105 and 2223, and FO 371/27891, F3682/17/23.

48 Halifax to FO, tel. 615, 9 Feb. 1941, FO 371/27886, F795/17/23.

49 In general on the question of an Anglo-Dutch pledge see Woodward, *British Foreign Policy*, II, 134–6, 178–9. For Churchill's comment, see CAB 65/17, WM 19 (41) 5, 20 Feb. 1941.

50 The Dutch had 144 aircraft in the Far East, including modern Glenn Martin bombers; the British had 156, all old models. The Dutch had 3 cruisers, 6 destroyers and 13 submarines; the U.S. Asiatic Fleet had 2 cruisers, 13 destroyers and 29 submarines; the British, until the arrival of Admiral Phillips' force in December, had 3 cruisers and 5 destroyers. (See Callahan, *The Worst Disaster*, p. 164; Gwyer, *Grand Strategy*, III/1, 267–8.)

51 These two paragraphs are based on Butow, *Tojo*, pp. 188–234, and also the essay on Matsuoka by Barbara Teters in Burns and Bennett (eds.), *Diplomats in Crisis*, pp. 275–96.

52 James Crowley points out that by April 1941 the justification for expansion had shifted from the goal of a New Order in Asia to that of pure self-defence—an indication of the increasingly embattled, encircled mentality in Tokyo. (See his essay in Morley (ed.), *Japan's Foreign Policy*, pp. 91–2.)

53 Feis, *Road to Pearl Harbor*, p. 268 and note 18. The following account of the U.S. oil embargo is taken from Anderson, *The Standard-Vacuum Oil Company*, pp. 168–92 (also to be found in his article 'The 1941 *de facto* embargo', pp. 215–31) and Utley, 'Upstairs, downstairs at Foggy Bottom', pp. 22–8. These authors reach very similar conclusions; Anderson's discussion is fuller and clearer. See also Acheson, *Present at the Creation*, pp. 21–7.

54 Anderson, *The Standard-Vacuum Oil Company*, pp. 175–6.

55 This paragraph draws particularly on Morton, *Fall of the Philippines*, chs. I–III; Russell F. Weigley, 'The role of the War Department and the Army', in Borg and Okamoto (eds.), *Pearl Harbor as History*, pp. 181–4; Harrington, 'A careless hope: American air power and Japan, 1941'.

56 Stimson Diary, 35: 62–3, 12 Sept. 1941.

57 This entailed a complete revision of existing B–17 production and allocation schedules—hence the shock the British Chiefs of Staff received at the Atlantic Meeting.

58 Welles, memo, 23 July 1941, *FRUS, Japan*, II, 525.

59 CAB 66/18, WP (41) 202.

60 Utley, 'Upstairs, downstairs', p. 24. Anderson, *Stan-Vac*, p. 179, note 55, says that a small shipment of 1,578 barrels did leave San Francisco in early August.

61 Utley, 'Upstairs, downstairs', pp. 24–5. Anderson, *Stan-Vac*, pp. 180–1 says that three licences were approved on 11 Aug., for fuel totalling $178,000. It is not clear whether these were separate from the licences Utley mentions. What *is* clear is that Roosevelt's written intention was for the FFCC to follow the policy adopted by Export Control. (Cf. Welles, memo, 31 July 1941, *FRUS, 1941*, IV, pp. 846–8, esp. last para.—memo approved by F.D.R.)

62 Anderson's and Utley's account of the 'oil embargo' is not without its problems (for some qualifications see Brune, 'Considerations of force', p. 398), but this would not have been the first or last occasion when F.D.R.'s tactics of 'divide and rule' or 'divide to decide' misfired because of his own inattention to detail. For another example—at the same time—see the 28 July draft of the Lend-Lease Consideration, discussed below, ch. 10 (c) and note 96.

63 For a general account of British policy see Medlicott, *Economic Blockade*, II, 103–23.

64 See FO 371/27663, F6022/9/61, esp. Clarke, min., 10 July 1941, and memos of 7 July by Eden (para. 4) and Dalton (paras. 2 and 11), CAB 66/17, WP (41) 155.

65 CAB 65/19, WM 76 (41) 6, 31 July 1941.

66 CAB 66/17, WP (41) 172, 20 July 1941. Cf. minutes by Sterndale Bennett, head of FO/FE, 19 and 20 July, FO 371/27972, F6472/1299/23 and FO371/27763, F6473/9/61.

67 CAB 65/19, WM 72 (41) 8, 21 July 1941. Dalton called the discussion 'long and not very conclusive' (Dalton Diaries, 25:24), which perhaps explains the terse account in the Cabinet conclusions. As Dalton and Cadogan (*Diaries*, p. 393) note, Harry Hopkins, then in London, had been invited to attend the Cabinet—a very rare honour for a foreigner, as distinct from a Dominions leader. However, his continued presence would have been embarrassing during the discussion of the Far East. A bogus agenda was therefore circulated, indicating that the meeting would end after item seven. When that point was reached Churchill declared the Cabinet adjourned and an impression was created of general movement. In fact only Hopkins left—ushered into the passage by Churchill with promises that he was always available. The Cabinet was then free to discuss the Far East without restraint. This elaborate little charade neatly illustrates both the reality of Anglo-American co-operation—Hopkins' very presence in Cabinet—and its limitations.

68 Cf. the comments by W.S.C. in early June and Eden on 18 July in Crozier, *Off the Record*, pp. 225, 228.

69 FO 371/27973, F7168/1299/23, esp. Canberra to DO, tel. 467, 23 July, and DO tel. 179, 25 July. See also ibid., F7071, F7072, F7169.

70 WP (41) 172, cited in note 66.

71 CAB 65/23, WM (41) 72/10 CA and 75/8 CA, 21 and 28 July 1941.

72 CAB 65/19, WM 76 (41) 7, 31 July 1941.

73 For background see Cadogan, memo, no date, PREM 3/156/1, p. 22.

74 Welles, memo, 10 Aug. 1941, *FRUS*, 1941, I, 354–6.

75 CAB 66/18, WP (41) 202. Lash, *Roosevelt and Churchill*, p. 406, suggests that F.D.R. 'might well have indicated his intention to give armed support to the British during one of the six meals that he had with Churchill'. This seems very unlikely. Even the slightest hint from Roosevelt would surely have been relayed by Churchill to the Cabinet, in view of the PM's anxiety to show some return from the conference. Furthermore, his policy throughout the autumn, as we shall see, assumed that U.S. intentions were still not certain. Once F.D.R. gave an assurance, in early Dec., Churchill's position changed completely.

76 WP (41) 202. For British and U.S. accounts of the 11 Aug. meeting, see FO 371/27909, F7995/86/23, and *FRUS*, 1941, I, 357–60.

77 *FRUS, Japan*, II, 556–7.

78 Generally see Langer and Gleason, *Undeclared War*, pp. 670–7, 693–8, and Woodward, *British Foreign Policy*, II, 140–50. Also Long, *War Diary*, 31 Aug. 1941, pp. 214–15.

79 PREM 3/163/3: esp. W.S.C. mins. of 25 and 29 August 1941, pp. 71–4, 60–3 (quotation from p. 61). Churchill reprinted the exchange in *Second World War*,

III, book 2, appendix E. 'The PM still does not think that the Japs will go to war with us.' (Dalton Diary, 25: 56, 26 Aug. 1941, following meeting with W.S.C.)

80 Cf. Roskill, *Churchill and the Admirals*, pp. 280, 298.

81 Points made by Callahan, *Worst Disaster*, pp. 149–55.

82 For background on Japanese policy in the autumn of 1941 see Butow, *Tojo*, chs. 9–11.

83 For detail see Butow, 'Backdoor diplomacy in the Pacific: The proposal for a Konoye–Roosevelt Meeting, 1941'. Butow has shown that the proposal was yet another casualty of the confusion created by the John Doe Associates. It was a pet scheme of Father Drought and had been included in the Associates' 9 April 'Draft Understanding'. The Japanese had ignored the idea when they responded to the 'Understanding' on 12 May, but revived it in August as a last-ditch effort to reach agreement. Since they erroneously believed that the 9 April document was an official *U.S.* proposal, the American failure to take the idea of a summit seriously in the autumn seemed further evidence that the U.S. position had hardened to the point of near-inflexibility.

84 Heinrichs, *Grew*, pp. 339–54, 384–5. Other accounts of the Tokyo Embassy stress its 'minimal role' in U.S. policymaking by this date. E.g. the essays by Akira Iriye, in Borg and Okamoto (eds.), *Pearl Harbor as History*, pp. 107–26, and by Edward M. Bennett, in Burns and Bennett (eds.), *Diplomats in Crisis*, pp. 65–89.

85 *FRUS, Japan*, II, 656–61.

86 Craigie to FO, tel. 2186, 1 Nov. 1941, FO 371/27911, F11672/86/23. See also Lowe, *Britain and the Origins of the Pacific War*, pp. 257–9, and Craigie tels. of 30 Sept. and 18 Nov. in FO 371/27883, F10117/12/23, and FO 371/27912, F12486/86/23.

87 FO mins. of 6 and 8 Sept. 1941, and R. I. Campbell to FO, tel. 4162, 9 Sept., FO 371/27910, F8929, F9173/86/23; also min. by Foulds, 3 Nov. 1941, F11672.

88 At this time there was still doubt in London about Russia's chances of survival into the winter. It seemed that Japan might be holding back in South-East Asia until Russia had been conquered, thereby removing any remaining anxiety about her north and west flanks. On these grounds it was argued by some in FO/FE that Britain should help force the issue before the Russian collapse. (See e.g. mins. by Clarke, 20 Aug. and 17 Sept., and by Foulds, 13 Sept., respectively FO 371/27909, F7883, and FO 371/27910, F9321 and F9173.)

89 Halifax to FO, tel. 4550, 4 Oct. 1941, and FO mins., FO 371/27910, F10329.

90 Eden, min., ?14 Oct. 1941, ibid., F10918.

91 For a recent examination of Hull's handling of the *modus vivendi* see Brune, 'Considerations of force'.

92 On 12 Oct. Churchill's roving eye had seen a telegram from Pound to the Mediterranean Fleet announcing the fleet movement. The PM immediately ordered Pound to take no action until the Defence Commt. had reached a decision. (See PREM 3/163/3, p. 55.)

93 DC(O) (41) 65/1 and 66/1, 17 and 20 Oct., in CAB 69/2 and CAB 69/8. See also Roskill, *War at Sea*, I, ch. xxvi, and Middlebrook and Mahoney, *Battleship*, ch. 3.

94 Callahan, *Worst Disaster*, pp. 146–7, 157.

95 After the Atlantic Meeting his staff had emphasized to Churchill that American military took ABC–1 as their 'strategic bible'. (See PREM 3/489/1, p. 3.)

96 W.S.C., min., 23 Nov. 1941, PREM 3/156/6, pp. 128–9. For FO and MEW comment see FO 371/27912, F12675.

97 CAB 65/24, WM 118 (41) 3 CA, 24 Nov. 1941; FO 371/27912, F12655.

98 In an interesting article on British handling of the *modus vivendi*, Richard Grace claims that 'the specter of Munich roamed the corridors of Whitehall with a presence so large that it blocked the perspective of men there' so that 'the mere question of compromising with an antagonist was received with indignation and disdain'. ('Whitehall and the ghost of appeasement', pp. 188, 189). This seems to me a distortion even of FO/FE's position. HMG wanted to gain time through diplomacy. The 'lessons of Munich' concerned the tactics of negotiation rather than the principle—start with one's maximum demands; don't conclude an agreement that would allow a potential enemy to increase his strength.

99 E.g. Welles, memo, 27 Nov. 1941, *FRUS*, 1941, IV, 667.

100 Hull only told Halifax in passing about the ten-point statement on 25 Nov., without making clear that State intended to present it along with the *modus vivendi*, and Halifax only obtained a copy on 2 Dec. In his memoirs Churchill remarked that the statement not only met British reservations 'but indeed went beyond anything for which we had ventured to ask'. (*Second World War*, III, 531.) Even allowing for some special pleading, there is much truth in his comment.

101 According to Hull, *Memoirs*, II, 1082. There is no extant record of this important meeting, and the chronology and precise reasons for the decision to abandon the *modus vivendi* remain unclear. There is a good discussion in Langer and Gleason, *Undeclared War*, ch. xxvii, esp. sec. 3. Hull's memo of explanation for F.D.R. on 26 Nov. (*FRUS*, 1941, IV, 665–6) is that of a man still convinced of the 'wisdom and benefit' of the *modus vivendi* but unwilling to fight any longer against what he perceived to be the encircling forces of ignorance, criticism and opposition at home and abroad. (See also note 115.)

102 Clarke, min., 27 Nov. 1941, FO 371/27913, F12859.

103 Dalton Diary, 25: 147, 26 Nov.; Harvey, *War Diaries*, 26 and 29 Nov., pp. 66–7; Clarke, min., 1 Dec. 1941, FO 371/27913, F12992.

104 CAB 65/24, WM 122 (41) 3 CA, 1 Dec. 1941.

105 CAB 65/24, WM 112 (41) 1 CA, 12 Nov. 1941. The PM made similar comments in private to an American intelligence officer in London, which got back to the White House. (See Whitney to Donovan, tel. 5392, 12 Nov. 1941, PSF 141: COI, Donovan.)

106 WM 122 (41) 3 CA; CAB 69/2, DC(O) 71 (41) 1, 3 Dec. 1941; cf. Crozier, *Off the Record*, 20 March 1942, p. 310. In his directive of 28 April 1941 Churchill told the military: 'it may be taken as almost certain that the entry of Japan into the war would be followed by the immediate entry of the United States on our side.' (PREM 3/156/6, p. 138.)

107 Churchill, *Speeches*, VI, 6475, 6504. After the second speech, at the Mansion House, Welles 'volunteered the opinion' to Halifax that it 'had been immensely helpful to the feeling in this country and had wiped out [the] last trace of bad feeling aroused in 1931'. (Halifax to FO, tel. 5139, 13 Nov. 1941, FO 371/27911, F12186.)

108 Cf. Harvey, *War Diaries*, 3 Dec. 1941, pp. 68–9; Harriman to Hopkins, tel. 0949, 6 Dec. 1941, Hopkins papers, Box 157: Harriman.

109 Cf. CAB 65/20, WM 125 (41) 1.

110 Cf. Miles to Marshall, and Stark to F.D.R., both 27 Nov. 1941, PSF 103: War Dept. and PSF 80: Navy Dept. The intelligence story is fully documented in Wohlstetter, *Pearl Harbor*.

111 Stimson Diary, 36: 58, 28 Nov. 1941; Halifax to FO, tels. 5441 and 5474, 28 and 29 Nov. 1941, FO 371/27913, F12959. Halifax found it 'very difficult

to believe the United States Government would not very soon support us in the event of hostilities. I know Hull, Stimson, Knox would wish to do so . . . The real question to my mind is how quickly the United States would join up.' (Tel. 5493, 30 Nov., ibid., F13001.)

112 Halifax to FO, tel. 5519, 1 Dec. 1941, ibid., F13114.

113 CAB 66/19, WP (41) 296; CAB 69/2, DC(O) 71 (41) 1, 3 Dec. 1941; Halifax to FO, tel. 5577, 4 Dec. 1941, FO 371/27914, F13219/86/23; CAB 65/24, WM 124 (41) 4 CA, 4 Dec. 1941. See also Esthus, 'Roosevelt's commitment to Britain'.

114 Their agreement is printed in U.S. Congress, 79/1, *Joint Commt. on the Investigation of the Pearl Harbor Attack* (Washington, 1946), part 4, pp. 1933–5. See also Roskill, *War at Sea*, I, 561–2.

115 There is a good account in Langer and Gleason, *Undeclared War*, pp. 911–37, which also shows that in early Dec. Hull and F.D.R. gave renewed consideration to the idea of a *modus vivendi*.

116 Themes discussed in Thorne, *Allies of a Kind*, and Storry, *Japan*, ch. 1.

117 Points made in Waldo Heinrichs' excellent biography of *Grew*, pp. 348–54, which also apply to Craigie. We still lack a study of Craigie's ambassadorship.

118 Cf. Lowe, *Britain and the Origins of the Pacific War*, pp. 284–7; Sato, 'Anglo–Japanese relations', esp. ch. VIII.

119 The best critique of U.S. policy from this angle is Schroeder, *The Axis Alliance and Japanese–American Relations*, esp. chs. IV and IX.

120 A point emphasized against Schroeder by Iriye, 'Japan's policies towards the United States', in Morley (ed.), *Japan's Foreign Policy*, p. 459. See also Iriye, *Across the Pacific*, pp. 216–22.

121 Craigie to Eden, 4 May 1943, and enclosed memo, FO 371/35957, F821/751/23; cf. Schroeder, *The Axis Alliance*, esp. pp. 202–5, 212–16; Gwyer, *Grand Strategy*, III/1, 260–5.

122 Wohlstetter, *Pearl Harbor*, p. 341.

123 A question raised tentatively by Anderson, 'The 1941 *de facto* embargo', pp. 230–1; cf. Herzog, *Closing the Open Door*, p. 238.

124 Dexterously, Eden tried to make a virtue of necessity. In a fulsome speech on Thanksgiving Day, to celebrate Anglo-American amity, he referred to Britain's exclusion from the Washington talks: 'We have complete confidence in the United States spokesmen: so much confidence that indeed we have never asked and shall not ask to be represented in these conversations. We trust our friends.' This was on 20 Nov., just as the *modus vivendi* crisis was beginning. (See text in FO 371/26180, A9832/101/45; and press report in *The Times*, 21 Nov. 1941, p. 2c.)

125 W.S.C., min., 19 Sept. 1943, FO 371/35957, F2602/751/23. As usual the British Establishment formed a united front against criticism. Craigie had insisted that his report be printed. It was only printed in conjunction with a counter-memo by FO/FE, and even then was given minimal circulation, on Churchill's instructions.

126 Halifax, for instance, recorded in his diary on 19 Nov. 1941 that he did not believe Japan would be at war with anyone new by 1 Jan. 1942. (Hickleton papers, A 7.8.9.) As late as 27 Nov. 1941 Stanley Hornbeck, Hull's special adviser on Far Eastern affairs, was imprudent enough to suggest odds of five to one that Japan would not be formally at war with the U.S.A. by 15 Dec., three to one that there would be no war by 15 Jan. and evens that the two countries would still be officially at peace on 1 March. (See memo in *FRUS*, 1941, IV, 673.)

127 Churchill's phrase, used at a talk with newspaper editors on 22 Aug. 1941, quoted in King, *With Malice Toward None*, 23 Aug. 1941, p. 140.

128 The news of their loss was a devastating blow to Churchill and it haunted him for the rest of his life. Although he had been responsible for the decision to send the small force straight to Singapore, the primary blame for the disaster was not his. Churchill and the Admiralty were well aware of the importance of air power. Under the original decision of 20 Oct. the carrier *Indomitable* had been scheduled to accompany Phillips east, but she had been delayed by an accident in the Caribbean. The RAF in Malaya had not been able to provide continuous air cover for Phillips' force, but a squadron of Buffalo fighters was on permanent alert at Singapore, ready to take off if requested. Phillips never sent a request, and it was the *Repulse*'s commander who sent a belated call—45 minutes after the first Japanese attack and 105 minutes after the British knew they had been sighted by Japanese reconnaissance planes. By this time the Buffalos arrived, the *Repulse* had sunk and the *Prince of Wales* was about to. For a good discussion see Mahoney and Middlebrook, *Battleship*, esp. ch. 15; also Roskill, *War at Sea*, I, 563–9.

129 5s *HC Debs.*, 377: 601. The rest of the sentence reads '. . . against the impact of a vast military Empire like Japan, with more than 70 mobile divisions, the third navy in the world, a great air force, and the thrust of 80 or 90 millions of hardy, warlike Asiatics'. That was not the Churchill of 1941!

130 Cf. Pownall, *Diaries*, II, 92, 25 Feb. 1942.

## Chapter Ten

1 Rexford G. Tugwell to Harold Ickes, 23 April 1941, Ickes papers (LC), 373/12; Halifax to Eden, desp. 976, 15 Oct. 1941, FO 371/26151, A9358/18/45.

2 For earlier discussion see chs. 1 (e) and 3 (b). For background see Range, *Roosevelt's World Order*; and Notter, *Postwar Foreign Policy Preparation*, chs. 1–3.

3 Cf. his comments recorded in Halifax to Scott, 24 April 1941, FO 371/26250, A3774/2215/45.

4 Henry Luce, 'The American century', *Life*, 17 Feb. 1941, pp. 61–5.

5 For a fascinating study of how America's changing conception of her place in the world was reflected cartographically, see Henrikson, 'The map as an "idea" '.

6 F.D.R., *Public Papers*, IX, 1940–41, p. 672. For earlier formulations see Lothian to Halifax, 14 Dec. 1939, FO 800/397, US/39/14; Lothian to FO, tel. 142, 2 Feb. 1940, FO 371/24417, C1839/285/18; Langer and Gleason, *Challenge*, p. 346; Presidential press conferences, 5 June and 5 July 1940, vols. 15: 498–500 and 16: 18–22.

7 Cadogan, min., 30 Jan. 1941, FO 371/28899, W6189/426/49.

8 For background see Addison, *Road to 1945*, chs. IV–VI; also Calder, *People's War*, ch. V.

9 'At the present time America is prepared to use British bodies to blast a way into the markets of the Continent and to re-establish the old financial system of Wall Street in these countries', Independent Labour Party MP John Mc-Govern of Glasgow told the Commons on 27 Nov. 1941 (5s *HC Debs.*, 376:920).

10 E.g., Laski to F.D.R., 20 Oct. 1940, PSF (C) 53: Great Britain, Laski; Attlee to Laski, 7 Nov. 1940, enclosed with Laski to F.D R., 18 Feb. 1941, in PPF 3014: Laski.

11 Halifax to Keynes, and Nicolson to Keynes, both 19 Nov. 1940, in, respectively, FO 371/25208, W11850/8805/49, and T 247/85. CAB 65/10, WM 292 (40) 8, 20 Nov. 1940.

12 CAB 65/17, WM 8 (41) 6, 20 Jan. 1941; cf. Halifax, memo, 13 Dec. 1940, printed in CAB 67/9, WP(G) (41) 1. Halifax later used this as the basis of a speech in New York in March 1941.

13 E.g., 5s *HC Debs.*, 368: 22, 1222–23, 21 Jan. and 11 Feb. 1941; Harvey, diary, 1 March 1941, B.L. Add. Mss. 56397 (ban); W.S.C. to Bevin, 25 Nov. 1940, PREM 4/83/1A, quoted in Lash, *Roosevelt and Churchill*, p. 279; W.S.C. to Eden, 24 May 1941, PREM 4/100/5, p. 182. Churchill made the latter point more memorably a year or so later: the would-be peace planners, he told Eden, should 'not overlook Mrs. Glass' Cookery Book recipe for Jugged Hare: "First catch your hare".' (W.S.C. to Eden, 18 Oct. 1942, quoted in Hughes, 'Churchill and the formation of the UN', p. 181, n. 17.)

14 Despite his ability to inspire them. In the spring of 1945 Churchill's wife told his doctor a revealing story. Winston, she said, knew 'nothing of the life of ordinary people'. He had never been on a bus and only once on the Underground. That was during the General Strike of 1926. She left him at Sloane Square and he travelled round and round on the Circle Line, not knowing where to get off, until he was eventually rescued. (Moran, *Churchill*, p. 247.)

15 Quotations from Laski to Frankfurter, 13 Aug. 1941, Frankfurter papers (LC), 75/1503, and W.S.C., *Speeches*, VI, 6695, address of 10 Nov. 1942.

16 Harvey Diary, 15 Jan. and 6 June 1941, B.L. Add. Mss. 56397.

17 Ibid., and also entries for 31 Jan., 20 Feb., 5, 12, 13 May 1941. Eden was also keen to strengthen Anglo-American contacts: Harvey and Law, unlike R. A. Butler, were keen Americophiles. David Scott, initially on Eden's hit list, was retained, and on closer acquaintance seemed 'very wise' and 'very good indeed' as Under-Secretary for the American Dept. (Harvey Diary, 14 July 1941, vol. 56398.) However, Ronald I. Campbell, one of the FO's best younger men, who had originally been scheduled to replace Scott, was sent to Washington as Minister, to provide some much-needed support for Halifax, whose performance was still causing the FO concern. Nevile Butler was brought back from Washington to head FO/A and Jock Balfour was moved to Lisbon.

18 Sargent, min., 1 Feb. 1941, FO 371/28899, W587/426/49. This vol., together with papers in PREM 4/100/5 and T 247/85, provides the material for the summary given in this paragraph.

19 See esp. Halifax to Hull, with enclosure, 23 May 1941, copy in OF 48/2: England; and Halifax to FO, tel. 2405, 28 May 1941, FO 371/28899, W6513/426/49. See also ibid., W6156, W6227, W6457. Harvey Diary, 6 June 1941.

20 Berle to F.D.R., and F.D.R. to Berle, 21 and 26 June, PSF 90: State Dept. For Berle's views on Britain and peacemaking see esp. Berle Diary, 6, 11, 14 Oct. 1940.

21 Welles, memo, 15 June 1941, *FRUS*, 1941, I, 759–61; cf. Berle Diary, 19 June 1941, p. 3, and 31 July, p. 3.

22 See Berle, memos, 1 and 2 Aug. 1941, Berle papers (FDRL), box 54: Allied commitments; Berle Diary, 2 Aug. 1941.

23 Berle to F.D.R., 9 July 1941, PSF 52: GB, Churchill.

24 Hickerson to Berle, 21 July 1941, Berle papers, 54: Allied commitments; Sherwood, *Roosevelt and Hopkins*, p. 311; Berle Diary, 11 July 1941; F.D.R. to W.S.C., 14 July 1941, Map Room papers, box 1.

25 Langer and Gleason, *Undeclared War*, pp. 680–1; Wilson, *First Summit*, pp. 22–3.

26 See *FRUS*, 1941, III, 176–81, quotation from Welles to Hull, 6 Aug. 1941. For background see Hess, *America Encounters India*, pp. 21–5, and Thorne, *Allies of a Kind*, pp. 60–2.

27 Cf. Wilson, *First Summit*, p. 123.

28 Robert Sherwood (*Roosevelt and Hopkins*, p. 350) claimed that during the voyage from Scotland Churchill and Hopkins 'discussed the phraseology of the Atlantic Charter which the Prime Minister was to present to the President'. Wilson, *First Summit*, pp. 76–7, cast doubt on this statement, and there is nothing to substantiate it in the British records. The first W.S.C. and Cadogan knew of the idea was when F.D.R. mentioned it at dinner on the 9th (Cadogan, *Diaries*, p. 398; CAB 66/18, WP (41) 202; Cadogan to Wilson, 26 Aug. 1941, T 160/1105, F17660/02/1); the first the FO knew of it was when a draft arrived for the Cabinet's consideration, early on 12 Aug. (cf. below, note 37).

29 For drafts see FO 371/28903, W10151/426/49; *FRUS*, 1941, I, pp. 354–69; and discussion in Wilson, *First Summit*, ch. IX and Woodward, *British Foreign Policy*, II, pp. 199–203. For 'Mr. Jorkins' see ch. 6 (c), and note 84.

30 Quotations from Sir Edward Grigg to Lloyd George, memo [Aug. 1941], Lloyd George papers, G/8/11/17 (b); Harvey Diary 12 Aug. 1941 (Bevin); Thorne, *Allies of a Kind*, p. 61 (Amery). An international lawyer, attached to the FO's semi-official research dept., pulled the Charter to bits clause by clause (Brierly, note, 3 Sept. 1941, FRPS RR I/59/iii in CAB 117/58). Sherwood was criticized in Britain when he wrote that the British regarded the Atlantic Charter as 'not much more than a publicity handout' (*Roosevelt and Hopkins*, pp. 362, 945). The evidence cited here largely substantiates his judgement.

31 CAB 66/18, WP (41) 202; Cadogan, min., 6 May 1943, quoted in Louis, *Imperialism at Bay*, p. 123, n. 5.

32 Such was the haste with which it was prepared that the Charter omitted any reference to 'freedom of religion'—one of F.D.R.'s Four Freedoms as stated in January.

33 Amery to W.S.C., 20 Aug. 1941, PREM 4/50/3, pp. 253–6; Moyne to Amery, 26 Aug. 1941, CO 323/1858, file 9057/4.

34 CAB 65/19, WM 89 (41) 3, 4 Sept. 1941; 5s *HC Debs.*, 374:69. In his full account of the episode Roger Louis (*Imperialism at Bay*, pp. 129–31) argues that W.S.C. sided unequivocally with Amery and that he 'had stated explicitly before Parliament that Britain was committed to self-government in the colonies, and, moreover, that these commitments were "complete in themselves" and "free from ambiguity".' As I read W.S.C.'s statement, he simply said that the Atlantic Charter was a separate topic from decolonization, and did not explain what HMG's supposedly unambiguous statements on the latter question contained. In short, it was a masterful piece of Whitehall obfuscation.

35 Presidential press conferences, 19:4, 155–6, 2 Jan. and 24 Feb. 1942; F.D.R., *Public Papers*, XI, 115, fireside chat of 23 Feb. 1942.

36 Avon, *The Reckoning*, p. 273, quoting diary entry for 21 July; Harvey Diary, 22 July 1941, B.L. Add. Mss., 56398; Peake to Harvey, dated 1 July but from content clearly 1 Aug. 1941, Harvey papers, Add. Mss. 56402, p. 11. For similar comments see Peake's letter of 10 Sept. 1941, in vol. 56398, p. 91.

37 Harvey Diary, vol. 56398, 12 Aug. and 6 Oct. 1941. Eden's feelings are indicated by his comment to Churchill a year later that if HMG did not formulate a basic post-war plan, the result would be 'that the U.S. makes a policy and we follow, which I do not regard as a satisfactory role for the British empire'. (Eden to W.S.C., 19 Oct. 1942, quoted in Barker, *Churchill and Eden*, p. 212.)

38 British failure to respond quickly may have been because F.D.R., as usual, presented a blunt demand in deliberately casual guise, telling W.S.C. in his 14 July cable that the question was 'not in any way serious at this time'. This probably encouraged the British to wait until the forthcoming Atlantic Meeting, where face-to-face discussion would be better than written communications.

Welles implies in his account that he raised the topic; Cadogan, in his, says that he brought it up himself, that Welles was quite satisfied with what he called Cadogan's 'heartening statement' of the situation, and that when he, Cadogan, raised the question again later in the conference and asked if F.D.R. wanted a formal statement by HMG Welles said that in view of the Declaration that would be entirely superfluous. See Welles, memo, 9 Aug. 1941, *FRUS*, 1941, I, 351–2, and Cadogan, memo, 20 Aug. 1941, FO 371/28904, W10301/426/49. For updates see e.g., Halifax to Welles and Welles to F.D.R., 18 and 21 Oct. 1941, PSF(S) 2: Atlantic Charter.

39 On 13 Sept. 1941 Berle had an interesting conversation with Ralph Skrine Stevenson, who had been Halifax's Principal Private Secretary until Harvey's return in late June. Berle asked Stevenson if the proposal for a loose Eastern European federation in close relationship with Russia 'did not really mean—to the Russians, at least—that they were to dominate that entire area. Stevenson said that, speaking frankly, the British Government had given half a promise to that effect. At all events, they had permitted the Russians to believe that the British would be favorable.' He added, however, that the British felt that conditions in Eastern Europe at the end of the war 'would be such as to make it virtually impossible to carry out the kind of thing that the Russians had in mind and from which the British had at least not dissented'. (Berle, memo, 15 Sept. 1941, Berle papers, 54: Allied commitments.)

40 Eden to Cripps, tel. 159, 17 Nov. 1941, FO 371/29471, N6575/3/38. The FO Northern Dept.'s original draft had been blunter, saying that the Americans 'have shown themselves most suspicious lest we should undertake . . . '.

41 Eden to Halifax, 22 Jan. 1942, FO 954/29A, p. 361.

42 Quotations from Eden, memo, 28 Jan. 1942, CAB 66/21, WP (42) 48. For details see Woodward, *British Foreign Policy*, II, ch. xxvi; Davis, *Cold War Begins*, ch. 1; Barker, *Churchill and Eden*, pp. 233–41; Mastny, *Russia's Road to the Cold War*, pp. 45–7.

43 To my mind this does more justice to both elements of F.D.R.'s thinking than Daniel Yergin's term 'renegade Wilsonian' (*Shattered Peace*, p. 44). See also Divine, *Roosevelt and World War II*, ch. 3. For the earlier, quasi-isolationist 'realism' of the State Dept., see above, ch. 1 (e).

44 Berle Diary, 23 July 1941, cf. 29 Dec. 1939 (Welles); Notter, *Postwar Foreign Policy Preparation*, pp. 458–60, and Berle Diary, 12 and 17 March 1941. Berle himself believed that the model for European security would be the Pan American system evolved by the Roosevelt Administration during the 1930s. (See Berle, memo, 21 June 1941, PSF 90: State.)

45 Dalton Diary, 24 Oct. 1940.

46 Keynes to Kingsley Wood, 2 June 1941, p. 8, T 160/1105, F17660/02/1; Halifax to Eden, desp. 382, 21 April 1941, FO 371/28899, W5382/426/49; *FRUS*, 1941, I, 363, 366 (Atlantic Meeting).

47 Harvey Diary, 1 March 1941. (Like Churchill, Macmillan had an American mother.) For other examples, see Josiah Wedgwood, 'America and the War', *Contemporary Review*, CLIX (Feb. 1941), 121–7, and Wedgwood to Nicholas Murray Butler, 2 Jan. 1941, Butler papers—'Wedgwood' file (Columbia Univ., New York); and the persistent efforts by William Craven-Ellis, MP, to organize an all-party 'Anglo-American Union' committee in the Commons (FO 371/26179, esp. A2752, A4217, A4965/101/45).

48 Streit's first statement of his idea was made in his book *Union Now*, published in March 1939. A revised version, adapted to suit the times and entitled *Union Now with Britain*, appeared two years later. His ideas were also outlined in numerous articles, e.g. 'For mutual advantage', *Atlantic Monthly*, 166/5 (Nov.

1940), 531–9 and 'An American expeditionary idea can win the war', *Look*, 5/15 (29 July 1941), 38–9.

49 Minutes by Whitehead and Balfour, 18 and 21 Oct. 1940, FO 371/25208, W11171/8805/49. On Cripps' ideas see above, ch. 4 (a) and note 27.

50 For the FO see Bell, *Certain Eventuality*, pp. 6–7; Shlaim, 'Prelude to downfall', pp. 31–2; Harvey, *Diplomatic Diaries*, pp. 337–8, 342, 345–6. For Churchill see CAB 65/8, WM 233 (40) 6, 23 Aug. 1940, and Hughes, 'Churchill and the formation of the UN', pp. 177–80.

51 Cadogan, min., 31 Oct. 1940, FO 371/28899, W11399.

52 *Speeches*, VI, 6327, 9 Jan. 1941. For his earlier opinions see above, ch. 3 (d).

53 Dalton Diary, 25: 57, 26 Aug. 1941.

54 CAB 66/18, WP (41) 202, p. 4.

55 Harvey Diary, 12 Aug. 1941.

56 E.g., mins. by Evans, 7 Jan. 1942, FO 371/28813, W15335/37/49; Latham, 16 April 1941, FO 371/26149, p. 136; Ronald, 20 Dec. 1940, FO 371/26419, C14/14/62.

57 Whitehead, min., 10 March 1941, FO 371/26170, A1450/44/45. See also mins. by Ronald and Whitehead, 18 and 19 Oct. 1940, FO 371/25208, W11042/8805/49. Whitehead, a professor of business psychology by training, saw isolationism as one manifestation of the basic tradition of 'rugged individualism'—the 'persistent failure to recognise the inevitable connexion between . . . privilege and responsibility'—which, he believed, permeated American life and thought, at home and abroad. (See min. of 21 March 1941, FO 371/26149, A1893/18/45.)

58 Scott, min., 16 Aug. 1940, FO 371/24259, A3958/3742/45.

59 Mins. by Whitehead, Balfour and Cadogan, 2 July 1940, FO 371/25206, W8602/8602/49; by Ronald, Balfour and Collier, 28 Sept. 1940, and by Whitehead, 18 Oct. 1940, FO 371/25208, W10484, W11171/8805/49.

60 Halifax to FO, tel. 1206, 18 March 1941, and min. by Whitehead, 21 March, FO 371/26149, A1893; similarly Whitehead, min. of 27 Feb. on tel. 870, 25 Feb. 1941, FO 371/26145, A1171/3/45.

61 Whitehead, min., 19 Aug. 1941, FO 371/28909, W14302/426/49.

62 Harvey Diary, vol. 56398, 14 Nov. 1941. For a more extreme statement of this view see the opinions of Lord Cecil, recorded in Crozier, *Off the Record*, 2 Oct. 1941, pp. 233–4.

63 Notes by Scott and Butler, no dates, FO 371/26149, p. 128.

64 FO/A mins. on FO 371/26171, A3060/44/45.

65 Harvey Diary, 11 Aug. 1941. See also above, chs. 7 (a) note 6 and 8 (a) note 28.

66 Harvey, min., and Eden's annotation, 24 Aug. 1941, Harvey papers, vol. 56402, pp. 16–18. Elisabeth Barker also notes Eden's inclination towards a semi-independent European policy, but suggests that this really dates from his disappointing meetings with F.D.R. in May 1943 (*Churchill and Eden*, p. 128, 211–17). The evidence cited in this book indicates that Eden's doubts and fears about the U.S.A. had a much longer history.

67 Harvey, min., 24 Aug. 1941.

68 Both Dill and Churchill remarked on the need for a proper inter-departmental committee structure and White House secretariat on the British model, to facilitate orderly decision-taking and implementation. (See Bryant, *Turn of the Tide*, pp. 292–3; CAB 65/25, p. 33, WM 8 (41) 1.) Keynes, like most British officials, was appalled at the lack of confidentiality in Washington—'There is practically no information you cannot get just by asking for it'—and was disconcerted to find that whenever he emerged from a meeting with Morgenthau or even the President he was immediately surrounded in the

ante-room by reporters wanting to know what had been said. His comments on the machinery of government are worth reproducing in full: 'To the outsider it looks almost incredibly inefficient. One wonders how decisions are ever reached at all. There is no clear hierarchy of authority. The different departments of the Government criticise one another in public and produce rival programmes. There is perpetual internecine warfare between prominent personalities. Individuals rise and fall in general esteem with bewildering rapidity. New groupings of administrative power and influence spring up every day. Members of the so-called Cabinet make public speeches containing urgent proposals which are not agreed as part of the Government policy. In the higher ranges of government no work ever seems to be done on paper; no decisions are recorded on paper; no-one seems to read a document and no-one ever answers a communication in writing. Nothing is ever settled in principle. There is just endless debate and sitting around. But this, I suppose, is their characteristic method. Suddenly some drastic, clear-cut decision is reached, by what process one cannot understand, and all the talk seems to have gone for nothing, being the fifth wheel to the coach, the ultimate decision appearing to be largely independent of the immense parlez-vous, responsible and irresponsible, which has preceded it.' (Keynes to Wood, 2 June 1941, p. 4, T 160/1105, F17660/02/1.)

69 A point emphasized by Nicholas, *Britain and the United States*, pp. 24, 166, 171–6.

70 Whitehead, mins., 27 March (quotation), and 25 April 1941, FO 371/26250, A2215/2215/45, and FO 371/26179, A3295/101/45. See also above, ch. 5 (a), notes 5–6.

71 E.g. Ronald, min., 20 Dec. 1940, FO 371/26419, C14/14/62.

72 Board of Education, *The Teaching of the History of the United States of America—I* (memo. no. 26 in series 'The schools in wartime', July 1941).

73 Butler, min., 3 April 1941, FO 371/26149, A1893/18/45.

74 Harvey, min., 24 Aug. 1941, Harvey papers, vol. 56402, p. 17; Scott, min., 13 May 1941, FO 371/28899, W5382/426/49.

75 Halifax to Eden, desp. 976, 15 Oct. 1941, para. 12, FO 371/26151, A9358/18/45.

76 See also discussion in ch. 1 (b). For background see e.g. Kindleberger, *World in Depression*; Rowland (ed.), *Balance of Power or Hegemony*.

77 *New York Herald-Tribune*, 31 March 1946, quoted in Rees, *White*, p. 138; Cleveland, in Rowland (ed.), *Balance of Power*, pp. 53–6; Strange, *Sterling and British Policy*, pp. 70–1.

78 Ashton-Gwatkin, memo, 6 Aug. 1941, FO 371/28904, W10371/426/49; cf. Shackle to Playfair, 11 July 1941, T 160/1200, F15994/2.

79 For a good statement, quoted here, see Amery, memo, 10 Dec. 1941, FO 371/28813, W15335/37/49. For other examples see memos of 29 Oct. 1940, FO 371/28899, W2311/426/49, and 12 Jan. 1942, CAB 66/21, WP (42) 23.

80 See esp. Keynes to Ashton-Gwatkin, 25 April 1941 and min. by Ronald, 6 June, FO 371/28899, W6635/426/49. For other examples see Sargent, min., 6 Jan. 1941, ibid., W426; Pinsent, memo, 27 March 1941, D/S 841.24/481½; Leith-Ross, note, April 1941, T 188/249.

81 Halifax to Eden, 5 Jan. 1942, FO 954/29A, p. 348.

82 Quotations from W.S.C. to Kingsley Wood, 28 Aug. 1941, PREM 4/71/1, p. 108. For his comments at the Atlantic Meeting see *FRUS*, 1941, I, 361–2. On 18 Sept. Mackenzie King, the Canadian premier, told Pierrepont Moffat, U.S. Minister in Ottawa, about his recent visit to Britain. He said that during a discussion of post-war economic policy 'Churchill had turned to Cranborne [the Dominions Secretary] and said, "Your grandfather, old Lord Salisbury,

would turn in his grave if he knew of the Ottawa Agreements, high tariffs and increasing preferences." Cranborne answered that his grandfather would have turned several times, but that conditions had made these Agreements inevitable and if they had to be done again Mr. Churchill would join in negotiating them. "I would not", snapped Churchill.' (Moffat Diary, vol. 47, 18 Sept. 1941.)

83 A point noted by Addison, *Road to 1945*, pp. 101–2, 235–6.

84 E.g. Welles to Representative Charles Eaton, 16 July 1941, D/S 841.24/749; Cox to Hopkins, 7 July, Hopkins papers 305: 'Lend-Lease Misuse'.

85 Text in *FRUS*, 1941, III, 32–4. For background see Sayers, *Financial Policy*, pp. 398–405, and Kimball, 'Lend-Lease', pp. 250–2.

86 See BT 11/1724: esp. letters from Robert Tucker & Co., 16 Sept., 13 Oct. and 25 Oct. 1941, from Richard Stokes, 28 Oct., and from Sir Patrick Hannon, as Pres. of the National Union of Manufacturers, to W.S.C., ? 27 Oct. British missions in South America reported that ill-feeling between British and U.S. firms was not widespread (see reports in FO 371/25975, A229/229/51) but British businessmen there claimed that the diplomats paid little attention to 'the determined efforts that American Interests are making to freeze Britain out of this continent'. (Quote from a letter from a Rio de Janeiro subsidiary of Metropolitan Vickers to Associated Electrical Industries, 18 Oct. 1941, BT 11/1438.) Further research is needed on this whole question.

87 Robertson to Playfair, 19 Aug. 1941, T 160/1369, F17660/08/2.

88 I hope to discuss the negotiations more fully in a future article. For earlier accounts see Penrose, *Economic Planning*, esp. pp 13–31; Gardner, *Sterling–Dollar Diplomacy*, chs. III–IV; Sayers, *Financial Policy*, pp. 405–13; and Kimball, 'Lend-Lease and the Open Door', based on the U.S. documents but published before the British archives were opened.

89 E.g. copy in Morgenthau Diary, 391: 300–5, sent to Hull on 25 April 1941; cf. Morgenthau Presidtl. Diary, 4: 849–52, and Diary, 381: 19–21.

90 See esp. Moffat Diary, 31 March 1941; quotation from Acheson, 7 April 1941, in Morgenthau Diary, 386:231.

91 *FRUS*, 1941, III, 15.

92 See Moffat Diary, 31 March 1941; Keynes to Treasury, tel. 2439, 29 May 1941, T 160/1105, F17660/02/1. Cf. Hull, *Memoirs*, II, 975. See also below, note 101.

93 E.g. Hopkins, memo, 9 June 1941, Hopkins papers 307: 'Period between 1st and 2nd London visits' (folder 2); Halifax to FO, tel. 3177, 8 July 1941, T 160/1105, F17660/02/1.

94 F.D.R., memo to Welles and Acheson, 18 July 1941, PSF 96: State Dept., Welles.

95 Keynes, memo of conversation with Acheson, 28 July 1941, PREM 4/17/3, p. 509, and min. to Wood, 2 Aug. 1941, ibid., p. 514 (quote).

96 State Dept. officials had followed F.D.R.'s 18 July instructions, except on the question of economic liberalization. Welles read F.D.R. the draft over the phone on 27 July, explained why they had stuck to their guns, and elicited the President's 'complete approval for Article VII as now drafted'. However, F.D.R. emphasized that this was not a final commitment on his part but only approval of the draft as a basis for negotiation with HMG. (See Welles, memo, 27 July 1941, and State Dept. memo on Art. VII, D/S 841.24/646 1/2.) Roosevelt may not have realized how far State's draft differed from his 18 July instructions, or he may have decided that there was no point in further intra-Administration argument until some British reaction had been ascertained. Probably there is truth in both these hypotheses.

97 'The Foreign Office view is that it would be desirable to postpone as long as possible any commitment in the general "consideration" field. Generally

speaking, it would appear expedient to play for time in the expectation that if America came into the war we should get much better terms than we could hope for now.' (Ronald to Waley, 30 May 1941, FO 371/28799, W6216/37/49.)

98 Keynes to Halifax, 12 June 1941, T 247/44.

99 See Keynes to Wood, 21 June, and Halifax tels. 3177 and 3178, 8 July 1941; FO tels. 3634, 29 June, and 4022–3, 14 July 1941, all in T 160/1105, F17660/02/1.

100 Keynes to Acheson, 29 July 1941, *FRUS*, 1941, III, 16–17. For other examples of how Keynes upset State Dept. officials see Hawkins, memos of 1 Aug. 1941, ibid., pp. 19–22, and 4 Aug., PSF 90: State Dept.; Opie, memos of 12 Aug. based on talks with Acheson, FO 115/3466.

101 Emphasis added. For the Charter see sources cited in note 29. For State's unhappiness see Wilson, *First Summit*, pp. 247–9. This was the point, in my judgement, when Hull became seriously involved. In the spring he had not been willing to force the British into firm economic commitments, but, now that a declaration *had* been made, he was distressed at its vagueness and wanted to make explicit that it covered both Imperial Preference and U.S. tariffs. British prevarication led him to support his officials' toughness on article seven.

102 Printed in *FRUS*, 1941, III, 41–2. For background see papers in T 160/1105, F17660/02/1.

103 Acheson, memo, 28 Oct. 1941, D/S 841.24/942½.

104 U.S. draft of 2 Dec. 1941, printed in *FRUS*, 1941, III, 45–6. The crucial section of article seven stated that the final terms of the Lend-Lease settlement 'shall include provision for agreed action by the United States of America and the United Kingdom, open to participation by all other countries of like mind, directed to the expansion, by appropriate international and domestic measures, of production, employment, and the exchange and consumption of goods, which are the material foundations of the liberty and welfare of all peoples; to the elimination of all forms of discriminatory treatment in international commerce, and to the reduction of tariffs and other trade barriers; and, in general, to the attainment of all the economic objectives set forth in the Joint Declaration [Atlantic Charter]. . . At an early convenient date, conversations shall be begun between the two Governments with a view to determining, in the light of governing economic conditions, the best means of attaining the above-stated objectives by their own agreed action and of seeking the agreed action of other like-minded Governments.' My interpretation of this redraft is similar to that of Penrose, *Economic Planning*, pp. 26–7, which was followed by Gardner, *Sterling–Dollar Diplomacy*, pp. 58–9. For a different view see Kimball, 'Lend-Lease and the Open Door', pp. 253–4.

105 CAB 65/25, WM (42) 14/8 and 17/4. For FO views see e.g. FO 371/28813, and /32491.

106 F.D.R. to W.S.C., 11 Feb. 1942, *FRUS*, 1942, I, 535–6. The crucial sentences read: 'What seems to be bothering the Cabinet is the thought that we want a commitment in advance that Empire preference will be abolished. We are asking for no such commitment, and I can say that Article 7 does not contain any such commitment.' Originally F.D.R. had favoured a revised interpretative note, but then changed his mind (see drafts and papers in Map Room 1).

107 Cf. Acheson, *Present at the Creation*, p. 33.

108 After reading the cable to the Cabinet on 12 Feb., the PM commented that in F.D.R.'s view 'Article 7 contained no commitment in advance to abolish Empire Preference, which should be excluded from our discussions.' (CAB 65/29, p. 41, WM 20 (42) 4 CA.) The first part of his comment was correct, the second quite wrong. The source of W.S.C.'s error may have been a hasty

reading of this sentence from the cable, where F.D.R. said: 'It seems to me the proposed note leaves a clear implication that Empire preference and, say, agreements between ourselves and the Philippines are excluded before we sit down at the table.' Roosevelt was referring to the proposed *British* note, to qualify article seven, and saying that it limited his principle of a totally comprehensive discussion, but Churchill may have taken 'the proposed note' to refer to the U.S. draft of article seven.

109 See Gardner, *Sterling–Dollar Diplomacy*, pp. 65–6. Gardner was unaware of the confusion in the British Cabinet records.

110 Waley to Wilson and Keynes to Wilson, 11 and 12 Feb. 1942, T 247/44 (see also T 160/1105, F17660/02/3).

111 E.g. Treasury note, 'Post-war trade and financial policy', 27 Sept. 1941, T 247/121, 7.

112 Keynes to Wilson, 19 Sept. 1941, T 160/1105, F17660/02/1.

113 Cf. Harrod, *Keynes*, pp. 525–6.

114 See esp. T 247/33 and /116.

115 See Harry White Papers, box 8 (see also above, ch. 3 (b) and note 43). For fuller discussion see Harrod, *Keynes*, ch. XIII; Rees, *White*, chs. 10 and 14; Blum, *From the Morgenthau Diaries*, III, ch. v; Gardner, *Sterling–Dollar Diplomacy*, chs. V and VII; and Van Dormael, *Bretton Woods*.

116 See Rowland (ed.), *Balance of Power or Hegemony*, esp. essays by Cleveland and Skidelsky; Strange, *Sterling and British Policy*, esp. chs. 1–2; and Katzenstein, *Between Power and Plenty*, pp. 591–5. For dissenting views, arguing that a 'balance of power' or pluralist system of interacting blocs is more desirable, see the essays by Brittain, Calleo and Rowland in the Rowland collection, and esp. Calleo and Rowland, *America and the World Political Economy*.

117 Kindleberger, *The World in Depression*, pp. 303, 292. Kindleberger's is the most forceful statement of this thesis.

118 A point emphasized particularly by Skidelsky, in Rowland (ed.), *Balance of Power*, pp. 150–1.

119 This is the term favoured by Calleo and Rowland, *America and the World Political Economy*, p. 251 (see also Rowland, in *Balance of Power*, p. xii). But neither accepts the notion of a responsible leader, let alone Skidelsky's concept of self-sacrifice, and Calleo's essay in *Balance of Power* argues that the instability of the 1920s and 1930s was caused by Britain's attempt to usurp a role she had never had in the first place.

**Conclusion**

1 Quoted in Howard K. Beale, *Theodore Roosevelt and the Rise of America to World Power* (Baltimore, 1956), p. 447; and in *Irrepressible Churchill: A Treasury of Winston Churchill's Wit*, comp. Kay Halle (Cleveland, Ohio, 1966), p. 157.

2 For these interpretations see, respectively, Allen, *Great Britain and the United States*, e.g. pp. 52, 781, 983 (but cf. his revised judgement nearly 25 years later in Allen and Thompson (eds.), *Contrast and Connection*, p. 153); and Barnett, *Collapse of British Power*, p. 592.

3 W.S.C. to F.D.R., 9 Dec. 1941, PREM 3/469, pp. 11–12.

4 Stettinius to Hopkins, 9 Dec. 1941, and memo by McCloy, 10 Dec., Hopkins papers 308: Post Dec. 7 (Lend-Lease); CAB 69/2, DC(O) 73 (41) 1, 19 Dec. 1941, and Abbazia, *Mr. Roosevelt's Navy*, p. 413 (Atlantic).

5 Brooke Diary, 8 Dec. 1941, quoted in Bryant, *The Turn of the Tide*, p. 282.

6 First draft of message to F.D.R., 5 Feb. 1942, PREM 4/17/3, p. 303.

7 Cf. Sherwin, 'The atomic bomb and the origins of the Cold War'; Hinsley *et al.*, *British Intelligence*, I, 311–14.

8 As Churchill himself was at pains to emphasize, cf. *Second World War*, II, 20–3.

9 See Villa, 'The atomic bomb and the Normandy invasion'; Van Dormael, *Bretton Woods*, ch. 20.

10 Leighton, 'The American arsenal policy', p. 251; Milward, *War, Economy and Society*, ch. 3, esp. pp. 63, 67.

11 E.g. Gaddis, *The U.S. and the Origins of the Cold War*; Yergin, *Shattered Peace*.

12 Which is often overlooked. For good discussion see the essay by Stephen Blank in Katzenstein (ed.), *Between Power and Plenty*, esp. pp. 676–9.

13 For a good recent discussion, see Henrikson, 'The creation of the North Atlantic alliance'. See also Osgood, *NATO*, esp. chs. 1–2; Manderson-Jones, *The Special Relationship*.

14 From the very beginning in 1942 the FO's official post-war planning papers stated this explicitly as the first assumption. See Woodward, *British Foreign Policy*, V, e.g. pp. 5, 10, 14.

15 See Blank, essay cited in note 12, pp. 680–3. There were dissenting voices, but usually on the fringe of policy-making circles. For example the merchant banker R. H. Brand referred in Oct. 1940 to 'the fundamental dilemma before this country—Can we still act as a sort of go-between between Europe and the rest of the world? Shall we not be forced to throw in our lot with Europe whether we are beaten or whether we win? . . . Or can we still play a great part in the world associated with the United States and the Dominions, together controlling the oceans? I do not think both roles . . . can be combined. It is one thing or the other . . .' (Brand, notes, 1 Oct. 1940, in Nancy Astor papers, 4/60, E). Significantly, Brand preferred 'to make one last effort to keep company with the English-speaking races'.

16 Gladstone, 'Kin Beyond Sea', cited in Intro., note 1.

17 David Scott, min., 22 March 1939, FO 371/23981, W4677/108/50.

18 'The P.M. has always gone in for appeasing the Americans', complained Cripps to Dalton on 30 May 1942 (Dalton Diary, 26:214).

19 This is the point of A. J. P. Taylor's tendentious comment, after noting the economic losses and human casualties sustained by Britain and particularly by Russia, that: 'Of the three great men at the top, Roosevelt was the only one who knew what he was doing: he made the United States the greatest power in the world at virtually no cost.' (*English History*, p. 577.)

20 Cf. Calleo and Rowland, *America and the World Political Economy*, p. 26; Amery, memo, 12 Jan. 1942, CAB 66/21, WP (42) 23.

21 In his stimulating book, *The Collapse of British Power*, Correlli Barnett argues that by fighting on in 1940 Britain inevitably became an 'American satellite warrior-state' (p. 592), and that she could have sought a compromise peace or fought a strictly limited war commensurate with the immediate security needs of the British Isles and with their long-term wealth and prosperity. Instead, he argues, Churchill quixotically tried to wage total war for total victory, believing that the U.S.A. was Britain's friend rather than her rival and failing to see the cost to British power of such a war effort (esp. pp. 8–15, 583–93). Although this is similar to my own argument in some respects, I feel that there were no real choices open to British leaders in 1940. As we saw in ch. 4 (b), most British leaders, and probably Churchill himself, did believe privately that a negotiated peace was all that could realistically be hoped for in mid-

1940. 'Victory at all costs' was morale-boosting rhetoric. But, after some disputes around the time of Dunkirk, a consensus emerged that Britain could only hope to secure acceptable terms by proving that she could not be invaded. Such proof required an all-out war effort, which necessarily depended on the U.S.A. Moreover, the invasion threat did not disappear in October 1940. It seemed as real in the spring of 1941, and brilliant German deception measures helped to keep it alive well into 1942. The only point at which there might have been hope of extracting a negotiated peace was when Hitler got bogged down in Russia. It is here that Barnett's strictures have most validity: by 1941–42 Churchill had removed the 'appeasers' and the idea of a special relationship had become an axiom of British policy. But even so, the case is highly arguable. Russian survival was far from certain throughout 1941 and early 1942—hence the continued fears of invasion. Despite Churchill's more romantic moments, we have seen that the FO had a hard-headed view of the Anglo-American relationship. And, fundamentally, after the events of the late 1930s, no one could place any trust in an agreement with Hitler. In short, from the summer of 1940 HMG had few choices open; it was Chamberlain's appreciation of that fact that led him to work so ardently in 1937–40 to avoid total war. For all his illusions about Hitler, Chamberlain was more realistic about the costs of all-out war than Churchill or Eden.

22 Points emphasized in Campbell, 'The U.S. and Britain', p. 439, n. 21; Bell, 'The "special relationship" ', p. 106.

23 'It has been going on now for three hundred years.' Lord Illingworth, in *A Woman of No Importance*, Act I, *Complete Works of Oscar Wilde* (London, 1968), p. 436.

24 It has been argued that both Britain and the U.S.A share a common tradition of seeing foreign policy in ideological and moral terms, permitted this luxury by their relative immunity from the realities—and consequent Realpolitik—of continental power politics. (See Arnold Wolfers' intro. to Wolfers and Martin (eds.), *The Anglo-American Tradition in Foreign Affairs*, esp. pp. xix–xxiii.)

25 Chatfield to Fisher, 6 June 1934, Chatfield papers, CHT/3/1, p. 62.

# BIBLIOGRAPHY

**I Manuscript Sources**

A. GREAT BRITAIN
A. V. Alexander (Churchill College, Cambridge).
Nancy Astor (University Library, Reading).
Waldorf Astor (University Library, Reading).
Beaverbrook (House of Lords Record Office, London).
British Government (Public Record Office, Kew):
  Admiralty (ADM).
  Cabinet Office (CAB).
  Colonial Office (CO).
  Board of Education (ED).
  Foreign Office (FO).
  Ministry of Information (INF).
  Prime Minister's Office (PREM).
  Board of Trade (BT).
  Treasury (T).
Caldecote, formerly Sir Thomas Inskip (Churchill College, Cambridge).
Neville Chamberlain (University Library, Birmingham).
Chatfield (National Maritime Museum, Greenwich).
Citrine (British Library of Political & Economic Science, London).
Lionel Curtis (Bodleian Library, Oxford).
Dalton (British Library of Political & Economic Science).
Elibank, formerly Sir Arthur Murray (National Library, Edinburgh).
Sir Warren Fisher (British Library of Political & Economic Science).
Sir Edward Grigg (Bodleian Library, Oxford).
Sir P. J. Grigg (Churchill College, Cambridge).
Halifax (Hickleton Papers at Churchill College, Cambridge and Garrowby Hall, York).
Hankey (Churchill College, Cambridge).
Sir Patrick Hannon (House of Lords Record Office).
Oliver Harvey (British Library Add. Mss.).
Keynes (King's College, Cambridge).
Lloyd George (House of Lords Record Office).
Lothian (Scottish Record Office, Edinburgh).
Ivison S. MacAdam (Bodleian Library, Oxford).
Kingsley Martin (Sussex University Library, Falmer).
Sir Walter Monckton (Bodleian Library, Oxford: Dep. Monck. Trustees).
Sir Charles Peake (private hands, East Molesey, Surrey).
Samuel (House of Lords Record Office).
Templewood, formerly Sir Samuel Hoare (University Library, Cambridge).
Euan Wallace (Bodleian Library, Oxford).
Sir Charles Webster (British Library of Political & Economic Science).

B. UNITED STATES
Joseph Alsop (Library of Congress, Washington, D.C.).
John Balderston (Library of Congress).
Hanson W. Baldwin (Sterling Library, Yale University).
Bernard Baruch (Seeley G. Mudd Library, Princeton University).
Ulric Bell (Private hands, New York).

Adolf A. Berle (Franklin D. Roosevelt Library, Hyde Park, N.Y.).
Nicholas M. Butler (Butler Library, Columbia University, N.Y.).
Carnegie Endowment for International Peace (CEIP) (Butler Library, Columbia University).
Committee to Defend America by Aiding the Allies (CDAAA):
    New York City HQ (Mudd Library, Princeton University).
    Hartford and Connecticut chapters (Sterling Library, Yale University).
Council on Foreign Relations (CFR offices, New York City).
Oscar Cox (F.D.R. Library).
Norman Davis (Library of Congress).
Fight for Freedom Committee (FFF) (Mudd Library, Princeton University).
Felix Frankfurter (Library of Congress).
Frank P. Graham (Southern Historical Collection, University of North Carolina, Chapel Hill).
Roger Sherman Greene (Houghton Library, Harvard University).
Admiral John Greenslade (Library of Congress).
Harry Hopkins (F.D.R. Library).
Cordell Hull (Library of Congress).
Harold Ickes (Library of Congress).
Herschel V. Johnson (Southern Historical Collection, Chapel Hill).
Tyler G. Kent (Sterling Library, Yale University).
Admiral Alan Kirk (Naval Historical Division, Washington Navy Yard).
Frank Knox (Library of Congress).
Arthur Krock (Mudd Library, Princeton University).
Thomas Lamont (Baker Library, Harvard Business School).
Walter Lippmann (Sterling Library, Yale University).
Admiral Charles Lockwood (Library of Congress).
Breckinridge Long (Library of Congress).
Roger B. Merriman (Massachusetts Historical Society, Boston).
Jay Pierrepont Moffat (Houghton Library, Harvard University).
Henry Morgenthau, Jr. (F.D.R. Library).
Edward R. Murrow (Fletcher School, Tufts University, Medford, Mass.).
Charles Parsons (Sterling Library, Yale University).
Frank L. Polk (Sterling Library, Yale University).
Franklin D. Roosevelt (F.D.R. Library):
    Map Room files (MR).
    Official files (OF).
    President's Personal files (PPF).
    President's Secretary's files (PSF).
    Presidential press conferences (PPC).
Whitney H. Shephardson (F.D.R. Library).
Henry L. Stimson (Sterling Library, Yale University).
General Carl Spaatz (Library of Congress).
United States Government:
    Department of State (D/S) (National Archives, Washington).
    U.S. Navy War Plans Division and Naval Forces Europe (Naval Historical Division, Washington Navy Yard).
Oswald G. Villard (Houghton Library, Harvard University).
Harry Dexter White (Mudd Library, Princeton University).
William Allen White (Library of Congress).
T. North Whitehead (Private hands, Cambridge, Mass.).
Sir Arthur Willert (Sterling Library, Yale University).
John G. Winant (F.D.R. Library).

## II Printed Sources

### A. OFFICIAL

*Germany*
Auswärtiges Amt, *Documents on German Foreign Policy, 1918–1945*, series D (London, 1949–54). (*DGFP*)

*Great Britain*
Foreign Office, *Documents on British Foreign Policy, 1919–1939*, 3rd series, eds. E. L. Woodward and Rohan Butler (London, 1949–55). (*DBFP*)
Foreign Office, *Confidential Despatches: Analysis of America by the British Ambassador, 1939–1945*, ed. Thomas E. Hachey (Evanston, Ill., 1974).
House of Commons, *Debates*, 5th series (London, 1934–42). (*HC Debs.*, 5s)
House of Lords, *Debates*, 5th series (London, 1938–41). (*HL Debs.*, 5s)

*United States of America*
Congress, *Congressional Record* (Washington). (*CR*)
Department of State, *Foreign Relations of the United States* (Washington). (*FRUS*); *Japan: 1931–41* (2 vols., 1943); *1937–42* (multi vols., 1954–63).
Department of State, *Peace and War: United States Foreign Policy, 1931–1941* (1943).

### B. DIARIES, PAPERS, SPEECHES, ETC.

George Bilainkin, *Diary of a Diplomatic Correspondent* (London, 1942).
Adolf A. Berle, *Navigating the Rapids, 1918–1971: From the Papers of Adolf A. Berle*, eds. Beatrice B. Berle and Travis B. Jacobs (New York, 1973).
William C. Bullitt, *For the President, Personal and Secret: Correspondence between Franklin D. Roosevelt and William C. Bullitt*, ed. Orville H. Bullitt (London, 1973).
Sir Alexander Cadogan, *The Diaries of Sir Alexander Cadogan, O.M., 1938–1945*, ed. David Dilks (London, 1971).
Sir Henry Channon, *'Chips': the Diaries of Sir Henry Channon*, ed. Robert Rhodes James (London, 1967).
Winston S. Churchill, *Collected Essays*, gen. ed. Michael Wolff (4 vols., London, 1976).
Winston S. Churchill, *Complete Speeches, 1897–1963*, vol. VI, 1935–42, ed. Robert Rhodes James (New York, 1974).
Winston S. Churchill, *Secret Session Speeches*, comp. Charles Eade (London, 1946).
W. P. Crozier, *Off the Record: Political Interviews, 1933–1943* (London, 1972).
George N. Gallup (ed.), *The Gallup Poll: Public Opinion, 1935–1971*, vol. I (New York, 1972).
Samuel Grafton, *An American Diary* (New York, 1943).
Oliver Harvey, *The Diplomatic Diaries of Oliver Harvey, 1937–1940*, ed. John Harvey (London, 1970).
Oliver Harvey, *The War Diaries of Oliver Harvey*, ed. John Harvey (London, 1978).
Harold L. Ickes, *The Secret Diary of Harold L. Ickes*, vols. II and III (New York, 1954).
Gen. Lord Ironside, *The Ironside Diaries, 1937–1940*, eds. Roderick Macleod and Denis Kelly (London, 1962).
Thomas Jones, *A Diary with Letters, 1931–1950* (London, 1954).
John Maynard Keynes, *Collected Writings*, eds. Elizabeth Johnson and Donald Moggridge (London, 1971–); vol. II, *The Economic Consequences of the Peace* (1919); vol. XXII, *Activities, 1939–1945: Internal War Finance;* vol. XXIII, *Activities, 1940–1943: External War Finance.*
Cecil H. King, *With Malice Toward None: A War Diary*, ed. William Armstrong (London, 1970).

Raymond E. Lee, *The London Observer: The Journal of General Raymond E. Lee, 1940–1941*, ed. James Leutze (London, 1972).

Charles A. Lindbergh, *The Wartime Journals of Charles A. Lindbergh* (New York, 1970).

David Lloyd George, *My Darling Pussy: The Letters of Lloyd George and Frances Stevenson, 1913–1941*, ed. A. J. P. Taylor (London, 1975).

Breckinridge Long, *The War Diary of Breckinridge Long. Selections from the War Years, 1939–1944*, ed. Fred L. Israel (Lincoln, Nebr., 1966).

Lord Lothian, *The American Speeches of Lord Lothian, July 1939 to December 1940* (London, 1941).

Jay Pierrepont Moffat, *The Moffat Papers: Selections from the Diplomatic Journals of Jay Pierrepont Moffat, 1919–1943*, ed. Nancy Harvison Hooker (Cambridge, Mass., 1956).

Harold Nicolson, *Diaries and Letters*, ed. Nigel Nicolson (London). vol. I, 1930–39 (1966); vol. II, 1939–45 (1967).

Mollie Panter-Downes, *London War Notes, 1939–1945*, ed. William Shawn (New York, 1971).

Sir Henry Pownall, *Chief of Staff: The Diaries of Lieutenant-General Sir Henry Pownall*, ed. Brian Bond (London, 2 vols., 1972, 1974).

Franklin D. Roosevelt, *Roosevelt and Churchill: Their Secret Wartime Correspondence*, eds. Francis L. Loewenheim, Harold D. Langley and Manfred Jonas (London, 1975).

Franklin D. Roosevelt, *Franklin D. Roosevelt and Foreign Affairs*, ed. Edgar B. Nixon (3 vols., Cambridge, Mass., 1969).

Franklin D. Roosevelt, *F.D.R.: His Personal Letters, 1928–1945*, ed. Elliott Roosevelt with Joseph P. Lash (2 vols., New York, 1950).

Franklin D. Roosevelt, *The Public Papers and Addresses of Franklin D. Roosevelt*, ed. Samuel I. Rosenman (New York, 1938–50).

A. J. Sylvester, *Life with Lloyd George: The Diary of A. J. Sylvester, 1931–1945*, ed. Colin Cross (London, 1975).

### III Printed Secondary Works: Books

Patrick Abbazia, *Mr. Roosevelt's Navy: The Private War of the U.S. Atlantic Fleet, 1939–1942* (Annapolis, Md., 1975).

Dean Acheson, *Present at the Creation: My Years at the State Department* (New York, 1969).

Anthony Adamthwaite, *France and the Coming of the Second World War, 1936–1939* (London, 1977).

Paul Addison, *The Road to 1945: British Politics and the Second World War* (London, 1975).

Herbert Agar, *Britain Alone: June 1940–June 1941* (London, 1972).

Derek Aldcroft, *The Inter-War Economy: Britain, 1919–1939* (London, pbk. edn., 1973).

H. C. Allen, *Great Britain and the United States: A History of Anglo-American Relations, 1783–1952* (London, 1952).

H. C. Allen and Roger Thompson (eds.), *Contrast and Connection: Bicentennial Essays in Anglo-American History* (London, 1976).

Irvine H. Anderson, Jr., *The Standard-Vacuum Oil Company and United States East Asian Policy, 1933–1941* (Princeton, 1975).

Maurice Ashley, *Churchill as Historian* (London, 1966).

Sidney Aster, *1939: The Making of the Second World War* (London, 1973).

Lord Avon, *Facing the Dictators* (London, 1967).
Lord Avon, *The Reckoning* (London, 1965).

Thomas A. Bailey and Paul B. Ryan, *Hitler vs. Roosevelt* (New York, 1979).
Phillip J. Baram, *The Department of State in the Middle East, 1919–1945* (Philadelphia, 1978).
Glen St J. Barclay, *Their Finest Hour* (London, 1977).
Elisabeth Barker, *British Policy in South-East Europe in the Second World War* (London, 1976).
Elisabeth Barker, *Churchill and Eden at War* (London, 1978).
Correlli Barnett, *The Collapse of British Power* (London, 1972).
Gloria J. Barron, *Leadership in Crisis: FDR and the Path to Intervention* (Port Washington, N.Y., 1973).
Joan Beaumont, *Comrades in Arms: British Aid to Russia, 1941–1945* (London, 1980).
Daniel R. Beaver (ed.), *Some Pathways in Twentieth Century History* (Detroit, 1969).
Coral Bell, *The Debatable Alliance: An Essay in Anglo-American Relations* (London, 1964).
P. M. H. Bell, *A Certain Eventuality: Britain and the Fall of France* (Farnborough, Hants., 1974).
Bernard Bellush, *He Walked Alone: A Biography of John Gilbert Winant* (The Hague, 1968).
Max Beloff, *Imperial Sunset: I, Britain's Liberal Empire* (London, 1969).
Michael R. Beschloss, *Kennedy and Roosevelt: The Uneasy Alliance* (New York, 1980).
Lord Birkenhead, *Halifax: The Life of Lord Halifax* (London, 1965).
John M. Blum, *From the Morgenthau Diaries*, 3 vols. (Boston, 1959–67).
Brian Bond, *France and Belgium, 1939–1940* (London, 1975).
Dorothy Borg, *The United States and the Far Eastern Crisis of 1933–1938* (Cambridge, Mass., 1964).
Dorothy Borg and Shumpei Okamoto (eds.), *Pearl Harbor as History: Japanese–American Relations, 1931–1941* (New York, 1973).
Kenneth Bourne, *Britain and the Balance of Power in North America, 1815–1908* (London, 1967).
John Braeman, Robert H. Bremner and David Brody (eds.), *Twentieth Century American Foreign Policy* (Columbus, Ohio, 1971).
John Braeman, Robert H. Bremner and David Brody (eds.), *The New Deal: I, The National Level* (Columbus, Ohio, 1975).
Henry N. Brailsford, *America our Ally* (London, 1940).
Arthur Bryant, *The Turn of the Tide, 1939–1943: A Study Based on the Diaries and Autobiographical Notes of Field Marshal the Viscount Alanbrooke, K.G., O.M.* (London, 1957).
James M. Burns, *Roosevelt: The Lion and the Fox* (New York, 1956).
James M. Burns, *Roosevelt: The Soldier of Freedom* (New York, 1970).
Richard Dean Burns and Edward M. Bennett, *Diplomats in Crisis: United States–Chinese–Japanese Relations, 1919–1941* (Santa Barbara, Ca., 1974).
J. R. M. Butler, *Grand Strategy, September 1939–June 1941* (London, 1957).
J. R. M. Butler, *Lord Lothian (Philip Kerr), 1882–1940* (London, 1960).
Robert J. C. Butow, *Tojo and the Coming of War* (Stanford, Ca., 1961).
Robert J. C. Butow, *The John Doe Associates: Backdoor Diplomacy for Peace, 1941* (Stanford, Ca., 1974).

Angus Calder, *The People's War: Britain, 1939–1945* (London, pbk. edn., 1971).
Raymond Callahan, *The Worst Disaster: The Fall of Singapore* (Newark, N.J., 1977).

David P. Calleo and Benjamin M. Rowland, *America and the World Political Economy: Atlantic Dreams and National Realities* (Bloomington, Ind., 1973).

A. E. Campbell, *Great Britain and the United States, 1895–1903* (London, 1960).

Joseph T. Carroll, *Ireland in the War Years* (Newton Abbot, 1975).

Lord Richard G. Casey, *Personal Experience, 1939–1946* (London, 1962).

Mark L. Chadwin, *The Warhawks: American Interventionists before Pearl Harbor* (New York, 1970).

Winston S. Churchill, *The Second World War* (6 vols., London, 1948–54).

Bernard C. Cohen, *The Public's Impact on Foreign Policy* (Boston, 1973).

Warren I. Cohen, *The American Revisionists: Lessons of Intervention in World War I* (Chicago, 1967).

Wayne S. Cole, *America First: The Battle against Intervention, 1940–1941* (New York, 1953).

Wayne S. Cole, *Senator Gerald P. Nye and American Foreign Relations* (Minneapolis, 1962).

Wayne S. Cole, *Charles A. Lindbergh and the Battle against American Intervention in World War II* (New York, 1974).

D. C. Coleman, *Courtaulds: An Economic and Social History* (2 vols., Oxford, 1969).

Basil Collier, *The Defence of the United Kingdom* (London, 1957).

Sir John Colville, *Footprints in Time* (London, 1976).

Ian Colvin, *The Chamberlain Cabinet* (New York edn., 1971).

James V. Compton, *The Swastika and the Eagle: Hitler, the United States, and the Origins of the Second World War* (London, 1968).

Stetson Conn and Byron Fairchild, *The Western Hemisphere: The Framework of Hemisphere Defense* (Washington, 1960).

Herbert Corkran, Jr., *Patterns of International Cooperation in the Caribbean, 1942–1969* (Dallas, 1970).

Maurice Cowling, *The Impact of Hitler: British Politics and British Strategy, 1933–1940* (London, 1975).

Charles Cruickshank, *Greece, 1940–1941* (London, 1976).

David H. Culbert, *News for Everyman: Radio and Foreign Affairs in Thirties America* (Westport, Conn., 1976).


Robert Dallek, *Franklin D. Roosevelt and American Foreign Policy, 1932–1945* (New York, 1979).

Hugh Dalton, *Memoirs 1931–1945: The Fateful Years* (London, 1957).

Forrest Davis and Ernest K. Lindley, *How War Came to America: From the Fall of France to Pearl Harbor* (London, 1943).

Lynn E. Davis, *The Cold War Begins: Soviet-American Confrontation over Eastern Europe* (Princeton, 1974).

Raymond H. Dawson, *The Decision to Aid Russia, 1941: Foreign Policy and Domestic Politics* (Chapel Hill, N.C., 1959).

Patrick Devlin, *Too Proud to Fight: Woodrow Wilson's Neutrality* (London, 1974).

Robert A. Divine, *The Illusion of Neutrality* (Chicago, pbk. edn., 1962).

Robert A. Divine, *The Reluctant Belligerent: American Entry into World War II* (New York, 1965).

Robert A. Divine, *Roosevelt and World War II* (Baltimore, pbk. edn., 1970).

Robert A. Divine, *Foreign Policy and U.S. Presidential Elections*, vol. I, 1940–48 (New York, 1974).

Justus D. Doenecke, *The Literature of Isolationism: A Guide to Non-Interventionist Scholarship, 1930–1972* (Colorado Springs, 1972).

Roy Douglas, *In the Year of Munich* (London, 1977).

Roy Douglas, *The Advent of War, 1939–1940* (London, 1978).

Ian S. Drummond, *British Economic Policy and the Empire, 1919–1939* (London, 1972).

Ian S. Drummond, *Imperial Economic Policy, 1917–1939: Studies in Expansion and Protection* (London, 1974).

T. Ryle Dwyer, *Irish Neutrality and the USA, 1939–1947* (London, 1977).

Jerome E. Edwards, *The Foreign Policy of Col. McCormick's Tribune, 1929–1941* (Reno, Nev., 1971).

John Erickson, *The Road to Stalingrad: Stalin's War with Germany*, vol. I (London, 1975).

Raymond A. Esthus, *From Enmity to Alliance: U.S.–Australian Relations 1931–1941* (Seattle, 1964).

Keith Feiling, *The Life of Neville Chamberlain* (London, 1946).

Barry Feinberg and Ronald Kasrils, *Bertrand Russell's America: His Transatlantic Travels and Writings*, vol. I, *1896–1945* (London, 1973).

Herbert Feis, *The Road to Pearl Harbor: The Coming of War between the United States and Japan* (Princeton, 1950).

George Q. Flynn, *Roosevelt and Romanism: Catholics and American Diplomacy, 1937–1945* (Westport, Conn., 1976).

Frank Freidel, *Franklin D. Roosevelt* (4 vols., Boston, 1952–).

Saul Friedländer, *Prelude to Downfall: Hitler and the United States, 1939–1941* (London, 1967).

John L. Gaddis, *The United States and the Origins of the Cold War, 1941–1947* (New York, 1972).

Lloyd C. Gardner, *Economic Aspects of New Deal Diplomacy* (Boston, pbk. edn., 1971).

Richard N. Gardner, *Sterling-Dollar Diplomacy: The Origins and Prospects of Our International Economic Order* (New York, rev. edn., 1969).

N. H. Gibbs, *Grand Strategy: I, Rearmament Policy* (London, 1976).

Martin Gilbert, *Winston S. Churchill*, vol. V, 1922–39 (London, 1976).

Philip Goodhart, *Fifty Ships that Saved the World: The Foundation of the Anglo-American Alliance* (London, 1965).

J. L. Granatstein, *Canada's War: The Politics of the Mackenzie King Government, 1939–1945* (Toronto, 1975).

J. M. A. Gwyer, *Grand Strategy*, vol. III, part 1 (London, 1964).

John M. Haight, *American Aid to France, 1938–1940* (New York, 1970).

Lord Halifax, *Fulness of Days* (London, 1957).

H. Duncan Hall, *North American Supply* (London, 1955).

W. K. Hancock and M. M. Gowing, *British War Economy* (London, rev. edn., 1975).

W. Averell Harriman and Elie Abel, *Special Envoy to Churchill and Stalin, 1941–1946* (New York, 1975).

Roy Harrod, *The Life of John Maynard Keynes* (Harmondsworth, pbk. edn., 1972).

Richard H. Heindel, *The American Impact on Great Britain, 1898–1914: A Study of the United States in World History* (Philadelphia, 1940).

Waldo H. Heinrichs, Jr., *American Ambassador: Joseph C. Grew and the Development of the United States Diplomatic Tradition* (Boston, 1966).

George C. Herring, Jr., *Aid to Russia, 1941–1946: Strategy, Diplomacy, the Origins of the Cold War* (New York, 1973).

James H. Herzog. *Closing the Open Door: American–Japanese Diplomatic Negotiations, 1936–1941* (Annapolis, Md., 1973).

379

Gary R. Hess, *America Encounters India, 1941–1947* (Baltimore, 1971).
Klaus Hildebrand, *The Foreign Policy of the Third Reich*, tr. by Anthony Fothergill (London, 1973).
F. H. Hinsley with E. E. Thomas, C. F. G. Ransom and R. C. Knight, *British Intelligence in the Second World War: Its Influence on Strategy and Operations*, vol. I (New York, 1979).
Michael J. Hogan, *Informal Entente: The Private Structure of Cooperation in Anglo-American Diplomacy, 1918–1928* (Columbus, Mo., 1977).
Michael Howard, *The Continental Commitment: The Dilemma of British Defence Policy in the Era of Two World Wars* (Harmondsworth, pbk. edn., 1974).
Cordell Hull, *The Memoirs of Cordell Hull* (2 vols., New York, 1948).
Graham Hutton, *Midwest at Noon* (Chicago, 1946).
H. Montgomery Hyde, *The Quiet Canadian: The Secret Service Story of Sir William Stephenson* (London, 1962).
H. Montgomery Hyde, *Neville Chamberlain* (London, 1976).

Akira Iriye, *From Nationalism to Internationalism: US Foreign Policy to 1914* (London, 1977).
Akira Iriye, *Across the Pacific: An Inner History of American–East Asian Relations* (New York, 1967).
Fred L. Israel, *Nevada's Key Pittman* (Lincoln, Nebr., 1963).

Robert Rhodes James, *Churchill: A Study in Failure, 1900–1939* (Harmondsworth, pbk. edn., 1973).
Robert Rhodes James, *Victor Cazalet: A Portrait* (London, 1976).
Donald B. Johnson, *The Republican Party and Wendell Willkie* (Urbana, Ill., 1960).
Walter Johnson, *The Battle Against Isolation* (Chicago, 1944).
Manfred Jonas, *Isolationism in America, 1935–1941* (Ithaca, N.Y., 1966).

Peter J. Katzenstein (ed.), *Between Power and Plenty: Foreign Economic Policies of Advanced Industrial States* (Madison, Wis., 1977). Published as vol. 31, no. 4 of *International Organization*.
Alexander Kendrick, *Prime Time: The Life of Edward R. Murrow* (Boston, Mass., 1969).
Milo Keynes (ed.), *Essays on John Maynard Keynes* (Cambridge, 1975).
Warren F. Kimball, *The Most Unsordid Act: Lend-Lease, 1939–1941* (Baltimore, 1969).
Charles P. Kindleberger, *The World in Depression, 1929–1939* (London, 1973).
S. Woodburn Kirby, *The War Against Japan, vol. I: The Loss of Singapore* (London, 1957).
David E. Koskoff, *Joseph P. Kennedy: A Life and Times* (Englewood Cliffs, N.J., 1974).
Richard N. Kottman, *Reciprocity and the North Atlantic Triangle, 1932–1938* (Ithaca, N.Y., 1968).

William L. Langer and S. Everett Gleason, *The Challenge to Isolation, 1937–1940* (New York, 1952).
William L. Langer and S. Everett Gleason, *The Undeclared War, 1940–1941* (New York, 1953).
Joseph P. Lash, *Roosevelt and Churchill, 1939–1941: The Partnership that Saved the West* (New York, 1976).
Barry A. Leach, *German Strategy against Russia, 1939–1941* (Oxford, 1973).

Bradford A. Lee, *Britain and the Sino-Japanese War, 1937–1939: A Study in the Dilemmas of British Decline* (Stanford, 1973).

Michael Leigh, *Mobilizing Consent: Public Opinion and American Foreign Policy, 1937–1947* (Westport, Conn., 1976).

Richard M. Leighton and Robert W. Coakley, *Global Logistics and Strategy, 1940–1943* (Washington, 1955).

William E. Leuchtenburg, *Franklin D. Roosevelt and the New Deal, 1932–1940* (New York, 1963).

James R. Leutze, *Bargaining for Supremacy: Anglo-American Naval Relations, 1937–1941* (Chapel Hill, N.C., 1977).

Ralph B. Levering, *American Opinion and the Russian Alliance, 1939–1945* (Chapel Hill, N.C., 1976).

N. Gordon Levin, *Woodrow Wilson and World Politics: America's Response to War and Revolution* (New York, 1968).

Gordon K. Lewis, *The Growth of the Modern West Indies* (London, 1968).

Arthur S. Link, *Wilson the Diplomatist: A Look at his Major Foreign Policies* (Chicago, 1957).

M. P. Lissington, *New Zealand and the United States, 1840–1944* (Wellington, N.Z., 1972).

R. H. Bruce Lockhart, *Comes the Reckoning* (London, 1947).

Norman Longmate, *The G.I.'s: The Americans in Britain, 1942–1945* (London, 1975).

W. Roger Louis, *British Strategy in the Far East, 1919–1939* (Oxford, 1971).

W. Roger Louis, *Imperialism at Bay, 1941–1945: The United States and the Decolonization of the British Empire* (Oxford, 1977).

Peter Lowe, *Great Britain and the Origins of the Pacific War: A Study of British Policy in East Asia, 1937–1941* (Oxford, 1977).

John Lukacs, *The Last European War: September 1939/December 1941* (London, 1977).

Charles E. Lysaght, *Brendan Bracken* (London, 1979).


Callum A. MacDonald, *The United States, Britain and Appeasement, 1936–1939* (London, 1980).

Keith D. McFarland, *Harry H. Woodring: A Political Biography of FDR's Controversial Secretary of War* (Lawrence, Kan., 1975).

Iain MacLeod, *Neville Chamberlain* (London, 1961).

R. B. Manderson-Jones, *The Special Relationship: Anglo-American Relations and Western European Unity, 1947–1956* (London, 1972).

Nicholas Mansergh, *Survey of British Commonwealth Affairs: Problems of Wartime Co-operation and Post-war Change, 1939–1952* (London, 1958).

Vojtech Mastny, *Russia's Road to the Cold War: Diplomacy, Warfare, and the Politics of Communism, 1941–1945* (New York, 1979).

Ernest R. May, *'Lessons' of the Past: The Use and Misuse of History in American Foreign Policy* (New York, 1973).

Ernest R. May and James C. Thomson (eds.), *American–East Asian Relations: A Survey* (Cambridge, Mass., 1972).

Robert J. Maddox, *William E. Borah and American Foreign Policy* (Baton Rouge, La., 1969).

Maurice Matloff and Edwin M. Snell, *Strategic Planning for Coalition Warfare, 1941–1942* (Washington, 1953).

W. N. Medlicott, *The Economic Blockade* (2 vols., London, 1952, 1959).

W. N. Medlicott, *Britain and Germany: The Search for an Agreement, 1930–1937* (London, 1969).

Keith Middlemas, *Diplomacy of Illusion: The British Government and Germany 1937–1939* (London, 1972).

Alan S. Milward, *War, Economy and Society, 1939–1945* (London, 1977).
Donald E. Moggridge, *Keynes* (London, 1976).
Lord Moran, *Winston Churchill: The Struggle for Survival, 1940–1965* (London, 1966).
James W. Morley (ed.), *Japan's Foreign Policy, 1868–1941: A Research Guide* (New York, 1974).
James W. Morley (ed.), *Deterrent Diplomacy: Japan, Germany and the USSR, 1935–1940* (New York, 1976).
James W. Morley (ed.), *The Fateful Choice: Japan's Advance into Southeast Asia, 1939–1941* (New York, 1980).
Louis Morton, *The Fall of the Philippines* (Washington, 1953).

Simon Newman, *March 1939: The British Guarantee to Poland. A Study in the Continuity of British Foreign Policy* (Oxford, 1976).
H. G. Nicholas, *Britain and the United States* (London, 1963).
H. G. Nicholas, *The United States and Britain* (Chicago, 1975).
Ian Nish, *Japanese Foreign Policy, 1869–1942: Kasumigaseki to Miyakezaka* (London, 1977).
Harley A. Notter, *Postwar Foreign Policy Preparation, 1939–1945* (Washington, 1949).

Arnold A. Offner, *The Origins of the Second World War: American Foreign Policy and World Politics, 1917–1941* (New York, 1975).
Arnold A. Offner, *American Appeasement: United States Foreign Policy and Germany, 1933–1938* (New York, pbk. edn., 1976).
Robert E. Osgood, *NATO: The Entangling Alliance* (Chicago, 1962).
Ritchie Ovendale, *'Appeasement' and the English Speaking World: Britain, the United States, the Dominions, and the Policy of 'Appeasement', 1937–1939* (Cardiff, 1975).

Carl P. Parrini, *Heir to Empire: United States Economic Diplomacy, 1916–1923* (Pittsburgh, 1969).
Edward B. Parsons, *Wilsonian Diplomacy: Allied-American Rivalries in War and Peace* (St. Louis, Mo., 1978).
James T. Patterson, *Congressional Conservatism and the New Deal: The Conservative Coalition in Congress, 1933–1939* (Lexington, Ky., 1967).
G. C. Peden, *British Rearmament and the Treasury, 1932–1939* (Edinburgh, 1979).
Henry Pelling, *America and the British Left: From Bright to Bevan* (London, 1956).
Henry Pelling, *Britain and the Second World War* (London, 1970).
Henry Pelling, *Winston Churchill* (London, 1974).
Ernest F. Penrose, *Economic Planning for the Peace* (Princeton, N.J. 1953).
Bradford Perkins, *The Great Rapprochement: England and the United States, 1895–1914* (New York, 1968).
H. C. Peterson, *Propaganda for War: The Campaign against American Neutrality, 1914–1917* (Norman, Okla., 1939).
J. W. Pickersgill, *The Mackenzie King Record*, vol. I (Toronto, 1960).
Forrest C. Pogue, *George C. Marshall* (2 vols., London edn., 1964–65).
David L. Porter, *The Seventy-sixth Congress and World War II, 1939–1940* (Columbia, Mo., 1979).
M. M. Postan, *British War Production* (London, 1952).
Jim Potter, *The American Economy Between the World Wars* (London, 1974).
Julius W. Pratt, *Cordell Hull, 1939–1944* (2 vols., New York, 1964).
Lawrence Pratt, *East of Malta, West of Suez: Britain's Mediterranean Crisis, 1936–1939* (Cambridge, 1975).

John Ramsden, *A History of the Conservative Party: The Age of Balfour and Baldwin, 1902–1940* (London, 1978).

Willard Range, *Franklin D. Roosevelt's World Order* (Athens, Ga., 1959).

David Rees, *Harry Dexter White: A Study in Paradox* (New York, 1973).

David Reynolds, *Lord Lothian and Anglo-American Relations, 1939–1940* (Philadelphia, 1982). Published as part of the American Philosophical Society's *Transactions* series of monographs.

P. A. Reynolds and E. J. Hughes, *The Historian as Diplomat: Charles Kingsley Webster and the United Nations, 1939–1946* (London, 1976).

Elliott Roosevelt and James Brough, *A Rendezvous with Destiny: The Roosevelts of the White House* (London, 1977).

Stephen Roskill, *The War at Sea*, vol. I (London, 1954).

Stephen Roskill, *Naval Policy Between the Wars* (2 vols., London, 1968, 1976).

Stephen Roskill, *Hankey: Man of Secrets*, vol. III (London, 1974).

Stephen Roskill, *Churchill and the Admirals* (London, 1977).

Benjamin M. Rowland (ed.), *Balance of Power or Hegemony: The Interwar Monetary System* (New York, 1976).

Peter Rowland, *Lloyd George* (London, 1975).

Bruce M. Russett, *Community and Contention: Britain and America in the Twentieth Century* (Cambridge, Mass., 1963).

Bruce M. Russett, *No Clear and Present Danger: A Skeptical View of the U.S. Entry into World War II* (New York, 1972).


R. S. Sayers, *Financial Policy, 1939–1945* (London, 1956).

R. S. Sayers, *The Bank of England, 1891–1944*, vol. 2 (Cambridge, 1976).

Arthur M. Schlesinger, Jr. (ed.), *History of U.S. Political Parties*, vol. III (New York, 1973).

Arthur M. Schlesinger, Jr. and Fred L. Israel (eds.), *History of American Presidential Elections, 1789–1968*, vol. III (New York, 1971).

Maxwell P. Schoenfeld, *The War Ministry of Winston Churchill* (Ames, Iowa, 1972).

Paul W. Schroeder, *The Axis Alliance and Japanese–American Relations, 1941* (Ithaca, N.Y., 1958).

Robert P. Shay, Jr., *British Rearmament in the Thirties: Politics and Profits* (Princeton, 1977).

Robert E. Sherwood, *Roosevelt and Hopkins: An Intimate History* (New York, 1948).

Robert Skidelsky (ed.), *The End of the Keynesian Era: Essays on the Disintegration of the Keynesian Political Economy* (London, 1977).

James D. Squires, *British Propaganda at Home and in the United States from 1914 to 1917* (Cambridge, Mass., 1935).

C. P. Stacey, *Arms, Men and Governments: The War Policies of Canada, 1939–1945* (Ottawa, 1970).

Richard W. Steele, *The First Offensive, 1942: Roosevelt, Marshall, and the Making of American Strategy* (Bloomington, Ind., 1973).

William Stevenson, *A Man Called Intrepid: The Secret War* (New York, pbk. edn., 1977).

Henry L. Stimson and McGeorge Bundy, *On Active Service in War and Peace* (New York, 1948).

Mark A. Stoler, *The Politics of the Second Front: American Military Planning and Diplomacy in Coalition Warfare, 1941–1943* (Westport, Conn., 1977).

Richard Storry, *Japan and the Decline of the West in Asia, 1894–1943* (London, 1979).

Susan Strange, *Sterling and British Policy: A Political Study of an International Currency in Decline* (London, 1971).
Cushing Strout, *The American Image of the Old World* (New York, 1963).

A. J. P. Taylor, *English History, 1914–1945* (Oxford, 1965).
A. J. P. Taylor, *Beaverbrook* (London, 1972).
Lord Templewood, *Nine Troubled Years* (London, 1954).
R. T. Thomas, *Britain and Vichy: The Dilemma of Anglo-French Relations, 1940–1942* (London, 1979).
Neville Thompson, *The Anti-Appeasers* (London, 1971).
Christopher Thorne, *The Limits of Foreign Policy: The West, the League and the Far Eastern Crisis of 1931–1933* (London, 1972).
Christopher Thorne, *Allies of a Kind: The United States, Great Britain and the War against Japan, 1941–1945* (London, 1978).
C. David Tompkins, *Senator Arthur H. Vandenberg: The Evolution of a Modern Republican, 1884–1945* (East Lansing, Mich., 1970).
Joseph Tulchin, *Aftermath of War: World War I and U.S. Policy Towards Latin America* (New York, 1971).

Martin L. Van Creveld, *Hitler's Strategy, 1940–1941: The Balkan Clue* (London, 1973).
Armand Van Dormael, *Bretton Woods: Birth of a Monetary System* (London, 1978).

Alan Watt, *The Evolution of Australian Foreign Policy, 1938–1965* (Cambridge, 1965).
Donald C. Watt, *Personalities and Policies* (London, 1965).
Donald C. Watt, *Too Serious a Business: European Armed Forces and the Approach to the Second World War* (London, 1975).
Mark S. Watson, *Chief of Staff: Prewar Plans and Preparations* (Washington, 1950).
Gerhard L. Weinberg, *The Foreign Policy of Hitler's Germany: II, Starting World War II, 1937–1939* (Chicago, 1980).
Sumner Welles, *The Time for Decision* (New York, 1944).
Sumner Welles, *Seven Major Decisions* (London edn., 1951).
Barton Whaley, *Codeword Barbarossa* (Cambridge, Mass., 1973).
Sir John Wheeler-Bennett, *King George VI: His Life and Reign* (London, 1958).
Sir John Wheeler-Bennett (ed.), *Action This Day: Working with Churchill* (London, 1968).
Sir John Wheeler-Bennett, *Special Relationships: America in Peace and War* (London, 1975).
Sir Arthur Willert, *Washington and Other Memories* (Boston, 1972).
Theodore A. Wilson, *The First Summit: Roosevelt and Churchill at Placentia Bay, 1941* (London, 1970).
John E. Wiltz, *In Search of Peace: The Senate Munitions Inquiry, 1934–1936* (Baton Rouge, La., 1963).
John E. Wiltz, *From Isolation to War, 1931–1941* (London, 1969).
John G. Winant, *A Letter from Grosvenor Square: An Account of a Stewardship* (London, 1947).
Roberta A. Wohlstetter, *Pearl Harbor: Warning and Decision* (Stanford, Ca., 1962).
Arnold Wolfers and Laurence W. Martin (eds.), *The Anglo-American Tradition in Foreign Affairs* (New Haven, 1956).
Sir Llewellyn Woodward, *British Foreign Policy in the Second World War* (5 vols., London, 1970–76).

Daniel Yergin, *Shattered Peace: The Origins of the Cold War and the National Security State* (London, 1978).

Kenneth Young, *Churchill and Beaverbrook, A Study in Friendship and Politics* (London, 1966).


## IV  Printed Secondary Works: Articles and Essays

Abbreviations:

| | |
|---|---|
| *AHR* | *American Historical Review* |
| *DH* | *Diplomatic History* |
| *EHR* | *English Historical Review* |
| *ESR* | *European Studies Review* |
| *HJ* | *Historical Journal* |
| *JAH* | *Journal of American History* |
| *JCH* | *Journal of Contemporary History* |
| *JEcH* | *Journal of Economic History* |
| *JICH* | *Journal of Imperial and Commonwealth History* |
| *JMH* | *Journal of Modern History* |
| *PHR* | *Pacific Historical Review* |

Robert D. Accinelli, 'The Roosevelt administration and the World Court defeat, 1935', *The Historian*, 40 (1978), 463–78.

Paul Addison, 'Lloyd George and compromise peace in the Second World War', in A. J. P. Taylor (ed.), *Lloyd George: Twelve Essays* (London, 1971).

Lloyd E. Ambrosius, 'The orthodoxy of revisionism: Woodrow Wilson and the New Left', *DH*, 1 (1977), 199–214.

Irvine H. Anderson, Jr., 'The 1941 *de facto* embargo on oil to Japan: A bureaucratic reflex', *PHR*, 44 (1975), 201–31.


F. A. Baptiste, 'The British grant of air and naval facilities to the United States in Trinidad, St. Lucia and Bermuda in 1939 (June–December)', *Caribbean Studies*, 16 (1976), 5–43.

Glen St J. Barclay, 'Singapore strategy: The role of the United States in Imperial defence', *Military Affairs*, 39 (1975), 54–9.

Glen St J. Barclay, 'Australia looks to America: The wartime relationship, 1939–1942', *PHR*, 46 (1975), 251–71.

Alan Beattie, 'Neville Chamberlain', in John P. Mackintosh (ed.), *British Prime Ministers in the Twentieth Century* (London, 1977), I, 219–71.

François Bédarida, 'France, Britain and the Nordic countries', *Scandinavian Journal of History*, 2 (1977), 7–27.

Coral Bell, 'The "special relationship" ', in Michael Leifer (ed.), *Constraints and Adjustments in British Foreign Policy* (London, 1972), pp. 103–19.

Max Beloff, 'The special relationship: An Anglo-American myth', in Martin Gilbert (ed.), *A Century of Conflict, 1850–1950: Essays for A. J. P. Taylor* (London, 1966), pp. 151–71.

Max Beloff, 'The Whitehall factor: The role of the higher civil service, 1919–39', in Gillian Peele and Chris Cook (eds.), *The Politics of Reappraisal, 1918–1939* (London, 1975), pp. 209–31.

Lester H. Brune, 'Considerations of force in Cordell Hull's diplomacy, July 26 to November 26, 1941', *DH*, 2 (1978), 389–405.

Kathleen Burk, 'The diplomacy of finance: British financial missions to the United States, 1914–1918', *HJ*, 22 (1979), 351–72.

Kathleen Burk, 'Great Britain in the United States, 1917-1918: The turning point', *International History Review*, 1 (1979), 228-45.
Robert J. C. Butow, 'The Hull–Nomura conversations: A fundamental misconception', *AHR*, 65 (1960), 822-36.
Robert J. C. Butow, 'Backdoor diplomacy in the Pacific: The proposal for a Konoye–Roosevelt meeting, 1941', *JAH*, 59 (1972), 48-72.

John C. Cairns, 'A nation of shopkeepers in search of a suitable France, 1919-1940', *AHR*, 79 (1974), 710-43.
Raymond Callahan, 'The illusion of security: Singapore, 1919-1942', *JCH*, 9 (1974), 69-92.
A. E. Campbell, 'The United States and Great Britain: Uneasy allies', in Braeman *et al.* (eds.), *20th Century American Foreign Policy*, pp. 471-501.
F. Coghlan, 'Armaments, economic policy and appeasement: Background to British foreign policy, 1931-7', *History*, 57 (1972), 205-21.
Frank C. Costigliola, 'Anglo-American financial rivalry in the 1920s', *JEcH*, 37 (1977), 911-34.

David Dilks, 'Appeasement revisited', *University of Leeds Review*, 15 (1972), 28-56.
David Dilks, 'Baldwin and Chamberlain', in Lord Butler (ed.), *The Conservatives: A History from Their Origins to 1965* (London, 1977), 271-404.
David Dilks, 'Great Britain and Scandinavia in the "Phoney War" ', *Scandinavian Journal of History*, 2 (1977), 29-51.
David Dilks, 'The twilight war and the fall of France: Chamberlain and Churchill in 1940', *Transactions of the Royal Historical Society*, 5s, 28 (1978), 61-86.
Justus D. Doenecke, 'Beyond polemics: An historiographical re-appraisal of American entry into World War II', *The History Teacher*, XII (1979), 217-51.
Roy Douglas, 'Chamberlain and Eden, 1937-1938', *JCH*, 13 (1978), 97-116.
Donald F. Drummond, 'Cordell Hull', in Norman A. Graebner (ed.), *An Uncertain Tradition: American Secretaries of State in the 20th Century* (New York, 1961), pp. 184-209.

P. G. Edwards, 'R. G. Menzies' appeals to the United States, May–June, 1940', *Australian Outlook*, 28 (1974), 64-70.
Lord Elibank, 'Franklin Roosevelt: Friend of Britain', *The Contemporary Review*, 188 (1955), 362-8.
William Emerson, 'Franklin Roosevelt as Commander-in-Chief in World War II', *Military Affairs*, 22 (1959), 181-207.
Raymond A. Esthus, 'President Roosevelt's commitment to Britain to intervene in a Pacific war', *Mississippi Valley Historical Review*, 50 (1963), 28-38.

Norman Gibbs, 'The naval conferences of the interwar years: A study of Anglo-American relations', *Naval War College Review*, 30 (1977), 50-63.
Richard J. Grace, 'Whitehall and the ghost of appeasement: November 1941', *DH*, 3 (1979), 173-91.
Fred Greene, 'The military view of American national policy, 1904-1940', *AHR*, 66 (1961), 354-77.
Thomas N. Guinsberg, 'Ebb tide of American isolationism: The Senate debate on the arms embargo, 1937-1939', *Historical Papers* (Ottawa), (1972), 313-34.

Thomas E. Hachey (ed.), 'Winning friends and influencing policy: British strategy to woo America in 1937', *Wisconsin Magazine of History*, 55 (1971-2), 120-9.
John M. Haight, 'France, the United States, and the Munich crisis', *JMH*, XXXII (1960), 340-58.

John M. Haight, 'Franklin D. Roosevelt and a naval quarantine of Japan', *PHR*, 40 (1971), 203–26.

Gerald K. Haines, 'Under the Eagle's wing: The Franklin Roosevelt Administration forges an American Hemisphere', *DH*, 1 (1977), 373–88.

Charles R. Halstead, 'Diligent diplomat: Alexander W. Weddell as American Ambassador to Spain, 1939–1942', *Virginia Magazine of History and Biography*, 82 (1974), 3–38.

Daniel F. Harrington, 'A careless hope: American air power and Japan, 1941', *PHR*, 48 (1979), 217–38.

Milan Hauner, 'Did Hitler want a world dominion?', *JCH*, 13 (1978), 15–32.

Alan K. Henrikson, 'The map as an "idea": the role of cartographic imagery during the Second World War', *The American Cartographer*, 2 (1975), 19–53.

Alan K. Henrikson, 'The creation of the North Atlantic alliance, 1948–1952', *US Naval War College Review*, 32 (May–June, 1980), 4–39.

Alan K. Henrikson, 'America's changing place in the world: From "periphery" to "centre"?', in Jean Gottmann (ed.), *Centre and Periphery: Spatial Variation in Politics* (London, 1980), pp. 73–100.

Edward L. Henson, Jr., 'Britain, America and the month of Munich', *International Relations*, II (1962), 291–301.

Holger H. Herwig, 'Prelude to *Weltblitzkrieg:* Germany's naval policy towards the United States, 1939–41', *JMH*, 43 (1971), 649–68.

James H. Herzog, 'Influence of the United States Navy in the embargo of oil to Japan, 1940–1941', *PHR*, 35 (1966), 317–28.

Stanley E. Hilton, 'The Welles mission to Europe, February–March 1940: Illusion or realism?', *JAH*, 58 (1971), 93–120.

Chihiro Hosoya, 'Miscalculations in deterrent policy: Japanese–U.S. relations, 1938–1941', *Journal of Peace Research*, 5 (1968), 97–115.

Chihiro Hosoya, 'The tripartite pact, 1939–1940', in James W. Morley (ed.), *Deterrent Diplomacy: Japan, Germany and the USSR, 1935–1940* (New York, 1976), pp. 191–257.

E. J. Hughes, 'Winston Churchill and the formation of the United Nations Organization', *JCH*, 9 (1974), 27–56.

Morton Keller, 'Anglo-American politics 1900–1930, in Anglo-American perspective: A case study in comparative history', *Comparative Studies in Society and History*, 22 (1980), 458–77.

Warren F. Kimball, 'Beggar my neighbor: America and the British interim financial crisis, 1940–1941', *JEcH*, 29 (1969), 758–72.

Warren F. Kimball, 'Lend-Lease and the Open Door: The temptation of British opulence, 1937–1942', *Political Science Quarterly*, 86 (1971), 232–59.

Warren F. Kimball, 'Churchill and Roosevelt: The personal equation', *Prologue*, 6 (1974), 169–82.

Donald Lammers, 'From Whitehall after Munich: The Foreign Office and the future course of British policy', *HJ*, XVI (1973), 831–56.

John D. Langer, 'The Harriman–Beaverbrook mission and the debate over unconditional aid for the Soviet Union, 1941', *JCH*, 14 (1979), 463–82.

Melvyn P. Leffler, 'Political isolationism, economic expansion, or diplomatic realism: American policy towards western Europe, 1921–1933', *Perspectives in American History*, 8 (1974), 413–61.

Richard M. Leighton, 'The American arsenal policy in World War II: A retrospective view', in Beaver (ed.), *Some Pathways*, pp. 221–52.

James Leutze, 'The secret of the Churchill–Roosevelt correspondence: September 1939–May 1940', *JCH*, 10 (1975), 465–91.

Arthur S. Link, 'President Wilson and his English critics: Survey and interpretation' (1959), reprinted in Link, *The Higher Realism of Woodrow Wilson and Other Essays* (Nashville, 1971), pp. 110–26.

Francis L. Loewenheim, 'An illusion that shaped history: New light on the history and historiography of American peace efforts before Munich', in Beaver (ed.), *Some Pathways*, pp. 177–220.

Hans-Dietrich Loock, '*Weserubung*—A step towards a Greater Germanic Reich', *Scandinavian Journal of History*, 2 (1977), 67–88.

Ralph M. Lutz, 'Studies of world war propaganda, 1914–1933', *JMH*, 5 (1933), 496–516.

Mark M. Lowenthal, 'Intrepid and the history of world war II', *Military Affairs*, XLI (1977), 88–90.

John M. McCarthy, 'Singapore and Australian defence, 1921–1942', *Australian Outlook*, 25 (1971), 165–80.

John M. McCarthy, 'Australia: A view from Whitehall, 1939–1945', *Australian Outlook*, 28 (1974), 318–31.

John M. McCarthy, 'The imperial commitment, 1939–1941', *Australian Journal of Politics and History*, 23 (1977), 178–81.

Callum A. MacDonald, 'Britain, France and the April crisis of 1939', *ESR*, 2 (1972), 151–69.

Callum A. MacDonald, 'Economic appeasement and the German "moderates", 1937–1939. An introductory essay', *Past & Present*, 56 (1972), 105–35.

Callum A. MacDonald, 'The Venlo affair', *ESR*, 8 (1978) 443–64.

Keith D. McFarland, 'Woodring vs. Johnson: F.D.R. and the great War Department feud', *Army*, 26 (1976), 36–42.

Barbara C. Malament, 'British Labour and Roosevelt's New Deal: The response of the left and the unions', *Journal of British Studies*, 17 (1978), 136–67.

Robert Manne, 'The British decision for alliance with Russia, May 1939', *JCH*, 9 (1974), 3–26.

Arthur Marder, 'Winston is back: Churchill at the Admiralty, 1939–1940', *EHR*, supplement 5 (1972).

Arthur Marwick, 'Middle opinion in the thirties: Planning, progress, and political "agreement" ', *EHR*, 79 (1964), 285–98.

Ernest R. May, 'An American tradition in foreign policy: The role of public opinion', in William H. Nelson (ed.), *Theory and Practice in American Politics* (Chicago, 1964), pp. 101–22.

Ernest R. May, 'Nazi Germany and the United States: A review essay', *JMH*, 41 (1969), 207–14.

M. Ruth Megaw, 'Undiplomatic channels: Australian representation in the United States, 1918–1939', *Historical Studies*, 15 (1973), 610–30.

M. Ruth Megaw, 'Australia and the Anglo-American Trade Agreement, 1938', *JICH*, 3 (1975), 191–211.

M. Ruth Megaw, 'The scramble for the Pacific: Anglo-United States rivalry in the 1930s', *Historical Studies*, 17 (1977), 458–73.

Arnold A. Offner, 'Appeasement revisited: The United States, Great Britain, and Germany, 1933–1940', *JAH*, 64 (1977), 373–93.

R. J. Overy, 'German pre-war aircraft production plans: November 1936–April 1939', *EHR*, 90 (1975), 778–97.

R. A. C. Parker, 'Economics, rearmament and foreign policy: The United Kingdom before 1939—a preliminary study', *JCH*, 10 (1975), 637–47.

R. A. C. Parker, 'Britain, France and Scandinavia, 1939–1940', *History*, 61 (1976), 369–87.

James T. Patterson, 'A conservative coalition forms in Congress, 1933–1939', *JAH*, 52 (1966), 757–72.

James T. Patterson, 'Eating humble pie: A note on Roosevelt, Congress and neutrality revision in 1939', *The Historian*, 31 (1969), 407–14.

R. H. Pear, 'The impact of the New Deal on British economic and political ideas', *Bulletin of the British Association for American Studies*, n.s., 4 (1962), 17–28.

J. H. Plumb, 'The historian', in A. J. P. Taylor *et al.*, *Churchill: Four Faces and the Man* (London, 1969), pp. 119–51.

Lawrence Pratt, 'The Anglo-American naval conversations on the Far East of January 1938', *International Affairs*, 47 (1971), 745–63.

Nicholas Pronay, 'The newsreels: The illusion of actuality', in Paul Smith (ed.), *The Historian and Film* (Cambridge, 1976), pp. 95–119.

Robert J. Quinlan, 'The United States fleet: Diplomacy, strategy and the allocation of ships (1940–1941)', in Harold Stein (ed.), *American Civil-Military Decisions: A Book of Case Studies* (Birmingham, Ala., 1963), pp. 153–201.

Stephen J. Rabe, 'Anglo-American rivalry for Venezuelan oil, 1919–1929', *Mid-America*, 58 (1976), 97–109.

Jorgen S. Rasmussen, 'Party discipline in wartime: The downfall of the Chamberlain government', *Journal of Politics*, 32 (1970), 379–406.

David Reynolds, 'FDR on the British: A postscript', *Proceedings of the Massachusetts Historical Society*, 90 (1978), 106–10.

David Reynolds, 'Competitive co-operation: Anglo-American relations in World War Two', *HJ*, 23 (1980), 233–45.

Benjamin D. Rhodes, 'Reassessing "Uncle Shylock": The United States and the French war debt, 1917–1929', *JAH*, 55 (1969), 787–803.

Benjamin D. Rhodes, 'Herbert Hoover and the war debts, 1919–1933', *Prologue*, 6 (1974), 130–44.

Benjamin D. Rhodes, 'The British royal visit of 1939 and the "psychological approach" to the United States', *DH*, 2 (1978), 197–211.

Floyd M. Riddick, 'American government and politics: The first session of the seventy-sixth Congress, January 3 to August 5, 1939', *American Political Science Review*, 33 (1939), 1022–43.

Emily S. Rosenberg, 'Anglo-American economic rivalry in Brazil during World War I', *DH*, 2 (1978), 131–52.

Hugh Ross, 'Roosevelt's third-term nomination', *Mid-America*, 44 (1962), 80–94.

Hugh Ross, 'Was the nomination of Wendell Willkie a political miracle?', *Indiana Magazine of History*, 58 (1962), 79–100.

M. L. Sanders, 'Wellington House and British propaganda during the First World War', *HJ*, 18 (1975), 119–46.

Arthur W. Schatz, 'The Anglo-American trade agreement and Cordell Hull's search for peace, 1936–1938', *JAH*, 57 (1970), 85–103.

Martin J. Sherwin, 'The atomic bomb and the origins of the Cold War: U.S. atomic-energy policy and diplomacy, 1941–1945', *AHR*, 78 (1973), 945–68.

Avi Shlaim, 'Prelude to downfall: The British offer of Union to France', *JCH*, 9 (1974), 27–63.

Robert Skidelsky, 'Going to war with Germany: Between revisionism and orthodoxy', *Encounter*, 39 (1972), 56–65.

Richard W. Steele, 'The pulse of the people: Franklin D. Roosevelt and the gauging of public opinion', *JCH*, 9 (1974), 195–216.

R. H. S. Stolfi, 'Equipment for victory in France in 1940', *History*, 55 (1970), 1–20.

Jonathan G. Utley, 'Upstairs, downstairs at Foggy Bottom: Oil exports and Japan, 1940–41', *Prologue*, 8 (1976), 17–28.

Martin Van Creveld, 'Prelude to disaster: The British decision to aid Greece, 1940–41', *JCH*, 9 (1974), 65–92.
Jane K. Vieth, 'The donkey and the lion: The ambassadorship of Joseph P. Kennedy at the Court of St. James's, 1938–1940', *Michigan Academician*, 10 (1978), 273–81.
Brian L. Villa, 'The atomic bomb and the Normandy invasion', *Perspectives in American History*, XI (1977–78), 461–502.

William V. Wallace, 'Roosevelt and British appeasement in 1938', *Bulletin of the British Association for American Studies*, n.s., 5 (1962), 4–30.
D. C. Watt, 'Appeasement: The rise of a revisionist school?', *The Political Quarterly*, 36 (1965), 191–213.
D. C. Watt, 'Roosevelt and Neville Chamberlain: Two appeasers', *International Journal*, 28 (1973), 185–204.
Gerhard L. Weinberg, 'Hitler's image of the United States', *AHR*, 69 (1964), 1006–21.
Bert R. Whittemore, 'A quiet triumph: The mission of John Gilbert Winant to London, 1941', *Historical New Hampshire*, 30 (1975), 1–11.
Francis O. Wilcox, 'American government and politics: The neutrality fight in Congress: 1939', *American Political Science Review*, 33 (1939), 811–23.

Lowell T. Young, 'Franklin D. Roosevelt and America's islets: Acquisition of territory in the Caribbean and in the Pacific', *The Historian*, 35 (1973), 205–20.

**V Unpublished Manuscripts** (Ph.D. dissertations unless otherwise stated)

Sir John Balfour, 'Diadems askew: A diplomatic cavalcade' (TS. memoirs, 1960, copy in FCO Library, London).
John Dizikes, 'Britain, Roosevelt and the New Deal, 1932–1938' (Harvard University, 1964).
Charles J. Errico, Jr., 'Foreign affairs and the presidential election of 1940' (University of Maryland, 1973).
Ernest Gilman, 'Economic aspects of Anglo-American relations in the era of Roosevelt and Chamberlain, 1937–1940' (University of London, 1976).
Richard A. Harrison, 'Appeasement and isolation: The relation of British and American foreign policy, 1935–1938' (Princeton University, 1974).
Tracy B. Kittredge, 'United States–British naval cooperation, 1939–1942' (Unpublished TS., U.S. Naval Archives, Washington Navy Yard).
Mary C. Kuhn, 'The activity of the foreign press service of the NSDAP in the United States, 1937–1941' (The Catholic University of America, 1964).
Kyozo Sato, 'Anglo-Japanese relations, 1939–1941: Japan's expansion and Britain's response' (Cambridge University, 1978).
Jane H. D. Schwar, 'Interventionist propaganda and pressure groups in the United States, 1937–1941' (Ohio State University, 1973).
Denis Smyth, 'Diplomacy and strategy of survival: British policy and Spanish non-belligerency, 1940–1941' (Cambridge University, 1978).
J. A. Thompson, '20th-century U.S. diplomacy: The British perspective' (OAH conference paper, Atlanta, 1977).

# INDEX